Voices of the Saints

Also by Bert Ghezzi

Everyday Encounters with God
(coauthored with Benedict J. Groeschel, CFR)

The Heart of a Saint

The Sign of the Cross

Mystics and Miracles

BERT GHEZZI

Voices of the Saints

A 365-Day Journey with our Spiritual Companions

LoyolaPress.
A Jesuit Ministry
Chicago

LoyolaPress.
A Jesuit Ministry

3441 N. Ashland Avenue
Chicago, Illinois 60657
(800) 621-1008
www.loyolapress.com

Originally published by DOUBLEDAY
a division of Random House, Inc.
1540 Broadway, New York, New York 10036

Cover design by Tracey Sainz
Interior design by Joan Bledig
Author photo by Mark Poulalion
Cover images: Left to right; Ignatius of Loyola *(Agnus Images);* Martin de Porres *(The Crosiers/ Gene Plaisted OSC);* Katherine Tekakwitha *(W.P. Wittman Limited);* Thomas *(iStock/Denis Radovanovic);* Thérèse of Lisieux *(iStock/Paul Hill); background image iStock/Anthony Rosenberg*

Library of Congress Cataloging-in-Publication Data
Ghezzi, Bert.
Voices of the saints : a 365-day journey with our spiritual companions / Bert Ghezzi.
p. cm.
Originally published: 1st ed. New York : Doubleday, 2000.
Includes bibliographical references (p.).
ISBN-13: 978-0-8294-2806-3
ISBN-10: 0-8294-2806-2
1. Christian saints—Prayers and devotions. 2. Devotional calendars—Catholic Church. I. Title.
BX4655.3.G49 2009
282.092'2--dc22
[B]

2009007250

Printed in the United States of America
First hardcover edition published September 2000 (ISBN 978-0-385-49181-5)

Printed in the United States of America
14 15 Versa 10 9 8 7 6 5 4 3

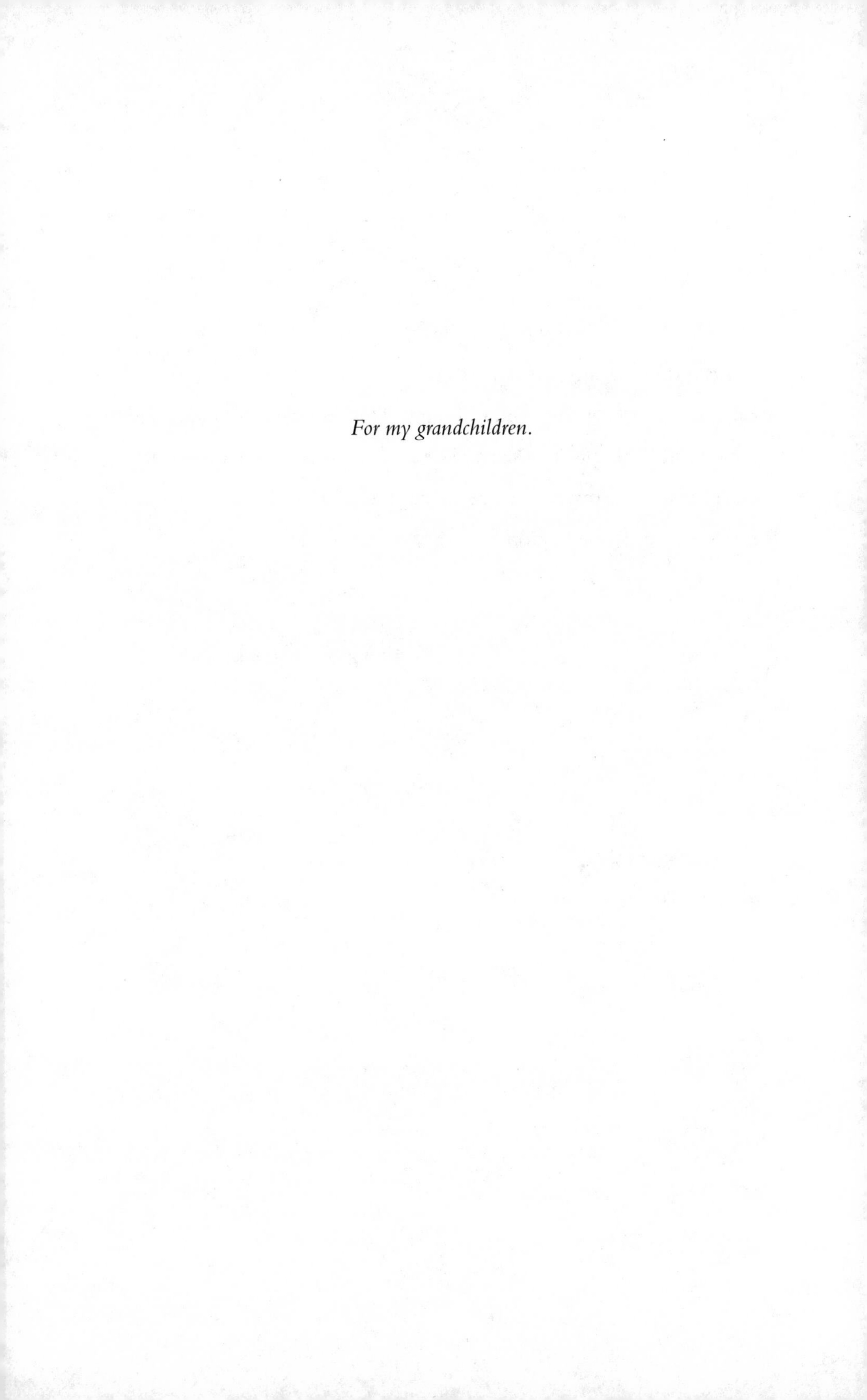

For my grandchildren.

IF YOU ARE A "SAINT WATCHER" this is the book for you, with a totally new arrangement permitting one to look up themes and calendars as well as the names of saints. This represents a unique step forward in biographies of saints. The quotations supplied are also fascinating and worthwhile for meditation. A book to keep where you make your daily meditations.

Father Benedict J. Groeschel, CFR
Author of *The Journey Toward God*

Contents

Acknowledgments

Thanks to all who aided me in researching and writing this book. I am grateful to the librarians of many institutions that served me well, especially the Winter Park Public Library for many interlibrary loans and the Hesburgh Library of the University of Notre Dame, my alma mater.

This book would not have been possible without the generosity of my friend and saint-watcher Don Fishel, who allowed me to root through and borrow many of his thousands of books by and about saints.

I am indebted to my friend and agent Joseph Durepos, whose vision, coaching, and encouragement made this a much better book. Thanks, too, to Evelyn Bence, my friend and an author in her own right, who with her characteristic thoroughness and persistence obtained the copyright permissions for this book. I am grateful to the publishing team at Loyola Press for their creativity and care in producing this revised edition. And my special thanks to all the booksellers who make my books available.

How to Use This Book

You can read *Voices of the Saints* in a variety of ways.

The book presents the saints in chronological order from Mary, the queen of all saints, to Mother Teresa. Following this arrangement will give you a sense of where the saints fit into the flow of church history.

1. You can read one selection each day through the year. To help you keep track, *Voices of the Saints* is numbered from 1 to 365.
2. You can also read *Voices of the Saints* by topic. Just choose a theme from the chart of ninety-six themes and go to the saints that are listed for each topic. You will find subjects of perennial interest such as Angels, Prayer, and Suffering. And you may be intrigued by such topics as Married Saints, Feisty Saints, and Twenty-Something Saints. The themes begin on page 733.
3. The book includes an alphabetical index so that you can find a saint that interests you. The index appears on page 785.
4. By using A Calendar of the Saints, you may read this book through the year from January to December. Note that while the calendar is based on the liturgical year of the Roman Rite of the Catholic Church, only saints presented in *Voices of the Saints* are listed. A Calendar of the Saints begins on page 747.

Voices of the Saints is cross-referenced. When the name of a saint who is treated in the book appears within a selection, I have printed it in semibold type. For example, when **St. Bernard of Clairvaux** appears thus in the article on St. Malachy, you will find related information in the article on St. Bernard.

The saint's feast day, canonization information, and patronage appears at the end of each daily reading.

Introduction

If they, why not I?—If these men and women could become saints, why cannot I with the help of him who is all-powerful?

—St. Augustine

Saints intrigue us. We recognize something special about them that seems to set them apart. They have achieved an excellence that we admire, but that we suppose we can never reach. "Virtue is our Everest," said saint-watcher Phyllis McGinley, "and those who climb highest are most worth admiring." So we honor the saints by mentally placing them on pedestals that distance them from us, believing them to be the exceptional and we the ordinary.

When we get to know the saints a little better, however, that imagined distance shrinks. Observing saints more closely reveals that they were ordinary people just like us. I am inspired by seeing St. Teresa of Ávila scarfing down a partridge instead of fasting and St. Lutgarde interrupting her Eucharistic devotion to get a snack. I like noting the inconsistency of St. Sabas, who punished a disciple for looking at a beautiful woman that he also had apparently eyed with appreciation. I am relieved to discover that St. Bertilla, with whom I share not only a name but a persistent problem with anger, once had to repent for cursing a young nun who crossed her. Even saints who lived with Christ and personally experienced his heavenly invasion stayed earthbound. Only a week after Christ's rising, for example, St. Peter got bored and said, "I'm going fishing," and six other saints tagged along (John 21:3).

What distinguishes saints from most people is their life purpose. Simply put, more than anything else, they wanted to be saints. "May God keep us in his grace," wrote fifteen-year-old Dominic Savio to a friend, "and help us to become saints." Young Thérèse of Lisieux resolved to become a saint. She said, "I am determined to find an elevator to carry me to Jesus, for I was too small to climb the steep stairs of perfection . . . It is your arms, Jesus, which are the elevator to carry me to heaven." And Ignatius of Loyola stated his intention in words that invite our imitation: "The saints were of the same frame as I. Why should I not do as they have done?" This compelling desire for sanctity motivated all the saints, and their resolve invited a divine touch.

But determination does not create saints. As the word *saint* indicates, only God makes saints. *Saint* comes from a Latin root that means "holy" or "reserved for God." The presence of the divine in human beings causes them to be holy and transforms them into saints. In fact, Scripture calls all Christians "saints" because God dwells in us. We share with those we call saints a union with God that makes us more like them than we may realize. Grace gives us all the potential to become saints like Teresa, Ignatius, Thérèse, and Dominic Savio. If we don't aim for it, we lose out. "The one sadness," said Léon Blois, "is not to be a saint."

Of the millions of saints who have preceded us, the church has formally identified some women and men to aid us on our journey. Over the centuries and throughout the world, it has in diverse ways recognized about ten thousand saints. The early church first recognized martyrs as saints—men and women who died for their faith. Christians began to remember the dates of the martyrs' deaths as their birthday into heaven, visit their tombs to ask for their intercession, write their stories, and enroll their names on lists called martyrologies. About the fourth century, when the persecutions subsided, the church started to recognize women and men who had not been martyred, but who would have given their lives for Christ had they had the chance. For the next six centuries, holy virgins, monks, lay theologians, widows, priests, and bishops had their names added to the lists of saints everywhere.

Today we call the church's way of making saints "canonization."

The term literally refers to adding a name to a "canon," or an official list of saints. But the term has come to refer more broadly to the process used to verify a person's reputation for holiness. Today only the pope proclaims a saint after the Congregation for the Causes of Saints, the church's official saint-making research group, completes a lengthy and rigorous examination of the person's life.

However, canonization evolved slowly. The first official canonization occurred in 993 when Pope John XV canonized St. Ulrich. Only in the twelfth century was the process of naming saints reserved to Rome by Pope Alexander III. Four centuries later, in 1588, Pope Sixtus V established a formal office in Rome to investigate the lives of candidates and conduct the saint-making process. The church still uses that system today, although it has been much reformed and improved, especially in the last century.

Persons under consideration for sainthood in the Roman Catholic Church pass through different stages. Early on they are declared "Venerable," meaning that they either had been martyred or had exercised Christian virtues to a heroic degree. Then the candidate may be beatified and given the title "Blessed." When the pope beatifies someone, he authorizes the limited public veneration of the saint within a diocese, religious order, or perhaps a country. Canonization is the final stage of the process and occurs when the pope decrees that a person has already entered eternal glory and that the saint may be venerated universally. Over the years the church has canonized about eight hundred saints.

The church gives us saints as exemplars. When a pope canonizes a saint, he identifies the person's life message so that we may imitate it. For example, in 1988, Pope John Paul II canonized Philippine Duchesne, a nineteenth-century French missionary to Native Americans. In the official decree, he recommended her "radical commitment to the poor and the outcast of society" as a "dynamic source of inspiration" and a "valid example for all" to follow. But the church also expects us to familiarize ourselves with the saints and to discern wisdom for our lives from their words and actions.

In these pages you will meet many people deserving of your imitation. Some you may know already, like St. Dominic and St. Jerome, both of whom once abandoned the study of the Bible in order to apply its teaching. When famine struck his town, Dominic sold his valuable parchments to aid the starving, saying, "I will not study on dead skins, when living skins are dying of hunger." And when refugees who were fleeing barbarian invaders overran the Holy Land, Jerome put away his books and served them. "Today," he said, "we must translate the words of Scripture into deeds, and instead of speaking saintly words, we must act on them."

You will encounter here other saints that you may not know. Like Anne-Marie Javouhey, the Mother Teresa of nineteenth-century France, who once at the government's request prepared six hundred slaves in Guiana for emancipation. You may become fascinated, as I am, with Roque González, a seventeenth-century Jesuit of Peru, who helped engineer thirty communities for thousands of Indians that provided them the precious gift of economic and political autonomy and prepared them for faith. And you will delight in Miguel Pro, a young priest and practical joker, who gave his life serving the persecuted poor in early twentieth-century Mexico. "If I meet any long-faced saints in heaven," he said, "I will cheer them up with a Mexican hat dance!" We cannot misinterpret the message that all these saints declare: the joyful service of those in need.

The church also gives us saints as intercessors and as patrons. We are encouraged to ask the saints to pray with us for our concerns and to invite them to protect and guide us on our journey. Intercession and patronage involve us personally with the saints that we believe now live in heaven with God. From the earliest days, Christians have spoken about this "communion of saints," as we still do when we recite the Apostle's Creed. We earthly saints are linked with heavenly saints, who constitute a vast, but invisible, sector of the Christian community. But as brothers and sisters who are joined with us in the church, we can rely on them for prayer and support.

The saints themselves expected to be doing the work of intercession once they got to heaven. St. Dominic assured his friars that he could accomplish more for them after his death than he could in life. On his way to execution, St. Thomas More stopped to assure a man he had always prayed for that death would not stop his interceding for him. St. Thérèse of Lisieux promised to respond to requests by asking God to flood the world with little miracles, and thousands testify that she has kept her word. The saint we turn to most often for intercession is the Queen of All Saints, Mary, who was influential enough with her Son to get him at Cana to adjust the timing of God's plan (John 2:4).

We still look to saints as patrons, but patronage for us has retreated considerably from its original meaning. In the early church, a patron acted as a protector and a guide. St. Paulinus of Nola believed that St. Felix, his patron, accompanied him through life, protecting him from dangers and ensuring his relationship with Christ. Our selecting a saint's name for a child is distantly patterned on this ideal of patronage, but we expect far less of the patron for the child than perhaps we ought. We should anticipate much more spiritual support from our invisible, but powerful, partners in the communion of saints.

Voices of the Saints offers stories of the saints, one for each day of the year, to help you relate to the saints as exemplars, intercessors, and patrons. The daily articles show the human side of the saints, taking them down from their pedestals so you can more easily identify with them. Uniquely, each story features a substantial quotation by or about the saint, giving you a feel for what he or she was really like. A brief reflection concludes each day's reading, either a Bible text, a quote from a saint, or a personal reflection by me.

A word on the selection of saints. I tried to include as many popular saints as possible, and I endeavored to include saints from many diverse backgrounds. Limiting my choices was the availability of material written by or about the saint. For some that I would like to have included, no quotable material was available. I also decided to include some not-so-well-known saints who are really worth knowing. While you may not choose to name a daughter "Syncletica" nor a son "Aelred," you may enjoy getting to know saints like them.

My hope is that you will read *Voices of the Saints* with interest and expectation. I recommend that you approach your reading with this advice of St. Philip Neri: *Imagine yourselves to be spiritual beggars in the presence of God and his saints. You should go round from saint to saint, imploring an alms with the same real earnestness with which the poor beg.*

Bert Ghezzi

The best preparation for prayer is to read the lives of the saints, not from mere curiosity, but quietly and with recollection a little at a time. And to pause whenever you feel your heart touched with devotion.

—St. Philip Neri

Daily Readings

1. Mary
(First Century)

My soul proclaims the greatness of the Lord
and my spirit rejoices in God my Saviour;
because he has looked upon the humiliation of his servant.
Yes, from now onwards all generations will call me blessed,
for the Almighty has done great things for me.
Holy is his name,
and his faithful love extends from age after age to those who fear him.
He has used the power of his arm, he has routed the arrogant of heart.
He has pulled down princes from their thrones and raised high the lowly.
He has filled the starving with good things, sent the rich away empty.
He has come to the help of Israel his servant, mindful of his faithful love
—according to the promise he made to our ancestors—
of his mercy to Abraham and to his descendants for ever.

—Mary's Magnificat (Luke 1:46–55 *NJB)*

Mary is the most significant woman in history. We honor her as the Virgin Mother of God, and we meditate on her unique role in God's plan of salvation. Yet Scripture gives us only a few details about her life: the Annunciation, the visit to Elizabeth, the birth of Jesus, the prophecies at his circumcision, the flight into Egypt, the finding of the twelve-year-old Jesus in the Temple.

Then Mary disappears until Christ's public ministry. We don't see her again until she accompanies him at the Cana wedding. At Capernaum, he held her up as the example of a person who does God's will. At the cross, he gave her to the beloved disciple, and she suffered with him there until his death. At Pentecost, she received the Holy Spirit with the other disciples. Tradition tells us further that at her death she was assumed bodily into heaven.

Among the many reasons we venerate Mary, three stand out: her submission, her intercession, and her collaboration with her Son.

Imagine Mary's confusion when Gabriel told her that God wanted her to bear his Son. Her pregnancy would seem to violate the law and disgrace Joseph. Yet even without understanding how things would work out, she said yes to God's invitation. Thus she is a model of submission for us, who often must wade through confusion and misunderstanding as we try to follow God's will.

Mary is the intercessor par excellence. No saint even comes close to her influence with her Son. Mary's intervention seems to have changed the timing of God's plan. A mere hint at the wedding of Cana caused Christ to work an early miracle. So we confidently ask her to present our petitions to the Lord.

Mary plays a unique role in God's saving plan. While Christ is the sole mediator between God and humanity, Mary is an extraordinary collaborator with him. At once she is the daughter and Mother of God, the Mother of the Redeemer, and the Bride of the Holy Spirit. Her cooperation allowed her Son to defeat our enemies—the devil, sin, and death.

The Lord gives Mary to us as the exemplar of a human being perfected by his grace. She who was to be the God-Bearer was born without sin. By anticipation of her Son's Resurrection, she was transformed into the glorious condition we were all meant to share. So we look to Mary as a sign of hope, as we long for deliverance from the limits of our present circumstances.

The knot of Eve's disobedience was untied by Mary's obedience; what the virgin Eve bound through her unbelief, the Virgin Mary loosened by her faith.

—Irenaeus

SEPTEMBER 8; JANUARY 1; AUGUST 22 (QUEENSHIP OF MARY) / PATRON OF THE UNITED STATES OF AMERICA

Grace; Intercession; Intimacy with the Divine; Simple Obedience

2. Joseph
(First Century)

This is how Jesus Christ came to be born. His mother Mary was betrothed to Joseph; but before they came to live together she was found to be with child through the Holy Spirit. Her husband Joseph, being an upright man and wanting to spare her disgrace, decided to divorce her informally. He had made up his mind to do this when suddenly the angel of the Lord appeared to him in a dream and said, "Joseph, son of David, do not be afraid to take Mary home as your wife, because she has conceived what is in her by the Holy Spirit. She will give birth to a son and you must name him Jesus, because he is the one who is to save his people from their sins." Now all this took place to fulfill what the Lord had spoken through the prophet:

> *Look! the virgin is with child and will give birth to a son*
> *whom they will call Immanuel, (see Isaiah 7:14)*

a name which means "God-is-with-us." When Joseph woke up he did what the angel of the Lord had told him to do: he took his wife to his home; he had not had intercourse with her when she gave birth to a son; and he named him Jesus.

—Matthew 1:18–25 *NJB*

A few verses in Matthew and Luke tell us all we know about St. Joseph. They provide just enough information to demonstrate why he was the divine choice to become the husband of **Mary** and the foster father of Jesus.

Joseph was genealogically perfect for these roles. A distant descendant of King David, he gave Christ the King his royal lineage. Joseph also came from the right hometown. He was from Bethlehem, the city that Scripture predicted would produce the messiah (see Micah 5:1). And as a carpenter (see Matthew 13:55), Joseph was poor—Christ's condition of preference.

Scripture portrays Joseph as open to God, obedient, upright, and, above all, kind. The saint displayed all of these qualities in his handling of Mary's surprise pregnancy. Imagine the confusion of emotions that must have flooded him when Mary confided that she was going to have a baby by the Holy Spirit!

As a devout observer of the law, Joseph knew that he might have to repudiate his betrothal. But his kindness and confidence in Mary prevented his taking such a harsh step, which would have shamed her. It may have even put her in danger of capital punishment (see Deuteronomy 22:20–21). Joseph must have agonized over his decision, praying intently about it. Finally he decided to divorce Mary quietly. But Joseph was open to God, and in a dream a divine messenger told him to take Mary home as his wife. Joseph did exactly as he was told. He showed the same virtues in his care for his family in the flight to Egypt and the return to Nazareth.

Devotion to Joseph became prominent in the Middle Ages when saints like **Bridget of Sweden, Ignatius Loyola,** and, especially **Teresa of Ávila,** promoted it. "I have never known anyone to be truly devoted to St. Joseph," said Teresa, "who did not noticeably advance in virtue, for he gives very real help to souls who commend themselves to him."

Joseph's wise dealing with Mary is a model for us when we face complex moral and personal issues. He subordinated his feelings to do what God required. He was open to whatever God wanted, and when he sensed the divine will, he obeyed.

MARCH 19 AND MAY 1 / PATRON OF FATHERS, THE CHURCH, WORKERS, CHINA, AND PERU
Dreams; Family; Kindness; Mere Christian Love

3. Joachim and Anne

(First Century)

Scripture does not mention **Mary**'s father and mother. But early Fathers like **St. Jerome** and **St. John Chrysostom** believed the second-century story that presented St. Joachim and St. Anne as Mary's parents. However, today scholars regard this work, the *Protoevangelium of James*, as unreliable. But for centuries the popular tradition about St. Joachim and St. Anne has inspired Christians with a message of God's tender love. It still inspires us today.

Joachim, a Galilean from Nazareth, married Anne from Bethlehem. They lived on one-third of their resources and donated the rest to the temple and to the poor. After twenty childless years, the couple promised God that if he would grant them a baby they would consecrate it to him.

Once when Joachim went to Jerusalem to celebrate a feast, he approached the altar to make his offering. However, the priest turned him away with an angry reproach. He said that no man subject to the Law's curse may offer sacrifice, nor may a sterile man stand with men who fathered sons. Ashamed because of this public rejection, Joachim decided to avoid his family and friends. So he went to live with his shepherds. Anne worried about his absence, fearing he might be dead.

Then as Jacob of Voragine, the medieval hagiographer, tells it, God intervened:

> An angel appeared to Joachim and said:
>
> "I am sent to announce to you that your prayers have been heard . . . I have seen how you were put to shame, and heard the reproach of childlessness wrongly put upon you. God punishes not nature but sin, and therefore, when he closes a woman's womb, he does this in order to open it miraculously later on. . . . So then, your wife will bear you a daughter and you will call her Mary. As you have vowed, she will be consecrated to the Lord from infancy and filled with the Holy Spirit from her mother's womb. . . . Miraculously, the Son of the Most High will be born of her. His name will be Jesus, and through him all nations will be saved. And let this be a sign to you when you arrive at the Golden Gate of Jerusalem, Anne your wife will be there waiting for you. . . .

> Meanwhile, Anne was weeping bitterly, not knowing where her husband had gone, when the same angel . . . revealed to her the same things he had told Joachim, and added that . . . she should go to Jerusalem's Golden Gate, where she would meet her husband. . . . So they met as the angel had predicted, and were happy to see each other and to be sure they were to have a child. They adored God and went to their home, joyfully awaiting the fulfillment of the divine promise. Anne conceived and brought forth a daughter and they called her name Mary.

Anne and Joachim took Mary at age three to dedicate her to God at the temple. They set the child down at the foot of the temple hill and she climbed the fifteen steps like a grown-up. When the saints had made their offering, they left Mary to be raised with the other temple virgins and returned home, glad because of God's great blessing to them. You know the rest of the story that continues when Mary became a teenager.

> *Faith is the unshaken stance of the soul and is unmoved by any adversity. The believing person is not one who thinks God can do all things, but one who trusts that he will obtain everything. Faith is the agent of things unhoped for. . . .*
>
> —John Climacus

JULY 26 / ANNE, PATRON OF CABINETMAKERS, CANADA, HOUSEWIVES, WOMEN IN LABOR
Angels; Married Saints; Perseverance

4. John the Baptist

(First Century)

One day an angel appeared to Zachary and announced that he was to have a son named John, who would prepare Israel for the messiah. Zachary doubted that Elizabeth, his aged wife, could bear a child. He asked for a sign, and the angel obliged. Zachary was struck dumb until John's birth. When the baby was born, the old man cuddled him and celebrated with this prophetic song:

> Blessed be the Lord, the God of Israel,
> for he has visited his people, he has set them free;
> and he has established for us a saving power
> in the House of his servant David,
> just as he proclaimed,
> by the mouth of the holy prophets from ancient times,
> that he would save us from our enemies
> and from the hands of all those who hate us,
> and show faithful love to our ancestors,
> and so keep in mind his holy covenant.
> This was the oath he swore
> to our father Abraham,
> that he would grant us, free from fear,
> to be delivered from the hands of our enemies,
> to serve him in holiness and uprightness
> in his presence, all our days.
> And you, little child,
> you shall be called Prophet of the Most High,
> for you will go before the Lord
> to prepare a way for him,
> to give his people knowledge of salvation
> through the forgiveness of their sins,
> because of the faithful love of our God
> in which the rising Sun has come from on high to visit us
> to give light to those who live in darkness and the shadow dark as death,
> and to guide our feet
> into the way of peace.

—Luke 1:68–79 *NJB*

St. John began his ministry about three decades later. He called people to repent and baptized them in water as a sign of purification. Jesus himself approached John for baptism "Behold the lamb of God," John declared to the crowds, "who takes away the sin of the world." He resisted baptizing Jesus, but acquiesced when Jesus explained that he wanted to set an example of righteous behavior.

Herod Antipas, the ruler of Galilee, arrested John because he feared the Baptist might foment a rebellion. John had also embittered Herod by condemning his marriage to Herodias, his half-brother's wife. While in prison, John was bothered with doubt about Jesus. He had expected the messiah to come more forcefully with a "winnowing fan in his hand to clear the threshing floor." Thus, he sent his disciples to ask Jesus if he was really the messiah.

Jesus responded that he fulfilled all the messianic signs, healing the blind, the deaf, the lame, and lepers, raising the dead, and preaching good news to the poor. Then Jesus praised John to the crowds as "more than a prophet" and as the greatest man who ever lived.

One evening Herod threw a party for Galilee's upper crust. Herodias's daughter entertained, dancing so beautifully that Herod offered to reward her with anything she desired. Her mother told her to ask for John the Baptist's head on a platter. Herod kept his promise. Without even a pretense of a trial, he gave the order and a soldier beheaded John at the prison.

John the Baptist expected people to act on their repentance by changing their behavior. "Produce good fruits as evidence of your repentance," he said (Luke 3:8 NAB*). He told all to clothe and feed the poor, tax collectors to stop cheating, soldiers to stop making false accusations. I know exactly what he might say to me. What do you think he might prescribe for you?*

JUNE 24 AND AUGUST 29, THE PASSION OF ST. JOHN THE BAPTIST
Doubt; Prophets; Repentance

5. Andrew

(First Century)

St. John's gospel (1:35–42) reported that one day Andrew heard **John the Baptist,** his master, designate Jesus as "the Lamb of God." Fascinated and curious, he and another of the Baptist's disciples caught up with Jesus and visited with him the entire day. The next morning Andrew announced to Simon, his brother, that he had found the messiah. Then he presented Simon to Christ, who renamed him **Peter. St. Mark** (1:16–20) gave a different account of Andrew's call. He says Jesus encountered Peter and Andrew fishing beside the Sea of Galilee. "Come after me," Jesus said, "and I will make you into fishers of people" (v. 17, *NJB*). Abruptly, the brothers abandoned all and took off after him.

However it happened, Jesus made Andrew one of his first disciples. Later he chose Andrew as one of the Twelve whom he prepared especially to carry on his work. Andrew appears to have emerged as a leader among them. Twice in the gospels we see him directly involved in Christ's ministry. He pointed out the lad with five loaves and two fishes at the feeding of the five thousand (see John 6:8–10). And at Jerusalem, Andrew presented to Jesus the Greeks who had asked to see him (see John 12:20–22).

Early sources, frequently judged as unreliable, disagree about St. Andrew's Christian work. However, **Gregory Nazianzen** and **Jerome** favor the view that he went to cities in Greece. A medieval legend that Andrew founded the see of Constantinople became popular in the East in an effort to counterbalance Rome's apostolic origins. A dubious tale that Andrew preached in Kiev justifies Russia's claiming him as patron. And Scotland regards Andrew as its patron because St. Rule supposedly transported his relics to the spot now called by his name.

An apocryphal account of Andrew's death says that sometime around AD 60 he was crucified at Patras in Achaia. Bound to an X-shaped cross, the apostle reportedly proclaimed the gospel from it for two days before he finally died.

Andrew's yes to Jesus' call has always inspired preachers. Here **St. Gregory the Great** stirs us from our apathy:

Dearest brethren, you have heard that at a single command Peter and Andrew, leaving their nets, followed the Redeemer. Up to that time they had not seen him perform any miracles. They had heard nothing from him concerning a reward of eternal joy, and still, at a single bidding of our Lord, they forgot about that which they seemed to possess. What great miracles have we seen, with how many scourges are we afflicted, by what great anxieties of threatening things are we disheartened, and yet we scorn him who calls us to follow!

He who counsels us in our manner of life already sits enthroned in heaven; . . . already, with the world's disasters increasing more and more, does he announce the approaching day of his severe judgment. And yet our proud mind still does not wish to abandon freely that which it is daily losing unwillingly.

. . . But perhaps someone will say in his silent thoughts: "What or how much did either of these fishermen, who possessed almost nothing, forfeit at the call of the Lord?"

In this matter . . . we must consider the disposition rather than the personal wealth. He forsakes much who keeps nothing for himself. He forsakes much who gives up every little thing, his all. But we, on the other hand, hold with love the things we have, and even out of desire seek those things which we do not have. Therefore, Peter and Andrew forsook much when both forfeited even their desire to possess.

NOVEMBER 30 / PATRON OF FISHERS, GREECE, RUSSIA, AND SCOTLAND
The Cost of Discipleship; Vocation

6. Peter

(D. 64?)

The New Testament leaves no doubt that St. Peter was preeminent among the Twelve. Upon meeting him, Jesus gave him the name of Cephas that means "rock." Later Christ unpacked the meaning of the name when he told Peter that he was the rock upon which he would build his church.

Peter heads every New Testament list of apostles. Jesus included him in the select group that witnessed the Transfiguration, the raising of Jairus's daughter, and the agony in the garden. After the resurrection, Peter led the early church. He guided the church in choosing a successor for Judas, preached at Pentecost, worked the first miracle, defended the apostles before the Sanhedrin, and condemned Ananias and Sapphira. Most significantly, he decided it was the divine will to welcome gentiles into the Christian community.

Thankfully, Scripture does not lionize Peter as a superhero, but portrays his weaknesses. Jesus had to rebuke Peter's attempt to dissuade him from the cross. We also see Christ rescuing him when he tried to walk on water and forgiving him for his threefold betrayal.

One of the last times we meet Peter in the Bible is Luke's account of his escape from prison. Herod had beheaded James, and had arrested Peter:

> On the night before Herod was to try him, Peter was sleeping between two soldiers, fastened with two chains, while guards kept watch at the main entrance to the prison. Then suddenly an angel of the Lord stood there, and the cell was filled with light. He tapped Peter on the side and woke him. "Get up!" he said, "Hurry!"—and the chains fell from his hands. The angel then said, "Put on your belt and sandals." After he had done this, the angel next said, "Wrap your cloak round you and follow me." He followed him out, but had no idea that what the angel did was all happening in reality; he thought he was seeing a vision. They passed through the first guard post and then the second and reached the iron gate leading to the city. This opened of its own accord; they went through it and had walked the whole length of one street when suddenly the angel left him (Acts 12:6–10 *NJB*).

Then Peter went to a house where members of the community had assembled to pray.

> He knocked at the outside door and a servant called Rhoda came to answer it. She recognized Peter's voice and was so overcome with joy that, instead of opening the door, she ran inside with the news that Peter was standing at the main entrance. They said to her, "You are out of your mind," but she insisted that it was true. Then they said, "It must be his angel!" Peter, meanwhile, was still knocking. When they opened the door, they were amazed to see that it really was Peter himself. He raised his hand for silence and described to them how the Lord had led him out of prison. He added, "Tell James and the brothers." Then he left and went elsewhere (Acts 12:13–17 *NJB*).

Tradition has it that "elsewhere" meant Antioch, where Origen says he founded the Christian community, and ultimately Rome, where he was crucified during the persecution of Nero, around AD 64.

> *The end of all things is near, so keep your minds calm and sober for prayer. Above all preserve an intense love for each other, since love covers over many a sin.*
>
> —1 Peter 4:7–8 *NJB*

JUNE 29 / PATRON OF THE FISHING INDUSTRY
Angels; Miracles Do Happen; Spiritual Warfare

7. James the Great
(D. 44)

Before Jesus called him as one of the Twelve, St. James worked with his brother **St. John** as a fisherman. The hard manual labor of rowing against the wind and hauling fish gave him both a rugged body and a rugged disposition. Jesus recognized James' roughness when he nicknamed him and his brother "Boanerges," the "Sons of Thunder" (Mark 3:17). Once when a Samaritan town rejected Jesus and his followers, James hotly desired to call down fire to destroy it, and Jesus had to rebuke him (Luke 9:52–55).

But flaws and all, Jesus made James a leader among the Twelve. Jesus included him in his inner circle along with **St. Peter** and St. John. James accompanied him when he raised a girl from the dead (Mark 5:37), when he was transfigured on Mount Tabor (Mark 9:2), and when he suffered his agony at Gethsemane (Mark 14:33). That's why we call him "the Great."

Shortly before the crucifixion, James and his brother boldly asked Jesus for places of honor in his kingdom (Mark 10:35–38). Reflecting on the event, **St. John Chrysostom** cautioned us not to be surprised at their perverse inclination as they had not yet received the grace of the Holy Spirit. Chrysostom then showed how Jesus seized the opportunity and gently prepared the Sons of Thunder for their transformation and deaths:

> I conjecture that they had heard that the disciples were to be seated on twelve thrones and they wished to ask for the place of honor in this assembly. They knew that at other times they were given precedence over the rest, but fearing that Peter might be put before them, they were bold enough to request, "Allow us to sit one at your right hand and the other on your left" (Mark 10:37 *NJB*). . . . And what did he say? That he might show that they sought nothing spiritual, and did not even know what they were asking—for had they known they would not have asked it—Jesus said to them, "You know not what you ask. You don't know how great, how admirable a thing this is! . . ."
>
> And he added further: "Can you drink the cup that I shall drink, or be baptized with the baptism with which I shall be baptized?" (Mark 10:38 *NJB*). Notice how he moves them from their present state of mind by bringing to their attention things entirely contrary. "For," he says, "you ask me for crowns and honors, but I speak to you of struggle

> and perspiration. This is not a time for rewards, nor will my glory appear at this time, but the present is the time of death and dangers." But observe how by his very manner of questioning he exhorts and consoles. He did not say, "Can you undergo suffering? Can you shed your blood?" But he said, "Can you drink the cup?" Then by way of consolation he adds, "that I shall drink." So that by their very union with him they might become more eager for hardships.

James said that he was ready to drink the cup, and Jesus promised him a share in his chalice of suffering and in his baptism in blood (Mark 10:39). Around AD 44, Jesus' prophetic words about James were fulfilled. Out to kill certain leaders of the Christian community, King Herod Agrippa chose James as his first victim and had him beheaded (Acts 12:2).

Perhaps Herod regarded James as dangerous because as a transformed Son of Thunder he preached powerfully and radiated a strength that attracted people to the church. May our transformation in Christ also make us dangerous.

JULY 25 / PATRON OF PILGRIMS
Martyrs

8. John
(First Century)

St. John, along with **St. James the Great**, his brother, and **St. Peter**, was part of Jesus' inner circle, disciples to whom he gave special attention and privileges. Jesus wanted John with him at significant moments. He invited John, for example, to be with him for the raising of Jairus's daughter and for his Transfiguration. And as Christ approached his passion, he sent John along with Peter to arrange for his final Passover and allowed him to witness his agony in the garden. Perhaps John's sense of being favored had prompted his presumptuous request for a place of honor next to Jesus in his kingdom (Mark 10:36).

Traditionally, Christian writers have identified John as the Beloved Disciple, who leaned on the Lord's breast at the Last Supper; stood by him at the foot of the cross; accepted responsibility to care for his mother; and was the first apostle to arrive at the tomb, realize what had happened, and believe in the resurrection. But Catholic Scripture scholars now say that the Beloved Disciple is an anonymous follower of Christ, left unidentified so that we could identify with him. I think John would like to see us placing ourselves as beloved disciples near the Lord during his passion, death and resurrection.

After the Lord's resurrection and the outpouring of the Spirit at Pentecost, John played a significant role in the early Christian community. For instance:

> Once when Peter and John were going up to the Temple for the prayers at the ninth hour, it happened that there was a man being carried along. He was a cripple from birth; and they used to put him down every day near the Temple entrance called the Beautiful Gate so that he could beg from the people going in. When this man saw Peter and John on their way into the Temple he begged from them. Peter, and John too, looked straight at him and said, "Look at us." He turned to them expectantly, hoping to get something from them, but Peter said, "I have neither silver nor gold, but I will give you what I have: in the name of Jesus Christ, the Nazarene, walk!" Then he took him by the right hand and helped him to stand up. Instantly his feet and ankles became firm, he jumped up, stood, and began to walk, and went with them into the Temple, walking and jumping and praising God. Everyone could see him walking and praising God, and they recognized him as the man

> who used to sit begging at the Beautiful Gate of the Temple. They were all astonished and perplexed at what had happened to him (Acts of the Apostles, 3:1–10 *NJB*).

From ancient times, Christian leaders have regarded St. John as the author of a gospel, three letters, and the book of Revelation. But some scholars now assert that the gospel and letters were probably written by someone informed by the witness of the Beloved Disciple. And they also say that another person named John wrote Revelation. This questioning of the authorship of St. John does not question the authority of these books and their inspiration by the Holy Spirit.

St. Irenaeus received a tradition from **St. Polycarp** that John lived at Ephesus until the time of the Emperor Trajan at the turn of the second century and that he died peacefully around the year 100.

When St. John was too feeble to preach, he used to be carried into the assembly at Ephesus where he always said the same thing: "My little children, love one another. When asked why, he said: "Because it is the word of the Lord and if you keep it you do enough."

DECEMBER 27
Mere Christian Love; Miracles Do Happen

9. Mary Magdalen

(First Century)

St. Mary Magdalen was a member of the community that traveled with Jesus. She had suffered with serious problems, which he cured by casting seven demons from her. After her healing, Mary Magdalen became an eminent disciple, one of his intimate companions alongside the Twelve. With other women, she took care of the Lord's practical needs on the road (see Luke 8:1–3).

We may customarily identify Mary Magdalen with the woman who washed Jesus' feet with her tears (Luke 7:39) and with the woman who anointed his head with expensive ointment (Matthew 26:6–8; Mark 14:3). And we may believe that she is Mary of Bethany, the sister of Lazarus. We may envision her sitting before Jesus as the first contemplative (Luke 10:39–42). We may also see her just before Christ's death, anointing his feet and wiping them with her hair, a preparation for his burial (John 11:2; 12:3). While these beliefs have ancient roots, today scholars say that the Bible does not support the identification of all these women with Mary Magdalen.

However, this interpretation need not diminish the saint's significance nor our admiration for her. Mary Magdalen was faithful to Christ to the end. She stood courageously beneath the cross (John 19:25) and lurked near the sepulchre (Matthew 26:61) to be sure she knew where he had been buried. With other women she prepared spices and ointments to anoint the Lord's body. She was the first to discover the empty tomb (Luke 23:55–24:11). And, appropriately, Jesus, risen from the dead, appeared first to her:

> But Mary was standing outside near the tomb, weeping. Then, as she wept, she stooped to look inside, and saw two angels in white sitting where the body of Jesus had been, one at the head, the other at the feet. They said, "Woman, why are you weeping?" "They have taken my Lord away," she replied, "and I don't know where they have put him." As she said this she turned round and saw Jesus standing there, though she did not realize that it was Jesus. Jesus said to her, "Woman, why are you weeping? Who are you looking for?" Supposing him to be the gardener, she said, "Sir, if you have taken him away, tell me where you have put him, and I will go and remove him." Jesus said, "Mary!" She turned round then and said to him in Hebrew, "Rabbuni!" —which

> means Master. Jesus said to her, "Do not cling to me, because I have not yet ascended to the Father. But go and find my brothers, and tell them: I am ascending to my Father and your Father, to my God and your God." So Mary of Magdala told the disciples, "I have seen the Lord," and that he had said these things to her (John 20:11–18 *NJB*).

We may know less about Mary Magdalen than we thought. However, what we do know is enough for us to honor her and to love her.

St. Mary Magdalen,
You come with springing tears
To the spring of mercy, Christ. . . .
What can I say, how can I find words to tell
About the burning love with which you sought Him
Weeping at the sepulchre
And wept for Him in your seeking? . . .
For the sweetness of love He shows Himself
Who would not for the bitterness of tears.

—Anselm of Canterbury

JULY 22 / PATRON OF REPENTANT PROSTITUTES AND HAIRDRESSERS
Courage; Intimacy with the Divine; Valiant Women

10. James the Just

(First Century)

Among first-century Jewish families, "James" was a very popular name. This has contributed to longstanding confusion about men named James in the New Testament. Here are the facts. When Jesus called his apostles, he chose James the son of Zebedee and James the son of Alphaeus (Matthew 10:2–3). Zebedee's son is now known as **James the Great.** There are four passing references in the gospels to a James whose mother is named Mary; Mark refers to him as James the younger or "the less" (Mark 15:40). Then there is the James that Scripture says was a "brother" of Jesus (Matthew 13:55). Christian writers have nicknamed him James the Just. And the author of a New Testament letter identifies himself as "James, a servant of God and of the Lord Jesus Christ" (James 1:1 *NJB*).

While James the Great has maintained his separate identity, early Christian writers lumped the other four into one James. But scholars now contend that James the son of Alphaeus, James the younger, and James the brother of Jesus were distinct individuals. They also assert from internal evidence in the letter of James that it is improbable that any of the three was the author of this letter. Once they are separated, we know next to nothing about all of them except for James the Just.

Catholics hold to the perpetual virginity of **Mary**, so we do not regard James the Just as the natural brother of Jesus. Following **St. Jerome**, some believe that James was Jesus' cousin, because the Hebrew and Aramaic words for "brother" could also mean "cousin." Others suggest that James was a son of **Joseph** from a previous marriage. Very likely, Mary and Joseph raised James and Jesus together as "brothers."

We bump into James the brother of the Lord several times in the New Testament. **Paul** mentions him in his letters to the communities at Galatia and Corinth. He says that he met James twice in Jerusalem. He also mentions him at Antioch when he confronted **Peter** about his refusing to dine with gentiles (Galatians 1:18, 2:9 and 12). Paul hints that James was married (1 Corinthians 9:5) and says that the risen Jesus appeared to him (1 Corinthians 15:7). Some spiritual writers speculate that shortly before his ascension, the Lord visited James to affirm his leadership in the early church.

We meet James in the Acts of the Apostles as the leader who governed the Christian community at Jerusalem. In AD 49, the apostles convened a council there to consider whether gentile converts had to become Jews. James presided over that important meeting and rendered its final judgment. Both Paul and Peter addressed the issue, and the apostles and elders engaged in a full discussion.

> When they had finished it was James who spoke. "My brothers," he said, "listen to me. Simeon has described how God first arranged to enlist a people for his name out of the gentiles. This is entirely in harmony with the words of the prophets, since the scriptures say:
>
> After that I shall return
> and rebuild the fallen hut of David;
> I shall make good the gaps in it
> and restore it.
> Then the rest of humanity,
> and of all the nations once called mine,
> will look for the Lord,
> *says the Lord who made this* known so long ago.
>
> My verdict is then, that instead of making things more difficult for gentiles who turn to God, we should send them a letter telling them merely to abstain from anything polluted by idols, from illicit marriages, from the meat of strangled animals and from blood" (Acts 15:13–20 *NJB*).

Eusebius, a fourth-century bishop, writes in his *History of the Church* that in AD 62, scribes and Pharisees martyred James for proclaiming Jesus, throwing him down from a parapet of the Temple and stoning him before beating him to death with a fuller's club.

> *Blessed is anyone who perseveres when trials come. Such a person is of proven worth and will win the prize of life, the crown that the Lord has promised to those who love him.*
>
> —James 1:12 *NJB*

MAY 3
Christian Unity; Mercy

11. Thomas

(First Century)

We feel great kinship for the apostle Thomas because, like him, most of us curiously combine faith and doubt. We sometimes share the enthusiasm St. Thomas expressed when upon Lazarus's death Jesus decided to go to Bethany. "Let's go too," Thomas said to the other disciples, "that we may die with him" (see John 11:16). But also like him we sometimes wonder where Jesus is headed and where he is taking us (see John 14:5).

However, we are most like Thomas because doubts occasionally rattle our brains and cloud our souls. So we all relate to the story of doubting Thomas (see John 20:25–29). Thomas was absent the first time Jesus appeared after his resurrection. The apostle swore he would not believe, "Unless I see in his hands the print of the nails, and place my finger in the mark of the nails and place my hand in his side" (v. 25 *RSV*). Eight days later Jesus appeared again and told Thomas to touch his wounds. "My Lord, and my God," Thomas exclaimed, recovering his faith (v. 28).

Some early Christian writers criticized Thomas's faithless behavior. But others praised him for helping us cure our doubts, as **Gregory the Great** does in this homily:

> . . . The divine goodness acted so that the doubting disciple, when he had touched the wounds of the flesh in his Master, might heal the wounds of infidelity in us.
>
> For the faithlessness of Thomas aids us in our belief more than does the faith of the disciples who believed. . . . When he is brought to believe by feeling with his own hand, every doubt having been removed, our own mind is confirmed in faith. Thus the Lord permits his disciple to doubt after his Resurrection, but he does not forsake him. . . . Just as before his birth he wished that Mary should have a spouse who did not come to wed her. For the disciple who doubted and touched was made a witness of the truth of the Resurrection, just as the spouse of his mother had been the guardian of her unspotted virginity. . . .
>
> The divinity cannot be seen by any mortal man. So Thomas saw man and confessed him to be God, saying, "My Lord, and my God." On seeing, then, he believed, and proclaimed him to be God whom he could not see. Then Jesus spoke these words that give us much joy: "Blessed are they who have not seen and yet have believed" (see

John 20:29). This sentence undoubtedly signifies to us who hold in our minds him whom we have not seen in the flesh. But we are signified only if we follow up our faith by works. For he really believes who carries out in deed what he believes.

We do not know for sure where Thomas conducted his missionary activity after Pentecost. Some claim he evangelized among the Parthians. But a stronger tradition says he carried the gospel to India. He is supposed to have recruited the Christians of Malabar and died a martyr by the spear at Mylapore, near Madras. An ancient stone cross there marks the place where his remains lay buried until they were removed to Edessa in 394.

Doubt is nothing but a trivial agitation on the surface of the soul, while deep down there is a calm certainty.

—François Mauriac

JULY 3 / PATRON OF ARCHITECTS AND THE EAST INDIES
Doubt

12. Matthew

(First Century)

Matthew, a Galilean Jew, worked as a publican, or tax collector, in Capernaum. One day Jesus stopped by his office and simply said, "Follow me." As St. Matthew himself tells it, he got up right away and followed him (Matthew 9:9). Jesus had lived for a time in Capernaum, so we might suppose that Matthew knew of him before his call. But no mere familiarity could explain the immediacy of his total response. Readers of the gospel sometimes doubt that Matthew actually responded right at that instant. Others regard such radical behavior as foolish. Listen to what **St. Jerome** said to critics of Matthew's decisiveness:

> Some commentators on the text about Matthew's abruptly following Jesus think the story is a lie. Others criticize the folly of those who immediately went after the Savior, as if they might have followed without reason any man at all who called to them.
>
> Certainly the splendor and the majesty of the hidden divinity that shone on his face could have drawn from the first glance those who looked at him. For if a magnet or an amber rod has such strength that they draw to themselves rings, straws, and splinters, how much more could the Lord of all creatures draw to himself those whom he called!

Right after Jesus called Matthew, we find him at a party in his new disciple's home, surrounded by other tax collectors and sinners. We cannot appreciate the shock and disgust of the Pharisees at this sight (Matthew 9:10–11), unless we realize why and how much Jews hated tax gatherers. Jews abhorred these officials because they cheated them and extorted money from them. So they excluded them from religious worship and shunned them at all civic and commercial affairs.

That's why Matthew insists on identifying himself as a publican. If God forgave him, he is saying, he will forgive anyone. Listen again to Jerome:

> The tax collectors and sinners who ate with Jesus saw that a publican had turned from his sins to better ways. They realized that he had found the way of penance. For that reason they also did not despair of salvation. They did not come to Jesus stuck in their former sins, but doing penance. As Jesus said, "I came not to call the righteous, but sinners"

> (See Matthew 9:13). The Lord attended the banquet of sinners so that he might teach and offer spiritual food to those who had invited him.

So one day Matthew collected taxes. The next, he served Christ as an apostle. After the resurrection, Matthew reportedly carried the gospel to Ethiopia, but no direct evidence supports this belief. On the testimony of Irenaeus and Papias, from early times the church has regarded Matthew as the author of the first gospel. Unsupported legends say that late in the first century Matthew died as a martyr either in Ethiopia or Persia.

> *The other Evangelists, out of respect for Matthew, did not call him by his common name, so they said Levi. But Matthew called himself Matthew and a publican, that he might show his readers that no one ought to despair of salvation if he is converted to better ways, since he himself suddenly changed from a publican to an apostle.*
>
> —Jerome

SEPTEMBER 21
Repentance; Saints and the Bible

13. Stephen

(First Century)

We encounter St. Stephen in the Acts of the Apostles as one of six young Hellenistic Jews chosen as deacons in Jerusalem. The Twelve assigned them to distribute alms in the Greek sector of the community. Stephen, however, described by **St. Luke** as full of faith and the Holy Spirit, did not stick to his job description. Armed with grace and power, he went about preaching the gospel and performing miracles and great signs. Thus he attracted the attention of all Jerusalem.

A party of foreign-born Jews engaged Stephen in debates about his beliefs. When he continually bested them, they jealously accused him of blasphemy before the Sanhedrin. Charged with elevating Jesus over Moses and denigrating the Temple, Stephen responded eloquently. Yes, he declared in effect, Moses and the other prophets subordinated themselves to Jesus when they pointed to his coming. Yes, he also said, the Temple was not God's exclusive dwelling place. He concluded his bold speech with these forceful words:

> "[David] won God's favor and asked permission to find a dwelling for the House of Jacob, though it was Solomon who actually built a house for God. Even so the Most High does not live in a house that human hands have built: for as the prophet says:
>
> With heaven my throne
> and earth my footstool,
> what house could you build me, says the Lord,
> what place for me to rest,
> when all these things were made by me?
>
> "You stubborn people, with uncircumcised hearts and ears. You are always resisting the Holy Spirit, just as your ancestors used to do. Can you name a single prophet your ancestors never persecuted? They killed those who foretold the coming of the Upright One, and now you have become his betrayers, his murderers. In spite of being given the Law through the angels, you have not kept it" (Acts 7:46–53 *NJB*).

That was enough. Like Jesus, Stephen had signed his own death warrant:

> They were infuriated when they heard this, and ground their teeth at him. But Stephen, filled with the Holy Spirit, gazed into heaven and saw the glory of God, and Jesus standing at God's right hand: "Look! I can see heaven thrown open," he said, "and the Son of man standing at the right hand of God." All the members of the council shouted out and stopped their ears with their hands; then they made a concerted rush at him, thrust him out of the city and stoned him. The witnesses put down their clothes at the feet of a young man called Saul (Acts 7:54–59 *NJB*).

Stephen was the first disciple to die a martyr like Jesus, and in his narrative Luke emphasized the similarity of their executions. Like Jesus, opponents accused Stephen to the Sanhedrin, false witnesses charged him with blasphemy, and he was taken outside the city and martyred. His final words also imitated Jesus' last utterances (see Luke 24:36 and 47):

> As they were stoning him, Stephen said in invocation, "Lord Jesus, receive my Spirit." Then he knelt down and said aloud, "Lord, do not hold this sin against them." And with these words he fell asleep (Acts 7:60 *NJB*).

Thus Stephen became the prototypical Christian martyr, honored and emulated throughout the centuries.

When Stephen saw people pick up stones to kill him, he must have been deathly afraid. But he took courage when he envisioned Jesus looking on him from above. When we fear the worst, we can also take courage, if in our heart's eye we envision Jesus nearby and realize that he is supporting us.

DECEMBER 26 / PATRON OF DEACONS AND HEADACHES
Defending the Faith; Martyrs

14. Paul

(D. 65?)

St. Paul pursued his convictions enthusiastically. As a religious Jew, he strove to weed Christians from the community. We first meet him in the Acts of the Apostles assisting at the stoning of **Stephen** (Acts 7:59). On his way to persecute Christians at Damascus, however, Jesus appeared to him and redirected his life (Acts 9). From the time of that mystical encounter, Paul believed Christ had commissioned him as an apostle to the gentiles.

First with **Barnabas** at Antioch and then on three missionary journeys in Greece and Asia Minor, Paul brought many non-Jews into the church. In 49, at a meeting in Jerusalem, he and **Peter** persuaded the other apostles that gentile converts need not become Jews (Acts 15).

Paul planted the church throughout the eastern Mediterranean world. He spent himself tending his communities at a great personal cost:

> Five times I have been given the thirty-nine lashes by the Jews; three times I have been beaten with sticks; once I was stoned; three times I have been shipwrecked, and once I have been in the open sea for a night and a day; continually traveling, I have been in danger . . . ; I have worked with unsparing energy, for many nights without sleep; I have been hungry and thirsty, . . . And, besides all the external things, there is, day in day out, the pressure on me of my anxiety for all the churches. (2 Corinthians 11:24–28 *NJB*).

Thirteen of the twenty-seven books in the New Testament are attributed to Paul—letters he wrote to deal with specific concerns of his communities. Through these foundational documents, he has shaped Christian pastoral practice and theology through the centuries.

Enthusiast, apostle, mystic, pastor, teacher, theologian—Paul was all of these. But what made him a saint was his selfless spirit of service that he modeled on Christ:

> If there is any encouragement in Christ, any solace in love, any participation in the Spirit, any compassion and mercy, complete my joy by being of the same mind, with the same love, united in heart, thinking one thing. Do nothing out of selfishness or out of vainglory; rather,

humbly regard others as more important than yourselves, each looking out not for his own interests, but [also] everyone for those of others.

Have among yourselves the same attitude that is also yours in Christ Jesus,

Who, though he was in the form of God,
did not regard equality with God something to be grasped.
Rather he emptied himself,
taking the form of a slave,
coming in human likeness;
and found human in appearance,
he humbled himself,
becoming obedient to death, even death on a cross.
Because of this, God greatly exalted him
and bestowed on him the name
that is above every name,
that at the name of Jesus
every knee should bend,
of those in heaven and on earth and under the earth,
and every tongue confess that Jesus Christ is Lord,
to the glory of God the Father.

—Philippians 2:1–11 *NAB*

Paul died a martyr, probably by beheading, during the persecution by Nero, around AD 65.

Paul's prayer for the Philippians is also his prayer for us: May your love for one another "grow more and more with the knowledge and complete understanding that will help you to come to true discernment, so that you will be innocent and free of any trace of guilt when the Day of Christ comes. [And may you be] entirely filled with the fruits of uprightness through Jesus Christ, for the glory and praise of God" (Philippians 1:9–11 NJB*).*

JUNE 29 / PATRON OF THE LAY APOSTOLATE, THE CURSILLO, AND GREECE
Imitation of Christ; Missionaries; True Humility; World Historical Saints

15. Barnabas

(First Century)

There are two ways of doctrine and authority, one of light, and the other of darkness. But these two ways differ greatly. For over one are stationed the light-bringing angels of God, but the angels of Satan are over the other.

This, then, is the way of light: Love God who created you. Glorify God who redeemed you from death. Be simple in heart, and rich in spirit. Hate doing anything unpleasing to God. Do not exalt yourself, but be of a lowly mind. Do not forsake the commandments of the Lord. Love your neighbor more than your own soul. Do not slay the child by procuring an abortion, nor destroy it after it is born. Receive your trials as good things. Do not hesitate to give without complaint. Confess your sins. This is the way of light.

But the way of darkness is crooked and cursed, for it is the way of eternal death with punishment. In this way are the things that destroy the soul: idolatry, overconfidence, the arrogance of power, hypocrisy, double-heartedness, adultery, rape, haughtiness, transgressions, deceit, malice, avarice, and absence of any fear of God. Also in this way are those who persecute the good, those who hate truth, those who do not attend to the widow and orphan, those who do not pity the needy, those who murder children, those who oppress the afflicted and are in every respect transgressors.

—The Epistle of Barnabas

We know nothing about St. Barnabas except what Scripture tells us. Luke says he was "a good man, filled with the Holy Spirit and faith" (Acts 11:24 *NJB*). No one could ask for a better recommendation!

The saint was born at Cyprus, a Jew of the tribe of Levi. His given name was Joseph, but the apostles called him Barnabas, which meant "son of encouragement" (Acts 4:36 *NJB*). That nickname suited him to a tee, for everywhere he went he seems to have played a major supportive role in establishing the Christian community. While he was not one of the Twelve, the early church recognized him as an apostle.

Wherever Barnabas saw a need he tried to meet it. For example, he sold his property and donated the money to the apostles for the poor. And when **Paul** arrived in Jerusalem, Barnabas authorized him to the community, overcoming their fears of the former persecutor (Acts 9:26–27).

Later the apostles sent him to care for the fledgling church at Antioch (Acts 11:20–22). He brought Paul from Tarsus to help him, and the community flourished under their leadership (Acts 11:25–26). Twice Barnabas and Paul traveled to Jerusalem on behalf of the church at Antioch (Acts 11:27–30; 15:2). He also accompanied Paul on his first missionary journey that began in Cyprus and circuited through Asia Minor (Acts 13:1–2, 7).

Before the next missionary journey, however, Paul and Barnabas quarreled over some personal and pastoral matters and decided to separate. Barnabas returned to Cyprus and evangelized the island. Paul's later references to Barnabas in his letters indicate that the two apostles were ultimately reconciled (see 1 Corinthians 9:6; Colossians 4:10).

Early Christians attributed an epistle to Barnabas, but modern scholars say he probably did not write it. Legend also says he died at Salamis in 61.

Barnabas himself walked in the way of light. He did not exalt himself, but saw himself as a servant. He was not full of himself, nor was his head swollen with big plans. He just did what needed to be done—an excellent model of service for us all.

JUNE 11
Christian Living; Love in Action; Purpose

16. Mark

(First Century)

Some speculate that St. Mark slipped a self-portrait into his gospel. He is supposed to be the young man who followed Jesus after his arrest. Mark says that he was wearing nothing but a linen cloth, and when the mob grabbed him, he left them holding his cloak, and fled naked (see Mark 14:51). Perhaps Mark recounted this vignette to confess a fault he felt deeply. But like **Peter,** whom Mark later served as an associate and interpreter, he became a faithful and hardworking disciple.

We usually identify the saint with John Mark, the son of Mary, whose house in Jerusalem was a gathering place for the Twelve (Acts 12:12 and 25). **Barnabas**, his cousin, was a Levite from Cyprus, and we may guess that Mark shared his roots. When **Paul** and Barnabas returned to Antioch from Jerusalem, they took Mark with them. And he joined them on their missionary journey to Cyprus.

Paul, however, lost confidence in Mark because he left the team and returned to Jerusalem. He opposed Barnabas's desire to take Mark on the next mission, and thus he became the issue that divided Barnabas and Paul. However, Paul later changed his mind about Mark, who had helped him during his first imprisonment (Colossians 4:10). Just before his martyrdom, Paul urged **Timothy** to "get Mark and bring him with you, for he is helpful to me in the ministry" (2 Timothy 4:11 *NAB*).

Mark may have written his gospel at Rome shortly before AD 70. He addressed a Gentile community to prepare them for an impending persecution (see Mark 13:9–13). His account of the Jesus story, the shortest of the four gospels, is simple and direct, and charged with reality. Consider, for example, his stark report of the resurrection (Mark 16:1–8 *NAB*):

> When the sabbath was over, Mary Magdalene, Mary, the mother of James, and Salome bought spices so that they might go and anoint him. Very early when the sun had risen, on the first day of the week, they came to the tomb. They were saying to one another, "Who will roll back the stone for us from the entrance to the tomb?" When they looked up, they saw that the stone had been rolled back; it was very large. On entering the tomb they saw a young man sitting on the right side, clothed in a white robe, and they were utterly amazed. He said to

> side, clothed in a white robe, and they were utterly amazed. He said to them, "Do not be amazed! You seek Jesus of Nazareth, the crucified. He has been raised; he is not here. Behold the place where they laid him. But go and tell his disciples and Peter. 'He is going before you to Galilee; there you will see him, as he told you.'" Then they went out and fled from the tomb, seized with trembling and bewilderment. They said nothing to anyone, for they were afraid.

Tradition says that Mark ended his life in Egypt, serving as bishop of Alexandria. Historians dispute the legend that he died a martyr there because they judge the documents reporting it as unreliable.

> *Jesus] summoned the crowd with his disciples and said to them: "Whoever wishes to come after me must deny himself, take up his cross and follow me. For whoever wishes to save his life, will lose it, but whoever loses his life for my sake and that of the gospel will save it. What profit is there for one to gain the whole world and forfeit his life? What could one give in exchange for his life?"*
>
> —Mark 8:34–35 *NAB*

APRIL 25
Saints and the Bible

17. Luke

(First Century)

We have only a few certain facts about St. Luke's life. We know him best as the author of the third gospel and of the Acts of the Apostles. A Greek himself, he wrote the story of Jesus and the Christian community for Gentile readers. He also accompanied **St. Paul** on some of his journeys and shared in his sufferings. Probably a physician, Luke may have pioneered as an early member of the church at Antioch. Highly improbable are the speculations that Jesus sent him out as one of the seventy-two disciples and that he was one who met Jesus on the road to Emmaus.

The saint's books reveal something about his character. Luke wrote excellent popular prose with an artist's skill at painting picture stories. Demonstrating an unusual commitment to accuracy, he appears to have fastidiously checked his facts. For example, archaeologists have confirmed many details that he reported in the Acts.

Some of Luke's main themes—prayer, the Holy Spirit, and mercy—suggest that he was a compassionate, spiritual man. For example, he seems to report Jesus' teaching on prayer and the Spirit with the confidence of one who spoke from personal experience:

> What father among you, if his son asked for a fish, would hand him a snake? Or if he asked for an egg, hand him a scorpion? If you then, evil as you are, know how to give your children what is good, how much more will the heavenly Father give the Holy Spirit to those who ask him (Luke 11:11–13 *NJB*).

Luke aimed in his books to persuade Gentiles that the Christian story was true. So he made it more accessible to them by filling his gospel with accounts of Christ's openness and mercy, like this one:

> He entered Jericho and was going through the town and suddenly a man whose name was Zacchaeus made his appearance; he was one of the senior tax collectors and a wealthy man. He kept trying to see which one was Jesus, but he was too short and could not see him for the crowd; so he ran ahead and climbed a sycamore tree to catch a glimpse of Jesus who was to pass that way. When Jesus reached the spot he looked up and spoke to him. "Zacchaeus, come down, Hurry, because I am to stay at your house today." And he hurried down and

> welcomed him joyfully. They all complained when they saw what was happening. "He has gone to stay at a sinner's house," they said. But Zacchaeus stood his ground and said to the Lord, "Look, sir, I am going to give half my property to the poor, and if I have cheated anybody I will pay him back four times the amount." And Jesus said to him. "Today salvation has come to this house, because this man too is a son of Abraham; for the Son of man has come to seek out and save what was lost" (Luke 19:1–10 *NJB*)

Tradition says Luke lived a long life without marrying and that he died at age eighty-four. But these assertions appeared centuries after his death and are not facts that we can check.

When we tell our stories we would do well to imitate Luke. In his prologue he says he wanted to give an ordered account of the Jesus story so that the reader can rely on what he has heard. Luke let the Holy Spirit speak through simple, unembroidered facts, a model for us who want to share God's mercy with family and friends.

OCTOBER 18
Mercy; Prayer; Saints and the Bible

18. Timothy

(D. 97)

St. Timothy grew up in the Christian community at Lystra in Laconia in present-day Turkey. Lois, his grandmother, and Eunice, his mother and a Jewish believer, formed him in the faith. They introduced him to the Hebrew Scriptures, which he studied from his youth. When **St. Paul** visited Lystra he recognized Timothy's gifts and made him his disciple. Paul circumcised Timothy in order to make him acceptable to Jewish Christians. Paul also did so because he wanted to demonstrate his respect for the law. From the first, Timothy was Paul's favorite son, one that he loved dearly and trusted unreservedly.

Timothy sometimes accompanied Paul on his travels as he did in Macedonia and Greece. And Paul sent him as his agent to offer support to the churches in places like Corinth, Thessalonica, and Ephesus.

Paul wrote two letters to Timothy that have found their way into the New Testament. He sent the second one from his prison in Rome as a tender and heartfelt encouragement to his beloved disciple. Thus he exhorts Timothy to persevere:

> As for you, my dear son, take strength from the grace which is in Christ Jesus. Pass on to reliable people what you have heard from me through many witnesses so that they in turn will be able to teach others.
>
> Bear with your share of difficulties, like a good soldier of Christ Jesus. No one on active service involves himself in the affairs of civilian life, because he must win the approval of the man who enlisted him; or again someone who enters an athletic contest wins only by competing in the sports—a prize can be won only by competing according to the rules; and again, it is the farmer who works hard that has the first claim on any crop that is harvested. Think over what I have said, and the Lord will give you full understanding.
>
> Remember the gospel that I carry, "Jesus Christ risen from the dead, sprung from the race of David"; it is on account of this that I have to put up with suffering, even to being chained like a criminal. But God's message cannot be chained up. So I persevere for the sake of those who are chosen, so that they, too, may obtain the salvation that is in Christ Jesus with eternal glory.
>
> Here is a saying that you can rely on:

If we have died with him, then we shall live with him.
If we persevere, then we shall reign with him.
If we disown him, then he will disown us.
If we are faithless, he is faithful still,
  for he cannot disown his own self.

—2 Timothy 2:1–13 *NJB*

Paul sent Timothy to Ephesus to correct false teaching and to establish good order in the community by appointing qualified men as elders and deacons.

The Acts of Timothy, a book probably written at Ephesus in the fourth or fifth century, claims that he was martyred in 97 while opposing a pagan festival. Marchers, each carrying both idols and clubs, used their handy weapons to pummel him to death.

I am reminding you now to fan into a flame the gift of God that you possess through the laying on of my hands. God did not give us a spirit of timidity, but a Spirit of power and love and self-control (2 Timothy 1:6–7 NJB*). Evidently, Timothy, like the rest of us, occasionally got cold feet and needed encouragement to fire him up.*

JANUARY 26, WITH ST. TITUS
Missionaries; Perseverance

19. Titus
(First Century)

St. Paul spoke with great affection and respect for St. Titus. He addressed him as "true child of mine in the faith that we share," suggesting that he had personally recruited Titus for Christ (see Titus 1:14). Paul told the Corinthians that at Troas he had no relief from anxiety because he had not found his "brother" Titus there. Paul also commended him as "my own partner and fellow-worker."

So Titus became one of Paul's most trusted colleagues, serving as his secretary, traveling companion, and ambassador. He accompanied Paul at the Council of Jerusalem that decided not to require circumcision of Jewish converts. To strengthen his case that gentile Christians need not become Jews first, Paul had refused to circumcise Titus, who was Greek.

When Paul discovered the sex scandal and subsequent dissension at Corinth, he sent Titus to deal with the situation. Apparently a gifted pastoral leader, he successfully brought the community through its ordeal. Afterwards Paul told the Corinthians of Titus's affection for them that was "all the stronger when he remembers how obedient you have all been, and how you welcomed him with fear and trembling" (2 Corinthians 7:15 *NJB*). Later he sent Titus back to Corinth to organize the collection in support of the Jerusalem community.

Paul sent Titus on mission to Crete, assigning him to consolidate the church there by appointing elders in every town. Paul had low regard for Cretans and accepted a popular view that generally they were "liars, dangerous animals, all greed and laziness" (Titus 1:12 *NJB*). So he gave Titus explicit instructions to take a firm stance with Cretan believers:

> Remind them to be obedient to the officials in authority; to be ready to do good at every opportunity; not to go slandering other people but to be peaceable and gentle, and always polite to people of all kinds. There was a time when we too were ignorant, disobedient and misled and enslaved by different passions and dissipations; we lived then in wickedness and malice, hating each other and hateful ourselves.
>
> But when the kindness and love of God our Savior for humanity were revealed, it was not because of any upright actions we had done

us, by means of the cleansing water of rebirth and renewal in the Holy Spirit which he has so generously poured over us through Jesus Christ our Savior; so that, justified by his grace, we should become heirs in hope of eternal life. This is doctrine that you can rely on.

I want you to be quite uncompromising in teaching all this, so that those who now believe in God may keep their minds constantly occupied in doing good works. All this is good, and useful for everybody. But avoid foolish speculations, and those genealogies, and the quibbles and disputes about the Law—they are useless and futile. If someone disputes what you teach, then after a first and a second warning, have no more to do with him: you will know that anyone of that sort is warped and is self-condemned as a sinner (Titus 3:1–11 *NJB*).

After many years of service-leadership, Titus died peacefully in Crete.

Paul depicted Titus in his specifications for the character of an elder: "a man of irreproachable character, . . . never arrogant or hot tempered, nor a heavy drinker or violent, nor avaricious; but hospitable and a lover of goodness; sensible, upright, devout and self-controlled; and he must have a firm grasp of the unchanging message of the tradition" (Titus 1:6–9 NJB*).*

JANUARY 26, WITH ST. TIMOTHY
Great Pastors

20. Clement I

(D. 100?)

We know only a little for sure about St. Clement. He wrote an important letter to the Corinthian church to calm dissension. Clement probably associated directly with the apostles. **St. Irenaeus** placed him with the apostles as a student of their teachings, and Origen called him "a disciple of the apostles." And Clement was possibly the coworker **St. Paul** mentioned to the Philippians (Philippians 4:3).

Other things alleged about Clement seem much less certain. An unreliable account identifies him as a Clement, cousin to Emperor Domitian, who was executed in the (AD) mid 90s. Another tradition, probably untrue, claimed that Clement died a martyr. A colorful fourth-century legend, however, has Clement exiled to the Crimea, where he was thrown into the sea with an anchor about his neck. The story said angels made him a bed in the sea that a low tide revealed annually. **Sts. Cyril and Methodius** claimed to have recovered his relics and the anchor. These were deposited at the San Clemente Church in Rome, which stood on the house of a man named Clement, perhaps this saint.

The early church held Clement's letter to the Corinthians in high regard. Sometimes communities included it with Scripture and read it during the liturgy. We don't know details about the disruption in Corinth that caused Clement to intervene. But his letter urges the Corinthian Christians humbly to repair the breach, to restore their submission to authority, and to care for one another again. He makes this eloquent appeal to the unitive power of love:

> Let him that has love in Christ keep Christ's commandments. Who can describe the bond of the love of God? . . . The height to which love raises us is unutterable. Love binds us to God. Love covers a multitude of sins. Love bears all things, is long suffering in all things. There is nothing vulgar in love, nothing overbearing. Love knows no schism, love is not seditious, love does all things in concord. By love all the elect of God were perfected. Without love nothing is pleasing to God. In love the Lord received us. Because of the love he had toward us, Jesus Christ Our Lord gave his blood for us by the will of God, and his flesh for our flesh, and his life for our lives.

> You see, beloved, how great and marvelous a thing love is. Of its perfection there is no telling. Who is able to be found in it except those whom God has counted worthy? Let us pray, therefore, and desire his mercy, that we may be found in love, spotless, without human partisanship. . . . Blessed are we, brethren, if we perform the commandments of God in the concord of love, that our sins may be forgiven through love. For it is written: "Blessed are those whose iniquities are forgiven and whose sins are covered. . . ." This blessedness came to those who were chosen by God through Jesus Christ Our Lord, to whom be the glory for ever and ever. Amen.

Clement's important letter gives us some clues about church life at the turn of the second century. Especially, it demonstrates the influence of the Roman community in the early church because Clement took the initiative to instruct and correct a distant Christian community.

> *Let not the strong neglect the care of the weak, and let the weak respect the strong. Let the rich distribute to the needs of the poor, and let the poor bless God who gives them people to supply their want. . . . The great can't subsist without the little, nor the little without the great.*
>
> —Clement I

NOVEMBER 23
Christian Unity; Mere Christian Love

21. Ignatius of Antioch
(37?–107?)

During the persecution by Trajan, St. Ignatius, bishop of Antioch, Syria, was condemned to death for his faith. In 107 a company of rough soldiers transported him to Rome, where he was to be thrown to wild animals in the amphitheater. His journey took him to several churches that welcomed him warmly. He stopped at Smyrna, where he became a friend of **St. Polycarp**. Along the way to his martyrdom Ignatius wrote letters to seven Christian communities. We know no details about his life except what he revealed in these messages.

Ignatius's preeminent concern in these letters was the healing of dissension among Christians. He insisted that the presence of Christ made the church one and that Christian unity required good relationships among believers. To ensure the practical expression of that oneness, Ignatius exhorted Christians to submit to the authority of their bishops. But most of all he taught that Christians were united in the Eucharist, where Christ received them into his presence. Thus Ignatius called himself "Theophorus," a God-bearer, and urged all to see themselves in the same way. "You are all bearers of God," he wrote to the Ephesians, "bearers of his temple, bearers of Christ."

Ignatius strove to conform to Christ and passionately desired to imitate him in a martyr's death. When the opportunity came, Ignatius was determined that nothing would prevent him from obtaining his crown of perfection, as he explained in his letter to the church at Rome:

> I am writing to all the churches, telling everyone that I freely die for God, unless you should prevent me. I exhort you not to perform any unwelcome kindness for me. Let me be given to the wild beasts, for through them I can attain to God.
>
> I am God's wheat. I am ground by the teeth of wild beasts so that I may be found the pure bread of Christ. I urge you to entice the wild beasts so that they may become my sepulcher. May they leave behind no part of my body, so that when I have fallen asleep I may not be a burden to anyone. Then shall I be truly a disciple of Jesus Christ, when the world shall not so much as see my body. Ask the Lord for me that through these instruments I may be found a sacrifice to God.

> I do not command you as Peter and Paul did. They were apostles, and I am a convict. They were free, but I am a slave to this very hour. Yet if I shall suffer, then I am a freed-man of Jesus Christ and I shall rise free in him.
>
> Now I am beginning to be a disciple. Come fire and cross and grapplings with wild beasts, cuttings and manglings, wrenching of bones, hacking of limbs, crushings of my whole body, come cruel tortures of the devil to assail me. Only may I attain to Jesus Christ.

When Ignatius arrived in Rome, he was taken directly to the Coliseum and thrown to lions. As he had prayed, he died instantly as they devoured him, a sacrifice like Christ.

In his letter to Smyrna, Ignatius made the first recorded use of the word catholic to designate the Christian community. "Where Christ Jesus is," he wrote, "there is the catholic church." Catholic means universal, and like Ignatius, we believe that what makes the church catholic is the omnipresence of the Lord of the universe.

OCTOBER 17
Christian Unity; Martyrs; Saints and Sacraments (Eucharist)

22. Justin

(100?–165)

One day the philosopher Justin was walking by the sea at Ephesus in Greece. He was probably meditating on his passionate quest—how a human being could come to know God. He had pursued it among the philosophical schools of his day—the Stoics, the Pythagoreans, and Platonists—but had not yet found a convincing answer. While strolling along the Aegean shore, however, he met a kind old man who told him about the Hebrew prophets and Christianity. As he listened, Justin's heart melted with excitement. Later, reflecting on the man's words, Justin decided that "his was the only sure and useful philosophy."

St. Justin's conversion to Christ occurred around 135. He continued to teach and write as a Christian philosopher. However, while other early teachers like **Ignatius** and **Polycarp** wrote theology for Christians, Justin addressed himself to pagans and Jews. He was convinced that a well-developed presentation of theology would win all thinking persons to Christ. For he believed that God himself drew all human beings to himself by planting universal truths in them. In the following selection, for example, he argued that God puts in everyone an understanding of good and evil:

> In every race of human beings God inserts an understanding of righteousness, that is, what is always and universally just. Every race knows that such things as adultery, and fornication, and homicide are sinful. For example, though they all fornicate, they do not escape from the knowledge that they are acting unrighteously—with the exception of those possessed by an unclean spirit, those debased by wicked customs and sinful institutions, and those who have quenched their natural ideas. For we observe that such persons refuse to endure the same things they inflict on others. They also reproach each other for the evil acts that they commit.
>
> Thus our Lord and Savior, Jesus Christ, spoke well when he summed up all righteousness in two commandments: "You shall love the Lord your God with all your heart, and with all your strength, and your neighbor as yourself" (see Matthew 22:37). For the one who loves God with all his heart and who is filled with a God-fearing mind will reverence no other god. And the person who loves his neighbor as himself will wish for him the same good things that he wishes for

> himself—and no one will wish evil things for himself. So a person who loves his neighbor would pray and work that others may possess the same benefits as himself.
>
> Therefore, since Scripture says all righteousness is divided into these two branches, whoever loves the Lord God with all his heart, and all his strength, and his neighbor as himself, would be a truly righteous person.

Around 150, Justin moved to Rome. He opened a school of philosophy and wrote many books, although only the two *Apologetics* and the *Dialogue with Trypho* have survived. An intense and dogged controversialist, Justin publicly debated all comers—Jewish rabbis, Roman philosophers, and heretics. His aggressive Christianity made him many enemies and brought him to the attention of the authorities. In 165, during the reign of the philosopher-emperor Marcus Aurelius, Justin, the great Christian philosopher, was scourged and beheaded because he confessed Christ and refused to worship the gods.

Justin was a layperson who bore witness to Christ in his everyday occupation as a philosopher. Today few Christians have full-time jobs that call on them daily for reasonable explanations of the Christian faith, as Justin's did. But the church expects laypeople to transform our worlds, so we must take every chance we get to show and tell others about Christ and his way.

JUNE 1 / PATRON OF PHILOSOPHERS
Conversion; Defending the Faith; Evangelization; Faith Seeking Understanding

23. Irenaeus

(130?–200?)

The name "Irenaeus" comes from a Greek word meaning peace, and appropriately St. Irenaeus's life was highlighted by peacemaking efforts. A disciple of **Polycarp,** he came via Rome as a priest to Lyons, Gaul's thriving trade center. Sometime after 170, Irenaeus went to Rome to beg the pope to be lenient with Christians in Phrygia (present-day Turkey) who had fallen under the influence of Montanist heretics. Even though Irenaeus himself disagreed with the excesses of these enthusiasts, he acted from his concern for unity among Christians.

Irenaeus became bishop of Lyons in 178. We know that he stayed close to his people, as he always used the language of Gaul instead of his native Greek. He also promoted evangelization throughout the countryside.

In his theological works, *Against Heresies* and *The Preaching of the Apostles,* Irenaeus significantly contributed to the refutation of the Gnostic heretics, who were very influential in Gaul. He opposed their esoteric and elitist notions with convincing arguments about the Trinity, the Incarnation, and the inclusiveness of God's love. Into his heady theological reflections, the saint tucked very practical advice about living in faith, as in the following excerpt:

> Since we consist of soul and body, both are involved in staying on the path. As either may cause us to stumble, we must attend to both: Bodily purity, the protective abstinence from all shameful things and wicked acts. And purity of the soul, keeping true faith in God, neither adding to nor subtracting from it. Godliness is dimmed when the body is soiled and loses its integrity when falsehood enters the soul.
>
> But our godliness maintains its beauty and integrity when the spirit sticks to the truth and the body keeps pure. What good is knowing the truth in words while polluting the body with evil deeds? What real good can purity produce if truth is not in the soul? These two rejoice with each other and unite as comrades-in-arms in the fight to bring us into God's presence.
>
> So to protect our virtue, we cling to the rule of faith without changing it at all. And we must also obey the commandments of God, believing in him, fearing him as Lord, and loving him as Father. Correct behavior is produced by faith because, as Isaiah says, "If you do not take your stand on me, you will not stand firm" (Isaiah 7:9 *NJB*).

> Further, faith itself is produced by truth, for faith must rest upon reality. When we believe in eternal realities, we hold to faith with confidence. Thus, since faith preserves our salvation, we must carefully sustain it by having a clear hold on reality.

In 190, Irenaeus went on another peacemaking mission. He successfully persuaded Pope Victor I to lift his excommunication of Christians in Asia Minor who traditionally celebrated Easter on the first day of Passover instead of on the Sunday following. Schism seemed imminent, but the saint's intervention preserved good relations and restored unity. Later, around the time of the Council of Nicea in 325, these Christians voluntarily adopted the Roman practice for celebrating Easter.

After two decades of service leadership, Irenaeus died around 200. No evidence exists to demonstrate the ancient legend that the saint died a martyr.

Truth and charity were the tools Irenaeus used to defend the faith and preserve Christian unity. With truth he demolished wrongheaded ideas. But he treated people he regarded as wrongheaded with love. Irenaeus is a model for the contemporary church, where we sometimes disagree vigorously on the truth and must learn to build peace and unity by loving brothers and sisters who we find disagreeable.

JUNE 28
Christian Unity; Defending the Faith; Passion for Purity; Peacemakers

24. Polycarp
(155? or 166?)

In the second century, St. Polycarp was the revered elder statesman of the church in the East. He was a second-generation apostle who had personal contact with the Twelve. **St. John** probably had appointed him bishop of Smyrna. For more than half a century Polycarp devoted himself to teaching sound doctrine and opposing heresy. Once on a visit to Rome he had snubbed the heretic Marcion. "Don't you know who I am, Polycarp?" he asked. "Oh yes," said the saint, "I know the firstborn of Satan when I see him."

At mid-century, governors began to require Christians to worship the emperor. At Smyrna mobs packed the amphitheater to watch as faithful Christians were forced to fight wild animals. One day when a Christian youth encouraged the beasts to devour him, the crowd went berserk. They began to chant, "We want Polycarp! We want Polycarp!"

Polycarp had hid himself on a farm outside of town. But a search party forced a servant to betray him. When they arrived to arrest him, he fed them and asked for a time to pray. Then they took the saint to the amphitheater. Here is the account as told in *The Martyrdom of Polycarp*, a circular letter the Smyrnean church distributed after his death:

> . . . A great shout arose when the people heard that it was Polycarp who had been arrested. As he was brought before him, the governor asked him: "Are you Polycarp?" And when he admitted he was, the governor tried to persuade him to recant, saying: "Have respect for your age . . . ; swear by the Genius of the emperor. Recant. Say, 'Away with the atheists!'"
>
> Polycarp, with a sober countenance, looked at all the mob of lawless pagans who were in the arena, and shaking his fist at them, groaned, looked up to heaven, and said: "Away with these atheists!"
>
> The governor persisted and said: "Swear and I will let you go. Curse Christ!"
>
> But Polycarp answered: "For eighty-six years I have been his servant and he has done me no wrong. How can I blaspheme against my king and savior?"

The governor continued to press Polycarp, but he did not flinch at the threat of the wild animals or of being burnt alive. Polycarp must have raised an eyebrow at the latter warning, as a few days before he had dreamt that he would die by fire. When the governor announced that Polycarp had declared himself a Christian, the frenzied mob gathered wood for his pyre.

Polycarp submitted peacefully to his death, even asking not to be nailed to the center pole. He prayed briefly and the fire was lit. Witnesses later reported that something miraculous happened to the flames, which:

> bellying out like a ship's sail in the wind, formed into the shape of a vault and thus surrounded the martyr's body as with a wall. And he was within it not as burning flesh but rather as bread being baked or like gold and silver being purified in a smelting furnace.

Since the fire was not consuming Polycarp, the governor had one of his men plunge a dagger into him. The death of the bishop climaxed and ended the Smyrnean persecution. And the report of his martyrdom engendered faith and courage throughout the still very young Christian church.

Jesus "said to all, 'If anyone wishes to come after me, he must deny himself and take up his cross daily and follow me. For whoever wishes to save his life will lose it, but whoever loses his life for my sake will save it.'"

—Luke 9:23–24 *NAB*

FEBRUARY 23 / PATRON OF EARACHE SUFFERERS
Defending the Faith; Martyrs

25. Perpetua
(181–203)

St. Perpetua was a delightful young woman we would like to have known personally. Clearheaded, courageous, and charming, she took control of every situation. Perpetua dazzled people with her pluck, and they would just let her have her way. And most remarkably, she was merry in the face of certain death.

When Perpetua became a Christian she was only twenty-two years old and the mother of an infant son. Shortly after her conversion in 203, the Emperor Severus decreed a persecution in Rome. Perpetua, her friend **Felicity**, and three others were arrested and held for trial. Her father, a good pagan, tried to persuade her to renounce her new faith. While Perpetua felt her dad's suffering, she could not reject Christ.

"Father," she said, pointing to a water jug, *"do you see this container? Can you call it by any other name than what it is—a jug?"*

"No," he replied.

"And in the same way, I cannot call myself by any other name than what I am—a Christian." Quivering with anger, he left in defeat.

You can imagine how Perpetua missed her baby and how she feared for his future. But her mother and brother, both Christians, brought him to her in prison, relieving her anguish. *"I spoke anxiously to my mother about my son,"* said Perpetua, *"and encouraged my brother. I commended my son to their care."*

Perpetua and her companions were tried before an angry mob. All refused to worship the emperor as a god and so were condemned to death by fighting wild beasts. Then at the emperor's birthday celebration, she and her companions were paraded into the arena, the crowd roaring for blood. An eyewitness gave this account:

> For Perpetua and Felicity, the devil had reserved a vicious cow. Perpetua was first thrown and landed on her side. When she sat up she noticed her dress had been torn, and she adjusted it to cover her thigh. Modesty was more on her mind than pain. And then she pinned up her disheveled hair because she didn't think it was right for a martyr to appear to be grieving at the moment of glory. She stood up, and when she saw Felicity struck down, she went over and helped her up.

At this point Perpetua and Felicity were moved from the field to an arena gate. The saint appeared to be dazed in an ecstasy, not even realizing that she had been gored.

> She did not believe she had been attacked until she saw the marks of mauling on her body and on her dress. Then she exhorted her brother and a catechumen, saying: "Stand fast in the faith, and love one another, and don't take offense at our suffering."

Soldiers were ordered to finish the women off by slitting their throats. Perpetua shrieked as a nervous soldier, a novice, awkwardly struck her with his sword. Then this extraordinary young woman took charge of her own martyrdom.

> And when the soldier's hand still wavered, she guided the sword to her own neck. Perhaps so great a woman, wrote the eyewitness, could not be dispatched unless she herself were willing.

The witness gave spiritual motives for Perpetua's demeanor in the arena. Modesty and glory, he said, caused her to cover her thigh and fix her hair after she was gored. Perhaps so, but I would rather attribute her behavior to the natural impulses of a twenty-two-year-old woman.

MARCH 7, WITH ST. FELICITY / PATRON OF COWS
Countercultural Witness; Martyrs; Twenty-Something Saints; Valiant Women

26. Felicity

(D. 203)

St. Felicity and her fellow slave, Revocatus—possibly her husband—were among the companions of **St. Perpetua**, all catechumens ready for baptism. In 203 they were arrested at Carthage because they refused to worship the Roman emperor as a god. Saturus, their catechist, voluntarily joined them in prison and baptized them, sealing the faith they were already demonstrating. Felicity was eight months pregnant at that time.

Shortly afterward Felicity, Perpetua, and their friends were tried in the public square. The judge had the men scourged and had Felicity and Perpetua hit in the face. Then he condemned them all to combat wild beasts on the emperor's birthday.

Felicity worried that her pregnancy might require her to suffer apart from her friends. However, they prayed for her, with a miraculous result, as Perpetua testified:

> As for Felicity, she too enjoyed the Lord's favor. . . . As the day of the spectacle drew near, she was very distressed that her martyrdom would be postponed because of her pregnancy; for it is against the law for women with child to be executed. Thus she might have to shed her holy, innocent blood afterwards along with others who were common criminals. Her comrades in martyrdom were also saddened. . . . They were afraid that they would have to leave behind so fine a companion to travel alone on the same road to hope. And so, two days before the contest, they poured forth a prayer to the Lord in one torrent of common grief. And immediately after their prayer the birth pains came upon her. She suffered a good deal in her labor because of the natural difficulty of an eight month's delivery.
>
> Hence one of the assistants of the prison guards said to her: "You suffer so much now—what will you do when you are tossed to the beasts? Little did you think of them when you refused to sacrifice."
>
> "What I am suffering now," she replied, "I suffer by myself. But then another will be inside me who will suffer for me, just as I shall be suffering for him."
>
> And she gave birth to a girl, and one of the sisters brought her up as her own daughter.

This account makes it all seem easier than it must have been. Felicity was strong and idealistic, but she was not inoculated against fear and immune to pain. Terrible questions must have preyed upon her confidence. What would become of her new baby? Would she also die a violent death? Perhaps Felicity even doubted that she was doing the right thing. Maybe she should offer a little incense to a conceited emperor and live to raise her daughter. But whatever painful thoughts might have distressed her, Felicity did not cave in.

On the day of the execution she marched proudly into the amphitheater alongside Perpetua and the others. A leopard and a bear mauled Revocatus to death. A wild heifer tossed the women to the ground but did not kill them. Perpetua helped Felicity up and they brushed themselves off. The crowd howled for their blood, and a soldier dispatched the brave young women with his sword.

We admire Felicity for her unequivocal commitment. But our modern minds don't really understand her martyrdom. How is it, we wonder, that one so new to the faith should eagerly desire such a horrific death, as Felicity did? And how is it that a new mother should prefer such a violent end to raising her baby daughter? These are terrible questions for us because we suspect we might not behave as selflessly as Felicity.

MARCH 7, WITH ST. PERPETUA
Facing Death; Martyrs; Saints and Sacraments (Baptism)

27. Clement of Alexandria

(150?–215?)

At the end of the second century, St. Clement headed the famous catechetical school at Alexandria. He began his career as a pagan philosopher, but upon his conversion to Christ he traveled throughout Greece, Italy, Egypt, and Palestine to study with the best Christian teachers. He became a disciple of Pantaenus at Alexandria, whom he esteemed as the greatest teacher of all. Around 190 he succeeded his master as head of the Alexandrian school. He taught there for a dozen years until persecution by Emperor Severus forced him into exile in 202.

Clement is regarded as a Father of the church, the author of the largest body of Christian writing surviving from the second century. In his three major works he exalts the living personal Christ, the Word made flesh: In *The Exhortation to the Heathen,* Jesus draws people from the corruption of paganism to faith. In *The Instructor* Jesus trains people in Christian living. And in the *Miscellanies*, he conducts them to a higher knowledge of the things of God. Clement also wrote a practical exposition of Mark 10:17–30, *Who Is the Rich Man That Shall Be Saved?* from which the following is taken:

> Whatever is done to a disciple, the Lord accepts as done to himself. He has not commanded you to wait to be begged. But you are to seek those who are to be benefited and are worthy disciples of the Savior. Excellent is the apostle's saying, "For God loves a cheerful giver" (2 Corinthians 9:7 *NAB*), who delights in giving, and spares not, sowing that he may also thus reap, without murmuring, which is pure beneficence. And this is above all a divine quality—not to wait to be asked, but to inquire oneself who deserves to receive kindness.
>
> God appoints such a reward for liberality—an everlasting habitation! O what an excellent trade, giving the perishable things of this world in exchange for an eternal heavenly mansion! Sail to this mart, if you are wise, O rich man!
>
> And don't judge who is worthy or who is unworthy of your gift because you may be mistaken in your opinion. It is better in ignorance to do good to the undeserving for the sake of the deserving, than to fail to serve the worthy by guarding against the unworthy. For by holding back and testing people for merit, you may neglect some that God loves. And the penalty for that is eternal fire. But by offering to

all in need you will necessarily find those who have power with God to save.

Open your compassion to all God's disciples. Don't be put off by appearance or age. Don't fret about those who seem to be penniless, ragged, ugly or feeble and turn away from them. For within their human form dwells hidden the Father and the Son who died for us and rose with us.

We don't know anything about the end of Clement's life, but he is thought to have died around 215.

Be gracious, O Instructor, to us your children. Grant to us who obey your precepts that we may with all our power know him who is the good God and not a harsh judge. And cause that all of us who have sailed tranquilly over the stormy waves of sin and have been moved forever into your commonwealth may always be wafted by the Holy Spirit—the ineffable wisdom—to the perfect day. Praise to the Father, Son, and Holy Spirit, all in one, to whom be glory now and forever. Amen.

—Clement of Alexandria

DECEMBER 5 / PATRON OF LIGHTHOUSES
Christian Living; Generosity; Serving the Poor

28. Hippolytus

(170?–236?)

Saints did not always get along with one another. In fact, sometimes they opposed each other bitterly. That was the case in the third century between St. Hippolytus and four consecutive sainted popes—Zephyrinus, Callistus, Urban, and Pontianus. Hippolytus disagreed vigorously with them over theological issues and pastoral practice.

As a prominent priest and theologian at Rome, Hippolytus took the lead in defending the faith against the heresy of Sabellius, who denied that God had three distinct persons. Hippolytus criticized Pope Zephyrinus (198–217) for not being quick enough to identify and censure heresy. He also thought the pope was too lenient in relaxing the penitential system to accommodate the large influx of converts from paganism. Upon the succession of Callistus I (217–222), Hippolytus went into schism and allowed himself to be set up as an antipope. He appears to have persisted in his opposition to Callistus's successors, Urban (222–230) and Pontianus (230–235).

History regards Hippolytus as the most important theologian of the early Roman church. In his principal book, *The Refutation of All Heresies*, he exposed as fallacious the philosophies that undergirded popular heresies. In the following excerpt from that book, he acclaims knowing the truth as the deliverer from the evils of damnation and the way into divine life:

> Do not devote your attention to the fallacies of artificial discourses, nor to the vain promises of heretics, but to the venerable simplicity of unassuming truth. By means of this knowledge you shall escape the approaching threat of the fire of judgment, and the rayless scenery of gloomy Tartarus, where never shines a beam from the irradiating voice of the Word!
>
> You shall escape the boiling flood of hell's eternal lake of fire and the menacing glare of fallen angels chained in Tartarus as punishment for their sins. And you shall escape the worm that ceaselessly coils for food around the body whose scum has bred it. You shall avoid such punishments by being instructed in a knowledge of the true God.
>
> You shall possess an immortal body, one placed beyond the possibility of corruption, just like the soul. And you who in this life knew the celestial king shall receive the kingdom of heaven. You shall be a companion of the deity and a co-heir with Christ, no longer enslaved

> by lusts or passions and never again wasted by disease. For you have "become" God: for God has promised to bestow on you whatever is consistent with God to impart, for you have been deified and begotten unto immortality. This constitutes the import of the proverb, "Know yourself," that is, discover God within yourself, for he has formed you after his own image.

In another important work, *The Apostolic Tradition*, Hippolytus presented the canon of the Mass as celebrated at Rome, one of the earliest accounts of the church's Eucharistic liturgy. It now acts as the basis for one of the canons of the renewed Roman liturgy.

During the persecution by Maximinus in 235, both Hippolytus and Pontianus were exiled to Sardinia, where they died as martyrs. Apparently Hippolytus had reconciled with Pontianus and the Roman church before his death, as his body was brought back to Rome and buried with honor.

As the saying goes, it takes two to tango. For his part in the controversies with the popes, Hippolytus seems to have been crusty, intransigent, and sometimes wrong. Today theologians regard his speculations on the Trinity as vague, defective, and tending toward the heretical. But he was a stalwart dissenter, and his dissent does not seem to have canceled his sanctity.

AUGUST 13

Defending the Faith; Eternal Perspective; Feisty Saints

29. Alban
(Third Century)

St. Alban, the first English martyr, was executed during an imperial persecution sometime in the mid-third century. A prominent Roman citizen of the ancient city of Verulamium, he was beheaded on a lovely hill thirty miles north of London. There his namesake church now stands, surrounded by the town of St. Albans.

Venerable Bede, writing in the mid-eighth century, gives us the fullest early version of Alban's story. Bede tells how Alban was converted while hiding a priest who was running from imperial soldiers:

> Alban, while he was still a pagan, hid in his house a certain priest, who was running from the persecutors. He observed his guest engaged in continual prayer and keeping vigil day and night. And prompted by a sudden infusion of divine light, he began to imitate the priest's example of faith and piety. Gradually instructed by his wholesome admonitions, Alban cast off the darkness of idolatry, and became a sincerely committed Christian. The wicked prince heard that the holy confessor of Christ was concealed at Alban's house. So he sent some soldiers to make a strict search for him. When they came to the martyr's house, St. Alban, dressed in the priest's long coat, immediately presented himself instead of his guest and master, and was led bound before the judge.

Enraged that Alban had substituted himself for the priest, the judge ordered him to profess his faith in the Roman gods. Alban stoutly refused, and during his interrogation provoked the ruler by saying that his gods were devils and that worshiping them would condemn him to hell. The judge tried to break the saint's adamantine will by having him flogged. But the saint endured through every torture, so the official condemned him to death.

Bede described the scene of Alban's martyrdom:

> Being led to execution, Alban came to a rapidly surging river which ran between the wall of the town and the arena where he was to be martyred. There a multitude had so obstructed the bridge that he would not be able to cross that evening. Almost the whole town had gone out so that no one attended the judge who remained in the city. St. Alban, eager for his martyrdom, approached the stream. And as he lifted his eyes to heaven, the channel immediately dried up, and he saw

> that the water had departed and made way for him to pass. The executioner observed this and, moved by divine inspiration, he hastened to meet Alban at the place of execution. Casting down the sword which he had carried ready drawn, he fell at Alban's feet, and prayed that he might suffer with the martyr or, if possible, instead of him.

Alban walked up a hill near the arena. To make it clear to all that his prayer had dried the river, Alban asked aloud that God would give him water and a spring bubbled up at his feet. Then he and his new Christian companion were beheaded. And as Alban's head fell, the eyes of his executioner dropped out on the ground. Bede observed that as a result of these miracles the ruler relented, canceled the persecution, and even began to honor the martyrs.

A beautiful church was built on the site of Alban's death, where centuries later Bede said, "sick folk are healed and frequent miracles take place to this day." Even now Alban's wondrous spirit still seems to linger there. Visitors to St. Alban's Church report that they sense a near palpable holiness at the place of his martyrdom and are drawn to God in prayer.

Greater love has no man than this, that a man lay down his life for his friends.
—John 15:13 *RSV*

JUNE 20 / PATRON OF CONVERTS AND VICTIMS OF TORTURE
Conversion; Evangelization; Martyrs; Miracles Do Happen

30. Cecilia
(Third Century?)

For centuries St. Cecilia has remained one of the church's most beloved saints. Singers, poets, and musicians honor her as their patron. Parents give their daughters her lovely name, which derives from Latin words that mean "lily of heaven."

However, all we know about Cecilia comes from a fifth-century legend that has no historical evidence to support it. Except that two young men featured in the story, Valerian and Tiburtius, were known to have been martyred in the third century and buried in the catacombs. However, no catacomb grave or contemporary writer validates the fascinating tale of St. Cecilia. Historians now speculate that it grew up to explain the dedication of a church in the Trastevere district of Rome by a woman named Cecilia.

However, the story still charms and inspires us. Cecilia, a patrician maiden, dedicated her virginity to Christ, but her father betrothed her to Valerian, a young pagan. Forced into marriage, Cecilia determined to keep her commitment. According to the legend:

> As the wedding day approached, she fasted for two or three days . . . , recommending her fears to God. On her nuptial day she wore a hair shirt next to her flesh, concealed by her gown of cloth of gold; and when the organs rang out, she sang in her heart to God alone, saying, "O Lord, let my heart and my body be undefiled, that I be not confounded."
>
> That night, when with her spouse she sought the secret silences of the bridal chamber, she spoke to him as follows: "O sweetest and most loving youth, there is a secret that I may confess to you, if only you will swear to guard it faithfully." Then Valerian swore that no necessity would make him betray it in any way. Then she said: "I have for my lover an angel of God, who guards my body with exceeding zeal! If he sees you but lightly touch me for sordid love, he will smite you, and you will lose the fair flower of your youth. But if he knows that you love me with a pure love, he will love you as he loves me, and will show you his glory!"
>
> Then Valerian, guided by the will of God, said: "If you will have me believe you, show me the angel! If I find that he is really an angel, I shall do as you ask me. But if your lover is another man, you shall both fall by my sword!"

We might wonder if bad breath from fasting and the stink of the hair shirt might not have been enough to protect Cecilia from Valerian's touch. However, the youth followed Cecilia's directions and sought baptism from Pope Urban I. Upon his return Valerian saw Cecilia's angel, who crowned both of them with floral wreaths. Then Valerian's brother, Tiburtius, was also converted. The two new Christians were soon beheaded for burying the bodies of those who had been martyred.

Cecilia herself was condemned for refusing to worship the gods. An attempt to suffocate her in her own bathroom failed. So a soldier was ordered to behead her, but he bungled the job. Cecilia lay dying for three days, during which she bequeathed her property to the church.

The Cecilia legend may be purely fictitious, but this fiction conveys truths that stimulate our faith. St. Cecilia testifies to the supernatural realities that penetrate our lives and invite us to live for God alone no matter what it costs.

NOVEMBER 22 / PATRON OF MUSICIANS, POETS, AND SINGERS
Angels; Martyrs; Twenty-Something Saints

31. Cyprian of Carthage

(200?–258)

Cyprian was a prominent man about town in early third-century Carthage. Well-known as a public speaker and lawyer, he reveled in the pagan world. But in 245 he was radically converted to Christ, renouncing all his ties to the profane culture, including his addiction to secular literature. Before his baptism St. Cyprian even made a vow of chastity that caused St. Pontius, his biographer, to exclaim: "Has anyone ever seen such a miracle?"

He transferred his skills to the study of Scripture and Christian writers, especially Tertullian, whom he regarded as his master. Not once in his own books did he quote a pagan author, so complete was his break with his former life. In 248 the Christians of Carthage acclaimed Cyprian as their bishop. Almost immediately, persecution by Emperor Decius forced him into hiding. He governed his flock by letter, instructing them in Christian fundamentals, as he did in this passage:

> The Lord taught us to pray not only in words, but also in actions. He prayed frequently himself and showed us by example what we must do. As Scripture says: "Rising very early in the morning, he left and went to a deserted place, where he prayed" (see Mark 1:35). But if the sinless one prayed, how much more ought sinners to pray.
>
> When we stand praying, we ought to be watchful and earnest with our whole heart, intent on our prayers. Let all carnal and worldly thoughts pass away. Don't let the soul think on anything except the object of its prayer. Thus the priest prepares the minds of the people by saying, "Lift up your hearts," so that upon the people's response, "We have lifted them up to the Lord," he may be reminded himself to think of nothing but the Lord.
>
> Moreover, those who pray should not come to the Lord with fruitless or naked prayers. Petition is ineffectual when it is a barren entreaty that implores God. For as every tree that bears no fruit is cut down and cast into the fire, so also assuredly words that do not bear fruit cannot deserve anything of God because they are not fruitful in any good action. Thus Holy Scripture instructs us, saying, "Prayer is good with fasting and almsgiving" (see Tobit 12:8). For he who will reward us on judgment day for our works and alms will even in this

> life listen mercifully to those who come to him in prayer combined with good works.

When the persecution subsided, the church debated over the situation of many believers who had abandoned the faith out of fear. St. Cyprian took a moderate position between the extremes of readmission to communion with no penitence on the one hand and complete and permanent exclusion on the other. And his approach to the lapsed prevailed at the Council of Carthage in 251. Cyprian's conviction that sacraments administered by schismatic priests were invalid forced him into an acrimonious controversy with Pope Stephen. That battle was resolved only after the death of both protagonists in favor of the tradition that the validity of the sacrament did not depend on the spiritual condition of the minister.

St. Augustine said that Cyprian's martyrdom atoned for his excesses during this conflict. He was beheaded in 258 during persecution by Valerian.

> *Let each of us pray to God not for himself only, but for all the brothers and sisters, according to the pattern that our Lord gave us, teaching us to pray as a community for all. When the Lord sees us humble, peaceable, unified and perfected by our sufferings, he will deliver us from the hands of our enemies.*
>
> —Cyprian of Carthage

SEPTEMBER 16
Almsgiving; Conversion; Fasting; Intercession; Prayer

32. Gregory the Wonderworker

(213?–270?)

In 1738, when Pope Clement XII was about to set the feast of **St. Gertrude** on November 17, he discovered that St. Gregory the Wonderworker already held that day. He decided that not even a pope should move a saint who reputedly had moved a mountain, so he assigned Gertrude to November 15. However, just as in his *Dialogues*, where **St. Gregory the Great** made a "mountain" out of a boulder Gregory once miraculously moved, legend has also enhanced Gregory's reputation for wonderworking.

Doubtless, Gregory had a gift of miracles. He used it well in his remarkable evangelization of Neocaesarea in present-day Turkey, the rich pagan city where he became bishop. The townspeople were immersed in vice and idolatry, but the saint's wonders caught their attention. With a touch of exaggeration, **St. Basil** reported that Gregory "through the cooperation of the Spirit had a formidable power over evil spirits. He altered the course of rivers in Christ's name. He dried up a lake that caused dissension between two brothers." When Gregory arrived in Neocaesarea, seventeen Christians lived there. At his death around 268, only seventeen of the city's pagans had not been converted to Christianity.

As a young man Gregory himself came to Christ because of the example and teaching of Origen, the great theologian who became his mentor. Origen taught Gregory to mine pagan philosophy and use it wisely in God's service, just as the Jews, he said, had applied the spoils of the Egyptians to build God's tabernacle. Gregory adapted this principle in his evangelistic methods. For example, he attracted pagans to the church by organizing secular entertainments to celebrate the annual feasts of Christian martyrs.

During the persecution by Decius in 250, Gregory advised his people to hide themselves from danger. Gregory himself was miraculously concealed. When informed that he and his deacon were living on a mountain, soldiers reported finding only two trees on the slope. The informer, checking his report, discovered that the "trees" were Gregory and his associate, and became a convert. Plague and barbarian invasions followed upon the persecution. Historians speculate that this grievous series of disruptions prevented Gregory from using his intellectual gifts to the full, as he wrote very little. Among his works, however, appears this moving creed that exalts the Trinity:

There is one God, the Father of the living Word, who is his coexistent Wisdom and Power and Eternal Image: perfect Begetter of the perfect Begotten, Father of the only-begotten Son.

There is one Lord, Only of the Only, God of God, Image and Likeness of Deity, Efficient Word, Wisdom comprehending the constitution of all things, and Power forming the whole creation, true Son of true Father, Invisible of Invisible, and Incorruptible of Incorruptible, and Immortal of Immortal, and Eternal of Eternal.

And there is one Holy Spirit, having his subsistence from God, and by the Son being made manifest to men: Image of the Son, Perfect Image of the Perfect; Life, the Cause of the Living; Holy Fount; Sanctity, the Supplier, or Leader of Sanctification. In whom is manifested God the Father, who is above all and in all, and God the Son, who is through all.

There is a perfect Trinity, in glory and eternity and sovereignty, neither divided nor estranged. Wherefore there is nothing either created or in subjection in the Trinity; nor is there anything in the Trinity that, nonexistent at some former period, was introduced at some later period. And thus neither was the Son ever wanting to the Father, nor the Spirit to the Son. But without variation and without change, the same Trinity abides forever.

NOVEMBER 17
Evangelization; Miracles Do Happen; Perseverance

33. Lawrence
(D. 258)

History affirms only a few facts about St. Lawrence, one of the church's most celebrated martyrs. In the mid-third century, he served as one of Rome's seven deacons. His duties included caring for the church's goods and almsgiving, which he administered generously. Lawrence was closely associated with Pope St. Sixtus II. And in 258, during the persecution by Valerian, he was martyred a few days after the pope. That's all we know for sure about him.

Popular legends tell us a lot more about Lawrence. However, historians say these tales are fanciful, probably borrowed in part from the *Acts* of **Vincent of Saragossa.** But over the centuries the Lawrence story has encouraged millions of Christians. The legend says that as Sixtus II was led off to die, he told Lawrence that he would also be martyred in three days. Delighted at the prospect, the deacon disposed all the money and goods he could to the city's poor. When the prefect of Rome heard of this, he gave Lawrence three days to bring him all the church's gold. Lawrence, however, decided to produce the church's real treasure. And on the third day he presented the prefect with a crowd of the poor, diseased, and homeless people that he served as deacon. Angered by what he regarded as a stunt, the prefect ordered Lawrence to die a slow death by roasting on a grill.

The fourth-century poet Prudentius spun these details of Lawrence's passion:

When slow consuming heat had seared
The flesh of Lawrence for a space,
He calmly from his gridiron made
This terse proposal to the judge:

"Pray turn my body, on one side
Already broiled sufficiently,
And see how well your Vulcan's fire
Has wrought its cruel punishment."

The prefect bade him to be turned.
Then Lawrence spoke: "I am well baked,
And whether better cooked or raw,
Make trial by a taste of me."

He said these words in way of jest;
Then raising shining eyes to heaven
And sighing deeply, thus he prayed
With pity for unholy Rome:

"Grant to your Roman people, Christ,
That they may wear the Christian name,
For through their city you did give
To others one religious faith."

Thus ended Lawrence's fervent prayer,
Thus ended too his earthly life:
With these last words his eager soul
Escaped with joy from carnal chains.

From the fourth century, Lawrence's story has captivated the imagination of Christians. Prudentius, **Ambrose,** and **Augustine** popularized the saint. And throughout Europe, stained-glass windows and frescoes depicted his martyrdom. Today we still remember his name in the canon of the Roman liturgy.

Lawrence was a deacon of the church at Rome. There he ministered the sacred blood of Christ. There for the sake of Christ's name he poured out his own blood. In his life he loved Christ. In his death he followed in his footsteps. Brothers and sisters, we too must imitate Christ if we truly love him.

—Augustine

AUGUST 10 / PATRON OF ROME, COOKS, AND SRI LANKA
Almsgiving; Martyrs

34. Felix of Nola
(D. 260?)

A hundred years after St. Felix's death, **St. Paulinus of Nola** told his story, adding without discernment appealing legends that had accumulated over the years. But we can trust the unadorned factual outline of Felix's life.

After Felix divested himself of all his possessions, St. Maximus, the bishop of Nola, a town near Naples, Italy, ordained him a priest and made him his right-hand man. In 250, when Emperor Decius decreed a ferocious persecution, Maximus installed himself in a desert hiding place from which he safely governed the church. Because soldiers could not find Maximus at Nola, they tortured and jailed Felix in his place. However, just as **St. Peter** had had a miraculous escape from prison, an angel is said to have released Felix. Then the angel guided Felix to rescue Maximus, who was near death.

The persecution subsided in 251. Upon the death of Maximus the people wanted to name Felix as bishop, but he declined. Instead he retired to a small farm, where for the rest of his life he raised crops to feed himself and provide alms for the poor. St. Felix died around 260.

Every year Paulinus wrote a poem to celebrate Felix's feast day. In one he said that while Felix did not die a martyr he was willing to offer his life as a sacrifice to God. Paulinus thus provided one of the earliest definitions of a "confessor":

> This festive day celebrates Felix's birthday, the day on which he died physically on earth and was born for Christ in heaven, winning his heavenly crown as a martyr who did not shed his blood. For he died as confessor, though he did not avoid execution by choice, since God accepted his inner faith in place of blood. God looks into the silence of hearts, and equates those ready to suffer with those who have already done so, for he considers this inward test as sufficient, and dispenses with physical execution in case of true devotion. Martyrdom without bloodshed is enough for him if mind and faith are ready to suffer and are fervent towards God.

Paulinus adopted Felix as his patron saint, a custom which had its roots in the early church. But for Paulinus, a patron was more than a namesake. Felix not only interceded for him in heaven. He also accompanied him spiritually as an encourager, guide, and protector, as Paulinus explained in the following passage:

> Father and lord, best of patrons to servants however unworthy, at last our prayer is answered to celebrate your birthday within your threshold. . . . You know what toils on land and sea have . . . kept me far from your abode in a distant world, because I have always and everywhere had you near me, and have called on you in the grim moments of travel, and in the uncertainties of life.
>
> . . . I never sailed without you, for I felt your protection in Christ the Lord when I overcame rough seas. On land and water my journeying is always made safe through you. Felix, I beg you, address a prayer on behalf of your own to that Embodiment of the calm of eternal love and peace, to him on whose great name you depend.

If patron saints can accomplish so much for us, we might find it advantageous to imitate Paulinus and rely more on ours.

> *The saints in each generation, joined to those who have gone before, and filled like them with light, become a golden chain, in which each saint is a separate link, united to the next by faith, works and love.*
>
> —Simeon the New Theologian

JANUARY 14
Intercession; Pursuit of Holiness

35. Christopher

(Third Century)

A martyr named St. Christopher suffered in Lycia in present-day Turkey under the Roman Emperor Decius in the mid-third century. After a failed attempt to burn him, he was shot with arrows and beheaded. Because we know nothing more about Christopher, the church removed him from the liturgical calendar. But the church has not denied St. Christopher's existence, nor demoted him.

In the Middle Ages a wonderful tale spread St. Christopher's fame. The legend says that Christopher, a magnificent giant, sought to serve the most powerful king. On his search, he pledged himself to a great Christian king and then to the devil, but was soon disappointed in both. As the story goes:

> Once a minstrel sang a song before the king in which he mentioned the devil. The king made the sign of the cross when he heard the devil's name. Christopher asked the king what the sign meant. Reluctantly, the king said, "When I hear the devil's name, I always defend myself with this sign because I fear the devil might get some power over me and do me harm!" Christopher said, "If you're afraid of being harmed by the devil, this proves that he is mightier and more powerful than you. So I'll go and seek him to be my lord, and become his servant!"
>
> On his way he saw a great company of knights, and one of them asked where he was going. Christopher answered, "I'm looking for the devil to be my master." The other said, "I'm the one you're seeking!" Christopher was glad to hear this and promised to serve him forever.
>
> As they went along the road they came upon a cross. When the devil saw it he was afraid and fled. Christopher marveled at this, and asked the devil what made him run. "There was a man called Christ who was hanged on a cross, and when I see his sign, I am terrified and flee from it!" Christopher said, "Then he is greater and mightier than you! And I see I have not found the greatest lord of the world! So I will serve you no longer. I will go to seek Christ!"

A hermit told Christopher that he might find Christ by carrying people across a certain river. One night Christopher ferried a child, who revealed himself as Christ and proved it by making Christopher's staff bear fruit and flowers.

Confirmed in the Lord's service, Christopher went to Lycia to encourage Christians who were being persecuted by a king. All the monarch's efforts to subdue Christopher failed, as he converted all who came to arrest him. Finally the king condemned Christopher because he refused to worship the gods. When his efforts to burn Christopher failed, he had hundreds of arrows shot at him, but they hung in midair. One of them strayed and blinded the king. Before Christopher was beheaded, he told the king to smear some of his blood on the wound and he would be healed. The story has it that the king did as Christopher instructed, received his sight, became a Christian, and from that time honored both God and Christopher.

Before his baptism, Christopher was called Reprobus, but after his baptism he was called Christopher, meaning Christ-bearer, because he bore Christ in four ways: upon his shoulders when he carried him, in his body by his mortifications, in his mind by his devotion, and in his mouth by professing and preaching him.

—Jacob of Voragine

JULY 25 / PATRON OF TRAVELERS AND MOTORISTS
The Sign of the Cross; Spiritual Warfare

36. Dionysius of Alexandria
(D. 265?)

As bishop of Alexandria from 247 to 265, St. Dionysius seemed to face nothing but trouble. Persecution, schism, plague, and violence followed one upon the other and doubled back again. Perhaps his fidelity through it all, as much as his top-notch theology, prompted **Basil** to call him Dionysius the Great.

Shortly after Dionysius became bishop of Alexandria, a local persecution erupted that was soon compounded by the anti-Christian decrees of Decius. In a confused set of circumstances, Dionysius was nearly arrested. When friends forcibly transported him on a donkey to safety in the Libyan desert, he resented that he had lost his chance for martyrdom.

After the persecutions subsided he returned to Alexandria, where he had to deal with schism and plague. He decried the rigorism of Novatian, who took a hard line toward Catholics who had lapsed under persecution. Dionysius uncompromisingly demanded that Novatian repair the disunity he had created by declaring himself pope. He wrote: "You ought to have suffered all things rather than have caused a schism in the church. To die in defense of its unity would be as glorious as laying down one's life for its faith."

During this period Dionysius wrote extensively, opposing heresy and interpreting Scripture. He exhibited a skillful approach to Scripture that other early Christian writers appreciated. Following is a sample from his exegesis of Jesus' application of "I am" to himself in John's Gospel:

> Now this word "I am" expresses his eternal substance. For if he is the reflection of the eternal light, he must also be eternal himself. For if the light subsists for ever, it is evident that the reflection also subsists for ever. And that this light subsists is known only by its shining. Neither can there be a light that does not give light.
>
> . . . If there is day, there is light. And if there is no such thing, the sun certainly cannot be present. If, therefore, the sun had been eternal, there would also have been endless day. Now, however, as it is not so, the day begins when the sun rises, and it ends when the sun sets. But God is eternal light, having neither beginning nor end.

> Along with him there is the reflection, also without beginning and end, and everlasting. The Father, then, being eternal, the Son is also eternal, being light of light. And if God is the light, Christ is the reflection. And if God is also a Spirit, as it is written, "God is a Spirit," Christ, again, is called analogously Spirit (see John 4:24).
>
> . . . The river which flows from the fountain is distinct from the fountain. For we cannot call either the river a fountain, or the fountain a river. However, we allow that they are both one according to nature, and also one in substance. We admit that the fountain may be conceived of as father, and that the river is begotten of the fountain.

Persecutions heated up again under Emperor Valerian in 257. When Dionysius balked at worshiping the gods, he was banished for two years. In 260 he returned to a city racked by violence and plague. It was safer, he said, to travel from east to west than to travel across Alexandria. But he patiently governed his flock there for five more years until his death in 265.

> *O God the Father: Origin of Divinity, good beyond all that is good, fair beyond all that is fair, in whom is calmness, peace, concord: Heal the dissensions that divide us from one another, and bring us back into the unity of love that resembles your divine nature.*
>
> —Dionysius of Alexandria

NOVEMBER 17
Christian Unity; Jesus Christ

37. Paul the Hermit

(233?–345?)

St. Jerome wrote, or at least translated from the Greek, a little biography of St. Paul the Hermit. Some speculate that he did so in order to establish St. Paul's reputation as the "first hermit" and to let the world know that the great **St. Anthony** had a predecessor. Others regard the story as so full of fables that they treat Paul as a type of a third-to-fourth-century hermit rather than as a historical individual.

A Christian from his youth, Paul was orphaned at age fifteen. In 250 the persecution by Decius forced him into hiding, first at a friend's house and then, fearing exposure, to a cave in the Egyptian desert. He had planned to return home after things quieted down, but the peaceful solitude of the desert seduced him to stay. A palm tree and a spring near his cave provided him food, clothing, and water until he turned forty-three. After that time, as it had happened for Elias, a raven brought him half a loaf of bread each day.

In Paul's ninetieth year in the desert his presence was revealed to St. Anthony, who immediately went to find him. Anthony met Paul in his cave, and the two hermits became friends overnight. They shared a whole loaf of bread brought by the raven, discussed world events, and prayed. Anthony thought he had found a companion, but Paul knew that God had sent Anthony to help him die. The biography described their meeting:

> Blessed Paul said to Anthony: "For a long time now, I have known that you dwelled in these regions. And for a long time God had promised you to me for a companion. Since my hour of eternal sleep has arrived, and because I have always desired 'to be dissolved and to be with Christ' (see Philippians 1:23), having 'finished the course, . . . a crown of justice' (see 2 Timothy 4:7–8) remains for me. You have been sent by God to bury my miserable body, rather to return earth to earth."
>
> Anthony listened to these words with tears and groans, begging Paul not to leave him behind, but to accept him as a companion on that journey. Paul answered: "You ought not seek your own interests but those of another. It is indeed profitable for you to cast off the burden of the flesh to follow the Lamb, but it is also profitable for the rest of your brethren that they may be the more instructed by your example. I beg of you, hasten, if is not too much to ask, and bring back the cloak which Athanasius the bishop gave you, to wrap about my wretched

> body." Now, blessed Paul made this request, not because he cared at all whether or not his body decayed covered up or naked, since for a long time now he had been wearing garments woven from palm leaves, but because he wanted to spare Anthony the grief of witnessing his death.

Anthony went to get the cloak. When he returned he found Paul kneeling with arms outstretched, but already dead. Two lions dug Paul's grave and Anthony buried him. But he kept Paul's outer garment woven from palm leaves, which he treasured from that time and which he always wore on great feast days.

Paul was spared a lonely death because he found a friend in Anthony. His experience suggests that we become friends with the sick and elderly and provide them companionship in their last days. And that we make friends with younger people ourselves as insurance against loneliness in the autumn of our lives.

JANUARY 15
Facing Death; Friendship; Solitude

38. Anthony of Egypt
(251–356)

At twenty, St. Anthony had inherited his parents' estate near Memphis, Egypt. One Sunday at mass, the gospel spoke directly to the wealthy young man: "If you wish to be perfect, go and sell your possessions and give the money to the poor, and you will have treasure in heaven; then come, follow me" (Matthew 19:21 *NJB*). The youth took Christ's words literally. He disposed of everything and moved to a hut outside of town. He stayed there fifteen years, practicing the asceticism he learned from hermits who lived nearby. Then, because he desired uninterrupted solitude, he withdrew to an isolated mountain in the Egyptian desert.

Anthony followed the same pattern every day. He ate only a little bread and water after sunset. He wore sheepskin garments with the hair against his body and never bathed. He supported himself by weaving mats from palm fronds. And Anthony prayed constantly. He especially liked to pray at night, complaining that the morning sun robbed him of the greater inner light of contemplation.

St. Athanasius, Anthony's biographer, says that the devil opposed the saint all through his life. Thus, he became adept at spiritual warfare. For example:

> One night while Anthony was praying, Satan sent wild beasts to terrify him. They surrounded him and were ready to pounce on him. He stared at them boldly and said, "If God gave you power over me, come quickly, for I'm ready for you. But if Satan sent you, you had better scatter, for I am a servant of Jesus the Conqueror." And the mere mention of the name of Christ instantly chased Satan away, like a sparrow before a hawk.
>
> On another day just outside his door, Anthony saw an animal that looked like this: from its head to its side it resembled a man and its legs and feet were those of an ass. When the blessed Anthony saw it, he simply made the sign of the cross over himself and said, "How can anyone imagine that the Evil One is crafty? And how can he frighten anyone more than once or twice? Doesn't he know that I regard these things as empty phantasms?" Then he said to the beast, "Now, if the one who sent you has any power at all, come here and do what he told you to do. But if Christ, who shall make an end of you, and in whom I hope, lives, and if he is true, may he destroy you and your master

> immediately." At the word "Christ," the creature began to quake and tremble, and he fled. And as he was running along terrified, he fell down not far from Anthony's hut and burst.

Anthony's reputation for holiness and spiritual power spread throughout Egypt. Many people interrupted his solitude to ask him for prayer, advice, and healing. At age fifty-five Anthony entered a more active phase in his spiritual career. He founded a community of monks who lived as hermits, but came together for worship and teaching. He had always maintained contact with the church at Alexandria. But now at the request of St. Athanasius, the patriarch and his friend, he visited the city to support Christians during persecutions and to wield his immense influence against heretics. St. Anthony died in 356 at the age of one hundred five years old.

The sign of the cross and the name of Jesus were potent remedies for Anthony, and today they have not lost any of their power. When irrational fears and phantasms of hopelessness cloud our minds, we can use these implements of spiritual warfare to dispel them.

JANUARY 17
Countercultural Witness; The Sign of the Cross; Solitude; Spiritual Warfare; Vocation

39. Pachomius

(292?–346)

The first monks were solitaries, but in the fourth century communities of men and women popped up in the Egyptian desert. We regard St. Pachomius as the founder of community monasticism because he was the first to provide his followers with a written rule of life.

As a conscript in the Roman army, Pachomius was deeply moved by the generosity some Christians showed him when he was being transported down the Nile River. So when he was discharged in 316 he became a Christian and endeavored to give his life entirely to God. For the next seven years he was a disciple of a hermit who trained him in prayer, fasting, and penitence. The saint also memorized the Psalms and many Bible passages, and while he worked he reflected on them.

According to legend, around 320 an angel directed Pachomius to gather monks into a community at Tabennesi, a desert wasteland along the Nile. The angel also gave him a simple rule of life, remarkable for its balance. Monks, for example, were allowed to eat or fast as they wished and were to work only as much as their strength allowed. Pachomius, however, was a strict disciplinarian, expecting total obedience and punishing offenders severely.

Pachomius organized his community into houses of thirty or forty who worked at the same trade. His monastery had gardeners, blacksmiths, bakers, carpenters, and makers of baskets, nets, mats, and sandals. Each house had a dean who supervised the work. The monks gathered in their units several times each day for liturgical prayer and meals.

Pachomius's knowledge and love for Scripture shaped the life of the community. In this meditation, for example, he exhorts his brothers to let the reality of death drive them to holiness:

> Let the soul, brothers, practice wisdom daily with respect to this material body of ours. When we come to our beds in the evening let it say to our members:
>
> "O legs, how much power have you to stand up and move before you die and become motionless? Will you not now willingly stand up for your Lord?
>
> "O hands, the time is coming when you shall be unable to move, and when you shall never be clasped in each other again. Why then,

before you come to that hour, do you not stretch yourselves out to the Lord?

"O body, before we are separated, rise up boldly to worship the Lord without resistance. And if you listen to me, we shall enjoy happiness together, inheriting the blessing. But if you don't listen to me, then cursed am I that I have ever been chained to you, for on your account I—a wretched thing—shall be condemned."

Now, if you do this daily and consecrate yourselves, you shall become real temples of God. And since God dwells in you, the cunning and wiles of Satan shall not be able to harm you.

Pachomius established nine communities for men and three for women, which attracted more than three thousand disciples. He died of plague in 346. His communities survived long after his death and his rule influenced the monastic tradition in both the eastern and western church.

Pachomius defies the notion that monks fled to the desert to escape civilization. He built large communities that ran prosperous businesses, so there was no escape from people or commercialism. With people and trade came sin, so there was no escape from evil either. Pachomius and other monks were not so much running away from the world, as they were running to God—together.

MAY 9
Angels; Community; Eternal Perspective; Prayer; Worship

40. Aphraates of Persia
(D. 345?)

After his conversion to Christ, St. Aphraates left his native Persia to live in Edessa, Mesopotamia, present-day Syria, because it was a stronghold of the faith. He decided that solitude offered the best opportunity to serve God perfectly. So he dwelt in a cell outside the city, giving himself over to penance, fasting, and contemplation. Later he moved to a hut at a monastery near Antioch, and there he gradually began to interrupt his solitude to counsel visitors.

When the Emperor Valens banished Bishop Meletius from Antioch, the Arians seized the city's churches. So the persecuted faithful were forced to conduct worship services on a military field near the Orontes River. Aphraates left his seclusion to come to their aid. Once as he was walking to meet them at the parade ground, he passed the emperor, who was watching from his porch. "Why does a monk like you wander so far from his cell?" asked Valens. Aphraates responded: "If I were a maiden secluded in my father's house, and saw it catch fire, would you recommend that I stay put and let it burn? You're the one who has kindled the flames that I am trying to extinguish." An imperial servant who threatened Aphraates was soon after accidentally scalded to death, persuading the superstitious emperor to protect the saint later when Arians sought his exile. Aphraates also apparently won Valens' favor by healing his favorite horse!

Many historians believe this saint is the Aphraates who wrote the twenty-three *Demonstrations* that are the earliest documents of the Syrian church. Some of these appear today in the western church's *Office of Readings*, such as the following discourse on true circumcision:

> God changed the first pact with Adam, and gave a new one to Noah. He gave another to Abraham and changed it to give a new one to Moses. . . . he gave another pact in this last age, a pact never again to be changed. . . .
>
> All these covenants were different from each other. Moreover, the circumcision that is approved by the giver of those covenants is the kind spoken of by Jeremiah: Circumcise your hearts. . . .
>
> . . . God is truthful and his commandments are most trustworthy. Every covenant was proved firm and trustworthy in its own time, and those who have been circumcised in heart are brought to life and

receive a second circumcision beside the true Jordan, the waters of baptism that bring forgiveness of sins.

Jesus, son of Nun, renewed the people's circumcision with a stone knife when he had crossed the Jordan with the Israelites. Jesus, our Savior, renews the circumcision of the heart for the nations who have believed in him and are washed by baptism: circumcision by the sword of his word, sharper than a two-edged sword.

Jesus, son of Nun, led the people across the Jordan into the promised land. Jesus, our Savior, has promised the land of the living to all who have crossed the true Jordan, have believed, and are circumcised in heart.

Blessed, then, are those who are circumcised in heart, and have been reborn in water through the second circumcision. They will receive their inheritance with Abraham, the faithful leader and father of all nations, for his faith was credited to him for righteousness (see Genesis 15:6).

Aphraates died around 345.

Perhaps Aphraates correctly decided that solitude was the best way to achieve perfect holiness before God. Certainly the loneliness of seclusion and the pain of asceticism made him humble and broke his willfulness. However, perhaps he approached God more perfectly when he set aside his preference in order to serve his distressed brothers and sisters.

APRIL 7
Saints and Sacraments (Baptism); Solitude

41. Hilarion

(291?–371)

Shortly after St. Hilarion's death, **St. Jerome** wrote about the life of this hermit who had introduced monasticism into Palestine. Jerome told of Hilarion's lifelong pursuit of solitude, where he could encounter God in prayer. And he wrote about the divine irony of the fame that denied it to him because his miracles attracted so many people.

In this brief excerpt, Jerome describes Hilarion's faith and a typical miracle:

> Once . . . when he was eighteen years old, brigands tried to find him at night. Either they believed that he had something to steal or they thought he would scorn them if they didn't intimidate him. . . . From evening till dawn, they hunted in every direction but couldn't find him. In the broad daylight, however, they came upon him and apparently as a joke asked him: "What would you do if robbers attacked you?" He answered: "A naked person does not fear robbers." "You could be killed." "I could," he said. "But I am not afraid of robbers because I am ready to die." Admiring his faith, they confessed their folly of the night before and their blindness, and promised to reform their lives. . . .
>
> A woman of Eleutheropolis, despised by her husband of fifteen years because of her sterility, . . . was the first who dared to intrude upon blessed Hilarion's solitude. While he was still unaware of her approach, she suddenly threw herself at his knees saying: "Forgive my boldness. . . . Don't regard me as a woman, but as a creature to be pitied," . . . for "they that are whole need not the physician, but they that are sick" (see Matthew 9:12). . . . Finally aware of the woman, he asked her why she had come and why she was weeping. When he learned the cause of her grief, raising his eyes to heaven, he commanded her to have faith and to believe. He followed her departure with tears. When a year had gone by, he saw her with her son.

Hilarion had become a Christian at age fifteen as a student in Alexandria. Then he lived two months in the Egyptian desert with **Anthony**, who taught him the disciplines of a monk. Disappointed by the vast number of people who came to Anthony for help, Hilarion returned to Palestine where he hoped to be alone with God. He gave away his inheritance and built a tiny tomb-like hut in the desert near a place called Majuma.

Like Anthony, Hilarion took only a little food once a day at sunset. When tempted sexually, he ate even less. "I'll see to it, you jackass," he said, "that you shall not kick." He never bathed nor changed his tunic until it wore out. He said, "It is idle to expect cleanliness in a hair shirt." Jerome relates that even though Hilarion suffered extreme dryness of spirit, he persevered in prayer and cured many people of sickness and demon possession.

The parade of petitioners and would-be disciples drove Hilarion to retire to more remote locations. But they followed him everywhere. First he visited Anthony's retreat in Egypt. Then he withdrew to Sicily, later to Dalmatia, and finally to Cyprus. He died there in 371.

Even for saints like Hilarion who steadfastly pursued God, life is a battle of wills. Hilarion desired solitude, believing it was God's will for him. But God had other ideas and sent crowds to disrupt his aloneness. Before we get too far along on our journey, we need to check to see if we are following God's road map, not our own. Or we may be like Yogi Berra, who once said, "We're making good time, but we're lost."

OCTOBER 21
Facing Death; Healing Touch; Miracles Do Happen; Solitude

42. Athanasius
(297?–373)

St. Athanasius served as the bishop of Alexandria in Egypt. He governed so effectively in a time of troubles that we must reckon him as one of the church's finest leaders. He cared well both for the churches of Alexandria and Ethiopia, and also for the burgeoning monastic communities in the Egyptian desert. But his main work was leading the fight against the Arian heretics.

Arius and his followers claimed that the Word of God was not eternal, was created in time, and was only figuratively the Son of God. In 325, Athanasius had led the Council of Nicea that condemned the heresy and excommunicated Arius. But the heresy was not easily expunged, and it began to spread anew in 327 just as Athanasius became bishop. For the rest of his life the saint waged an aggressive war of teaching and writing against the Arian movement. In turn, the Arian party continually hassled Athanasius by dragging him into imperial courts to defend himself against trumped-up charges.

For a time it appeared that the Arians might win. Between 338 and 365, Emperor Constantine and his successors alternatively deposed, reappointed, and banished the saint. Off and on, Athanasius spent seventeen and a half years in exile.

In 355, at the height of the controversy, Athanasius had to flee to the desert, where monks protected him for six years. During that time he may have written his *Life of St. Anthony*, the biography that popularized the monastic movement in the western church. This excerpt from that book gives us a glimpse of the practical wisdom that endeared him to his people and that got him through his daily battles:

> Let's continue to be strenuous in pursuing virtue. Let's not grow tired of seeking it, for our Lord has become a guide for us and for every person who has a desire for the virtues. And so that it might not be tedious for us, St. Paul became our example when he said, "I die daily" (see 1 Corinthians 15:31). Now, if we were to think each day that we had to die that day, we would never sin at all. This is the explanation of Paul's saying. If in the morning we imagined that we would never last till evening, and if at evening we thought that we would never see morning, we would never sin.

> If we were to keep the imminence of our death in mind, we would never be overcome by sin: lust which is fleeting would not reign over us; we would never harbor anger against another human being; we would not love the possessions which pass away; and we would forgive every person who offended us. Therefore, beloved, let's be zealous in carrying out the work we have committed ourselves to, and let's travel to the end on the road on which we have begun our journey.

Athanasius was able to return to Alexandria in 365. He dedicated his last seven years to building up the orthodox party which would eventually triumph over Arianism at the Council of Constantinople in 381. Athanasius died in Alexandria on May 2, 373, having traveled to the end on the road on which he began his journey.

Meditating on saints like Athanasius helps me to minimalize my trials. Every morning when Athanasius awakened, he faced the possibility that Arianism might prevail, but he did not flinch or waiver. Every morning when I wake up I face much lesser difficulties. Sometimes I flinch or waiver. But I pray that Athanasius will intercede for me, asking God to give me spiritual spine.

MAY 2

Applied Christianity; Defending the Faith; Doctors of the Church; Facing Death; Pursuit of Holiness; Temptation

43. Nicholas
(Fourth Century)

Sometime in the fourth century a man named Nicholas was elected bishop of Myra, now called Mugla in southwestern Turkey. After his death he was buried in his cathedral. These two sentences tell all that we know for sure about St. Nicholas.

Yet from ancient times Nicholas has been among the most celebrated saints. Somehow during the sixth century a cult of Nicholas's devotees grew extensively throughout the East. And in the ninth century a fictitious biography spread his following westward to Europe. When Muslims invaded Myra in 1087, Nicholas's body was taken surreptitiously to Bari, Italy. Pope Urban II presided at the ceremony that enshrined his relics in a newly constructed church. From that time St. Nicholas has been universally venerated. For example, it is said that in the Middle Ages he was the saint most frequently depicted in art, second only to the Virgin Mary. Today this saint about whom we have so few facts durably maintains his worldwide popularity.

However, we all enjoy the legends about St. Nicholas. All know, for example, the story of the generosity of young Nicholas to an impoverished neighbor. Here it is told by Jacob of Voragine in his famed thirteenth-century book of saints, *The Golden Legend:*

> One of his neighbors, a nobleman, was so poor that he planned to deliver his three daughters to prostitution in order to make a living from the profits of their shame.
>
> When Nicholas heard of this, he was horrified at the thought of such a sin. Wrapping a lump of gold in a cloth, during the night he threw it through a window in his neighbor's house. Then he fled without being seen. The next morning the man found the bundle of gold. Thanking God, he immediately arranged for his eldest daughter's marriage.
>
> A while later, St. Nicholas did the same thing a second time. Finding the gold, the neighbor broke out into great songs of praise. He determined in the future to watch and discover who was thus coming to the relief of his poverty.
>
> A few days later a bundle of gold twice as large was thrown into his house. He heard the noise it made falling and set out in pursuit of Nicholas. He begged him to stop so he could see his face. He ran so fast that he caught up with the young man and recognized him. Throwing himself before him, he tried to kiss his feet. But Nicholas declined his

thanks. He exacted a promise that the man would keep the secret of his deed until after his death.

"Threes" also play a role in other St. Nicholas legends. Nicholas is said to have personally obtained at Myra the release of three innocent men. And he miraculously appeared to the Emperor Constantine to rescue from death three falsely accused imperial officers. These latter reportedly had witnessed his intervention for the three men at Myra and had prayed for God to send Nicholas to their aid. Historians today regard as preposterous the tale that Nicholas resurrected three children that an innkeeper had beheaded and pickled in brine. The story may have been started by people who mistook three bags of gold in pictures for three childrens' heads.

The legends of the three gold bundles and the three children are probably behind the tradition of giving gifts on Nicholas's feast day and at Christmas, which originated in Germany, Switzerland, and the Netherlands. Dutch settlers in the United States transformed Saint Nicholas into the Santa Claus who now helps us celebrate the birth of Christ.

DECEMBER 6 / PATRON OF GREECE, RUSSIA, CHILDREN, BRIDES, PAWNBROKERS, MERCHANTS, SAILORS, TRAVELERS
Generosity; Kindness

44. Apphian
(Fourth Century)

Put Christ first, because he put us first and let nothing deter us from loving him.

—St. Cyprian of Carthage

In his *Church History*, Eusebius of Caesarea tells the story of St. Apphian, sometimes called Epiphanius, a young man of nineteen, who put God's honor ahead of his own life.

As a boy his wealthy parents had sent Apphian to Beirut for a classic Greek education. Eusebius reported that he navigated a virtuous course through the allurements of the big city and the bad influences of his friends. When he returned to his home in Lycia, he found he could not stand his family's irreligious lifestyle. So Apphian ran away to Caesarea, where Eusebius welcomed him into his home. He had spent only a short time there, studying Scripture with his host, when a general persecution of Christians erupted in the empire.

Around 306, the Emperor Maximinus decreed that local governors should see to it that all the people participated in public sacrifices to the gods. Urbanus, the governor of Caesarea, was quick to obey, occasioning Apphian's brave defiance. Eusebius gave this account:

> Throughout Caesarea, by command of the governor, heralds were summoning men, women, and children to the temples of the idols. Officials were also taking roll of all those in attendance. An immense crowd of the wicked were converging from all over town. Then this youth eluded both of us who lived in the house with him and the whole band of soldiers that surrounded the governor. He had not confided his intention to anyone. Fearlessly, he rushed up to Urbanus who was pouring a libation to the gods, grabbed his right hand and restrained him. "Stop this foolishness," he shouted. "We must not abandon the one true God to worship lifeless idols and demons! It will be our doom!"

Soldiers immediately seized Apphian. They beat him until his face was unrecognizable. Then they stretched him on a rack and imprisoned him in a dungeon overnight. The next day the guards tortured Apphian. They ripped open his body, exposing his bones and intestines, but he courageously endured everything. To the soldiers' taunts, he simply replied, "I am Christ's servant." He did not falter even when his tormentors set fire to his feet and burned his flesh to the bone. Because Apphian refused to renounce Christ and offer sacrifice, a magistrate ordered that he be drowned. When the frustrated guards happily implemented the sentence, something extraordinary happened. Eusebius was an eyewitness:

> Although I realize that those who did not see it will scarcely believe what happened next, I must report it. All the people of Caesarea, young and old alike, witnessed the marvelous event. For as soon as the soldiers cast the body of the holy youth into the water, a violent disturbance agitated the sea and the shore around it. An earthquake shook the whole city. And during this tumult, the sea, as though it could not hold the martyr's body, threw it ashore before the city gates.

Apphian loved God so passionately that he resolutely refused to accommodate himself to any evil. Nothing, not even fear of death, could make him betray the one he loved above all. Apphian's radicalism pricks our conscience and compels us to ask disturbing questions. For example: How much do I love God? What are my real priorities? Does material comfort mean more to me than spiritual reality? Would a little pain and humiliation be enough to divert me off course? Do I accommodate evil because I fear the consequences? Oh, St. Apphian, pray for us.

APRIL 2

The Cost of Discipleship; Countercultural Witness; Martyrs; Miracles Do Happen; Twenty-Something Saints

45. Pelagia the Penitent

(Date Unknown)

Like **St. Mary Magdalen** and **St. Mary of Egypt,** St. Pelagia inspired Christians of the Middle Ages as an enchanting icon of repentance. Storytellers probably spun her winsome tale from an anonymous factual illustration embedded in one of **John Chrysostom**'s homilies on **St. Matthew**'s Gospel. He told of a nameless actress of Antioch, famous for her glamour and notorious for her wickedness, who suddenly repented, was baptized, and afterwards embraced the austere life of a hermit.

Later a gifted writer who pretended to be James, a deacon working for St. Nonnus of Edessa, named the actress Pelagia and created the story that still speaks to our spirit. As he told it: One day Pelagia, dressed provocatively and surrounded by an entourage of her fans, passed by a group of bishops sitting at St. Julian's tomb near Antioch. All but one bishop were scandalized by her evil charms. But Pelagia's carefully appointed beauty touched Nonnus and led him to a spiritually disturbing conclusion. He said to the other bishops:

> In this prostitute we should reprove ourselves: we believe that we have a bridal chamber in heaven that will not pass away; . . . we have a fiancé who will neither die nor become corrupted; we have in heaven an inheritance to which the entire world cannot be compared; a happiness whose joy and felicity cannot be described is ours; ours too is the fragrance that never fades away: "eye has not seen, nor ear heard, nor has the mind of man imagined what God has prepared for those who love him" (see 1 Corinthians 2:9).
>
> What more need I say: we have vast promises in the supernal heights stored up with our hidden Lord who cannot be seen. It is he we should please, but we fail to do so; it is for him that we should adorn our bodies and souls, but we totally fail to do so. We should take pains over ourselves in order to scrub away the dirt of sins, to become clean from evil stains; but we have paid no attention to our souls in the attempt to adorn them with good habits so that Christ may desire to dwell in us. What a reproach to us, seeing that we have not taken pains to make ourselves pleasing to God nearly as much as this prostitute . . . has taken pains to please men—in order to captivate them, leading them into perdition by her wanton beauty. . . . Maybe we should even go and become the pupils of this lascivious woman.

The next day, the story continues, Pelagia made a rare appearance in church where she heard Nonnus preach on judgment and salvation. His words stabbed her heart. On the spot Pelagia repented and was converted to Christ. Then she demanded that Nonnus baptize her, a request he happily obliged. A deaconess named Romana took Pelagia under her wing until one day she slipped away. She hid herself in Jerusalem, where disguised as a man, she became a hermit on the Mount of Olives. Word about the holiness of the monk "Pelagios" spread throughout the Holy Land. And when it was discovered upon her death that the hermit was the repentant prostitute Pelagia, she was honored and loved even more.

Repentance came as a surprising gift to Pelagia and made her glad to trade her glamour for sanctity. Today Pelagia's story promises that a gift of repentance may also surprise us, making us glad to exchange the glamour of sin for simple holiness.

OCTOBER 8
Care of the Soul; Conversion; Sin

46. George of Lydda
(D. 303?)

We know St. George as the legendary dragon slayer. He is said to have come upon a young woman in a bridal gown about to be sacrificed to appease a dragon. He wounded the beast, dragged it to the town with the bride's belt, and killed it when the populace agreed to be baptized. The story is more fiction than fact: The dragon appeared late on the scene in the thirteenth-century *Golden Legend*, almost nine hundred years after George's death.

But George was truly a soldier who gave his life for Christ in the early fourth century. Some scholars stiffly contend that no further facts are known about him. Popular historians, however, accept more traditional details, such as this account from a fifth-century panegyric by Theodotus of Ancyra:

> Shortly after the death of St. George's father, a great lover of God named Justus replaced him as the governor of Palestine. When he came into Lydda, he fetched the youth, St. George, and grieved with him over his father's death. Afterwards, Justus entreated his mother to entrust St. George to him as a son. He said that he wanted to give the young man military training and make him a general over his armies. And she agreed to the request. So when George was of age, Justus sent him to the Emperor Diocletian with one hundred soldiers. The emperor was very pleased with St. George and in a short time appointed him general over five thousand men. Then the Emperor sent him back to the governor with much royal pomp.

It is possible that Diocletian appointed George a military tribune and that the saint served under Galerius in a campaign against Persia. He may also have resided for a time in Beirut in Lebanon. Some say Diocletian sent him on expedition to Britain, but the evidence for such a visit is slim.

George probably left the army in 298, when the emperor required all soldiers to participate in the public worship of the Roman gods. In 303, when Diocletian outlawed Christian assemblies and ordered the destruction of churches and Scriptures, George is said to have traveled to the imperial court at Nicomedia to plead for his fellow believers.

Some historians identify George as the hero described by Eusebius in his *Church History:*

> Immediately on the publication of the decree against the churches in Nicomedia, a certain prominent and highly honored man seized the edict and tore it to pieces as a profane and impious thing. He was motivated to this act by zeal for God and incited by ardent faith. And he did this while Diocletian and Galerius were in Nicomedia. After distinguishing himself in such a manner, he then suffered those things that were likely to follow such daring. And he kept his spirit cheerful and undisturbed until death.

For his crime, George was brutally tortured and beheaded, probably in 303.

Christian lore esteems George as one of the greatest martyrs. He became a popular figure in England during the Crusades, which called on his protection for soldiers. In 1415, after the battle of Agincourt, King Henry V solidified George's popularity by declaring him the patron saint of England.

Perhaps Christians have celebrated St. George as the slayer of the legendary dragon because we hope that through his intercession he can help us triumph over the very real dragons we find inside. St. George the Dragon Slayer, pray for us.

APRIL 23 / PATRON OF ENGLAND AND PORTUGAL
Countercultural Witness; Martyrs; Spiritual Warfare

47. Agnes

(D. 304?)

"A new kind of martyrdom!" exclaimed **St. Ambrose,** bishop of Milan. The assembly cheered and applauded. He was celebrating St. Agnes because she was a virgin, a martyr—and a child. She was executed at Rome in 304 during the Emperor Diocletian's vicious persecution. Here are Ambrose's observations on her death:

> St. Agnes is said to have suffered martyrdom at age twelve. The cruelty that did not spare so young a child was hateful, but the power of faith in the child was greater. Was there room for a wound in that small body? The sword could barely strike her, yet she had the inner strength to strike back. Girls of her age usually can't even bear a parent's angry glance. They cry at needles' pricks as though they were wounds. Agnes, however, faced her persecutors fearlessly. When they attempted to force her to worship at the pagan altars, she stretched out her hands and made the sign of the cross over the sacrificial fires. She was not fazed by the heavy weight of the chains they wrapped around her. And she freely offered her body to the executioner's sword.
>
> The executioner used both threats and allurements to try to change her mind. He encouraged young men to beg her to marry them. But she answered, "I already have a spouse, and I will not offend him by pretending that another might please me. I will give myself only to him who first chose me. So, executioner, what are you waiting for? Destroy this body that unwanted eyes desire."
>
> Agnes stood and prayed. Then she bent down her neck. The executioner trembled as though he himself had been condemned. His right hand shook and his face grew pale, but the virgin showed no fear at all.
>
> So in one victim we have a twofold martyrdom of purity and faith, for Agnes both remained a virgin and also obtained martyrdom.

Historians say that legends have embroidered the few facts we know about Agnes. But the stories are rooted in actual events and convey kernels of truth about her. These legends tell that Agnes was a beautiful and soon-to-be-marriageable young woman. Many eager young men pursued her, but she rebuffed them because she had consecrated her virginity to Christ.

One spurned suitor took revenge by reporting to the authorities that Agnes was a Christian. She was brought before a judge who tried to persuade her to recant. He threatened her with fire and torture, but she did not flinch. Then he had her stripped at a brothel and urged young men to seduce her. "You may stain your sword with my blood," she said, "but you will never profane my body that I have consecrated to Christ." All were so stunned by her presence that only one boy tried to touch her. Legend says he was struck blind, and that Agnes healed him.

Exasperated and egged on by her first accuser, the governor ordered her execution. Agnes was taken to the Stadium of Domitian, where she courageously faced a nervous soldier who hacked her to death with his sword. Over the centuries the little virgin martyr became one of the most popular saints in Christian history.

> *St. Agnes's death was "a new kind of martyrdom!" She taught us adults the meaning of valor while she was still a child. Agnes hurried to the place of her execution more joyfully than a bride goes to her wedding. And she was adorned not with plaited hair, but with Christ himself.*
>
> —St. Ambrose

JANUARY 21 / PATRON OF GIRLS
Child Saints; Courage; Passion for Purity

48. Eulalia of Mérida

(D. 304?)

St. Eulalia died a martyr at Mérida, Spain, during the persecution of Diocletian. In the early Middle Ages, her story captivated the hearts of Catholics throughout Europe. People admired her because they believed that she was only twelve when she submitted to a monstrous death. And the church in Spain now celebrates Eulalia as its greatest virgin martyr.

Around 405, Prudentius wrote a hymn in Eulalia's honor, which popularized her story. In the poem she appears as a child mature beyond her twelve years. Because she seemed determined to defy the decree requiring worship of the gods, her mother hid her at a home in the countryside. But Eulalia slipped off at night and the very next morning fearlessly confronted the judge. Prudentius wrote:

"Miserable men, for the Christians you search!
Lo, I am one of that odious race,
Foe to your fiendish idolatrous rites.
Witness to Christ with my heart and lips,
Under my feet I will trample your gods. . . ."

The judge tried bribery and gentle persuasion to win her, suggesting that she need only let her finger touch a little salt and incense. But Eulalia rebuffed him and she tramped on the offering cake. Losing all patience, the judge threatened her with instruments of torture. As Prudentius tells it:

Forthwith two slaughterers seize her and rend,
One on each side, her innocent breasts,
Cutting her virginal flesh to the bone
With clawlike instruments, cruelly sharp.
Counting her wounds, thus Eulalia speaks:
"Lo, thou has written, O lord, on my flesh
Beautiful letters I joy to read,
Telling thy triumph, O Christ, to the world.
Streams of red blood that pour forth from my wounds
Utter thy holy, all-powerful name."

When the executioners touched flames to her wounds, Eulalia's hair caught fire and she was burned alive. Prudentius says that as she died a miraculous sign of her innocence amazed the onlookers:

> Then of a sudden a snowy-white dove
> Springs from the martyr and flies
> Forth to the stars in the sight of the crowd.
> It was Eulalia's innocent soul,
> Winging its way to celestial heights.

Snow fell, covering Eulalia's remains until the Christians buried them nearby. Later, to mark the spot where she died, they constructed a church that became a popular shrine for pilgrims. **Augustine, Jerome,** and **Venantius Fortunatus** wrote about Eulalia, establishing her fame. And the earliest known French poem celebrated her courageous sacrifice.

> *By their eloquent and attractive example of a life completely transfigured by the splendor of moral truth, the martyrs light up every period of history by reawakening its moral sense.*
>
> —Pope John Paul II

DECEMBER 10 / PATRON OF SAILORS, RUNAWAYS, AND VICTIMS OF TORTURE
Child Saints; Martyrs

49. Vincent of Saragossa

(D. 304)

At the turn of the fourth century, St. Vincent, a young deacon, served under Valerius, his mentor and bishop of Saragossa in Spain. The two men gave courageous witness to the Christian faith during the general persecution by Diocletian.

In order to prevent Christian subversion of the state, in 303 the emperor forbade priests to offer Christian worship and he required all to sacrifice to the pagan gods. Dacian, the governor of Spain, enforced the decree in Saragossa. In 304, he arrested Valerius and Vincent and imprisoned them at Valencia. He allowed them to linger in prison, hoping that deprivation would open them to submission. But when the two men finally appeared before him, they remained stalwart in their Christian conviction. So Dacian exiled the elderly Valerius. But he decided to break Vincent with torture.

Our details about Vincent's martyrdom come from a fifth-century poem by Prudentius. Because the poet wrote so long after Vincent's death, historians are cautious about his story, as he may have embroidered it. But the main outlines of Prudentius's tale are probably true.

When Dacian ordered Vincent to adore the gods, he defiantly refused. Prudentius imagined that the young man ensured his suffering with this eloquent speech:

> To him the martyr answer made:
> "Come then, put forth your utmost strength,
> Use every force at your command,
> And I will still defy your laws.
>
> "Hear you the creed that we profess:
> Christ and the Father are one God,
> Him we confess, and him we serve;
> Destroy this faith, if you have power.
> Your tortures are to Christians sweet,
> The iron hooks and prison chains,
> The hissing flames and red-hot grates,
> And even death, the final doom.
>
> How senseless are your false beliefs,
> How stupid Caesar's stern decree!

You order us to worship gods
That match your own intelligence. . . .

"Well do they know and understand
That Christ still lives and reigns on high,
And that his kingdom soon to come
Shall to the wicked terror strike.

"They loudly cry as they confess
That by the power and name of Christ
They are cast out of men possessed,
These demons foul, who are your gods."

Famous for his brutality, Dacian had Vincent stretched on the rack, raked with iron hooks, roasted on a grill, and rubbed down with salt. All to no avail, as Vincent stood firm. Then the governor had him thrown into a dungeon whose floor was covered with broken pottery that opened his wounds. Prudentius says angels came to minister to the young man. Reportedly the jailer saw a divine light hovering around Vincent and was converted on the spot. At last Dacian seems to have relented. He allowed Christians to visit and comfort Vincent before he died from his terrible agony.

Vincent's story spread rapidly throughout the church, strengthening the faith of many Christians throughout the Middle Ages.

The blood of the martyrs is the seed of the church.

—Tertullian

JANUARY 22 / PATRON OF PORTUGAL AND OF VINTNERS IN BURGUNDY
Angels; Countercultural Witness; Martyrs

50. Methodius of Olympus
(D. 311?)

At the turn of the fourth century St. Methodius served as bishop of Olympus in present-day Turkey. But we know him better as a theologian who defended orthodoxy amid the controversies that swirled in the late-third-century Eastern Church. We also remember him as a teacher of Christian doctrine who believed that through the ministry of the church and the exercise of the spiritual disciplines, the radiance of God's image could be restored in sinful human beings.

Methodius vigorously, but respectfully, opposed Origen, the great lay theologian of Alexandria. He refuted the Origenist ideas of the eternity of the world and the preexistence of the soul. Especially, he debunked Origen's view that a person's resurrected body was not the same one he had during life on earth. Methodius also debated the Gnostics, holding against their fatalism the view that redeemed human beings had recovered enough freedom of the will to choose to do good.

In *The Symposium*, patterned on Plato's dialogue of the same name, Methodius displays the pastoral side of his teaching. He takes us to a banquet in the garden of virtue and allows us to eavesdrop on the conversation of ten maidens who are celebrating virginity. In their voices the saint presents his view that through its liturgy and teaching the church refurbishes the divine image in the souls of believers.

Methodius concluded this dialogue with one of the earliest liturgical hymns. The ten virgins are escorting Christ, the Bridegroom, and his Queen, the church, in a marriage procession:

Refrain: Chastely I live for you,
And holding my lighted lamp
My Spouse, I go forth to meet you.

From on high, there has come, O virgins, the sound of the cry that wakes the dead, bidding us to go to meet the Bridegroom in the east with all speed in white robes and with our lamps. Awake, before the King enters within the gates.

Flying from the riches of mortals that bring only wealth of sorrow, from love, from the delights and pleasures of this life, I desire to be sheltered in your lifegiving arms and to gaze forever on your beauty, Blessed One.

O Queen arrayed in beauty, receive us too with open doors within the bridal bower, O Bride of unsullied body, gloriously triumphant, breathing loveliness! At Christ's side we stand in robes like yours, singing, O youthful maiden of your blessed nuptials.

Chanting the new strain, our virgin choir escorts you, our Queen, to heaven, bathed in light. And garlanded with white lily cups, we bear in our hands light-bearing flames.

O Blessed One, who dwells in heaven's pure seat from all eternity, and governs all with everlasting sway, behold, we have come! Receive us too, O Father, with your Servant, within the gates of life.

Methodius was a prolific writer, but his other works have disappeared or have survived only in small fragments. Around 311 he died a martyr during the last general Roman persecution.

When we disagree with someone about religion, we should take the example of Methodius as a warning. We should respect people with whom we differ, as Methodius honored Origen, while refuting his doctrines. Humility preserves both truth and peace.

SEPTEMBER 18
Defending the Faith; Passion for Purity

51. The Forty Martyrs of Sebaste
(D. 320)

After 316, the emperor Licinius decreed a persecution of Christians in the East. He threatened death if they failed to renounce their faith. In 320, forty young Christian Roman soldiers refused to sacrifice to idols and were tried before the tribunal at Sebaste, Cappadocia. The governor tried threats, bribery, and torture to persuade the young men, but they stood firm. He put the forty in prison, where it is said that Christ appeared and encouraged them to persevere.

Incensed by the soldiers' obstinacy, the governor ordered that they be stripped and left to die standing on a frozen lake. He arranged a fire and warm bath on the shore to tempt them to apostatize. All forty signed a will, drafted by St. Meletius, the youngest, that expressed their faith, unity, and courage:

> When we by God's grace and the common prayers of all shall finish the strife set before us, and come to the rewards of the high calling, we desire that then this will of ours may be respected . . . : that our relics be conveyed to our father the presbyter Proidos . . . so that they may be deposited near the city of Zela at the spot called Sarin.
>
> For although we come from different localities, we have chosen one and the same resting-place because we have set before ourselves one common strife for the prize. These things have seemed good to the Holy Spirit and have pleased us. Therefore we . . . brothers in Christ beseech our honored parents and relatives to have no grief or distress, but to respect the decision of our brotherly fellowship, and to consent heartily to our wishes, so that you may receive from our common Father the great recompense of obedience and of sharing in our sufferings. . . .
>
> And if the boy, Eunoikos, by God's favor shall be brought to the same end . . . , he has requested to share our dwelling-place. But if he should be preserved unhurt by the grace of God and should be further proved in the world, we charge him to look liberally to our chapel. And we exhort him to keep the commandments of Christ, that in the great day of resurrection he may obtain part in our happiness. . . .
>
> We pray with our souls and with the Divine Spirit that we may all obtain the eternal good things of God and his kingdom, now and forever and ever. Amen.

The young men did not wait to be stripped, but removed their clothes themselves. And together they prayed, "Lord, we are forty engaged in this contest. Grant that forty may receive crowns and that we may not fall short of that sacred number." After one night's ordeal, however, one soldier caved, but died of extreme heat in the bath, losing his martyr's crown. But an off-duty guard, prompted by the martyrs' courage and a dream, professed himself a Christian and took his place, thus preserving their number.

After three days the governor had the survivors' limbs broken and their bodies burned. Officials hoped that young Meletius would save himself, but his mother herself lifted him onto the wagon, not wanting him to lose his prize. The governor had the ashes of the forty martyrs scattered into a river, but Christians secured some that became treasured relics, inspiring many throughout the Middle Ages.

The young martyrs of Sebaste have fascinated me since my youth. And their idealism and brotherhood may also intrigue today's young people and invite them to consider seriously a commitment to Christ. "Young people," says journalist Paul Lauer, "have enough energy to climb tall mountains of faith, hope, and love. If all we offer them are little molehills, they'll simply go elsewhere for their challenges."

MARCH 10
Martyrs; Purpose; Twenty-Something Saints

52. Alexander

(D. 326)

Trouble dogged St. Alexander from the moment he became bishop of Alexandria in 312. Immediately, he had to deal with opposition from Meletius of Lycopolis, whose rigorism toward lapsed Catholics had led him into schism. He also had problems with Kolluth, a priest who had usurped the power to ordain deacons and priests.

Alexander's biggest difficulty, however, was his controversy with the priest Arius. Arius viewed Alexander as a rival, and Alexander's choice as bishop frustrated his ambition. In a greathearted gesture, Alexander put Arius in charge of an important parish. Then Arius began to preach errors that rocked the church for decades. He taught that Christ was not truly God, that the Son was a creature who at some time did not exist and was capable of sinning.

At first Alexander tried to use gentle persuasion to correct Arius. But when discussions with local clergy failed to convince him of his error, Alexander had a synod of Egyptian bishops condemn and excommunicate him. Afterwards, Arius flooded the East with propaganda in his defense. To counteract it, Alexander wrote numerous letters explaining his actions and exposing Arius's error. The following passage comes from one of two such letters that have survived:

> Oh, the new and ineffable mystery! The Judge was judged. He who absolves from sin was bound. He was mocked who once framed the world. He was stretched upon the cross who stretched out the heavens. He was given up to the tomb who raises the dead. The powers were astonished, the angels wondered, the elements trembled, the whole created universe was shaken, the sun fled away . . . because it could not bear to look upon the crucified Lord. . . .
>
> . . . But when our Lord rose from death and trampled it down, when he bound the strong man and set man free, then every creature wondered at the Judge who for Adam's sake was judged, . . . at the immortal dead, at the celestial buried in the earth. For our Lord was made man. He was condemned that he might impart compassion. He was bound that he might set free. . . . He suffered that he might heal our sufferings. He died to restore life to us. . . .
>
> . . . For this cause he came down upon earth, that by pursuing death he might kill the rebel that slew men. For one underwent the judgment, and myriads were set free. One was buried, and myriads rose

> again. He is the mediator between God and man. He is the resurrection and salvation of all. He is the guide of the erring, the shepherd of men who have been set free, the life of the dead, the charioteer of the cherubim, . . . and the king of kings, to whom be the glory for ever and ever. Amen.

After Emperor Constantine conquered the East in 324, he intervened in the controversy. He sent Hosius of Cordoba, his adviser, to attempt to reconcile Alexander and Arius. However, when Hosius understood the issues at stake, he joined forces with Alexander. Together they called a general council at Nicea in 325. Alexander and his colleague, **St. Athanasius,** led the orthodox party at the council, which condemned the Arian heresy.

Two years later Alexander died after naming Athanasius as his successor.

> *We were made for action, and for right action—for thought, and for true thought. Let us live while we live, let us be alive and doing; let us act on what we have, since we have not what we wish. Let us believe what we do not see and know. Let us forestall knowledge by faith.*
>
> —John Henry Newman

FEBRUARY 26
Defending the Faith; Jesus Christ

53. Ammon

(D. 350?)

A wealthy uncle forced St. Ammon to marry at age twenty-two. However, **St. Paul's** praise of virginity inspired the couple to live as brother and sister, which they did for eighteen years. His uncle's death finally released Ammon to embrace the life of a hermit. With his wife's permission, he withdrew to Nitria, and became the first monk to dwell in that Egyptian wasteland. His wife invited a few nuns to live with her and Ammon came to give them spiritual direction twice a year.

When numerous other hermits began to gather in Nitria, **St. Anthony** advised Ammon to form them into a community. So at a center ten miles south of Nitria, Ammon organized his disciples into a loose-knit monastery that came to be called Kellia. The monks lived apart in their own cells under very light pastoral supervision. They assembled on Saturdays and Sundays to celebrate the hours and mass, and to share a common meal.

Ammon's teaching on the Christian ideal created a sense of unity among his brothers. In the following letter, for example, he urged them to yield to the Holy Spirit:

> If anyone has been stripped of the heavenly garment of the new life, he must plead tearfully with the Lord until he clothes his soul in the power from above. For God and his saints turn their faces away from those who are not clothed in the Holy Spirit. If Adam felt shame when he saw that he was naked, how much more shame is felt by the soul which is stripped of its Lord? Let him blush for his nakedness. Let his spirit cry out loudly to God until the heavenly glory comes to clothe him.
>
> When the woman suffering from a flow of blood believed and touched the hem of the Lord's clothing, her flow of blood dried up. In the same way, every soul wounded by sin and punished by a flood of evil thoughts will be saved if it draws near to the Lord in faith. And the stream of its evil thoughts will be dried up through the power of Jesus Christ, the Lord of the world.
>
> You must ask day and night for this divine power to be granted to you. It will cleanse and purify the eyes of your heart, enabling them to contemplate God in all purity. This power will also purge your soul of all worldly cares. So you must this instant implore God to send the

> Paraclete down to you from above. For the Lord has promised to send the Holy Spirit to all who ask it of him.

For many years Ammon disciplined himself to eat meals of bread and water only several times a week. He believed severe mortification helped him restrain evil thoughts and focus more tightly on God in prayer. He died around 350 at the age of sixty-two. Fifty years after his death, about six hundred hermits were living in Kellia.

In The Life of St. Anthony, ***St. Athanasius*** *tells this story about Ammon. Once he and Theodore, his disciple, had to cross a flooded river. They separated to undress, but even alone Ammon was too shy to swim across naked. While he hesitated, he found himself miraculously transported to the other shore. Our culture has so desensitized us to nudity that we may think Ammon a bit of a prude. But like other desert fathers, Ammon avoided physical nakedness to preserve his purity. And to cover his spiritual nakedness, he clothed himself with the Spirit.*

OCTOBER 4
Community; Holy Spirit; Passion for Purity; Repentance; Temptation

54. Eusebius of Vercelli

(D. 371)

In 345 the clergy and people of Vercelli in north Italy chose St. Eusebius as their bishop. **St. Ambrose** reported that he was the first bishop in the West to live in a monastic community with some of his priests. Life together with his clergy gave the bishop personal support as well as an opportunity to strengthen his brothers. Eusebius believed that the spiritual health of his flock depended on the quality of his clergy. So he invested himself in training his priests, ensuring their faith, and improving their pastoral care. Impressed by his success, many other bishops asked his help in the formation of their clergy.

Pope Liberius commissioned Eusebius to work for the wider church in 354. Eusebius persuaded the emperor Constantius to call a council at Milan in 355 to settle the Arian controversy. The meeting exploded in confusion when Eusebius stoutly opposed an attempt to condemn **Athanasius.** Outraged, the emperor banished Eusebius. Arian jailers imprisoned him in various locations in the East, where they abused him and humiliated him by dragging him naked through the streets. They also made it difficult for him to receive support from his friends, but he managed to write the following letter to his community at Vercelli:

> When I receive a letter from one of you and see in your writings your goodness and love, joy mingles with tears, and my desire to continue reading is checked by my weeping. . . . Days pass in this way as I imagine myself in conversation with you, and so I forget my past sufferings. . . .
>
> Dearly beloved, I rejoice in your faith, in the salvation that comes from faith, in your good works, which are not confined to your own surroundings but spread far and wide. Like a farmer tending a sound tree, untouched by ax or fire because of its fruit, I want not only to serve you in the body, good people that you are, but also to give my life for your well-being.
>
> Somehow or other I have managed with difficulty to complete this letter. I asked God constantly to keep the guards away hour by hour, and to allow the deacon to bring you some kind of greeting in writing, not simply news of my suffering. So I beg you to keep the faith with all vigilance, to preserve harmony, to be earnest in prayer, to remember me always, so that the Lord may grant freedom to his church which

is suffering throughout the world, and that I may be set free from the sufferings that weigh upon me, and so be able to rejoice with you.

I also ask . . . you in God's mercy, that each one of you should add his own name to the greeting in this letter. . . .

When Constantius died in 361, Eusebius obtained release for himself. Then he undertook new missions to Alexandria to consult with Athanasius and to Antioch on a failed effort to quell a schism. Finally, he collaborated with **Hilary of Poitiers** in opposing an Arian bishop of Milan.

A scholar saint, Eusebius may have taken part in composing the Athanasian Creed. He may also have copied the Vercelli Gospel Book, the earliest surviving manuscript of the Old Latin version of the Gospels. We don't know anything about his last years, except that he died in Vercelli in 371.

When you receive a letter from a friend, you should not delay to embrace it as a friend. For it is a fine consolation among the absent that if a loved one is not present, a letter may be embraced instead.

—Isidore of Seville

AUGUST 2

Community; The Cost of Discipleship; Defending the Faith; Great Pastors

55. Ephrem

(306?–C. 373?)

Syrians have nicknamed St. Ephrem "the Harp of the Holy Spirit" for his spellbinding preaching and especially for his beautiful hymns. While Christians have sung hymns from earliest times, we owe to Ephrem their extensive introduction into the church's public worship and their use as tools for instruction.

Heretics employed songs to spread false teachings, so Ephrem decided to imitate their success. He composed Christian hymns and set them to the tunes of the heretical songs. Ephrem had a women's choir sing his hymns in church. In a short time the saint's superior compositions had replaced all of his opponents' hymns.

Ephrem filled his poetry with great empathy for people's hurts. Here is one of his eighty-five surviving funeral hymns. He wrote it to diffuse a parent's sorrow over the death of a child.

Oh my son, tenderly beloved!
Whom grace fashioned
In his mother's womb,
And divine goodness completely formed,
He appeared in the world
Suffering like a flower,
And death put forth a heat
More fierce than the sun,
And scattered its leaves
And withered it, that it ceased to be.
I fear to weep for thee,
Because I am instructed
That the Son of the Kingdom hath removed thee
To his bright habitation.
Nature, in its fondness
Disposes me to tears,
Because, my son, of thy departure.
But when I remember the bright abode
To which they have led thee,
I fear lest I should defile
The dwelling place of the King
By weeping, which is adverse to it;
And lest I should be blamed,
By coming to the region of bliss

With tears which belong to sadness;
I will therefore rejoice,
Approaching with my pure offering.

Ephrem was baptized at eighteen. For a quarter of a century he headed up a school for his mentor, St. Jacob, the bishop of Nisidis, Syria. When Nisidis fell to the Persians in 350, Ephrem fled to the mountains near Edessa and lived in a cave. From this base, the saint made frequent sorties into the city to serve the church. Biographers say that his preaching on the end times moved his listeners so deeply that their sobs often competed with his eloquence.

Ephrem was a prolific writer of apologetics, theology, and commentaries on Scripture, for which he has been recognized as a doctor of the church. He was ordained a deacon late in life. He died in 373, shortly after he had spent several years in Egypt administering the distribution of food, money, and medical relief to the poor.

In the funeral hymn, Ephrem says awareness of the bright place to which Christ has taken the child comforts the parents and mollifies their sense of loss. I have never lost a child, but I remember the pain I felt at my mother's death. And I recall once shortly after her death, groaning loudly, and then singing a little verse about Christ wiping away my tears. As I sang, in my mind's eye I saw my mother, dressed in gold, dancing in a circle of light. Ephrem was right—singing of heaven heals a grieving heart.

JUNE 18
Defending the Faith; Doctors of the Church; Facing Death; Poets

56. Macarius the Great

(300?–390)

As a young man in upper Egypt, St. Macarius adopted the lifestyle of a hermit. He lived quietly until a woman falsely accused him of rape. Her relatives and friends beat him and dragged him through the streets, which he endured without complaint. However, the woman suffered in labor, unable to deliver her child until she cleared his name. Then Macarius became so popular for his virtue, that he had to withdraw to the wilderness of Scete in the Egyptian desert.

A large colony of hermits gathered around Macarius and he became their mentor. Widely known for his wisdom in his own day, we still benefit from his sayings. For example, consider his teaching on prayer: "You don't need to use many or high-sounding words. Just repeat often, 'Lord, show me mercy as you know best.' Or 'God come to my assistance.' "

Many legends about his pastoral care for other hermits have survived. Once, for example, he met Satan on his way to tempt some brothers in another part of the desert. The devil bragged that one brother, Theopemptus, especially obeyed him. So Macarius visited Theopemptus to help him conquer his temptations. As the story goes,

> Theopemptus received him with great joy. When he was alone with him, the old man asked him, "How are you getting on?" Theopemptus replied, "Thanks to your prayers, all goes well." The old man asked, "Don't your thoughts war against you?" He replied: "Up to now, it is all right," for he was afraid to admit anything.
>
> The old man said, "See how many years I have lived as an ascetic, and am praised by all. And though I am old, the spirit of fornication troubles me." Theopemptus said, "Believe me, abba, it is the same with me." The old man went on admitting that other thoughts warred against him, until he had brought him to admit them about himself.
>
> Then he said: "How do you fast?" He replied, "Till the ninth hour."
>
> "Practice fasting a little later. Meditate on the Gospel and the other Scriptures. If an alien thought arises within you, never look at it but always look upwards, and the Lord will come at once to your help." . . . The old man then returned to his solitude.

The next time Macarius encountered Satan, the devil complained about his failure to succeed in seducing the brothers. The story continues:

> When Satan returned, the old man asked him, "How are the brothers?" . . . He replied, "They are all obdurate, and the worst is the one friend I had who used to obey me. I don't know what has changed him, but not only does he not obey me any more, but he has become the most resistant of them all. So I have promised myself not to go down there again at least not for a long time."

When Macarius was very old, Lucius, the Arian usurper of the see of Alexandria, banished him to an island in the Nile delta. Before Lucius relented and allowed him to return to the desert, his holy example had converted many pagan inhabitants of the island. Shortly after his return to Scete, Macarius died at about ninety years of age.

> *Once Macarius directed a young seeker to go to a cemetery and upbraid the dead. Then to go and flatter them. "What answer did the dead give you?" he asked. "None at all," said the youth. "Then go and learn never to let abuse or flattery move you. If you die to the world and yourself, you will begin to live for Christ."*

JANUARY 15
Leading Men; Prayer; Sexual Temptation; Spiritual Warfare

57. Cyril of Jerusalem

(315?–386)

A gentle and conciliatory man, Cyril was not built for controversy. But he was bishop of Jerusalem in the heyday of the Arian heresy that denied Christ's divinity. Although condemned at the Council of Nicea in 325, with the support of several emperors Arianism flourished for another half century. Thus for most of his episcopacy, St. Cyril of Jerusalem was locked in conflict with the Arians.

Nicea had denounced Arianism's teaching that the Word was not eternal but rather a created being. Cyril does not seem to have been entirely happy with council's choice of the word "homousios" to describe the Son's "consubstantial" equality with the Father. He did not like it because it was not a biblical term. But while the saint appeared occasionally to lean toward watered-down versions of Arianism, he always remained orthodox. Exiled three times by Arian opponents, Cyril spent sixteen of his thirty-seven years as bishop away from his see. And in 381, Cyril stood with the orthodox party at the Council of Constantinople that pulled down the final curtain on Arianism.

Chief among Cyril's surviving writings are his *Catechetical Lectures*, sometimes described as the earliest systematic presentation of Catholic theology. Annually he presented two teaching series, one preparing catechumens for baptism and the other instructing the newly baptized in basic Christian living. Listen to him proclaim God's mercy to his catechumens:

> God loves human beings, and loves them in no small measure. Don't say, "I have fornicated and committed adultery. I have done dreadful things not only once, but often. Will he ever forgive me?"
>
> Listen to the psalmist: "How great is the abundance of your goodness, O Lord!" (see Psalm 31:19 or 20). Your accumulated offenses do not surpass the abundance of God's mercies. Your wounds are not greater than the Physician's skill. Just give yourself up in faith. Tell the Physician your ailment. With David, say: "I said, 'I will confess my sin to the Lord,' and you forgave the wickedness of my heart"—and the same shall be done to you (see Psalm 32:5).
>
> My new catechumens, would you like to see the loving-kindness of God and the abundance of his long-suffering? Then hear about Adam. When Adam, God's first-formed man, sinned, could he not at once have killed him? But consider what the Lord does in his great love for

Adam. He cast him out of Paradise because his sin made him unworthy to live there. However, God made him live close to Paradise so that, seeing from what and into what a state he had fallen, he might afterwards be saved by repentance.

Cain, the firstborn man, murdered his brother. Yet after slaying his brother, to what is he condemned? "You shall become a restless wanderer on the earth" (see Genesis 4:12). How great the offense, how light the sentence!

Brothers and sisters, make your heartfelt confession to the Lord. So you will both receive forgiveness for your former sins and also be counted worthy of the heavenly gift. You will thus inherit the heavenly kingdom with all the saints in Christ Jesus.

With Arianism's demise, for the last six years of his life Cyril cared for his flock in relative peace. He died in Jerusalem in 386.

We proclaim the Crucified and the devils quake. So don't be ashamed of the cross of Christ. Openly seal it on your forehead that the devils may behold the royal sign and flee trembling far away. Make the sign of the cross when you eat or drink, when you sit, lie down or get up, when you speak, when you walk—in a word, at every act.

—Cyril of Jerusalem

MARCH 18
Doctors of the Church; Mercy; The Sign of the Cross

58. Hilary of Poitiers
(315?–368?)

Much ink has been inconclusively spilled debating whether reason can prove the existence of God. But without doubt reason can carry a person to faith, as it brought St. Hilary of Poitiers to Christianity. A gifted pagan rhetorician, Hilary observed that human beings had been placed on earth to live virtuously and be rewarded for it. Such thinking led him to make a rational inquiry about God. He dismissed polytheism as illogical and determined that God was one and eternal. Then reading Scripture, especially the Pentateuch and John, brought him to Christ. He was baptized around 350.

Twenty-first-century readers may lift an eyebrow when they learn that Hilary, a married man with a daughter, was acclaimed bishop of Poitiers, France, in 353. But at that time, while bishops were normally selected from among the priests, an outstanding layman was sometimes chosen by popular demand. Hilary proved himself an excellent choice. Not only did he administer his diocese well, but he emerged in the West as the chief opponent of Arianism.

In 325, the Council of Ephesus had condemned the Arian heresy that the Son was a created being and not consubstantial with the Father. But with the support of several emperors, Arianism continued to flourish in the fourth century. At synods and in the public forum, Hilary fought the heresy aggressively, pitting himself against the powers of the day. In 356, because he refused to sign a document that deposed **Athanasius,** the champion of orthodoxy in the East, Hilary was banished to Phrygia. He used his three years' exile to write *De Trinitate*, his major treatise against the heresy. Modern readers would find it heavy reading. But occasional passages like the following can enlighten and inspire us:

> We must understand the Father and the Son according to the teaching of the divine scriptures, so that, when we have learned to know them and become familiar with them, our words may become clearer. The eternity of God transcends places, times, appearances and anything conceivable by the human mind. He is outside of all things and within all things. He comprises all things and is comprised by none. He does not change either by increase or decrease. He is invisible, incomprehensible, complete, perfect and eternal. He does not know anything

from elsewhere, but he himself is sufficient unto himself to remain what he is.

The unbegotten one brought forth the Son from himself before all time. Not from any pre-existing matter, because all things are through the Son. Nor from nothing, because the Son is from him. Nor as an ordinary birth, because there is nothing changeable or empty in God. Nor as a part that is divided, cut off or extended, because God is incapable of suffering and is incorporeal. Such things are characteristic of the flesh, and according to the apostle: "In Christ dwells all the fullness of the Godhead bodily" (see Colossians 2:9).

He is, therefore, the perfect Son of the perfect Father, the only-begotten offspring of the unbegotten God, who has received everything from him who possesses everything. He is God from God, Spirit from Spirit, Light from Light. And he proclaims with assurance: "I am in the Father and the Father is in me" (see John 14:10).

Hilary continued to battle for orthodoxy until his death in Poitiers around 368.

O God, may all my thoughts and words speak of you. Fill with wind the sails I have hoisted for you, and carry me forward on my course. Breathe your Spirit into my faith and the way I confess it. Enable me to continue the preaching I have begun.

—Hilary of Poitiers

JANUARY 13
Defending the Faith; Doctors of the Church; Married Saints

59. Basil the Great

(329–379)

Once the Emperor Valens, a supporter of Arianism, sent his agent Modestus to compel Basil, the influential bishop of Caesarea, to accommodate the heretics. Basil flatly refused. "No one talks to me like that," Modestus objected. "Perhaps," Basil said icily, "you have never yet had to deal with a bishop." On the strength of Modestus' report that only force could prevail against such a man, the emperor let the issue die. Thus we have one reason why Basil is called "great" —he successfully defended the freedom of the church from the overreaching power of the state.

Basil and his best friend, **Gregory Nazianzen**, effectively opposed Arianism as bishops and theologians. In their apologetics they significantly contributed to the development of Catholic doctrine, Gregory on the Trinity and Basil on the Holy Spirit. In the following passage, Basil describes the workings of the Spirit:

> As warmth cannot be separated from fire, nor brilliance from light, so the power to sanctify and to give life, together with the qualities of goodness and righteousness, cannot be separated from the Spirit. For as the Father is one and the Son is one, so too the Holy Spirit is one.
>
> The Spirit is spread throughout all creation and yet gives of his essence without ever being diminished. He distributes his grace to everything, yet he is never dispersed in particular situations. But he is constantly replenishing those he has visited without losing anything himself. For just as the sun shines on various things, giving of itself but never being diminished in the process, so the Spirit lavishes his gifts while remaining complete and undivided.
>
> He lightens the path to God for all who seek it. He inspires prophets. He gives wisdom to legislators and spiritual guidance to priests. He gives strength to kings and confidence to the honest and just. He heals the sick and revives the dead, releases those in chains and adopts those without a family. Through the working of the Spirit, the weak can escape the strong, the poor become rich and the ignorant surpass the wise.
>
> The Spirit is in heaven, but he fills the world with his presence that cannot be constrained. He is wholly present in each, and yet wholly with God. Let us pray that he is always at our side and that he never abandons us.

The Spirit had touched Basil as a young man through the influence of **St. Macrina**, his older sister. She persuaded him to forsake his promising secular career to devote himself to Christ. After a systematic tour of the monasteries of the East, Basil started a monastic community near the family estate in Pontus. Gregory and other young men soon joined him. Basil wrote a shorter and a longer *Rule* for his brothers that, through **St. Benedict**, shaped western monasticism for centuries and influenced the course of the monastic way in the East—another reason we call him "great." Unlike the individualistic hermits of the eastern desert, Basil insisted that monks share in community life. The purpose of monasticism, he taught, was to help monks find salvation by loving one another.

For a long time Basil endured a serious stomach ailment. He died on January 1, 379, at the age of forty-nine.

Basil taught a "social" Catholicism, building on his conviction that mutual love is the essence of Christianity. And he lived it. As bishop, for example, he personally manned a soup kitchen, cared for reformed prostitutes and thieves, and built and staffed a hospital complex for the people of Caesarea.

JANUARY 2, WITH ST. GREGORY NAZIANZEN
Community; Defending the Faith; Doctors of the Church; Holy Spirit; Saints and Politics; Serving the Poor

60. Macrina

(327?–379)

With charm and grace, St. Macrina ruled the roost in a family of saints. St. Basil the Elder and St. Emmelia, her parents, had ten children including the younger **St. Basil, St. Gregory of Nyssa,** and St. Peter of Sebaste. As the eldest child, Macrina exercised a formative influence on her more famous brothers and even on her mother.

A beautiful young woman, Macrina had been betrothed at age twelve. But when her fiancé died, she chose to remain single to devote herself to Christian service. Emmelia had given her daughter a Christian version of a classic education, training her in Scripture instead of Greek literature. In turn, Macrina conducted the early education of her younger brothers and sisters and formed them in piety.

Gregory of Nyssa, her biographer, reported that when Basil returned from Athens University all puffed up with self-importance, Macrina put him in his place—as only an older sister can. Apparently she persuaded her extremely talented brother to become a monk and subordinate his gifts to God's purposes.

When Naucratius, the handsome and athletic family favorite, died suddenly, Macrina supported Emmelia through her grief. Later she persuaded her mother to join her in renouncing their high standard of living and embracing the simpler life of their servants. Together they formed a small monastic community of nuns under the younger Basil's direction on the family estate at Annesi in Pontus in present-day Turkey.

In 379, shortly after Basil died, Macrina fell ill. Gregory came to visit her and found her in a very weakened condition, lying on two planks. Even though Macrina could barely talk, she spoke eloquently with her brother about death and the future life. Just before she died she prayed as follows:

> "O Lord, you have freed us from the fear of death. You have made the end of life here the beginning of a true life for us. For a time, you give rest to our bodies in sleep and you awaken us again with the trumpet. The dust from which you fashioned us with your hands you give back to the earth for safekeeping. And you will recall it, transforming with immortality and grace our mortal and graceless remains.

"O God everlasting, towards whom I have directed myself from my mother's womb: Send a shining angel to lead me to the place of refreshment where restful waters flow near the bosom of the holy fathers. You who compassionately gave paradise back to the man crucified with you, remember me also in your kingdom. For I too, have been crucified with you, having nailed down my flesh through fear of your judgments. Don't let the terrible abyss separate me from your chosen ones. Don't let the slanderer stand in my way. If I have committed sins in word, deed or thought because of the weakness of our nature, don't let your eyes discover them. You who have power on earth to forgive sins, forgive me so that I may be refreshed. May I be found before you once I have put off my body, having no fault in the form of my soul. May my soul be received into your hands, blameless and spotless, as an offering before you."

St. Gregory of Nyssa expanded his sister's deathbed reflections on the future life in his book, *On the Soul and the Resurrection.*

St. Emmelia and St. Basil the Elder have given us a superior model for Christian family life. They handed on the faith to their children in a loving household, and the children led by Macrina encouraged one another in the faith.

JULY 19
Eternal Perspective; Facing Death; Family

61. Gregory Nazianzen
(329?–390)

As a young man at school in Athens, St. Gregory Nazianzen became best friends with **St. Basil**, his polar opposite. Basil was the practical activist and Gregory the intellectual mystic. They complemented each other, and together their works influenced the shape of Christian spirituality for many centuries.

Gregory's life theme was the union with God that Christ had come to bestow on human beings. In the following sermon excerpt, he celebrates baptism, the sacrament through which Christ dispenses that incomparable gift of divine illumination.

> Illumination is the splendor of souls, the conversion of life, the aid to our weakness, the renunciation of the flesh, the following of the Spirit, the fellowship of the Word, the improvement of the creature, the overwhelming of sin, the participation of light, the dissolution of darkness. It is the carriage to God, the dying with Christ, the perfecting of the mind, the bulwark of faith, the key of the kingdom of heaven, the transformation of life, the removal of slavery, the loosing of chains, the remodeling of the whole person.
>
> Why should I go into further detail? Illumination is the greatest and most magnificent of the gifts of God.
>
> And as Christ the Giver is called by many various names, so too is this gift. We call it the gift, the grace, baptism, anointing, illumination, the clothing of immortality, the bath of regeneration, the seal and everything that is honorable.
>
> We call it the gift because it is given to us in return for nothing on our part. Grace because it is conferred even on debtors. Baptism because sin is buried with it in the water. Anointing as priests and kings for such were they who were signed with oil. Illumination because of its brilliance. Clothing because it hides our shame. The bath because it washes us. The seal because it preserves us and is moreover the indication of lordship. The heavens rejoice in the gift. The angels glorify it because of its kindred splendor. The gift is the image of the heavenly bliss. We long to sing out its praises, but we cannot worthily do so.

Gregory Nazianzen should be named patron saint of all who want one thing and have to settle for another. All his life Gregory longed for the solitude where he could simply rest in God. Instead, circumstances constantly dragged him into the public arena where he had to use his considerable gifts to serve God's people. At thirty he wanted to retire as a monk with Basil at Pontus. But he was ordained over his protests and for fifteen years reluctantly served as coadjutor to his father, who was the bishop of Nazianzus.

In 380, several bishops persuaded Gregory to come to Constantinople to help turn the tide against Arianism. He turned his house into a church named *Anastasis*, denoting a place where the true faith would revive. There he preached his celebrated sermons in which he defined the characteristics of the Trinity. With his friend **St. Gregory of Nyssa**, in 381 he presided over the Council of Constantinople that put the nails in Arianism's coffin.

Worn down by stress and controversy, in 384 Gregory retired to his estates at Nazianzus. He finally enjoyed a few years of solitude there before he died in 390.

> *Be purified that you may be like lights in the world, a quickening force to all others. May you stand as perfect lights beside that great Light. And may you learn the mystery of the illumination of heaven, enlightened by the Trinity more purely and clearly.*
>
> —Gregory Nazianzen

JANUARY 2, WITH ST. BASIL
Defending the Faith; Doctors of the Church; The Light of Christ; Saints and Sacraments (Baptism)

62. Gregory of Nyssa

(330?–395?)

St. Gregory was born into a family of saints: **St. Basil** and **St. Macrina**, Gregory's older brother and sister, raised him and his brother, St. Peter of Sebaste, after the death of his parents, also saints. Young Gregory became a lector in the church and married Theosebia, who was a strong Christian. He briefly flirted with a career as a rhetorician until **St. Gregory Nazianzen**, his friend, urged him to renounce it. Gregory returned to Christian ministry and was ordained a priest. As celibacy was not yet required, he may have stayed with his wife. But it's also possible that Theosebia joined St. Macrina's convent.

In 372, St. Basil appointed Gregory bishop of Nyssa, expecting him to counteract the influence of Arians in Armenia. But unskilled in diplomacy, Gregory failed in his tactless efforts to curb the heretics. They trumped up charges against him and drove him into exile until 378. Later, Gregory achieved prominence throughout the empire as a defender of orthodoxy. In 381 he played a significant role at the Council of Constantinople, which ended the Arian controversy.

The church of Gregory's day esteemed him as an apologist, honoring him as "the Father of the Fathers." His major writings include a catechetical discourse, Bible commentaries, and ascetical treatises. Gregory traveled extensively in his later years, preaching sermons that combined theological profundity with practical application. For example, in the following excerpt from a homily on Jesus' baptism, he offered a helpful strategy for dealing with temptation:

> After the dignity of our adoption the devil plots more vehemently against us, pining away with envy, when he sees the beauty of the new-born person, earnestly tending towards that heavenly city, from which he fell. And he raises up against us fiery temptations, seeking eagerly to despoil us. But when we are aware of his attacks, we ought to repeat to ourselves the apostolic words, "As many of us as were baptized into Christ were baptized into his death" (see Romans 6:3). Now if we have been conformed to his death, sin in us is surely now a corpse, pierced through by the javelin of baptism, as that fornicator was thrust through by the zealous Phinehas (see Numbers 25:7–8).
>
> Flee therefore from us, ill-omened one! For you seek to despoil a corpse, one long ago joined to you, but one who long since lost his

senses for pleasures. A corpse is not enamored of bodies, a corpse is not captivated by wealth, a corpse slanders not, a corpse lies not, snatches not at what is not its own, reviles not those who encounter it. My way of living is oriented to another life. I have learned to despise worldly things—to pass by the things of earth, to hasten to things of heaven—even as Paul expressly testifies, that the world is crucified to him, and he to the world (see Galatians 6:14).

These are the words of a soul truly regenerated. These are the utterances of the newly-baptized person, who remembers his own profession, which he made to God, when the sacrament was administered to him, promising that he would despise for the sake of love towards God all torment and all pleasure alike.

Gregory of Nyssa died around the year 395.

Once Gregory tried to resolve a family conflict by forging letters to Basil from an uncle, who was a bishop and a heretic. Basil uncovered the deceit, and with a touch of humor rebuked his younger brother. It's nice to know that a person can do dumb things and still become a saint.

MARCH 9
Defending the Faith; Married Saints; Spiritual Warfare; Temptation

63. Monica
(332–387)

Most often we think that what made Monica a saint was her long-suffering prayer for the conversion of her son, **St. Augustine.** But that's only a small part of the story of her sanctity.

In his *Confessions* and other writings, Augustine tells us all we know about St. Monica. Wisely, he described both her flaws and her strengths, so that we get a picture of her willingness to change and grow in Christ. As a young adult, for example, she broke a serious drinking habit when an angry servant girl called her a drunk.

Monica also dealt heroically with challenging family circumstances at the family home in Tagaste, North Africa. Her husband, Patricius, was volatile and unfaithful, but she related to him patiently. Monica's overbearing mother-in-law also lived with the family, making her marriage even more difficult. But Monica wove good relationships out of these evil possibilities. And she ultimately led both her husband and mother-in-law to Christ and the church.

Perhaps the virtue that contributed most to her holiness was her peacemaking. Augustine said:

> Among people who were quarreling or at discord she showed herself, whenever she could, very much of a peacemaker. She might hear very many bitter things said on both sides. This kind of outpouring of swelling and undigested malice very likely takes place when a person talks to a friend who is present about an enemy who is absent. On these occasions hatred is expressed in its very real crudity and in the bitterest terms possible. But my mother would never report to one person what another had said to her, unless what had been said might help to bring the two together again.
>
> Ordinary humanity ought to make us feel that we have not done enough if we merely refrain from increasing and exacerbating ill feeling among people by our evil tongues. We ought to go further and try to use our tongues well so as to put an end to ill feeling. This was what my mother was like, and you, Lord, were the master who, deep in the school of her heart, taught her this lesson.

For thirty years Monica prayed and schemed for Augustine's deliverance from his immorality and philosophical confusion. She alternated between faith and worry for him, surrendering him to God, yet traipsing after him to Milan. There finally in 386 Monica watched as **St. Ambrose** baptized her son. Then she spent a little time living in community with him and his Christian friends. However, she took sick in 387 and died at Ostia on the way home to North Africa.

St. Monica told Augustine just before her death that she felt she no longer had any reason to live:

> *My son, as to me, I no longer find any pleasure in this life. What more I have to do here and why I am still here I do not know, since I have no longer anything to hope for in this world. There was only one reason why I wanted to stay a little longer in this life, and that was that I should see you a Catholic before I died. Now God has granted me this beyond my hopes. For I see that you have despised the pleasures of this world and have become his servant. So what am I doing here?*

AUGUST 27 / PATRON OF ALCOHOLICS, DIFFICULT MARRIAGES, MOTHERS, VICTIMS OF UNFAITHFULNESS, AND WIDOWS
Difficult Marriages; Family; Intercession; Peacemakers

64. Martin of Tours
(336?–397)

One wintry day, young Martin, soldier and catechumen, met a shivering beggar in the streets of Amiens, France. Everyone knows the story. He cut his cape in two, giving half to the man. That night in a dream St. Martin saw Jesus wearing it and heard him say, "Martin is still only a catechumen, but has covered me with this garment." Stunned, soon afterward Martin presented himself for baptism.

Martin's father, a Roman tribune, had arranged for his son's conscription into the army at age fifteen. So Martin performed military service until he decided that it contradicted his Christian commitment. Sulpicius Severus, the saint's first biographer, described the day that Martin became the first Christian conscientious objector:

> . . . The barbarians were invading the Gallic provinces. Assembling an army at the city of the Vangiones, Emperor Julian prepared to distribute a bonus to his troops. The men were called up in the customary manner, one by one, until Martin's turn came. He recognized that moment as a suitable time to ask for his discharge, and he did not think it would be honest for him to accept the bonus when he did not intend to fight. "I have fought for you up to this point," he said to Caesar. "Now let me fight for God. As for your bonus, let someone who is going to join the battle receive it. I am a soldier of Christ: combat is not permitted me."

Julian exploded with rage and threatened Martin, calling him a coward.

> "If my act is set down to cowardice rather than to faith," he said, "I shall stand unarmed tomorrow before our lines. In the name of the Lord Jesus and protected only by the sign of the cross, without shield or helmet, I shall penetrate the enemy's ranks and not be afraid." The order was given that he should be put under guard: he was to make good his promise to be exposed, unarmed, to the barbarians.
>
> The next day, the enemy sent an embassy to sue for peace, handing over themselves and all that was theirs. From this can anyone doubt that the victory was due to the blessed man—a grace granted to prevent his being sent unarmed into combat?

As there was now no war to fight, Martin got his discharge.

In 360, **St. Hilary**, the bishop of Poitiers, gave Martin some land at Ligogé where he tried to live as a hermit. But disciples assembled around him and together they pioneered the first monastery in western Europe.

Circumstances prevented Martin from withdrawing entirely from an active life. The people of Tours acclaimed Martin bishop in 372. As bishop, he continued to live as a monk, establishing a monastery for eighty men on the outskirts of town. Martin was eager to Christianize rural areas so he invented a rudimentary parish system, faithfully visited village churches, and planted monasteries as educational centers.

Martin was renowned as a miracle worker, performing many cures and even raising a dead man. Once, for example, he healed **St. Paulinus of Nola's** diseased eye by touching it lightly with a fine paintbrush. Martin died on November 11, 397. Because of his reputation, promulgated by his biographer, he became one of the most admired saints of the Middle Ages.

Martin was a proponent of separation of church and state, but not in the contemporary sense. He wanted to prevent the state from interfering with the freedom of the church. Once, for example, he opposed the government's efforts to execute the heretic Priscillian because it was the church's business to deal with heresy, not the state's.

NOVEMBER 11 / PATRON OF SOLDIERS AND BEGGARS
Community; Countercultural Witness; Dreams; Healing Touch; Miracles Do Happen

65. Ambrose

(339–397)

"Ambrose for bishop!" someone shouted, and the whole assembly picked up the chant. St. Ambrose was flabbergasted. He was only a catechumen, thus not yet baptized, and had no desire to become bishop. As the governor he had come to church to pacify the Catholics and the Arian party as they chose a new bishop for Milan. Ambrose tried to evade the election, but the people prevailed. He was first baptized, then a week later consecrated bishop on December 7, 374.

Ambrose's first action as bishop was to divest himself of his wealth. He gave his money to the poor and his property to the church. He appointed St. Satyrus, his brother, to be his administrator, so that he could focus on the spiritual welfare of his people. Realizing that his Christian education was incomplete, he immersed himself in the study of Scripture and the church Fathers.

As bishop, Ambrose modeled prayer, kindness, and holiness for his flock. His door was always open, and every day people lined up to receive his help and counsel. When **St. Augustine** visited Milan in 386, Ambrose was instrumental in his conversion, probably as much by his witness as by his words. In his extensive writings in defense of the faith, Ambrose successfully used his classical education to give rational explanations of Christian truths. But his teaching always had a practical side, as the following selection shows:

> Perhaps you wonder, "Why are the wicked joyous? why do they live in luxury? why don't they have to strive like I do?" The reason is that they who have not signed up to strive for the crown are not required to undergo the labors of the contest. Those who haven't gone down to the track don't smear themselves with oil, nor get covered with dust. Trouble comes only to those on their way to glory. The perfumed spectators prefer to watch, not to join in the struggle, nor to endure the sun, the heat, the dust, and the rain.
>
> So those who have devoted themselves to pleasures, luxury, robbery, gain or honors are spectators rather than combatants. They have the profit of labor but not the fruits of virtue. They love their ease. By cunning and wickedness they heap up riches. But they will pay the penalty of their iniquity, though it be late in coming. Their rest will be in hell, yours in paradise. Thus, Job said beautifully that they watch in

the tomb (see Job 21:32), for they cannot have the calm of quiet rest that he enjoys who shall rise again.

Ambrose was embroiled in the high politics of the Roman Empire. He resisted the attempts of powerful Arians to get control of church buildings. And within a decade he had purged the Arian heresy from Milan. In 383, the Empress Justina sent him on a diplomatic mission to prevent the usurper Maximus from attacking Rome. Ambrose successfully persuaded him to confine himself to Gaul, Spain, and Britain. When the Christian emperor Theodosius had seven thousand Thessalonians executed as a reprisal, Ambrose required him to do public penance. He once said, "The emperor is in the church, not over it," and he stuck by it.

Ambrose died on Good Friday, 397.

O God, Creation's secret Force,
Yourself unmov'd, all motion's source,
Who from the morn till evening's ray,
Through all its changes guid'st the day:
Grant us, when this short life is past,
The glorious evening that shall last:
That by a holy death attain'd
Eternal glory may be gain'd.

—Ambrose

DECEMBER 7 / PATRON OF LEARNING AND CANDLEMAKERS
Applied Christianity; Defending the Faith; Doctors of the Church; Enduring Trials; Saints and Politics

66. Amphilochius

(339?–400?)

St. Amphilochius may have become a more familiar writer among the Fathers, but most of his works have not survived. We know about him mostly from the letters of his cousin, **St. Gregory Nazianzen,** and of his friend, **St. Basil.** Amphilochius began his career as a rhetorician at Constantinople. But he got into financial difficulty and moved near Nazianzus, where he grew close to Gregory. In a charming note we learn from Gregory that the cousins exchanged vegetables from their gardens, with Gregory joking that he always seemed to get the worst of the deal.

In 374, probably at St. Basil's initiative, Amphilochius became bishop of Iconium. Just after his consecration, he visited Basil and preached for his people, who claimed that they benefited more from his sermons than from any other visitor. Amphilochius preached with a charismatic flair, as this excerpt from his sermon for Holy Saturday demonstrates:

> Death has seized Our Lord Jesus Christ; but shall not keep its hold on Life. It swallowed him, not knowing him: but with him, it will give up many. . . . Tomorrow, he shall rise again, and hell shall be emptied. Yesterday, on the cross, he darkened the sun's light, and behold in full day it was as night. Today death has lost its dominion, suffering itself a kind of death. Yesterday the earth mourned, . . . and in sadness clothed itself in a garment of darkness. Today, "the people that walked in darkness have seen a great light" (Isaiah 9:1 *NJB*).
>
> O new and unheard-of happening! He is stretched out upon a cross who by his word "stretched out the heavens" (see Isaiah 51:13). He is held fast in bonds who has set the sand a bound for the sea (see Jeremiah 5:22). . . . He is crowned with thorns who has crowned the earth with flowers. With a reed they struck his head who of old struck Egypt with ten plagues, . . . That countenance was spat upon at which the Cherubim dare not gaze. Yet, while suffering these things he prayed for his tormentors saying: "Father, forgive them; they do not know what they are doing" (Luke 23:34 *NJB*).
>
> He overcame evil by goodness. Christ undertook the defense of those who put him to death: eager to gather them into his net; annulling the charge, and pleading their ignorance. Made the sport of their

> drunken frenzy, he submitted without bitterness. . . . What more could he do?

During his two decades as bishop, Amphilochius aggressively combated heresies. In 376, he held a council at Iconium that condemned the Macedonian heresy that denied the divinity of the Holy Spirit. St. Basil supported Amphilochius in this effort by writing a treatise on the Holy Spirit at his request. Later when Emperor Theodosius refused his demand to ban the Arians from meeting, Amphilochius resorted to a ploy by deliberately slighting the emperor's son. When the emperor reproached him, he said, "You can't stand an offense to your son, but you tolerate those who dishonor God's Son!" Persuaded, the emperor forbade Arians to assemble privately or publicly.

Amphilochius died around 400.

Turning with contrite hearts to the Lord our God, the Father Almighty, let us give thanks with all our hearts, asking him by his power to drive evil from our thoughts and actions, increase our faith, guide our minds, grant to us his holy inspirations and bring us to joy that is without end, through his Son, Our Lord and Savior Jesus Christ. Amen.

—Amphilochius

NOVEMBER 23
Defending the Faith; Great Preachers; Jesus Christ

67. Fabiola
(D. 399)

St. Fabiola belonged to the group of highborn women of Rome who fell under the influence of **St. Jerome.** However, unlike **Paula** and **Marcella**, who embraced the religious life, Fabiola pursued her Christian calling in the world. A gifted and competent woman, she seems to have been driven by a restlessness that she directed into Christian social activism.

Fabiola's friendship with Jerome cooled over the issue of her divorce and remarriage. Because her husband was abusive and unfaithful, she obtained a civil divorce. However, Fabiola remarried while he was still alive, a violation of church law. When her second husband died, she reconsidered her behavior, repented, and reconciled herself to the church. After she performed public penance at the Lateran cathedral, the pope restored her to full communion. Jerome tells us that Fabiola, typically passionate and headstrong, then channeled her energies into important Christian service:

> When she was restored to communion, what did Fabiola do? Having once suffered shipwreck, she was unwilling again to face the risks of the sea. Therefore, instead of reembarking on her old life, she sold all that she could lay hands on of her property (it was large and suitable to her rank). And she converted it into money so she could give it to the poor. She was the first person to found a hospital, where she might gather sufferers from the streets and where she might nurse the unfortunate victims of sickness and want.
>
> She often carried on her own shoulders persons infected with jaundice or covered with filth. She also often cleansed the revolting discharge of wounds which others, even men, could not bear to look at. She fed her patients with her own hand, and moistened the scarce breathing lips of the dying with sips of liquid. I know of many wealthy and devout persons who, unable to overcome their natural repugnance to such sights, perform this work of mercy by the agency of others. They give money instead of personal aid. I do not blame them and am far from construing their weakness of resolution into a want of faith. While, however, I pardon such squeamishness, I extol to the skies the enthusiastic zeal of one who is above it. A great faith makes little of such trifles. Fabiola so wonderfully alleviated the disease of the suffering poor that many healthy people began to envy the sick.

Fabiola's redirecting of her life bore significant fruit. She made history by founding the first public hospital on record in the West.

In 395, Fabiola visited Jerome in Bethlehem. She had hoped to spend the rest of her days there, but she could not tolerate the lifestyle of Paula's religious community. Jerome quipped that her only idea of solitude was stopping at an inn, like Mary at Bethlehem, then continuing on her fast-paced journey. So Fabiola returned to Rome where she continued her works of private and public charity. With St. Pammachius, for example, she founded a large hostel for sick and poor pilgrims that became world-famous.

St. Fabiola died in 399. Jerome said that all the people of Rome gathered at her funeral to acknowledge her generous contributions.

Mother Teresa loved this verse that describes Fabiola, who seems to stand as a distant forebear of the saint of Calcutta:

Love has a hem to her garment
That reaches the very dust.
It sweeps the stains
From the streets and lanes,
And because it can, it must.

DECEMBER 27 / PATRON OF DIFFICULT MARRIAGES, THE DIVORCED, VICTIMS OF PHYSICAL ABUSE AND UNFAITHFULNESS, WIDOWS
Innovative Saints; Care of the Sick; Difficult Marriages; Generosity

68. Syncletica

(D. 400?)

The poignant sayings of the desert fathers have charmed many of us. But fewer among us have encountered the desert *mothers*. These dedicated women of the fourth and fifth centuries left the world for simplicity and solitude in the wilderness. When the church scans the centuries for women who could be named doctors of the church, it should take a good look at these desert "ammas." Their grace-filled writings rival in wisdom those of the fathers. Consider, for example, St. Syncletica, a beautiful and gifted woman who lived at Alexandria, Egypt, in the fourth century.

As the daughter of wealthy Macedonian parents, marriage into a high-society family was Syncletica's expected course. But as a young girl she had pointed her life in a different direction by promising to live single for Christ. When Syncletica's parents died, she inherited their fortune and responsibility for her blind sister. Like **Anthony,** she distributed her wealth to the poor and abandoned the seductions of the world. Together with her sister she went to live in an unused burial chamber on a relative's estate. With a priest as her witness, she cut her hair to signify her break with ordinary society and renewed her vow of virginity.

Many women sought Syncletica's counsel. Although reticent at first to give much advice, as she matured in holiness she felt freer to teach others. Here is a sampling of her very practical sayings that she characteristically illustrated with homey metaphors:

> Amma Syncletica said:
>
> In the beginning there are a great many battles and a good deal of suffering for those who are advancing towards God and afterwards, ineffable joy. It is like those who wish to light a fire; at first they are choked by the smoke and cry, and by this means obtain what they seek. As it is said, "Our God is a consuming fire" (see Hebrews 12:24): so we must kindle the fire in ourselves through tears and hard work.
>
> If you have begun to act well, do not turn back through constraint of the enemy, for your endurance destroys the enemy. Those who put out to sea at first sail with a favorable wind. Then the sails spread, but later the winds become adverse. Then waves toss the ship, and the rudder no longer controls it. But when in a little while there is calm, and

> the tempest dies down, the ship sails on again. So it is with us, when we are driven by the spirits who are against us. We hold to the cross as our sail and so we can set a safe course.
>
> It is dangerous for anyone to teach who has not first been trained in the practical life. For someone who owns a ruined house and receives guests there does them harm because of the dilapidation of the dwelling. That one causes loss to those who come. By words a person may convert them to salvation, but by evil behavior, he injures them.

In Syncletica's eightieth year, a disease infected her lungs and cancer began to devour her larynx and mouth. Gradually she lost her speech, but her biographer says her calm endurance of excruciating pain spoke plainly to all. She died around 400 at the age of eighty-four.

> *We have a most experienced pilot at the helm of our vessel, Jesus Christ, who will conduct us safe into the haven of salvation, if our sluggishness does not cause our own ruin.*
>
> —Syncletica

JANUARY 5
Christian Living; Leading Women; Spiritual Warfare

69. John Kolobos

(D. 409?)

St. John's Greek nickname "Kolobos" meant "small," and the English-speaking world sometimes calls him John the Dwarf. An intense person with an angry disposition, he humbly subdued his passions and became renowned as one of the wisest of the desert fathers.

When John first went into the desert at Scete in Egypt, his mentor ordered him to plant a dry stick in the ground and water it daily until it bore fruit. Without complaint, John daily walked a long distance to carry water for the stick. After three years, the stick had taken root and borne fruit. Then John's mentor presented the fruit to other hermits. "Take," he said, "and eat the fruit of obedience."

On his own, however, John did not always behave so prudently. Once, for example, he walked naked into the desert, telling a brother hermit that he was going to live like an angel. He returned a week later and knocked on the door of the hut. "It's John," he said, "let me in." But his brother said, "You can't be John, he's an angel now, not a man." The hermit let John stand outside until morning, when the saint repented of his folly.

John disconnected himself completely from current events and never spoke of the "news." He saturated himself so thoroughly in God's presence that he was often distracted and forgetful. Yet the following winsome story has John giving an old hermit advice about correcting forgetfulness:

> There was an old man at Scete, very austere of body, but not very clear in his thoughts. He went to see Abba John to ask him about forgetfulness. Having received a word from him, he returned to his cell and forgot what Abba John had said to him. He went off again to ask him and he returned with the same word. As he got near his cell, he forgot it again. This he did many times; he went there, but while he was returning he was overcome by forgetfulness.
>
> Later, meeting Abba John he said to him, "Do you know, abba, that I have forgotten again what you said to me? But I did not want to overburden you, so I did not come back."
>
> Abba John said to him, "Go light a lamp." He lit it. He said to him, "Bring some more lamps and light them from the first." He did so.

Then Abba John said to the old man, "Has that lamp suffered any loss from the fact that other lamps have been lit from it?"

"No."

"So it is with John. Even if the whole of Scete came to see me they would not separate me from the love of Christ. So whenever you want to, come to me without hesitation."

So, thanks to the endurance of these two men, God took forgetfulness away from the old man. The monks of Scete do violence to themselves to win others to do good.

John built a monastery near the Wadi Natrun to care for the disciples who had assembled around him. When Berbers invaded Scete around 400, he retreated across the Red Sea and reestablished his base at Clysma, near the place where **Anthony** had dwelt. He died there in his seventies with his brothers around him. When they asked him for a final word of wisdom, he said:

I never followed my own will, nor did I ever teach another what I had not first practiced myself.

OCTOBER 17
Kindness

70. John Chrysostom

(347–407)

History has given St. John the nickname "Chrysostom," or "Goldenmouthed," because he was an unusually gifted speaker. Like Archbishop Fulton Sheen, a twentieth-century "Chrysostom," he employed secular wisdom to reinvigorate the faith of Christians and attract people to Christ. From his platform as patriarch of Constantinople, John wielded significant influence throughout the fourth-century Roman Empire.

Even as a youth at Antioch he excelled in oratory. Libanius, his mentor, said that he would have named John his successor "had the Christians not snatched him from us." Baptized at twenty, John tried monasticism in the wilderness for six years. But his extremes nearly killed him, and he returned to the city in 381.

Bishop Flavian of Antioch ordained John a priest in 385. For the next dozen years he served as the bishop's deputy, assigned as an ombudsman for the poor. In these years John earned his reputation as one of Christianity's most outstanding pastors, preachers, and expositors of the faith. He delivered extensive series of sermons on Mark, John, and Romans, using his skill as an exegete to help people apply biblical teaching correctly.

John's constant theme was God's inexhaustible mercy. He often coaxed sinners to repent, as he does here:

> Suppose that a believer who once was pleasing to God becomes full of wickedness and commits grievous sins that exclude him from the kingdom. I will not allow even a person like that to despair, although he may have grown old practicing his unspeakable wickedness.
>
> Now if the wrath of God were a passion, a person might well despair of quenching the flame that his many sins kindled. However, because the divine nature is passionless, God never punishes nor takes vengeance with wrath, but with tender care and much lovingkindness. So we must be of much good courage and trust in the power of repentance.
>
> God does not punish for his own sake even those who have sinned against him, for nothing can harm that divine nature. Rather, to our advantage he acts to prevent our perverseness from worsening by our habitually neglecting him.
>
> Even a person who places himself outside the light inflicts no loss on the light. But shut up in darkness, he suffers the greatest loss himself.

> Similarly, he who habitually despises that almighty power, does no injury to the power, but inflicts the greatest possible injury on himself. And for this reason God threatens us with punishments—and often inflicts them—not as avenging himself, but by way of drawing us to himself.

In 397, Emperor Arcadius had John appointed patriarch of Constantinople. Immediately he set out to renew the church. Starting with himself, he cut his personal expenses, giving his savings to the poor. He imposed strict discipline on the clergy and called for the moral reform of the imperial court and the people. John's efforts made him many enemies, including Empress Eudoxia, who resented his condemnation of the frivolous behavior of women at court. Twice she conspired to have him banished. The second time imperial officials forced John to walk in bad weather to a location in Pontus. He died en route of exhaustion on September 14, 407.

I have always been ambivalent about administering punishment. And I have never liked being on the receiving end, even when I deserved it. But if I can appropriate John's view of punishment as an act of lovingkindness, maybe I can begin to take it and give it in the right spirit.

SEPTEMBER 13 / PATRON OF PREACHERS
Doctors of the Church; Great Preachers; Mercy

71. Jerome
(341?–420)

In the Apocalypse a book is shown sealed with seven seals, which if you hand to an educated person saying, "Read this," he will answer, "I can't because it's sealed." Today many people claim to be educated, yet the Scriptures are a sealed book to them, one which they cannot open except through him who has the key of David, "he that opens and no one shuts; and shuts and no one opens" (see Revelation 3:7).

In the Acts of the Apostles, Philip asked the holy eunuch who was reading Isaiah, "Do you understand what you are reading?" He answered: "How can I unless someone should guide me?" (see Acts 8:30–31). Yet although he had the book in his hand and took the words of the Lord into his mind, and even had them on his tongue and pronounced them with his lips, he still did not know the one he unknowingly worshiped in the book. Then Philip came and showed him Jesus, who was concealed beneath the letter. What a wonderful teacher! In the same hour the eunuch both believed and was baptized. He became one of the faithful and a saint. He was no longer a pupil, but a master.

I have touched on this instance to convince you that you can make no progress in the holy scriptures unless you have a guide to show you the way.

—Jerome

At age eighteen, St. Jerome went to Rome where in six years he mastered Greek and Roman literature. He took Cicero, the Roman senator, as a model for his rhetoric. He was also baptized at Rome, but claims that worldly distractions diluted his Christianity. For several years after 366 he lived as a monk near Aquilea, his hometown on the Adriatic. When Jerome traveled to Antioch in 374, he fell ill with a high fever. In a delirium he dreamed he saw himself before Christ's judgment seat:

"Who are you?" a voice asked.

"I'm a Christian," Jerome said.

"No, you're a liar. You're Cicero's disciple, not mine."

Jerome responded by withdrawing into the Syrian desert. For five years he trained himself by prayer and fasting to obey God. Sexual temptations plagued him at that time, but he distracted himself by studying Hebrew vocabulary and grammar.

Afterwards Jerome undertook biblical studies with **St. Gregory Nazianzen** at Constantinople. He was then fully equipped to launch his life project of producing an accurate Latin Bible. Over several decades he translated afresh most of the Old Testament and corrected the text of the New Testament. His edition of Scripture, called the Vulgate, for fifteen centuries was the benchmark translation of the Bible in the western church.

Jerome's sharp tongue and curmudgeonly disposition made him many enemies. His nastiness and broken relationships marred his reputation. Once a pope viewing a painting of Jerome striking his breast with a stone, said: "If it were not for that rock the church would have never declared you a saint." During a three-year stay at Rome he antagonized so many pagans and Christians that he had to relocate to Bethlehem in 385.

St. Paula and other highborn women that Jerome had influenced at Rome joined him. Together the two saints founded a monastery for men, a convent for women, and a hospice for visitors to the Holy Land. St. Jerome died there in 420.

After 404 barbarians overran Rome, and many Christians fled to the Holy Land. At Bethlehem, Jerome dropped all of his biblical studies. "Today," he said, "we must translate the words of Scripture into deeds, and instead of speaking saintly words, we must act them."

SEPTEMBER 30 / PATRON OF SCRIPTURE SCHOLARS
Feisty Saints; Repentance; Saints and the Bible; Sexual Temptation

72. Marcella

(325?–410)

St. Marcella seems to have been one of those warm, gracious but tough and forthright Italian women who are fun to know.

Like **St. Paula**, we know her exclusively from **St. Jerome's** letters. We have sixteen of them in which Jerome answers her questions on religious topics. Marcella, not a very docile student, often pushed Jerome, making him defend his answers. But he liked her feistiness. He praised her for it in this eulogy, which he wrote upon her death to Principia, her beloved pupil:

> As I was looked on as a person of some reputation in the study of the Scriptures, she never met me without asking some question about them. Nor did she immediately agree with my explanations. . . . To the contrary she would dispute them, not for the sake of argument, but in order to learn the answers to the objections which she saw might be raised. . . .
>
> How much virtue, ability, sanctity and purity I found in her I am afraid to say, so that I don't exceed the bounds of belief and increase your sorrow as you recall how much goodness you have lost. I will say only this, that whatever had been assembled together in me through long study and had . . . been transformed into my nature through daily meditation, this she tasted, learned and made her own. As a result, after my departure, if a dispute arose concerning some testimony of the Scriptures, it was brought to her as judge.

Marcella had been married only seven months when her husband died. She spurned all suitors, and instead of marrying again she chose to live a simple ascetic life. From **St. Athanasius**, who had visited Rome, she had learned about **St. Anthony** and the desert monks. Captivated by the idea, Marcella and Principia undertook to live a monastic regimen at a country house. Soon several domestic monasteries of women popped up among her friends, and Jerome took them under his wing. Thus, Marcella established the first monastic communities for women in the West.

Marcella also fought for Christian orthodoxy. She took a lead, for example, in opposing Rufinus, who had translated Origen's *On the First Principles*. Origen, a theologian from Alexandria, taught there that the Son was divine but only in a lesser sense than the Father. And

Rufinus was spreading Origen's heretical view of the Trinity in Rome. According to Jerome, Marcella

> originated the condemnation of the heretics. She it was who produced witnesses who . . . had been cured of their heretical error. She it was who showed how large a number had been deceived by them and who brought up against them the impious books On the First Principles, which were allegedly "improved" by the scorpion, Rufinus. She it was, lastly, who called on the heretics in frequent letters to defend themselves. They did not dare to come, for they were so conscience-stricken that they preferred to be condemned in their absence than to be convicted of their guilt in person.

When Alaric the Goth sacked Rome in 410, his agents abused Marcella, looking for treasures that she had long before distributed to the poor. Finally the soldiers relented and gave Marcella and Principia sanctuary in a church. Shortly afterward, however, Marcella died in Principia's arms.

The truly capable woman—who can find her?
She is far beyond the price of pearls. . . .
Many women have done admirable things,
But you surpass them all!
Charm is deceitful, and beauty empty;
the woman who fears Yahweh is the one to praise.

—Proverbs 31:10, 29–30 *NJB*

JANUARY 31
Community; Defending the Faith; Study

73. Paula

(347–404)

In his letters, **St. Jerome** tells us all we know about St. Paula. He says that when he came to Rome in 382, he found her leading a group of dedicated Christian women. Descended from the famous Gracchi and Scipios, she had married well and borne four daughters and a son. She was only thirty-two when her husband died. In her grief she experienced a conversion that propelled her to simplify her life. The ascetical Jerome was a novelty among Rome's genteel clergy, and Paula and her circle came under his influence.

In 385, Jerome left Rome to settle in Bethlehem. Paula, accompanied by her daughter Eustochium, soon set out to join him there. Jerome met her at Antioch, and together they made a pilgrimage to the holy places in Palestine and the monasteries in Egypt.

At Bethlehem, Jerome and Paula established a monastery for men, a convent for women, and a hospice for visitors. Jerome says Paula governed her sisters with charity and discretion. Under her leadership they embraced severe poverty and generously cared for the poor and guests.

At the heart of Paula's vocation was her passion for the Bible. A diligent student of Scripture, the saint even learned some Hebrew, as Jerome explained in this letter:

> No mind was ever more docile than hers. She was slow to speak and swift to hear, remembering the precept: "Be silent, Israel, and listen." (Deuteronomy 27:9 NJB). The holy Scriptures she knew by heart, and said that the history contained in them was the foundation of the truth. But even though she loved this, she preferred to seek for the underlying spiritual meaning. And she made this the keystone of the spiritual building raised within her soul.
>
> She asked . . . that she and her daughter might read through the Old and New Testaments under my guidance. Out of modesty, I first refused compliance, but as she persisted . . . and frequently urged me to consent . . . , I at last did so. I taught her what I had learned, not from myself—self-confidence is the worst of teachers—but from the church's most famous writers. Wherever I was stumped and honestly confessed myself at fault, she would by no means rest content. But she would force me by fresh questions to point out to her which of many possible solutions seemed to me the most probable.

> . . . Beginning as a young man, I have with much toil and effort partially acquired the Hebrew tongue. Now I study it unceasingly lest if I leave it, it also may leave me. Paula, however, made up her mind that she too would learn it. She succeeded so well that she could chant the psalms in Hebrew and could speak the language without a trace of the pronunciation peculiar to Latin.

With her wealth and knowledge of Scripture and languages, Paula was able to assist Jerome in his scholarly work. In turn, Jerome helped her, especially by overseeing the education of her granddaughter Paula, who came to succeed the saint at the Bethlehem convent.

Generosity consumed all of Paula's resources and in her final years she endured impoverished circumstances. She died in Bethlehem in 404.

> *Thanks be to the gospel, by means of which we also, who did not see Christ when he came into this world, seem to be with him when we read his deeds.*
>
> —Ambrose

JANUARY 26
Leading Women; Saints and the Bible

74. Olympias

(361?–408)

Throughout church history holy widows have become friends with priests and bishops, supporting them spiritually and materially. Examples include **Paula** and **Jerome**, **Jane de Chantal** and **Francis de Sales, Louise de Marillac** and **Vincent de Paul.** And less well-known but no less significant, Olympias and **John Chrysostom**. A member of Constantinople's wealthy elite, St. Olympias enjoyed a happy marriage to the prefect, Nebridius. However, when her husband died young, the lovely widow decided to remain single. She refused all suitors, including one advanced by the emperor Theodosius himself. He punished her by placing her estate under public administration. But she made a striking appeal in 391, and he restored her control over her fortune.

Olympias had already decided to live simply, and she began to divest herself, giving everything away to the needy and to the church. Her biographer described her largesse in this way:

> Olympias distributed all of her immense wealth and assisted everyone simply and without distinction. She surpassed in generosity to all the Samaritan whose story is told in the gospels.
>
> Immediately after the distribution of all her goods, she gave to the archbishop, John Chrysostom, for the cathedral church of the royal city, ten thousand pounds of gold, twenty thousand of silver and all of her real estate situated in all the provinces.
>
> Then by the divine will she was ordained deaconess of this holy cathedral of God. And she built a monastery at an angle south of it. John also ordained as deaconesses of the cathedral her three relatives, Elisanthia, Martyria and Palladia. Thus the four deaconesses could stay together in the convent that Olympias had founded.
>
> All were amazed at the holiness of these women: their constant praise and thanksgiving to God, their "charity which is the bond of perfection" (see Colossians 3:14), and their stillness. No man or woman from the outside was permitted to visit them. The holy patriarch John, the only exception, came regularly to sustain the women with his wise teaching.
>
> Olympias, like the women who served Christ, prepared the archbishop's daily meals and sent them to him. Only a wall separated his residence from the convent. She fed him not only before the plots

> against him, but also after he was banished. Up to the end of his life, she provided for all his expenses as well as for those who were with him in exile.

Olympias also constructed a hospital and orphanage near the convent. She regularly provided hospitality to Christian leaders from all over the East, including **Gregory of Nyssa.**

When John Chrysostom fell afoul of the empress and was banished, she supported him. He reciprocated by encouraging Olympias when officials persecuted her. Optatus, the prefect of Constantinople, twice banished her for refusing to accept Arsacius and his successor, Atticus, the usurpers who had replaced John as archbishop. Atticus finally disbanded her community and ended her charitable works. Olympias died in exile in 408, a year after the death of John Chrysostom.

St. John Chrysostom wrote these uplifting words to Olympias in exile:

I cannot cease to call you blessed. You have borne your sorrows with patience and dignity. You have managed delicate affairs with prudence and wisdom. You have thrown a veil over the malice of your persecutors with charity. Thus you have won a glory and reward that in the future will make all your sufferings seem light and passing in the presence of eternal joy.

DECEMBER 17
Friendship; Generosity; Married Saints

75. Gaudentius of Brescia

(D. 410?)

Apparently an accomplished but shy young priest, St. Gaudentius went on pilgrimage to Jerusalem in 386, as much to escape attention as to visit the holy sites. However, while he was gone from Brescia, Italy, St. Philastrius, the bishop who had educated him, died. The people immediately chose Gaudentius as his successor. They were so determined to have Gaudentius as bishop that they took an oath that they would accept no other. Gaudentius tried to shirk the appointment, but other bishops of the region threatened to excommunicate him if he did not accept the office as a call from God. So he relented, and around 390 **St. Ambrose** consecrated him.

Twenty-one of St. Gaudentius's sermons survive. He delivered ten of these during Easter week in 404, and Benevolus, a leading citizen, had them transcribed because he was too ill to attend church. Gaudentius taught about such topics as the divinity of Christ, faith, the church, Mary's perpetual virginity, and martyrdom, in all showing himself to be a skillful theologian. In the following excerpt from a sermon on the feast of **St. Peter** and **St. Paul**, he described the three birthdays of a Christian:

> There are three birthdays bestowed by the eternal Trinity on humankind. One is that of the body, which is common to all people. There are two that are spiritual, in proportion to the merit of each one's faith.
>
> Our first birth is that in which we are brought forth from nothingness into the life of this world. Our second is that in which we are born again in baptism, from sin and from errors, into the reality of charity. The third is that in which the most blessed martyrs who, because of their confession of Christ's name, are born again of their torments into the kingdom of heaven.
>
> This sequence first had place in Christ, who was born of the Virgin, born again in the Jordan, and upon the gibbet of the cross was baptized in the stream of his own precious blood. For following on that baptism which he had received in the Jordan, he said to his apostles concerning his passion: "There is a baptism I must still receive" (Luke 12:50 *NJB*). From this baptism of his passion he rose again to a life which no boundary will bring to a close: He returned to his kingdom, "and his reign will have no end" (Luke 1:33 *NJB*).

> In the footsteps of this master his faithful disciples Peter and Paul have followed, and on this day all the churches of the whole world are celebrating with fitting honor the birthday of their passion.

In 406, Pope Innocent I commissioned Gaudentius as one of the western bishops he sent to the emperor in Constantinople to plead in defense of **St. John Chrysostom,** who had been exiled. The mission failed, and evidently imperial agents tried to kill the bishops by arranging their return on a ship that was not seaworthy, but they arrived home safely. Gaudentius returned to Brescia, where he died about four years later.

The cult of martyrs in the early church grew up around their tombs, where nearness to their sacred corpses prompted many miracles. But Gaudentius believed that a small portion of a saint's relics had the same efficacy as the whole body. He said, "Therefore that we may be helped by the patronage of so many saints, let us come and pray with full confidence and earnestness, that by their intercession we may deserve to obtain everything we ask for, and glorify Christ our Lord, the giver of so much grace."

OCTOBER 25
Intercession; Saints and Sacraments (Baptism)

76. Nicetas of Remesiana

(D. 414)

Twice St. Nicetas left the icy winters of Yugoslavia to visit **Paulinus of Nola** in sunny south Italy. Although Nicetas was about twenty years older than Paulinus, the two became great friends. Paulinus dedicated two poems to Nicetas. One written as a farewell began tenderly, "Go, if you must, but leave your heart behind."

Paulinus revered Nicetas as a missionary and as a writer. From around 370 as bishop of Remesiana, now Bela Palanka in Serbia, his preaching converted many untamed tribes. For example, Paulinus said he brought the wild and marauding Bessi tribe like lambs into Christ's peaceful fold.

In the *Lives of Illustrious Men*, Gennadius says Nicetas "composed in simple and clear language" six books for new Christians. Among them were books on right conduct for catechumens, faith, and the creeds. Many scholars believe that he authored the *Te Deum*, one of Christianity's greatest hymns. He also wrote a little inspirational treatise on the names of Christ, in which the following selection appears:

> If you would learn of the Father, listen to the Word. If you would be wise, ask him who is Wisdom. When it is too dark for you to see, seek Christ, for he is the Light. Are you sick? Have recourse to him who is both doctor and health. . . .
>
> Are you afraid of this or that? Remember that on all occasions he will stand by your side like an angel. If you find it hard to meet face to face the high majesty of the Only-begotten, don't lose hope. Remember he was made man to make it easy for us to approach him. . . .
>
> Take courage if you are persecuted. Remember that he went like a lamb to the slaughter. And he is a priest who will offer you as a victim to the Father. . . . If you do not know the way of salvation, look for Christ, for he is the road for souls. If it is truth that you want, listen to him because he is the Truth. Have no fear whatever of death, for Christ is the Life of believers. Do the pleasures of the world seduce you? Turn all the more to the Cross of Christ to find solace in the sweetness of the vine that clustered there.
>
> Are you a lost sinner? Then you must hunger for justice and thirst for the Redeemer, for that is what Christ is. Because he is bread, he takes away all hunger. . . . If anger is tormenting you . . . , appeal to

Christ, who is peace. Then you will be reconciled to the Father and will love everyone as you would like to be loved yourself.

In 414, Pope Innocent I mentioned Nicetas in a letter to the bishops of Macedonia. As that was the last time the saint's name appeared, historians assign that year as the probable date of his death.

You overcame the sting of death
and opened the kingdom of heaven to all believers.
You are seated at God's right hand in glory.
We believe that you will come and be our judge.

Come, then, Lord, sustain your people,
bought with the price of your own blood,
and bring us with your saints
to everlasting glory.

—Te Deum

JUNE 22
Applied Christianity; Friendship; Jesus Christ; Missionaries

77. Maximus of Turin
(350?–415?)

"Sometimes I think I shouldn't bother to preach a sermon," grumbled Bishop Maximus to his flock near Turin, Italy. "I don't think some of you give a second thought to applying my teaching. How many of you go home from worship and say, 'Today the bishop spoke about almsgiving. Let's see what we can give to the poor? You know, he also warned us about idols. Let's get rid of anything in the house that even came near an idol.'" St. Maximus reprimanding his flock near Turin in the fourth century sounds very much like a twentieth-century Italian pastor scolding his immigrant congregation near Philadelphia.

Facts about Maximus are scarce, but we can learn a little about him from his sermons, 106 of which have survived. On most Sundays for about twenty years he preached to his rural community—except on occasion when he refused to speak because too few had shown up for the liturgy.

Unlike his contemporaries **St. Ambrose** and **St. Leo the Great,** Maximus was not an outstanding preacher. His strength lay in his directness and in tailoring his message to the spiritual needs of his hearers. Maximus maintained personal relationships with members of his church and so could pinpoint their needs. Once, for instance, he admonished people who were not keeping the strict Lenten fast. "Think about it," he said. "You will get your reproof during the liturgy if I smell food on your breath at the kiss of peace."

Paganism was still alive and well in the northern Italian countryside, and Maximus regularly warned his people to shun it. "I can't believe that you would leave the sacred banquet," he would complain, "and go off to a wild party honoring an idol! Don't you know that if you want to reign with Christ you can't rejoice with the world?"

Prominent among the saint's themes were the spiritual disciplines, especially almsgiving. In the following excerpt, for example, he declares that giving alms cleanses the soul:

> Sacred scripture says: As water extinguishes a fire, so almsgiving extinguishes sin (see Sirach 3:30). Everyone should apply this great truth. Giving alms promises refreshment to people withered near to death by sin, like moisture revives what has been dried up. Miserable people

who had been languishing in death because of their sins will come back to life through almsgiving.

Mercy will be a fountain of salvation for those to whom avarice had been a fiery death. By freely giving, they may quench the flames that their sin had enkindled. And by a more profitable business transaction, a person who paid to commit adultery now pays to stop being an adulterer. The person who used to purchase sin now purchases innocence.

For the Lord tells his disciples: "Give alms from what you have, and look, everything will be clean for you" (Luke 11:41 *NJB*). If you give alms, then you have begun to be innocent even though you may still be unclean and hedged in by numerous crimes. For almsgiving purifies what avarice polluted. You remove the stain of seizing another's property by giving away your own. See then what the grace of mercy is—a virtue that alone is the redemption of all sins!

Maximus died at Turin around 415.

A jewel demands a setting of gold, and a pearl should only be placed in precious necklaces. Be, then, the finest sort of gold! Be a precious necklace, so that the spiritual pearl can be set in you! For Christ the Lord is the pearl that the rich merchant in the gospel hastened to buy.

—Maximus of Turin

JUNE 25
Almsgiving; Celebration of Discipline; Great Pastors; Sin

78. Honoratus of Arles

(D. 429)

Born to an aristocratic Roman family in Gaul, Honoratus received a top-shelf pagan education. But he became a Christian and also converted his older brother,Venantius.Their father opposed their efforts to flee the world as monks. So taking the hermit St. Caprasius with them as their mentor, the young Christians escaped to Greece to look for a desert retreat. However,Venantius died on the way, and St. Honoratus became ill and had to return to Gaul with Caprasius.

For a time Honoratus lived as a hermit in the hills above the Côte d'Azur, where he apparently became familiar with the *Rule* of **St. Pachomius**, the originator of community monasticism. Then around 405, with Caprasius, he founded a monastic community on the island of Lérins off the French Riviera, now called St. Honorat. Honoratus governed the monastery largely according to the *Rule* of St. Pachomius. Some monks lived in total community in the main buildings, others as anchorites in cells nearby.

Honoratus attracted strong young men of rank to his community and transformed them into outstanding Christian leaders. In the following passage, **St. Hilary of Arles**, his biographer, praised his skill at producing virtue in others:

> How often did he seem to turn savage beasts into gentle doves? . . . His exhortations drove out many a plague of souls. Bitterness, harshness, and fierce anger gave way to the freedom of spirit brought by Christ, . . .
>
> Where was a workshop of the virtues so effective in refining the souls of men? If he could not move a man to his salvation by his lively exhortations, he would constrain God by his prayers.
>
> He looked on everyone's sufferings as his own, and lamented them as his own. . . . Knowing how to rejoice with those that rejoiced, and weep with those that wept, he transferred both the vices and the virtues of all into the store of his own merits. For, as virtue incites to virtue, so compassion spent upon the wretched bears fruit. For it will reap a greater harvest from each one than each one reaps for himself. . . .
>
> Ready, quick, tireless, he pressed on persistently, according to his insight into the nature and character of each. One he would approach in secret, the other openly. This one with severity, the other with soft words. In order to work a change in one who was to be corrected, he

> often changed the very appearance of the correction. Thus, we could not easily find anyone who was so much loved or so much feared. These two feelings toward him were so deeply implanted in each of his followers that love of him brought a dread of transgression, and fear brought a love of discipline.

Within twenty years Lérins was significantly influencing the shape and quality of Christianity throughout the West, as many of its monks became bishops. And **St. Patrick** probably spent years there, training for his mission to Ireland.

In 426, Honoratus himself became the bishop of Arles. He overworked himself with pastoral care and died there three years later.

As a parent of teenagers, I have sometimes felt, like Honoratus, that I have had to deal with "strangers," made so by our secularized culture. With faith in his example and much hope, I imitate his approach. I try to stab hard young hearts with exhortations. Imitating his compassion, I try to put myself in the young person's shoes. Like him, I attempt to give correction creatively, sometimes gently, sometimes severely. However, usually none of these things that Honoratus did so admirably seem to work for me. So I content myself with "constraining God" by my prayers.

JANUARY 16
Care of the Soul; Celebration of Discipline; Community; Leading Men

79. Augustine
(354–430)

In his *Confessions,* St. Augustine described himself as a serious sinner. From age seventeen he had indulged in sexual immorality. And although **St. Monica**, his mother, had raised him Christian, he had abandoned his faith at nineteen. For nine years at Tagaste and Carthage in North Africa, he taught Manichaeism, a religious dualism that believed ascetical practices could release the spirit from matter.

But in 383, Augustine moved to Milan to open a school of rhetoric, and in the next few years his life gradually turned about. He fell under the influence of **St. Ambrose**, whose sermons removed his intellectual objections to Christianity. By 386 all that remained was his sexual addiction. "Make me chaste," he would pray, "but not yet." The "yet" came after a visitor told Augustine and his friend, Alypius, how two men had experienced dramatic conversions by reading the *Life of* ***Anthony***. The story threw Augustine into turmoil. As he testified in the *Confessions*, he grieved and sought to break immediately with his besetting sin:

> Because solitude seemed more appropriate for weeping, I stole away from Alypius. He was astonished to see me choked up, so he remained where we had been sitting. I flung myself down under a fig tree and released my tears. Streams gushed from my eyes, an acceptable sacrifice to you, my God. And I poured out my heart to you, saying, "How long? How long? Why not put an end to my uncleanness right now?"
>
> Then I heard the voice of a boy or girl coming from a house nearby, chanting repeatedly. "Take up and read! Take up and read!" I knew such words were not part of any children's game, nor had I ever heard anything like it. So I interpreted it as a command from heaven to open the book and read the first chapter I should come upon. For I had heard about Anthony who was converted by hearing a gospel reading and taking it as a personal admonition.
>
> So I quickly returned to the place where Alypius was sitting and picked up the book of Paul's letters. I opened it and read silently the first paragraph that my eyes fell upon: "Not in orgies and drunkenness, not in promiscuity and licentiousness, not in rivalry and jealousy. But put on the Lord Jesus Christ, and make no provision for the desires of the flesh" (Romans 13:13–14 *NAB*). I did not need to read any

> further. Instantly as the sentence ended, all my gloomy doubt vanished, dispelled by a saving light infused into my heart.

All Christians must give thanks for Augustine's conversion because he has exercised a defining influence on Christian practice and thought. As bishop of Hippo, Augustine led the North African church for four decades. He built monastic communities, giving them a rule that many religious orders adopted over the centuries. Augustine also marshaled the church's defense against heresies. His apologetical books written in these controversies laid a foundation for Christian philosophy and theology through the Middle Ages, the Reformation, and down to the present.

After Rome fell to the Vandals in 410, Augustine wrote his masterful *On the City of God* to defend Christianity against the charge that it had undermined the empire. Twenty years later, Augustine died as the same Vandals were laying siege to his city.

> *Too late have I loved you, O Beauty so ancient and so new, too late have I loved you! You were with me, but I was not with you. You cried out and pierced my deafness. You enlightened my blindness. I tasted you and I am hungry for you. You touched me, and I am afire with longing for your embrace.*
>
> —Augustine

AUGUST 28 / PATRON OF THEOLOGIANS, PRINTERS, AND BREWERS
Doctors of the Church; Intimacy with the Divine; Passion for Purity; Repentance; Sexual Temptation

80. Paulinus of Nola

(354?–431)

As the son of a Roman patrician, Paulinus had it all—money, social position, power, education, and savoir-vivre. Educated by the poet Ausonius and owner of estates in Aquitaine, Spain, and Italy, successful attorney and public servant, he was well known in the Roman world. Gradually, however, he stripped himself of all the trappings of aristocracy to embrace a life of prayer and service. His example invites us to join him on the road to simplicity.

Turning points in Paulinus's life included his marriage to Theresia, a Spanish woman, and their conversion to Christ sometime before 390. Another occurred that year when the couple's only child died as an infant. From that time they began to divest themselves of their properties and dispense their wealth to needy people. In 393 the bishop of Barcelona responded to popular demand and ordained Paulinus a priest.

Then St. Paulinus and Theresia moved to Nola, a village near Naples. There they lived on the second floor of a building and housed financially ruined and homeless people downstairs. Daily with a few friends, the couple prayed the liturgy of the hours. They opened a guest house where they entertained numerous visitors, including **St. Melania** and **St. Nicetas.** And Paulinus and Theresia continued their philanthropy, building an aqueduct for Nola and churches for nearby towns.

Paulinus wrote many letters and poems, a handful of which have survived. The following excerpt celebrating the resurrection of the body comes from a funeral poem he wrote to cheer the parents of a deceased child:

> It is right for us to strengthen our spirits, raise our minds and thrust cowardly fears from our hearts. For, as you see, the Son of God laid down his life for us and took it up again, while remaining God in every way. God victoriously celebrated a triumph over our death and conveyed our human body with him to the stars.
>
> He considered it insufficient to have drained the entire cup of mortal life for us, removing our wounds by means of his own. He also rose again with the body in which he fell, so that the troubled anxiety of a hesitant mind should not keep me in uncertainty. He appeared after his death just as he was before it, and thus the evidence was made

crystal-clear to our eyes. For he showed himself of his own accord to his doubting disciples to be inspected by their eyes and hands.

It was not without divine purpose that the apostle doubted. It was so that none might be dubious of life after death. By his doubting, he strengthened faith. When the doubting Thomas was refuted face-to-face, all of us were given instruction. Because Thomas was bidden to see and feel in person, I learn to believe unswervingly and with steady faith that human death was overcome by the death of Christ crucified. And that the hope of resurrection resides in our bodies because Christ rose again victorious in the flesh which I bear and in which I die.

In 409, Paulinus became Bishop of Nola, but we know nothing about his administration except that he reportedly ruled with wisdom and liberality.

Paulinus punctuated his life of generous giving with a final donation. In 431, just before he died, he dispensed fifty silver pieces to buy clothes for the poor.

Paulinus lived near the tomb of St. Felix, his patron saint, and annually wrote a poem in Felix's honor. For Paulinus, Felix was more than his intercessor or protector. Felix was a presence in Paulinus that ensured his relationship to Christ.

JUNE 22
Eternal Perspective; Facing Death; Generosity; Married Saints; Poets; Serving the Poor

81. John Cassian

(360?–433?)

Around 380, John Cassian migrated from Romania to Bethlehem, where he embraced the monastic life. After 385 he wandered the Egyptian desert, the heart of eastern monasticism. He visited abbots at monasteries and hermits in their caves, absorbing their teachings about the Christian life.

The year 400 found him on the staff of **St. John Chrysostom** in Constantinople. When Chrysostom was unfairly deposed and exiled, Cassian was among his defenders who traveled to Rome to plead his case before the pope. At that time he was ordained a priest.

John Cassian never returned to the East. In 415 he founded two monasteries at Marseilles, one for men and another for women. His foundations were cenobia, community schools that formed candidates for a life of solitude. To instruct his monks and nuns, Cassian wrote two significant books. The *Institutes* described the eastern pattern of monastic life and the virtues required of monks. The *Conferences* presented the wisdom of the Egyptian desert in the form of discourses by famous abbots. In the following sample we hear "Abbot Isaac" on the practice of the presence of God:

> "To keep the thought of God always in your mind you must cling totally to this formula for piety: 'Come to my help, O God. Lord, hurry to my rescue' (see Psalm 70:2).
>
> "With good reason this verse has been chosen from the whole of Scripture as a device. It bears all the feelings that human nature can experience. It can be adapted to every condition and deployed against every temptation. It carries a cry to God in the face of every danger. It piously confesses humility. It conveys our sense of frailty, our assurance of being heard, our confidence in help that is always and everywhere present. Someone forever calling out to his protector is very sure of his nearness.
>
> "This short verse is an indomitable wall for all those struggling against the onslaught of demons. Whatever the disgust, the anguish, or the gloom in our thoughts, it keeps us from despairing of our salvation since it reveals to us the One to whom we call, the One who sees our struggles and who is never far from those who pray to him.
>
> "If things go well for us in spirit, this verse is a warning. We must not get puffed up at being in a good condition that we cannot retain

> without the protection of God for whose continuous and speedy help it prays. This little verse, I am saying, proves to be necessary and useful to each one of us in all circumstances."

Cassian's *Institutes* and *Conferences* interpreted Egyptian monasticism for the western church. **Benedict** advocated that monks read Cassian second only to the Bible, and **Augustine** and **Gregory the Great** also recommended his works. Through their influence Cassian shaped the practice of monasticism in the West through the Middle Ages and even into the present.

The eastern church recognizes Cassian as a saint. But the western church did not canonize him, probably because he was regarded as the leading proponent of a teaching called Semi-Pelagianism. In a controversy over salvation, he challenged Augustine's view of predestination and minimized the role of grace in the first steps of the Christian life. But historians now say that Cassian had adopted an "anti-Augustine" position rather than a heretical one. The saint died at Marseilles around 433.

Today laypeople cannot practice the presence of God with the constancy that Cassian demanded. But we can frequently remind ourselves of God's nearness and draw on his grace by praying "Come to my help, O God. Lord, hurry to my rescue."

FEBRUARY 29
Christian Living; Intimacy with the Divine; Prayer; Temptation

82. Melania

(383–439)

As the heiress of a high-ranking and extremely wealthy Roman family, St. Melania could anticipate great power and influence. From childhood, however, she hoped for the religious life, but her father forced her to live according to the family's status. Thus he married her to Pinian, a young Roman noble.

Melania pleaded with Pinian to trade wealth and sex for simplicity and prayer. At first he refused, but when Melania nearly died in childbirth, he acquiesced and agreed to give up conjugal relations. After her father's death, Melania, Pinian, and her mother withdrew to a country villa where many others joined them in an informal Christian community. At last Melania could embrace simplicity and divest herself of her wealth:

> First of all she bestowed all her silk upon the holy altars. Then she shipped her gold to the East: ten thousand gold pieces to churches and monasteries in Egypt and the Thebaid; ten thousand to those in Antioch and nearby countries; fifteen thousand gold pieces to those of Palestine; ten thousand each to churches in the islands and to the people in exile. In the West she personally distributed four times as much in money gifts to churches, monasteries, guest hostels and the poor. She released eight thousand of her slaves who chose to be free. To others who wished to remain in the service of her brother-in-law, she gave three thousand gold pieces.

In 406, Melania, Pinian, and their group fled the invading Goths. They stayed briefly in Campania with **St. Paulinus of Nola** before going to North Africa, where they met **St. Augustine** and St. Alypius. In Africa, Melania endowed two monasteries, one for men and another for women. She lived with the women, studying Greek and Latin and copying manuscripts. In contrast to contemporaries who went to extremes, Melania moderated the asceticism of her sisters. Fearing that too much fasting, for example, would lead to pride, she said:

> The devil can imitate all the righteous acts that we appear to do but he is splendidly defeated by love and humility. . . . We fast, but he eats absolutely nothing. We keep watch, but he does not sleep at all. Let us

> therefore hate pride because, through it, he fell from heaven, and again, because, through it, he wants to drag us down with him.

In 417 Melania and company withdrew to Jerusalem. Inspired by a tour of the monastic settlements in the Egyptian desert, she and Pinian returned to Jerusalem to imitate the spiritual discipline of the monks. There she became friends of St. Paula, her cousin, and St. Jerome. After fourteen years her mother died and Pinian died a year later. Melania buried them near the Mount of Olives. Nearby she had a hut built for herself, and soon a large assembly of nuns gathered there under her leadership.

At Christmas, 439, Melania had a premonition of her death and began to make her farewells. "I think the Enemy himself," she told her sisters, "will not at the last judgment accuse me of ever having gone to sleep with bitterness in my heart." Melania died on December 31, 439, at the age of fifty-six.

> *Just as a bride decked out in full finery cannot wear black sandals, but adorns her feet in the same way as her body, so the soul needs fasting, accompanied by all the other virtues. If anyone is eager to practice fasting apart from the other virtues, she is like a bride whose body is naked, and who adorns only her feet.*
>
> —Melania

DECEMBER 31
Celebration of Discipline; Fasting; Generosity

83. Mary of Egypt
(Fifth Century)

In the Middle Ages the story of St. Mary of Egypt was a popular icon of repentance, intercession, and grace. She was a prostitute whose life was transformed through **Mary's** intercession. People loved this sainted harlot because her example demonstrated that God's mercy was wide enough to encompass any sin, no matter how serious. The core of her story is factual, but legend has embroidered it with some fictional details.

At age twelve, Mary ran away from home to Alexandria. For seventeen years she sold herself on the streets, driven more by lust than money. One day out of curiosity she joined a group of pilgrims traveling to Jerusalem to celebrate the feast of the Holy Cross. Her sinful behavior seems to have been compulsive, as she seduced a dozen young men on the way.

At Jerusalem the pilgrims swarmed into the church of the Holy Sepulchre, but an invisible force prevented Mary from entering. After trying to go in and being pushed back several times, she realized that her sinful actions were blocking her entry. That inspiration prompted her to ask the Virgin Mary to help her repent:

> And then I saw in the place where I was standing, a picture of the holy Mother of God. Gazing directly into her eyes, I said, "Virgin and Lady, who gave birth to the Word of God according to the flesh, I see now that it is not suitable or decent for me, defiled as I am, to look upon this picture of you, ever immaculate Virgin, who always kept your body and soul chaste and clean from all sin. Indeed, it would be right for you in your purity to reject and loathe my impurity. But God to whom you gave birth became man, as I have heard, to save sinners and to call them to repentance.
>
> "So help me, for I am alone and without any other help. Receive my confession, and give me leave to enter the church and do not deprive me of the sight of that most precious wood upon which was fixed God made man, whom you carried and bore as a Virgin and where he gave his blood for my redemption. O Lady, let the doors be opened to me so that I may adore the divine cross. I beg you, from whom Christ took flesh, to guarantee my promise, which is, that I will never again defile my flesh by immersing it in horrifying lusts.

> As soon as I have seen the cross of your Son, holy Virgin, I will go wherever you as my mediator for salvation shall order and lead."

After this prayerful repentance, Mary was able to enter the church. She prostrated herself before the cross. After leaving the building, she returned to the picture of Mary and prayed for guidance. A voice seemed to say, "If you cross the Jordan, you will find rest." Thus Mary wandered into the desert east of Jerusalem, which had been home to Elijah and **St. John the Baptist,** where she lived as a penitent for eighteen years.

> *It is proof of God's own love for us, that Christ died for us while we were still sinners. How much more can we be sure, therefore, that, now that we have been justified by his death, we shall be saved through him from the retribution of God.*
>
> —Romans 5:8–9 *NJB*

APRIL 2
Conversion; Intercession; Mary; Repentance

84. Shenoute

(348?–466)

St. Shenoute is revered as a hero in the Coptic Church, but western Christians have mixed feelings about him. Admirers appreciate his charismatic leadership: he recruited and governed a community of 2,200 monks and 1,800 nuns. But his violent temper and extreme punishments appall his critics. Even minor infractions enraged him, and he had offenders severely beaten on the soles of their feet. However, with his sins, severity and all, many in the East still venerate Shenoute as a saint.

In 385, Shenoute became the abbot of White Monastery in Upper Egypt, ruling for about eighty years. He tightened the monastery's already strict rule. A major innovation was his requirement that every monk and nun sign an oath to adhere to a strict pattern of life that led to holiness. Any violation of the covenant or monastery rules was punishable by beating or expulsion.

Shenoute is credited with eliminating the vestiges of paganism in Upper Egypt. He and bands of his monks made sorties throughout the desert destroying pagan sanctuaries. Shenoute was also a fierce opponent of heretics. Most notably, in 431 he accompanied **Cyril of Alexandria** to the Council of Ephesus, which condemned Nestorius. Legend has it that Shenoute met the heretic and struck him on the chest.

Mixed with his vehement pursuit of justice, however, was a streak of compassion. For example, his biographer, Besa, reported his merciful treatment of men who had been captured by the Blemmyes, nomads who marauded desert settlements:

> Once the Blemmyes came north, captured some of the cities, and took captive the men and their beasts of burden. They went south with all that they had captured and camped in the district of Psoi. Then my father, Abba Shenoute, decided to go to them for the sake of the captives. When he crossed the river to go east to them, those he first met raised high their spears intending to kill him. Their hands immediately became stiff and dry like wood, fixed unbendably at full stretch, and they were crying out in great distress. The same thing happened to the rest of these people until Abba Shenoute arrived at the seat of their king.

> The king realized that they could not overcome the power that was with him. So he arose and bowed to the ground before him, saying: "I beg you, restore my men's hands!" When Shenoute made the sign of the cross over them, their hands were immediately restored to health. When the king promised him gifts, he did not take them, but said only this: "Give me the men; take for yourself all the spoils." The king freely gave all of them to him. He crossed over to the west bank of the water with them and brought them to the monastery. He provided them with expenses and sent them away in peace, each to his own house, glorifying God and his holy prophet Abba Shenoute.

If we can believe Besa, Shenoute lived to be 118 years old, a longevity comparable to that of Moses and **St. Anthony,** one of the founders of monasticism. He died in 466.

Shenoute does not appeal to us as much as "nicer" saints like ***Thérèse of Lisieux*** *or even other combative saints like* ***Don Bosco****. But his example shows us that sanctity is possible for a person with big character flaws and faults. Thus, those of us who aspire to holiness but still stumble over our sins can draw encouragement from his example.*

JULY 1
Miracles Do Happen; Feisty Saints

85. Cyril of Alexandria
(376–444)

"Truly, truly, I say to you, if you ask anything of the Father, he will give it to you in my name. Up to now you have asked nothing in my name: ask and you will receive, that your joy may be full" (see John 16:23, 24).

In this way Christ urges his disciples to ask for spiritual gifts. At the same time he gives them confidence that they will not fail to obtain them, should they ask for them. He says further, "Truly, truly," to confirm their belief that should they ask the Father for anything they would receive it. . . . For he will act as their mediator and relay their request, and as one with the Father, grant it.

This is what he means by "in my name." For it is only through the Son that we draw near to the Father. As it is written, it is through him we have access in the one Spirit to the Father (see Ephesians 2:18). On this account he said, "I am the door" (see John 10:9) and "I am the way; no one comes to the Father, but by me" (see John 14:6). For, as the Son is God, he, one with the Father, gives good things to those he has made holy and is found to be generous out of his abundant goodness to us." . . .

Let us offer our prayers, then, in Christ's name. The Father will most readily agree to them when they are made in this way.

—Cyril of Alexandria

St. Cyril, the patriarch of Alexandria from 412 to 444, sustained his flock with very practical teaching on Christian living, as the above quote shows. A stalwart defender of the faith, we esteem Cyril for his thoroughgoing opposition to Nestorianism, a heresy that eroded the doctrine of the Incarnation. He said he based all of his apologetical writing exclusively on church Fathers like **Athanasius**, **Basil**, and **Gregory Nazianzen**.

But not on **John Chrysostom**, whom he had implacably opposed. As a young priest, Cyril had assisted his uncle Theophilus, then the patriarch, to harass Chrysostom on petty, trumped-up charges.

Cyril succeeded his uncle in 412 and exercised his office with firmness and vigor. Depending on their point of view, some praise Cyril for his unbending orthodoxy and flinty leadership. Others criticize him for his inflexibility, intransigence, and inclination to violence.

Cyril pursued orthodoxy at all costs. He drove the Jews from Alexandria. Next he appropriated the churches of the followers of the antipope Novatian. A rigorist who insisted on permanent excommunication for Christians who compromised with paganism, Novatian had been consecrated as a rival bishop of Rome around 251. Then Cyril quarreled with Orestes, the imperial prefect, who objected to his treatment of the Jews. During the latter controversy, a mob cruelly killed Hypatia, a popular woman philosopher and adviser to the prefect. They lynched her without Cyril's knowledge, but his behavior had probably influenced their violence.

The church especially honors St. Cyril of Alexandria because he led the assault against Nestorianism. In 431 he presided at the Council of Ephesus that condemned the teaching of Nestorius, then the patriarch of Constantinople, and excommunicated him. Nestorius refused to recant and led his followers into schism. Opinions are also mixed on Cyril's role in the controversy. Some celebrate him as a champion of orthodoxy. Others wonder if a little more forbearance on his part could have prevented the schism.

With the same firm hand, Cyril governed his see until his death in 444.

Cyril of Alexandria holds a prime spot among "porcupine" saints. Holy throughout but sometimes prickly on the outside, we respect these sainted men and women. But even though their sanctity illumines their darker sides, we may find them hard to like.

JUNE 27
Defending the Faith; Doctors of the Church; Intercession; Feisty Saints; Prayer

86. Proclus

(390?–446)

Christ manifested himself to the world and, adorning the chaotic world, obtained beauty and happiness for it. He took upon himself the sin of the world and drove out the enemy. He sanctified the spring, enlightened the souls of men and worked miracles upon miracles.

Indeed, today on this feast of the Epiphany . . . the whole world was filled with joy, for it offers us a greater number of miracles than the festivity just passed. . . . On Christmas, we had placed before our eyes a still small baby signifying our immaturity. But in today's feast we contemplate Christ as a perfect man. Now, the king has put on the purple of the body. Now, the spring surrounds and inundates the river. . . .

Contemplate, then, the new and stupendous miracles: the sun of justice who washes in the Jordan, the fire immersed in the waters, and God sanctified in the mystery of humanity. Today all people extol and acclaim: "Blessed is he who comes in the name of the Lord" (see Matthew 21:9). . . .

Contemplate a wondrous and new flood, greater . . . than the one that occurred at the time of Noah. The water of the flood brought death to the human race. Here instead the water of baptism—by the power of him who was baptized—restores life to the dead. At Noah's time, the dove, bearing an olive branch in its beak, prefigured the fragrance of Christ the Lord. Here the Holy Spirit, descending in the form of a dove, shows us the merciful Lord.

—Proclus

St. Proclus exemplifies for us the right approach for Christians caught up in controversy. In his dealings with Nestorius and his followers, for example, he showed us how to hate errors while loving the people who hold them.

As a young man the church marked Proclus for leadership. In 425 he was appointed bishop of Cyzicus, but the people of that church refused to accept him. So he remained in Constantinople, where he came to be admired as an inspiring preacher. As he does in the homily for the Epiphany quoted above, Proclus popularized dogmas, especially the Incarnation.

When Nestorius, the patriarch, began to teach that there were two persons in the incarnate Christ, Proclus, the priest, courageously spoke against his views. In 429 he delivered his famous sermon attacking Nestorius's teaching. "We do not proclaim a deified man," he said, "but we confess an incarnate God."

As patriarch of Constantinople from 434 until his death in 446, he continued steadfastly to refute the Nestorian heresy, but made it easy for heretics to return to the church. Later, the Armenian bishops asked Proclus to judge the work of their hero, Theodore of Mopsuestia, who had died in communion with the church. With his typical moderation, Proclus refuted Theodore's errors about the Incarnation, but did not mention his name out of respect for the Armenians who revered him as a saint.

Proclus's friend, the Greek historian Socrates, wrote:

> He was always gentle to everyone, for he was convinced that kindness advances the cause of truth better than severity. He therefore determined not to irritate and harass heretics, and so restored to the church in his own person that mild and benignant dignity of character that had so often been unhappily violated. He was a pattern for all true prelates.

Proclus died on July 24, 446.

> *Tolerance is the bond of all friendship, and unites people in heart and opinion and action, not only with each other, but in unity with our Lord, so that they may really be at peace.*
>
> —Vincent de Paul

OCTOBER 24
Christian Unity; Defending the Faith; Great Pastors; Kindness

87. Germanus of Auxerre

(378?–448)

In 408 Germanus of Auxerre experienced a sudden change. At thirty, the young attorney was on track for secular success—wealthy, married, and ruling as governor of the Amorican provinces in Gaul. But that year, against his will, he was chosen bishop of Auxerre in France. Profoundly touched by the seriousness of his new office, St. Germanus radically transformed his life. He embraced poverty, began to live austerely, and personally tended to the needs of the poor. He used his money to endow churches and cathedrals in the provinces. He also founded a monastery at Auxerre, where **St. Patrick** would train for his mission to Ireland.

In 429, Germanus and Lupus of Troyes were sent to England to oppose Pelagianism, which taught that grace was not necessary for salvation. Their mission succeeded in renewing Catholic life in Britain. They bested heretics in public debates, and their preaching generated a revival. Germanus's biographer described the bishops' effectiveness in the following passage:

> It was not long before these apostolic priests had filled all Britain . . . with their fame, their preaching, and their miracles. As they were daily hemmed in by crowds, the word of God was preached, not only in the churches, but at the crossroads, in the fields, and in the lanes. Everywhere faithful Catholics were strengthened in their faith and the lapsed learned the way back to the truth. Their achievements . . . followed the pattern of the apostles themselves. They ruled through consciences, taught through letters and worked miracles through their holiness. Preached by such men, the truth had full course, so that whole regions passed quickly over to their side. . . .
>
> Once a military officer and his wife put their ten-year-old blind daughter into the arms of the bishops. They told him to take her to their opponents. But . . . stung in conscience, the heretics also begged the bishops to cure the little girl. The bishops, seeing that the people were expectant and their opponents in a humbler frame of mind, offered a short prayer. Then Germanus, filled with the Holy Spirit, took from his neck the reliquary that always hung at his side. In full view of everybody he touched it to the eyes of the child.
>
> Immediately it expelled their darkness and filled them with light and truth. The parents were overcome with joy at the miracle and

> the onlookers with awe. From that day onward the false doctrine was so completely uprooted from people's minds that they looked to the bishops for teaching with thirsty souls.

Not exactly, as Germanus had to return to Britain in 440 to combat Pelagianism a second time. On this visit he seems to have successfully purged the heresy. To insure its defeat, he founded schools to teach true doctrine.

Germanus also gained a reputation as a peacemaker. Once in Britain he stopped an attacking barbarian army by having Britons shout "Alleluia" in a mountain pass. The echo persuaded the invaders that they faced a massive force and they quit the field. And in 448, he went to Ravenna to beg the emperor to call off an army that had been sent to quell a rebellion in his provinces. His effort failed because a new uprising broke out in Amorica. Ironically, Germanus's very successful life ended on this downstroke, as he died in Ravenna on July 31, 448.

Through the ages a "cross pollinating" evangelization seems to have made the church resilient. For example, Germanus, a "Frenchman," strengthened the church in England by eliminating heresy, by preaching and teaching, and by establishing schools. A few centuries later, Boniface, an "Englishman," revived the church in France and established it in Germany.

JULY 31
Defending the Faith; Evangelization; Peacemakers

88. Hilary of Arles
(400–449)

St. Hilary, a young relative of **St. Honoratus of Arles** in France, was gifted, well-educated, and headed for a successful career. However, Honoratus, who dearly loved Hilary, had determined to bring him into Christ's service as a monk. In his old age, Honoratus made a difficult journey from his island monastery at Lérins in the French Riviera to confront the young man. But Hilary turned a deaf ear to him, and the abbot left, putting the matter entirely in God's hands. Hilary himself reported what happened:

> Meantime, while I recall Honoratus's great service to all, I pass over the infinite care he spent on me. For his care certainly brought me salvation in Christ. . . . Even in those years, when I was too close a friend of the world and obstinate toward God, as an honest seducer, he turned me with his gentle hand to the love of Christ. . . .
>
> When his pious words made little impression on my ears, he turned to his accustomed refuge of prayer. His loving cries entered the most holy ears of God, appealing for mercy. . . .
>
> But for the time being I won a disastrous victory. Then the right hand of God took me up to torment me and tame me, for he had handed me over to God. . . . What storms of diverse and conflicting desires were stirred up in my heart! How often did willingness and unwillingness succeed each other in my mind! Thus, while Honoratus was absent, Christ did his work within me. In two days, by his prayers and the mercy of God, my obstinacy was conquered.
>
> While the Lord was calling me, all the world's pleasures stood nearby. As though holding deliberations with a friend, my mind pondered what course to take, which to abandon. Thanks be to you, good Jesus, who, moved by the holy entreaties of your servant, broke my bonds and cast upon me the bonds of your love. If I continue to be held in them, the bonds of sin will never regain their strength.

So Hilary went to Lérins to become a monk with Honoratus. However, he did not stay there long. When Honoratus became bishop of Arles he took Hilary with him. Upon Honoratus's death in 429, the church at Arles chose Hilary, then only twenty-nine years old, as their bishop.

For twenty years Hilary served as bishop while continuing his monastic observances. He even performed manual labor to earn money for the poor and he sold liturgical vessels to ransom captives. However, in an overzealous and somewhat autocratic spirit, he made bad decisions about other bishops that backfired. Once he wrongheadedly deposed a bishop on allegations that he had been ordained illicitly. Another time, when an ailing bishop was about to die, he precipitously appointed a replacement. But the bishop recovered. So two men claimed the see, and Hilary stood by his appointee. Both cases were appealed to **Pope Leo the Great**. In both instances, the pope decided against Hilary. He censured Hilary, forbade him to appoint any more bishops, and stripped him of the dignity of metropolitan. Perhaps Honoratus should have left Hilary at Lérins for a few more years' formation before advancing him.

Hilary died at Arles in 449, after apparently being reconciled with Leo.

All saints have flaws and problems, but in many cases their admirers have piously concealed them. However, in Hilary of Arles we meet a saint whose weaknesses stick out for all to see because his uppity behavior brought him into conflict with a pope. We can be glad, not for Hilary's bad judgments, but for a chance to see in his life that we can be wrong and still be holy.

MAY 5
Conversion; Feisty Saints; Vocation

89. Eucherius

(D. 449?)

The church has honored as saints husbands and wives who have left their spouses to become anchorites or religious leaders. I study such saints to figure out what motivated them, but often the sources give little information. St. Eucherius of Lyons is a case in point.

A member of a prominent Gallo-Roman family, Eucherius married a woman named Galla. They had two sons, Salonius and Veranus, whom they had educated at the monastery of Lérins. Both later became bishops and saints.

At some point Eucherius himself entered the monastery at Lérins, where according to **John Cassian** he became a model of holiness. As is often the case, the sources do not tell us what happened to his wife. Just as the New Testament itself does not reveal anything about **Peter**'s wife. After a while Eucherius left the monastery to live alone on a nearby island. He seemed to have had an overpowering desire for solitude, where he expected to find God. That compulsion may help explain his decision to leave home for the monastery. Here is an illustrative excerpt from his book, *In Praise of the Desert:*

> The desert is truly the limitless temple of our God. For he who inhabits silence must be pleased with such a dwelling. There he often has manifested himself to his saints. In the shelter of that solitude he has stooped to speak with men. In the desert Moses, his face bathed in light, saw the Lord. It was in the desert that Elijah veiled his face, afraid of contemplating the Lord.
>
> With good reason then I shall call the desert the abode of faith, the ark of virtue, the sanctuary of love, the treasure of piety, the tabernacle of justice. In a big house the most precious treasures are kept under key and guard. Just so, the obstacles raised by nature itself protect the magnificence of holy things hidden in the desert. They are locked in the solitude, so as not to be lost among the crowds of men.
>
> What meetings, what gatherings of saints have I not seen there, dear Lord! While seeking the life of bliss their life is already blissful. While pursuing it already they enjoy it. They wish to be removed from sinners? Already they are far from them. They seek a chaste life? They live it. They intend to give all their time to praising God? Already they give it. They wish to enjoy the society of the saints? They do already. They long to possess Christ? Already they possess Christ in their heart.

Against his wishes, around 434, Eucherius left his desert to become bishop of Lyons. The hermit proved to be an excellent pastor, teaching and preaching eloquently, founding churches and religious centers, and administering alms generously. Friends like **Paulinus of Nola** visited Eucherius and sought his advice. He died at Lyons about 449.

> *I have seen men raised to the highest point of worldly honor and riches. Fortune seemed to be in their pay, throwing everything to them without their having the trouble of asking or seeking. Their prosperity in all things outdid their very desires. But in a moment they disappeared. Their vast possessions were fled, and the masters themselves were no more.*
>
> —Eucherius

NOVEMBER 16
Intimacy with the Divine; Pursuit of Holiness; Solitude

90. Vincent of Lérins

(D. 450?)

Many books have been written about St. Vincent of Lérins's seminal dictums about orthodoxy and the development of doctrine. But only a few sentences have been recorded about the man himself. Vincent was a native of Gaul, possibly the brother of St. Loup, bishop of Troyes. After a career as a soldier he became a monk and priest at the monastery of Lérins on an island opposite Cannes, France.

An excellent scholar and writer, Vincent set out to devise for himself a general rule to distinguish Christian truth from heresy. So he studied Scripture, the fathers of the church, and the general councils, and he says that in order to reinforce his memory he summarized his findings in a little book, the *Commintory* or "Reminder." Early in the treatise he established his oft-quoted and influential principle on tradition as the test of orthodoxy—the true Catholic faith is that which has been "believed everywhere, always and by all." Listen to Vincent's voice on the subject:

> I have often earnestly inquired of many holy and learned men how and by what sure and universal rule I may distinguish the truth of the Catholic faith from the falsehood of heresy. In almost every instance I have received this answer: All who wish to detect the frauds of heretics and to stay rooted in the Catholic faith must, with the Lord's help, fortify their own belief in two ways: first by the authority of Scripture, and then, by the tradition of the Catholic Church.
>
> Since the canon of Scripture is complete and more than sufficient of itself for everything, you might ask what need is there to join with it the authority of the church's interpretation. For this reason: Because owing to the depth of holy Scripture, all do not accept it in one and the same sense. But one understands its words in one way, another differently, so that the Bible seems to be capable of as many interpretations as there are interpreters. Thus it is very necessary that the rule for the right understanding of the prophets and apostles should be framed in accordance with the standard ecclesiastical and Catholic interpretation.
>
> Moreover, in the Catholic Church itself, all possible care must be taken that we hold that faith which has been believed everywhere, always and by all.

> This rule we shall observe if we follow universality, antiquity and consent. We follow universality if we confess that one faith as true that the whole church throughout the world confesses. Antiquity, if we never depart from those interpretations manifestly held by our holy ancestors and fathers. Consent, if in antiquity itself, we adhere to the definitions and determinations held by all, or at least by almost all priests and teachers.

In Vincent's view, however, doctrine was not static. But doctrinal development, like the polishing of metal, brought greater clarity to truth without warping or disfiguring it. Christian truth could evolve so long as the inner reality remained unchanged, like an infant evolving into a youth, then into a man, or a seed growing into a plant.

Ironically, Vincent himself is sometimes suspected of semi-Pelagianism, the heresy that attacked **Augustine**'s doctrine of predestination. But the evidence is circumstantial. And if the charge were true, Vincent's lapse occurred before the issue was settled, and he was in the company of other saints like **John Cassian.**

Vincent died at Lérins around 450.

Think back on the days of old,
think over the years, down the ages.
Question your father, let him explain to you,
your elders and let them tell you!

—Deuteronomy 32:7 *NJB*

MAY 24
Defending the Faith; Saints and the Bible

91. Peter Chrysologus
(406–450?)

Around 433, St Peter Chrysologus became Archbishop of Ravenna, Italy. An unreliable legend says that a vision directed Pope St. Sixtus III to appoint him instead of the popularly acclaimed candidate. More probably, however, **St. Leo the Great** elevated Peter to the see at the request of Emperor Valentinian III, who seems to have been the saint's friend.

The little information we have tells us that as archbishop Peter Chrysologus worked hard to remove the lingering traces of paganism from his diocese. With the support of Galla Placidia, the emperor's mother, he also engaged in an ambitious building program. For example, he constructed a baptistery and church at a nearby port.

Peter's practical sermons earned him the title "Chrysologus" or "golden-worded." Perhaps he was effective as a preacher because he believed in speaking simply and directly so that every member of the community could benefit from his words. As he once said, "Ordinary language is dear to simple souls and sweet to the learned."

Peter used his sermons to ground his flock in the basics of sound Christian living. He corrected their abuses and taught them the tools of piety. In the following sermon he explains the importance of prayer, fasting, and almsgiving:

> There are three things through which faith stands firm, devotion abides and virtue endures: prayer, fasting and mercy. What prayer knocks for on the door, fasting successfully begs and mercy receives. These three are one and give life to one another. For fasting is the soul of prayer. And mercy is the life of fasting.
>
> Let no one cut these three apart—they are inseparable. If a person has only one of them, or if he does not have them all simultaneously, he has nothing. Therefore, he who prays should also fast. And he who fasts should also be merciful. He who wants to be heard when he petitions should hear another who petitions him.
>
> Let prayer, mercy and fasting be one threefold petition for us before God. These three hold fast the citadel of heaven, knock at the private chamber of God our judge, follow up the cases of men before the tribunal of Christ, beg indulgence for the unjust, win pardon for the guilty. The person who does not have these as his aiding advocates in heaven does not have a secure position on earth.

> Since these have so high a post in heaven they influence events on earth. They guide prosperity and ward off adversity. They extinguish vices and enkindle virtues. They render bodies chaste and hearts pure. They bring peace to the body and ease to the mind. They make the senses a school for disciplinary control. They enable human hearts to become temples of God.

Peter Chrysologus also championed orthodoxy and the unity of the church. In 448, for example, Eutyches, a heretic condemned for denying Christ's humanity, defended himself in a circular letter to many bishops. Peter responded by exhorting Eutyches to adhere to the divinely revealed mystery of the Incarnation and to cease causing dissension in the church.

Peter Chrysologus died at Imola, his hometown, on July 30, probably in the year 450.

> *When mercy dries up, fasting suffers drought, for mercy is to fasting what rain is to the earth. The one who fasts may prepare his heart, cleanse his flesh, pull out his vices and sow virtues. But if he does not sprinkle his plants with streams of mercy, he does not gather his harvest. O faster, when your mercy fasts, your field fasts too.*
>
> —Peter Chrysologus

JULY 30
Almsgiving; Celebration of Discipline; Doctors of the Church; Fasting; Great Preachers

92. Euthymius
(378?–473)

St. Euthymius loved to be alone with God. He pursued solitude by wandering ever farther into the wilderness of Palestine. Paradoxically, fame followed him there as he became widely known as a spiritual counselor, miracle worker, evangelist to the Arabs, and defender of the faith.

The bishop of Melitene, Armenia, had ordained Euthymius and made him governor of the local monasteries. At twenty-nine, however, he withdrew to a monastery near Jerusalem and lived there five years as a hermit. Then he retreated into the desert toward Jericho, where a community of disciples gathered around him. He appointed his associate Theoctistus as his vicar and governed his monastery from a distant cave, receiving people only on weekends. A wise abbot, he insisted on strict discipline, but prohibited unusual penances that might foster pride.

Once Euthymius healed Terebôn, an Arab child, and as a result hundreds of Bedouins converted to Christianity. Cyril of Scythopolis, oral historian of the Palestinian monks, tells how the boy and his father approached Theoctistus, looking for the saint:

> At his father's bidding the boy said, "I received this affliction in Persia some time ago. I have passed through all medical science and magic arts, and these have not helped me in any way but have rather increased the disorder. . . . Reflecting on my condition in godly compunction, . . . one night I turned to prayer and besought God with tears, saying, 'O God, . . . creator of heaven and earth, . . . if you rescue me from this dire disorder, I will become a Christian. . . .'
>
> ". . . I suddenly fell asleep and saw a grizzled man with a great beard, who said to me . . . , 'Are you going to fulfill the pledge you have made to God. If so, he will cure you.' I said I would if I were healed. Then he said, 'I am Euthymius, who resides in the eastern desert near Jerusalem. . . . If you wish to be healed come to me without delay, and God will cure you through me.'"

Even though it was not yet the weekend, Theoctistus brought the boy to Euthymius:

> Euthymius, judging it preposterous to oppose visions from God, came down to them. By praying fervently and sealing Terebôn with the sign of the cross, he restored him to health. The barbarians, astounded at so total a transformation and so extraordinary a miracle, found faith in Christ. And casting themselves on the ground they all begged to receive the seal in Christ. The miracle-working Euthymius, perceiving that their faith in Christ came from the soul, ordered a small font to be constructed in the corner of the cave. . . . After catechizing them, he baptized them all in the name of the Father and of the Son and of the Holy Spirit.

So many Arabs became Christians through Euthymius's ministry that the patriarch of Jerusalem consecrated him as a bishop to care for them.

Around 459, Eudoxia, the widow of Emperor Theodosius II, sought the saint's counsel about serious family problems. Euthymius predicted that her situation would improve if she would abandon Monophysitism, which denied Christ's humanity, and return to orthodox Christianity. She followed his advice, returning to the church along with many of her followers.

After sixty-eight fruitful years in the desert, Euthymius died in 473 at age ninety-five.

> *Just as bread is never eaten without salt, so it is impossible to achieve virtue without love. For each virtue is made secure through love and humility, with the aid of experience, time and grace. While humility exalts to a height, love prevents falling from this height, since "he who humbles himself will be exalted" (see Luke 18:14) and "love never fails" (see 1 Corinthians 13:8).*
>
> —Euthymius

JANUARY 20
Dreams; Evangelization; Healing Touch; Humility; The Sign of the Cross; Solitude

93. Simeon Stylites
(390–459)

Once, at age thirteen, Simeon heard the beatitudes read at Mass and was awestruck. He asked an elderly hermit how he might obtain the happiness promised in these declarations. A solitary life, he was told, with continual prayer, fasting, humiliation, and enduring persecution was the way to real happiness. Hearing this, Simeon prostrated himself and asked God to put him on the road to virtue. Prompted by a vision, he entered a monastery in Cilicia, near the borders of Syria. Even though he was still a youth, the other monks admired him for his austerity and charity.

Today we may be astounded—and sometimes appalled—by the enormity of St. Simeon's self-inflicted penances. For example, he almost died from constricting his waist with a rough rope of palm leaves. Every Lent he abstained from food altogether. Once he had to be revived from near-death at Easter with a little water, a consecrated host, and some lettuce.

He lived for three years in a roofless hut. Then, atop a mountain, he tethered himself to a rock with a thirty-foot chain in order to force himself to remain faithful. But a friend persuaded him that his strong will was sufficient to make him endure, so he cut the chain.

However, Simeon was not allowed to enjoy solitude. So many people lined up for his prayer that he invented standing on a pillar as a novel way of keeping them at a distance. As Theodoret, his biographer, wrote:

> The visitors could not be counted. They all tried to touch him and reap some blessing from his garments of skins. At first he thought the excess of honor absurd. Later when he grew tired of it, he originated the idea of standing on a pillar. First he ordered the cutting of a nine-foot pillar. Then one of 18 feet, afterwards of 33 feet, and now of 54 feet—for he yearns to fly up to heaven and to be separated from life on earth.
>
> I do not think that this standing has occurred without God's dispensation. Thus, I ask faultfinders to curb their tongue and to consider how often the Master has contrived such things for the benefit of the more easygoing. He ordered Isaiah to walk naked and barefoot (Isaiah 20:2). Hosea to marry a harlot (Hosea 1:2) and again to love an adulterous woman (Hosea 3:1). Ezekiel to lie on his right side for 40 days and on

> his left for 150 (Ezekiel 4:4–6). The Ruler of the universe ordered each of these unique spectacles to attract those who would not heed words and could not bear hearing prophecy, and make them listen. So God has also ordained this new and singular sight in order by its strangeness to draw all to look and to make the proffered exhortation persuasive to those who come. A person who comes out of curiosity departs instructed in divine things.

Simeon dwelt on a pillar or *stylus* for thirty-seven years and is recognized as the first pillar-saint or "stylite." His unenclosed platform was only six feet in diameter. There he stood in prayer, daily prostrating himself as many as twelve hundred times. Twice a day he addressed the crowds. He did not call people to imitate his mortification, but urged them to pray and to work for justice. He died on his pillar in 459 at age sixty-nine.

Perhaps Simeon was to the fifth-century world what Teresa of Calcutta was to the twentieth century—a sacrament calling all people to look beyond earthly things to heavenly realities. And then to return to the world bringing love, justice, and hope to their neighbors.

JANUARY 5
Pursuit of Holiness

94. Valerian

(D. 460?)

Around 455, St. Valerian served as bishop of Cimiez on the Mediterranean coast of southern Gaul. The town was the capital of Rome's Maritime Alps province, and he saw it as a wild scene that endangered his flock. Debauchery, drunkenness, sexual immorality, feuds, and corruption contaminated Christians under his care, who apparently were only superficially evangelized. In his sermons, Valerian regularly condemned pride, covetousness, gluttony, drunkenness, and other capital sins. And he taught his people practical ways to avoid these evil snares. In the following sermon, for example, he corrects Christians who relaxed their Lenten discipline to celebrate Easter with uncontrolled revelry:

> I sometimes find myself displeased with Easter merrymakers because many think they may now freely do anything they had put under discipline during Lent. But your devotions only result in disorder if you fail to preserve what you gained for the purification of your soul by your difficult fasts and vigils. If we don't heed spiritual duties and give in to bodily desires, we swiftly destroy everything we have acquired.
>
> However, I am not saying that we should refrain extensively from food or abstain completely from drinking. Even if our bodies have been fashioned for the cross, they should nevertheless be sustained. This alone is what displeases me during these days: insatiable appetite, purposeless gorging of the stomach or a banquet profuse with drunkenness and scoffing all night long.
>
> What does it profit you if you display your goodness to the Lord for forty days, and on one day offend him by a frenzy of wicked cruelty? What good is it to preserve your chastity for a long period, if afterward you let yourself be drawn into a base sin? What benefit is there in cheating covetousness for a time, if you then delight in other people's losses? Whatever grace a person has acquired by good works through many years obviously perishes if he is depraved by deviation to base living for one hour.
>
> So here is the way to preserve disciplinary control: foster your integrity, love chastity, promote peace, check under the fear of punishment everything that serves evil.

In all of his sermons Valerian taught that true Christian discipline involved doing good even more than avoiding evil. "If you desire to see God," he said, "seek out the beggar, receive the pilgrim, visit the sick, hasten to the prison."

We don't know anything about Valerian's background except that he was probably a monk. A monastic martyrology claims that he came from Lérins, the island monastery on the French Riviera. Valerian also wrote a letter to monks that betrays an insider's tender kinship to the monastic way. In it he warmly encourages his brothers to embrace the ideals of the New Testament letters—the faith of Romans, the love of Corinthians, the freedom of Galatians, the truth of Ephesians and so on.

As bishop, Valerian participated in several provincial councils that strove to shore up the disorganized church of southern Gaul. He looked to the pope to support his efforts and those of his fellow bishops against the persistent influence of Arian heretics. In 452, **Pope Leo I** wrote a letter praising Valerian for his orthodoxy. The saint's name appears in no records after 460, so historians guess that he died around that time.

Without doubt the world would still be in darksome fetters if it were not illumined by the shining examples of the saints. It would be struggling for obscure and uncertain objectives if the crown of martyrdom, shedding its light throughout the world, were not confounding the unbelieving minds of men.

—Valerian

JULY 23

Celebration of Discipline; Pursuit of Holiness

95. Patrick

(389–461)

Christ with me, Christ before me,
Christ behind me, Christ within me,
Christ beneath me, Christ above me,
Christ at my right, Christ at my left,
Christ in my lying down, Christ in my sitting, Christ in my arising.
Christ in the heart of everyone who thinks of me,
Christ in the mouth of everyone who speaks to me,
Christ in every eye that sees me,
Christ in every ear that hears me.

—Patrick's Breastplate, or The Deer Cry

As a youth Patrick was carried off as a slave from Roman Britain to northern Ireland, where he tended his master's pigs. He spent his days praying, and so he grew both in closeness to God and in Christian maturity. Aided by divine voices and miracles, after six years he escaped and returned to his family. But Patrick had fallen in love with the Irish, and sensed that he should return to them:

> One night in a dream I had a vision of a man named Victoricus coming from Ireland and carrying a bundle of letters. He gave one of them to me. I read the beginning of the letter that claimed to be the "Voice of the Irish." At the moment I was reading the letter, I thought I heard the voices of those who dwelt beside the wood of Focluth, which is by the western sea. With one voice they cried: "We beg you, holy youth, to come and walk once more among us."

St. Patrick was convinced that he had a divine commission to establish the church in Ireland. He spent twenty-one years preparing himself for that formidable task. At two monasteries in France, Lérins and Auxerre, Patrick mastered the spiritual disciplines and acquired practical construction skills. He wanted to follow up his evangelization by building churches for his converts.

In 432, Patrick returned to Ireland as a bishop. He proceeded strategically, first winning protection from rulers by directly confronting the Druids, the pagan priests. Then he traversed the island, making thousands of converts. Everywhere he equipped his new Christian communities with church buildings and liturgical vessels. Patrick also founded monasteries which became centers of learning and sources of a native Irish clergy.

Patrick accomplished his mission in the face of daily mortal dangers. Legend has it that the song quoted above was first heard at the outset of his ministry. A powerful king was set to ambush Patrick and his fellows, but miraculously they became invisible. All the king saw was some deer passing by and voices chanting "Christ be in me. . . ." Thus the prayer is sometimes called the "Deer Cry."

Patrick died in 461. In twenty-nine years he had transformed Ireland, replacing an ancient paganism with a vibrant Christian church.

Near the end of his life Patrick wrote about his time as a slave: "My love and fear of God increased greatly, and my faith grew, and my spirit was stirred up. Before dawn, in snow and frost and rain, I used to be aroused in prayer. Nor was there any tepidity in me, such as I now feel, because then the spirit was fervent within me." Perhaps what Patrick felt was not so much "tepidity" as exhaustion from his apostolic labors. Still, his words console me and others, who in the autumn of our lives feel that our early fervor has somehow grown strangely cool.

MARCH 17 / PATRON OF IRELAND
Celtic Saints; Spiritual Warfare; World Historical Saints

96. Leo the Great
(D. 461)

St. Leo is called "Great" because of his significant ecclesiastical, theological, and political achievements. Leo solidified the office of the pope, formulated the doctrine of the Incarnation, and sustained Rome when the walls were tumbling down.

Leo was elected bishop of Rome in 440. As pope he exercised his authority more widely than any predecessor, taking a concern, for example, for the church in Africa, France, and Spain. In his letters and sermons he developed the belief that, as the heir of Peter, the bishop of Rome exercised a supreme and universal authority over the church and a primacy over all other bishops. Not every bishop accepted his authority without question, but Leo's teaching and behavior definitively shaped the papacy.

At the Council of Chalcedon in 451, six hundred bishops condemned the Monophysite heresy, which held that the incarnate Christ was only divine, not human. The decisive moment at the council came with the reading of Leo's letter to Bishop Flavian of Constantinople. In the following selection, he clearly describes the dual nature of Christ:

> Without detriment to the properties of the divine and the human that came together in one person, majesty took on humility, strength weakness, eternity mortality.
>
> Then the Son of God entered the lower parts of the world—descending from his heavenly home and yet not quitting his Father's glory, begotten in a new order by a new birthing. Invisible in his own nature, he became visible in ours. And he whom nothing could contain was content to be contained.
>
> Abiding before all time, he began to be in time. The Lord of all things, he obscured his immeasurable majesty and took on the form of a servant. Being God who cannot suffer, he did not disdain to be man that can suffer and, immortal as he is, to subject himself to the laws of death.
>
> The Lord assumed his mother's nature without faultiness. Nor does the marvel of his birth make his nature unlike ours. For he who is true God is also true man. In this union there is no deceit, since the humility of humanness and the loftiness of the Godhead both meet there.
>
> To be hungry and thirsty, to be weary and to sleep is clearly human. But to satisfy five thousand men with five loaves, to walk on the surface

> of the water with feet that do not sink and to quell the risings of the waves by rebuking the winds is without any doubt divine. For as God is not changed by the showing of pity, so man is not swallowed up in the dignity of the divine.

"Peter has spoken through Leo," acclaimed the assembly, and it accepted Leo's letter as defining the doctrine of the Incarnation.

When Attila the Hun was about to sack Rome in 452, Leo personally turned him away by persuading him to accept payment of a tribute. Three years later, however, Leo tried the same tack on the Vandals, but they ravaged the city and took many prisoners to Africa. Beaten but not defeated, Leo sent priests and aid to the captives. At this time of momentous change, the saint led the church and society with a hopeful spirit, restoring buildings, organizing relief for the hungry and the sick, and defending the faith.

Leo the Great died on November 10, 461.

> *Grant to us, O Lord, not to mind earthly things, but rather to love heavenly things, that while all things around us pass away, we even now may hold fast those things that abide forever.*
>
> —Leo the Great

NOVEMBER 10
Defending the Faith; Jesus Christ; Saints and Politics

97. Prosper of Aquitaine

(390?–465?)

Are human beings saved by grace or by works? Must we seek God, or does God come after us? Are some predestined to damnation or are all free to embrace salvation? Such questions that still divide Christians today embroiled St. Prosper of Aquitaine in lifelong controversies on the issue of grace versus freedom of the will.

We first meet Prosper Tiro around 425 as a participant in the Semi-Pelagian controversy that rocked the church in southern France. Semi-Pelagians minimized the role of grace in the first steps of becoming a Christian. **John Cassian** and others vigorously opposed **Augustine**'s strict views that special grace was required for salvation and thus many were predestined to damnation. Prosper, a monk and lay theologian, championed Augustine. And in 428, a letter from Prosper prompted Augustine to write a major book on predestination.

In 431, Prosper went to Rome and obtained a letter from Pope Celestine I that affirmed Augustine and his views, and urged the French bishops to quell the dispute peacefully. But it raged on. For several more years Prosper wrote extensively, defending and popularizing Augustine's teaching.

In his book *The Call to All Nations*, Prosper seems to have mellowed somewhat, allowing that God mercifully made the grace of salvation available to all human beings. In the following excerpt Prosper describes the interplay of grace and free will:

> When the word of God enters the ears through the ministry of preachers, the action of the divine power fuses with the sound of the human voice. The Inspirer of the preacher's office is also the strength of the hearer's heart. Then the food of the word becomes sweet to the soul. The new light expels the old darkness. The interior eye is freed from the cataracts of the ancient error. The soul passes from one will to another will. Although the will that is driven out lingers on for a while, the newborn will claims for itself all that is better in human beings. Thus the law of sin and the law of God do not dwell in the same way and together in the same person.
>
> Then the tempter tries to ambush a person through external things, but the mind strong with God's help prevails. For there are occasions for struggle, and these greatly benefit the faithful. Their weakness is buffeted so that their holiness may not yield to pride.

> All good things, especially those conducive to eternal life, are obtained, increased and preserved through God's favor. With this faith firmly fixed in our hearts, our religious sense ought not be disturbed by the problem of the total or only partial conversion of humankind. It is impossible that he who wills all people to be saved would, for no reasons whatever, not save the greater part of them.

Prosper spent the last part of his life in Rome where he served as secretary to **Pope St. Leo the Great.** During that time he wrote the *Chronicle*, a universal history from Adam's fall to the Vandal's conquest of Rome in 455. He died in Rome around 465.

> *Let the Good Shepherd find his erring sheep and not disdain to bear it, sick and tired of wandering trackless wilds, on his shoulders. Let him save it not only by calling it back, but also by carrying it along. Let the Lord seek his human image, wash away from it all accumulated uncleanness that has stained it and so brighten up the mirror of the human heart.*
>
> —Prosper of Aquitaine

JUNE 25
Faith Seeking Understanding; Grace

98. Severin of Noricum

(D. 480)

In the 450s, St. Severin arrived at Noricum in modern-day Austria, preaching repentance, spiritual renewal, and works of mercy. At that time advancing armies of Huns threatened Roman towns along the Danube River that were already dominated by barbarian conquerors.

A lay itinerant preacher whose background was shrouded in mystery, Severin seems somewhat exotic, a sort of spiritual ancestor of the Lone Ranger: With charismatic gifts of prophecy and healing he warned towns of danger, warded off enemies, put an end to famines, and healed the sick. But he kept his background a secret, though we know he came from the East, probably having spent time with the desert monks. People speculated that a profound humility prompted him to hide his noble origins.

Eugippus, his disciple, tells how Severin, responding to God's call, came first to the town of Asturias, now Stockerau. He went straight to the church to tell the townspeople how to ward off the threatening Huns:

> He asked the priests, the clergy and the layfolk to be called together, and then . . . foretold them how, with prayer, fasting, and fruits of mercy, they might prevent the imminent attack of the enemy. But they . . . judged the warnings of the prophet by the standard of their unbelief.

So Severin left the church and stayed briefly with an old sacristan, to whom he foretold the exact day and hour of the coming attack. Then he went to Comagenis, a nearby Roman town chafing under barbarian rule.

> He went to the church at once, and urged the whole population, which had already given up all hope, to arm themselves with fasting, prayer, and almsgiving. He held up to them the ancient examples of salvation from danger when the protection of God had miraculously freed his people contrary to all expectation.

But they did not believe him, until the elderly sacristan from Asturias arrived and told how Severin's predicting the day and time of the invasion of the town had saved him.

> When the inhabitants . . . heard this, they begged pardon for their unbelief and carried out the holy works which the man of God had urged, observed fasts, and, gathering in the church for three days, made up for their past faults with sighs and tears. On the third day, when the evening sacrifice was being celebrated, there suddenly started an earthquake.

Terrified, the town's barbarian conquerors panicked and fled from the gates.

> Swarming out in a hurry in every direction—they imagined that they were . . . besieged by their hostile neighbors, and their terror was still increased by the power of God—and straying in the dark of night they killed each other with their swords. The people freed through God's aid by this mutual destruction of their enemies, learnt from the holy man to fight with heavenly arms.

Severin repeated similar wonders in towns all along the Danube. For example, when the people of Faviana responded to his call for penance, they averted a famine. And in other places, he saved crops from swarms of locusts, stopped floods, warned of attacks, and healed the sick. But Severin did not rely exclusively on spiritual means. Apparently he had the clout to demand that better-off churches in Austria tithe grain and clothing, which he distributed to the poor or used to ransom captives.

Severin also established several monasteries in Austria, the main one at Faviana, where he died around 480.

> *In order to become an instrument in God's hands we must be of no account in our own eyes.*
>
> —Angela Merici

JANUARY 8
Almsgiving; Miracles Do Happen

99. Daniel the Stylite

(409–493)

At age fifty-one, St. Daniel ascended a pillar, or *stylus*, where he lived for thirty-three years. We might dismiss him as bizarre, but that would be a mistake. Daniel certainly was extreme, but he wasn't weird.

Daniel was an ascetic, an "athlete" training to win the prize of spiritual perfection. Like all monks, he identified his enemies as the temptations of the flesh and the harassments of the devil. To subdue both the body and demons, Daniel practiced rigorous penitential disciplines atop his column. He literally took a *stand* against these enemies, never sitting or lying down.

Daniel was a disciple of **St. Simeon**, the first stylite, who stood for many years on a pillar without any shelter. Daniel also began his stand on an unsheltered column. But once he nearly froze and was persuaded to move to a pillar with an enclosure.

From this column on the Bosporus near Constantinople, Daniel maintained a lively involvement in both church and state. Emperors and patriarchs frequently climbed the pillar to consult him. Admiring monks became his disciples and erected huts nearby. The faithful flocked there to hear him teach, or to beg him to intercede for them. The pillar served the practical purpose of allowing Daniel to decide who could approach him.

For example, Daniel's anonymous biographer tells of a goldsmith who brought his crippled son to him for healing:

> Throwing himself and his child in front of the column, he besought the holy man, saying, "Oh servant of God have pity on my young child who longs to stand up but cannot do so, for nature conceived him unnaturally. . . . Do not send me away with my petition unfulfilled."
>
> The holy man replied: "Do not speak so impatiently; for your zeal towards God, if accompanied by faith and patience, will release your son from his misfortune. Do not be discouraged, but go with the child and remain by the relics of Simeon [Stylites]. . . . Anoint the child's feet with the holy oil, bring him back here when prayer is being offered, and we trust in God that he will give him healing."
>
> The man did as the holy man had ordered him. And on the seventh day, when prayer had been offered in the enclosure, the boy suddenly jumped on to the steps of the pillar and went up and embraced the column. All marveled and glorified God for this wonderful happening.

> And his parents gave thanks to God and to the holy man and took home the boy in health. When the boy grew to be a man he frequently visited the holy man, received a blessing and returned home.

Over the years thousands of seekers came to the pillar to see Daniel. The Emperor Leo I even built a monastery at the site to care for his visitors, as today we build motels near the sites of apparitions. The saint was a beacon of hope and holiness for all. When he died in 493 he was perhaps the most revered person in the eastern Roman Empire.

Daniel the Stylite, like many other saints, was a literalist, who took at face value Jesus' commands to be perfect and to pray always. However, he did not impose his rigors on others. And his message was not at all eccentric. He constantly exhorted his hearers to love God, to love one another, and to care for the poor, the great commandments we all should take more literally.

DECEMBER 11
Healing Touch; Saints and Politics; Spiritual Warfare

100. Faustus of Riez
(403?–493?)

To those who see only with the outward eye, all these events at Cana are strange and wonderful; to those who understand, they are also signs. For . . . the very water tells us of our rebirth in baptism. One thing is turned into another from within, and in a hidden way a lesser creature is changed into a greater . . . [At Cana] water was suddenly changed; later [at baptism], it will cause a change in man.

By Christ's action in Galilee, then, wine is made, that is, the law withdraws and grace takes its place; . . . the old covenant with its outward discipline is transformed into the new. For, as the Apostle says: The old order has passed away; now all is new! (See 2 Corinthians 5:17). The water in the jars is not less than it was before, but now begins to be what it had not been; so too the law is not destroyed by Christ's coming, but is made better than it was.

When the wine fails, new wine is served: the wine of the old covenant was good, but the wine of the new is better. The old covenant . . . is exhausted by its letter; the new covenant, which belongs to us, has the savor of life and is filled with grace.

The good wine, that is, good precepts, refers to the law. Thus we read: You shall love your neighbor but hate your enemy (see Leviticus 19:18; Matthew 5:43). But the Gospel is a better and a stronger wine: My command to you is: love your enemies, pray for your persecutors (see Matthew 5:44).

—Faustus of Riez

As at Cana, where one thing became something better, Faustus himself was probably an attorney who became a monk, an abbot, and a bishop. In 426 he entered the monastery at Lérins on an island off the French Riviera. **St. Honoratus,** the abbot, once remarked that the quality of his monastic observance rivaled the fathers of the desert. St. Sidonius Apollinaris praised Faustus as an excellent extemporaneous preacher. He wrote in a letter: "I shouted myself hoarse at Faustus's sermon!" Apparently interactive sermons complete with "Amens!" and "Hallelujahs!" can trace their roots at least as far back as the fifth century.

Around 433, Faustus became the abbot at Lérins and ruled the famous abbey for a quarter of a century. Then he was elevated to the nearby see of Riez in Provence, succeeding Maximus, who had also served as abbot of the island monastery. "Lérins," he wrote, "has sent two successive bishops to Riez. Of the first she is proud. For the second she blushes."

But Lérins had no need to be ashamed, as Faustus proved to be a very good bishop. In addition to managing his diocese well, he played a significant role in combating Arianism and Pelagianism, the latter of which denied the freedom of the will in choosing to receive salvation. In treatises on the subject, however, Faustus brought criticism on himself by expressing—in good faith—ideas that could be labeled as semi-Pelagian and that were ultimately condemned in 529.

In 478, Faustus's opposition to Arianism angered Visigoth King Euric, who exiled him. He later returned to Riez, where he continued to serve his flock until he died at about age ninety.

> *If teaching and preaching is your job, then study diligently and apply yourself to whatever is necessary for doing the job well. Be sure that you first preach by the way you live. If you do not, people will notice that you say one thing, but live otherwise, and your words will bring only cynical laughter and a derisive shake of the head.*
>
> —Charles Borromeo

SEPTEMBER 28
Defending the Faith; Great Preachers; Saints and Sacraments (Baptism)

101. Epiphanius
(D. 496)

At the end of the fifth century the church in Europe weathered a period of great political turmoil. Waves of barbarian invaders had crushed imperial Rome and hastened its implosion. The pagan German and Ostrogoth conquerors of Italy had made life miserable for the people, imposing unbearable taxes on them and reducing them to starvation. In these confused times, when civil institutions could no longer guarantee any security, bishops like St. Epiphanius provided people a measure of safety and relief.

In 483 the church at Pavia chose Epiphanius as its bishop. The people recognized him as a man of mettle and integrity who patterned his behavior on the counsels of the gospel. Ennodius, his successor and biographer, portrayed him as living a simple and disciplined Christian life.

Epiphanius labored tirelessly to improve the welfare of his flock. He spearheaded the reconstruction of Pavia, which the German king Odoacer and his armies had leveled. An indefatigable campaigner for rights, he negotiated the release of many prisoners that the invading armies had captured. And he intervened successfully to modify oppressive laws and taxes.

Twice popes sent Epiphanius as an ambassador to disentangle ecclesiastical matters with Odoacer and Theodoric, king of the Ostrogoths. Later as a polished negotiator, he was sent on several peacekeeping missions. Once, when Ricimir, a patrician of Milan, and Emperor Anthemius were about to go to war, Epiphanius intervened to avert the conflict. The following passage from his biography describes his appeal to the emperor to reconcile with Ricimir:

> Venerable emperor, the Lord has ordained that the governance of so great a state be entrusted to one who, adhering to the dogmas of the Catholic faith, recognizes in God the author and lover of charity. And through whom the arms of peace break the fury of war. . . .
>
> Through the ages excellent kings like David have learned to be godlike in extending grace to the suppliant. In view of this, Italy and the patrician Ricimer have entrusted to my humbleness the task of intercession. Doubtless he is convinced that a Roman would not refuse to God the gift of peace which even a barbarian seeks. Moreover, a

> victory without bloodshed will be a triumph which will add great glory to the annals of your reign.
>
> I know of no manner of warfare in which you can better prove your valor than by contending against your own anger and shaming the fierce Goth by your kindness. For he who previously considered it a disgrace to make supplication will suffer even a greater humiliation if you grant what he asks. Then you must also consider that for you the outcome of this war will entail a twofold loss or gain. If wrong prevails, the losses endured on both sides will be losses to your realm. But with Ricimer as your friend whatever he holds intact will be yours as well as his. Remember also that he who is the first to offer peace looks to his own best interests.

The emperor relented and the war threat fizzled. Around 496, Epiphanius went to Burgundy to obtain the release of prisoners taken by yet another invading army. Peacemaker to the end, he died of fever upon his return to Pavia.

> *Remember that the Christian life is one of action, not of speech and day-dreams. Let there be few words and many deeds and let them be done well.*
>
> —St. Vincent Pallotti

JANUARY 21
Peacemakers; Saints and Politics

102. Genevieve

(422?–500?)

On his way to combat heresy in Britain, **St. Germanus of Auxerre** made an overnight stop at Nanterre, France. In the crowd that gathered to hear him speak, Germanus spotted Genevieve (or Genovefa), a beautiful seven-year-old girl, and he foresaw her future holiness. When he asked little St. Genevieve if she wanted to dedicate her life to God, she enthusiastically said yes. So he laid hands on her with a blessing, thus launching the spiritual career of one of France's most admired saints.

At fifteen Genevieve formally consecrated herself as a virgin, but continued to live as a laywoman. Because of her generous giving to the poor, she became widely known in the vicinity around Paris. At first, however, for some unknown reason Genevieve met great hostility. But St. Germanus defused it by authorizing her with public signs of his support.

Once when the Franks were besieging Paris, Genevieve rescued the city from starvation by leading a convoy of ships up the Seine to Troyes to obtain food. In this selection from her biography, we learn that she had to work a miracle to bring it home safely:

> During the return voyage, however, their ships were so buffeted by the wind . . . that the high holds fore and aft in which they had stored the grain tipped over on their sides. And the ships filled with water. Quickly Genovefa, her hands stretched toward heaven, begged Christ for assistance. Immediately the ships were righted. Thus through her our God . . . saved eleven grain-laden ships. . . .
>
> When she returned to Paris, her sole concern was to distribute the grain to all according to their needs. She made it her first priority to provide a whole loaf to those whose strength had been sapped by hunger. Thus when her servant girls went to the ovens they would often find only part of the bread they had baked. . . . But it was soon clear who had taken the bread from the ovens for they noticed the needy carrying loaves throughout the city and heard them magnifying and blessing the name of Genovefa. For she put her hopes not in what is seen but in what is not seen. For she knew the Prophet spoke truly who said: "Whoever is kind to the poor is lending to Yahweh" (Proverbs 19:17 *NJB*). For through a revelation of the Holy Spirit she had once been shown that land, where those who lend their treasure

> to the poor expect to find it again. And for this reason, she was accustomed to weep and pray incessantly: for she knew that as long as she was in the flesh she was exiled from the Lord.

From that time Genevieve enjoyed a heroine's status, and used her influence and wonders on the city's behalf. For example, she persuaded Childeric, who had conquered Paris, to release many captives. And in 451, when Attila the Hun was advancing on the city, she got the populace to pray and fast for their safety. The invader changed his course and Paris was spared. She also became a trusted adviser to Clovis, the king of the Franks.

When Genevieve died around 500, she was buried in the church of Sts. Peter and Paul at Paris. So many miracles occurred through her intercession there that it became a pilgrimage spot and came to be called St. Genevieve.

> *Extend mercy toward others, so that there can be no one in need whom you met without helping. Just consider how much we ourselves are in need of mercy. For what hope is there for us if God should withdraw his mercy from us?*
>
> —Vincent de Paul

JANUARY 3 / PATRON OF PARIS, DROUGHT, DISASTERS, AND FRENCH SPECIAL FORCES

Love in Action; Miracles Do Happen; Serving the Poor

103. Sabas
(438–532)

By the fourth century, monasteries had appeared in Palestine. Aspiring ascetics sought to be like Elijah, **John the Baptist**, and Jesus himself, who had found solitude in the desert east of Jerusalem.

St. Sabas, a leader of that early monasticism, founded seven monasteries, three lauras and four cenobia. A laura is a settlement of hermits living in caves and huts around a church. A community of monks who live, worship, and work together is a cenobium. Sabas built well as his chief monastery, the Mar Saba, still exists after fifteen centuries.

The saint dwelt in monasteries most of his life. At age eight he ran away from abusive relatives to a monastery in Cappadocia. Ten years later he went to the monastery of **St. Euthymius** at Jerusalem, hoping to become a hermit. But Euthymius judged him too young for absolute solitude and placed him in a cenobium nearby. When he was thirty Sabas was allowed to spend five days a week alone in the wilderness. After Euthymius's death, Sabas finally became an anchorite, dwelling in a cave on the face of a cliff. So many monks came desiring to live under his direction that he had to establish his first monastery, which became the Mar Saba.

Sabas did not give his disciples a written rule, but he expected them to follow certain basic guidelines. He did not micromanage their conduct. But he seized "teachable moments" to test his disciples' fidelity, as he did on the occasion described in this account:

> Once when journeying with a disciple from Jericho to the Jordan, this champion of piety Sabas fell in with some people of the world among whom was a girl of winning appearance. When they had passed by, the elder, wishing to test the disciple, asked, "What about the girl who has gone by and is one-eyed?"
>
> The brother replied, "No, father, she has two eyes."
>
> The elder said, "You are wrong, my child. She is one-eyed." The other insisted that he knew with precision that she was not one-eyed but had indeed extremely fine eyes. The elder asked, "How do you know that so clearly?"
>
> He replied, "I, father, had a careful look, and I noted that she has both her eyes."
>
> At this the elder said, "And where have you stored the precept that says, 'Do not fix your eye on her and do not be captured by her

> eyebrows?' (See Proverbs 6:25). Fiery is the passion that arises from inquisitive looks. Know this: from now on you are not to stay with me in a cell because you do not guard your eyes as you should." He sent him to the cenobium at Castellium and, when he had spent sufficient time there and learnt to keep a careful watch on his eyes and thoughts, he received him as an anchorite into the laura.

The patriarch of Jerusalem ordained Sabas in 491, and two years later appointed him head over all the monks of Palestine who were hermits. When the saint was old, other patriarchs sent him on diplomatic missions representing the church's interests to the emperors at Constantinople. Sabas died after a brief illness in 532.

For Sabas, the "desert" was not merely the wilderness, but it was also his encounter with God in his aloneness. My soul also craves that divine experience of solitude. But city-dweller that I am, I must create my own "desert." So, early in the morning when my family is still asleep, I go alone into the "wilderness" of my living room and open myself to God.

DECEMBER 5
Celebration of Discipline; Community; Passion for Purity; Solitude

104. Brigid

(450?–525)

Historians say we know a lot more about St. Brigid than we have facts, a polite way of saying that legends swirl about Ireland's most celebrated woman. But even legends may have cores of truth. And some miracle stories are not legends at all, but true accounts of God's interventions.

Brigid was the daughter of a slave woman and a chieftain, who liberated her at the urging of his overlord. As a girl she sensed a call to become a nun, and St. Mel, bishop of Armagh, received her vows. Before Brigid, consecrated virgins lived at home with their families. But the saint, imitating **Patrick,** began to assemble nuns in communities, a historic move which enriched the church in Ireland.

In 471, Brigid founded a monastery for both women and men at Kildare. This was the first convent in Ireland, and Brigid was the abbess. Under her leadership Kildare became a center of learning and spirituality. Her school of art fashioned both lovely utensils for worship and beautifully illustrated manuscripts. Again following Patrick's model, Brigid used Kildare as a base and built convents throughout the island.

Brigid's hallmark was uninhibited, generous giving to anyone in need. Many of the saint's earliest miracles seem to have rescued her from punishment for having given something to the poor that was intended for someone else. For example, once as a child she gave a piece of bacon to a dog, and was glad to find it replaced when she was about to be disciplined. Brigid exhibited this unbounded charity all her life, giving away valuables, clothing, food—anything close by—to anyone who asked.

The saint's unrestrained hospitality is the context in which we should read this famous Celtic poem attributed to her:

I should like a great lake of ale
 For the King of the kings.
 I should like the family of heaven
 To be drinking it through time eternal.
I should like the viands
 Of belief and pure piety,
 I should like [scythes]
 Of penance at my house.

I should like the men of heaven
　　In my own house;
　　I should like [tubs]
　　of peace to be at their disposal.
I should like vessels
　　Of charity for distribution.
　　I should like [vessels]
　　Of mercy for their company.
I should like cheerfulness
　　To be in their drinking;
　　I should like Jesus,
　　Too, to be there among them.
I should like the three
　　Marys of illustrious renown;
　　I should like the people
　　Of heaven there from all parts.
I should like that I should be
　　A rent-payer to the Lord;
　　That, should I suffer distress,
　　He would bestow on me a good blessing.

We should beware of reading twenty-first century notions into a fifth-century poem. Ale in Brigid's Ireland, for example, was a nutritious malt drink brewed and served in every household. You could not get drunk on it, and our tea is a much stronger stimulant. The poem celebrates bountiful larders, which Brigid never knew. She always had to scrounge for something to give. She expected heaven to be different, overflowing with goodness and satisfying everyone's deepest hungers.

One of the most appealing things told of Brigid is her contemporaries' belief that there was peace in her blessing. Not merely did contentiousness die out in her presence, but just as by the touch of her hand she healed leprosy, so by her very will for peace she healed strife and laid antiseptics on the suppurating bitterness that foments it.

—Alice Curtayne

FEBRUARY 1 / PATRON OF IRISH WOMEN
Celtic Saints; Community; Generosity; Leading Women; Serving the Poor

105. Severinus Boethius

(480?–524)

History remembers St. Severinus Boethius as the last of the Roman philosophers and the first of the scholastic theologians. A well-educated member of one of Rome's most influential families, he made it his life goal to translate all of Plato and Aristotle into Latin and to reconcile their thought. Boethius fell short of his objective, but his translations of these two, as well as of Pythagoras, Ptolemy, Euclid, and Archimedes, became the main source of these authors for medieval philosophers and theologians.

Boethius entered public life because he believed with Plato that philosophers made the best governors. Theodoric appointed him consul in 510 and made him most proud twelve years later by appointing both of his sons to the same office. Although Theodoric trusted Boethius with the highest responsibilities, he soon fell into disgrace. Boethius's support for the ideal of a united empire may have threatened Theodoric. And when he defended a condemned senator, the emperor had Boethius arrested and, after nine months, tortured and executed.

While in prison awaiting execution, Boethius wrote his most famous work, *The Consolation of Philosophy*. In a dialogue between Philosophy and himself, she comforted him by declaring the impermanence of earthly success and the eternal value of things of the mind. Boethius found his consolation in the truth that through knowledge the soul finds its way to God. In this selection from the conclusion of the book, Boethius celebrates human freedom and divine providence:

> And if human and divine present may be compared, just as you see certain things in this your present time, so God sees all things in his eternal present. So that this divine foreknowledge does not change the nature and property of things; it simply sees things present to it exactly as they will happen some time as future events. It makes no confused judgments of things, but with one glance of its mind distinguishes all that is to come to pass whether it is necessitated or not. . . .
>
> Since this is so, man's freedom of will remains inviolate and the law does not impose reward and punishment unfairly, because the will is free from all necessity. God has foreknowledge and rests a spectator from on high of all things; and as the ever present eternity of his vision

> dispenses reward to the good and punishment to the bad, it adapts itself to the future quality of our actions. Hope is not placed in God in vain and prayers are not made in vain, for if they are the right kind they cannot but be efficacious. Avoid vice, therefore, and cultivate virtue, lift up your mind to the right kind of hope, and put forth humble prayers on high. A great necessity is laid upon you; if you will be honest with yourself, a great necessity to be good, since you live in the sight of a judge who sees all things.

Medieval Christians venerated Boethius as a martyr probably because Theodoric, who was an Arian, executed the philosopher unjustly. More recently, however, scholars deprived Boethius of his martyr's crown, saying that the reasons for his death were purely political. However, the same writers uphold the saint's Christianity against those who challenge it because his last book seems devoid of Christian content. Boethius was undoubtedly a Christian to the end, believing that reason and faith both led to God and Christian truth.

> *He who bears his sufferings with patience for God's sake, will soon arrive at high perfection. He will be master of the world and will already have one foot in the other world.*
>
> —Giles of Assisi

OCTOBER 23 / CULT CONFIRMED IN 1897
Faith Seeking Understanding; Saints and Politics; World Historical Saints

106. Fulgentius of Ruspe

(468?–533)

Let not considering the atrocity of any sin cause anyone to despair of the mercy of God. Nor still should anyone remain in his sins on the pretext of hoping for the mercy of God at death. But let a hopeful person confidently seek the harbor of penance without faltering so that his humility may avoid the deadly shipwreck of despair. And may he so love God's mercy that, although fearful, he may also take into consideration his justice. Let him hope that everything can be forgiven him when he turns from his sin. But let him think that nothing is forgiven a stubborn person. Let the wicked person change his life now and he will not find punishment. Let him flee guilt and he will receive mercy.

Now let a person who does not wish to suffer endless misery seek the mercy of the Lord. Now let a person who does not wish eternal death seek eternal life. Now let a person who does not wish to be damned with eternal punishment hurry to confess before the face of God.

For now is the time when doing penance bears fruit. Now the forgiveness of sins is granted to the person who does penance. Now to the converted is not denied possession of the Kingdom of Heaven in which we live and rejoice without end. And where neither death can take life away from the happy nor sadness take away happiness from the living.

—Fulgentius of Ruspe

As a young nobleman of Carthage, Fulgentius became well-known as a gifted civil servant. And he won respect for competently managing the affairs of Mariana, his widowed mother. But while reading **Augustine**'s commentary on Psalm 36, Fulgentius was convinced of the emptiness of worldly success and decided to become a monk. At age twenty-two, he entered a monastery at Carthage. He made Augustine his ideal, and like him, Fulgentius defended the faith against heresy, fostered monastic communities, and became a model bishop. From the beginning of Fulgentius's life as a monk to its end, trials, opposition, and suffering stalked him. First, he withstood his mother's protest that the church was robbing her of a widow's due support. Then Arian persecutions and invasions drove him from one monastery to another. Once at Sicca Veneria, an Arian priest had him scourged for defending the Catholic faith. In 500, at Byzacena near Carthage, he built a monastery and, although governing it as abbot, lived nearby in a cell.

Fulgentius was appointed bishop of Ruspe in 508. However, he had barely begun his work when the Arian king Thrasimund exiled him and sixty other bishops to Sardinia. There he founded a monastery, became the spokesman for the persecuted bishops, and wrote treatises against Arianism. At Thrasimund's invitation he returned to Carthage, where he eloquently defended orthodoxy against Arian debaters. Upon the king's death in 523, Fulgentius returned to his flock at Ruspe. He devoted the rest of his life to renewing the spiritual life of his people. His gentle leadership earned him broad fame as a pastor and preacher. As the quote above shows, he proclaimed mercy to people whose life circumstances had caused them great fears.

In 532, Fulgentius tried to retire to solitude on the island of Circinia. However, he returned to Ruspe at the pleading of his flock. He died there in 533 at sixty-five years of age.

Christ made love the stairway that would enable all Christians to climb to heaven. Hold fast to love, therefore, in all sincerity, and give one another practical proof of it."

—Fulgentius of Ruspe

JANUARY 1
Defending the Faith; Enduring Trials; Mercy; Sin

107. Caesarius of Arles

(470–543)

For forty years as bishop of Arles in southern France, St. Caesarius held his people to a high Christian standard. He made his life theme the correlation between worship and behavior. When he became bishop in 503, he immediately brought the liturgy to the people. He modified the liturgy of the hours for laypeople and had them celebrated in public daily. Caesarius insisted that worship must not be a mere external observance, but rather a lifting of the heart to God that had life-changing consequences. "Match your behavior to the words you sing" became his motto. He also urged his people to receive communion often.

Perhaps the first popular preacher in the western church, Caesarius frequently addressed the local church, admirably never speaking longer than fifteen minutes. You get a sample of his practical idealism in the following sermon excerpt:

> Consider more carefully why we are Christians and why we bear the cross of Christ on our forehead. It's not enough that we have received the name of Christian, if we do not perform the works of a Christian. As the Lord said: "What does it profit you to call me, 'Lord, Lord,' when you do not practice the things that I say?" (see Luke 6:46).
>
> You may say a thousand times that you're a Christian and continually sign yourself with the cross of Christ. But if you do not give alms according to your means, your title of Christian can profit you not at all. The sign of Christ and his cross are a great thing, and for this reason should signify something great and precious.
>
> What is the good of putting the sign of Christ on our forehead and lips, when we hide sins and offenses within our soul? When many men go out to commit theft or adultery, if they strike their foot they sign themselves, but they do not withdraw from their evil deed. But if a person endeavors with God's help to reject sins, and always attempts to think and do what is right, he justly makes the sign of the cross, for he tries to do things which merit the sign of Christ. Therefore, in order that we may bear the name Christian as a remedy, not unto judgment, let's turn to good works while the remedies are still within our power.

Caesarius had his sermons copied and disseminated widely throughout western Europe, possibly making him one of the earliest Christian publishers and best-selling authors. Some say that Caesarius also may have laid the groundwork for the rule of **St. Benedict** by providing rules for a cloister of women he had founded and later another for monks in his diocese.

When Visigoths herded Burgundian prisoners into Arles, Caesarius melted down gold communion vessels to aid them. He reminded critics that the "Lord celebrated his last supper on earthenware, not on plate. And we need not scruple to part with his vessels for those whom he has redeemed with his own life."

Barbarian kings esteemed Caesarius. When he was exiled on suspicion of sympathizing with the Burgundians, Alaric II cleared him of the charge and restored him. And Caesarius stopped him from executing his accusers. Theodoric, the Ostrogoth conqueror of Provence, honored him with gifts and allowed him to remain in his office. But when the Franks conquered the land in 536, Caesarius retired to a monastery. He died at Arles in 543.

A person worships whatever captivates his mind during prayer. Whoever in his prayers thinks of public affairs, or the house he is building, worships them rather than God.

—Caesarius of Arles

AUGUST 27
Almsgiving; Christian Living; Great Preachers; Prayer; The Sign of the Cross; Sin

108. Vedast

(D. 539)

St. Vedast appeared on history's stage as the priest who catechized Clovis, King of the Franks. In 496, Clovis promised to become a Christian if Christ would help him defeat his enemy, the Alamanni, a Germanic tribe who had the upper hand in a battle. When he prayed, his opponents suddenly turned heel. So Clovis set out to be baptized at Rheims, where **St. Clotilda,** his wife, and St. Remigius, the archbishop, awaited him.

At Toul the king met Vedast, who joined the entourage in order to instruct him in the faith and to prepare him for the sacrament. Along the way a significant event occurred at a bridge over the Aisne River. There Vedast prayed for a blind beggar to receive his sight, and the resultant healing seems to have strengthened Clovis's resolve to become a Christian. And it also opened some of his recalcitrant chiefs to embrace the faith.

The conversion of Clovis opened the Frankish kingdom to evangelization. In 499, Remigius appointed Vedast as bishop of Arras and assigned him to reestablish Christianity in that region. When the saint arrived in his see, he found a dilapidated church overgrown with brush and inhabited by a bear. Repeated invasions by marauding tribes had eliminated every trace of Catholicism, except in the memory of a few old people.

Vedast's task was not easy, as the Franks were not clamoring to become Catholic. "He was unable," said his biographer, "to induce the Franks as a nation to leave their profane errors. But only little by little could he convert them." Vedast, however, seized every opportunity to attract them to Christ, especially their leaders. For example, once after Clothaire had succeed his father, Vedast made a scene for the gospel at a dinner party:

> A certain Frank named Hocinus invited King Clothaire to dinner. Among the king's courtiers, he also invited Bishop Vedast. He consented to attend the feast not to endorse the crowd's gluttony, but to instruct them in true doctrine and with the king's authority to bring many to be baptized.

When he entered the house, he noticed a number of barrels of beer. "Why are these barrels standing in the middle of the house?" he asked.

"Some are for the Christian guests. Others have been offered in sacrifice to the gods."

When Vedast heard this, he made the sign of the cross over the barrels and calling on the name of Almighty God, prayed a blessing. And when he made the sign of the cross and blessed the barrels that had been sacrificed to the pagan gods, they burst. Beer flowed out all over the pavement.

Astonished at the miracle, the king and the crowd asked Vedast why he had done it. "O King, the devil wanted to use this beer to cause the hearts of the faithful to stray out of the right way into the path of sin. But now the power of God has routed the devil's craft. So all should renounce their heathen superstitions and turn to the wholesome medicines of faith in Christ."

This miracle benefitted the guests, for many of them came to the grace of baptism and bowed their heads to the true religion.

No teetotaler, Vedast seems to have preserved the Christians' beer!

For forty years at Arras, Vedast patiently gathered new believers and formed them into a faith community. He died at Arras in 539, leaving behind a restored and flourishing church.

Today under vastly different circumstances, Christians still find evangelization to be a Sisyphean task, requiring the patience and persistence of a St. Vedast.

FEBRUARY 6
Evangelization; Lights in the "Dark Ages"; Miracles Do Happen; Perseverance; Saints and Politics

109. Clotilda

(D. 545)

In 491, Clovis, the king of the Franks, married Clotilda, a Burgundian princess. Either the two were deeply in love, or Clovis regarded his queen with unusual tolerance and a measure of fear. While she seems to have supported her husband, she also stood up to him. A Catholic in a heathen court, the queen did not shrink from giving her husband a forthright argument for her faith. For instance, in his *History of the Franks*, Gregory of Tours reported that while Clovis resisted St. Clotilda's desire to have her infant sons baptized, he acquiesced to her demands:

> King Clovis had a firstborn son by Queen Clotilda. She urged Clovis to allow the boy to be baptized, saying: "The gods you worship are nothing. They are stone, wooden or metal images who can't help anyone, themselves or others. You even give them the names of men and not of gods. Jupiter, for example, the lewdest practitioner of all debaucheries and unnatural vice; the abuser of the women of his own family, who could not even abstain from intercourse with his own sister. But you should rather serve him who created out of nothing the heavens and the earth, the sea and everything in it. You should adore the one who created the human race and gave it charge over all other creatures."
>
> Clovis objected. "Your God," he said, "is not even proven to belong to the race of gods." Clotilda, however, presented the child for baptism, hoping the ceremony might persuade Clovis to believe. But the boy died that day still in his baptismal clothes. Enraged, Clovis bitterly reproached the queen: "Had the child been dedicated to my gods, he would have survived."
>
> Clotilda was undaunted. "I know that my child, called home in his baptismal robe, will be nurtured in the sight of God."
>
> Afterward she bore another son, who was also baptized. When he fell ill, the king feared that the child would die like his brother. But Clotilda prayed and God ordained that the boy should recover.

Clovis would have nothing to do with Christ until his gods failed him. In 496 he defended his kingdom against an invasion by the Alamanni, a fierce Germanic tribe. When defeat seemed imminent, Clovis appealed to Clotilda's God: "I have called upon my gods and they are powerless. If you deliver me from my enemies, I promise I'll be baptized in your name." Suddenly the Alamanni abandoned the field, leaving the Franks victorious.

Clovis kept his word. Clotilda with the help of St. Remi arranged a gala celebration for his baptism at the church at Reims. Shortly afterward, Remi also baptized three thousand of Clovis's warriors and their families. With the support of Clotilda and Clovis, Remi organized the evangelization of the whole Frankish kingdom.

Clovis died in 511. Clotilda survived him by thirty-four years, her later life marred by violent family feuds. She died in 545.

Clotilda's courageous behavior as a wife had world historical significance. She and her king were the only Catholic rulers in Europe. All the kings in Italy, Spain, France, and North Africa were Arians, heretics who claimed that Jesus was merely human and not divine. Thus, the planting of the church in Europe came in part from the seeds of St. Clotilda's faith.

JUNE 3 / PATRON OF ADOPTED CHILDREN, DEATH OF CHILDREN, AND PARENTS OF LARGE FAMILIES

Courage; Difficult Marriages; Lights in the "Dark Ages"; Married Saints; World Historical Saints

110. Gall of Clermont

(486?–551)

Bishop Gall of Clermont, France, raised his nephew, Gregory of Tours, who later wrote his uncle's story in his *Lives of the Fathers*. The famous hagiographer depicted Gall as one of those unusual wealthy noblemen who discerned true spiritual realities. And who "like birds escaping from a trap and rising up, have freed themselves" and who "forsaking and despising earthly goods . . . have turned with all their might toward heavenly things."

St. Gall's father was a senator, the head of the first family of Clermont. He had planned to marry his handsome son into another senatorial family. But Gall chose the religious life and asked the abbot of a monastery nearby to admit him. The abbot, however, recognizing the importance of Gall's family, insisted on getting his father's approval. Surprisingly, Gall's father acquiesced without resistance, apparently seeing that his son had a divine call.

Gall had an excellent singing voice, which opened many doors for him. First he became a cantor at the monastery. Then Quintian, the bishop of Clermont, adopted him as a spiritual son, making him the cantor at the cathedral. Finally, King Theodoric took a liking to the young singer and brought him to serve in the church at Trèves.

When Quintian died, Gall replaced him as bishop. Gregory of Tours said that his uncle's defining characteristic as bishop was the patience with which he bore injuries. Once, for example, a priest struck him during a meal, but Gall showed no anger or resentment. Another time, when Evodius, a priest from a high-ranking family, provoked him at a banquet, Gall simply left the building. When Evodius publicly asked Gall's forgiveness, kneeling in the street, the bishop gently raised him and pardoned him.

Gregory recorded several miracles that Gall worked in behalf of Clermont. Once his intercession stopped a fire that engulfed the city. And the following report tells how he saved Clermont from the plague:

> When the bubonic plague was raging in various regions and ravaging the province of Arles worst of all, St. Gall feared not so much for himself as for his people. And, he prayed to the Lord night and day, asking that in his lifetime he might not see his people devastated. Then

an angel of the Lord appeared to him in a dream, with hair and garment white as snow, and said to him, "O priest, the Divine Goodness regards favorably your supplication for your people. Do not fear, for your prayer has been heard, and see! You will be free from this infirmity with your people. While you live, no one will perish in this land from this epidemic. Do not be afraid now, but after the completion of eight years you will depart from this world." Indeed, this came to pass. . . .

Gall awakened and thanked God for this consolation with which he had comforted him by the heavenly messenger. Then Gall instituted those rogations which are performed in mid-Lent as, singing psalms, they go on foot to the basilica of blessed Julian the Martyr. There are about 5 miles in this route. So then, while the plague was ravaging these parts, as we have said, through the prayers of St. Gall, it did not touch the city of Clermont. And I think it no little grace which he merited, that this shepherd did not see his flock devoured by the epidemic because the Lord protected it.

Gall died at Clermont around 551.

Those are patient who would rather bear evils without inflicting them, than inflict them without bearing them.

—Augustine

JULY 1

Angels; Intercession; Perseverance; Vocation

111. Benedict

(480?–550?)

At age twenty, revolted by Rome's degeneracy, St. Benedict left his studies to become a hermit. He settled in a rocky cave in Italy near Subiaco where he spent his days in prayer and fasting. After several years, disciples gathered around him. He organized them into twelve small communities and for two decades governed them by his teaching and example.

Around 525, Benedict suddenly left Subiaco, probably to protect his monks from persecution directed only at him. He relocated at Monte Cassino, where he founded a monastery that as a center of worship and learning would come to influence European culture for centuries.

At Monte Cassino, Benedict wrote his *Rule*, a flexible and moderate pattern of life that became the norm for monastic life in the West. In it he called on monks to deny their own will and take up "the strong and bright armor of obedience to fight under the Lord Christ, our true king." A monastery was to be a school of Christian service where monks devoted themselves to prayer, study, manual labor, and community living, directed by a spiritual father. In the following selection from the *Rule*, Benedict describes the qualities necessary for an abbot, that we may read as the saint's self-portrait:

> An abbot who is worthy to have charge of a monastery ought always to remember what he is called and show it in his actions. He represents the person of Christ because he is called by his name. As the apostle says, "You received the spirit of adoption, enabling us to cry out, 'Abba, Father!' " (Romans 8:15 *NJB*). Therefore, God forbid that the abbot teach, ordain or require anything that does not conform to the Lord's commands.
>
> Let the abbot remember always that in the dreadful judgment of God he must give an account of both his doctrine and of his disciples' obedience. So he ought to govern his followers with a twofold doctrine. He must show them all virtue and sanctity more by deeds than words. Then let him demonstrate by his actions that they ought not do anything that he has taught them to be unfitting.
>
> Let the abbot make no distinction of persons in the monastery. Let not one be loved more than another, except he be found to surpass the rest in good works and in obedience. Let no one of noble parentage

> be put before him who is of servile extraction, except there be some other reasonable cause for it. Only on one condition are we preferred by God: if in good works and humility we are better than others. So let the abbot bear equal love to all. And let all be subject to the same discipline according as they deserve.

St. Gregory the Great says that Benedict reached out to the local populace, preaching, distributing alms, feeding the poor, and working miracles. Once, for example, he miraculously restored and repaired a workman's scythe. But perhaps his greatest "miracle" was getting the sons of noblemen to perform manual labor shoulder to shoulder with commoners.

St. Benedict died around 550. Other saints like **Augustine of Canterbury** and **Boniface** installed his *Rule* in monasteries throughout Europe, making him the father of western monasticism.

If Benedict thought his cave was an escape from Rome's debauchery, he was mistaken. An image of a sexy woman continued to plague him. For relief, he rolled naked in a thornbush. Gregory says that the procedure cured his lust once and for all. Perhaps Gregory was wrong, and when lust resurfaced, Benedict found less sharp ways to refuse it.

JULY 11 / PATRON OF EUROPE AND CAVE EXPLORERS
Celebration of Discipline; Leading Men; Sexual Temptation; World Historical Saints

112. Scholastica
(D. 547)

Our scant information about St. Scholastica comes from the *Dialogues* of **St. Gregory the Great.** She was the sister of **St. Benedict** and sometimes believed to have been his twin. Gregory tells us that she consecrated herself to God as a child. When Benedict founded his monastery at Monte Cassino in Italy, Scholastica settled about five miles to the south at Plombariola. There she gathered some women into a convent that she headed under her brother's oversight.

Once a year Benedict visited his sister. Since women were not allowed in the monastery, he and a few brothers met Scholastica at a house nearby. Gregory gives us this appealing account of their last visit:

> They spent the whole day praising God and conversing about spiritual matters. As night drew near they continued their reflection. They lingered at table, stretching their precious time together with more conversation. Then his sister begged him to stay, saying, "Brother, don't leave me tonight. Let's talk until morning about the joys of life in heaven."
>
> "What are you saying?" he replied. "There's no way that I can stay out of my monastery."
>
> At this moment the sky was serene. Not a cloud was to be seen in the air. But when her brother refused her, the holy woman clasped her hands together on the table. She bowed her head on them and prayed to God. As she raised her head from the table, vehement lightning and thunder announced such a great downpour of rain that Benedict and his brothers could not even set foot outside.
>
> For the saintly woman, when she leaned her head upon her hands, had poured forth a flood of tears by which she changed the fair weather into foul and rainy. For the storm followed immediately after her prayers. The two coincided so perfectly, that as she lifted her head, the thunder cracked and in the same instant she brought down the rain.
>
> Realizing that the violent storm prevented his return to the monastery, the man of God was disappointed and began to complain. "God Almighty forgive you, sister!" he said. "What have you done?"
>
> "I asked you to stay," she said, "and you would not hear me. So I prayed to God and he heard me. So now leave me and go to your monastery, if you can." But he could not go and was forced to stay against his will.

> So it happened that they spent the night watching and speaking to their heart's content about heavenly things. Contrary to what Benedict wanted, he found a miracle worked by the courage of woman in the strength of God. No wonder the woman was more powerful than he, since she had long desired to see her brother. As St. John said, "God is love." So with good reason she was more powerful who loved more.

Perhaps Scholastica asked God to prolong the visit because she had some premonition of her death. For three days later she died. Gregory says that while standing in his cell, Benedict saw the soul of his sister depart from her body, ascending to heaven in the form of a dove. He had her body brought to the monastery and buried her in the tomb he had prepared for himself. "Thus," wrote Gregory, "as their minds were always one in God, so also their bodies were not to be separated in burial."

> *If you . . . evil as you are, know how to give your children what is good, how much more will your Father in heaven give good things to those who ask him!*
>
> —Matthew 7:11 *NJB*

FEBRUARY 10 / PATRON OF CONVULSIVE CHILDREN
Family; Intercession; Miracles Do Happen

113. Maurus

(Sixth Century)

Several years after **St. Benedict** had established himself in Subiaco, Italy, many highborn Romans asked him to take their children into his monastic community. They wanted him to train their boys to put God first and live virtuously. Thus **St. Gregory the Great** reported that Equitius, a Roman noble, confided his twelve-year-old son, Maurus, to Benedict's care. Because Maurus was innocent and gifted, after he matured a little, Benedict appointed his youthful disciple as his personal aide.

St. Gregory the Great reports only two instances of St. Maurus assisting Benedict, both of them miracle stories.

Once Benedict gave a new monk a sickle and told him to clear the brush from an area that was intended for a garden. The monk went to work vigorously. As he swung the tool, the iron slipped off the handle and flew into a nearby lake. The water was so deep that he had no hope of recovering the blade. Trembling with fear, he explained the loss to Maurus, who reported the situation to the abbot. Benedict went down to the shore. He touched the handle to the water. Immediately the blade swooped up from the lake bottom and reattached itself to the handle. "Here is your sickle," Benedict said to the monk. "Get back to work and stop worrying."

Gregory also told this story about Maurus:

> One day the boy Placid, a noble youth in Benedict's care, went out to fetch water from the lake. But he was careless and when he dipped his pitcher into the water, he fell in. The waves immediately carried him out about a hundred yards. Back in his cell, the saint knew instantly about the sad accident. He called Maurus, his disciple, and said: "Brother Maurus, run quickly. Placid went to get water and has fallen into the lake. The waves have already carried him off a long distance."
>
> A thing wonderful and unheard of since that instance of the apostle, Peter! Maurus asked the abbot for a blessing. Then he ran to the lake to carry out his order. Assuming that he was running on dry land, he sped to the spot where the waves had carried the boy. He grabbed him by the hair and hurried back to the shore with him in tow.
>
> Once on the shore, Maurus thought about what he had done. He glanced back and saw that he had been running over the waves. He was

astonished that he had done something he would not have dared, had he realized what he was doing.

When he returned to the monastery, he told the abbot everything that had happened. St. Benedict attributed the miracle to his disciple's obedience, rather than to his own merit. Maurus, however, said he was only doing what he was told. So he denied that he had any part in a miracle that he unconsciously performed.

Maurus may have eventually become the abbot at Subiaco. In the past, many believed he also migrated to France and served as the abbot at Glanfeuil. However, historians have shown that Odo, an abbot of Glanfeuil, apparently concocted this tale as a way of attracting pilgrims to his community.

We know nothing else about Maurus's life or his death.

Here's what Gregory the Great said to people who doubt the miraculous:

Everyone wondered to see the water turned into wine. Every day the earth's moisture being drawn into the root of a vine, is turned by the grape into wine, and no one wonders. Full of wonder then are all the things that people never think to wonder at.

JANUARY 15
Miracles Do Happen; Simple Obedience

114. John the Silent
(454–558)

St. John the Silent, named for his love of solitude, came from a prominent Armenian family. At eighteen, he built a monastery and for a decade led ten young companions in a life of devotion and hard work. Because of his reputation as a leader, at age twenty-eight and over his protests, he was made bishop of Colonia in Armenia. For nine years he faithfully performed his office. In 490, however, John went to Constantinople to secure the emperor's intervention to quell a local persecution. When the mission was accomplished, he decided not to return to Colonia, but slipped away into the desert in search of quiet.

A vision of a bright cross led John to the Mar Saba, the monastery of **St. Sabas** in Palestine. For several years Sabas subjected his novice to tests of hard labor and service. Judging John to be a serious candidate for holiness, around 494 he finally allowed him to embrace the solitary life of a hermit. John reveled in his new pattern of life: alone five days a week to contemplate God and mortify his flesh, joining the other hermits for worship only on Saturdays and Sundays.

However, John left the Mar Saba in 503, when factious monks forced Sabas to abandon his monastery. At that time John's disciple, Roubâ, lived with him. The young man's bullheadedness occasioned the following episode. Roubâ, expecting fine food, wanted to celebrate Easter at the monastery. John, however, as a test of his obedience, said no:

> "Let us stay calm, brother, and have faith that he who nourished six hundred thousand in the desert for forty years will himself provide us with not only necessary nourishment but a surplus as well. . . . 'So do not worry; do not say "What are we to eat? What are we to drink?" . . . Your heavenly Father knows you need them all. Set your hearts on his kingdom first, and on God's saving justice, and all these other things will be given to you as well' (Matthew 6:31–33 NJB). Have patience, my child, and prefer the narrow path to the broad one. For self-indulgence in this world begets eternal punishment, while present mortification is a preparation for the enjoyment of good things."
>
> Unconvinced . . . the brother departed . . . to the monastery. After his departure a man totally unknown came to the elder with an ass loaded with . . . hot white loaves, wine, oil, fresh cheeses and eggs, and a jar of honey.

> He unloaded and went away . . . John rejoiced in spirit at this divine visitation, while the brother who had left, after losing his way . . . returned on the third day hungry and exhausted, having enjoyed the fruits of his own disobedience. When he found such good things in the cave, he recognized his own lack of faith and stubbornness and prostrated himself shamefacedly before the elder, begging to receive forgiveness. The elder, sympathizing with human weakness . . . raised him up and admonished him, saying: "Recognize precisely that God is able to prepare a table in the desert" (see Psalm 78:19).

Six years later, when the monks welcomed Sabas back, John also returned to the monastery. He lived forty more years in his coveted silent adoration and died in his hermitage at 104 years of age.

> *Our chief labor in prayer must be to . . . set our hearts on fire with fervent love of God, and then to spin our prayer, so long until we have attained unto this end. But when through weariness of our frail body we find this fervor grows cold, then we must desist and pray no longer, but then apply ourselves to some other works of virtue.*
>
> —St. John Fisher

MAY 13
Prayer; Solitude

115. Brendan the Navigator

(486?–575?)

One of the most popular Celtic saints, St. Brendan lived and worked during the sixth century in western Ireland. Raised by St. Ita (next to **St. Brigid**, the Emerald Isle's most famous woman saint) Brendan became a monk, a priest, and an abbot. Around 559 he established an abbey at Clonfert. From that center he founded numerous other monasteries, including Annadown, Inishdroum, and Ardfert.

Like his contemporary, **St. Columba**, whom he once visited at Argyll, Brendan traveled extensively, undertaking many missionary journeys. Reportedly, Brendan founded a monastery in Scotland, became the abbot of a Welsh monastery, and sailed to Brittany with St. Malo.

A charming romance of the eighth and ninth centuries, *The Navigation of St. Brendan* made him one of the most celebrated saints of the Middle Ages. An expatriated Irish monk in Germany created this fascinating legend of St. Brendan the Navigator. He transformed a rather pedestrian missionary abbot into a mystical and mythical seafarer. This delightful and still readable story tells how Brendan and a band of monks voyaged the Atlantic Ocean in quest of an island of promise. The events of Brendan's magical journey coincided with the liturgical seasons, and everywhere he ventured, birds joined him in chanting the liturgy of the hours. Along the way he encountered huge sea monsters, as in the following excerpt from the romance:

> One day from a lofty crag on the island Brendan saw two sea monsters coming from the depth of the sea, and fighting desperately together, each of them trying to drown the other. Then one of the monsters tried to fly, and the other pursued it. And the flying monster said with a human voice: "I beg you in the name of St. Brigid to let me be." The other monster at once left it and went into the depth of the sea.
>
> Brendan marveled greatly at this, and came to his company and said to them: "Let's depart quickly for Ireland, that we may speak with St. Brigid." . . .
>
> When he reached the place where Brigid was, he told her of the conversation of the two monsters. And he asked her: "What good do you do for God more than I, when the monsters entreated you, though absent, and me, though present, they did not invoke?" Brigid said to Brendan: "Make your confession." "I declare," said he, "that I never

crossed seven furrows without turning my mind to God. Make your confession." "I confess," said Brigid, "that since I fixed my mind on God, I have never taken it off, and never will, till doom. You, however, are so constantly incurring great danger by sea and land, that you must give attention to it. So it is not because you forget God that your mind is fixed on him only at every third furrow."

The Navigation of St. Brendan has survived in 116 medieval Latin manuscripts and numerous versions in vernacular languages. Brendan died around 575.

Just as we learn about the power of persistent prayer in the tale above, The Navigation of St. Brendan used other fabulous events to teach spiritual truths. In another story, for example, Brendan met a poor man who was enslaved to a cruel monarch. The saint thrust his staff into the sod and found a pound of gold that brought freedom to both the servant and the king. "This gold is Christ's," said the king, "not to me does it belong but to God's own servants. And I grant freedom to you and to your children in honor of God and Brendan."

MAY 16 / PATRON OF SAILORS
Celtic Saints; Missionaries; Prayer

116. Martin of Braga
(D. 579)

About 550, St. Martin arrived in Galicia, now northern Portugal, aboard a ship transporting pilgrims from the Holy Land. We know little about Martin's background, except that he had received a Greek education in the East and training as a monk in the tradition of the Egyptian desert. The young monk seems to have come to Galicia as a missionary to a church infected with heresy.

The Suevi, a Germanic tribe that controlled Galicia, had adopted Priscillianism, a version of gnosticism that denied Christ's humanity. Martin took a strategic approach to winning the Suevi to the Catholic Church. First he became the friend of King Theodomir and won the admiration of the royal family. Then, building on his personal relationships, Martin converted the king and his court. With Theodomir's support he preached throughout the province, reconciling many Priscillianists to the church.

Martin founded a monastery at Dumium, which served as his missionary base. Out of respect for him, the Suevian monarchs made him bishop of Dumium. Later they appointed Martin as archbishop of Braga, which established him as the preeminent leader of the Galician church. In that position he held several councils that condemned Priscillianism and he promulgated teaching that restored its adherents to the church.

Gregory of Tours declared Martin the greatest scholar of his age. His writings included a guide to the Christian life, a description of superstitious peasant customs, a set of moral maxims, and a version of the sayings of the Egyptian fathers. Listen to Martin's voice in the following selection from his little essay on vanity:

> A person desires nothing more than to be praised, nor is there a single thing that he would consider it more agreeable to receive than someone's admiration for him as a person of renown. . . .
>
> Hence arises that sacrilege of the blasphemous, which is the most wicked deed possible, that since we seize everything pertaining to praise, all that is left to offer God is blame. The human race has exceeded its limit when you cannot find a person who does not want to be admired as God. . . .

> For those who have usurped the things above, all that is left, so it seems to me, is the things below. They have no higher place to which to ascend, for the result of their constant ascending is that all they have left is to descend. . . . Everyone everywhere strives to spread his own fame, and therefore the cure for such vanity is most difficult, because it mingles not only with vices, but also with virtues. It does not allow a person to be recognized by himself for what he is. For when he rejoices in other people's praises his joy is followed by exalted triumph, and his triumph, in turn, by pretentiousness and overestimation of himself. . . . This is that deadly vice of which the Lord spoke in the gospel thus to the Jews: "How can you believe, who receive glory from one another and do not seek the glory which is from the only God?" (see John 5:44).

Martin of Braga served the Christians of Galicia for nearly a quarter of a century. He died at his monastery at Dumium in 579.

> *He is the true gospel-bearer that carries it in his hands, in his mouth and in his heart. A person does not carry it in his heart that does not love it with all his soul. And nobody loves it as he ought, that does not conform to it in his life.*
>
> —Desiderius Erasmus

MARCH 20
Christian Living; Christian Unity; Evangelization

117. Radegund
(518–587)

St. Radegund shone like a beacon of peace amid the dark violence of sixth-century France. Kidnapped at twelve from Thuringia in central Germany by Frankish raiders, she was married to the wild and abusive King Clothaire. As queen she lived a life of prayer and Christian service, but she also made a priority of supporting her husband.

Clothaire, however, mocked Radegund's fervor and mistreated her. When he murdered her beloved brother, she asked to be released from court. Grudgingly the king allowed her to withdraw to Poitiers in France, where she became a nun and was ordained a deaconess. She founded the monastery of Holy Cross, the first in Europe for both men and women, and appointed her friend Agnes as its abbess.

Radegund valued learning and required her followers to study two hours daily. And the saint herself became an exemplary student, as her biographer reported:

> Whenever as servant of God visited, she would question him closely about his manner of serving the Lord. If she learned anything new from him which she was not used to doing, she would immediately impose it first upon herself and then she would teach her congregation with words what she had already shown them by her example.
>
> When the antiphonal singing of the Psalter ended, her reading would continue. By day or by night it never stopped, not even while she gave her body its meager refreshment. When the lesson had been read, she would say. . . . "If you do not understand what is read, why don't you search for it diligently in the mirror of your souls." There may have been a little irreverence in presuming to ask this question, but from pious and maternal love, she never ceased to preach on what the readings offered for the salvation of the soul. Just as the bee chooses various flowers from which to make its honey, so was she careful to pluck little spiritual flowers from the clerics she had to visit her. So from them she could bring forth the fruit of good works in herself and those who followed her. Even at night or whenever she seemed to snatch an hour's sleep, she had the lesson read to her. Sometimes the reader began to feel drowsy and, thinking that Radegund was resting for a while, she might stop. But Radegund would ask, "Why are you silent? Read on, don't stop."

Radegund also became well known for her peacemaking. When word of war reached her, for example, she wrote to the combatants urging them to settle their differences peaceably. But the din of battle often drowned out her gentle voice. Once she found herself in grievous danger when Clothaire tried forcibly to take her back. But Bishop Germanus of Paris interceded for her so persuasively that Clothaire repented and even became a benefactor of Holy Cross.

Radegund had a church built at the monastery and secured for it a relic of Christ's cross, which she viewed as her crowning achievement. **St. Venantius Fortunatus,** her friend and confessor, wrote his celebrated hymn about the cross to mark the event.

Radegund died peacefully in 587, surrounded by two hundred of her sisters.

Once a friend told Radegund that if she kept on kissing lepers, no one would dare to kiss her. "If you don't want to kiss me," she snapped, "I won't mind at all." She also drove a fearful bishop to action with these fighting words: "If you refuse to consecrate me a deaconess, you fear man more than God, and he will require you to account for my soul." Clothaire oppressed his gentle queen, but that did not keep this valiant woman from asserting herself.

AUGUST 13
Difficult Marriages; Study; Valiant Women

118. Kentigern
(518?–603)

"Facts about St. Kentigern are lost in Celtic mists of time," *Butler's Lives* says with an unexpected humorous touch. But in those mists swirl wonderful, typically Celtic miracle stories.

One story tells of Kentigern's marvelous birth. Supposedly, Princess Thaney, his mother, became pregnant to an unknown man. As punishment she was cast from a cliff on the shore of the Firth of Forth, but landed unhurt. Then a small boat floated her across the Firth, where she gave birth to her son. St. Serf reportedly welcomed mother and son and became so fond of the lad that he nicknamed him "Mungo," which means "darling."

Now some facts. Kentigern grew up to become a monk, adopting traditional Celtic practices of solitude and self-denial. He established a community of disciples at Glasgow. Later the church there chose him as bishop. Feuds among local chiefs, however, caused Kentigern to flee, some say to Wales, but more probably to Cumbria.

Another quaint story makes Kentigern something of a romantic. A queen allegedly presented to a knight as a love token a ring that her king had given her. The king slipped the ring from her lover's finger while he slept and tossed it into the sea. Then he challenged the queen to show it to him in three days. She begged Kentigern's help. He sent a monk fishing who found the ring in the belly of a salmon. Perhaps the event caused the queen to repent of her dalliance. This story accounts for the appearance of a ring and a fish on Glasgow's coat of arms. He is honored in Scotland as the first bishop of Glasgow, where the cathedral claims to house his relics.

Other outlandish claims have attached themselves to Kentigern. Legend says, for example, that he prayed the entire Psalter every day, usually standing in an icy stream. If that were true, hypothermia would probably have claimed him long before the *185* years his medieval biographer assigned to him. But it is probably true that Kentigern once met the great **St. Columba** and exchanged crosiers with him.

Kentigern died, most likely at age eighty-five, in 603. His biographer recreated the details of his last hour in the following passage:

Worn out by exceeding old age, the blessed Kentigern began sensing by his frequent falls that the destruction of his earthly dwelling-place was at hand, yet the foundation of his faith set upon a rock continued to comfort his soul. By this faith he was confident that he had a dwelling, not made by hands, prepared in heaven after the dissolution of this earthly habitation. He, beloved of God and men, being aware then that the hour was drawing near for his passing from this world to the Father of lights, fortified himself with the sacred anointing—effective of the remission of sins—and with the life-giving sacrament of the Lord's Body and Blood, so that the ancient serpent, lying in wait for his heel, would be unable to sink-in a poisoned fang and inflict a lethal wound, but would depart confounded with his head crushed. . . .

Then, as far as his strength allowed, he reminded his disciples, gathered together before him, about the following of our holy religion, about the preservation of mutual love and peace, of the grace of hospitality, of application to prayer and reading. . . . Then he gave to each, humbled before him on bended knees . . . the kiss of peace; and, having lifted up his hands as best as he was able, he blessed them. And, making his last farewell, entrusting them all to the tutelage of the Blessed Trinity and the protection of the holy mother of God, he composed himself on his noble bed of stone. . . .

JANUARY 14
Celtic Saints; Miracles Do Happen

119. David

(520?–589?)

Unfortunately, history has given us few facts about St. David (or Dewi in Welsh), one of Britain's most celebrated saints. Rhygyfarch, his biographer, told David's story five centuries after his death. While Rhygyfarch claims to have consulted ancient documents, he was primarily concerned with defending the primacy of the see of St. David's, Wales, against Canterbury. So historians regard his biography mainly as propaganda. But Rhygyfarch wove a creative tale, and from his pleasant legends we can glean a rough sketch of David's later life. Stories of his youth, however, such as his miraculously healing his teacher's blindness, seem to be entirely fictitious.

David established a monastery at Menevia (now St. David's) and used it as a base to found other communities in eastern Wales. Rhygyfarch believed that an angel had indicated Menevia to David as a land of promise. And he said that when David claimed it, he met the opposition of Baia, a local landowner, just as Joshua had encountered opposition in the Promised Land. But David and his monks waged spiritual warfare and won:

> Another day, Baia's wife, afire with a jealous spite, called her maids and said: "Go where the monks can see you. Take off your clothes, play suggestive games and use lewd words." The maids obeyed, playing seductively and imitating erotic intimacies and sexual intercourse. They enticed the minds of some monks to lust and they irritated the minds of others.
>
> The monks wanted to abandon the place. But the holy father David, steadfast with a long-enduring patience, said to them: "You know that the world hates you. But you must realize now that when the children of Israel, accompanied by the Ark of the Covenant, entered the Promised Land, they were beaten down in prolonged and dangerous battles. But they were not overthrown. They destroyed the uncircumcised people who were settled in the land and owned it. That struggle clearly foreshadows our victory. For he who seeks a promised heavenly country must be wearied by adversities, but without being overcome. With Christ as his ally, he must finally conquer the evil blemishes of his sins. We must therefore not let evil overcome us, but we must overcome it with good. Because if Christ is for us, who can be against us? So be strong with irresistible warfare so that your enemy may not rejoice in

> your flight. We must stand fast. Baia himself must give way." With these words he fortified the resolution of his disciples.

Rhygyfarch reported that later Baia's wife went mad after killing her daughter and that an enemy surprised and destroyed Baia himself.

David built a community at Menevia patterned on the extreme austerity of the Egyptian monks. Sustained only by bread, vegetables, and water, they practiced continuous prayer, diligent study of Scripture, and hard manual labor. David's own favorite mortification was total immersion in iced water. But he balanced that unusual penitential act with extensive mercies to the poor of the neighborhood.

Rhygyfarch claimed that St. David preached so dynamically at a synod at Brevi, that his peers unanimously chose him as archbishop and Menevia as the primary see of Wales. Apparently, the biographer invented the elevation of David as metropolitan in order to enhance his propaganda.

David died surrounded by members of his community at Menevia around 589.

> *Be joyful, brothers and sisters. Keep your faith, and do the little things that you have seen and heard with me.*
>
> —David

MARCH 1 / PATRON OF WALES
Perseverance; Sexual Temptation; Spiritual Warfare; Temptation

120. Columba

(521?–597)

Monk, priest, warrior, teacher, poet, pastor, missionary, apostle—St. Columba filled all these roles. The title "warrior" puzzles us because the notion of a warrior monk seems contradictory. But Columba had descended from two royal Celtic lines and the Celts resolved conflicts by fighting. And Columba's remorse over his leadership in a battle had far-reaching consequences.

In his youth Columba became a monk under the tutelage of St. Finnian of Clonard. For fifteen years he preached and established several monasteries. Columba appreciated the importance of study for Christian growth and aggressively sought after books. So when Finnian brought an edition of **St. Jerome's** Psalter to Ireland, Columba made himself a copy. Finnian, however, claimed ownership of the copy. King Diarmaid, overlord of Ireland, ruled against Columba, requiring that he give his Psalter to Finnian.

Later King Diarmaid's men killed a man who had found sanctuary with Columba. Over this issue, war broke out between the king and Columba's clan. Columba led and won a battle in which three thousand died. He got his Psalter back, but allegedly was so grieved over the deaths that he undertook the severest of punishments for a Celt: he banished himself from Ireland.

In 565 he and a dozen relatives sailed to the island of Iona off the coast of Scotland. Columba founded a monastery there that became his missionary base. From Iona the saint strengthened the Irish community in Scotland and evangelized the Picts to the north. The Scots celebrate him as their apostle.

Columba, however, sorely missed Ireland. The following poem attributed to him expresses his longing for home:

Delightful would it be to me to be in Uchd Ailiun
　　On the pinnacle of a rock,
That I might often see
　　The face of the ocean;
That I might see its heaving waves
　　Over the wide ocean,
When they chant music to their Father
　　Upon the world's course;
That I might see its level sparkling shore
　　It would be no cause for sorrow,

That contrition might come upon my heart
    Upon looking at her;
That I might bewail my evils all,
    Though it were difficult to compute them;
That I might bless the Lord
    Who conserves all,
Heaven with its bright orders,
    Land, shore and flood;
That I might search the books all,
    That would be good for my soul;
At times kneeling to beloved heaven;
    At times psalm singing;
At times contemplating the King of heaven,
    Chief of all the holy ones;
At times at work without compulsion,
    That would be delightful.
At times giving food to the poor;
    At times in solitude.
The best advice in the presence of God
    To me has been graciously giv'n.
The King whose servant I am will not let
    Anything deceive me.

Under the saint's governance, Iona became a classic center of learning. Monks came from as near as England and as far as Egypt to study with him. Like the Irish monks before them, Iona's scholars copied thousands of books, preserving the wisdom of the ancients for future generations.

Columba, a giant of a man who in his youth was somewhat gruff and rigid, mellowed in his old age. He died after a long illness in 597.

Some say Columba's self-imposed exile was his version of the early monks' exile to the desert. Other Celtic and Anglo-Saxon monks followed his example, leaving their monasteries to carry the gospel and learning to continental Europe. So Columba's repentance had world historical consequences. He launched the monastic migrations of the seventh and eighth centuries that laid the foundations of our western civilization.

JUNE 9 / PATRON OF IRELAND
Celtic Saints; Lights in the "Dark Ages"; Missionaries; Poets; Repentance; Study; World Historical Saints

121. Venantius Fortunatus

(530?–610?)

The hymns of St. Venantius Fortunatus that are still sung during the liturgies of Holy Week have moved many of us. A talented author, the saint published ten books of poems, hymns, and biographies. He came to be widely known throughout the kingdom of the Franks, the sixth-century equivalent of a best-selling author.

Around 565, Fortunatus made a pilgrimage from Lombardy to the shrine of **St. Martin of Tours** in thanksgiving for the healing of an eye problem. He settled at Poitiers in France, where he was ordained a priest. He became a close friend of **St. Radegund** and Agnes, the abbess at Holy Cross, and served as chaplain to their monastery.

Fortunatus affectionately regarded Radegund as his "mother," and wrote her playful letters. Once he urged her to go easy on herself during Lent and not to shut herself up so much. "Even though the clouds have gone and the sky is serene," he wrote, "the day is sunless when you are absent." In a refreshingly frank thank-you note for food and advice, he confessed a weakness: "You told me to eat two eggs in the evening. To tell the truth, I ate four. I wish I could find my mind always as prepared to submit as my stomach is prepared to obey your directions."

In 569, Emperor Justin II sent a relic of the true cross to Radegund. For the occasion of the solemn presentation of the relic at Holy Cross, Fortunatus wrote the following hymn that may be appropriately sung during the Good Friday liturgy:

The royal banners forward go;
The cross shines forth in mystic glow;
Where he in flesh, our flesh who made,
Our sentence bore, our ransom paid. . . .

O tree of beauty! Tree of light!
O Tree with royal purple bright!
Elect on whose triumphal breast
Those holy limbs should find their rest!

On whose dear arms, so widely flung,
The weight of this world's ransom hung:

The price of human kind to pay,
And spoil the spoiler of his prey.

In addition to composing many hymns for Christian feasts, Fortunatus also wrote lives of saints in prose and verse, all of which Gregory of Tours encouraged him to publish. Late in his life he was elected bishop of Poitiers. He served in that office a short time before his death around 610.

Faithful cross! Above all other,
One and only noble tree!
None in foliage, none in blossom,
None in fruit thy peers may be:
Sweetest wood, and sweetest iron!
Sweetest weight is hung on thee.

—Venantius Fortunatus

DECEMBER 14
Mere Christian Love; Poets

122. Leander of Seville

(534?–600?)

St. Leander of Seville dedicated his life to reclaiming Spanish Arians to the Catholic Church. As an early champion of Christian unity, he used intercessory prayer, gentle persuasion, dynamic preaching, and brilliant arguments to bring the Visigoths back to the fold.

With great diplomatic skill, Leander worked to press Catholic truths on Visigothic King Leovigild (a committed Arian) and on the Arian bishops. As bishop of Seville, through prayer and preaching he made many converts, including Hermenegild, the king's eldest son. But in 586, Leovigild executed his son because he had refused to take communion from an Arian bishop. Then he exiled several bishops, including Leander. The saint used this time to write three persuasive treatises against Arianism.

When he returned from exile, Leander patiently continued to influence the king and finally achieved success. On his deathbed, Leovigild asked the bishop to instruct Reccared, his son and successor, in the Catholic faith.

Recarred became a well-formed Catholic and allowed Leander the freedom to convert his people. With sheer force of reasonable argument he persuaded the Arian bishops to embrace Catholicism. In 589 and 590 Leander held councils in Toledo and Seville, respectively, to seal the restoration of the nation to the church.

Among the few surviving works of St. Leander is his sermon celebrating the reunion of the Spanish church. We can take the following excerpt as a hopeful manifesto for Christian unity:

> How sweet is love and how delightful is unity you know well through the foretelling of the prophets, through the divine word in the gospels, through the teachings of the apostles. Therefore, preach only the unity of nations, dream only of the oneness of all peoples, spread abroad only the good seeds of peace and love. Rejoice, therefore, in the Lord that you were not cheated of your desire. For now, after the winter's ice . . . like the fruit which is the delight of the fields and the joyous flowers of springtime . . . , you have suddenly and joyously recovered those whom you embraced so long with constant mourning and continual prayers.
>
> Therefore, brethren, let us be glad in the Lord with the full joy of our hearts and let us be jubilant in God our Savior. From now on, we

> may use the fulfillment of the past as proof that the things that are still awaited shall come true. This has already been said by the Lord in the words: "Other sheep I have that are not of this fold. Them also I must bring, and there shall be one fold and one shepherd" (see John 10:16). Behold, we see that this has been fulfilled. . . . If, then, there remain any part of the world or any barbarian race upon whom the faith of Christ has not yet shone, we need never doubt that it will believe and will come into one church, if we reflect on the truth of what the Lord has said.

Leander's friend **Pope Gregory the Great**, whom he had met in 583 on a diplomatic mission to Constantinople, sent him a congratulatory letter and made him an archbishop.

In his ministry to his flock, especially to monks and nuns, Leander promoted the ideal of continual prayer and he conducted a reform of the Spanish liturgy. He also introduced the eastern practice of reciting the Nicene Creed at Mass, which Rome itself later adopted.

Leander died around 600 and his brother, **St. Isidore,** succeeded him as bishop of Seville.

> *May they all be one, just as, Father, you are in me and I am in you, so that they also may be in us, so that the world may believe it was you who sent me.*
>
> —John 17:21 *NJB*

FEBRUARY 27
Christian Unity; Evangelization

123. Gregory the Great
(540?–604)

We call Pope Gregory I "the Great" because in his short thirteen-year reign he completed a series of world-historical accomplishments. An outline of his achievements leaves us breathless: He made himself the political leader of the West, rebuilt Rome, rescued its population from famine and plague, conducted a reform of the church, withstood the arrogant power of the Byzantine emperor, initiated the temporal power of the papacy, stopped the Lombard invasions, promoted Benedictine monasticism, sponsored the creation of "Gregorian" chant, and engineered the conversion of the English to Christianity.

In the city of Rome that barbarians had ravaged, young Gregory emerged as a significant civic leader. But in 573 he followed his heart's desire. He sold his vast estates and founded St. Andrew's Monastery at his house. But he was allowed only a few years of monastic life. Then the pope engaged his service as one of Rome's seven deacons and as ambassador to Byzantium. Elected pope himself in 590, Gregory immediately faced crises—floods, plague, and invasions. Amid the general breakdown of the empire, he virtually assumed the role of emperor. For example, he unilaterally appointed governors in Italian cities. In 593, ignoring the representative of the eastern emperor, he concluded a separate peace with the Lombard invaders. With such decisive actions, Gregory established for all time the power of the bishop of Rome, virtually founding the powerful medieval papacy.

Gregory was also a prolific writer whose works handed on the tradition of the Fathers to the newly converted barbarians. Two of his books were medieval "bestsellers": the *Dialogues* that told of saints' lives, and the *Pastoral Care* that for centuries set the standards of preaching and discipline for bishops and priests. Gregory himself was a gifted preacher whose homilies made hearers think twice, like the following selection:

> When our hearts are reluctant we often have to compel ourselves to pray for our enemies, to pour out prayer for those who are against us. Would that our hearts were filled with love! How frequently we offer a prayer for our enemies, but do it because we are commanded to, not out of love for them. We ask the gift of life for them even while we are afraid that our prayer may be heard. The judge of our souls considers

our hearts rather than our words. Those who do not pray for their enemies out of love are not asking anything for their benefit.

Jesus, our advocate, has composed a prayer for our case. And our advocate is also our judge. He has inserted a condition in the prayer that reads: Forgive us our trespasses as we forgive those who trespass against us. Sometimes we say these words without carrying them out. Thus our words bind us more tightly.

What are we to do then, my friends? We must bestow our love on our brothers and sisters. We must not allow any malice at all to remain in our hearts. May almighty God have regard for our love of our neighbor, so that he may pardon our iniquities! Remember what he taught us: Forgive, and you will be forgiven. People are in debt to us, and we to them. Let us forgive them their debts, so that what we owe may be forgiven.

Gregory the Great died in 604. His last act was to send a warm coat to a poor bishop who suffered from the cold.

Gregory suffered daily from gastritis and gout. But his personal discomfort never caused him to lose focus. He referred to himself as the "servant of the servants of God"—a name that popes still use—and patterned his life according to the phrase.

SEPTEMBER 3 / PATRON OF MUSICIANS, SINGERS, AND TEACHERS
Forgiveness; Mere Christian Love; Saints and Politics; World Historical Saints

124. Augustine of Canterbury

(D. 604?)

St. Augustine began his service as prior of St. Andrew's monastery in Rome, which **St. Gregory the Great** had founded before he became pope. When Gregory decided to implement his dream of evangelizing the Anglo-Saxons, he chose Augustine for the job. In 596, he sent him and thirty monks to take the gospel to southern England. Fear stalled the party in Provence, but Gregory reassured them through Augustine, who had returned to Rome to seek his advice. So the group continued on its way and at Arles the archbishop consecrated Augustine bishop for England.

In 597, Augustine's team landed at Kent, the strongest of the seven Anglo-Saxon kingdoms. King Ethelbert received him beneath an oak tree because he feared the saint might use magic spells that were believed powerless out of doors. But the king listened patiently to Augustine's message, part of which follows:

> Your everlasting peace, O king, and that of your kingdom, is the object we desire to promote in coming here. We bring you news of never-ending joy.
>
> Do not regard us as superstitious because we have been at pains to come from Rome to your dominions for the sake of your salvation and that of your subjects. Do not see us as coming to force upon an unknown people benefits against their will. Be assured that only a great love constrains us to do this. For we long, beyond all the desires and glory of the world, to have as many fellow citizens with us as we can in the kingdom of God. We strive with all our efforts to prevent those from perishing, who may be advanced to the company of the holy angels.
>
> The loving-kindness of Christ has everywhere infused goodwill into preachers of his truth. Thus without thought of themselves they burn with zeal for the salvation of all nations. Moved, too, by such love as this, Gregory, the present father of all Christendom, thirsts ardently for your salvation. He would have come to you himself had he been able, but he cannot leave the care of so many souls committed to his charge. Therefore, he has sent us in his place to open to you the way of everlasting light and the gate of the kingdom of heaven. You will reign there forever if you reject the idols of the devil and decide to enter through Christ.

Ethelbert gave Augustine permission to convert anyone who would listen and provided him an ancient church in Canterbury. But did not embrace the faith himself, explaining that he needed to think about it. However, by 601 Augustine and his associates had baptized the king and many of his leading subjects.

Augustine chose to consolidate a localized base for evangelization rather than disperse missionaries over a large area. He built the first cathedral at Canterbury. He also founded a monastery just outside the town's walls. In 601, Gregory appointed Augustine archbishop and articulated a plan for the future organization of the church in England. While Gregory allowed Augustine considerable freedom in his creating the Anglo-Saxon church, the saint mostly imitated Roman patterns.

In the last of Augustine's short seven years in Kent he consolidated the faith he had planted there. He died on March 26, probably in 604, just two weeks after Gregory's death in Rome.

At Gregory's direction, Augustine implemented creative missionary techniques that still serve the church well. Move gradually, said the pope, and incorporate into church life whatever is innocent in pagan customs. So Augustine, after destroying idols, transformed their temples into churches and he replaced pagan celebrations with martyr's feasts.

MAY 27
Evangelization; Missionaries

125. Columban

(542?–615)

Young Columban pursued a classical education in Latin literature, Scripture, and the church Fathers. But adolescent lust for a pretty girl distracted him from his studies. Advised by a woman hermit, he fled to a monastery. All three—the education, the flight from the world, and the monastic life—predicted the thrust of St. Columban's life. For he would flee Ireland to establish in Europe strictly disciplined monasteries and renowned centers of learning.

After many quiet years at the monastery of Bangor in Northern Ireland, around 590 Columban joined twelve companions in a traditional Celtic voluntary exile to proclaim the gospel on the continent. He and his associates founded monasteries in Burgundy at Annegray, Luxeuil, and Fontes. Columban's rule for his brothers was harsh, prescribing punishment for the smallest faults. His monasteries preserved Celtic Christian practices in a land that had adopted Roman customs, so he ran afoul of the local bishops. Several times he stood up to them and simultaneously professed his loyalty to the pope, yet asking him to permit his houses to maintain their Celtic ways.

Every Sunday at church, Columban instructed his monks with short talks that drove home some practical truth. In the following address, for example, he called them to self-knowledge and hatred of sin:

> Don't consider what you are, but what you will be. What you are only lasts a moment, what you will be is eternal. Don't indulge yourself in laziness, but rather acquire in a short time what you will possess forever. Overcome your dislike for exertion in the present by thinking of the reward to come.
>
> If the world lures you, remember that your pursuit of it is vain. What does it profit you to gaze at a shadow reflected in the water? How do you benefit from joy and happiness tasted in a dream? All dreams, no matter how long they last, are short-lived. And life's joys are like dreams in a dark night.
>
> Awake, therefore, out of the night and seek the light so that you may see and be seen. Your life is a wheel that is ever turning and never waits for you. You must keep up with it. You have nothing on earth. And you will die as naked as you were when you were born. You have only the prospect of heaven, your inheritance, provided you do not forfeit it.

> But if you have lost it already, sell yourself to regain it. What do I mean by "sell yourself" ? Sell your vices and buy life. Do you want to know what those vices are? Above all, sell pride, the root-vice, and buy humility. Then you will be like Christ who says, "Learn from me, for I am gentle and humble in heart" (Matthew 11:29 *NJB*).

When Columban reprimanded Theodoric II of Burgundy for his concubinage and refused to bless his illegitimate sons, the king put him on a boat back to Ireland. However, a storm drove Columban back to the continent. He worked for a while in Austrasia, present-day Switzerland, but Theodoric conquered that territory, forcing him to flee to Lombardy. Then Columban founded a monastery at Bobbio, near Genoa, Italy, where at age seventy he personally helped to construct the buildings. Bobbio became a great educational center and housed one of Europe's finest libraries during the Middle Ages. Columban died at Bobbio in 615.

Only he lives well who never has to repent or is ever repenting.

—Columban

NOVEMBER 23
Celtic Saints; Eternal Perspective; Humility; Missionaries

126. Theodore of Sykeon

(D. 613)

St. Theodore spent his childhood at his mother's inn that doubled as a brothel at Sykeon in Asia Minor. When Theodore was about six years old a wonderful cook arrived at the inn who created so much business that his mother stopped her prostitution. The cook became Theodore's spiritual director, teaching him to visit churches, to pray and fast, and to use the sacraments.

In his teens Theodore lived as a hermit in a cave near Sykeon. Then he shut himself up in a mountainous cave to practice extreme mortification. But Theodore also became well known for serving his neighbors with his gifts of healing, exorcism, and prophecy. For example, once he helped the treasurer of Heliopolis, who came to him with this tearful story:

> "Have pity on me, oh servant of God, for the tragedy which has befallen me! I sent my elder son to collect the church-taxes from the villages and he has taken the whole sum and made off! And though I have . . . searched for him everywhere I have not been able to find him. I therefore implore your holiness to pray to God to restore him to me, because all my substance is insufficient to pay back to the church the large sum he has taken."
>
> And the holy man sent this reply . . . "If you will agree that when he is found you will not give him a beating nor compel him to give up more money than the amount he stole, God will be entreated and restore your son to you;" . . . Then the father agreed to these terms on oath. . . .
>
> Then the holy man prayed to the Lord to hold up the man who had committed the theft in whatsoever place he might be and to make known with all speed where he would be found. . . .
>
> Now the holy man's prayer reached the son in a place close to the city of Nicea and did not allow him to depart thence, but he kept wandering about in a circle. . . . Some men who knew him and the treasurer . . . recognized him and . . . laid hold on him and sent word to the treasurer. The latter came and took the stolen gold away from him and returned to the holy man giving thanks to God.

At the young age of eighteen Theodore was ordained a priest. And he made a pilgrimage to Jerusalem to observe the hermits of Palestine.

Upon his return he adopted some weird ascetical practices. Annually from Christmas to Palm Sunday he had himself suspended from a rock in a cage. He also wrapped himself in an iron breastplate, iron collar, rings, and chains. His reputed holiness attracted many disciples, and he developed a large monastic settlement at Sykeon.

When the church at Anastasiopolis chose Theodore as bishop, he reluctantly accepted the office. About his administration we know very little as his biography records only a long series of his miracles. After ten years he resigned because he was neglecting his prayer and his monks at Sykeon. Theodore retired to an oratory near Heliopolis. There he exercised a ministry of healing and miracles until his death in 613.

Theodore once punished his body so severely that, ill and vermin-infested, he had to be rescued. Many other saints also indulged in such excessive spiritual asceticism. But we may agree with St. Charles of Sezze, who wrote: "God does not command us to live dressed in hair-shirts and chains, or to chastise our flesh with scourges, but to love him above all things and our neighbor as ourselves.

APRIL 22
Miracles Do Happen

127. Kevin

(D. 618)

All Ireland honors St. Kevin as the founder of the celebrated abbey of Glendalough and patron of Dublin. Kevin is the anglicized form of Coemgen, meaning "fair-begotten." His biographers wrote at least four hundred years after his death and laced his story with fanciful legends.

Raised in a monastery at Kilmanach and ordained a priest there, Kevin retired to live as a solitary in the district of Glendalough, probably to a cave now called St. Kevin's Bed. But he also reached out to local people, as he gathered blackberries and apples for the sick and dying, apparently as part of a ministry of healing.

Kevin customarily subjected his body to harsh penances. In the following passage, a biographer romanticized his extreme mortification with verses from the poet Solomon:

> Coemgen was accustomed all his life through the severity of his asceticism to spend every Lent in a . . . pen, and a grey flag-stone under him as a bed, and his only food was the music of the angels. And he would spend a month and two weeks like this. One Lent when he was acting in this way, a blackbird came from the wood to his pen, and hopped on his palm as he lay on the flag-stone with his hand stretched out. He kept his hand in that position, so that the blackbird built its nest in it and hatched its brood.
>
> The angel came after this to visit Coemgen, and bade him leave the penance in which he was, and return to the society of men once more. Coemgen said that the pain of his hand being under the blackbird till she hatched her clutch was little compared with the pain which his Lord suffered for his sake. As Solomon says . . . of the words of Coemgen:
>
> > Alas! A pain greater than the requital
> > My hand like a log under the blackbird;
> > The blood of his hands, of his side, of his feet
> > The King of heaven shed for my sake.
>
> However, the angel bade Coemgen go out of the pen, and revealed to him that God had promised to him that he should run no risk of danger of the judgment or doom. . . . So Solomon says:

God gave power to Coemgen
Such as he gave not to every saint in the world,
In the doom to be strong in the assemblies
Where the children of Adam will be trembling.

Kevin's severe asceticism ruined his health. He had to be carried from the cave on a litter to Disert-Coemgen, where he and a few disciples settled. It is said that every day an otter brought Kevin a salmon with which he fed his monks. But the otter fled in fear when it sensed that one of the monks hankered for otter-skin gloves. Probably because of an actual food shortage, Kevin moved his community to the upper reaches of Glendalough and established there a permanent center that became the core of the famous abbey.

Once Kevin made a pilgrimage to Rome and brought back relics and soil from the holy city. And he made Glendalough one of Ireland's main pilgrimage spots, seven visits there being regarded as one to Rome itself. Reportedly Kevin lived to be 120 years old.

If you have fasted for two days, don't think yourself better than one who hasn't fasted. You fast and are peevish. The other eats and is pleasant. You work off your irritability and hunger by quarreling. The other eats and gives thanks to God.

—Jerome

JUNE 3 / PATRON OF DUBLIN
Angels; Celtic Saints; Fasting

128. Isidore of Seville

(560?–636)

St. Isidore of Seville is sometimes called "the schoolmaster of the Middle Ages" because his books and schools helped shape the education and culture of medieval Europe, and so, of western civilization. For ten centuries, Isidore's voluminous works were among those most quoted by other writers. And his establishment of cathedral schools laid a foundation for the medieval universities and for education in the West.

In 599, Isidore became bishop of Seville and for thirty-seven years led the Spanish church through a period of intense religious development. He continued the conversion of the Visigoths from Arianism, a process that had started when their king, Reccared, embraced orthodoxy in 587. Isidore also organized representative councils that established the structure and discipline of the church in Spain. At the Council of Toledo in 633 he obtained a decree that required the establishment of a school in every diocese. Reflecting the saint's broad interests, the schools taught every branch of knowledge, including the liberal arts, medicine, law, Hebrew, and Greek.

Isidore wrote many books, the most famous being the *Etymologies*, an encyclopedia of grammar, rhetoric, theology, history, medicine, and mathematics. He also wrote a dictionary of synonyms, brief biographies of illustrious men, treatises on theological and philosophical subjects, a history of world events since the creation, and a history of the Goths, which is our only source of information about them.

Throughout his long life, Isidore lived austerely so that he could give to the poor. Even in the last years of his life, they queued up daily at his door. But while Isidore had compassion for needy, he thought they were better off than their oppressors, as he explains in this selection:

> We ought to sorrow for people who do evil rather than for people who suffer it. The wrongdoing of the first leads them further into evil. The others' suffering corrects them from evil. Through the evil wills of some, God works much good in others.
>
> Some people, resisting the will of God, unwittingly do his purpose. Understand then that so truly are all things subject to God that even those who oppose his law nevertheless fulfill his will.

> Evil men are necessary so that through them the good may be scourged when they do wrong. Thus the Lord declares the Assyrian to be the rod of his anger. Through such men, God in his indignation wreaks his anger on those whom he would amend by chastisement. God works in this with a will of perfect justice, but his instruments often with the intent of cruelty, as the prophet says of the same Assyrian: "His heart is set on destruction."
>
> Some simple men, not understanding the dispensation of God, are scandalized by the success of evil men. They say with the prophet: "Why does the way of the wicked prosper?" Those who speak thus should not wonder to see the frail temporal happiness of the wicked. Rather they should consider the final end of evil men, and the everlasting torments prepared for them. As the prophet says: "They spend their days in wealth, and in a moment they go down to hell."

Shortly before his death, Isidore had two friends clothe him in sackcloth and rub ashes on his head so that he could come before God as a poor penitent. He died peacefully at Seville in 636.

> *The pleasure that a person seeks by gratifying his own inclinations quickly changes into bitterness and leaves nothing behind but the regret of having been ignorant of the secret of true beatitude and of the way of the saints.*
>
> —Isidore of Seville

APRIL 4 / CANONIZED IN 1598 / PATRON OF THE INTERNET
Innovative Saints; Doctors of the Church; Study; World Historical Saints

129. Gall

(550?–640?)

St. Gall became a monk at Bangor, Northern Ireland, where **St. Columban** supervised his education in Scripture and classical studies. In 590, Gall joined Columban on his famed missionary voyage to take Christianity to continental Europe. There he emerged as the most famous disciple of the great Celtic leader. Together they founded monasteries first at Annegray and then at Luxeuil, both in northeastern France, where they stayed twenty years. However, in 610 Columban and his monks were driven from the area, probably because he had rebuked the royal court. The exiles settled in Switzerland, building huts near Lake Constance, where St. Gall occupied himself with preaching against idolatry. And with fishing!

Once at the end of a sermon denouncing idol worship, Gall broke statues of the pagan gods and threw them into the lake. Then apparently he went fishing, which occasioned this charming story in his biography:

> One night, as Gall was casting his nets into the lake, he heard a demon calling with a loud voice from a nearby mountain to a fellow demon who inhabited the water. "Rise and help me," he said, "that we may cast out these strangers who have expelled me from my temple, shattered my images and drawn away my followers. Let's unite our strength and drive these enemies from our borders."
>
> "Alas," replied the second demon, "I know from experience what you are going through. For one of them imprisons me in the lake and exploits my domains. I can't damage his nets or stop him because he always has the divine name on his lips. By its protection and his ceaseless vigilance he avoids my traps. . . ."
>
> When he heard this, Gall protected himself with the sign of the cross and said to them, "In the name of our Lord Jesus Christ I command you to depart from this place and forbid you to injure anyone here."
>
> Then he went to tell Columban what he had heard. The abbot immediately summoned the brethren to the church. But before they finished chanting the psalms, they heard the awful voices of the demons passing from mountain to mountain in mingled tones of despair and fear, as they took their departure. Then the servants of God prostrated themselves in prayer, asking the Lord to protect them and offering him thanks because he had delivered them from the terror of the fiends.

In 612 a barbarian invasion persuaded Columban to migrate to Italy. When Gall declined to go along because he was ill, Columban unfairly judged that he was being too easy on himself. So he forbade Gall to celebrate Mass until his (Columban's) death. Committed to obedience, Gall humbly submitted to the unjust punishment. He remained in Switzerland and set up a hermitage on the Steinach River. Gall declined many invitations to become a bishop or abbot. He preferred to maintain simplicity and solitude with a few disciples, living with them under the Rule of St. Columban. Gall died on a preaching expedition around 640.

Walahfrid Strabo, St. Gall's biographer, made too much of the saint's miracles, but also assured us that Gall had "plenty of practical sense." Later the renowned medieval monastery, famous as a center of learning, library, and scriptorium, was developed on the Steinach River site and came to be called St. Gall's.

I arise today:
in the might of God for my piloting;
Power of God for my upholding;
Wisdom of God for my guidance; . . .
Word of God for my utterance; . . .
Shield of God for my protection; . . .
against snares of demons;
against allurements of vices; . . .
against every person that wishes me ill, far and near; . . . .

—Patrick

OCTOBER 16
Humility; The Sign of the Cross; Spiritual Warfare

130. John Climacus
(579?–649?)

St. John took his name Climacus or "ladder" from his book, *The Ladder of Divine Ascent,* which became one of the most widely read spiritual works of the Middle Ages. The reader who climbed *The Ladder* ascended thirty steps to holiness. According to St. John, the goal was to reach a state of apatheia or passive disinterestedness in earthly life so as to anticipate the wonders of heaven. Each step communicated some practical insight into Christian living that twenty-first-century readers will still find beneficial. Consider, for example, the tenth step on avoiding slander and judging others:

> Slander is the offspring of hatred, a subtle yet crass disease, a leech escaping notice, wasting and draining away the lifeblood of love.
>
> I have rebuked slanderers, and in self-defense these evildoers claimed to be acting out of love. My answer was, "If, as you insist, you love that person, then don't make a mockery of him, but pray for him in secret, for this is the kind of love that is acceptable to the Lord. Do not start passing judgment on the offender—Judas was in the company of Christ's disciples and the robber was in the company of killers. Yet what a turnabout there was when the decisive moment arrived!"
>
> Do not allow human respect to get in your way when you hear someone slandering his neighbor. Instead, say: "Brother, stop it! I do worse things every day, so how can I criticize him?" You accomplish two things when you say this. You heal yourself and you heal your neighbor with the one bandage.
>
> Do not make judgments, and you will travel no quicker road to the forgiveness of your sins. "Do not judge, and you will not be judged" (Luke 6:37 *NJB*). If a man commits a sin before you at the very moment of his death, pass no judgment because God's judgment is hidden from us. Men have sinned greatly in the open but have done greater good deeds in secret. Their detractors have been fooled with smoke instead of sunlight in their eyes.

A native of Palestine and possibly a disciple of **St. Gregory Nazianzen,** at sixteen, John entered a monastery in the Palestinian desert. After four years of training in a community, he lived forty years as a hermit. Like other desert fathers, he broke his near-total solitude only on

Saturdays and Sundays to worship with other hermits and counsel his followers.

Early in his monastic career John decided that as a mark of submission to God he would receive all criticism as true. Once, for example, some monks reproached him for wasting time in idle conversation. So to correct what he regarded as a serious fault, for a year John observed absolute silence. Only when his disciples insisted that they needed his spiritual teaching did the saint start speaking again.

When John was seventy he was elected abbot of the monastery at Mount Sinai. That was an appropriate choice, for many monks saw John as a Moses who had received Christian commandments from God and recorded them in his *Ladder*. After four years in office, John retired to his cell and died there around 649 at eighty years of age.

> *Someone who does not trip up in speech has reached perfection and is able to keep the whole body on a tight rein. Once we put a bit in the horse's mouth, to make it do what we want, we have the whole animal under our control.*
>
> —James 3:2–4 *NJB*

MARCH 30
Applied Christianity; Pursuit of Holiness

131. Braulio

(D. 650)

St. Isidore recognized the young nobleman Braulio as an outstanding graduate of his college at Seville in Spain and took him under his wing. He made Braulio his colleague, a peer to whom he submitted his books for editing. Isidore ordained him and appointed him bishop of Saragossa in 631.

St. Braulio maintained the pattern of life he had learned earlier as a monk. He lived simply, dressed in rough clothes, ate sparingly, and gave alms generously. He collaborated with Isidore in completing the conversion of the Visigoths from Arianism and in renewing church order in Spain.

Forty-four of Braulio's letters that have survived give us a good picture of the saint and his ministry. He counseled priests on liturgical and pastoral questions. Sometimes he discussed complex theological matters like the resurrection of the body. Often he consoled relatives and friends on the death of loved ones. In his most famous letter he defended the Spanish bishops to Pope Honorius I, who had accused them of laxity. Braulio's sense of humor bursts forth in letters requesting manuscripts, teasing friends who failed to visit, and lightly reprimanding an arrogant young priest who was to succeed him.

Braulio is remembered as an eloquent preacher. We can almost hear the power of his voice in this letter to his brother Frominian, who wanted to resign his office as abbot:

> I am shocked that you are so upset by all these routine scandals that you prefer to spend your life in silence rather than to stay in the duties entrusted to you.
>
> Where will your blessed perseverance be if your patience fails? Remember the apostle who said: "All who want to live piously in Christ Jesus will suffer persecution" (see 2 Timothy 3:12). Endurance exists not only in confessing the name of Christ by sword and fire and various punishments. But differences in customs, insults of the disobedient and barbs of wicked tongues and various temptations are also included in this kind of persecution.
>
> There is not a single occupation that is without its dangers. Who will guide the ship if the pilot quits his post? Who will guard against wolves if the shepherd does not watch? Or who will drive away the robber if the watchman sleeps? You must stick by the work entrusted to

> you and the task you have undertaken. You must hate the sins, not the people. Even though tribulation brings us more than we can endure, let us not be afraid as if we were resisting with our own strength. We must pray with the apostle that God give us "the way out with the temptation" (see 1 Corinthians 10–13), that we may be able to withstand, for Christ is both our courage and our counsel, "without him we can do nothing" (see John 15:5) and "with him we can do all things" (see Philippians 4:13).

Braulio also wrote a life of St. Emilian, a patron of Spain. He prepared a list of the works of St. Isidore and reportedly completed some of his master's unfinished works. St. Braulio went partially blind in 650 and died in the same year.

> *He more rightly mourns the miseries of human life who expects that he will die each day. Thus it isn't so much having departed from the world as having lived with the world that is full of sadness. Moreover, living so as to serve Christ is to have conquered the world and not to have lived with it.*
>
> —Braulio

MARCH 26 / PATRON OF ARAGON
Facing Death; Great Pastors; Perseverance

132. Martin I

(D. 655)

Because of his obvious gifts and reputation for holiness, St. Martin's star rose fast in Rome. When he was a deacon, Pope Theodore I sent him as his nuncio to Constantinople, the chief city of the Byzantine Empire. Upon Theodore's death in 649, Martin himself was elected pope.

Immediately the new pope plunged into a dangerous whirlpool of religious and political controversy. In October 649, he chaired a synod at the Lateran Cathedral that condemned Monothelitism, a heresy that denied that Christ had a human will. The synod fathers also censured two imperial edicts because they favored that heresy over orthodoxy. "The Lord," they said, "commanded us to shun evil and do good, but not to reject the good with the evil. We are not to deny at the same time both error and truth."

The emperor, Constans II, responded with rage. He sent an agent to kidnap the pope. The lieutenant found the pope sick and lying on a cot before the altar at the Lateran. He arrested Martin, who made no resistance, and secretly carried him off to Constantinople. So began the saint's slow and humiliating martyrdom.

At Constantinople the emperor jailed the pope under the most miserable circumstances. Martin wrote in a letter:

> I have not been allowed to wash, even in cold water, for forty-seven days. I am wasted away and frozen through, and have had no respite from dysentery. The food that is given me makes me feel sick. I hope that God, who knows all things, will bring my persecutors to repentance after he will have taken me out of this world.

In a kangaroo court where Martin was allowed no defense, the imperial senate condemned him as a traitor, a capital offense. However, at the request of the patriarch of Constantinople, the court spared Martin's life and sent him instead into exile at Kherson in the Crimea. There the pope slowly wasted away from hunger and sickness. Perhaps his greatest suffering, however, was his sense of being abandoned by his friends. In 654, he wrote:

> I am surprised at the indifference of all those who, though they once knew me, have now so entirely forgotten me that they do not even seem to know whether I am in the world. I wonder still more at those who belong to the church of St. Peter for the little concern they show for one of their body. If that church has no money, it wants not corn, oil or other provisions out of which they might send me a small supply. What fear has seized all these men that it hinders them from fulfilling the commands of God in relieving the distressed? Have I appeared such an enemy to the whole church, or to them in particular?
>
> However, I pray God, by the intercession of St. Peter, to preserve them steadfast and immovable in the orthodox faith. As to this wretched body, God will have care of it. He is at hand. Why should I trouble myself? I hope in his mercy that he will not prolong my course.

Martin may have felt that the answer to his prayer was no, as his suffering continued for two years. He died in 655, the last pope to be recognized as a martyr.

The emperor's vicious and violent treatment of the pope should not surprise us. When politics mixes with religion it tends to drive charity away. But what should shock us is the failure of Martin's community to care for him during his agony. May no fear or forgetfulness keep us from supporting sisters and brothers who are suffering.

APRIL 13
Defending the Faith; Martyrs; Suffering

133. Ildefonsus of Toledo

(607?–667)

Spanish Catholics esteem St. Ildefonsus as one of their greatest saints, second only to **Isidore of Seville.** As archbishop of Toledo, he led the Spanish church from 658 to 667. Like Isidore, Ildefonsus contributed to the creation of the collaborative union of church and state that came to typify medieval Europe. For example, he presided over a council in 653 that granted secular leaders the right to participate in ecclesiastical decisions. But at the same time, bishops participated in the election of kings and joined with state officials in publishing secular laws and pardoning traitors. Thus the saint helped forge medieval political relationships well ahead of their time.

Pastorally, Ildefonsus aimed to raise the faith level of the laypeople in Toledo, so he set about to educate them in Christian truth. For example, he wrote *On Understanding Baptism* to elevate their ideals. Here is a quote from that popular book:

> We come to the font as to the Red Sea. Moses was the leader in saving Israel; Christ was the leader in redeeming man. The former left Egypt; the latter left the world. The Egyptians pursued the Israelites; sin pursued man. The sea is colored by the red of its shore; baptism is consecrated with the blood of Christ. The vast sea is divided by a rod; the entrance to the font is opened with the sign of the cross.
>
> Israel enters the sea; man is washed in the font. Israel passes on a dry path between the waters without hindrance; through the waters man journeys the way of salvation. The pursuing Egyptians are drowned with Pharaoh; sins are destroyed in baptism together with the devil in a destruction not of life but of power. The children of Israel left Egypt in the spring of the year and passed through the sea; in the same season we celebrate the Pasch of our Lord Jesus Christ.
>
> In baptism, souls cross from vices to virtues. They pass from the lusts of the flesh to grace and sobriety of spirit. And they escape from the leaven of malice and wickedness to truth and sincerity. Thus we say to those born again: "This month shall be to you the beginning of months: it shall be the first of the months of the year" (see Exodus 12:2). For he who is washed abandons Pharaoh, the leader of this world, with all its works.

Veneration of the Virgin Mary runs deep in the Hispanic Catholic tradition. That stream of Marian devotion can trace its roots in part to Ildefonsus. He loved Mary and honored her in his landmark book, *On the Perpetual Virginity of Holy Mary*. Its themes inspired the Marian "breastplate" songs of Irish monks in Europe, and through many centuries copyists placed quotes from it in books of hours. Ildefonsus's work may have influenced the long-standing practice of celebrating mass on Saturdays in honor of Mary.

El Greco and Velásquez have memorialized in paintings a story about Ildefonsus that became popular around the twelfth century. Once when he was seated in his episcopal chair, Mary is reported to have appeared and presented him with a chasuble as a token of gratitude for his devotion.

Ildefonsus died on January 23, 667.

The Holy Spirit heated, inflamed and melted Mary with love, as fire does iron, so that the flame of the Spirit was seen and nothing was felt but the fire of the love of God.

—Ildefonsus of Toledo

JANUARY 23

Mary; Saints and Politics; Saints and Sacraments (Baptism)

134. Hilda
(614–680)

In his *History of the English Church and People*, **Bede** celebrated the competence and holiness of St. Hilda. A grandniece of St. Edwin, king of Northumbria, at age thirteen she was baptized with him by St. Paulinus, the archbishop of York. According to Bede she spent the next twenty years "most nobly in secular occupations." Unfortunately he does not satisfy our curiosity about how a sainted laywoman might have lived in the seventh-century world, as he is silent about Hilda's early career. Given her later accomplishments in the religious life, however, we can conjecture that whatever she did, she did it well.

At thirty-three, Hilda decided to devote the rest of her life to divine service. Her intention was to join her sister, Queen Hereswith, at Chelles in France, but St. Aidan gave her a small plot in Northumbria in northern England where she began to live a monastic life with a few companions. Then she became an abbess, first at Hartlepool and then at Streanaeshalch, later called Whitby.

At Whitby, Hilda governed a mixed monastery, where monks and nuns worshiped together, but lived separately. Bede said she approached her leadership there with great energy:

> Hilda put this monastery under the same regular discipline as she had done the former. And she taught there the strict observance of justice, piety, chastity, and other virtues, particularly of peace and charity.
>
> After the example of the primitive church, no person there was rich, and none poor, all being in common to all, and none having any property. Her prudence was so great, that not only indifferent persons, but even kings and princes asked and received her advice. She obliged those who were under her direction to attend so much to reading of the Holy Scriptures, and to exercise themselves so much in works of justice, that many might be found there fit for ecclesiastical duties, and to serve at the altar.
>
> We afterwards saw five bishops taken out of that monastery, and all of them men of singular merit and sanctity. . . .
>
> The Lord's servant Abbess Hilda, whom everyone who knew her called Mother because of her marvelous piety and grace, was not only an example of holiness to members of her own community. For she also brought about the repentance and salvation of many living afar, who heard the inspiring story of her industry and goodness.

In 663, Hilda hosted the Synod of Whitby that settled a troublesome dispute over the date for celebrating Easter. Hilda favored the traditional Celtic practice, but yielded to **St. Wilfrid,** whose argument for the Roman custom won the day. However, some say she may have evened the score fifteen years later. At that time **St. Theodore,** the archbishop of Canterbury, arbitrarily partitioned St. Wilfrid's diocese and appointed two of Hilda's monks as bishops of the newly formed sees. Hilda sided with Theodore, who prevailed over Wilfrid's futile resistance.

Hilda was sick for the last seven years of her life, but her illness did not slow her down. Although often weakened by a fever, she continued to rule the monastery, especially to teach publicly and one-on-one. She died at Whitby on November 17, 680.

I find it refreshing and instructive to discover that a saint could vigorously disagree with another saint and both still be holy. Charity seems to stretch far enough to cover a diversity of opinions, as well as a multitude of sins.

NOVEMBER 17
Celtic Saints; Community; Lights in the "Dark Ages"; Valiant Women

135. Caedmon

(D. 680?)

Sometimes we may scratch our heads and doubt the value of wonders like weeping statues and bleeding crucifixes. But we readily appreciate the miracle that changed St. Caedmon's life. He received a charism of song and poetry that inspired faith and love in the Celtic world. And his gift made him the first recorded English-speaking poet.

Caedmon worked as a herdsman near the abbey of Whitby. Already an elderly man, he knew nothing about poetry and could not sing. At parties, for example, guests were expected to entertain when the harp was passed to them, but Caedmon, because of his reticence, would exit before the instrument reached him. **Bede** described such an event, the one that occasioned Caedmon's divine gift:

> Having . . . gone out of the house, where the entertainment was underway, to the stable where he had to take care of the horses that night, there he settled himself down to rest. A person appeared to him in his sleep and, greeting him by name, said:
>
> "Caedmon, sing some song to me."
>
> "I cannot sing," he answered. "That was the reason why I left the entertainment and came to this place. . . ." The other replied, "But you shall sing."
>
> "What shall I sing?" he asked.
>
> "Sing of the beginning of created things," said the other.
>
> And at once Caedmon began to sing verses in praise of God, which he had never heard, on this theme:
>
> Now must we praise the Maker of the heavenly kingdom,
> the might of God and the thought of his mind,
> the glorious Father of men,
> How he, the Lord everlasting, wrought the beginning of all wonders,
> He, the holy Creator, first fashioned
> the heavens as a roof for the children of earth;
> then this middle-earth the Master of mankind,
> the Lord eternal, afterwards adorned,
> the earth for men, the Ruler almighty. . . .
>
> Awaking from his sleep, he remembered all that he had sung in his dream, and soon added much more to the same effect in verse worthy of God.

Caedmon reported his dream to **St. Hilda,** the abbess at Whitby.

She tested the spirit of his gift by having him sing his creation song for a group of monks. All agreed that the saint had been divinely inspired. Hilda was delighted and persuaded Caedmon to become a monk. She had him instructed in Scripture so that he could sing about all the events of sacred history. Apparently he composed an extensive collection of poems on subjects ranging from creation to the last judgment. Bede says Caedmon wanted his songs "to turn his hearers from delight in wickedness and to inspire them to love and do good." Recited and sung all over northern England, his poems confirmed the faith of Christians and attracted new converts. Sadly, all of his poetry is lost except the few lines above preserved by Bede.

One day in 680, after two weeks of feeling somewhat ill, Caedmon had a premonition of his death. He surprised his friends by preparing himself to die, as they were sure he would recover. But after reconciling with all of them and receiving the Eucharist, that night the saint died peacefully in his sleep.

The advent of Caedmon must have been hailed by Christian teachers much as if a native Milton were in our days to arise in some Hindu or Chinese mission to propagate the truth among his countrymen whom the preacher could not reach.

—Charles Hole

FEBRUARY 11

Celtic Saints; Dreams; Lights in the "Dark Ages"; Miracles Do Happen; Poets

136. Balthild

(D. 680)

On the surface, St. Balthild's life seems to have been a parabola—up from slave girl to queen and regent and down again to humble nun. But the woman herself was consistently Christian and competent, a model for anyone whose life seems to flip-flop unpredictably. A beautiful and gifted Anglo-Saxon girl, Balthild was sold as a slave to an officer of the imperial court of the Frankish king, Clovis II. She caught the monarch's eye, and he married her in 649. Clovis must have prized his queen, for in seven years she bore him three healthy sons, all of whom would someday wear his crown. The youngest son was only five when the king died in 657, so Balthild served as regent. She had a rocky time of it, defending declining royal authority against nobles who were growing in power. But as this excerpt from her biography shows, she was able to take a firm stand on some religious and social issues:

> Then following the exhortations of good priests, by God's will working through her, Lady Balthild prohibited the impious evil of the simoniac heresy, a depraved custom that stained the church of God, whereby episcopal orders were obtained for a price. She proclaimed that no payment could be exacted for receipt of a sacred rank.
>
> She, or God acting through her, ordained that yet another evil custom should cease, namely, that many people determined to kill their children rather than nurture them, for they feared to incur the public exactions that were heaped upon them by custom which caused great damage to their affairs. In her mercy, that lady forbade anyone to do these things.
>
> And let it be remembered, since it increases the magnitude of her own reward, that she prohibited the sale of captive Christian folk to outsiders and gave orders through all the lands that no one was to sell captive Christians within the borders of the Frankish realm. What is more, she ordered that many captives should be ransomed, paying the price herself. And she installed some of the captives she released and other people in monasteries, particularly as many men and women of her own people as possible and cared for them.

Balthild made generous contributions to several abbeys and founded monasteries at Corbie and Chelles, where she planned to retire. That came sooner than expected, as a palace revolution forced her out of her office as regent in 665. Thus in her declining years as a humble nun at Chelles, she lived obediently under the direction of **St. Bertilla**, whom she had personally chosen as abbess. Her biographer says Queen Balthild deported herself as the lowest among the nuns. As evidence he says she cherished the most demeaning chores:

> She valiantly took care of the dirtiest jobs, personally cleaning up the dung from the latrine. She did this gladly, performing such humble service for Christ's sake. For who would believe that one so sublime in power would take care of things so vile.

Balthild fell seriously ill with a disease that caused her great pain. But she concealed the extent of her suffering from the other nuns to keep them from worrying about her. Balthild—slave, queen, nun, and saint—died at Chelles in 680.

Yahweh makes poor and rich,
He humbles and also exalts.
He raises the poor from the dust,
he lifts the needy from the dunghill
to give them a place with princes,
to assign them a seat of honor.

—1 Samuel 2:7–8 *NJB*

JANUARY 30
Married Saints; Saints and Politics; True Humility

137. Cuthbert

(634?–687)

St. Cuthbert's youth as a shepherd foreshadowed his life as a monk, bishop, and missionary. Tending his flock in the Northumbrian fields, he learned to appreciate solitude and quiet communion with God. And as he roamed the countryside from village to village, he was unconsciously preparing himself for his later missionary journeys to the people of northern England.

Fifteen-year-old Cuthbert entered Melrose Abbey and became a monk. Early in his monastic career a plague struck Northumbria, driving many Christians back to pagan practices. Cuthbert himself almost died of the disease. But when he heard that the monks had prayed all of one night for him, he jumped up. "What am I doing in bed?" he asked. "Can God close his ears to such men?"

While he never fully recovered his strength, Cuthbert threw himself aggressively into missionary journeys. As the prior of Melrose and later, of Lindisfarne, he traversed Northumbria to aid stricken people and revive their Christian faith. He went from house to house, teaching, counseling, and healing. So many miracles occurred in his ministry that he became known in his lifetime as the "Wonder Worker of Britain."

Cuthbert's anonymous biographer tells of a miracle that happened on his sea voyage to the country of the Picts in northern Scotland:

> He set out from the monastery of Melrose with two brothers and sailed to the country of the Picts. They remained there for some days afflicted with hunger, while a stormy sea prevented them from sailing on their way. The man of God, having prayed the whole night on the shore, came to them on the morning of the feast of the Epiphany and assured them, "Let us go look for food, begging of God in accord with his promise, 'Ask, and it will be given to you; search and you will find' (Matthew 7:7 *NJB*). For I believe that the Lord will make us a present of something on this day on which the Magi paid him homage with their gifts."
>
> So the three rose and went searching, with Cuthbert in the lead, as though he were a guide. They went to the seashore and, looking about there, immediately discovered three portions of dolphin flesh that a human hand seemed to have cut off with a knife and washed with water. Then the man of God threw himself to his knees, thanking

> the Lord, and said to his companions, "Take them up and bring them away, and let us bless the Lord. Three pieces, you see, will be sufficient for three men for three days and nights. And on the fourth day the sea will be calm for sailing." So they carried the food away and cooked it. They enjoyed the marvelous sweetness of the meat. They remained then three days through the storm. On the fourth day they sailed away in bright weather—as he had said they would—and happily arrived at a safe landing place.

After 676, Cuthbert lived for nearly a decade as a hermit, though petitioners constantly interrupted his solitude. He became bishop of Lindisfarne in 685 and resumed his missionary journeys in pastoral visits to his people. After two years of vigorous leadership, he died on March 20, 687.

Contemporary gurus tell us that we must love ourselves before we can truly love others. What would have become of Cuthbert had he been given that advice? He might never have risen from his sickbed. And if he had coddled himself, many would have missed his loving care and touch.

MARCH 20 / PATRON OF SAILORS
Celtic Saints; Lights in the "Dark Ages"; Miracles Do Happen; Missionaries

138. Theodore of Canterbury
(602–690)

St. Theodore, archbishop of Canterbury, accomplished a series of important "firsts" for England. Under his episcopacy from 668 to 690, for the first time all the churches of Anglo-Saxon England willingly obeyed the archbishop of Canterbury. In 673, Theodore convened at Hertford the first national council of the English church. And at that historic meeting, the bishops accepted decrees that organized the English church, an action that is regarded as the first legislation, civil or ecclesiastic, for the whole English people.

In 667, the pope named Theodore, a Greek monk from Tarsus, to Canterbury and in 668 ordained him deacon, priest, and bishop. Theodore was sixty-six years old when he arrived in England. Immediately he set about unifying the very divided English church. Theodore visited the churches of the island, consolidating pastoral and liturgical practices on the pattern of Rome. The council at Hertford enforced the Roman custom for dating Easter and structured the English church on the diocesan system. Theodore, himself a scholar, also founded an excellent school at Canterbury that trained many future leaders of the English church.

After 678, Theodore was embroiled in a controversy with **St. Wilfrid** that resulted in a model reconciliation. Wilfrid fell into disfavor with King Egfrid and was forced into exile. Theodore took advantage of the situation to extend his authority northward. In a highhanded fashion he divided Wilfrid's vast Northumbrian diocese into three and appointed new bishops. Later he acknowledged his wrongdoing in the matter and asked Wilfrid's forgiveness in this letter:

> My greatest remorse is for the crime I have committed against you, most holy bishop, in consenting to the will of the king when they robbed you of your possessions and sent you into exile without any fault of yours. I confess it to God and St. Peter, and I take you both to witness that I will do what I can to make up for this sin, and to reconcile you with all the kings and nobles among my friends, whether they wish it or not. God has revealed to me that I shall die within a year. Therefore, I entreat you, by the love of God and **St. Peter**, to consent that I establish you during my life as heir to my episcopal see, for I

> acknowledge that of all your nation you are the best instructed in all knowledge and in the discipline of Rome.

In response, Wilfrid graciously received Theodore's offer of reconciliation:

> May God and St. Peter pardon you for your controversy. I shall always pray for you as your friend. Send letters now to your friends that they may be aware of our reconciliation, and the injustice of the robbery of which I have been the victim, and that they may restore to me at least a part of my goods, according to the command of the Holy See, after which we will examine with you in the great council of the country, who is worthy to become your successor.

But even though Theodore attempted restitution, Wilfrid was never appointed to Canterbury. Theodore continued to govern the English church until 690 when he died at age eighty-seven.

> *St. Theodore's great achievement was to give unity, organization and outstanding scholarship to a divided church on the edge of the civilized world at an age when most men had reached retirement or infirmity.*
>
> —David Hugh Farmer

SEPTEMBER 19
Peacemakers; Repentance

139. Benedict Biscop
(628–689)

Biscop Baducing, a Northumbrian nobleman, served Oswiu, his king, until 653. Then at age 25 he renounced his secular involvements, intending to become a monk. But first he accompanied **Wilfrid** on a pilgrimage to Rome. The see of St. Peter seems to have drawn him like nectar attracts a bee, as he subsequently traveled there five more times. A while later he took Oswiu's son on his second trip to Rome. On his return he stopped at Lérins, where he finally became a monk and took the name Benedict.

After two years of monastic training, St. Benedict went a third time to Rome. There the pope had just appointed **Theodore** as archbishop of Canterbury and Benedict accompanied him to England. Then Theodore appointed Benedict as abbot of St. Augustine's in Canterbury.

In a short while Benedict developed a vision for a foundation of his own. So in order to observe the best monasteries, he went off again to Rome a fourth time. He visited seventeen monasteries there and in Europe in order to skim the cream of monastic teaching and practice. In 674 he founded Wearmouth Abbey on land donated by King Ecgfrith. He brought in masons from Europe to construct the first stone Romanesque church in northern England.

On his fifth visit to Rome in 678, Benedict obtained treasures that significantly shaped England's Christian heritage. **Bede**, his disciple, gave this account:

> First of all, he brought back a vast number of books of every kind. Secondly, he brought a rich treasury of relics of the apostles and martyrs of Christ for the benefit of many a church yet-to-be built in the land of the Angles.
>
> Thirdly, he introduced in his monastery the manner of singing and chanting and conducting the church ceremonies in accord with the Roman usage by obtaining from Pope Agatho the arch-chanter of the church of the blessed Apostle Peter and abbot of the monastery of St. Martin, named John. . . .
>
> Fourthly, Benedict brought back as a gift of no mean value a letter of privilege which he had received from the venerable Pope Agatho with the permission, consent, desire and even the urging of King Ecgfrith,

> and which guaranteed that the monastery he had founded should be absolutely and forever secure from all outside intrusion.
>
> Fifthly, to adorn the church of St. Peter the Apostle which he had built, he brought back painted representations of the saints. . . . This he did so that all those entering his church, even those unable to read, could gaze on the dear face of Christ and his saints wherever they looked, even though only in representation. Or so that they could call more vividly to mind the grace of the Lord's incarnation. Or so that having the perilous moment of the Last Judgment as though it were happening before their eyes, they might remember to keep a stricter watch over themselves.

In 682, Benedict founded a second monastery at Jarrow. On a sixth and final trip to Rome he obtained even more books and paintings. In 683 paralysis struck Benedict and for three years he lay bedridden, with his monks tending him and listening to his teaching. He died in 689.

Benedict Biscop laid the foundation for England's continuance of the ancient tradition of learning. Abbot John, for example, trained his monks in the script with which they copied many manuscripts, including a one-volume Latin Bible. And Benedict tutored Bede, who came to him at age seven. With his mentor's treasured books as resources, Venerable Bede wrote his masterpieces that stand near the beginnings of English literature.

JANUARY 12
Innovative Saints; Study

140. Bertilla
(D. 700?)

Sometime in the mid-seventh century, as a girl St. Bertilla entered the convent at Jouarre, near Meaux, France. Her biographer says that she advanced rapidly in holiness and obedience, and that as a young woman she assumed responsibilities second only to the abbess. In 660, when **St. Balthild,** the English queen of Clovis II, founded a monastery at Chelles, she chose Bertilla as its first head. Following the Irish monastic pattern, she ruled there over the spiritual lives of both women and men.

Bertilla's eighth-century biographer presented her as a model of perfect obedience for nuns and monks. He fashioned the story of her impeccable conduct to encourage them to conform eagerly to their rule of life. But he heaped so much praise on Bertilla's virtuous behavior that she seemed to be more angelic than human. He did not succeed, however, in concealing completely the real Bertilla. He could not resist telling the following miracle story that inadvertently revealed the saint's besetting sin:

> Once, when a troubled sister spoke angry words to her, Bertilla called down divine judgment upon her. Although the fault was forgiven, Bertilla worried about her curse. Then the sister died unexpectedly, choked by asthma. Not having heard the signal for the funeral, Bertilla asked the reason for the resounding chorus of psalms. When she learned of the sister's death, she trembled fearfully. She hurried to the place where the little body lay lifeless and with great faith laid her hand on the dead nun's breast. Bertilla ordered her receding soul through Jesus Christ, the Son of God, not to leave, but before she spoke with him, to forgive her anger against her. And God permitted the spirit that had left the body to return to the corpse. To the amazement of all, the revived cadaver drew breath. Looking at the servant of God, she said: "What have you done, sister? Why did you retrieve me from the way of light?"
>
> "I beg you sister," said Bertilla humbly, "to give me words of forgiveness, for once I cursed you when you had a troubled spirit."
>
> "May God forgive you," said the nun. "I harbor no resentment in my heart against you now and I love you. Please entreat God for me and permit me to go in peace and don't hold me back. For I am ready for the bright road and now I cannot start without your permission."

"Go then in the peace of Christ," said Bertilla, "and pray for me, sweet sister."

Nestled among Bertilla's virtues was a problem—anger so strong that it could cause her to damn a sister. Her unpredictable behavior endeared the saint to her charges, but also made them wary. They loved her, writes the biographer cryptically, "when she was angry and feared when she laughed." These little slips of the biographer are refreshing signs that sanctity may cover a multitude of sins.

Bertilla governed the abbey at Chelles for forty-six years. Two queens submitted themselves to her care—Hereswith, queen of East Anglia, and, after her husband died, St. Balthild herself. As the saint aged she apparently overcame her flaw, as her reputation for humility and gentleness spread widely. She died around the year 700.

Bertilla's story has a special interest for Christians who are fascinated with near-death experiences. The nun she called back from death spoke of "the way of light" and of "the bright road." So this ancient account seems to corroborate the testimony of many twentieth-century witnesses who say they "died" and traveled along a pathway to the Light.

NOVEMBER 5
Lights in the "Dark Ages"; Repentance

141. Wilfrid
(633?–709)

Today we might call St. Wilfrid a "brick and mortar" bishop, comparing him to the Spellmans and Stritchs who built the American church. He believed a bishop needed a large territory, wealth, and political power to allow him to plant new churches and found monasteries and schools. But Wilfrid was also a courageous evangelist and pastor who personally converted thousands of pagans and reared them in the faith.

A Celtic monk of Lindisfarne and abbot of the new Celtic monastery at Ripon, nonetheless Wilfrid championed Roman influence in Anglo-Saxon England. In 663 he persuaded the famous Synod of Whitby to settle the controversy over the date of Easter by choosing the Roman method of calculation. A few years later he became bishop of Northumbria, a vast arena for his mission of expanding and consolidating the church. He planted many new Catholic communities. Among them was the new monastery at Hexam, where Wilfrid had constructed the largest church north of the Alps.

Three times in Wilfrid's long episcopacy kings exiled him, and each time he appealed to the pope, who upheld his claims. Thus he strengthened the Anglo-Saxon pattern of maintaining close ties with the church at Rome. During his first exile in 678, Wilfrid was sidetracked on his way to Rome and spent some months preaching to pagans in Frisia, establishing the Anglo-Saxon mission to Germany. During his second forced exile, Wilfrid took the Christian faith to the people of Wessex and Sussex. His biographer, Eddius Stephanus, reported on his successful mission:

> Directed by God after human help had failed him, our holy bishop fled to the pagans of Sussex. He sought out their king, Aethiwalh, and told him the bitter tale of his exile. The king gave his solemn promise of a strong compact of peace and friendship between them. He swore that no enemy would terrorize the bishop with threats nor persuade him with bribes to break this pact.
>
> The holy man of God rejoiced at these consoling words. And after thanking God, he began to preach the gospel. On the king and queen first he gently urged the word of God and the splendor of his kingdom. Then with the king's consent, Bishop Wilfrid assembled the pagan

> people, who had never yet heard the word of God. Standing in their midst, he spoke like our Lord Jesus Christ and his precursor: "Repent, for the kingdom of heaven is at hand" (Matthew 3:2 *NAB*) and, "Be baptized every one of you in the name of God the Father, and the Son and the Holy Spirit" (see Acts 2:38).
>
> For many months the evangelical preacher spoke eloquently, the long sweep of his words covering everything Almighty God did to put idolatry to shame. Then Wilfrid found grace in the sight of the king and a great gateway of faith opened for him. On one day he baptized many thousands of pagans (as the Apostle Peter did) of both sexes who forsook idolatry and professed faith in Almighty God.

After his third exile from 692 to 703, Wilfrid returned to end his controversial life as bishop of Hexam. He died in 709 at Oundle, a monastery he had founded in Mercia.

Wilfrid may seem too triumphalistic for our modern tastes. But he directed his grandiose ideals and exalted view of the bishop's office to the spread of the gospel and establishment of the church. And that in a half-pagan land governed by powerful and arbitrary rulers.

OCTOBER 12
Celtic Saints; Great Preachers; Lights in the "Dark Ages"; Missionaries; Saints and Politics

142. Flannan

(Seventh Century)

Ireland and Scotland both honor St. Flannan. He was educated by monks, stayed close to nature, made a pilgrimage to Rome, was appointed bishop, wandered about preaching, and worked miracles. All that makes him a classic Celtic saint.

The son of Turlough, a Celtic chieftain, Flannan was educated by a monk who also taught him farming. His biographer says he learned how to "till, sow, harvest, grind, winnow, and bake for the monks." Against the advice of relatives, Flannan decided to undertake a pilgrimage by sea to Rome. Following the lore of other saints in Celtic literature, legend says that he floated miraculously to Rome on a stone. There the pope consecrated him as the first bishop of Killaloe.

Flannan led his diocese by traveling about teaching and preaching. His charismatic eloquence even persuaded his elderly father to become a monk under St. Colman. When Turlough asked Colman to bless his family, the abbot predicted that seven of his descendants would be kings. Fearing that kingship might fall on him, Flannan prayed for a physical deformity that might prevent it. His biography says that his face became disfigured with scars and rashes.

As bishop, Flannan sometimes forcefully intervened to pacify petty clan wars. Once he had negotiated a truce between two chiefs, which one of them broke a year later by invading and destroying the other's land. Flannan addressed the robber chief in the following no-nonsense fashion:

> "What, falsest of men, do you intend to do? Why have you deceitfully broken faith? Turn back! Repent!"
>
> The faithless chief bent obstinately on plunder replied: "If the fleetness of my horse enables me to outstrip you I will neither wait for you nor obey you."

So Flannan cursed the horse and it died. Then he said:

> "Most perfidious prince, because you have violated your promise and have trampled on all laws, human and divine, none of your family shall survive you."

> The saint's curse terrified the robber-prince, who flung himself at the feet of St. Flannan and begged pardon. The saint did not deny to the robber-chief the pardon he always extended to expressed sorrow for an offense and promise of amendment. But this pardon given to himself personally did not satisfy him. He was uneasy because of the utterance of the saint against his posterity. Weeping and bowed down, he addressed St. Flannan thus: "My father, you have often preached that all crimes are forgiven through repentance. I beg you not to have my family become extinct with me. Take back the prophecy pronounced against my children and descendants. And I promise to pay you a yearly tribute and to devote myself and mine to your service and that of your successors for ever."
>
> In the spirit of forgiveness and mercy, the saint blessed the children so that they should not suffer for their father's sins. But he did so on condition that they should observe the promise of their father.

The exact date of Flannan's death is not known, but it probably fell in the last quarter of the seventh century.

Flannan often recited the liturgy of the hours immersed in icy water, one of the practices of Celtic saints that understandably has not experienced a revival.

DECEMBER 18
Celtic Saints; Peacemakers

143. Germanus of Constantinople
(634?–732)

St. Germanus, patriarch of Constantinople from 715 to 730, holds an important place in the development of Catholic doctrine about the Virgin Mary. His sermons speak of her perpetual purity in language that suggests the Immaculate Conception. And in the following sermon he dramatically celebrated her Assumption into heaven:

> When Christ had willed that his Mother, she who had borne Life Itself within her, should be taken upwards to himself, he told her through an angel who was already known to her, that the time of her falling asleep was now at hand. And this he did so that through the intimation of her coming death, she might not be troubled at her departure from the living. . . . For we know that the separation of the body can bring distress to the spirit of even strong men. Therefore . . . , he who knows all things sent an angel to her, to give her strength of soul by such words as these, coming from Christ himself through him:
>
> "It is time for me . . . to take to myself, you my Mother. As you have filled the earth . . . with joy, so shall you now bring joy to heaven. You will gladden the mansions of my Father and delight the spirits of his saints. For beholding the honor the angels give you . . . at your translation to me, they shall be confirmed in their belief that through you their members also shall dwell in my light, oh Full of Grace!
>
> "Come therefore with exceeding great joy! Hail and again rejoice as once before. For you above all creatures are worthy of being hailed "full of grace." As when you were about to conceive me, you received tidings of great joy, so now rejoice that once more you are sought for, to be received by me."

Germanus lived more than ninety years, but most of his significant work, mainly as a spokesman for orthodoxy, occurred in the last third of his life. In the 690s, as bishop of Cyzicus, now Kapidagi, Turkey, he battled Monothelitism, a heresy that said Christ had only a divine and not a human will. After he became patriarch of Constantinople in 715, one of his first major acts was to hold a synod that condemned Monothelite teachings.

In 725 the emperor Leo the Isaurian issued a decree in support of the Iconoclasts against the veneration of images, opening a fierce controversy that lasted for nearly a century. Germanus boldly rebuked the emperor, reminding him that at his coronation he had taken an oath to defend the Catholic faith. But Leo persisted. When Leo ordered the destruction of icons and statues, Germanus wrote other bishops to rally them against the Iconoclastic heresy. "Pictures are history in figure," he wrote, "and tend to the sole glory of the Heavenly Father. When we show reverence to representations of Jesus Christ, we do not worship the colors laid on the wood. We are venerating the invisible God who is in the bosom of the Father: him we worship in Spirit and in truth." For five years Germanus spearheaded resistance to the emperor's decrees, but he did not prevail. In 730, Leo forced him to resign, and Germanus died two years later.

No one draws closer to a knowledge of the truth than he who has advanced far in the knowledge of divine things, and yet knows that something always remains for him to seek.

—Leo the Great

MAY 12
Defending the Faith; Mary

144. Willibrord

(658–739)

St. Willibrord's career exemplified the cross-pollination of the gospel between England and Ireland, and between these islands and the continent. From age seven, **Wilfrid** raised him at the monastery of Ripon in Northumbria. Around 678 he migrated to Ireland, where he spent twelve years studying with St. Egbert and St. Wigbert. Then after his ordination, imitating Celtic predecessors like **Columba,** Willibrord set out with eleven disciples for the continent. They became missionaries to the Frisians who lived on the coast of what is now the Netherlands.

In his evangelistic work Willibrord relied on the collaborative support of the Frankish king and the pope. Pepin of Herstal had just wrested Lower Frisia from its king, Radbod. Pepin encouraged Willibrord because he saw the Christianization of the Frisians as a way of integrating them into his kingdom. Twice Willibrord went to Rome to secure the authorization of Pope Sergius I. On the second trip the pope made him an archbishop, renamed him "Clement," and commissioned him to establish the church in Friesland.

Like all evangelists, Willibrord experienced many setbacks. For example, his effort to convert the Danes failed, except for his purchase of thirty young slaves, whom he immediately baptized. On the way back from Denmark he was shipwrecked on Heligoland, an island controlled by Radbod. There he confronted pagan superstitions by slaughtering sacred animals and by loudly baptizing three people in a pool where absolute silence was required. To appease his god, an angry Radbod martyred one of Willibrord's party. Then the king summoned Willibrord and upbraided him. According to **Alcuin:**

> The king demanded to know why he had violated their sacred places and insulted their god. The herald of truth answered him with steady courage: "O king, you do not adore God but the devil. He has foully deluded you so that he can thrust your soul into everlasting fire. For there is no God but one. He created sky, earth, sea, and everything that is in them. Whoever worships him with true faith will have life forever. As the servant of that God, I here today bear witness to you of the truth. I urge you finally to renounce that foolish delusion of your ancestors, and to believe in the one Almighty God and Our Lord Jesus

> Christ. I call on you to be baptized in the font of life and wash away all your sins. Then with all wickedness and wrongdoing cast away from you, you may live as a new man in all reasonableness, righteousness and holiness. If you do this you will win an eternal life of glory with God and his saints. But if instead you reject the path of salvation, then be most assured that you will suffer eternal tortures and hellish flames along with the devil to whom you pay court."
>
> Astounded, the king replied: "I see that you truly had no fear of our threats, and that your words match your deeds." Although he refused to believe in the truth that Willibrord preached, still he respectfully sent him back to Pepin.

In 715, Radbod regained Lower Frisia and temporarily undid much of Willibrord's work. However, after the king's death in 719, Willibrord with the aid of **Boniface** repaired the damage. In his remaining years he planted the church there so firmly that he earned the title "Apostle of the Frisians." Willibrord died in 739 on retreat at Echternach, Luxembourg, a monastery that he had founded.

> *There is no failure so great that a Christian cannot rise from it, there is no defeat so final that he cannot convert it into a victory.*
>
> —Helen C. White

NOVEMBER 7

Celtic Saints; Evangelization; Missionaries; Success in Failure

145. Andrew of Crete

(660?–740)

Hagiographers often hide saints' flaws, as if acknowledging their weaknesses might somehow make them less admirable. But watching a saint rise up holy after a fall inspires us. Such examples encourage us, like Andrew of Crete, who briefly flirted with heresy, hoping that God might also pick us up when we fail.

In 680 the Council of Constantinople had condemned monothelitism. Adherents of that heresy believed that Jesus, having only a divine will, was not fully human. Five years later, Theodore, patriarch of Jerusalem, sent his young subdeacon Andrew to Constantinople to profess his church's adherence to the council's decrees.

Andrew stayed in Constantinople where, because of his gifts, he quickly ascended the ecclesiastical ladder. Ordained deacon, he accepted the responsibility for an orphanage and a hospice for elderly men. Then he became archbishop of Gortyna, the metropolitan see of Crete.

In 711, Philippicus Bardanes, a usurper of the imperial throne, resurrected monothelitism. He burned the decrees of the council and called a synod in 712 to rubber-stamp his action. Temporarily muddleheaded or numbed by fear, St. Andrew participated in that synod and supported the heresy. However, he recovered his senses a year later when the orthodox Anastasius II took the throne and deposed the heretical usurper. He associated himself with a letter of apology and explanation that the patriarch sent to the pope.

Andrew resumed leadership of his archdiocese, where he won a reputation as a spellbinding preacher. Following, for example, is a selection from his Palm Sunday sermon. He began by exhorting his hearers to greet Christ with the words, "Hosanna! Blessed is he who comes in the name of the Lord!":

> Let us offer him our songs of praise, symbolizing palms, before his passion. Let us acclaim him not with olive branches but by honoring one another in charity. Let us strew the desires of our hearts like garments at his feet that he may direct his steps toward us and make his home in us. May he place us wholly in him, and himself wholly in us.
>
> Let us shout to Zion the words of the prophet: "Courage, daughter of Zion, fear not: Your king shall come to you humble and riding on an

> ass" (see Zechariah 9:9). He comes who is present everywhere and fills the universe. He comes who has "not come to invite the self-righteous to a change of heart, but sinners" to rescue them who are immersed in sin (see Luke 5:32).
>
> Therefore, do not fear, "God is in your midst, you shall not be disturbed" (see Psalm 46:6). Raising your hands, welcome him whose hands have designed your walls. Welcome him who has accepted in himself all that is ours, sin alone excepted, that he might take us with him. Rejoice, Mother, city of Zion, and fear not. Give glory to him who comes to you, for his mercy. Rejoice, greatly, daughter of Jerusalem, sing and dance with joy. With the trumpet of Isaiah we shout to you: "Rise up in splendor! Your light has come, the glory of the Lord shines upon you" (see Isaiah 60:1).

Some of Andrew's homilies appear in the Liturgy of the Hours. He also wrote a large number of hymns, some of which worshipers sing during the Byzantine Liturgy.

Andrew of Crete died in 740 on the island of Lesbos.

> *I may err, but I will never be a heretic.*
>
> —Augustine

JULY 4
Great Preachers; Jesus Christ; Repentance; Worship

146. Bede

(673–735)

St. Bede lived a routine and uneventful life. His long years in the monastery unfolded daily at praying the hours in church and studying Scripture in his cell. Yet from his remote spot on civilization's edge, with his scholarship he enriched his world and ours by helping to establish Christianity in the West.

His family entrusted seven-year-old Bede's education to **Benedict Biscop** at Wearmouth Abbey in northern England. Then he was placed under the tutelage of Ceolfrith at Jarrow, where he spent the rest of his life as a monk.

Bede regarded prayer as a discipline, but study, teaching, and writing as a delight. *I have worked*, he wrote, *both for my own benefit and that of my brethren, to compile short extracts from the works of the venerable fathers on Holy Scripture and to comment on their meaning and interpretation*. He wrote twenty-five commentaries on the Bible, always striving to uncover the spiritual meaning of the text. In the following passage he explained his method of interpretation:

> All scripture is interpreted in a fourfold way—historically, or allegorically, tropologically (morally) or anagogically.
>
> It is history when something is recorded clearly as it was literally said or done. For example, the people of Israel are reported to have made a tabernacle of the Lord in the wilderness.
>
> It is allegory when the presence of Christ or the sacraments are designated by mystical words or events. For example, when Isaiah says, "A shoot will spring from the stock of Jesse, a new shoot will grow from his roots" (11:1 *NJB*), he means the Virgin Mary shall be born of the root of David and Christ shall be born out of her stock.
>
> It is tropology when in either literal or figurative language, it appertains to moral instruction and correction. For example, as when John warns, "Let us not love in word or speech, but in deed and in truth" (1 John 3:18 *RSV*).
>
> It is anagogy, that is, a form of speech looking to higher things which discusses, plainly or mystically, future rewards and the future life of heaven. For example, plainly: "Blessed are the pure in heart: they shall see God" (Matthew 5:8 *NJB*). But in mystical words: "Blessed are those who will have washed their robes clean, so that they will have the right to feed on the tree of life" (Revelation 22:14 *NJB*), which means

> blessed are they who cleanse their thoughts and actions so that they may have the power to see the Lord Christ.

Without leaving his cell, Bede exerted a wide missionary influence. His teaching equipped Anglo-Saxon monks and nuns to carry the Christian faith to the people of England and Germany. Today we still read with profit his Bible commentaries, but we value even more his *History of the English Church and People.*

Bede fell ill before Easter in 735, but continued to teach his brothers and complete his translation of John. On Tuesday after the Ascension he gathered his brothers around him to bid farewell. The young man who served as his scribe announced that his last book was finished. The lad helped Bede sit on the floor facing the place where he had always prayed and the saint died singing the doxology. "The candle of the church," wrote **St. Boniface**, "lit by the Holy Spirit, was extinguished."

> *I pray you, noble Jesus, that as you have graciously granted me joyfully to imbibe the words of your knowledge, so you will also of your bounty grant me to come at length to yourself, the fount of all wisdom, and to dwell in your presence forever.*
>
> —Venerable Bede

MAY 25

Doctors of the Church; Saints and the Bible; Study; World Historical Saints

147. John Damascene
(675?–749?)

Think of St. John Damascene as a Greek forerunner of **St. Thomas Aquinas**. Like him, John studied Aristotle, wrote a renowned summary of theology, and composed hymns that are still sung today.

John inherited his father's post as chief financial officer for the caliphs of Damascus, serving in that position until 716. Then he became a monk at Mar Saba, the monastery of **St. Sabas** near Jerusalem, where he was also ordained a priest. The Iconoclast heresy reached its height just after John entered Mar Saba. Championed by the Byzantine emperors, Iconoclasts denounced the veneration of images. John wrote three treatises against the heresy that were widely circulated. They won him the reputation as Iconoclasm's main opponent. The following selection presents his view:

> Since some criticize us for honoring images of our Savior, our Lady and other saints, let them remember that in the beginning God created us after his own image. On what grounds then do we show reverence to each other unless because we are made after God's image? For as St. Basil says, the honor given to the image passes over to the prototype. Now a prototype is the original from which the derivative is obtained. Didn't the people of Israel prostrate themselves before the tabernacle that bore the image of heavenly things? Didn't God himself direct Moses to make those images exactly according to the pattern revealed to him on the mountain?
>
> The use of images was not common in the Old Testament because it is foolish to try to give a form to the invisible God. But when God became man for our salvation, many people saw the things that he did. He lived among us, worked miracles, suffered, was crucified, rose again and was taken back to heaven. These things were written down for the instruction of us who were not yet alive, so that by hearing and believing, we might still obtain the Lord's blessing. But for the sake of those who were illiterate, the Fathers permitted the depiction of these events in images as concise memorials. Thus when we see the crucifix, we remember Christ's saving passion. We fall down to worship not the piece of wood, but the One who is imaged, Christ crucified.

John's influential arguments enraged the emperors. But, ironically, they could not harm him because he lived in Muslim territory.

At Mar Saba, John Damascene also wrote a major theological work, *On the Orthodox Faith.* His "summa theologica," however, made no pretense of originality, but presented a summary of the teachings of the Greek fathers. In addition to treating principal Christian doctrines such as the Trinity and the Incarnation, he touched notably on topics such as the Real Presence, the Assumption of Mary, and the Immaculate Conception. John also wrote hymns that his spiritual director sometimes regarded as a distraction from his spiritual discipline. Once the older monk was so displeased with John's hymnody that he made him pick up the filth from the monastery grounds with bare hands. But he soon relented, saying that Mary had appeared and directed him to give John free reign to write anything he wanted.

John Damascene, the last of the Greek fathers of the church, died in 749.

Come, and let us drink of that New River,
Not from barren rock divinely poured,
But the Fount of Life that is forever
From the Sepulcher of Christ the Lord.
Yesterday with Thee in burial lying,
Now today with Thee aris'n I rise;
Yesterday the partner of Thy dying,
With Thyself upraise me to the skies.

—John Damascene

DECEMBER 4
Defending the Faith; Mary; Poets

148. Fridiswede

(680?–727)

From the Middle Ages, St. Fridiswede has been honored as the patron of Oxford University. An elaborate legend says that she fled to Oxford to protect her virginity from an amorous young king who desperately wanted to marry her. In the early twelfth century William of Malmesbury wrote about Fridiswede's flight and how she came to found a convent at Oxford:

> In ancient times there was in the town of Oxford a convent of nuns in which the most holy virgin Fridiswede lived.
>
> She, the daughter of a king, despised marriage with a king, consecrating her virginity to the Lord Christ. But the young king had determined to marry the virgin. When he found all his proposals and flatteries of no avail, he decided to resort to force.
>
> When Fridiswede discovered this she fled into the woods. However, she could not keep her hiding-place a secret from her would-be lover. And the king did not lack the courage to pursue her.
>
> Hearing about the young man's renewed passion, the virgin, with God's help, traveled at night through obscure paths to Oxford. The next morning her anxious lover also hurried there. Then Fridiswede despaired of finding safety in flight. And she was too weary to run any further. So she invoked the aid of God for herself and punishment for her persecutor. As the young king and his companions approached the gates of the city, the hand of heaven suddenly struck him blind. Later he admitted the fault of his obstinacy and sent messengers to beg Fridiswede to relent. Then he received back his sight as suddenly as he had lost it. Thus a dread has arisen amongst all the kings of England which has made them wary of going to that city because it is said to be fraught with destruction. Every one of the kings has declined to test the truth for himself by incurring the danger.
>
> In that place, where the maiden gained the triumph of her virginity, she established a convent. And when her days were over and her Spouse called her, she died there.

Historians have clarified some of the facts behind St. Fridiswede's legend. In the late seventh century, her father, Dida of Enysham, ruled as king over the territory west of Oxfordshire. He endowed monastery churches at Enysham, Bampton, and Oxford. And Fridiswede was chosen as the first abbess of the double monastery at Oxford, a community including both men and women. The convent rested on what is now the site of Christ's Church, and the city of Oxford grew up around it.

In the fifteenth century Oxford University officially adopted Fridiswede as its patron saint. Twice a year, once in Lent and again at the Ascension, the chancellor and other members of the university conducted ceremonies at her shrine.

During the volatile period of the Reformation in England, Fridiswede's buildings were destroyed. But the discovery of building fragments in a well at Christ's Church has allowed a partial reconstruction of her shrine. And as they did in ancient times, pilgrims today come to Fridiswede's burial place looking for a blessing.

A pure soul is like a fine pearl. As long as it is hidden in the shell at the bottom of the sea, no one thinks of admiring it. But if you bring it into the sunlight, this pearl will shine and attract all eyes. Thus, the pure soul that is hidden from the eyes of the world, will one day shine before the angels in the sublime sunlight of eternity.

—John Vianney

OCTOBER 19
Lights in the "Dark Ages"; Passion for Purity; Valiant Women

149. Boniface
(680?–754)

St. Boniface was the **St. Paul** of the Dark Ages, a blazing light in that badly misnamed epoch. In thirty-five years this English missionary established the church in Germany and revived it in the kingdom of the Franks, the medieval ancestor of France.

Boniface, who was baptized Winfred, became a monk in his youth and was ordained a priest at age thirty. He was renowned among the Anglo-Saxons for his Latin scholarship and Bible-based preaching and teaching. The saint made friends easily, using his exceptional personal magnetism to win others to Christ's service. Had we been alive at the time, he may very well have captured our hearts and put us to work in his missions.

In 715, Winfred recognized a divine call to spread the gospel in Germany, a mission which he pursued strategically. Three years later, Pope Gregory II commissioned him to evangelize in Germany and also changed his name to Boniface. The saint's first mission in Hesse was so successful that in 722 the pope made him a bishop with jurisdiction over Germany. He also persuaded Charles Martel, the leader of the Franks, to give protection to Boniface.

Armed with the authority of church and state, Boniface continued his work in Hesse. He established his authority with a bold frontal attack on local paganism. Willibald, his first biographer, tells the story:

> At Geismar, surrounded by his companions, the saint decided to fell a gigantic oak, revered by the pagans as Jupiter's Oak. A big crowd of pagans watched him cut the lower notch, cursing him in their hearts as an enemy of the gods. But when Boniface had scarcely chipped the front of the sacred tree, a divine blast from above crashed it to the ground with its crown of branches shivering as it fell. And as if by the gracious dispensation of the Most High, the oak also burst into four equal parts. The bystanders could see four huge trunks, uniform in length, that had not been cut by Boniface or his associates. At this sight the pagans who had been cursing the saint, now, on the contrary, believed. They blessed the Lord and stopped their reviling. Then after consulting his companions, the holy bishop used the timber of the tree to construct an oratory there, which he dedicated to St. Peter, the apostle.

That dramatic event gave Boniface momentum. He moved systematically to establish the church in Germany and renew it in France. He founded monasteries throughout Germany that became centers of education and evangelization. He staffed them with his Anglo-Saxon friends, who eagerly responded in unprecedented numbers to his invitation to serve. After 731, he founded dioceses throughout Germany, appointing his Anglo-Saxon companions as bishops. Later, supported by the Frankish kings, he called councils to reform the decadent church in their kingdom. In 747 the pope appointed Boniface the archbishop of all Germany and located his see at Mainz.

Boniface "retired" in 753 but did not stop working. He went to Friesland to recover lapsed Christians and win new converts. On Pentecost eve, 754, as he was preparing for an open-air confirmation ceremony, a band of marauders martyred him and his companions.

With heroic fortitude, doggedness, and vision, St. Boniface changed his world. His strategic establishment of the church throughout Germany and France created the first European unity, the basis for western civilization, and the forerunner of the European Economic Community. My sights are somewhat lower. Maybe with a little fortitude, doggedness, and vision, I can influence my family, friends, and neighbors for Christ.

JUNE 5 / PATRON OF ENGLAND
Lights in the "Dark Ages"; Missionaries; Spiritual Warfare; World Historical Saints

150. Leoba
(D. 779)

The last thing we might expect to find in the "Dark Ages" is an educated and holy woman who was a world-renowned leader in the church. But such was Leoba, an Anglo-Saxon missionary, scholar, abbess, counselor to monks and bishops, confidant of kings and queens—and a saint.

Aebba, St. Leoba's mother, dreamt that her womb bore a church bell which, when delivered, chimed merrily. So when her daughter Thrutgeba was born, she dedicated the baby to serve Christ. She nicknamed the girl "Leoba," which means "beloved." At age seven, Leoba was sent to the monastery at Wimbourne, where two other outstanding women, Tetta and Eadburga, taught her the liberal arts and Scripture.

Rudolf, Leoba's biographer, reported that once she had a dream that revealed her vocation:

> She had a dream in which one night she saw a purple thread issuing from her mouth. It seemed to her that when she took hold of it with her hand and tried to draw it out there was no end to it. And as if it were coming from her very bowels, it extended little by little until it was of enormous length. When her hand was full of thread and it still issued from her mouth, she rolled it round and round and made a ball of it.

An elderly nun at Wimbourne with a prophetic gift explained that the dream announced Leoba's great work:

> By her teaching and good example she will confer benefits on many people. The thread coming from her mouth signifies the wise counsels that she will speak from the heart. The fact that it filled her hand means that she will carry out in her actions whatever she expresses in her words. Furthermore, the ball which she made by rolling it round and round signifies the mystery of the divine teaching. It is set in motion by the words and deeds of those who give instruction. And it turns earthwards through active works and heavenwards through contemplation, at one time swinging downwards through compassion for one's neighbor, again swinging upwards through the love of God. By these signs God shows that she will profit many by her words and example,

and the effect of them will be felt in other lands afar off wherever she will go.

The dream came to be when **St. Boniface,** a cousin of Leoba, invited her to assist his church-planting work in Germany. He wanted Leoba to care for women in his communities. So around 733, Leoba left Wimbourne and Boniface made her the abbess at Bishofscheim, where she led hundreds of nuns.

At the monastery, Leoba trained many young women in both secular and Christian studies. She herself became an accomplished scholar of Scripture, the fathers, and canon law. St. Boniface arranged for her to be an adviser to the elders at Fulda, the main center of his work. And Charlemagne and Hiltigard, king and queen of the Franks, sought her advice.

Thus, for nearly four decades Leoba served the infant church in Germany. She died at Bishofscheim in 779.

Dreams with divine messages startled both Leoba and her mother. God seems to have worked in their imaginations to orient them for his service. I doubt that these women were focused on their dreams, recording them dutifully and hoping to find their life's direction in them. More likely, they kept their lives, minds, and spiritual ears open to God, and he spoke to them. Their example is a good one for anyone who longs for guidance from God.

SEPTEMBER 28
Dreams; Leading Women; Lights in the "Dark Ages"; Study

151. Sturm
(D. 779?)

As a boy, Sturm caught the eye of **St. Boniface,** who recognized his gifts. Perhaps Boniface foresaw that the lad would grow up to become his chief collaborator in his mission to Germany. He took Sturm under his care and had him trained at the abbey of Fritzlar.

Boniface planned to have St. Sturm establish a monastic base from which he could evangelize the Saxons. So after his ordination, Sturm spent three years on mission in Westphalia. Then Boniface had him set up a hermitage at Hersfeld. But after a short time marauding Saxons forced him to abandon it.

However, in 744, under Boniface's supervision, Sturm founded the monastery at Fulda in central Germany and became its first abbot. Now Boniface had the base he desired as the engine for his German mission. Under Sturm's leadership, Fulda would become the model monastery and the seminary for all Germany.

Sturm and Boniface wanted to plant Fulda securely in the tradition of **St. Benedict**. So, as Sturm's biographer tells it, a plan evolved to send observers to Monte Cassino, the source of Benedictine monasticism:

> The brothers had a burning desire to follow the rule of the holy father Saint Benedict. And they strove to conform their ideas and actions to the discipline of the monastic life. Thus, they formed a plan to send some of their members to well-established monasteries in other places so that they could become informed about their customs and observances. Bishop Boniface heartily approved of the scheme and he commanded Sturm to undertake the experiment himself. When all the necessary preparations were made for the journey, two other brothers were chosen to accompany him. And so, four years after the foundation of the monastery, Sturm set out for Rome. There he visited all the monasteries, spending a whole year inquiring into the customs, observances, and traditions of the brothers who lived in them. In the following year, spiritually strengthened by the holiness he had met, he returned home.
>
> And he set out to visit Bishop Boniface. On seeing him the bishop was greatly pleased. Thanking God for his safe return, he interrogated Sturm about the places he had seen. When he noticed how shrewdly Sturm had investigated the manners of the people and the monks' observances, he said: "Go back to Fulda and as far as possible establish

> monastic discipline on the pattern of the monks you observed." Sturm begged the bishop's blessing. He set off immediately to his solitude and reached it after four days, full of joy at seeing his brothers once again.

Fulda flourished under Sturm's direction, but not without serious controversy with St. Lull, the local bishop. For several years he engaged Sturm in a bitter struggle over control of the monastery. In 763, Lull got the king to expel Sturm from Fulda. However, Sturm returned when one of his disciples became abbot and persuaded the king to reverse his decision.

Sturm's mission to the Saxons was only partially successful. The Frankish wars against them poisoned the opportunity for evangelism. The Saxons resisted conversion because they felt that their enemies were forcing Christ's message on them. In 779 the Saxons drove the monks from the monastery. But Charlemagne, the Frankish king, soon restored them. However, Sturm did not live to resume his work. He died on December 17, 779.

Sturm and Boniface developed strategies for evangelization that we should consider for the church today. Early identification of gifted youths, mentoring and training, field experience, developing educational centers as bases for outreach—such things could make a significant difference in proclaiming the gospel.

DECEMBER 17 / CANONIZED IN 1139
Evangelization; Lights in the "Dark Ages"; Missionaries

152. Alcuin

(730?–804)

In the last half of the eighth century, Charlemagne presided over a revival of learning in the Frankish empire. Alcuin of York, a scholar saint, was largely responsible for generating this cultural renewal now called the Carolingian Renaissance. In 767, Alcuin became the rector of the minster school at York, where he had studied. An innovative educator, he improved the school, made its library one of England's best, and attracted outstanding students.

Charlemagne brought Alcuin to Aachen in 781 and appointed him as his ecclesiastical and educational adviser. Later, even though Alcuin was not a priest and probably was not a monk, Charlemagne installed him as the abbot of the monastery of St. Martin at Tours. As head of the palace school, Alcuin elevated the culture at court and sponsored educational enterprises throughout the realm. And under his guidance the abbey at Tours became famous as a center of learning. Most renowned among his many students was **Venantius Fortunatus.**

Alcuin also won his reputation as a theologian and liturgist. He wrote and spoke against the Adoptionists, heretics who claimed that Jesus was God's adopted son. And Alcuin conducted a liturgical reform that left its mark on the Roman style of worship. He revised the Roman lectionary, the book of readings used in worship, and put together a new sacramentary, the book of formulas for baptism and other sacraments. He also wrote verse, textbooks, and innumerable letters. As adviser to Charlemagne, he played a special role in the education of the royal family. As the following letter to one of Charlemagne's sons shows, he held his heirs to a high Christian ideal:

> I rejoice my dearest son, in your devoted good will regarding both your generous almsgiving and your gentle rule. All this surely pleases God and deserves the mercy of his perpetual blessing. Always work to the utmost for the honor of God Almighty. In goodness and piety, follow the example of your most excellent father so that by Christ's divine clemency you may inherit his blessing.
>
> Listen faithfully to the poor and judge their cause with absolute justice. Do not permit the judges under you to judge for presents and gifts. For Holy Scripture says gifts blind the hearts of the wise and subvert the words of the just. Hold in honor those who are true servants

> of God, for some come in sheep's clothing but inwardly are ravening wolves. The Truth says that by their fruits shall you know them. Have as counselors wise men, who fear God. Not flatterers, for a flatterer is a bland enemy and often seduces those who consent to him. Be prudent in thought and cautious in speech. Always set your hope on God, for he never fails them whose hope is set on him.
>
> My greatest joy is hearing about a good manner of life on your part. For God prospers a kingdom where the rulers of a Christian people live most strict lives, and conduct their relationships among men in a way pleasing to him. Thus a blessing from heaven is certain to come on the nation and kingdom.

For his vast efforts as an educational reformer, history recognizes Alcuin as "the schoolmaster of Europe." He died at the abbey of Tours in 804.

Holy Scripture is the table of Christ,
from whence we are nourished,
from whence we learn what we should love
and what we should desire,
to whom
we should have our eyes raised.

—Alcuin

MAY 19
Innovative Saints; Saints and the Bible

153. Benedict of Aniane

(751–821)

Next to **St. Benedict** himself, St. Benedict of Aniane influenced the shape of Benedictine monasticism in the West more than anyone else. Allied with Holy Roman emperors Charlemagne and Louis the Pious, he promulgated a strict and idealistic monastic reform that lasted nearly two centuries. And Benedict's work influenced later reforms, including the Cluniac Reform movement of the eleventh and twelfth centuries.

Of noble Visigothic descent, Benedict first served as a cupbearer in the Frankish court. But at age twenty he resolved to live for God alone and became a monk at an abbey near Dijon. When the monks wanted to make him abbot, he left because he felt that they would not accept the severe pattern of life he had adopted. So he returned to his own estate on the river Aniane in Languedoc, where he built a small hermitage. Later he built a monastery from which he exercised influence over many other abbeys in France and Germany that he had reformed. Eventually Benedict became the overseer of all the monasteries in the Frankish empire.

Louis the Pious compelled Benedict to build a monastery at Inde, Belgium, near the court at Aachen. Then Louis had Benedict generate a monastic reform throughout the empire. Benedict presided at councils that reinforced discipline, he codified all extant monastic regulations, and he worked with other abbots to improve monastic observance. He standardized monastic practice on the pattern of Inde. Benedict aimed to have monks "pass from faith to sight" through prayer, study, meditation, and reading. He believed that as their understanding increased, they would grow into a contemplative love for God.

Benedict of Aniane died in 821. He never achieved the uniformity he intended because it depended on the unity of an empire that soon disintegrated. But he did elevate the idealism and observance of western monasticism. Benedict of Aniane's impact was more structural than inspirational, but as his biographer indicated in the following passage, his spirituality touched his brothers profoundly:

Benedict had great concern not only to refresh his own people with food of preaching, but also to nourish with heavenly bread whomever he happened to encounter. That they might not lose the salutary food through forgetfulness, he was accustomed to impress upon them to cling tenaciously to it in their hearts. This he did with such words as, "Let it be with chaste body and humble heart, because proud chastity and vain humility are not acceptable to God." On some he was in the habit of stressing this, "If most precepts are impossible for you to remember, keep at least this short one, 'Depart from evil and do good.'" (See Psalm 37:27). That sentence was so habitual to him that near the time of his death, when he had assembled statements from all the Fathers, he proposed to produce one book about it alone. At every hour, whether at nocturn, in chapter or in refectory, he provided the food of life for all those subject to him.

Benedict possessed an unusual gift: as soon as anyone with disturbed thoughts in his mind approached him, the tumultuous crowd of thoughts dissipated at his wholesome counsel. Often indeed when bombarded by unsafe thoughts . . . a person would say to himself, "I will go and reveal you to Lord Benedict." At that very moment the unsuitable confusion left him. If anyone was hindered by severer faults, he received soothing consolation when he opened up his heart to Benedict.

FEBRUARY 12
Catholic Reformers; Leading Men; Pursuit of Holiness

154. Theodore the Studite
(759–826)

Never has anyone been nearer to God than the blessed and most wonderful Virgin Mary. Who could be purer? Who more sinless? She was loved so ardently by God, the divine, infinitely pure light, that he made himself one in substance with her through the power of the Holy Spirit. He was born of her as perfect man, while keeping entire his own unchangeable and unblended nature. How marvelous this is! In his immense love for us, God was not ashamed to take for his mother her who was his handmaid. What condescension! In his infinite goodness he did not hesitate to become a child of her whom he himself had made. He was truly in love with the most gracious of his creatures and he took her who was of greater worth than the heavenly powers.

Rejoice, House of God, land on which God has stepped, you who have contained in your body him whose divinity overflows all bounds. From you he who is simplicity itself has taken our complex nature. The Eternal has entered into time and the Infinite into limits. Rejoice, House of God, resplendent with the light of divinity. Rejoice, Full of Grace, your deed and your name are more joy-giving than all joy. From you immortal joy, Christ, has come into the world, the cure for the sadness of us all. Rejoice, paradise happier than the garden of Eden, where all virtue has grown and where the tree of life has flourished.

—Theodore the Studite

The eastern church reveres Theodore as one of its greatest saints. He is called the "Studite" because he headed the monastery of Studion at Constantinople. As a model of courage and meekness, St. Theodore's life speaks relevantly to twenty-first-century western Christians. He took zealous public stands for what he knew was right and patiently bore the consequences. For example, twice Theodore suffered exile because he denounced the adulterous marriage of Emperor Constantine VI. In 799, Theodore became the abbot at Studion, which had fallen into spiritual and material disrepair. He introduced a reform based on the rule of St. Basil. Theodore required a healthy moderation in ascetical practices. "Don't cultivate a self-centered austerity," he once told a monk. "Eat bread, drink wine occasionally, wear shoes, especially in winter, and take meat when you need it." His gentle leadership increased the abbey's population from twelve to more than a thousand within a few years. And his influence spread to Mt. Athos and from there to Bulgaria, Serbia, and Russia. Thus, like Benedict in the West, Theodore set a pattern for monasticism throughout the East.

Theodore's preaching gift helps explain his effectiveness and popularity. The inspiring tone of the homily quoted above illustrates his power as a speaker.

During the Iconoclastic controversy, Theodore defended the orthodox view. The Iconoclasts outlawed the veneration of all images. Theodore fiercely opposed the heresy because he believed icons both helped many ordinary Christians understand the faith and drew them to God. He wrote and spoke against the Iconoclasts and paid the price of imprisonment and exile. Even after the Emperor Michael II pacified the controversy, Theodore was not restored to Studion because he refused to accept the emperor's conditions for his return. He died on November 11, 826, at a little monastery on the Akrita Peninsula.

> *Costly grace is the treasure hidden in the field. For the sake of it a man will gladly go and sell all that he has. It is costly because it costs a man his life, and it is grace because it gives a man the only true life.*
>
> —Dietrich Bonhoeffer

NOVEMBER 11
The Cost of Discipleship; Courage; Leading Men; Mary

155. Rabanus Maurus

(C. 776–856)

Come, Creator, Spirit, come
from your bright heavenly throne,
come take possession of our souls,
and make them all your own.

You who are called the Paraclete,
best gift of God above,
the living spring, the vital fire
sweet christ'ning and true love. . . .

O guide our minds with your best light,
with love our hearts inflame;
and with your strength, which ne'er decays,
confirm our mortal frame.

Far from us drive our deadly foe;
true peace unto us bring;
and through all perils lead us safe
beneath your sacred wing.

Through you may we the Father know,
through you th'eternal Son
and you the Spirit of them both,
thrice-blessed Three in One. . . .

—Rabanus Maurus

St. Rabanus Maurus had three careers. He was a schoolmaster, then an abbot, and finally an archbishop. He lived during the reign of Charlemagne when Christianity was being established in Europe. We are indebted to Rabanus and saints like him, for they built the church from which most of us received our gift of faith.

Rabanus was a scholar saint. He was a lifelong student of Scripture, the great Christian writers, and Catholic teaching. He used his mind to explore the faith, and his study drew him closer to Christ. We should take him for a model, for study is essential to our Christian growth.

Young Rabanus was sent to school at Fulda in central Germany, the chief monastery founded by **St. Boniface**. Rabanus astounded his teachers with his quickness to learn. He also spent a year studying at Tours with **Alcuin**, Charlemagne's adviser. Rabanus learned Greek, Hebrew, and Syriac so that he could better understand Scripture. He also read the church Fathers and wrote summaries of their works.

In 799 he was ordained deacon and in 815 became a priest. Sometime during that period he was appointed master of Fulda's school. In that office he had the opportunity to form young monks who would help create a tradition of Christian learning in the West.

Rabanus became the abbot at Fulda in 822. During this, his second career, he probably wrote most of his works, including a martyrology and numerous commentaries on Scripture. He was in constant demand as an expert at synods and councils. However, care for the monks caused him to hone his pastoral and administrative gifts. He completed Fulda's buildings and founded other monasteries.

After a brief retirement, Rabanus unexpectedly took up a third career. In 847, at age seventy-one, he was appointed archbishop of Mainz. He undertook the job aggressively. With a team of priests, Rabanus went about the diocese teaching, preaching, and administering the sacraments. He held synods that called Christians to a stricter observance of church laws and that condemned a local heresy. Once during a famine he fed three hundred people a day from his house. With great energy he led the diocese and continued his writing until his death in 856.

Special among Rabanus's gifts to the church is the Veni, Creator Spiritus. Monks carried the hymn to communities throughout the continent and it became part of the Pentecost liturgy. Praying the Come, Creator Spirit seems to have occasioned life-changing moments for numerous saints, including ***Lutgarde****, Clare, and* ***Teresa of Ávila****. Apparently, Rabanus's hymn is extraordinarily effective in releasing the gifts of the Spirit, so when we pray it we can expect God to act.*

FEBRUARY 4
Faith Seeking Understanding; Lights in the "Dark Ages"; Poets

156. Flora
(D. 851)

St. Flora was raised in Cordoba, Spain, by a Christian mother in a Muslim household. After her father died, her mother formed her in the faith. But her older brother, a totally committed follower of Mohammed, forced her to go through the motions of practicing Islam.

One day, however, Flora slipped away from home and sought to live as a Christian. Her influential brother had her priest friends arrested and punished. Because she saw that her flight had caused suffering in the church, she came out of hiding and boldly confronted her brother. She said:

> "I know how eagerly you seek me and how keen you are about it. Well, now you have me! I come, like a good Christian, armed with the sign of the cross. Now, tear this faith from me, separate me from Christ if you can. I think it will be very difficult, for I am ready to suffer every torture for him. I speak strongly—do I not? Well, during martyrdom, I shall speak more strongly."

Hoping to compel her to change her mind, her brother accused her before the cadi. He said:

> "Judge, this is my youngest sister who always practiced our holy religion with me. But the Christians have perverted her, making her hate our prophet and believe that Christ is God."

The judge turned to Flora and asked:

> "Does your brother tell the truth?" And she replied, "Do you call that wicked man my brother? Everything he said was a lie. I have never been a Muslim. From my infancy I have known none but Christ. He is my God and I have consecrated myself to him as his bride."

The judge decided that severe punishment would correct such an intelligent young woman. So he had her scourged until she fainted under the blows. Then he turned her over to her brother, charging him to make her into a good Muslim.

However, soon Flora escaped again and withdrew to a town in the mountains. There one day in church she met a woman named Mary, whose younger brother had recently been martyred in Cordoba. Together they decided to give themselves up as martyrs and presented themselves to the cadi. Flora said:

> "I was ill-treated some time ago in the most cruel manner by the Muslims because I refused to renounce Christ. Since then I have been weak enough to hide myself. But today, full of confidence in my God, I am not afraid to come forward to declare, as resolutely as before, that Christ is God. . . ."

When the judge threatened to sell both Flora and Mary as prostitutes, they considered backing down. **St. Eulogius,** himself in prison, heard of their temptation and wrote Flora an encouraging letter. Even if their bodies were violated, he said, their souls would remain pure. So the two women gathered their strength and endured shameful suffering in a brothel until their captors finally beheaded them. They promised that in heaven they would pray for the release of all the other prisoners. And a week after Flora and Mary died, those prisoners were freed.

Eulogius wrote a celebratory piece about the martyrdom of Flora, his spiritual daughter. He frankly described her weakness and fears that almost caused her to compromise her faith in order to avoid shame and death. I appreciate his report because it showed that Flora was cut from the same human cloth of which I am made. Her superior faith did not eradicate her natural fear. She wavered and trembled on her way to glory.

NOVEMBER 24
Courage; Martyrs

157. Eulogius of Cordoba

(D. 859)

St. Eulogius's friend and biographer Paul Alvarez affectionately described him as gentle, reverent, well educated, steeped in Scripture, and so humble that he freely submitted to opinions of others less informed than he. He said that Eulogius had a pleasant demeanor and conducted his relationships with such kindness that everyone regarded him as a friend. A gifted leader, the most prominent among his charisms was the ability to give encouragement. As a priest serving in an occupied country, he used this gift to strengthen his friends in the face of danger.

In the ninth century, the Muslim conquerors of Spain made Cordoba their capital. They allowed Christians to live in relative peace and, subject to a monthly tax, permitted them to worship. Some, like Eulogius's younger brother, even rose to high positions in the government.

However, in 850 the Muslims began to persecute Christians because some had spoken against Mohammed and converted Muslims to Christianity. They imprisoned the bishop and priests of Cordoba, including Eulogius. In jail, the saint read the Bible to his companions, exhorting them to faithfulness. He wrote to **Flora** and Mary, two young women who were threatened because they were converts. In the letter quoted below, he assured them that nothing done to their bodies could harm their souls:

> They threaten to sell you as slaves and dishonor you, but be assured that they cannot injure the purity of your souls, whatever infamy they may inflict on you. Cowardly Christians will tell you, in order to shake your constancy, that the churches are silent, deserted, and deprived of the sacrifice on account of your obstinacy: that if you will but yield temporarily you will regain the free exercise of your religion. But be persuaded that, for you, the sacrifice most pleasing to God is contrition of heart, and that you can no longer draw back or renounce the truth you have confessed.
>
> You spoke against Mohammed, and you spoke well. . . . If you were to deny it now, you would commit a double sin. But such a thing is not possible. You are caught in the net. Do not be one of the worthless fish that the apostle throws back into the sea, but be reserved for the heavenly banquet. . . . You must fight till death and leave God to defend

his church: you must fight till death because in such a struggle as this victory is won by death alone.

The maidens faced death courageously. Shortly after their martyrdom the Muslims released the other captives. But in 852 things heated up again and martyrdoms resumed. In 859, Eulogius himself was arrested because he had protected and hidden Leocritia, a young convert. He was charged before a judge, who offered to let him off if he would soften his views. But Eulogius began to proclaim the Gospel to the court, so to silence him the judge hastily condemned him to death. He was taken out and beheaded on the spot.

During this persecution, Eulogius wrote the following to instill hope in his fellow Christians:

You, brothers and holy sisters, leap for joy, for you have sent to God's granary the sheaves of your harvest. The fruit from your seed is in the blessed city of Zion. The heavenly Jerusalem has already peacefully received your triumphant brethren. Travel in safety, hasten on. No one will obstruct your path. When you reach your fatherland, there will go forth to meet you not only this phalanx of the blessed, but all the multitude of the elect as well, among whom will be these brothers of ours, the first fruits of martyrdom.

MARCH 11
Eternal Perspective; Martyrs; Pursuit of Holiness

158. Nicholas I

(820?–867)

"God has raised up a second Elijah!" declared one observer of Pope Nicholas I. "He gave orders to kings and rulers as though he were lord of the world. To good bishops and priests, to religious laypeople, he was kind, gentle and modest. To evildoers, he was terrible and stern." History has affirmed this assessment by naming St. Nicholas "the Great."

Noticed for his gifts as a young man, Nicholas served for eleven years in the administration of two popes. Then in 858, at age thirty-six, he was elected pope, an office he filled with great energy and integrity. Nicholas strengthened the papacy by steadfastly asserting the rights of the church against the state. Listen as he explains the separation of the ecclesiastical and secular powers:

> Just as he on whom is laid the charge of worldly government should keep carefully aloof from sacred matters, so should clerics, who belong to the divine army, keep themselves free from entanglement in civic affairs. And how can he whose privilege it is to be at the head of human interests presume to judge the ministers of things divine?
>
> Christ Jesus, the mediator between God and men, desired to separate the offices of the two powers. So he designated specific acts and distinct dignities appropriate to each. He desired that, steeped in the medicine of his own humility, they might rise up without risk of falling again into the depths because of pride. This is why Christian emperors need pontiffs in order to obtain eternal life. And pontiffs, in their turn—but in the conduct of temporal matters only—need to have recourse to the imperial laws. This necessary line of demarcation safeguards the spiritual domain from exposure to the incursions of the flesh.
>
> Let him, therefore, who is of the army of God, entangle himself very little in secular business. And let not him who is already so entangled be seen presiding over divine matters. If each is careful to keep modestly his own order and neither vaunts himself over the other, both will be able by the quality of their actions to fulfill his special commission.

In practice, Nicholas had to work hard to assert the papal primacy. He had to deal with nobles who had usurped the right to appoint bishops, and young, and often corrupt, bishops who abused their power. He repeatedly disciplined two recalcitrant archbishops,

Hincmar of Rheims and John of Ravenna, until they finally accepted his authority.

Nicholas stood up to strong rulers in defense of the indissolubility and freedom of marriage. For example, he reversed the decision of the Frankish bishops to approve the divorce of King Lothair II of Lorraine. He also defended the freedom of Judith, daughter of King Charles the Bald of France, to marry without her father's consent.

All during his nine-year reign, Nicholas struggled to maintain papal primacy in the East. The emperor had deposed Ignatius, the patriarch of Constantinople, and replaced him with Photius, a layman. In the ensuing ecclesiastical dogfight, Nicholas asserted his authority but failed to subordinate the church of the East to Rome. The conflict continued after his death and contributed significantly to the division of the church into eastern and western communities.

In 867, Nicholas became so painfully ill that he could not even dictate replies to letters. He died in Rome on November 13.

Involvement in ecclesiastical politics did not distract Nicholas from the care of his own flock. For example, he had a list drawn up of the disabled poor of Rome and saw to it that each was fed daily.

NOVEMBER 13
Saints and Politics; World Historical Saints

159. Cyril and Methodius

(826–869) and (815?–884)

We honor the brother team of St. Cyril and St. Methodius for introducing Christianity into eastern Europe, translating the Bible into the Slavic language, pioneering the celebration of the liturgy in the vernacular, and founding Slavonic literature. So the church has named them the Apostles of the Slavs and, with **Benedict,** the patron saints of Europe.

Cyril (baptized as Constantine and not called Cyril until just before his death) and Methodius were ordained priests in Thessalonica and then moved to Constantinople. Around 863, the emperor sent them as missionaries to Moravia. Rotislav, the local ruler, wanted them to teach in the vernacular, which the brothers were well equipped to do as they had learned Slavonic as boys. With great enthusiasm, Cyril and Methodius plunged into the work, translating some of the Bible and the liturgy into Slavonic. In the process they created an alphabet, later developed into the Cyrillic alphabet, which laid the foundations for all Slav literature.

When German missionary bishops refused to ordain their candidates, Cyril and Methodius headed toward Byzantium for help. But when they reached Venice, the pope summoned them to Rome. They presented him with the alleged relics of **St. Clement I**, and he received the brothers with great honor. However, after becoming a monk, Cyril died in Rome in 869. In the following passage, his biographer reconstructed his last moments, including his celebrated prayer for Christian unity:

> When the time came for him to set out from this world to the peace of his heavenly homeland, he prayed to God with his hands outstretched and his eyes filled with tears: "O Lord, my God, you have created the choirs of angels and spiritual powers; you have stretched forth the heavens and established the earth, creating all that exists from nothing. You hear those who obey your will and keep your commands in holy fear. Hear my prayer and protect your faithful people, for you have established me as their unsuitable and unworthy servant.
>
> "Keep them free from harm and worldly cunning of those who blaspheme you. Build up your Church and gather all into unity. Make your people known for the unity and profession of their faith. Inspire

the hearts of your people with your word and your teaching. You called us to preach the Gospel of your Christ and to encourage them to lives and works pleasing to you.

"I now return to you, your people, your gift to me. Direct them with your powerful right hand, and protect them under the shadow of your wings. May all praise and glorify your name, the Father, Son and Holy Spirit. Amen."

Once he had exchanged the gift of peace with everyone, he said: "Blessed be God, who did not hand us over to our invisible enemy, but freed us from his snare and delivered us from perdition." Then he fell asleep in the Lord at the age of forty-two.

The pope consecrated Methodius the archbishop of Sirmium, empowering him to build a native Slavonic clergy. He returned to Moravia where he labored for sixteen years, opposed at every turn by his German counterparts. He had to fight to maintain the vernacular liturgy, but won his battle in 880 with the support of the pope. And before his death in 884, Methodius had translated almost the entire Bible into Slavonic.

Like Cyril and Methodius, who made the gospel understandable by putting it in the vernacular, today we must find ways of translating the gospel, already in our vernacular, into language that our friends can understand.

FEBRUARY 14 / PATRONS OF EUROPE AND CHRISTIAN UNITY
Christian Unity; Evangelization; Missionaries; World Historical Saints

160. Odo of Cluny
(879–942)

When Odo, a cleric at Tours, read *The Rule of St. Benedict*, he was stunned. Judging that his Christian life did not measure up to **Benedict**'s standard, he determined to become a monk. In 909, Odo went to Beaume, a reformed monastery where the rule was strictly observed, and Abbot Berno received him into the community.

That same year Berno started a new monastery at Cluny in Burgundy. He established it on the pattern of Beaume, insisting on a rigorous conformance to the Benedictine rule. In 927, St. Odo succeeded Berno as Cluny's abbot and spread its influence to monasteries all over Europe. He encouraged lax monasteries to return to the original pattern of the Benedictine rule of prayer, manual labor, and community life under the direction of a spiritual father. Under his influence, monasteries chose more worthy abbots, cultivated a more committed spiritual life in the monks, and restored the solemnity of daily worship. Thus the saint helped lay the foundation for a renewal movement that in two centuries reformed more than a thousand monastic communities.

Installing higher ideals was not easy at monasteries where monks had grown comfortable in their laxity. Odo, however, seemed to blend just the right measure of firmness and grace to pull it off. When the monks at Fleury, for example, violently resisted his entry, he first spoke to them gently. Then he waited three days and, with his strength under control, meekly rode a donkey into the abbey.

And in the following passage, John of Salerno, Odo's biographer, says he combined his power with wry humor to compel members of his entourage to behave charitably:

> The blind and the lame, Odo said, would be the doorkeepers of heaven. Therefore no one ought to drive them away from his house, so that in the future they should not shut the doors of heaven against him. So if one of our servants, not being able to put up with their shameless begging, replied sharply to them or denied them access to the door of our tent, Odo at once rebuked him with threats. Then in the servant's presence he used to call the poor man and command him, saying, "When this man comes to the gate of heaven, pay him back in the same way."

> He said this to frighten the servants, so that they should not act in this way again, and that he might teach them to love charity.
>
> If he found an old or feeble man by the roadside, he used to get down and set the poor man upon his horse, ordering all to go on a little distance ahead. He would command a servant to stay back and support the man so he didn't fall. He himself continued on foot in the midst of us on horseback. And always singing the psalms himself, he made us sing with him. If out of shame, or respect of him, anyone wished to get off his horse, Odo immediately ordered him to stay where he was, knowing that it was reverence for him and not for the poor man that made him want to dismount.

At the pope's request, Odo traveled to Rome three times to pacify relations between Hugh, king of Italy and Alberic, called the Patrician of the Romans. On each of these trips Odo took the opportunity to introduce the Cluniac reform to monasteries en route. On his return from the third venture in 942, he died at Tours, shortly after celebrating the feast of St. Martin.

Perhaps Odo's notion was not fictitious—that the poor we refuse or people we snub will be our greeters after death. Imagine that the person meeting us at heaven's gate will be the person we have offended most, now empowered to welcome or to reject us. That thought should make us hurry to be reconciled with anyone we have hurt.

NOVEMBER 19
Catholic Reformers; Leading Men; Meekness; Serving the Poor

161. Wenceslaus
(905?–929)

When St. Wenceslaus became king of Bohemia in 922, he instituted a Christian rule over a people who were only partially converted to Christianity. Thus, a cadre of powerful pagan nobles opposed him and ultimately conspired to have him murdered.

Earlier these nobles had murdered St. Ludmilla, Wenceslaus's grandmother. She had introduced Christianity into Bohemia and raised the king in the faith. They killed her because she was maneuvering to install young Wenceslaus as king. She wanted him to replace Drahomira, his mother, who as regent had instituted anti-Christian policies. Later, however, an uprising deposed Drahomira. Thus Wenceslaus ascended the throne, declaring that he would support God's law and the church. His biographer describes his governance as justice balanced with compassion:

> He was the honor of the clergy, the joy of the poor, the father of orphans, the defender of widows, the visitor of prisoners, the liberator of captives, and the pious consoler of all in need. For in the heart of the blessed man, there burned the glorious fire of charity.
>
> . . . So that none of the Christians be evilly punished by calumny, he destroyed all the prisons throughout his duchy. He cut down the gallows, and reduced all kinds of torment to nothing. When indeed anyone caught in criminal vice was brought to his judgment, he dismissed him. . . . The saint corrected him with fatherly words or with motherly chiding and warned him to make satisfaction by suitable penance for his sins.
>
> He never sentenced anyone to death or assented to such a sentence. If, however, he was unable to free a man from a death sentence because either of the great guilt of his crimes, or of the insistence of his nobles or the traditional justice of the land, he begged from the judges a time for him to do penance and make his confession. If he could not help the guilty one in this way, . . . he would rise from his throne and leave the place of council, so that he should not see the blood of his condemned neighbor. Then he would send messengers to the judges and ask for one or two days' stay of execution. And secretly approaching the condemned person at night, he consoled him persuasively and gave him money, that he might buy himself off. For he always kept in mind this saying of the Lord, "Be merciful and do not judge, so that you be

> not judged, and do not condemn and you will not be condemned" (see Luke 6:36–37).

In 926, Wenceslaus acknowledged German King Henry the Fowler as his overlord. This was the last straw for his opponents among the nobility, who were already annoyed because he severely checked their oppression of his people. They conspired with his jealous brother, Boleslaus, to kill him. Boleslaus invited the king to celebrate the feast of Sts. Cosmos and Damian at his palace. The morning after the party, he and his friends met Wenceslaus on the way to Mass. Wenceslaus said, "Brother, you were a good subject to me yesterday." "And today," said Boleslaus, "I intend to be a better one." And he struck Wenceslaus with his sword. The two grappled, but then friends of Boleslaus finished off the king. As Wenceslaus fell, he said, "Brother, may God forgive you."

While Wenceslaus was not killed purely for his faith, a popular cult that regarded him as a martyr developed shortly after his death.

Therefore, Christian men, be sure
Wealth or rank possessing,
Ye who now will bless the poor,
Shall yourselves find blessing.

—"Good King Wenceslaus"

SEPTEMBER 28 / PATRON OF BOHEMIA
Mercy; Saints and Politics; Social Justice; Twenty-Something Saints

162. Dunstan of Canterbury
(909–988)

As a trendsetting monastic reformer, archbishop, and collaborator of kings, St. Dunstan is acclaimed for his influence on the course of English history. Through his fruitful alliance with Edgar, who became king of Wessex at sixteen, Dunstan spawned a general renewal of the English church, which was driven by reformed monasteries.

Before Dunstan became abbot of the ancient monastery of Glastonbury in 939, the Danish invasions and local magnates had all but eradicated monastic life in England. Over the next thirty years, especially with Edgar's support, he revived Glastonbury and five other monasteries. In these communities, he restored the Rule of **St. Benedict** adding prayers for the king to the liturgy and requiring monks to copy manuscripts and to acquire a practical skill. Dunstan's reform of English monasticism spilled over into the church at large and lasted six centuries.

King Edgar appointed Dunstan archbishop of Canterbury in 960, an office he performed zealously. He reconstructed churches, insisted on observance of the marriage laws and fasting, and often acted as a judge. He influenced Edgar's legislation, including a law in which king and archbishop together required payment of the tithe. An accomplished metalworker himself, Dunstan also influenced one of Edgar's laws that commanded the practice of some handicraft on every priest.

Despite their friendship, Dunstan postponed Edgar's coronation for fourteen years, probably because the monarch had tried to entrap and forcibly marry St. Wulfhilda when she was a novice. But in 973, Dunstan finally presided at Edgar's coronation, using a liturgy which he largely wrote and which became the basis for the coronation ceremony of the English monarchs. Here is an excerpt:

> God, who of your goodness takes thought for your peoples and governs them with love, give your servant Edgar the spirit of wisdom with the exercise of discipline. Devoted in all his heart to you, may he ever be found apt in the ruling of his realm. . . .
>
> In his days may justice and mercy arise for all men, aid for our allies, hindrance for our enemies, solace for the lowly, rebuke for the proud, learning for the rich, loyalty for the poor, friendship for the alien, peace and security for our own in our Fatherland. May he govern discretely

> each person according to his measure. May he learn zealously to know himself; so that, with conscience given by God to enliven him, he may hold up to all his people the pattern of a life well-pleasing to you. Walking with his flock in the way of truth, may he reap harvest of plenteous fruit and receive in all things the health that you give of body and of soul. So may he conceive in you every counsel of the mind that he may ever appear in peace and in wisdom the just deviser of rule for his people. So by your help may he attain length of days in this present life, and through a goodly course come to full count of age. When this frailty has reached its end, may he find release from all bonds of sin and receive unending reward in the joyous company of angels forever.

After Edgar's death, Dunstan fell out of favor with the king's successors, but he continued faithfully to administer his diocese. He died at the age of eighty in 988.

Dunstan's popular reputation as a blacksmith sometimes overshadows his reputation as a reformer. A story still circulates, often depicted in art, that Dunstan once used his blacksmith's pincers to grab and deter the devil, who was tempting him.

MAY 19 / PATRON OF GOLDSMITHS, JEWELERS, MUSICIANS, AND BLACKSMITHS
Catholic Reformers; Saints and Politics; World Historical Saints

163. Simeon the New Theologian
(949–1022)

St. Simeon acquired the nickname "New Theologian" because his teaching revived the experiential Christianity of the "old" mystical theologians, such as **St. John** and **St. Gregory Nazianzen.** In Simeon's view, many Christians at the turn of the second millennium had the form of the faith but lacked the divine relationship that made it live. He held that all believers, laypeople and monks alike, must strive to experience God personally. "*God is fire,*" he taught in this typical *Discourse*,

> and he is so called by all the inspired Scripture (see Hebrews 6:4; 12:29). The soul of each of us is a lamp. Now a lamp is wholly in darkness, even though it be filled with oil, until it receives fire and is kindled. So too the soul, though it may seem to be adorned with all virtues, yet has not received the divine nature and light, is still unkindled and dark. And its works are uncertain.
>
> So see to it, brethren, that when we seem to be in God and think that we have communion with him, we should not be found excluded and separated from him, since we do not now see his light. If that light had kindled our lamps—our souls—it would shine brightly in us, just as our God and Lord Jesus Christ said, "If your whole body is full of light, having no part dark, it will be wholly bright, as when a lamp with its rays gives you light" (see Luke 11:36).
>
> Let us strive and increase the divine fire within us by practicing the commandments, that fire that makes the divine light shine more brightly and brilliantly.

At age fourteen, Simeon had already decided to become a monk. He took as his spiritual director another Simeon, a simple monk of the Studion, the famous monastery in Constantinople. But the mentor made his disciple wait thirteen years before allowing him to fulfill his vocation. During the days the saint kept busy with secular work. At night, however, he trained himself in prayer and asceticism.

Finally at age twenty-seven Simeon entered the Studion. But after three short months the abbot dismissed him because his outspoken radicalism aggravated other monks who enjoyed a comfortable worldliness. Then Simeon joined the monastery of St. Mamas that Nicetas, his biographer, described as a "cemetery for a great number of dead."

By age thirty he was elected abbot. And during the next quarter century Simeon transformed Mamas from a refuge for worldly monks into a center of spiritual renewal. Prominent leaders from the city came to him there for counsel.

Like all prophets, Simeon also attracted vigorous opponents. Once thirty of his monks rebelled against him, but the patriarch at Constantinople ruled against them. Later, Stephen of Nicomedia, the emperor's official theologian, discredited him because his charismatic theology seemed to demean hierarchical authority. In 1009, Stephen had Simeon exiled to Asia Minor.

The patriarch quickly lifted the ban and even offered Simeon an archbishopric as recompense. But the saint preferred to live the rest of his life in voluntary exile. He and a few friends founded a small monastery at a dilapidated chapel near Chrysopolis. Simeon savored his solitude there until his death in 1022.

> *Oh what swirlings of the flame in me—miserable one that I am—coming from you and your glory!*
> *I fall down in adoration before you.*
> *I thank you that you have made me worthy to know, however little it may be, the power of your divinity.*
>
> —Simeon

MARCH 12
The Light of Christ; The Secrets of Spiritual Success; A Soul Afire

164. Stephen of Hungary
(975–1038)

At the turn of the second millennium, St. Stephen succeeded his father as leader of the Magyars in Hungary. Looking to strengthen his authority, he determined to consolidate the state and extend Christianity throughout the land. In 1001 he arranged to have Pope Sylvester II name him king of Hungary. The pope obliged. As an additional sign of support, Sylvester had a special crown fashioned for Stephen that has become world famous.

Stephen extended his control over Hungary by restricting the power of the nobles. Then he replaced the country's tribal structure with counties governed by his appointees. By creating dioceses and establishing monasteries, Stephen strengthened the church and positioned it for expansion. Politically, he aggressively used his power to establish Christianity as Hungary's religion. He ruthlessly abolished pagan customs, outlawing adultery and blasphemy. Stephen ordered everyone to marry, except religious, and forbade marriages between Christians and pagans.

But Stephen had a kinder, gentler side. Like **St. Louis IX,** he made himself accessible to his people. He also took personal concern for the poor. He used to walk the streets in disguise so he could give alms to needy people. Once he barely escaped when some beggars beat and robbed him. But he refused to stop the practice.

Stephen was a family man. In 1015 he had married Gisela, the sister of emperor St. Henry II. The couple had one son, Emeric, whom Stephen groomed as his successor. In the following letter to his son, Stephen lays out his vision of what a Christian monarch must be:

> My dearest son, if you desire to honor the royal crown, I advise, I counsel, I urge you above all things to maintain the Catholic and apostolic faith with such diligence and care that you may be an example for all those placed under you by God and that all the clergy may rightly call you a man of true Christian profession. Failing to do this, you may be sure that you will not be called a Christian or a son of the Church. . . .
>
> However, dearest son, even now in our kingdom the Church is proclaimed as young and newly planted; and for that reason she needs more prudent and trustworthy guardians lest a benefit which the

divine mercy bestowed on us undeservedly should be destroyed and annihilated through your idleness, indolence or neglect. . . .

Finally, be strong lest prosperity lift you up too much or adversity cast you down. Be humble in this life, that God may raise you up in the next. Be truly moderate and do not punish or condemn anyone immoderately. Be gentle so that you may never oppose justice. Be honorable so that you may never voluntarily bring disgrace upon anyone. Be chaste so that you may avoid all the foulness of lust like the pangs of death.

All these virtues I have noted above make up the royal crown and without them no one is fit to rule here on earth or attain to the heavenly kingdom.

Sadly, Emeric died in a hunting accident, leaving Stephen no successor. After the saint's death in 1038, a series of Magyar kings undid much of his work.

Laypeoples' field of Christian service is the vast world of politics, society and economics, as well as the world of culture, sciences, arts, international affairs and mass media. It also includes human love, the family, the education of children, professional work, and suffering. The more gospel-inspired laypeople that engage in these areas, the more these areas will be at the service of the Kingdom of God.

—Pope Paul VI

AUGUST 16 / CANONIZED IN 1083 / PATRON OF HUNGARY, KINGS, DEATH OF CHILDREN, AND STONEMASONS
Married Saints; Saints and Politics

165. Olaf

(995–1030)

Violence marked St. Olaf's youth. He had spent his youth as a pirate, and in 1013, he fought in England with King Ethelred against the Danes. Two years later he returned to Norway, drove out the Swedes and Danes, and set himself up as king. Then, although a fairly new Christian himself, he undertook to Christianize Norway.

To aid in the work, Olaf imported priests and monks from England. He appointed one of these, Grimkel, bishop of Nidaros, his capital. With Grimkel's wise counsel, the king abolished many old laws and customs that contradicted the gospel and promulgated good laws that advanced it.

However, the young king's faith had not tamed his violence, and he vigorously used forceful methods in his efforts to evangelize his people. For example, Sigrid Undset described an important meeting of the king with heathen landowners at which he presented the gospel menacingly. At the assembly, the king spoke first and the leading landowner responded:

> Olaf . . . told them that in the northern valleys the folk had broken down their heathen temples. He ended: "Now they believe in the true God who has made heaven and earth and who knows all things." . . . Dale-Gudbrand answered him.
>
> "We do not know him of whom you speak. You call God one whom neither you nor anyone else has ever seen. But we have a god we can see every day. . . ."
>
> Olaf then listened while Dale-Gudbrand's son told of the image of Thor, who every day received his offering of meat and who devoured it during the night.

Then Olaf had a bishop explain the gospel to all at the meeting. Impressed by miracle stories, one landowner challenged Olaf to a contest between Christ and Thor to see which one could make the sun come out on a cloudless day. Next morning the heavens were cloudless and Dale-Gudbrand dragged up a gigantic gold-plated statue of Thor. The king took the initiative:

> So Olaf stood up and began to speak, until the moment when the first ray of sunlight flashed across . . . the edge of the hills. . . . He cried, "look towards the east, where comes our God surrounded by light."
>
> The farmers looked toward the sun slowly rising above the horizon, and Olaf's henchman gave one mighty blow with his club and broke in pieces the image of the god. Mice and rats and snakes came tumbling out. . . .
>
> "I do not know what all this trouble and commotion is about, but now you can see what good your god is made of and who it was who had the benefit of all the food you took to him. Gather up the gold and treasures which lie here on the ground and take them home to your women, but do not offer them again to stocks and stones."

Then Olaf gave the landowners his usual ultimatum—either become Christians or fight with him. So the landowners caved in.

Not surprisingly, Olaf made many enemies, and in 1029 with the aid of Canute, King of England and Denmark, they defeated and exiled him. With a small army he tried to regain his power a year later, but was killed in battle.

As Catholics in an age when evangelization is done by friendship, few may be able to stir up much admiration for this warrior saint, let alone devotion. But which is worse: Olaf's aggressively compelling people to confront Christ or our timid failure to even tell others about him?

JULY 29 / CANONIZED IN 1164 / PATRON OF NORWAY
Saints and Politics

166. Peter Damian
(1007–1072)

Already an austere ascetic, in 1035 St. Peter Damian left his secular professorship at Ravenna in Italy to embrace the eremitical life with the reformed Benedictines at Fonte Avellina. He soon became head of that community, governing with a strictness gloved in kindness that prepared him for his wider service in the church.

A series of popes recruited Peter Damian to help them reform the church that at the turn of the second millennium was suffering from immorality and corruption. He reproved bishops, spoke at synods against simony and clerical marriage, and rebuffed monasteries for laxity. As bishop of Ostia and a cardinal after 1057, he vigorously opposed antipopes and went on diplomatic missions throughout Europe supporting the cause of church renewal. He was firmly convinced that a reformed papacy was essential for the future of the church. Thus he helped prepare the way for the work of **St. Gregory VII.**

Peter Damian was also concerned with revitalizing the faith of ordinary believers. One of his prescriptions for a revitalized Christian life was frequent reception of the Eucharist, as he once wrote to a friend:

> Receive the body and blood of Christ very frequently that you may deserve to hear his words:
>
> "Your lips, my promised bride,
> distil wild honey. Honey and milk
> are under your tongue" (Song of Songs 4:11 *NJB*).
>
> For the sight of a Christian's lips red with the blood of Christ terrifies the Enemy. He immediately recognizes the sign of his own ruin. He cannot stand the instrument of divine victory by which he was taken captive and cast down. Let Christ, therefore, through his mysteries be present on your tongue and let him always abide in your heart by the fire of his love.

And he often preached on the real presence of Christ in the believer's heart, as in this sermon:

> The Blessed Virgin alone conceived Christ in her womb, yet all the elect carry him in the devotion of their hearts. Happy and most blessed the woman who bore him for nine months in her womb. Happy also we, if we diligently strive to bear him in our thoughts. It was indeed wondrous that Christ was conceived in a womb, but it is no less striking that he be borne in the prison of the heart.
>
> Consider, dearly beloved, what a dignity is ours, and what a likeness there is between us and Mary. Mary conceived Christ in her womb, and we bear him about in our heart. Mary fed Christ when she gave milk from her breasts to his tender lips, and we feed him with the varied delights of our good works.

In 1069 at the pope's request the saint persuaded the emperor Henry IV not to divorce his wife, Bertha, though Henry hated her all the more thereafter. Then Peter Damian, always the monk, retired to Fonte Avellina where he pursued God through spiritual disciplines which he did not relax in the least in his old age. He died on February 22, 1072, on his way home from one last embassy to reconcile factions in the diocese of Ravenna.

Writers uniformly characterize Peter Damian as "stern," "vehement," and "intransigent." They seem to be warning us that we may not find him very attractive. But if Peter Damian was a hard-nosed reformer, the deteriorated condition of the church in his day demanded it. And had he upbraided us for some favorite fault or comfortable sin, as he often did, we may not have liked him very much.

FEBRUARY 21
Mary; Saints and Sacraments (Eucharist)

167. Gregory VII

(1025?–1085)

In his twelve years as pope, St. Gregory VII had few dull moments. From the start he escalated the efforts of previous popes to reform the clergy and free the church from state control. He clashed with recalcitrant bishops and priests who resisted his proscription of the sale of church offices and sexual misconduct. But he fought most bitterly with kings and emperors who refused to surrender their power over the church. Through it all he modeled heroic fortitude, perhaps the main reason we venerate him as a saint.

Born into Tuscany's lower class and baptized Hildebrand, he went to Rome as a youth. As he matured he became well known for his piety and giftedness. Tapped by Pope Gregory VI as his personal chaplain, Hildebrand subsequently served as the power behind the throne for a series of five reforming popes.

Elected pope himself in 1073, Gregory VII set out to release the church from the state's grip. He decreed that secular rulers could no longer choose bishops and invest them in their office. Many kings and princes simply ignored his order, but Emperor Henry IV of Germany opposed him violently. Twice during the conflict Gregory excommunicated Henry IV, thus undermining his position as emperor. Once Henry IV repented, standing three days in snow at Canossa waiting to receive the pope's absolution. The second time, however, he turned to force and lay siege to Rome itself. Embattled and threatened, Gregory VII wrote the following letter to rally all clergy and laity who were faithful to him:

> We are sure, beloved brethren, that you sympathize with our sufferings and that you pray for us. Do not doubt that we have the same mind toward you—and with good reason. For the Apostle says: "If one member suffers, the other members suffer with it" (see 1 Corinthians 12:26). We believe too that God's love is in our hearts because we have one will, one desire and one goal. We wish that all the wicked may repent and return to their Creator. We desire that the holy church, now trampled, confused and divided, may return to its former unity. We have as our goal that God may be glorified in us and that all, including our persecutors, may be worthy to share eternal life.

> We provoke the world against us by opposing its desires and condemning its works. No wonder the princes of this world hate us, Christ's poor, when we resist their evil doing. Yet up to the present very few of us have suffered death for Christ's sake. How many mercenaries give their lives daily for their lords? And we, what do we do or suffer for our Supreme King? What shame is put on us because they aren't afraid to suffer death for a trifle while we avoid persecution whose reward is heavenly treasure?
>
> Lift up your hearts then with strength. Keep your hope alive. Have ever before your eyes the banner of our leader, the King Eternal, bearing his watchword: "Your perseverance will win you your lives" (Luke 21:19 *NJB*).

Ultimately Gregory VII called on Robert Guiscard, who ruled Norman Sicily, to break the siege. But the Norman rescuers instead sacked the city, forcing the pope into exile at Salerno, where he died in 1085.

In the past, some discredited Pope Gregory VII because of his power struggle with Emperor Henry IV. Now, however, he is generally admired as a courageous reformer. The saint saw himself as the successor of ***St. Peter****, charged with securing and preserving the spiritual welfare of the church. His dying words were: "I have loved justice and therefore die in exile!"*

MAY 25 / CANONIZED IN 1606
Courage; Saints and Politics

168. Margaret of Scotland

(1046–1093)

As one of the last survivors of the Anglo-Saxon royal family, St. Margaret was no longer safe in England after the Norman Conquest in 1066. So she fled to Scotland to the court of King Malcolm III. Attracted by Margaret's beauty and intelligence, Malcolm married her around 1070. The couple enjoyed nearly a quarter century of happy marriage and had six sons and two daughters. Three sons—Edgar, Alexander, and St. David—ruled as kings of Scotland and a daughter, Matilda, became the queen of Henry I of England.

Because of her excellent education and good taste, Margaret exercised a civilizing influence on the Scottish court and enhanced its reputation. And the saint brought the best out of her husband, as Turgot, her biographer, noted:

> She made the king himself most attentive to works of justice, mercy, almsgiving, and other virtues. The king seemed to fear to offend a queen whose life was so venerable. What she refused he refused, and what she loved, he loved for the love of her love. Thus the king—though unable to read—often handled affectionately her devotional books and examined their illustrations and bindings.

Margaret used her royal position to advocate church reform. She revived various observances, including the Lenten fast, abstinence from work on Sundays, and Easter communion. At one ecclesiastical council, for example, Margaret was appalled at the excuse given for refraining from receiving communion at Easter. Delegates told her they did not approach the altar out of fear because Paul had said *He that eats and drinks unworthily, eats and drinks judgment to himself (see 1 Corinthians 11:29).* The saint replied heatedly:

> "What! Shall all who are sinners not taste that holy mystery? Then no one ought to receive it, for everyone is stained with sin.
>
> "And if no one ought to receive it, why did the Lord say: If you do not eat the flesh of the Son of man and drink his blood, you have no life in you (John 6:53 *NJB*)? But the Apostle does not say that all sinners are unworthy to receive the sacraments of salvation. For after saying 'he eats and drinks judgment to himself,' he adds, 'not discerning the body of our Lord.'

> "So only he eats and drinks judgment to himself, who without confession and penance, and with the defilement of his sins presumes to draw near to the sacred mysteries. But we who have confessed our faults, on the day of the Lord's resurrection receive the body and blood of the Immaculate Lamb not to judgment, but to remission of sins and the salutary preparation of our souls for eternal blessedness."

Margaret also renewed the monastery at Iona and constructed Dunfermline Abbey, inspired by Westminster Abbey as a burial place for Scottish royalty.

Margaret of Scotland died in 1093, shortly after learning that Malcolm and one of her sons had died during a skirmish in England.

Okay, married readers, let's take this rare chance to celebrate a married saint! At the beginning of the third millennium we have much to learn from this saint from the early part of the second millennium. We don't have many details about their relationship, but refined and educated Margaret and rough-hewn, illiterate Malcolm seem to have enjoyed their marriage. Perhaps Margaret's message for us is that mutual respect between husband and wife fosters a lasting, and even a pleasant, marriage.

NOVEMBER 16 / CANONIZED IN 1250 / PATRON OF THE DEATH OF CHILDREN, PARENTS OF LARGE FAMILIES, WIDOWS, AND QUEENS
Married Saints; Saints and Sacraments (Eucharist)

169. Bruno

(1035?–1101)

As it happened for **St. Francis Xavier** and many other saints, St. Bruno's life did not work out according to plan. A wealthy canon of Cologne cathedral and distinguished director of the school at Reims, France, his career seemed cast in bronze.

But after eighteen years at Reims everything suddenly changed. He became chancellor of the diocese of Reims under an unworthy bishop. Bruno unsuccessfully challenged the bishop, and the experience seems to have persuaded him to abandon all worldly pursuits.

Bruno gave up all wealth and position. With a few friends, he went to live near St. Robert at the Cistercian abbey of Molesmes. But seeking a more severe solitude, Bruno and his companions went to Grenoble, where his former pupil, St. Hugh, gave them a remote valley called La Chartreuse. There Bruno built a chapel and cells that became the origin of the Carthusian Order.

The first Carthusians practiced a strict solitude, coming together only for Matins and Vespers. They fasted perpetually, eating no meat. And they occupied themselves with constant prayer, study, and the manual work of copying manuscripts.

The regimen of severe solitude may have enervated Bruno's body, but it seems to have enriched his soul. In the following letter to his friend, Raoul, the provost at Reims, he celebrated its blessings:

> Only those who have experienced the solitude and silence of the wilderness can know what benefit and divine joy they bring to those who love them.
>
> There strong men can be recollected as often as they wish, abide within themselves, carefully cultivate the seeds of virtue, and be nourished happily by the fruits of paradise. There one can try to come to clear vision of the divine Spouse who has been wounded by love, to a pure vision that permits them to see God. There they can dedicate themselves to leisure that is occupied and activity that is tranquil. There, for their labor in the contest, God gives his athletes the reward they desire: a peace that the world does not know and joy in the Holy Spirit.
>
> Remember lovely Rachel. Although she gave Jacob fewer offspring than Leah, he preferred her to the more fruitful one, whose vision was dim. The offspring of contemplation are more rare than the offspring

> of action; so it was that their father had more affection for Joseph and Benjamin than for their other brothers. . . .
>
> Remember the lovely Sunamitess, that virgin who was the only one in the land of Israel found worthy to attend to David and warm him when he was old. I should like for you, too, dear brother, to love God above all, so that warmed by his embrace you may be aflame with divine love.

Bruno was not to enjoy his solitude for long, as another former pupil, Pope Urban II, brought him to Rome as his counselor. He aided the pope in his controversy with an antipope at Ravenna and later declined an appointment as bishop of Reggio. However, Bruno took the opportunity of his time in Italy to establish other monasteries on the model of La Grande Chartreuse. He died at one of these, La Torre, in 1101.

> *St. Bruno provided the basis of a universally valuable spiritual theology with its stress on love, self-knowledge, and the true vision that comes from delighting in the world as God's creation, but seeing beyond its attractions through study, prayer, humility, and asceticism. With that vision, Carthusians could become involved in secular affairs, as Bruno himself had been, without being distracted by them.*
>
> —Butler's *Lives of the Saints*

OCTOBER 6
Intimacy with the Divine; Solitude; A Soul Afire

170. Anselm
(1033–1109)

In his life and work, St. Anselm seems to have blended perfectly the Christian essentials of prayer, thought, and action. As a monk he learned the discipline of prayer and won respect as a gifted preacher. As abbot of Bec in Normandy (1078–93), he formed others in the spiritual life and wrote theological treatises that are still read with profit today. As archbishop of Canterbury (1093–1109) he plunged into English politics and defended the church against the incursions of Kings William II and Henry I. We would do well to imitate his balance even in small ways, assuring our attention to spirituality, study, and service.

History applauds Anselm as the best theologian between **St. Augustine** and **St. Thomas Aquinas**. He preferred to defend the faith by using reasonable arguments instead of relying on the authority of Scripture. "Faith seeking understanding" was his life theme. In the *Monologion* and the *Proslogion*, Anselm offered rational proofs for God's existence. And the *Cur Deus Homo?*, his most famous book, explained that the Incarnation was necessary to atone for humankind's outrageous offense of God's majesty.

As a pastor and teacher, Anselm held forward-looking views. For example, his biographer, Eadmer, tells how the saint chided another abbot for his brutish treatment of boys:

> "Now tell me, if you plant a tree shoot in your garden, and straightway shut it in on every side so that it has no space to put out its branches, what kind of tree will you have after years when you let it out of its confinement?"
>
> "A useless one, certainly, with its branches all twisted and knotted."
>
> "Without doubt this is what you do with your boys. They are planted in the garden of the church, to grow and bring forth fruit for God. But you so terrify them and hem them in on all sides with threats and blows that they are utterly deprived of their liberty. And being thus injudiciously oppressed, they harbor evil thoughts like thorns. They cherish these thoughts so passionately that they doggedly reject everything that could minister to their correction. Thus, feeling no love or pity, good will or tenderness in your attitude towards them, they have in the future no faith in your goodness but believe that all your actions proceed from malice against them. The deplorable result is that as they

grow in body so their hatred increases, together with their apprehension of evil. They have been brought up in no true charity towards anyone, so they regard everyone with suspicion and jealousy."

Also forward-thinking in his opposition to slavery, in 1102, Anselm got an ecclesiastical council at Westminster to pass a resolution against it.

No diplomat, Anselm knocked heads with Kings William II and Henry I over their insistence on investing bishops with the staff and ring, the spiritual signs of the episcopal office. Twice over this issue he was forced into exile. Ultimately Pope Paschal arranged a compromise that became a model for settling the issue in other countries: the king would have the right to choose the bishop and the church would invest him with the spiritual signs of office.

Anselm died at Canterbury on April 21, 1109. He was named a doctor of the church in 1720.

> *My soul, have you found what you are looking for? You were looking for God, and you have discovered that he is the supreme being, and that you could not possibly imagine anything more perfect. You have discovered that this supreme being is life itself, light, wisdom, goodness, eternal blessedness and blessed eternity.*
>
> —Anselm

APRIL 21
Innovative Saints; Doctors of the Church; Faith Seeking Understanding; Raising Christian Youth

171. Norbert
(1080–1134)

For his first thirty-five years Norbert enjoyed the easy life of a young nobleman. He had an appointment as a canon at Xanten in the duchy of Cleves in modern Belgium, but he lived somewhat frivolously at the imperial court.

In 1115, however, while Norbert was riding through Westphalia during a storm, lightning frightened his horse. The terrified animal tossed him to the ground, knocking him unconscious. Upon awakening, he prayed, "Lord, what would you have me do?" "Turn away from evil," said an inner voice, "and do good. Seek peace and pursue it."

St. Norbert responded as completely as **Paul** had after his experience on the Damascus road. During a retreat at Xanten he determined to live a simple, evangelical life. He was ordained a priest and donned a monk's habit. Offended by his austere behavior and unauthorized preaching, other canons denounced him to the pope. So Norbert renounced his canonry, sold his possessions, and walked barefoot to humble himself before Pope Gelasius II. The pope gave him permission to proclaim the gospel anywhere. And he soon became famous as an itinerant preacher in northern France.

Influenced by his friend, **Bernard of Clairvaux**. Norbert undertook to reform the Canons Regular. In 1120, with thirteen companions he founded a monastery at Prémontré that quickly became a center for renewal.

Norbert's reform was Bible-based. For example, he expected members of his order to pattern their lives on the gospel. Listen to his exhortation on applying Scripture to life:

> Never be tired of studying these writings where you find a short exhortation to remain faithful in serving God. For the word of God is fiery. It is inflamed with the fire of the Holy Spirit. It consumes vices and promotes virtue. It bestows wisdom on well-disposed people and provides for them heavenly food.
>
> Therefore, Christ said, "Blessed are they who hear the word of God and keep it" (see Luke 11:28). So, **Mary Magdalene**, by listening attentively to the word of God, chose the best part that Martha, busy with her activities, couldn't obtain (see Luke 10:38–42). Listen cheerfully to the word of God, keep it judiciously and observe it faithfully.

> Thus at the end of time you may rejoice to hear Christ's consoling words: "Come, you whom my Father has blessed, take as your heritage the kingdom prepared for you since the foundation of the world" (Matthew 25:34 *NJB*).

In 1125, after Norbert had founded eight abbeys and two convents, the pope gave official approval to his order. The next year, however, Norbert was appointed archbishop of Magdeburg and had to bid farewell to his beloved Prémonstratensian communities.

As archbishop he courageously confronted people who had usurped church property and enforced strict celibacy on the clergy. As a result he made many enemies, some who threatened his life. So he went into voluntary exile until the people of Magdeburg freely demanded his return.

As Bernard did in France, in Germany Norbert championed Pope Innocent II against an antipope. Both saints accompanied the emperor and an army to Rome to restore Innocent. Afterwards the emperor appointed him chancellor of Italy, but Norbert took ill and died at Magdeburg in 1134.

When Count Theobald of Champagne applied to join Norbert's order, the saint said no. He had discerned that the nobleman did not have a vocation. Instead he encouraged him to adopt the order's pattern of life as a layperson. And he gave Theobald a small white scapular to wear beneath his clothes. For the first time on record a layman living in the world associated himself with a religious order. Thus Norbert had instituted the first Third Order.

JUNE 6 / CANONIZED IN 1582 / PATRON OF MAGDEBURG AND BOHEMIA
Conversion; Saints and the Bible

172. Malachy
(1098–1148)

In 1123, Archbishop Celsus of Armagh ordained St. Malachy and commissioned him to help introduce in Ireland the reforms of **Gregory VII.** Getting his countrymen to replace Celtic customs with the requirements of canon law was a tall order. But Malachy wisely tempered his zeal with careful reserve.

That same year the energetic young priest rebuilt the defunct monastery at Bangor and renewed community life there. And in 1124 he was appointed bishop of Connor and Down, where the religious practice of Christians was at a low ebb. Within three years, through pastoral visits and sound teaching, Malachy had revived faith and renewed sacramental life in his church. But in 1127 a local chieftain invaded Down and drove him off.

On his deathbed in 1129, Archbishop Celsus rejected the ancient Celtic practice of hereditary sees by appointing Malachy to succeed him. But instead his relatives installed Murtagh, his cousin. To keep the peace, for three years Malachy declined to occupy his see. Finally he persuaded Celsus's kinsmen to accept his governance for a short time on condition that he would soon resign. In 1137 he appointed a mutually acceptable abbot to Armagh and retired to Down. Thus, through his patience, Malachy both restored harmony to the church and terminated the unwise custom of hereditary bishoprics.

Two years later Malachy traveled to Rome to visit the pope. On the way he stopped at Clairvaux and became a friend of **St. Bernard**. In 1148, Malachy again set out on ecclesiastical business to meet the pope in France. But the pope had already returned to Rome, so Malachy paid a return visit to Bernard at Clairvaux. During his stay Malachy took ill suddenly and died in his friend's arms on November 2.

Bernard loved and esteemed Malachy and became the saint's first biographer. Among numerous anecdotes about Malachy's spiritual prowess, he tells about the following remarkable healing:

> A spirit of temper and fury so dominated a woman that her neighbors and relatives avoided her. Even her own children could hardly bear to live with her. She was foolhardy, outrageous, quick-tempered, formidable in both tongue and hand, impossible to live with and despised. Her children ached for her and for themselves. Weeping, they took her

to Malachy and explained their sad situation. The holy man took pity both on the mother and on her children's troubles. Calling her aside he carefully inquired whether she had ever confessed her sins.

"Never," she replied.

"Confess," he told her.

She obeyed. Then he assigned a penance to her when she confessed. Over her he prayed that the Lord Almighty should give her the spirit of meekness. In the name of the Lord Jesus he commanded her never to lose her temper again.

Such great meekness followed that it was clear to everyone that this was nothing other than a miraculous change brought about by the right hand of the Most High. They say that she is still alive today. Reportedly, she exercises such patience and gentleness that while she used to exasperate everyone, she herself is now never angered by any injuries or abuses or torments.

St. Bernard made a mind-clearing observation about this healing: "In my opinion," he wrote, "this must be put ahead of the miracle of Malachy's raising up of a dead woman. The former was an exterior act, but here the inner person was brought back to life."

NOVEMBER 3

Catholic Reformers; Christian Unity; Great Pastors; Miracles Do Happen; Perseverance

173. Bernard of Clairvaux

(1090?–1153)

In the age of knighthood and crusades, St. Bernard of Clairvaux viewed himself as a soldier for Christ. Ironically both warrior and peacemaker, he opposed everything that he saw as evil an simultaneously strove to maintain peaceful relations in the church.

Bernard's intelligence and charm equipped him for great worldly success, but in 1112 he decided to become a monk at the reformed Benedictine monastery at Cîteaux. And he enthusiastically persuaded thirty-one friends, including some of his brothers, to join him, giving a burst of new life to the Cistercian community. Perhaps he had his own life choice in mind when later in his famous book, *On Loving God*, he wrote about the folly of worldliness:

> Today you see many people who already have great possessions still laboring day by day to add one field to another with greed that knows no bounds. And you see those who have houses worthy of a king, nevertheless adding house to house every day (see Isaiah 5:8). And do we not see people in high positions striving mightily for still higher positions? There is no end to it all because the highest and best is not to be found in any of these things. If a person cannot be at peace until he has the highest and best, is it surprising that he is not content with inferior and worse things? It is folly and extreme madness always to be longing for things that cannot only never satisfy but cannot even blunt the appetite. However much you have of such things you still desire what you have not yet attained. You are always restlessly sighing after what is missing.
>
> The wicked therefore walk round in this circle (see Psalm 11:9), naturally wanting what will satisfy their wants, and foolishly thrusting away the means of attaining it—that is, of attaining not consumption but consummation. Thus, they wear themselves out with pointless effort and do not reach the end of happy fulfillment. They delight in the beauty of the creature rather than of the Creator (see Romans 1:23). They lust for each and every experience more than they desire to come to the Lord of all.

Bernard quickly emerged as a leader at Cîteaux, and in 1115 the abbot sent him with twelve monks to start a new monastery in Champagne. They settled in a sunny valley that they called Clairvaux.

Within two years the magnetism of the young Abbot Bernard had attracted one hundred thirty new members.

Although the saint preferred the solitude and brotherhood of Clairvaux, his renown as a reformer and theologian put him in constant demand. For example, he wrote the rule for the new Order of the Knights Templars and secured ecclesiastical recognition for these soldiers who were both to fight the church's battles and to serve the sick, the poor, and pilgrims. In the interest of preserving Christian unity, in 1130 he traversed Europe, championing Pope Innocent II against the claims of an antipope. In the next decade he was busy writing, preaching, debating theologian Peter Abelard, and evangelizing Albigensian heretics in Languedoc. At the request of Pope Eugenius III, who had been one of his monks, in 1145 he preached the disastrous Second Crusade. Roundly criticized for its failure, he said that he had launched it for a divine cause and that the sins of the armies had ruined it.

Bernard had also recruited a peaceful army. By his death in 1153, thousands of young men filled the sixty-eight monasteries that Clairvaux had founded or reformed.

Jesus is honey in the mouth, music in the ear and a shout of joy in the heart.

—Bernard of Clairvaux

AUGUST 20 / PATRON OF CANCER VICTIMS AND GIBRALTAR

Doctors of the Church; Leading Men; A Passionate Love; Pursuit of Holiness

174. Ubald of Gubbio
(D. 1160)

The call to serve as bishop seems to have rested on St. Ubald from his youth. After his parents died, his uncle, the bishop of Gubbio in Italy, raised him in his household. When Ubald completed his studies, the bishop appointed him dean of the cathedral. Although quite young for the job, he managed to bring a group of disorderly canons into line. He persuaded several of them to live with him in community and gradually introduced a rule of life for all of them.

Ubald hankered for solitude, but could not escape the duty imposed by his gifts for leadership. Elected bishop of Perugia in 1126, he finagled the pope to excuse him. However, two years later the pope directed the clergy of Gubbio to choose Ubald as their bishop.

Ubald governed the church of Gubbio for thirty-two years. He developed close and friendly relationships with his people and grew to be much loved by them. Theobald, his immediate successor and biographer, praised Ubald as possessing the virtues of the ancient apostles. Above all, said Theobald, Ubald was remarkably mild and gentle.

Once, for example, a workman was thoughtlessly damaging some of Ubald's vines. When the saint respectfully asked the man to be more careful, he pushed the bishop into a pool of cement. Ubald ignored the offense, but the townspeople brought the worker to trial. However, Ubald appeared in court and claimed that, since the offense was against a cleric, the jurisdiction was his as bishop. Then he embraced his offender with a kiss of peace, prayed for him, and set him free.

Two years before his death the saint was afflicted with painful diseases that often restricted him to bed. On Easter Day, 1160, his flock begged him to leave his sickbed and celebrate the feast with them. Theobald gave this account:

> After the people of Gubbio had been sorrowfully expecting for a long time that the bishop might die at any time, they met at Easter and said: "Today our holy bishop should celebrate mass for us. . . ." . . . A delegation went to the bishop's house. But their request met with a negative answer, . . . as the bishop had not a scrap of energy left.
>
> Then Bambo, the governor of Gubbio, spoke directly to Ubaldo. "Dearest father, 'Christ loved his own unto the end' (see John 13:1),

and although you also to this day have lived not for yourself but for us, now do you not pay attention to your children when you are on the threshold of eternity? . . . Despite your dire condition, . . . celebrate mass for us today!"

"Son," replied the bishop, ". . . by reminding me of Christ, you have persuaded me. Prepare what is necessary. Carry me in your arms to the cathedral. . . ." Everyone was overjoyed. The entire city rushed up at the pealing of the bells. . . . That day Ubaldo sang his last mass as he had never before sang it.

That day he spoke of eternal life, paradise for the blessed and for the wicked, hell, . . . preaching for a longer time than usual and enlightening us like some star from heaven. All agreed that this was his beautiful swan song as he was about to die and ascend to heaven. When mass was ended, the bishop was taken back to his bed—or rather, to his cross to end his life.

Ubald died a few weeks later at Pentecost, 1160.

Spread love everywhere you go. Be the living expression of God's kindness. Kindness in your face. Kindness in your eyes. Kindness in your smile. Kindness in your warm greeting.

—Teresa of Calcutta

MAY 16 / CANONIZED IN 1192
Forgiveness; Great Pastors; Kindness

175. Hildegard of Bingen
(1098–1179)

A shaft of light of dazzling brilliancy came from the opened heavens and pierced my mind and heart like a flame, that warms without burning as the sun heats by its rays. And suddenly I knew and understood the . . . Catholic books of the Old and New Testaments.

—Hildegard

Visions, prophecies, and premonitions thrust themselves lifelong on St. Hildegard. As a girl, they so embarrassed her that she once said, "I would have killed myself had that been possible." However, Hildegard as an adult became comfortable with her extraordinary gifts, using them for the instruction and reform of the Christian people.

In 1141 a divine light seemed to illumine Hildegard with an understanding of all salvation history. Aided by a monk named Volmar, Hildegard recorded this vision in a book of twenty-six revelations that she called the *Scivias*, or *Know God's Ways*. The last vision contains the prototype for her *Play of Virtues,* the first known morality play:

> THE SOUL: O soldiery of the Queen Humility, look gently upon me! O Humility, who are true healing, help me. For Pride has broken me with many vices, and wounded me with many scars. Now I fly to you; oh, receive me!
>
> HUMILITY (to the virtues): O virtues all, for the sake of Christ's wounds receive this mourning sinner and bring her to me.
>
> VIRTUES (to the soul): O unhappy daughter, I will embrace you; for the great Physician for your sake suffered deep and bitter wounds.
>
> THE DEVIL (whispering to the soul): You embraced me, and I led you forth. And now you return and confound me! But I will throw you down in battle.
>
> THE SOUL (to the devil): I recognized that all your ways are evil. So I fled from you. And now, O imposter, I fight against you!
>
> HUMILITY (to Victory and the other virtues): O Victory! You conquered the Devil in Heaven; run now with your companions, and all bind the Devil.
>
> VICTORY (to the virtues): O strong soldiers, help me conquer this deceiver!

VIRTUES (to Victory): O you crowned with glory, we gladly fight with you against the deluder of souls!

VICTORY: Rejoice, comrades! The ancient serpent is bound!

In 1147, Hildegard founded a monastery at Rupertsburg, near Bingen in central Germany. She oversaw the construction of a center for fifty nuns "with water piped to every room." Like an Old Testament prophet, from 1152 to 1162 the abbess preached reform to lax churches and monasteries throughout the Rhineland. Still extant are several hundred of Hildegard's letters, many containing prophetic warnings to civic and religious leaders. Often the center of controversy, she disclaimed responsibility, saying "I am a poor earthen vessel, and say these things not of myself but from the serene Light."

Indefatigably creative, highly musical, Hildegard also wrote liturgical hymns and two books of medicine and natural history. She died in 1179 at the age of eighty-one. Today Hildegard of Bingen has emerged as a most popular saint. Time has dissolved all controversy and criticism, and has enhanced our appreciation of this remarkable woman.

Hildegard unites vision with doctrine, religion with science, charismatic jubilation with prophetic indignation, and the longing for social order with the quest for social justice in ways that continue to challenge and inspire.

—Barbara J. Newman

SEPTEMBER 17

The Light of Christ; Prophets; Pursuit of Holiness; Visions and Visionaries

176. Aelred of Rievaulx
(1110–1167)

How good, how delightful it is to live as brothers together!

—Psalm 133:1 *NJB*

Although St. Aelred lived a millennium ago, his life and writings have a distinctively contemporary feel. An extremely competent administrator of Rievaulx, a vast Yorkshire abbey in Northern England, yet even more a spiritual father to hundreds of men, had we met Aelred we would identify him with Pope John XXIII or Carlo Martini, the archbishop of Milan, Italy. Like these beloved shepherds of the modern church, Aelred loved his flock and was much loved in return. *As I was walking around the cloisters,* he said, *all the brothers were sitting together. And in the whole throng I could not find one whom I did not love and by whom I was not loved.*

As a writer, too, Aelred seems to address our modern concerns and sensibilities. In his teaching that the interior life is communal—that we move from self and sin to find God in community—we might imagine we are hearing Henri J. M. Nouwen or Dorothy Day. Consider, for example, Aelred's reflections on how spiritual friendship leads us to Christ:

> It is no small consolation in this life to have someone who can unite with you in an intimate affection and the embrace of a holy love. Someone in whom your spirit can rest, to whom you can pour out your soul, to whose pleasant exchanges, as to soothing songs, you can fly in sorrow. To the dear breast of whose friendship, amidst the many troubles of the world, you can safely retire. A person who can shed tears with you in your worries, be happy with you when things go well, search out with you the answers to your problems, whom with the ties of charity you can lead into the depths of your heart. A person who, though absent in body, is yet present in spirit, where heart to heart you can talk to him, where the sweetness of the Spirit flows between you, where you so join yourself and cleave to him that soul mingles with soul and two become one.
>
> And so praying to Christ for your friend, and longing to be heard by Christ for your friend's sake, you reach out with devotion and desire to Christ himself. And suddenly and insensibly, as though touched by

> the gentleness of Christ close at hand, you begin to taste how sweet he is and to feel how lovely he is. Thus from that holy love with which you embrace your friend, you rise to that love by which you embrace Christ.

From 1147 to 1167, Aelred governed 150 choir monks and 500 lay brothers at the Cistercian abbey at Rievaulx. He ruled firmly, but with kindness. In two decades he did not dismiss even one person from the monastery. Although constantly suffering from kidney stones, Aelred visited many other abbeys, extending his gentle influence throughout western monasticism. Encouraged by **St. Bernard of Clairvaux,** he wrote numerous books, including *The Mirror of Charity* and *On Spiritual Friendship.* For the last four years of his life, illness confined him to a cell attached to the abbey where small groups of monks daily sought his counsel. He died on January 12, 1167.

I shall no longer call you servants,
because a servant does not know
the master's business;
I call you friends,
because I have made known to you
everything I have learnt
from my Father.
You did not choose me,
no I chose you;
and I commissioned you to go out and bear fruit,
fruit that will last . . . .
My command to you
is to love one another.

—John 15:15–17 *NJB*

JANUARY 12
Friendship; Leading Men; Mere Christian Love

177. Thomas Becket
(1118–1170)

In 1162, English King Henry II appointed his loyal friend Thomas Becket as archbishop of Canterbury. For seven years Becket had served him well as his chancellor. Thus the king expected that Thomas would continue to favor him. But Thomas had warned Henry that he would hate him as archbishop: "Several things," he said, "that you do in prejudice of the rights of the church make me fear you would require of me what I could not agree to." And things went as Thomas predicted.

The appointment drew a line across Becket's life. The elegant, flinty statesman unexpectedly changed into a responsible churchman. Daily he celebrated mass, studied Scripture, distributed alms, and visited the sick. He dressed simply and wore a hair shirt. However, the character flaws that made Thomas a powerful chancellor—excessive self-confidence and obstinacy—persisted in the "new" Thomas. They also made him a powerful archbishop.

Inevitably king and archbishop clashed. Thomas opposed Henry on issues of taxation, punishment of clerics by secular courts, and the right of appeal to Rome. Henry harassed Thomas with petty persecutions. The tension finally boiled over in 1164. After appealing to the pope, Thomas exiled himself to France.

By 1170, Thomas had repaired relations with Henry enough to return to England. But serious unresolved issues remained. Thomas complained to Henry in this letter:

> Christ, the judge of souls, knows how sincerely and affectionately I have made peace with you, believing that good faith and guilelessness were being shown to me. What other conclusion could I draw from your words. For whether you were agreeing or disagreeing with me, your speech expressed kindness toward me. And what other note, if not one of benevolence, peace and security, is sounded in the letters you sent to my lord the king, your son, ordering restitution to me and my men of all we held before we departed from England? But the guilelessness and good faith I heard in your words is not apparent in deeds. And this, God knows, grieves me less for the disadvantages to me than for the possible slur upon your honor.
>
> It is plain that the holy church of Canterbury, the mother in Christ of the Britons, is perishing because of the hatred directed at me. Rather than let her perish, I shall expose my head to the blows of

> my persecutors. I am ready not only to die for Christ, but to endure a thousand deaths and all manner of torments, if he by his grace will grant me the strength to suffer. I had wished, my lord, to call on you once more; but necessity draws me, afflicted as I am, to my afflicted church. With your permission, I shall return to it, perhaps to perish that it may live, unless you in your goodness come swiftly to my rescue.

Thomas excommunicated several bishops who had coronated young Henry III without respect to his rights as archbishop of Canterbury. For Henry II that was the last straw. "Who will rid me of this turbulent priest?" he shouted angrily. Feeling commissioned by the king, four knights went to Canterbury cathedral to kill Thomas. Bullheaded to the end, Becket resisted vigorously. He threw one knight to the ground. Another struck him with a sword. "For the name of Jesus," said Becket, "and in defense of the church, I am willing to die." Then Thomas submitted to their blows and they butchered him, giving him in death the sanctity his flaws had denied him in life.

Although Thomas Becket had not always lived like a saint, he certainly died like one.

—David Hugh Farmer

DECEMBER 29
Martyrs; Feisty Saints; Saints and Politics

178. Hugh of Lincoln

(1140?–1200)

Legend says that squirrels befriended St. Hugh outside his cell at the Grande Chartreuse. They probably did, as his gracious personality and strength of character made him attractive to every creature from babies to kings. Hugh's successful leadership through several decades deserved the high praise of King Richard I of England, who said, "If all the prelates of the church were like him, there is not a king in Christendom who would dare to raise his head in the presence of a bishop." With charismatic skills and good-humored friendliness, Hugh established the Carthusians in England, reformed the diocese of Lincoln, personally protected Jews, and stood up to three kings, defending the church's rights.

At about age twenty-five, Hugh joined the Carthusians, embracing their rugged but deep spiritual life at the Grande Chartreuse, near Grenoble, France. For a decade he steeped himself in contemplation that prepared him for his later very active service. In 1175, King Henry II brought Hugh to England and appointed him prior of the Carthusian abbey at Witham, which he had founded in reparation for the murder of **Thomas Becket.** Before Hugh assumed the post, he compelled the king to compensate people he had displaced to make way for the monks. Under his leadership, the once foundering monastery flourished. Then in 1186 the king appointed Hugh to the see of Lincoln, which had been vacant for eighteen years. Assisted by a team of gifted young priests, he renewed the spiritual life of the diocese.

With extraordinary courage and a light touch, Hugh once rebuked King Richard I when he had confiscated the property of a fellow bishop who had refused money to support a war with France. The king, softened by Hugh's meekness, backed down. And once at Lincoln he also single-handedly stopped an armed crowd from killing local Jews.

In 1200, King John sent Hugh on a diplomatic mission to France, where he visited the Grande Chartreuse, Cluny, and Cîteaux. He returned to London with a fatal illness and died there on November 16.

We can read this excerpt from one of Hugh's sermons as a comment on his own death:

The most striking proof of God's love for us are the gifts bestowed either before birth or after death. For each person now being born or now dying God the Son has given the price of his death. And the Trinity instituted the sacraments by which soon after his birth he is cleansed, strengthened and protected.

When death cuts short a person's life, God immediately sends his angels to guard the soul on its return to its creator. And he also sends his earthly ministers, priests and other clerics, to bury him, giving these instructions:

"See this my creature whom I have always loved and for whose sake I did not spare my only Son but made Him the sharer in mortality and death. Go to meet him as his soul flies to me. Take up this image of my Son with incense and candles. Toll the bells of my church and open wide its doors and its inner sanctuary with solemn chants. Lay the remains of my brother near the altar where my Son's body rests. Renew my Son's acceptable sacrifice and prepare the communion feast so that the restless soul, still weary from its mortal condition, may recover its vigor. Let the body, now emptied of its former principle of life, be cherished in the lap of mother earth and be watered by this hallowing. Thus, on the last day, being happily reunited with its soul, it will blossom again, to enjoy forever eternal renewal."

—Hugh of Lincoln

NOVEMBER 17 / CANONIZED IN 1220
Facing Death; Meekness; Saints and Politics

179. Dominic
(1170–1221)

St. Dominic's spirituality was both simple and strategic. He simply held to the New Testament basics of prayer, Scripture study, community, and action. And he strategically understood the needs of the thirteenth-century church and created communities that brought it new life.

Dominic's adult life falls into two periods. A predominantly contemplative phase from 1184 to 1204 prepared him for an intensely active period from 1204 until his death in 1221. At fourteen he entered the University of Palencia in Castile, where for a decade he undertook secular and theological studies. Dominic immersed himself in Scripture, writing notes in the margins of his parchment copy of the Bible. But when famine struck Palencia, he sold all of his possessions, including his precious parchments and used the money to aid his starving neighbors. "I will not study on dead skins," he said, "when living skins are dying of hunger." In 1195 he became a canon of the cathedral at Osma and for nine years grew in prayer and spiritual fundamentals.

In 1204, Dominic accompanied Diego, the bishop of Osma, on a diplomatic mission that took them through Languedoc in southeast France, the base of the Albigensian heretics. The Albigensians were a religious sect that taught a dualism affirming two eternal principles of good and evil. Dominic shrewdly observed that he could effectively oppose these highly organized idealists by forming communities of disciplined men and women. By 1206 he had established a group of women in Prouille, France, and assigned them to the education and evangelization of girls. He also gathered there a group of carefully chosen men whom he trained as preachers.

Thus Dominic laid the groundwork for his strategic contribution to the church—communities of preachers and teachers who would revive the spiritual life of many Christians. And the secret of his effectiveness was his insistence on the basics. For example, contemporaries recorded the following observation about his practice and teaching on prayer:

> Saint Dominic used to pray by throwing himself outstretched upon the ground, lying on his face. He would feel great remorse in his heart and call to mind these words of the Gospel, saying sometimes in a voice loud enough to be heard: "God, be merciful to me, a sinner" (Luke 18:13 *NJB*). . . .
>
> Wishing to teach his brothers to pray reverently, he would sometimes say to them: "When those devout Magi entered the dwelling they found the child with Mary, his mother, and falling down they worshiped him. There is no doubt that we too have found the God-Man with Mary his handmaid." . . .

He would also exhort the young men, and say to them:

> "If you cannot weep for your own sins because you have none, remember that there are many sinners who can be disposed for mercy and charity. It was for these that the prophets lamented; and when Jesus saw them, he wept bitterly."

In October 1216, Rome recognized Dominic's order of Friars Preachers. Ten months later Dominic convoked a meeting of his sixteen brothers at Prouille. To everyone's surprise, at that assembly he dispersed his little community throughout Europe. "Leave it to me," he said, "I know what I am about. We must sow the seed, not hoard it." Time proved him right. By Dominic's death in 1221, he had sixty friaries organized into eight provinces. The Friars Preachers were in France, Italy, Spain, and England and had traveled as far as Poland, Scandinavia, and the Holy Land.

Were Dominic alive today, he might diagnose needs in the church similar to those he saw in the thirteenth century. His prescription for us might also be the same as it was then: return to Christian fundamentals and build small communities committed to high gospel ideals.

AUGUST 8 / CANONIZED IN 1234 / PATRON OF ASTRONOMERS
Community; Intercession; Leading Men; Prayer; Saints and the Bible; Worship

180. Francis of Assisi
(1181–1226)

You are holy, Lord, the only God, and your deeds are wonderful.
You are strong.
You are great.
You are the Most High,
You are almighty.
You, holy Father, are King of heaven and earth.
You are Three and One, Lord God all Good.
You are Good, all Good, supreme Good, Lord God living and true.
You are love,
You are wisdom.
You are humility,
You are endurance.
You are rest,
You are peace.
You are joy and gladness,
You are justice and moderation.
You are all our riches, and you suffice for us.
You are beauty.
You are gentleness.
You are our protector,
You are our guardian and defender.
You are courage.
You are our haven and our hope.
You are our faith, our great consolation.
You are our eternal life, great and wonderful Lord,
God almighty, merciful Savior.

—Francis of Assisi

The popular image of St. Francis of Assisi is warped with romantic notions. Many see him as a sweet simpleton who picked flowers and talked with animals. Francis *was* gentle and loved God's creation, but he was not naive. Just the opposite. As a youth he went to war eagerly, patiently endured imprisonment and illnesses, embraced Lady Poverty as his bride, and gave up everything to follow Christ. The real St. Francis of Assisi was a courageous spiritual warrior.

Francis's vocation cost him dearly. Decision by decision he stripped himself of attachments so as to be more like Jesus. Once en route to a war in southern Italy, Francis heard a divine voice invite him to stop serving the servant and dedicate himself to the master. He responded by committing himself to live for God alone. In his early twenties Francis decided to become like the poor he met in Assisi's back streets and took "Lady Poverty" as his bride. Then one day when Francis was praying in the dilapidated church of St. Damian, he heard a voice from the crucifix say, "Go and repair my church." At first Francis literally worked to fix the building, but later understood that his real call was to renew people spiritually. From that day Francis devoted himself to Christ crucified. Francis's father took him to the bishop's court, demanding that his son repay the money he had used to repair St. Damian's church building. The saint submitted, but then stripped naked, returning his clothes to his father as a sign that he forsook his family and his inheritance.

Then Francis began his itinerant ministry in central Italy, attracting young followers as he went. Once in 1209 at Mass he heard the gospel about Jesus sending his disciples to preach, to heal, and to do spiritual warfare. He took it literally as a life pattern for him and his band of men (see Matthew 10:7–10). In 1210, Francis got formal approval for his community of Friars Minor from Pope Innocent III, and by 1221 he had hundreds of brothers and had established friaries all over Europe.

In 1224 at his retreat on Mount Alvernia, Francis had a vision of a seraph, a great angel, nailed to a cross. As he watched, Francis himself received the stigmata. Replicas of the Savior's wounds appeared in his hands and side, acknowledging the saint's intimacy with Christ.

The movement Francis launched has reverberated through the centuries, touching millions of souls. He died in 1226.

What are the servants of God but his singers whose duty it is to lift up the hearts of men and women and move them to spiritual joy?

—Francis of Assisi

OCTOBER 4 / CANONIZED IN 1228 / PATRON OF ECOLOGISTS AND ANIMALS
The Cost of Discipleship; Leading Men; Purpose; Stigmata

181. Anthony of Padua
(1195–1231)

The ideal preacher should be hard as flint. From him must spring the spark that gives light to the soul and enkindles in it the fire of divine love.

Society wounded with the sores of evil is Lazarus. We are the dogs who must draw near to cure with our tongues—our preaching—by which we lick with the milk and honey of kindness and gentleness, healing—not aggravating—the evils that afflict humankind.

—Anthony of Padua

St. Anthony intrigued people because his personality was a balance of contradictory, yet complementary, qualities. He was a remarkable series of "boths" and "ands." Anthony of Padua was both physically unimpressive and personally dynamic. Both reticent and charismatic, both learned and practical, both high-minded and down-to-earth. This combination of opposing attributes made the saint resilient, and equipped him for his mission of sparking a new wave of spiritual renewal in Europe. Above all, Anthony was both firm and gentle, which on his own terms, cited above, made him an ideal preacher. His over-arching concern was his passion for souls, and he characteristically pursued them with both strict justice and tender mercy:

> Should an ass fall by the wayside, how quickly people run to lift him up. Yet, alas! souls perish and no one is moved. The devil besieges the city of the spirit, setting a light to the fires of concupiscence, massacring the virtues, the good works just begun, the holy resolutions. And how few weep for that calamity!
>
> Some show a compassion, merely sensual in origin, for a neighbor's physical needs. At least it shows that they have some good will. Others are too hard and severe, making no excuse for human weakness. Both end up by remaining indifferent. With a fallen brother we must show ourselves neither too tender nor too hard, neither soft as flesh nor hard as bone. In him we must love our own human nature while hating his fault.

In 1210, Anthony entered an Augustinian monastery near Lisbon, Portugal. Over the next decade he acquired an extensive knowledge of Scripture and the church Fathers that later enriched his preaching. At age twenty-five he joined the Franciscans, hoping to go to a foreign mission where he might be martyred. In 1221 he was sent to Morocco, but fell seriously ill and had to return to Italy.

The saint's reticence temporarily hid his gifts from the Franciscans, who assigned him to kitchen duty at St. Paul's monastery in Forli, Italy. But one evening at a celebration, Anthony's companions called on him to speak extemporaneously. The dishwasher held them spellbound, and when word reached his superiors, they assigned him to preach in central Italy.

Anthony became the "Billy Graham" of the thirteenth century. Thousands turned out to hear him. Everywhere he spoke he generated a spiritual renewal. The Franciscans wanted other men to imitate his successful methods, and **St. Francis** himself appointed him to teach theology in the community.

Many people pray to Anthony to recover lost items. Perhaps the practice stems from the occasion when a young friar stole one of Anthony's valuable manuscripts. Anthony prayed for its return, and a menacing vision stopped the fleeing youth, who immediately returned it to the saint.

Anthony spent his last five years preaching and spearheading social reforms in Padua. He died there in 1231.

Poverty is true riches. So precious is poverty that God's Only-Begotten Son came on earth in search of it. In heaven he had superabundance of all goods. Nothing was lacking there but poverty.

—Anthony of Padua

JUNE 13 / CANONIZED IN 1232 / PATRON OF LOST ARTICLES
Great Preachers; Intercession; Mercy

182. Elizabeth of Hungary
(1207–1231)

St. Elizabeth and Louis of Thuringia were friends, lovers, a married couple with children—and saints. For today's married Christians, who may feel that sanctity is reserved for celibates, they are a refreshing sign of hope.

Louis was heir to the Central European duchy of Thuringia and Elizabeth was the daughter of the king of Hungary. Their royalty distances them from us, but their mutual tenderness makes them accessible. In 1211, when Louis was eleven and Elizabeth was four, they were betrothed. Elizabeth was brought to the Wartburg, the Thuringian castle, to be raised with her future husband. Louis seems always to have cherished his bride-to-be, and Elizabeth doted on him. As they grew up they became the best of friends. Biographers report little signs of their affection. When the young man was away on the hunt or on business, Elizabeth pined for him. And on his return Louis always brought his beloved a gift—a brooch, a necklace, a coral rosary. They were married in 1221, and in the next six years they had a son and two daughters.

Louis may be a saint because of the gracious way he cared for his wife. A lesser man may not have tolerated Elizabeth's ascetical practices. Once, however, he almost exploded when she used their bed to nurse a leper. But he calmed down when he saw in his mind's eye not the sick man, but an image of Christ crucified. Incidents like this persuaded Louis to let Elizabeth build a hospital for the poor at the Wartburg.

Louis was also patient with his wife's habit of waking at night to pray. Montalembert, a nineteenth-century biographer, described how he indulged her:

> The Duchess, so as not to oversleep nor to disturb her husband, ordered Ysentrude, her most trusted maid, to awaken her by grabbing her foot. Once, however, Ysentrude accidentally shook the Duke's foot. Louis awoke suddenly, but guessing Ysentrude's mistake, he lay down again without showing the least sign of impatience. "He saw," said Theodoric, Elizabeth's first biographer, "that she loved God with her whole heart, and that thought comforted him. And because Elizabeth trusted her husband's wisdom, she did not conceal from him any of her penitential

exercises. She knew well that he would never interfere between her and her Savior."

To their frequent expressions of their mutual tenderness both added gentle exhortations to advance together in the way of perfection. This mutual desire for holiness strengthened them and preserved them in the service of God. It taught the couple to draw even from the ardent affection which united them, the charm and feeling of the Supreme Love.

In 1227, Louis died of plague en route to a crusade. Elizabeth had recently delivered her third child when she heard the tragic news. Nearly mad with her loss, she was beyond comfort. "O God," she cried, "now the world is dead to me and all it contained of happiness."

Elizabeth's grief, however, did not untrack her. Under difficult circumstances she continued her growth in prayer and her uninhibited service to the poor. But she survived her beloved Louis only by four years, and died of illness in 1231 at the age of twenty-four.

Neither my wife, nor I for sure, rise in the middle of the night to pray, and that's not because we have no maid to rouse us. And our generosity to the poor could use some loosening up. But maybe our affection and desire to please God will help us imitate the kindness of Elizabeth and Louis toward each other, which may have been their greatest strength.

NOVEMBER 17 / CANONIZED IN 1235 / PATRON OF NURSING HOMES AND BAKERS
Care of the Sick; Celebration of Discipline; Generosity; Kindness; Married Saints; Twenty-Something Saints

183. Jordan of Saxony

(D. 1237)

With hard-edged discipline and brilliant confrontation, **St. Dominic** established the Friars Preachers to proclaim the gospel and revitalize the church. Jordan of Saxony, his successor, took a different tack to advance the work of the Dominicans. He used gentleness and charm to attract new members and expand the order throughout Europe. A divine hand seems to have arranged this succession, tapping the right man at the right time.

Jordan's meteoric rise to head the Dominicans measures his exceptional leadership ability. Two months after he entered the order in 1220 he was one of a select group invited to participate in the first general chapter at Bologna. And just two years later, after Dominic's death the community chose Jordan as its second master-general.

Sometimes called the first university chaplain, Jordan had a gift for evangelizing college-age youth. When he preached at universities he enthralled his hearers. He personally brought a thousand young men into the order, including **St. Albert the Great**. During his tenure, he sent friars throughout Germany, Switzerland, and Denmark.

Following Dominic, Jordan believed that the prayer of contemplatives fueled the activism of the friars. So he fostered the development of the Dominican sisters, who devoted themselves to intercession. He personally directed the spiritual career of **Diana d'Andalo**, who headed a cloister in Bologna. Jordan loved Diana, and his letters to her have a lyrical charm. In the following selection he exhorts her and her sisters to keep heaven in mind:

> Apply yourselves with all your might to the life of virtue and the practice of the godliness that the apostle says is profitable to all things (see 1 Timothy 4:8). And do not work so much at bodily penances that can so easily exceed the limits of prudence and wisdom. Let your hearts be always filled with a burning desire for the blessed city of the saints in paradise, that glorious storeroom of perfect joy and gladness, that abode of light, radiant with the splendor of utter beauty, far exceeding the understanding of man: a realm truly divine, worthy to be the dwelling place of him who is created in the image and likeness of God (see Genesis 1:26).

> Let the loving thought of the Bridegroom be constantly in your minds. And as his eyes are upon you, do all you can to make your beauty perfect before him. Rid yourselves of any stain or blemish however small that might sully it and offend his divine gaze. Let there be purity in your hearts and innocence in your lives. In all that you do, be of one mind and one heart, in peace and concord, in unshakable love, and in that loving humility that is the guardian of all good things. So that, while your souls find deep and lasting delight in the life of holiness, they may themselves be a source of delight to the Son of God who is blessed for ever and ever. Amen.

Jordan wrote a life of St. Dominic that has become the main source of information about the founder and the early Dominicans. In 1237, while on the way to the Holy Land, he and two friars died in a shipwreck off the coast of Syria.

Once when Jordan was at evening prayer with some novices, a fit of giggles broke out among the young men. An older brother gestured them to stop. Jordan asked the senior friar, "Who made you novice master?" Turning to the youths, he said, "Go ahead and laugh! Laugh all you want, for you have escaped from the devil who used to hold you captive."

FEBRUARY 15 / BEATIFIED IN 1827
Eternal Perspective; Evangelization; Kindness; Leading Men

184. Diana d'Andalo

(1201?–1236)

Many celibate saints of the opposite sex became close friends. **Paula** and **Jerome, Clare** and **Francis, Jane de Chantal** and **Francis de Sales**, to name a few such relationships. But none of these friendships was touched by the romance that St. Diana d'Andalo seems to have shared with **Jordan of Saxony**. Apparently the two saints fell in love, but faithfully maintained their vows of celibacy.

From the very first time Diana d'Andalo heard **St. Dominic** preach she wholeheartedly desired to live like the friars. When Dominic decided to establish a base near the University of Bologna, Diana played a significant role. The d'Andalo family, who owned the land he wanted, strongly opposed him until Diana prevailed upon her father to give in. Then she persuaded Dominic privately to receive her vows in religion, which he did on condition that she would enter a convent as soon as possible.

Diana thought she would be able to persuade her family to set up a Dominican convent on their property. However, when her father adamantly refused, she ran away to join an Augustinian community nearby. But her brothers forcibly removed her, breaking one of her ribs in the process. When she left again, the family finally acquiesced. Jordan of Saxony, Dominic's successor, used gentle persuasion to convince d'Andalo and his sons that Diana had a real vocation. Finally they helped Jordan open a small convent nearby, where Diana and four companions were installed as nuns in 1222.

Somewhere along the way Diana and Jordan gave their hearts to each other, becoming more than mere friends. But their commitment to Christ took precedence over their human love. And they suffered dearly for it, as this tender letter of Jordan shows:

> I cannot, beloved, see you in the flesh as often as you and I would wish and enjoy the comfort of our meeting. But my heart's desire receives some alleviation when I can visit you by letter and inform you how things are going with me, even as I long to hear how you are faring. . . .
>
> Unhappy, Diana, is our present lot. Here below our love cannot be without sorrow and care. For you grieve . . . that you cannot see me constantly, I too that I may so seldom have the joy of seeing you. Who

> will lead us into the citadel, the city of the Lord of hosts . . . where we shall have nothing more to desire from him or from each other? Here we are tormented every day, our heartstrings wrung and our griefs draw from us the cry: "Who will free us from the body of this death?" (see Romans 7:24). But we must bear these things patiently and, so far as the necessities of daily life permit, fix our minds on him alone who is able to set us free from our afflictions, in whom alone rest can be found. Apart from him whatever we see will prove a source of suffering and much sorrow. Meantime we must accept joyfully any unhappiness we may meet. For the measure of our sufferings will be the measure of the joy we shall receive from Jesus Christ, the Son of God, to whom be honor, glory, power and majesty for ever and ever.

Diana and her sisters interceded daily for the mission of the Dominicans, and Jordan attributed the great success of his outreach to their prayers. Diana died in 1236 and Jordan followed her a year later.

Diana and Jordan's love testifies to the genuine humanity of the saints who remain subject even to romantic inclinations. And to the way divine love subsumes all our human loves.

JUNE 9 / BEATIFIED IN 1891
Eternal Perspective; Friendship

185. Hedwig
(1174–1243)

At age twelve, St. Hedwig, the daughter of a Bavarian count, was married to Henry, Duke of Silesia, then eighteen years old. Together they raised seven children. As a couple, but strongly influenced by Hedwig's concerns, they presided over a spiritual renewal in Silesia, now a part of present-day Poland, founding religious houses, establishing hospitals, and caring for the poor.

Hedwig's biographer characterized her as a woman of prayer and action, which he summed up in the following passage:

> She afflicted herself with continual mortification of the flesh, but she did so with prudent discretion. The more attentively she kept watch, the more she grew in the strength of the spirit [sic] and in grace, and the more the fire of devotion and divine love blazed within her. She was often borne aloft with such ardent desire and impelled toward God that she would no longer be aware of the things that were around her.
>
> Just as her devotion made her always seek after God, so her generous piety turned her toward her neighbor, and she bountifully bestowed alms on the needy. She gave aid to colleges and to religious persons dwelling within or outside monasteries, to widows and orphans, to the weak and the feeble, to lepers and those bound in chains or imprisoned, to travelers and needy women nursing infants. She allowed no one who came to her for help to go away uncomforted.
>
> And because this servant of God never neglected the practice of all good works, God also conferred on her such grace that when she lacked human means to do good, and her own powers failed, the divine power of the sufferings of Christ strengthened her to respond to the needs of her neighbors. And so through divine favor she had the power to relieve the bodily and spiritual troubles of all who sought her help.

In 1202, at Hedwig's urging, the couple founded the great convent of Cistercian nuns at Treibniz in Silesia. Over the years they opened numerous other religious houses that fostered the spiritual life of their people and spread German culture throughout their territories. Henry and Hedwig also took a close personal interest in hospitals they had built.

In 1209, Hedwig persuaded Henry that they should live celibately and separately for the rest of their lives. Hedwig moved near the Treibniz convent, often joining in the nun's observances and devoting herself to works of mercy. Once, for example, she took a poor, learning-disabled woman into her own room for ten weeks in order patiently to teach her to pray the Our Father. And once she prayed for a blind nun, making the sign of the cross, and the woman regained her sight.

Hedwig saw herself as a peacemaker in her combative family. When her sons Henry and Conrad fought over their lands, she tried to reconcile them but failed. Later, however, she brought her husband and another duke to terms, preventing them from going to war.

After Henry's death in 1238, Hedwig took the habit at Treibniz. But she did not take religious vows, so that she could remain free to dispense her property as alms for the poor. St. Hedwig died in 1243 and was buried at Treibniz.

If God allows some people to pile up riches instead of making themselves poor as Jesus did, it is so that they may use what he has entrusted to them as loyal servants, in accordance with the Master's will, to do spiritual and temporal good to others.

—Charles de Foucauld

OCTOBER 16 / CANONIZED IN 1267 / PATRON OF SILESIA
Almsgiving; Care of the Sick; Contemplatives in Action; Peacemakers; Serving the Poor

186. Lutgarde of Aywières
(1182–1246)

When Lutgarde was twelve, her parents placed her in the care of the Benedictine sisters at St. Catherine's monastery near Liège, Belgium. The convent allowed visitors, and young men came to court the beautiful young woman. Once when an ardent fellow and Lutgarde were talking, Christ appeared to her. Thomas de Cantimpré, Lutgarde's biographer, described the scene:

> Opening his garment, Christ showed Lutgarde the wound in his side bleeding as if recently opened, and he said to her, "Do not seek any longer the caresses of unseemly love. Contemplate here what you should love and why you should love it. Here, I pledge to you are the delights of total purity, which will follow it."

When the confused young man tried to resume their conversation, Lutgarde chased him off. "Get away from me, you fodder of death," she said, "for I have been overtaken by another lover."

St. Lutgarde made unusually rapid progress in the spiritual life. She opened herself fully to Christ in prayer, and he favored her with an intimate experience of his presence. He gave her gifts of healing and of understanding the convent's Latin prayers. But she asked him to take them back because both kept her from focusing on loving him.

> Then the Lord said to her, "What do you want?"
>
> "I want your heart," she said.
>
> "No, rather it is your heart that I want," replied the Lord.
>
> "So be it, Lord," said Lutgarde, "so long as your heart's love is mingled with mine, and I have and hold my heart in you. For with you as my shield, my heart is secure for all time."

In 1205, Lutgarde was elected prioress of St. Catherine's, a job she abhorred because it interfered with her prayer. So a year later she moved to a French-speaking Cistercian convent at Aywières, near Brussels. Since the saint spoke only Flemish, she figured she had little chance of being chosen for offices in that community!

Lutgarde believed Christ put his own concerns on her heart. Three times she fasted for periods of seven years, subsisting only on bread and liquids. The saint dedicated each fast for the Lord's purposes: once for the conversion of heretics, a second time for the salvation of sinners, and a final time for Emperor Frederick II, who was threatening the church. Before her death she prophesied the latter's demise, which occurred in 1250.

Biographers sometimes speak so much about spiritual phenomena that they make a saint appear to be abnormal. But occasionally, Lutgarde's biographer slips and lets us see her charming humanness:

> One Sunday after receiving the Body of Christ in the Eucharist, Lutgarde was meditating on her Savior. But she was torn because while she was enjoying her closeness to Christ, she was also feeling weak from hunger and wanted to eat something. So she said, "Lord Jesus, now is not the right time for me to be occupied with your delights. Go instead to Elizabeth, who is so weak that she must be fed every hour. Take possession of her heart, and let me go to take some food to restore my strength."

And that's exactly what happened. Lutgarde got her meal and Christ healed Elizabeth, who was able to resume normal life in the convent. St. Lutgarde spent four decades at Aywières entirely devoted to the heart of Christ. She died in 1246.

No one expected Lutgarde to remain a virgin, let alone become a nun, a mystic, and a saint. Her life sings of a fundamental Christian reality we easily forget: it's God who seeks after us, not vice versa.

JUNE 16
Conversations with God; Intercession; Miracles Do Happen; A Passionate Love

187. Clare of Assisi

(1193–1253)

Clare was already a faithful Christian when she first met **St. Francis of Assisi** in 1211, but his total dedication to Christ sealed her convictions. Clare decided that she also wanted to live by the gospel as simply as possible.

She determined to compare herself to Jesus as though looking in a mirror. She expected to conform her behavior to his image, and she taught others to do the same. For example, she exhorted Queen Agnes of Bohemia to look at herself in Christ-the-mirror:

> Happy the soul to whom it is given to attain this life with Christ, to cleave with all one's heart to him whose beauty all the heavenly hosts behold forever;
>
> whose love inflames our love;
> whose contemplation is our refreshment;
> whose graciousness is our delight;
> whose gentleness fills us to overflowing;
> whose remembrance gives sweet light;
> whose fragrance revives the dead;
> whose glorious vision will be the happiness of all the citizens of that heavenly Jerusalem. For he is the brightness of eternal glory (see Hebrews 1:3), the splendor of eternal light, the mirror without spot (see Wisdom 7:26).
>
> Look into that mirror daily, O queen and spouse of Jesus Christ. Always study your face in it, so that within and without you may adorn and clothe and gird yourself with all manner of virtue. So by God's grace you can contemplate blessed poverty, holy humility and sacred charity, which are reflected in that mirror.

Francis invited Clare to lead a community of women who would live like his friars. On Palm Sunday, 1212, Clare met him and his brothers at a chapel where she committed herself to live by the gospel in poverty and chastity. Clare's family was outraged because they felt she had disgraced them. Relatives even tried to bring her home forcibly, but she held firm. In a short time things calmed down, and many prominent women of Assisi, including her sister and mother, joined her.

Francis gave Clare a house near the church of San Damiano outside the walls of Assisi. There she and her sisters happily followed a severe pattern of life. The women wore rough habits, went barefoot, fasted often, slept on the floor, abstained from meat entirely, and spoke only when necessary.

Like Francis, Clare was determined to imitate Christ's poverty. She wanted her sisters to own nothing and live on daily contributions. *O blessed poverty!* she wrote to her friend Queen Agnes,

> to those who love and embrace her she gives eternal riches. O holy poverty!
>
> To those who possess and desire her, God promises the kingdom of heaven and bestows eternal glory and the blessed life. O poverty whom the Lord Jesus Christ deigned to embrace so completely!
>
> Rejoice and be glad that so great and good a Lord, on coming into the Virgin's womb willed to appear despised, needy and poor in this world, so that men who were in dire poverty and suffering great need of heavenly food might be made rich in him.

Within a few years, convents of Clare's followers popped up in Italy, France, and Bohemia. Clare seems to have had a gift of healing which blessed her sisters and neighbors. But she herself was ill for twenty-seven years before she died in 1253.

> *The saints differ from us in their exuberance, the excess of our human talents. Moderation is not their secret. It is in the wildness of their dreams, the desperate vitality of their ambitions, that they stand apart from ordinary people of good will.*
>
> —Phyllis Mcginley

AUGUST 11 / PATRON OF TELEVISION

Care of the Soul; Imitation of Christ; Leading Women; Pursuit of Holiness; A Soul Afire

188. Fina

(D. 1253)

St. Fina is the heroine of the old northern Italian town of San Geminiano. Unlike other great women such as **St. Clare** or **St. Teresa of Ávila**, Fina is not remembered for anything she did. She is celebrated for having patiently—even joyfully—endured a lengthy, grievous illness without complaint. For people like me, who don't handle even little pains well, meditating on Fina is worthwhile.

We don't know much about Fina. John DiCoppo, the saint's thirteenth-century biographer, tells more about miracles she worked after her death than he does about her life. Apparently Cambio and Imperiera, her father and mother, were from well-established families but poor. Imperiera instructed her daughter in the faith and in household crafts. Even as a child Fina seems to have been a recluse. Perhaps she was kept at home because she was already fragile and given to illness.

In her teen years Fina became a beautiful young woman. "It pleased God," says DiCoppo, "that she had a lovely face, was tall of stature and well-proportioned." But illness struck and ruined all her loveliness. DiCoppo described Fina's unthinkable response to her horrible condition:

> **St. Paul** teaches that suffering makes us strong in spirit. For this reason, when Fina was at her prettiest and most attractive, it pleased Jesus Christ, our master, to allow her to suffer a serious illness. She was paralyzed from her neck down through all of her body. She could not get up from her couch, or even move a hand or a foot.
>
> As God permitted this affliction, she decided not to rest her body on anything soft or comfortable. Instead, she chose an oak plank for her bed. And because one side of her body was afflicted with the sickness and wearied her greatly, she slept on the other. Thus, for five years she lay on that side. She would not allow anyone to move her or to change her clothes. This holy virgin spent so many days lying only on one side, that her flesh rotted with sores. . . . Even though she was so grievously afflicted, she never complained or groaned. But she kept a joyful countenance and gave thanks to God.

Imperiera cared for Fina as best she could. But she had to leave her alone for long hours when she went out to work or beg. One day, however, Imperiera was assaulted on the street and died at her doorstep. From that time Fina had to depend upon the casual attention of neighbors, many of whom were repulsed by her sores. Thus, her condition rapidly worsened.

Fina was devoted to **St. Gregory the Great,** who persevered while severe gastritis enervated his body. She frequently asked him to intercede for her endurance. Just before she died, St. Gregory appeared in a vision to comfort her and told her that she would die eight days later on his feast. And so it happened that Fina's torments ended on March 12, 1253, the anniversary of St. Gregory the Great.

Townspeople said that when she was lifted from her plank, it was found to be covered with white violets. Several friends who approached her bier were healed. These were the first of thousands of miracles that have occurred through her intercession. Thus, Fina, who was alone and neglected in her suffering, became a popular hero.

May all Christians who are impatient in their smallest afflictions and infirmities be ashamed and follow the example of Saint Fina.

—John Dicoppo

MARCH 12
Enduring Trials; Miracles Do Happen; Suffering

189. Giles of Assisi

(D. 1262)

Young Giles admired **Francis of Assisi**, but kept a safe distance from the radical saint. However, when Peter and Bernard, his good friends, became friars, Giles also decided to embrace a life of poverty. He met Francis, and while they were speaking, a woman approached them, begging. "Give her your coat," said Francis. Without hesitating, Giles gave it to her. He had passed the little test. Next day Francis clothed Giles with the habit. From that time Giles became his dearest brother.

At first, Francis took St. Giles along on his evangelistic tours of central Italy. But then Giles ventured out on his own. He journeyed to Compostella and to the Holy Land, working along the way so that he could give to the poor he encountered. Once he traveled to Tunis to evangelize the Saracens. However, local Christians felt endangered by Giles' enthusiasm and sent him back to Italy. He spent the rest of his life there in places like Rieti and Perugia.

Giles had very little formal schooling. But he possessed a remarkable spiritual gift of wisdom. Collected in *The Golden Sayings of Brother Giles*, his practical teaching on Christian living still helps us today. Listen, for example, to Giles' counsel to friars who complained that they did not experience any consolation in prayer:

> I advise you to go slowly. For if you had a glass of good wine with some sediment at the bottom, would you shake the glass and mix the wine with the sediment? That is not the thing to do.
>
> And if the grindstone sometimes does not make good flour, the miller does not immediately smash it with a hammer. But he repairs that grindstone gradually, and afterwards it makes good flour. Do likewise yourself. Reflect that you are not at all worthy to receive any consolation from God in prayer. For if someone had lived from the beginning of the world until now and were to live on until the end of the world, and every day while he prayed his eyes shed a dishful of tears, he would not be worthy that God should give him one single consolation.
>
> Labor faithfully, because the grace that God does not give you at one time he may give you at another. And what he does not give you one day or one week or month or year, he could give you another day or another week or month or year. Place your labor humbly in

> God, and God will place his grace in you as it may please him. A metal worker making a knife strikes many blows on the iron before he finishes the knife. But finally he finishes the knife with one blow.

Giles became known throughout Europe as a mystic. Once **St. Louis IX** on his way to the Holy Land stopped at Perugia to see Giles. The two met, embraced, and knelt in silent prayer. Then the king departed, without having exchanged a word with Giles.

However, despite his reputation, Giles himself did not have an easy time with prayer. Temptations constantly interrupted him and he called his spiritual combat a "martyrdom of contemplation." He believed the devil was trying to hinder his divine relationship. But Giles persisted, believing he would ultimately win. As he once said, "the more the devil tries to interfere by troubling me, the lower he descends and is tortured in hell because he is resisting God."

Giles died at Perugia in 1262.

> *The word of God does not belong to him who bears or speaks it, but to him who puts it into practice.*
>
> —Giles of Assisi

APRIL 23
Evangelization; Prayer; Spiritual Warfare

190. Raymond of Penyafort
(1175–1275)

As a lawyer, priest, and preacher, St. Raymond of Penyafort made a significant mark on the history of Spain and the church. His preaching helped re-Christianize Spain after the Moors were overthrown. And his compilation of papal and conciliar decrees was the main source of canon law for seven centuries.

An accomplished lawyer and scholar, Raymond joined the Dominicans at Barcelona in 1222. The forty-seven-year-old novice was assigned to develop a book of case studies for confessors that helped to shape the medieval church's penitential system. Also a gifted preacher, Raymond had remarkable success evangelizing Moors and Jews. And he traveled throughout Spain rejuvenating the spiritual life of Christians that the Moors had enslaved. Among his main themes were spiritual combat and standing firm in trials. Listen to his voice in this letter:

> The preacher of God's truth has told us that all who want to live righteously in Christ will suffer persecution. . . . the only exception to this general statement is, I think, the person who either neglects, or does not know how, to live temperately, justly and righteously in this world.
>
> May you never be numbered among those whose house is peaceful, quiet and free from care; those on whom the Lord's chastisement does not descend; those who live out their days in prosperity, and in the twinkling of an eye will go down to hell.
>
> Your purity of life, your devotion, deserve and call for a reward; because you are acceptable and pleasing to God your purity of life must be made purer still, by frequent buffetings, until you attain perfect sincerity of heart. If from time to time you feel the sword falling on you with double or treble force, this also should be seen as sheer joy and the mark of love.
>
> The two-edged sword consists in conflict without, fears within. It falls with double or treble force within, when the cunning spirit troubles the depths of your heart with guile and enticements. . . .
>
> The sword falls with double and treble force externally when, without cause, persecution breaks out from within the church, where wounds are more serious, especially when inflicted by friends.

> This is that enviable and blessed cross of Christ . . . the cross in which alone we must make our boast, as **Paul**, God's chosen instrument, has told us.

In 1230, Pope Gregory IX brought Raymond to Rome as his confessor. There Raymond collected all the decrees of popes and councils since 1150. Because they were so well arranged, canonists relied on Raymond's *Decretals* until the new codification of 1917.

Characteristically, Raymond tried to dodge ecclesiastical appointments. In 1236, illness saved him from becoming archbishop of Tarragona. But he could not avoid his election as the third general of the Dominicans in 1238. But when he reformed the Dominican rule, he slipped in a clause allowing early retirement of officeholders. And he used it to retire in 1240.

But he continued to work thirty-five more years, focusing on bringing Jews and Moors to Christ. To equip Catholics for this work he introduced the study of Hebrew and Arabic among Dominicans and persuaded **Thomas Aquinas** to write his *Summa Contra Gentes* as an evangelistic tool. Raymond told his general that ten thousand Moors had been baptized through the efforts of the Dominicans. He died at one hundred years of age in 1275.

> *May God shelter you from disturbance in the hidden recesses of his love, until he brings you at last into that place of fullness where you will repose forever in the vision of peace, the security of trust and the restful enjoyment of his riches.*
>
> —Raymond of Penyafort

JANUARY 7 / CANONIZED IN 1601 / PATRON OF CANON LAWYERS AND LIBRARIANS
Leading Men; Suffering

191. Louis IX
(1214–1270)

Had history not left us an accurate record of King Louis IX's reign, we might be tempted to regard his story as religious fiction. Imagine a king who put God first, who would rather die a leper than commit one mortal sin, who prayed the liturgy of the hours daily, who often personally waited table for his poor guests, and who waged war only to build peace—and you would have a snapshot of St. Louis IX.

During his long reign in France from 1235 to 1270, Louis IX presided over a religious and cultural renaissance. For example, he established three monasteries, supported the foundation of the Sorbonne University in Paris. and sponsored the construction of great Gothic cathedrals. Twice Louis went to war against Henry III of England, but instead of pressing for total victory, he negotiated a settlement that he believed would guarantee peace.

If we could ask John of Joinville, his biographer, to name the king's defining trait, I think he would say "just judgment." In the following selection, for example, Joinville describes the king's practice of personally settling his subjects' cases:

> Often in the summer he went after Mass to the wood of Vincennes and sat down with his back against an oak tree, and made us sit all around him. Everyone who had an affair to settle could come and speak to him without the interference of any official. The king would ask, "Is there anyone here who has a case to settle?" All those who had would then stand up and he would say, "Quiet, all of you, and your cases will be dealt with in turn."
>
> Then he would call my Lord Peter of Fontaines and my Lord Geoffrey of Villette and say to one of them, "Now give me your judgment in this case."
>
> When those who spoke for him or for the other part said anything which he saw needed correction, he corrected it himself.

In 1234, Louis IX married Margaret of Provence, to the great displeasure of his mother, Blanche of Castile. She detested the young queen and did all she could to make the couple miserable. For many years, for example, she forced them to live in separate apartments, one situated above her own rooms and another below. But that did not seem to stop their meeting, as Margaret bore Louis IX eleven children. Relief came only when Blanche died in 1254.

Louis IX led two disastrous crusades against the Muslim invaders of Palestine, but we must not be too quick or too harsh in judging him. His sole motive seems to have been to bring aid to Christians suffering under their Saracen conquerors. And he tried, though unsuccessfully, to restrain the violence of the crusading army. On the second expedition, Louis IX caught typhoid fever at Tunis and died on August 24, 1270.

Louis IX had an easier time ruling an entire kingdom with justice than the mayor of a city like Miami has governing today. Things moved more slowly in the thirteenth century, fewer people were alive, and events were somewhat more manageable. But even though everything is bigger now and impossible to control, contemporary governors would do well to imitate the saint-king's love of God and his justice. The results just might seem too good to be true.

AUGUST 25 / CANONIZED IN 1297 / DEATH OF CHILDREN, DIFFICULT MARRIAGES, PARENTS OF LARGE FAMILIES, PRISONERS, SICKNESS
Love in Action; Married Saints; Saints and Politics

192. Bonaventure

(1218?–1274)

From 1248 to 1257, St. Bonaventure taught Scripture and theology at the Franciscan school at Paris. His teaching and writing there established him as a leading scholastic theologian. Bonaventure's books about Christian realities dispel the false contemporary opinion that medieval theologians were dry-as-dust rationalists who wasted time counting angels on the heads of pins. In this excerpt from *The Tree of Life*, Bonaventure lyrically urges the soul to seek God:

> You soul devoted to God, . . .
> run with living desire
> to this Fountain of life and light
> and with the innermost power of your heart cry out to him:
> O eternal and inaccessible,
> clear and sweet stream from the fountain
> hidden from the eyes of all mortals, . . .
> From this Fountain
> flows the stream of the oil of gladness,
> which gladdens the city of God, . . .
> Anoint us with this sacred oil
> and refresh with the longed-for waters of this torrent
> the thirsting throat of our parched hearts
> so that amid shouts of joy and thanksgiving
> we may sing to you
> a canticle of praise,
> proving by experience that
> with you is the fountain of life,
> and in your light we will see light (see Psalm 36:10).

After 1257, as master-general of the Franciscans, Bonaventure governed the friars gently but firmly. He reorganized the order, whose numbers had increased enormously, and he renewed the friars' zeal. However, Bonaventure could not resolve the dissension between rigorists who put poverty above all and moderates who wanted a less-severe rule. His insistence on serious study departed from **St. Francis's** teaching and required the possession of buildings and books. He saw the friars' mission as preaching and giving spiritual direction, complementing the work of parish priests who often were not skilled in these areas.

In 1273, Pope Gregory X appointed Bonaventure cardinal-bishop of Albano. His legates came bearing the red hat and other symbols of office only to find Bonaventure washing the dishes. The saint told his visitors to hang the hat on a tree and wait in the garden until he was finished with his task. "A constant fidelity in small things," he once wrote, "is a great and heroic virtue."

The pope summoned Bonaventure to Rome, charging him to prepare for the Council at Lyon that he had called at the Greek emperor's request to restore unity with the Orthodox churches of the East. In 1274, Bonaventure played a major role at the meeting, even addressing the assembly in Greek, and the delegates agreed on reunion. Bonaventure preached at the mass of reconciliation. The saint must have felt exhilarated at making peace in the church. But he died shortly afterward, not surviving long enough to see his work dashed when Constantinople repudiated the reunion.

No one can be made happy unless he rise above himself,
not by an ascent of the body,
but of the heart.
But we cannot rise above ourselves
unless a higher power lifts us up.
And divine aid is available
to those who seek it from their hearts,
humbly and devoutly.

—Bonaventure

JULY 15 / CANONIZED IN 1482
Christian Unity; Doctors of the Church; Prayer; True Humility

193. Humbert of Romans
(1200?–1277)

By 1254, when Humbert of Romans became the fifth master-general of the Dominicans, the order had grown very large. Dominican convents of friars and nuns all over Europe lived in diverse patterns and used different standards for the admission of new members. So the condition of the order seemed somewhat chaotic, but Humbert was just the right leader to deal with it. A lawyer by training, he was a stickler for detail. However, at the same time he appreciated that the friars' ministry of preaching depended upon an element of charismatic freedom.

First, he achieved a measure of unity in the order by revising and standardizing the Dominican liturgy. Then he developed structures for all Dominican houses and institutions that gracefully improved discipline. These included a single set of constitutions for all Dominican nuns, a revised constitution for the friars, and a statute governing the order's academic life. He also revitalized the order by opening new apostolic ventures. For example, fascinated by the East, he had friars trained in oriental studies to prepare them to carry the gospel to Arabs and Tartars.

Throughout the nine years of his administration, Humbert had to defend the order against a vicious assault by the secular clergy at the University of Paris, who were out to destroy both the Dominicans and the Franciscans. Among the actions Humbert took was his effort to repair long-standing poor relations with the Franciscans. He promulgated a joint letter with the Franciscan minister-general that exhorted the two communities to collaborate in their struggle for survival. But the vexatious controversy that divided the orders persisted long after his death.

Ill health caused Humbert to resign his office in 1263. He filled his time with writing books, notably *On the Formation of Preachers*, a treatise that still offers valuable teaching. Here is an excerpt:

> There are many people whose spirits are in their bodies like corpses in their tombs. And, just as God will, at the end of time, raise up dead bodies by his word, so he now gives life to dead spirits by the power of his word. "The hour is coming—indeed it is already here—when the

dead will hear the voice of the Son of God, and all who hear it will live" (John 5:25 *NJB*).

Again, there are many who, spiritually, have nothing to live on. But it is the word of God which sustains man's spiritual life. "Man does not live by bread alone, but by every word which comes from the mouth of God" (see Matthew 4:4). Poor people who have nothing with which to keep themselves alive come running for alms. Similarly people who are spiritually poor ought to come running to sermons, to receive the word of God in their spirit, to keep themselves alive.

Again, there are many who, in the darkness of this world, do not know how to hold to the right path. But the word of God is like a torch by night, showing them the right way. "Your word is a lamp for my feet, a light on my path" (Psalm 119:105 *NJB*).

Again, there are some medicines which work against some kinds of sickness, but not against them all. But the word of God works against every kind of spiritual sickness. "Your word is all powerful, Lord, it cures everything" (see Wisdom 18:15; 16:12).

Humbert died at Romans, his hometown near Valence, France, in 1277.

Preaching is performed by means of the tongue, and the tongue goes astray extremely easily, unless it is directed by the power of God.

—Humbert of Romans

JULY 14
Leading Men; Saints and the Bible

194. Albert the Great
(1206–1280)

St. Albert's friends at the universities of Paris and Cologne called him "the Great" and the "universal doctor," apt nicknames for this scholar-saint. Not only did he lay a foundation for scholasticism, the avantgarde philosophy of the Middle Ages that integrated faith and reason, driven by his irrepressible curiosity, Albert also mastered the natural sciences. Often compared to his contemporary, Roger Bacon, he wrote authoritatively about biology, chemistry, physics, astronomy, and geography. Two centuries before Columbus, for example, he held that the earth was not flat, but spherical.

St. Albert the Great was also a practical spiritual guide, as this passage from his treatise on union with God shows:

> He who enters into the secret place of his own soul passes beyond himself and truly ascends to God.
>
> Therefore, banish from your heart the distractions of earth. Turn your eyes to spiritual joys so that you may learn at last to rest in the light of the contemplation of God. Indeed, the soul's true life and repose are to abide in God, held fast by love and refreshed by divine consolations.
>
> In your spiritual ascent and your search for a closer union with God, you must allow yourself no rest, no slipping back. You must go forward till you have obtained the object of your desires. Follow the example of mountain climbers. If your desires turn aside after objects that pass below, you will lose yourself in byways and your mind will be drawn in all directions. Your progress will be uncertain. You will not reach your goal. And you will not find rest after your labors.
>
> But if your heart and mind, led by love and desire, withdraw from the distractions of the world, you will grow strong. Your recollection will deepen the higher you rise on the wings of knowledge and desire. Little by little as you abandon baser things to rest in the one true and unchangeable Good, you will dwell there, held fast by the bonds of love.

Against the wishes of his noble Swabian parents, Albert became a Dominican friar at age sixteen. The community recognized his ability and for twenty years assigned him to teach at various German universities and at Paris. In 1248, Albert organized the house of study at

Cologne. During four years there, he became the mentor and friend of **St. Thomas Aquinas,** who later erected his philosophical system on his teacher's foundation.

From 1254 to 1262, Albert held various church offices, serving as a Dominican provincial, theologian to the pope, and bishop of Regensburg. Temperamentally unsuited for flinty ecclesiastical politics or tough-minded pastoral leadership, he was not successful as a bishop and resigned his see in 1262. He spent the autumn of his life teaching at Cologne. In 1277 he went to Paris to defend the work of Thomas Aquinas, who had died in 1274, but was not able to prevent his friend's posthumous condemnation. Albert seems to have succumbed to Alzheimer's disease in 1278 and he died in 1280.

An egg given during life for love of God is more profitable for eternity than a cathedral full of gold given after death.

To forgive those who have injured us in our body, our reputation, our goods, is more advantageous to us than to cross the seas to go to venerate the sepulcher of the Lord.

Knowledge of divine things is imprinted on our minds by union with God, who is Wisdom itself, just as the wax molds itself into the seal—not the reverse.

—Albert the Great

NOVEMBER 15 / CANONIZED IN 1931 / PATRON OF STUDENTS OF NATURAL SCIENCE

Innovative Saints; Prayer; Study

195. Thomas Aquinas
(1225?–1275)

When St. Thomas Aquinas decided in 1244 to join the Dominicans, his brothers imprisoned him in a castle. They even tempted him with a prostitute, trying unsuccessfully to untrack his vocation. As Dominicans were looked down on as beggars, the family preferred that Thomas at least become a Benedictine. Then perhaps he might become abbot of prestigious Monte Cassino, where he had gone to school.

But after a year Thomas escaped and became a Dominican. At Paris and Cologne he studied philosophy and theology with **St. Albert the Great.** Probably referring to Aquinas's physical bulk, Albert accurately predicted that "the lowing of this dumb ox would be heard all over the world."

For the next two decades Thomas divided his time between Paris and Italy, teaching and writing prodigiously. Between 1259 and 1264 he developed one of his major works, the *Summa Contra Gentes.* Using Aristotle, who was popular among Muslim, Jewish, and pagan scholars, Aquinas strove in this book to give these peers rational arguments for Christianity. In the following selection, for example, he explains reasonably how an unchangeable God can answer prayer without changing:

> The immutability of providence does not mean that prayer is unprofitable, any more than it means that there is no room for contingency within the domain of providence. Prayer is not made to God in order to get the eternal plan of providence changed, because this is impossible. Its purpose is that people should obtain what they desire from God.
>
> It is appropriate that God should assent to the pious desires of rational creatures. Not as if our desires moved the immovable God, but it is a consequence of his own goodness that he brings about what they desire in a suitable way. All things naturally desire the good. And it belongs to the excellence of God's goodness to distribute being and well-being to everything in an ordered way. It follows that, in line with his own goodness, he fulfills the pious desires which are unfolded in prayer.
>
> God loves his creatures, and he loves each one the more, the more it shares his own goodness, which is the first and primary object of his love. Therefore he wants the desires of his rational creatures to be

fulfilled because they share most perfectly of all creatures the goodness of God.

And his will is an accomplisher of things because he is the cause of things by his will. So it belongs to the divine goodness to fulfill the desires of rational creatures which are put to him in prayer.

In 1266, Thomas began to write his most important work, the *Summa Theologica*. In five hefty volumes he developed a systematic statement of his mature thought on all Christian doctrine. But Thomas left the *Summa* unfinished. An experience at mass in December 1273 persuaded him to stop writing. "All I have written," he said, "seems to me like straw compared to what I have seen and what has been revealed to me."

Thomas Aquinas died a year later. For a half-century after his death the saint was under a cloud of suspicion because of his innovation. But through the centuries he has come to be esteemed as one of the greatest Catholic theologians of all time.

We remember Thomas Aquinas most as a high-powered theologian, whose stature we could never equal. But Aquinas is a saint, not because of his accomplishments, but because he lived a committed Christian life of humble prayer and service. That we can imitate, no matter what we do for work.

JANUARY 28 / CANONIZED IN 1323 / PATRON OF STUDENTS AND SCHOOLS
Faith Seeking Understanding; Intercession; Prayer; Study

196. Mechtild of Magdeburg

(1210–1297)

God says to the soul:
I come to my love
As dew on the flowers.

Welcome sweet dove!
You have flown so long over the earth
That your wings have grown strong enough
To carry you up to heaven!

—Mechtild of Magdeburg

Mechtild's century, the thirteenth, was the golden age of chivalry. Troubadours sang of romance between lords and ladies. It was also a golden age of saints, including **Francis, Clare**, **Dominic,** and **Gertrude.** Mechtild takes her place among them as a mystic and poet. She was a troubadour of the love that binds the soul to God.

Thus, in *The Flowing Light of the Godhead,* Mechtild describes the union of the soul with God in the imagery of courtly love:

> When the poor soul comes to Court, she is discreet and modest. She looks at her God with joyful eyes. Ah! how lovingly she is there received! She is silent but longs above everything to praise him. And he, with great desire, shows her his divine heart. It glows like red gold in a great fire. And God lays the soul in his glowing heart so that he, the great God, and she, the humble maid, embrace and are one as water with wine. Then she is overcome and beside herself for weakness. And he is overpowered with love for her, as he always was. Then she says, "Lord! you art my beloved! My desire! My flowing stream! My sun! and I am your reflection!"
>
> Thus does the loving soul who cannot exist without God, come to Court.

At twenty-three, Mechtild moved from her village to Magdeburg, Thuringia, in central Europe. She lived there many years as a Béguine and later became a Dominican tertiary. Béguines were women without religious vows who formed communities to serve the poor.

Mechtild exhausted herself with austerities because she believed she had to conquer her self in order to achieve oneness with God. Later she wrote this beautiful dialogue between God and the soul about curbing desires and orienting them to God:

> God: You hunt ardently for your love,
> What do you bring to me, my Queen?
> Soul: Lord! I bring you my treasure;
> It is greater than the mountains, . . .
> More glorious than the sun,
> More manifold than the stars,
> It outweighs the whole earth!
> God: O image of my Divine Godhead, . . .
> What is your treasure called?
> Soul: Lord! it is called my heart's desire!
> I have withdrawn it from the world, . . .
> Where, O Lord, shall I lay it?
> God: Your heart's desire shall you lay nowhere
> But in my own divine heart
> And on my human breast.
> There alone you will find comfort
> And be embraced by my Spirit.

Bothered by persecution for her outspoken criticism of church abuses and laxity, Mechtild retired to the convent at Helfta in 1285. Welcomed there by St. Gertrude the Great, she spent her last twelve years in the hospitable environment of that famous monastery.

> *If it had not been for the delighted reports of the mystics, their insistence on Reality's overwhelming actuality and their heroic self-dedication to that which they have seen, we little half-animal creatures could never have supposed that the life of conscious correspondence with this all-penetrating Perfection was possible for the human soul.*
>
> —Evelyn Underhill

NOVEMBER 19
Conversations with God; Intimacy with the Divine; Poets; A Soul Afire

197. Philip Benizi
(1233–1285)

On May 24, 1276, St. Philip Benizi, the head of the order of Servites, arrived in Pistoia, Italy, for a general chapter. Word zipped through the city that the famous preacher would be speaking to all at the Servite church. At the time civil war was gnawing at Pistoia, and violent men and criminals from both sides came to hear the saint.

Before a hushed, standing-room-only crowd, Philip read from Psalm 137: "By the rivers of Babylon we sat and wept at the memory of Zion" (Psalm 137:1 *NJB*). Then with prophetic courage he spoke directly to the warriors about their wicked behavior:

> Like the psalmist, we weep over the barbarous feuds by which you seem hell bent on destroying each other.
>
> I beg you to check this fury. Remember, God created you in his image and wants you to aspire to heavenly things, not to grovel on the earth like senseless creatures.
>
> Your city is cursed like ancient Babylon. Our Lord no longer reigns here, but wicked Nabucodnosor. I mean the Evil One to whom you continually sacrifice human lives. There is really cause to weep over this wretched Babylon.
>
> Remember, he who shed his blood for you forbids you to shed the blood of your neighbor. You are not sons of the Prince of Peace, but of Esau, for you are men of blood. Your songs are all of mourning and lamentation and woe. You have forgotten the Lord your God. You don't call upon him in the day of trouble. No, you only blaspheme his name. And the sword and shield that he put into your hands you have used to spread destruction.
>
> O unhappy daughter of Babylon, the judgment of God condemns you, "Raze it, raze it to the ground!" But we will intercede with the Blessed Virgin Mary. We will beg her to obtain for you from God the blessings of peace and unity. Brethren, lay aside your dissensions so that the Lord does not let you fall into the hands of the wicked. Seek peace and the God of peace will be with you.

Philip's eloquence did not stop the war, but reportedly many of the worst offenders repented and put down their arms. Among them was Bonaventure Buonaccorso, so touched by Philip's sermon that he publicly sought forgiveness of his enemies. Later Bonaventure became a Servite and a saint. Philip's preaching in other cities produced many other remarkable conversions of mercenaries into saints, including St. Peregrine Laziosi, once a ringleader of the sedition.

Philip Benizi had joined the Servites in 1255. In order to humble himself, he worked as a gardener, hiding his talents and education. But his gifts were soon discovered and despite his resistance he rapidly ascended to leadership in the community. Elected superior general in 1267, he governed the Servites for eighteen years. He visited the order's houses throughout Europe, codified their rules, sent the first Servite missionaries to their martyrdom in Russia, and founded the Servite third order. In 1285, realizing that his health was rapidly declining, Philip retired to the poorest Servite house at Todi, where he died on August 15.

When rumor reached Philip that he was a serious candidate to be elected pope, he did the only sensible thing a person could do in the face of such a possibility. He hid in a cave in the mountains for three months until the danger had passed.

AUGUST 23 / CANONIZED IN 1671
Conversion; Great Preachers; Peacemakers; Prophets

198. Margaret of Hungary
(1242–1270)

Margaret was born to Béla IV, king of Hungary, at a moment when the country was threatened by enemies. So the king promised God that if things reversed in his favor he would dedicate his little princess to the religious life. The prayer was answered, and Béla put Margaret in the care of the Dominican Sisters at Veszprém. When Margaret was twelve, Béla built a convent for her on an island in the Danube near Buda. There the young teenager professed her vows.

A young woman of extraordinary beauty, St. Margaret attracted the attention of suitors even though she was a nun. Ottokar, the king of Bohemia, was determined to marry her. For political reasons, Béla liked the idea. He asked Margaret to get released from her commitments and marry Ottokar. Béla had not bargained for the steely resistance of his strong-willed daughter. She responded to his request with defiance:

> When I was only seven years old, you tried to espouse me to the Polish Duke. You will remember my answer then. I said that I wished to serve him only to whom you had espoused me at my birth. As a child, I would not yield to your will in opposition to God's claims on me. Do you think that I am likely to give in to you now that I am older and wiser? And am more capable of grasping the greatness of the divine grace that has been given me? Then, my Father, stop trying to turn me from my determination to remain a religious. I prefer the heavenly kingdom to that which has been offered me by the King of Bohemia. I would rather die than obey these commands of yours that will bring death to my soul.
>
> As often as you command what is pleasing to God I will obey you as my parent and master. But if you command me to do what is contrary to God's will, then you are neither my parent nor my master. I will never obey you. I would rather cut off my nose and my lips than consent to such a thing. Mark my words. If matters ever come to such a pass and I am driven to it, I will surely put an end to the whole affair by mutilating myself, so that I shall never again be desirable to any man.

So Béla backed down. Witnesses say that had he persisted, gritty Margaret would likely have fulfilled her threat.

Margaret punished herself with extreme self-abnegation that some observers call "self-crucifixion." She undertook the most menial and repugnant tasks. *Butler's Lives of the Saints* says that she performed "marvelous" service to the sick, so nauseating that its "details cannot be set out before the fastidious modern reader." Out of sympathy for the poor, Margaret also imitated their squalor. She so neglected all personal hygiene, for example, that she repulsed her sisters. And for long periods she denied herself food and sleep. Since she was a princess and the convent was built for her, no one seems to have been able to temper her excesses. Her utter disregard for her body certainly shortened her life. Margaret died on January 18, 1270 at the age of twenty-eight.

The church recognizes Margaret of Hungary as a saint in spite of the traces of willfulness and pride that seem to have marked her life. But she excelled in charity, and "love covers over many a sin" (1 Peter 4:8 NJB*). Those of us who want to be holy, but have many "in-spite-ofs" to contend with, can be glad for that.*

JANUARY 18 / CANONIZED IN 1943
Feisty Saints; Vocation

199. Margaret of Cortona
(1247?–1297)

Rejected by her stepmother and hungry for affection, twelve-year-old Margaret was seduced by a young Italian knight of Montepulciano. For nine years she lived scandalously as his mistress and bore him a son. One day, however, she found him dead, butchered by an assassin. Margaret interpreted her lover's tragic demise as God's judgment. Repentant and afraid, she fled home with her boy, but her stepmother rebuffed her. So she sought the help of Franciscans at Cortona, who cared for her and tried to moderate her remorse.

St. Margaret tried to appease what she believed to be divine vengeance by severely abusing her body. She did public penance, wore a hair shirt, beat herself until she bled, and even scarred her beautiful face. As part of her misguided penitence, she even seems to have treated her son with severity.

She longed to feel reconciled with God, but believed her past sexual sins were an insuperable obstacle to any peaceful union with him. But she begged Christ to receive her as a daughter. Finally, after a general confession and receiving the Eucharist, within her heart she heard him say: *My daughter!* And Margaret responded with this prayer:

> O my infinitely and sovereign sweet Lord! Here at last is the day which my Jesus promised me! At last, in this intoxicating moment, he has given me the sweet name of daughter, that word which I had yearned and prayed for with all my heart's fervor. My God has said to me: My daughter! My Jesus has called me: My daughter!

Later she is reported to have had this conversation with Christ:

> "My daughter, one day I will place you among the Seraphs, among the virgins whose hearts are flaming with love for God."
>
> "How can that be, Lord, after I have soiled myself with so many sins?"
>
> "My daughter, your many penances have purified your soul from all the effects of sin to such a degree that your contrition and your sufferings will reintegrate you into the purity of a virgin.
>
> "My daughter, you are a rose among flowers. You are pure. And for your love of chastity. I have placed you among the virgins."
>
> "O Lord, you are the life of my life! You are a treasure to me, without which all wealth seems utter poverty. With joy dear Lord, I offer

> myself to suffer anything for love of you. You know that I seek and want nothing but you, who are infinitely sweet and without whom I would feel as though I was in hell."

After several years of careful supervision, the Franciscans allowed Margaret to join the Third Order. By the time her son was grown and in the Franciscan novitiate, Margaret had given herself over to nursing the sick poor. She founded a community of like-minded women at a hospital in Cortona. She continued her course of severe self-discipline, directing her prayer and penances toward the conversion of sinners. In the last years of her life she felt led to call others to repentance and persuaded many to reform their lives. Margaret, the Magdalen of the Franciscans, died in 1297 at age fifty.

For the last twenty-nine years of her life, guilt feelings and sexual temptations tortured Margaret of Cortona. We may empathize with her misery as guilt and lust are still with us, strong as ever. But few can tolerate or even understand the ever-increasing self-punishments and occasional self-mutilations, the unimaginable means she chose to subdue her torments.

FEBRUARY 22 / CANONIZED IN 1728 / PATRON OF THE FALSELY ACCUSED, HOMELESS, MIDWIVES, SINGLE LAYWOMEN, AND TERTIARIES
Conversations with God; Passion for Purity; Repentance; Sexual Temptation

200. Mechtild of Helfta
(1241?–1298)

Little seven-year-old Mechtild von Hackeborn accompanied her mother to the monastery at Rodarsdorf, Saxony, to visit Gertrude, her sister—and she never left. The child went from nun to nun, begging them to keep her there. Mechtild's pleading and the nuns' intercession persuaded her mother to let her stay. Gertrude, who was soon elected abbess, took Mechtild under her care and saw to it that she received an excellent education.

In 1258, St. Mechtild moved with the nuns to Helfta, Saxony, where the monastery became renowned as a center of spirituality and education. As a young woman she served as the teacher of the children in the monastery school. In 1261, a five-year-old girl, also named Gertrude, came under her care. Over the years teacher and pupil became closest friends, together growing deep in the spiritual life. And history regards Mechtild and **Gertrude the Great** as two of the church's outstanding women mystics.

Mechtild had such a beautiful singing voice that Gertrude nicknamed her "the nightingale of Christ." As the chantress at Helfta, for forty years she led the community in the celebration of the liturgy of the hours. But she regarded prayer itself as her most important service. Sometime she was so caught up in her meditation that she lost contact with reality. Gertrude tells us, for example, that once Mechtild was so distracted with divine thoughts that to the disgust of all at table, she unknowingly ate a rotten egg.

Typically, Mechtild carried on mystical conversations with Christ and reported his revelations as counsels to her sisters. Today we still benefit from the practical insight of her messages on Christian living:

> "Christ is more easily possessed than a bit of thread or straw. A single wish, a sigh, is sufficient."
>
> "You can never be in so large a crowd that you are not alone with me [Christ] if you turn to me with your whole heart."
>
> "If any obstacle arises in our service of God, we should take it as a messenger from God, sending it back to him with praise and thanksgiving."
>
> "Temptations cannot hurt you any more than gnats can destroy a mountain."

"God permits persons to keep certain faults that humiliate and discipline them, but make them advance every day in the way of salvation. I would not wish to change by one iota what the Lord's wisdom and mercy had planned for each one."

Over the years St. Gertrude secretly recorded her mentor's messages. As Mechtild lay dying, Gertrude set about editing her revelations into *The Book of Special Grace*. Initially distressed by the idea of the collection, Mechtild accepted it after she sensed Christ's assurance that he wanted it done. Mechtild of Helfta died in 1298 at the age of fifty-seven.

Once Jesus said to Mechtild:

Seek me through your five senses, just as a host awaiting the arrival of a very dear friend looks through the doors and windows to see if the expected guest is coming. The faithful soul ought to watch for me unceasingly through the senses that are the windows of the spirit. If he sees beautiful or lovable things, let him think how beautiful, lovable, and good is the One who made them. When he hears an enchanting melody or an excellent discourse, let him say to himself: "O how sweet will be the voice that will one day call me!" And when he hears conversation or something read aloud, let him seek his beloved in it.

—Mechtild of Helfta

NOVEMBER 16
Conversations with God; The Secrets of Spiritual Success

201. Gertrude the Great

(1256–1302)

If St. Gertrude were alive today, we would esteem her as a spiritual guide. We would woo her out of her cloister—a feminine version of Thomas Merton—to speak at conferences on soul care. Publishers would be hounding her. When she declined their offers, they would scrounge around, collecting her scribbled notes and prayers. This thirteenth-century cloistered nun, scholar, and mystic has a timeless quality which twenty-first-century readers find appealing.

Gertrude came as a five-year-old to the Benedictine convent in Helfta, Saxony. Nothing is known of her background, but the saint herself once hinted that she was an orphan. Gertrude became the pupil and friend of **St. Mechtild**, who was in charge of children at the monastery. By age twenty-five, Gertrude was an attractive and intelligent young professional woman who had become a proficient student of Latin literature and taken her vows as a nun.

In Gertrude's twenty-sixth year, Christ appeared to her in a life-changing vision. One evening when she was about to go to bed, she seemed to see Jesus in the form of a handsome youth. She wrote:

> You attracted my heart and my eyes by the infinite light of your glory. Then with tenderness you said to me, "Your salvation is near. Why are you consumed with grief?" Although I knew I was standing bodily in our dormitory, it seemed to me that I was in the corner of the choir where I usually offered up my tepid prayers. There I seemed to hear these words: "I will save you. I will deliver you. Don't be afraid." Afterward I saw you place your right hand in mine, as if to ratify your promise.
>
> Then I heard you say, "You have licked the dust with my enemies, and you have sucked honey from thorns. But return now to me—I will receive you and my divine delights will be like wine for you." My soul melted within me.

Gertrude wanted to draw nearer to the Lord, but a vast, impenetrable hedge of thorns prevented her. She saw the obstacle as a figure of her faults and sins. Jesus, however, took her by the hand and instantly placed her at his side.

> Then in that hand which you had extended to me as a pledge, I recognized your radiant wounds, which have made to no effect the handwriting that was against us (see Colossians 2:14).

This conversion experience initiated Gertrude's lifelong career as a mystic and visionary. We have an inspiring and instructional record of her intimate relationship with the Lord in the book commonly called the *Revelations of St. Gertrude*. The saint wrote only part two of this five-part treatise, which compares favorably with the works of **Teresa of Ávila**. An anonymous colleague compiled the other parts. After her extraordinary encounter with the Lord, Gertrude turned from her secular studies and devoted herself to prayer and the study of Scripture and the fathers of the church. Gertrude died after a decade of illness in 1302.

Few of us will ever fly the mystical heights with Gertrude. If we see visions at all, I suspect they will be of the impenetrable hedge of our thorny sins and faults that keep us from the Lord. However, we should let this great woman remind us that we don't have to muscle our way through our self-constructed blockade. As Jesus did for Gertrude, he will lift us over it and instantly bring us to himself.

NOVEMBER 16 / PATRON OF THE WEST INDIES
Conversations with God; Intimacy with the Divine; Mercy; Visions and Visionaries

202. Jacopone da Todi
(1230?–1306)

Jacopo Benedetti seems to have invented a peculiar way to lose his life for Christ in order to gain it (see Matthew 10:39). In 1268, Vanna, his beautiful wife of one year, was killed at a party when a balcony collapsed. That tragedy prompted Jacopo's conversion to Christ that he first expressed in most unusual ways. A well-established attorney in Umbria, Italy, he renounced his profession. And for a decade Jacopo performed strange public penances in the streets of Todi. Once, for example, he crawled through the center of town wearing a donkey's harness. Children made fun of him, calling him "Jacopone," which means "Big Jimmy," a nickname that stuck for life.

Perhaps Jacopone went temporarily insane because of his wife's death. Or perhaps an overwhelming sense of sin accounts for his conduct. Or perhaps, as he says in the following poem, the unfathomable love of Christ overcame him with a divine "madness":

> Love [Jesus] is nailed on the cross, that has seized him and will not let him go. I go running to it and am nailed there too so that I cannot go astray, for to flee from it would make me disappear and not be inscribed among the beloved.
>
> O cross, I am hanging on you and am nailed to you, so that I, dying, may taste the life with which you are adorned. O honeyed death, sad for one who has not undergone it! O my soul, so burning to receive its wound that I may die with my heart overcome with love.
>
> O love of the lamb, greater than the wide sea, who can tell of you? Whoever is drowned in it and has it on all sides does not know where he is, and madness, walking driven mad with love, seems the straight way to him.

In 1278, Jacopone became a lay brother in a Franciscan community in Umbria. At the time a heated controversy divided the order between the Spirituals, who practiced a strict observance of **St. Francis**'s life pattern and the Conventuals, who took a moderated approach to the founder's way. Jacopone became a spokesperson for the Spirituals. Apparently in good conscience, with pointed satire he vigorously opposed Pope Boniface VIII, the champion of the Conventuals. Thus, when the pope suppressed the Spirituals in 1297, Jacopone landed in prison, where he stayed six years.

While in jail, in contrast to his vitriolic satires, Jacopone composed lovely songs in his native Umbrian. For example, listen as he celebrates the love of Christ in this poem:

> Sweet, incomparable love, you are, Christ, to love. You are the love that often joins friends who fight; you anoint every wound and cure it without ointment. Love, you do not abandon but pardon the one who offends you and crown with glory the one who knows how to humble himself.
>
> Great, sweet and delicate love, you are the uncreated divine, you who make the seraph flame with glory. Cherubim and other singers, apostles and doctors, virgins—you make them all happy. Patriarchs and prophets you draw from the devil's net. They have such thirst for you, love, that it will never be slaked.

After Pope Boniface VIII died in 1303, Jacopone was released. He lived the rest of his life quietly at a convent of Poor Clares near Todi. He died there on Christmas Day in 1306.

> *He became a fool for Christ's sake, and having deceived the world by a new artifice, took heaven by storm.*
>
> —Inscription on the Tomb of Jacopone da Todi

DECEMBER 25
A Passionate Love; Poets

203. Aldobrandesca
(1245–1310)

St. Aldobrandesca was a mystic in thirteenth-century Siena, Italy. She was a popular curiosity in the town because of her many visions, ecstasies, and miracles. Once, for example, a hospital maid came upon Aldobrandesca when she was in a trance. The saint appeared to be cataleptic—muscles rigid, unconscious, and without feeling. Aldobrandesca's biographer says the woman screamed in fear,

> summoning everyone to see her whom she thought was dead. Some were amazed, others amused. They began to punch and pinch her, to prick her with pins and to burn her fingers with candle flames. When she returned to her senses and felt her entire body in excruciating pain, she simply said: "May God forgive you."

That act of forgiveness tells us more about Aldobrandesca than all of her paranormal experiences. Visions and ecstasies may be evidence of a supernatural touch, but mercy expressed to others is a sure sign of divine love. We honor Aldobrandesca as a saint for her charity, not for her trances.

As a young woman Aldobrandesca had reluctantly acquiesced to the marriage her parents arranged, but she seems to have grown to love her husband. However, he died young, leaving her a childless widow. Aldobrandesca decided to remain celibate and dedicate herself to a life of prayer. She associated herself with the Humiliati, an order of penitents who served the poor and the sick. For a while she lived in Siena, but later sought solitude on a small farm outside the town.

Aldobrandesca's biographer says she had to fight persistent sexual temptations. Erotic memories of relations with her husband bothered her, and she tried to fight them off by wearing a hair shirt. Aldobrandesca's biographer assures us that it worked, but her ever more extreme bodily penances suggest that the temptation never faded.

Gradually, Aldobrandesca simplified her life, giving away her money and belongings. In her old age she moved to a hospital, where she could care for the sick and the poor. She comforted widows and orphans, and she evangelized prostitutes. Aldobrandesca also made good use of her spiritual gifts:

A certain boy who suffered great pains throughout his body was cured as soon as Aldobrandesca made the sign of the cross over him. No other remedy than the saint's sign of the cross was needed for a girl whose face was so puffed up that one eye was entirely closed. Physicians had scheduled her for surgery the next day, but it wasn't necessary. Nor was any other remedy needed for a woman who was gravely ill with breast cancer.

The doctor had recommended surgery to another woman with breast cancer, but Aldobrandesca reached the poor woman first. When the saint anointed the woman with blessed oil and made the sign of the cross over her, the tumor disappeared. Another woman with cancer put a grape leaf on her breast, invoked Aldobrandesca's name and made the sign of the cross. And she was soon healed.

Aldobrandesca performed her charitable works daily right up to her death on April 26, 1310.

Mystics like St. Aldobrandesca of Siena fascinate us. They are so penetrated by the supernatural that they make visions appear to be as natural as visits with grandma. They seem to be touched by the divine, and we also long for God to rest his hand upon us.

APRIL 26

Contemplatives in Action; Forgiveness; Healing Touch; Sexual Temptation; The Sign of the Cross; Temptation

204. Angela of Foligno
(1248?–1309)

Angela of Foligno is a model for people who want to simplify their lifestyle. As a young adult she reveled in luxury and sensuality. She married a rich man of Foligno, Italy, and used his wealth to indulge herself in possessions. And her impetuous temperament nudged her into sinful behavior.

However in 1285, Angela made a surprising about-face. One day she wept bitterly and confessed a serious sin to a friar, who absolved her. Then she embarked on a life of prayer and penance. Over the next six years, step-by-step she divested herself of her attachments to people and things.

In 1288 her mother, husband, and sons died of a plague. As a widow, Angela was free to concentrate on her pursuit of holiness. She modeled herself on **St. Francis of Assisi** and joined the Franciscan Third Order in 1291.

Like Francis, Angela expected to meet Christ in the poor. For instance, on Holy Thursday, 1292, she and a companion went to care for lepers at the hospital in Foligno. After they had washed a man who was badly decomposed, they drank some of the bathwater. The experience so moved Angela that she says all the way home she felt "as if we had received Holy Communion."

Angela of Foligno was a visionary who, like **St. Catherine of Siena,** at the drop of a hat might fall into a trance. From 1292 to 1296 she dictated her revelations to Brother Arnold, her confessor. Angela recorded thirty steps of her tortured spiritual journey, which always seemed to blend awareness and absence of God, certitude and doubt, and joy and agony.

A small band of disciples gathered around the saint. She led them wisely, instructing them in basic Christian living. This excerpt from her *Instructions* advocates prayer and meditation on Scripture:

> No one can be saved without divine light. Divine light causes us to begin and to make progress, and it leads us to the summit of perfection. Therefore if you want to begin and to receive this divine light, pray. If you have begun to make progress, pray. And if you have reached the summit of perfection, and want to be super-illumined so as to remain in that state, pray.

If you want faith, pray. If you want hope, pray. If you want charity, pray. If you want poverty, pray. If you want obedience, pray. If you want chastity, pray. If you want humility, pray. If you want meekness, pray. If you want fortitude, pray. If you want any virtue, pray.

And pray in this fashion: always reading the Book of Life, that is, the life of the God-man, Jesus Christ, whose life consisted of poverty, pain, contempt and true obedience.

At Christmas, 1308, Angela told her companions she would die shortly. A few days later Christ appeared to her, promising to come personally to take her to heaven. She died in her sleep on January 3, 1309.

I was inspired with the thought that if I wanted to go to the cross, I would need to strip myself in order to be lighter and go naked to it. This would entail forgiving all who had offended me, stripping myself of everything worldly, of all attachments to men and women, of my friends and relatives, and everyone else, and likewise, of my possessions and of my very self. Then I would be free to give my heart to Christ from whom I had received so many graces, and to walk along the thorny path, that is, the path of tribulation.

—Angela of Foligno

FEBRUARY 28

Contemplatives in Action; Prayer; Repentance; Visions and Visionaries

205. Odoric of Pordenone
(1285?–1331)

We are all familiar with the voyages of Marco Polo, the fourteenth-century Venetian who traveled throughout East Asia. But we may have never heard of his equally adventuresome contemporary, Friar Odoric of Pordenone, the Franciscan saint who also journeyed to the Orient. The young man was motivated by missionary zeal, as he explained later in his memoir: "I desired to travel to the land of the pagans to win the fruit of some souls." But he seems also to have shared Polo's spirit of adventure.

At fifteen, Odoric became a Franciscan at Udine, Italy. For some years he was allowed to live as a hermit in a remote place. Then he returned to Udine where he became well-known for his preaching. But around 1316, apparently struck by missionary wanderlust, St. Odoric set out for India.

Odoric journeyed first to Constantinople. Then staying at Franciscan houses, he traveled through Armenia and sailed down the Persian Gulf and on to Malabar, Sri Lanka, and to the shrine of **St. Thomas** near modern Madras.

While in India he collected the relics of four Franciscan martyrs. As he explained in the following passage from his memoir, a little miracle helped him bring them home safely:

> I was voyaging by sea with these bones to a city called Polumbum, where pepper grows in abundance. The wind slacked off completely. The idolaters aboard began to petition their gods to grant them a favorable breeze—which their gods were utterly unable to produce.
>
> Finally they ordered my companion and me to beseech our God to grant us the wind. The captain of the ship, speaking in Armenian so the others would not understand, said, "But if we don't get the wind, overboard with those bones of yours."
>
> With the captain's words in our ears, my companion and I prayed to God for wind. When we saw the wind was still not forthcoming, we promised many Masses in honor of the glorious Virgin, just so we might have a little wind. But not even then did we have any success.
>
> As a final resort, I took one of the bones of the martyrs and gave it to our servant. I instructed him to hurry to the bow of the ship and quickly throw the relic into the sea.

As soon as the bone was cast in to the sea, a favorable wind began to blow. It did not slack off until we reached port. It was only by the merits of our martyred brothers that we arrived in safety. God withheld his assistance and the Virgin her aid because it was the divine will to draw attention to the holiness of the murdered Franciscans.

Leaving India, Odoric sailed to Sumatra and Java and then northward to China. He spent three years in Peking at a church that had been founded by Archbishop John of Montecorvino, another adventurous Franciscan missionary. Strangely—perhaps out of modesty—Odoric tells us nothing about his evangelistic activities in the East. Later biographers say he converted twenty thousand people, but no source verifies the claim.

He returned home through Tibet, the first European to cross that land. At Udine he was planning another missionary voyage to the East when he died in 1331. He was only about forty-six years old.

Like Odoric, today thousands of Christians—Catholic, Protestant, and Orthodox alike—travel the earth to proclaim the good news message. And we stay-at-home Christians, who do not share their call, can participate vicariously in their adventures by remembering to intercede for them.

JANUARY 14 / CULT CONFIRMED IN 1755
Miracles Do Happen; Missionaries

206. Gregory of Sinai

(D. 1346)

Originally from Cyprus, St. Gregory migrated to Palestine where he joined a monastic community on Mount Sinai. There he immersed himself in the tradition of contemplative prayer that had descended from **St. John Climacus** and **St. Simeon the New Theologian**. Later he moved to Mount Athos in northern Greece, where he developed his own method of contemplation that has influenced Christians worldwide. If, for example, you have ever prayed the Jesus Prayer, then the heritage of St. Gregory of Sinai has probably touched your life.

Like his spiritual forebears, Gregory sought union with God by disciplining the body and quieting the mind. He taught that repetition of the Jesus Prayer opened the soul to the divine presence and led to the highest forms of contemplation. In the following passage, he gives instruction about practicing this prayer:

> Some of the fathers taught that the prayer should be said in full: "Lord, Jesus Christ, Son of God, have mercy upon me." Others advised saying half, thus: "Jesus, Son of God, have mercy upon me"; or "Lord Jesus Christ, have mercy upon me," or to alternate, sometimes saying it in full and sometimes in a shorter form. Yet it is not advisable to pander to laziness by changing the words of the prayer too often, but to persist a certain time as a test of patience.
>
> Again, some teach the saying of the prayer with the lips, others with and in the mind. In my opinion both are advisable. For at times the mind, left to itself, becomes wearied and too exhausted to say the prayer mentally; at other times the lips get tired of this work. Therefore both methods of prayer should be used—with the lips and with the mind. But one should appeal to the Lord quietly and without agitation, so that the voice does not disturb the attention of the mind and does not thus break off the prayer, until the mind is accustomed to this doing and, receiving force from the Spirit, firmly prays within on its own. Then there will be no need to say the prayer with the lips; indeed, it will be impossible, for he who reaches this stage is fully content with mental doing of the prayer and has no wish to leave it.

Gregory taught his method to monks on Mount Athos and made it a source of contemplative prayer for the church of the East. He traveled to monasteries and dioceses throughout Greece and Macedonia, inviting monks and religious to practice the Jesus Prayer. In Macedonia he also established three colonies of anchorites who were devoted to contemplative prayer.

Harassed by invasions of Ottoman Turks, Gregory moved to Mount Paroria in Bulgaria. Around 1325 he founded a monastery there that became the center for spirituality and learning in the Balkan countries.

Gregory wrote extensively, including tracts on asceticism, verses on the nature of God, liturgical hymns, and theological treatises. His most significant work, *The 137 Chapters or Spiritual Meditations*, spread the practice of disciplined contemplative prayer throughout the East and Europe.

Gregory of Sinai died at Mount Paroria in 1346.

Souls without prayer are like people whose bodies or limbs are paralyzed: they possess feet and hands but they cannot control them. In the same way there are souls so infirm and so accustomed to busying themselves with outside affairs that they seem incapable of entering into themselves at all.

—Teresa of Ávila

NOVEMBER 27
Prayer

207. Richard Rolle
(1300?–1349)

The church should proclaim Richard Rolle the patron of college dropouts. At nineteen he quit Oxford, abandoning a professional career to take the path of a hermit. Judged a failure by some, the saint, however, achieved spiritual success. He served the Christian community as a counselor, teacher, and writer. And as a contemplative he witnessed to all of the Christian's union with God.

"My brother has gone mad," screamed Richard's sister as she watched him don an outfit fabricated from her dresses. Young Rolle wore this homemade habit to launch his vocation as a hermit. Over the next thirty years he seems to have ascended the stages of mysticism, but left no record of visions or physical manifestations. Today he is one of the most respected of medieval mystics.

Richard wrote prolifically about the spiritual life and practical Christian living, much of it as advice to women religious. The following, for example, is typical of *The Form of Living* that he wrote for his friend, Margaret Wolfe, who lived as an anchoress:

> Love is an ardent yearning for God, with a wonderful delight and security. God is light and burning. Light illuminates our reason. Burning ignites our yearning so that we can desire nothing except him. Love is one life, coupling together the one loving and the one beloved. Meekness makes us sweet to God, purity joins us to God, and love makes us one with God.
>
> We must strive to clothe ourselves in love, as iron or as charcoal do in fire, as the air does in the sun, and as the wool does in the dye. The charcoal is so imbued with fire that the whole is fire. The air so clothes itself in the sun that the whole is light. The wool so essentially adopts the dye that it totally matches it. In this fashion a real lover of Christ is to act: his or her heart is to burn in love to such an extent that it will be turned into a fire of love, and be, so to speak, entirely fire. And he or she will so shine in virtues that no part of Christ's lover will be darkened by degenerate behavior.

Like an Old Testament prophet, Richard openly criticized lax clergy and bishops, for which he won their resentment. The saint was serious, but not dour. He seems to have been merry, with a subtle sense of humor. Once, for instance, when Margaret Kirkby was suffering a seizure, he held her calmly against his shoulder. "Even if you had been the devil," he quipped, "I would have held you." He wrote about the role of humor in a saint's life and it reads like a self-portrait:

> During this earthly exile, the holy lover of God shows himself neither too merry nor too serious, but he expresses a mature cheerfulness. Indeed, some reprove laughter and others praise it. I disapprove of laughter that stems from empty-headed foolishness. But I praise laughter that comes from gladness of conscience and spiritual merriment. Only the righteous enjoy this mirth in the love of God.

Late in his life Richard settled near the Cistercian convent at Hampole, where he acted as a spiritual director for the sisters. He died there in 1349, probably a victim of the plague.

Jesus, my soul now mend: your love into me send,
That I with you life spend in joy that has no end.
In love wound now my thought, my heart lift up in glee;
My soul you dearly bought: make it your lover be.

—Richard Rolle

SEPTEMBER 29
A Passionate Love; A Soul Afire; Success in Failure

208. Gertrude of Delft

(D. 1358)

While working as a servant-girl at Delft in the Netherlands, Gertrude was engaged to be married. But her fiancé broke with her and married another woman. Broken-hearted at first, Gertrude gradually overcame her anguish and chose a new direction for her life. She joined the Béguines at Delft, spending the rest of her life among them. The Béguines were sisterhoods of celibate women who lived in common households, prayed together, and dedicated themselves to works of mercy. Béguines could hold property and leave the community to marry. But as Gertrude immersed herself in her new life, all thoughts of marriage evaporated. She even befriended the woman who had stolen her fiancé.

As St. Gertrude opened herself to God in prayer, he seems to have touched her soul very personally. In the following note, she records her response to his comforting interventions:

> As I was occupied after Vespers with my evening prayers before retiring to rest, this passage of the gospel came suddenly to my mind: "Anyone who loves me will keep my word, and my Father will love him, and we shall come to him and make a home in him" (John 14:23 *NJB*). At these words my worthless heart felt your presence, O my most sweet God and my delight. And although my mind takes pleasure in wandering after and in distracting itself with perishable things, yet when I return to my heart I find you there. So I cannot complain that you have left me, even for a moment, from that time until this year, the ninth since I received this grace.
>
> Only once I felt that you left me for a period of eleven days. It seemed to me that this happened on account of involvement with the world. Then your sweetest humanity and stupendous charity prompted you to seek me. I had reached such a pitch of madness that I thought no more of the greatness of the treasure I had lost. I don't even remember feeling at the time any grief for having lost it, nor any desire of recovering it.
>
> Draw and unite me entirely to yourself. May I remain inseparably attached to you even when I am obliged to perform external duties for my neighbor's good. And afterwards may I return to seek you within me when I have accomplished them.

On Good Friday, 1340, images of Christ's wounds appeared on Gertrude's body. For a time these painful marks bled seven times a day. Word of Gertrude's stigmata spread throughout the country. So many people interrupted her prayerful solitude in order to view the phenomena that she asked God to do something about it. So the bleeding stopped, but the marks and pain remained with her for the rest of her life.

For the next eighteen years Gertrude suffered patiently every day. She leavened her spiritual anguish with hope by singing hymns. She repeated a favorite Dutch chorus so often that she came to bear the surname *van der Oosten* after its first line: The day is breaking *in the East.*

Gertrude of Delft died on the feast of Epiphany, 1358, whispering, "I am longing to go home."

> *Acquire the habit of speaking to God as if you were alone with God. Speak with familiarity and confidence as to your dearest and most loving friend. Speak of your life, your plans, your troubles, your joys, your fears. In return, God will speak to you—not that you will hear audible words in your ears, but words that you will clearly understand in your heart.*
>
> —Alphonsus Liguori

JANUARY 6
Conversations with God; Intimacy with the Divine; Stigmata

209. Henry Suso
(1298?–1366)

Anyone who endures dryness at prayer or feels abandoned by God will find instruction, and perhaps some relief, in the experience of Henry Suso. A mystic who called himself the "servant of Eternal Wisdom," he endured long stretches of spiritual darkness interrupted only by occasional bursts of brightness. Henry's life says to us that in apparent barrenness the soul draws closest to God. And we see him only by learning to look deep within.

Henry Suso was born at Constance, Switzerland, and became a Dominican there at thirteen. Five years later an extraordinary divine encounter launched him on his lifelong mystical pursuit of God. For the next decade, however, Suso suffered severe depression and doubt. Finally, counsel with Meister Eckhart, the patriarch of fourteenth-century German mysticism, delivered him from the worst of it.

Like many other mystics, at midlife Henry threw himself into active Christian work. For nearly two decades he traveled throughout the Rhineland preaching, teaching, and giving spiritual direction. He also wrote extensively about the inner life. His work on prayer, *The Little Book of Eternal Wisdom*, became the most popular Christian book in Europe before *The Imitation of Christ* appeared. In this excerpt he asks God, the Eternal Wisdom, why he seems to forsake those he loves:

> Eternal Wisdom: When I hide myself, only then do you become aware of who I am or who you are. I am eternal Good, and so when I pour myself forth so lovingly, everything I enter becomes good. One can thus detect my presence as one detects the sun by its brightness since one cannot see its essence.
>
> Servant: Lord, I find within myself a great unevenness. When I feel forsaken, my soul is like a sick person to whom everything is repugnant. But when the bright morning star bursts forth in my soul, all gloom disappears. Quickly, however, it is all snatched away and I am again forsaken. But then after intense sadness it returns. What is going on?
>
> Eternal Wisdom: I am causing it, and it is the game of love. As long as love is together with love, love does not know how dear love is. But when love departs from love, then truly love feels how dear love was.
>
> Servant: Dear Lord, teach me how to conduct myself in this game.
>
> Eternal Wisdom: On good days you should consider the bad days, and on the bad days consider the good days. Then neither exuberance

> at my presence nor despondency can harm you. To find joy on earth, it is not enough that you give me a certain period of the day. You must constantly remain within yourself if you want to find God, hear his familiar words and be sensitive to his secret thoughts.

Suso's individualistic piety and his association with Meister Eckhart, who was suspected of heresy, won him many enemies. He was accused of theft, sacrilege, fathering a child, poisoning, and heresy, but he was completely cleared of all charges. Toward the end of his life he served as the prior of the Dominican house at Ulm in central Germany. Henry Suso died there in 1366.

> *My soul has longed for you all night, O Eternal Wisdom! And in the early morning I turn to you from the depths of my heart. May your holy presence remove all dangers from my soul and body. May your many graces fill the inmost recesses of my heart, and inflame it with your divine love.*
>
> —Henry Suso

MARCH 2 / BEATIFIED IN 1831
Contemplatives in Action; Conversations with God; Doubt; Prayer; Suffering

210. John Ruysbroeck
(1293–1381)

Throughout the fourteenth century a renewal movement touched the hearts of many in northern Europe. The *Devotio Moderna* or Modern Devotion brought people both to a personal commitment to follow Christ and to a deeper life in the Spirit. The movement's leaders included popular writers like Thomas à Kempis, author of *The Imitation of Christ,* still a best-seller today, and John Ruysbroeck, less famous now than à Kempis, but a very influential spiritual writer in his own time.

As a young priest in Brussels, John Ruysbroeck associated himself with two contemplatives, John Hinckaert, his uncle, and Franco van Coudenberg. Between 1317 and 1343 he devoted himself to prayer and publishing several books on the spiritual life. In order to reach as broad a readership as possible, Ruysbroeck wrote in Flemish rather than the traditional Latin of scholars. In the following selection he invites people engaged in an active life to open themselves to God in prayer. Like Zacchaeus (see Luke 19:1–10), an active person *must run before the crowd, that is, the multiplicity of created things. These make man so little that he cannot perceive God. Then he must climb up the Tree of Faith that grows from above downwards because its root is in the Godhead. The upper branches reveal the Trinity of persons and the unity of the divine nature. Man must cling to the unity at the tree top because here Jesus will pass by with all his gifts.*

> Then Jesus comes. He sees man and in the light of faith shows him that by virtue of his divinity he is unlimited, incomprehensible, inaccessible and fathomless. Thus the highest knowledge of God that man can acquire in the active life is to recognize by faith that God is inconceivable and unknowable.
>
> In this light God says to the desire of man: "Come down quickly, for I would dwell in your house today." This is a quick descent by love and desire into the abyss of the Godhead to which no intellect can attain by its created light. When the soul thus leans upon God by intention and love—beyond all her understanding—then she rests in God, and God in her. Stretching by desire towards this incomprehensible God, she meets Christ and is fulfilled with his gifts. And loving and resting above all things, she dwells in God and God in her. In this way, Christ may be encountered upon the summit of the active life.

In 1349, Ruysbroeck, his uncle, and von Coudenberg founded a monastery at Groenendael in present-day Belgium. Franco served as the provost and administered the community. As prior of the monastery, John provided spiritual leadership for the brothers. John's presence at Groenendael made it a renewal center for the Modern Devotion. Hundreds of people made pilgrimages there to hear him and obtain his advice. For example, Ruysbroeck oriented the life of Gerard de Groote, the founder of the Brethren of the Common Life, whose schools disseminated the renewal movement throughout northern Europe.

John Ruysbroeck, weakened by old age, spent the last few years of his long life of service confined to his cell. He died at Groenendael in 1381 at the age of eighty-eight.

It is the nature of love ever to give and to take, to love and to be loved, and these two things meet in whomsoever loves. Thus the love of Christ is both avid and generous. If he absorbs us utterly into himself, in return he gives us his very self again.

—John Ruysbroeck

DECEMBER 2
Care of the Soul; Conversations with God; Prayer

211. Bridget of Sweden
(1303–1373)

In 1372, St. Bridget visited the royal court at Naples. There, with a spirit reminiscent of Jeremiah, she prophesied the following warning, and priests proclaimed it from every pulpit. Bridget spoke for Christ:

> O my enemies, why do you so boldly commit such sins and do other things contrary to my will? Why have you neglected my passion? Why do you not attend in your hearts to how I "stood" naked on the cross and cried out, full of wounds and clothed in blood?
>
> But your eyes and hearts forget and neglect all these things. And so you behave like prostitutes, who love the delight of the flesh, but not its offspring. For when they feel a living infant in their womb, at once they procure an abortion so that without losing their fleshly pleasure, they may always engage in their foul intercourse. This is also how you behave. For I, God, your Creator and Redeemer, visit all with my grace, knocking at your hearts, because I love all. But when you feel in your hearts any knock of a inpouring of my Spirit or any compunction; or when through hearing my words, you conceive any good intention, at once you procure spiritually an abortion. You excuse your sins, delight in them and are even damnably willing to persevere in them. For that reason, you do the devil's will, enclosing him in your hearts and expelling me in this contemptible way.
>
> My mercy, however, is that none of my enemies is so thorough or so great a sinner that I would deny him my forgiveness if he were to ask for it humbly and wholeheartedly.

Such revelation flowed through Bridget like a river. She prophesied condemnation and guidance to popes, kings, and nations. Individuals queried her about their spiritual state, and she spoke God's answers to them. From childhood, Bridget also received personal revelations detailing the sufferings of Jesus and Mary. Once at age ten, she stood beneath a crucifix and thought she heard Christ say, "Look upon me, my daughter."

"Who treated you like this?" she asked.

"Those who despise me, and spurn my love for them," he replied. From that time Bridget focused her spirituality on Christ's passion.

Bridget was married to Ulf Gudmarsson, a Swedish landowner, for twenty-eight years, and they had eight children. In 1335 she became a lady-in-waiting to Queen Blanche, wife of young Swedish King Magnus II. The royal couple loved the saint but ignored her inspired pleas to reform their worldly lives.

When Ulf died in 1344, Bridget committed herself to celibacy and austerity. At Vadstena she founded a monastery for women and men with an innovative structure: As abbess she ruled over all temporal affairs and the men only over spiritual matters. The community developed into the religious order called the Brigittines.

For two decades after 1350, Bridget campaigned with three popes to return from their refuge in Avignon to Rome. She did not spare them her prophetic denunciations, calling one pope "a murderer of souls, more unjust than Pilate and more cruel than Judas." But they did not heed her words.

Prompted by a revelation, Bridget made a pilgrimage to Jerusalem in 1371. On her return she paid her prophetic visit to Naples. She died in Rome on July 23, 1373.

Yahweh himself sent me to prophesy against this Temple and this city all the things you have heard. So now amend your behavior and actions, listen to the voice of Yahweh your God, and Yahweh will relent about the disaster that he has decreed for you.

—Jeremiah 26:12–13 *NJB*

JULY 23 / PATRON OF SWEDEN AND CO-PATRON OF EUROPE / CANONIZED IN 1391
Great Preachers; Mercy; Prophets; Sin; Valiant Women

212. Raymond of Capua
(1333–1399)

At age thirty-seven, Dominican Father Raymond of Capua met **St. Catherine** at Siena. He quickly recognized the authenticity of this unusually gifted laywoman. For the last six years of Catherine's life Raymond became her spiritual director. And he collaborated with Catherine in her mission as peacemaker for souls and the church.

In the early 1370s, Raymond worked with Catherine, caring for plague victims in Siena. When the disease struck him, Catherine prayed with him and the next morning he woke up well. During these years Catherine converted so many people that Raymond some of the times had to spend twelve hours a day hearing their confessions.

In the mid-1370s, Raymond and Catherine worked to bring peace between the cities of northern Italy and the pope at Avignon, France. In 1378 the Great Western Schism erupted with two rivals claiming to be pope. Catherine supported Pope Urban VI at Rome and sent Raymond on a futile mission to preach against the pope at Avignon. Much ado is made about the two saints' efforts to resolve the schism, but they accomplished less than is popularly believed.

After Catherine's death in 1380, Raymond was elected master-general of the Dominicans, who were loyal to Pope Urban VI. For the next nineteen years he conducted a reform of the order, requiring a strict observance of St. Dominic's life pattern. In the following letter we can sample Raymond's wisdom as he warns his brothers against pride:

> I thank God that you have been brought by the Holy Spirit to a regular observance of the rule. And that you imitate our saintly predecessors who followed St. Dominic's straight path. I beg you not to allow yourselves to be terrified by a few opponents or by a few threats. Nor to be turned aside from the holy manner of life that you have undertaken. You know, my brothers, how all holy enterprises meet with obstacles from Satan and his agents so that they may be made perfect enough to offer to the Lord.
>
> Moreover, brothers, I don't want you to feel pride. Nor do I want you to despise those who live differently from yourselves, because God is powerful enough to give them his Holy Spirit. Besides, they may be more pleasing to God than you are, for bodily penances are worth

> far less than piety. The kingdom of God is not food and drink, but the love of God and neighbor. So if these others, while eating meat and drinking wine, abound more in piety, they will be better than you in the Lord's eyes.
>
> So guard yourselves, brothers, from the wild beast of pride and self-esteem that enervates and destroys all good works. And to open all my heart to you, I will say that I dread nothing so much for you as this malignant plague. Nothing that I so much wish you to avoid by your care and watchfulness.

Raymond's renewal of the monastic side of the order's life was so extensive that he is sometimes called its second founder. He died in 1399 at Nuremberg, where he was conducting a reform of the German Dominican community.

On the day before Catherine died, Raymond heard in his mind these words: "Tell him never to lose courage. I will be with him in every danger. If he fails, I will help him up again." Later he learned that on her deathbed Catherine had said this to those standing by. She apparently intended to continue from heaven her collaboration with Raymond on earth.

OCTOBER 5 / BEATIFIED IN 1899
Friendship; Humility

213. Julian of Norwich
(1342?–1423?)

It is an act of sovereign friendship on the part of our courteous Lord that he tenderly preserves us while we are in sin, and that, furthermore, he touches us most secretly, showing us our sin by the sweet light of mercy and grace. But when we have seen how foul we are, we imagine that God must be angry with us for our sin. Then we are stirred by the Holy Spirit, by means of contrition, to pray and desire to amend our lives, and with all our powers, to lessen God's wrath until such time as we can find rest of soul and relief in confession. Then we hope that God has forgiven us our sins, and that it is true.

Then our courteous Lord shows himself to the soul most merrily and with a glad expression. With a friendly welcome, as if the soul had been in pain and imprisoned, he says sweetly, "My darling, I am glad you have come to me. In all this misery I have ever been with you. Now you see my loving, and we are made one in bliss."

—Julian of Norwich

We don't know much about this fourteenth-century recluse because she deliberately hid herself. We don't even know her name, so we identify her with the Church of St. Julian in Norwich in England, where she had attached her hut. Julian believed God had given her a revelation for all Christians, so she didn't want readers to think about her, but urged them to focus on God alone.

Once in her youth Julian asked the Lord—if it were his will—to grant her three requests: a deeper personal understanding of Christ's sufferings; a severe illness, short of death, that would purge her worldliness; and three enduring "wounds" of compunction for sin, compassion toward others, and longing for God. Julian says she soon forgot the first two petitions but never lost sight of the third. God remembered, however, and granted all of them.

When Julian was thirty years old she contracted a fatal disease. After seven days, she felt death closing in. But suddenly all her pain left and she was restored to health. Then, in the early morning hours of that day, May 8, 1373, Julian received fifteen revelations or "showings" and a sixteenth on the following day. The revelations mainly concerned aspects of Christ's passion.

The visions had satisfied Julian's desire for contrition for sin and rewarded her with a lasting sense of peace. But she continually mulled them over, seeking to understand them fully. Many years later, when she finally wrote the *Revelations of Divine Love*, she had grasped their significance:

> From the time it was shown, I often desired to know what was our Lord's meaning. And fifteen years and more after, I was answered in spiritual understanding, with this saying: "Would you know your Lord's meaning in this thing? Know it well: love was his meaning. Who showed it to you? Love. What did he show you? Love. Why did he show it to you? For love. Hold yourself in love and you shall know and learn more in the same vein."

Julian says that she burst out in laughter during the fifth revelation when she was shown how Christ's passion reduced the devil's power to nothing. If only we could see the demise of Satan more clearly, we might also laugh at his vain efforts to snare us. And so, with the recluse of Norwich, revel in God's love.

MAY 13
A Passionate Love; Solitude; Visions and Visionaries

214. Catherine of Siena

(1347–1380)

Offer your bodies as a living sacrifice, dedicated and acceptable to God.

—Romans 12:1 *NJB*

St. Catherine of Siena was a peacemaker. By prayer and personal diplomacy, she labored to make peace between popes and Italian city-states. On her knees and with her letters, she sought peace for the church by influencing the pope to return from Avignon to Rome.

Most of all, Catherine sacrificed herself for the peace of souls. The following passage from her *Dialogue* epitomizes her life. Here God responds to her offer to suffer for others:

> The sufferings you endure will, through the power of charity, suffice to win both atonement and reward for you and for others. For you they will win the fruit of life. The stains of your foolishness will be blotted out, and I will no longer remember that you had ever offended me. As for others, because of your loving charity, I will pardon them in proportion to their receptivity.
>
> The willing desire to suffer every pain and hardship even to the point of death for the salvation of souls is very pleasing to me. The more you bear, the more you show your love for me. In loving me you come to know more of my truth, and the more you know, the more intolerable pain and sorrow you will feel when I am offended.
>
> You asked for suffering, and you asked me to punish you for the sins of others. You were, in effect, asking for love and light and knowledge of the truth. For suffering and sorrow increase in proportion to love: When love grows, so does sorrow. Patience is not proved except in suffering, and patience is one with charity. Endure courageously, then. Otherwise you will not show yourselves to be—nor will you be—faithful spouses and children of my Truth, nor will you show that your delight is in my honor and in the salvation of souls.

Catherine gathered a band of disciples who served Siena's poor and lived in poverty themselves. Daily the saint begged and baked bread to feed the hungry, but her real concern was for hungry souls. Catherine evangelized the whole town. No one escaped her attention. Through her intercession belligerent inmates in the jails repented. She even confronted local crime bosses, causing them to abandon their plots and transforming their lives. It is said that she kept three priests busy with the confessions and pastoral care of her penitents.

For most of the fourteenth century, the popes resided in Avignon, France, kept there by politics and civil strife. In 1376, Catherine visited Gregory XI and helped him decide to return to Rome. Two years later, however, a schism divided the church when two men claimed to be pope, one at Rome and another at Avignon.

This scandal wore heavily on Catherine. Urban VI required her to advise him in Rome, and she exhausted herself with prayer and advocacy on his behalf. In 1380 her health deteriorated rapidly, and she could not eat or drink water. She had a vision of the church as a great ship that was crushing her. And she offered her suffering as a living sacrifice for the sake of the church. On April 29, 1380, she died of a stroke.

> *God: I have placed you in the midst of your fellows that you may do to them what you cannot do to me, that is to say that you may love your neighbor freely without expecting any return from him, and what you do to him I count as done to me.*
>
> —Catherine of Siena

APRIL 29 / CANONIZED IN 1461 / PATRON OF ITALY AND NURSING SERVICES
Contemplatives in Action; Conversations with God; Doctors of the Church; Intercession; Suffering

215. Vincent Ferrer
(1350–1419)

Brilliant and devout, Spanish-born Vincent Ferrer joined the Dominicans in 1367. As a young priest he taught philosophy at the universities of Lérida and Barcelona. In 1379 he served as prior of the Dominican house at Valencia, the only office he ever held. But for most of his life, St. Vincent Ferrer worked as an indomitable activist. He was renowned as a preacher, miracle worker, adviser to popes and kings, and champion of Christian unity. However, he founded his tireless work on a deeply personal spirituality:

> You must open the interior eyes of your soul on this light, on this heaven within you, a vast horizon stretching far beyond the realm of human activity, an unexplored country to the majority of men. The ordinary observer sees in the ocean only the realm of storms, and never guesses that a few feet below the surface its waters are always limpid, and in a scintillating clarity is found vegetation and living creatures of wondrous diversity, marvelous in beauty and structure, mysterious depths where the pearl is formed.
>
> Such is the depth of the soul where God dwells and shows himself to us. And when the soul has seen God, what more can it want? If it possesses him, why and for whom can it ever be moved to abandon him?
>
> So, at any price, preserve yourself in that calm through which the soul sees the eternal Sun. This vision of God will also show you yourself. The heights of greatness will show you the depths of misery. But fear nothing. . . . When you have realized your true worth you will be able to judge your faults sanely, your own crimes will come home to you in full light, and the faults of your neighbor will remain in shadow.

This sense of peace with God steadied Vincent for his service in the stormy fourteenth century, when plague, famine, and war devastated Europe, and heresy and division racked the church. His life spanned the Great Western Schism, when popes rivaled each other at Rome and at Avignon, France. Vincent was loyal to the Avignon popes, but he pressured them to cooperate with efforts to restore unity.

The schism reached its nadir after 1409, with three men claiming to be pope. At the Council of Constance in 1414, the bishops resolved to depose one claimant and ask the other two to resign, so that a new pope could be elected. The pope at Rome was willing to abdicate, but Benedict XIII, Vincent's friend, adamantly refused. Vincent then declared publicly that because Benedict was blocking the unity vital to the church, the faithful could justly withdraw their allegiance. Thus, the saint's vast popularity significantly contributed to ending the schism. Benedict was ultimately deposed, the Roman pope stepped down, and a new pope was chosen.

Vincent Ferrer's main work, however, was revitalizing faith at the grass roots. In 1398 the saint was deathly ill and prayed for recovery so that he might continue preaching. Vincent said that Christ appeared and healed him. "You will preach repentance throughout the world," Jesus had said, which the saint took as a commission.

For twenty years after 1399, Vincent crisscrossed Europe four times on foot. Everywhere large crowds gathered to hear his message about the folly of sin, the need for repentance, and the imminence of the end of the world. Like **St. Paul** and many other saints, Vincent expected Jesus to come soon to wrap up history. In response to his ministry thousands revolutionized their lives. Thousands also were miraculously healed during his missionary visits. Thus, Vincent Ferrer brought new life to people who had been battered by disease and war in the world and by confusion and division in the church.

You can only give what you yourself possess. In fact, you must have much more than you attempt to give, to enable you to give without despoiling yourself.

—Vincent Ferrer

APRIL 5 / CANONIZED IN 1455 / PATRON OF BUILDERS
Care of the Soul; Catholic Reformers; Defending the Faith; The Light of Christ; Great Preachers; Prophets

216. Rita of Cascia

(1377–1457)

Blessed by God,
you were a light in darkness
through your steadfast courage
when you had to suffer such agony
upon your cross. You turned aside from this vale of tears
to seek wholeness for your hidden wounds
in the great passion of Christ. . . .
You were not content with less than perfect healing,
and so endured the thorn for fifteen years
before you entered into the joy
of your Lord. 1457

This poem was engraved on the casket of St. Rita of Cascia and is one of the few contemporary sources that tell us about her.

St. Rita received her "hidden wounds" in an unfortunate marriage. For eighteen years she endured the abuses and infidelities of a violent husband. She also suffered the rascality of two sons who were strongly influenced by him. She was delivered from these miserable circumstances in a horrific way: one day her husband was brought home dead, brutally slashed by his enemies. Her rambunctious sons planned to get revenge, but died before they could obtain it.

Rita was then free to pursue her lifelong dream of becoming a nun. She applied to enter the Augustinian convent at Cascia of Italy, in 1407. But her suffering was not over. Even though orders customarily received widows, the Augustinians three times refused Rita because she had been married. Only after six years did they acquiesce and install her as a nun.

The poem said Rita "sought wholeness" in the passion of Christ. In her meditations she preoccupied her imagination with his agony. On Good Friday, 1441, she prostrated herself before a crucifix and begged Christ for some small share of his suffering. As though punctured by a crown of thorns, a single wound opened on Rita's forehead. For fifteen years it caused her daily pain and embarrassed her, as its putrid odor frequently offended her sisters. In 1450, when she was preparing to visit Rome for the jubilee year, the wound temporarily healed.

But it reappeared when she returned to Cascia and remained until her death.

Rita died of tuberculosis on May 22, 1457. Three days later, Domenico Angeli, a notary of Cascia, recorded eleven miracles that occurred upon the saint's death. He left us this brief profile of her religious life:

> A very honorable nun, Lady Rita, having spent forty years as a nun in the cloister of the Church of Saint Mary Magdalene of Cascia by living with charity in the service of God, followed the destiny of every human being. God, in whose service she persevered for the aforementioned time—desiring to show all the faithful a model of life, so that as she had lived serving God with love by fasting and prayer, they too, all faithful Christians, would live also—worked many wonderful miracles and through the merits of Saint Rita, especially on 25 May 1457.

At every stage of her life, Rita seems to have bravely endured unendurable circumstances: frustration because her parents overrode her wish to become a nun; married an abuser; refused three times by the Augustinians; afflicted with the pain and embarrassment of the stigmata. None of these things, however, prevented her from serving God and her sisters. We can pray for her intercession in our desperate need, but we should also imitate her love-in-action.

MAY 22 / CANONIZED IN 1900. / PATRON OF DESPERATE SITUATIONS
Difficult Marriages; Enduring Trials; Stigmata

217. Bernardino of Siena
(1380–1444)

At age twenty-three, St. Bernardino had completed a classical education and capped it with a degree in canon law. In 1403 he joined the Friars of the Strict Observance, a new branch of the Franciscans.

For more than a dozen years he lived quietly and unremarkably in Fiesole, Italy. But in 1417, a novice prophesied three times to Bernardino. "Brother Bernardino," he exclaimed, "stop hiding your gifts. Go to Lombardy where all await you!" The saint went obediently to Milan, not knowing what to do. But he soon discovered that his vocation was preaching when his eloquence began to draw huge congregations. Thousands came to hear this entertaining friar who used his personable humor and wisdom to penetrate their souls with truth. For nearly a quarter of a century he crisscrossed Italy on foot, calling people to repentance in exhortations like this:

> A sinner who repents learns to be prudent. He is like an ass that, once he has fallen in a spot, afterwards looks more carefully where he sets his foot. For fear of punishment he takes care not to fall into those sins again, or into any others.
>
> O great idiot who keeps on sinning! Why don't you consider what the ass teaches you about saving your soul? The ass doesn't fall again, but you always do. If you would only turn to God with love, you would learn much about prudence.
>
> O children, don't you know that when you are learning to write with a pen you make blots? And you who want to ride a horse, don't you know you will never learn unless you fall sometimes?
>
> Now I want to ask older people about this. Old man and old woman, are you there?
>
> "Yes."
>
> Tell me, have you fallen into sin over and over again?
>
> "Yes."
>
> Well, have you returned to God?
>
> "Yes."
>
> See, you would never have learned what sin is unless you had tried it. *In antiquis est prudentia.* In the old is prudence, and do you know why? Because they have experience. They have fallen often, and so they walk more gingerly. They think about how they had better set their feet. As they see death approaching, they thank God that they

have had time to turn to him. And they do not trust themselves not to fall, but always ask God to help them not to fall again.

Bernardino popularized devotion to the name of Jesus. At the end of every sermon he blessed the crowd, holding a placard marked "IHS," an acronym for the name "Jesus." And everyone wanted a copy of the sign. A maker of playing cards whose business Bernardino had ruined by denouncing gambling made more money than ever by manufacturing the placard.

In 1437 the Observants elected Bernardino as their general. In six years he reformed the order, sending friars from their enclosures to service in the world. Overcoming the traditional Franciscan fear of learning, he required his men to study theology and canon law. During his period of leadership, he attracted so many new recruits that membership increased tenfold. He resigned in 1443 to return to preaching. But he died in 1444 shortly after delivering at his hometown a series of fifty sermons in as many days.

God has two arms—an arm of love and an arm of fear. With both arms he embraces the sinner who desires to return to him. If you want to be loved by him, love him and he will prosper you. And if you fear him, he will protect you from every danger.

—Bernardino of Siena

MAY 20 / CANONIZED IN 1450
Catholic Reformers; Great Preachers; Repentance

218. Frances of Rome
(1384–1440)

As a girl, St. Frances thought she was called to be a nun. Instead, however, she lived forty happy years as a married woman. An exceptionally competent person, Frances conducted herself according to clear priorities. She expressed her commitment to Christ first in her affectionate care for her husband and children, then for her extended household, and finally for Rome's sick poor. "Sometimes," she said, "a wife must leave God at the altar to find him in her household management."

At twelve, Frances married Lorenzo Ponziano, a nobleman who loved her tenderly. She drew close to Vannozza, her sister-in-law, who lived in the same house and shared her zeal. Together they tended the sick, seeking out Rome's worst cases. In 1400, Frances gave birth to a son, the first of four children, all of whom she tended personally. A year later she became mistress of the Ponziano family estate, which she managed skillfully even during the ravages of the plague and the turbulence of civil wars.

Frances made everyone feel like a best friend, and thus attracted many people, especially younger women who idealized her. In 1424, with Lorenzo's full support, she organized a group of women as the Oblates of Mary. They lived at home under the Rule of **St. Benedict** without vows and shared Frances's mission to the sick. But seven years later, Frances acquired an old building and called the women to live in community. A biographer reported her invitation, as follows:

> My dear companions, I have gathered you to impart the direction that I have received from the Lord and his blessed Mother regarding our congregation. For seven years we have been especially consecrated to her service. We have bound ourselves to live in chastity and obedience, and to observe the rules prescribed to us. I have long thought that as we have been united in spirit, so we ought to be in our mode of life.
>
> For a while I imagined that my desire might only be the result of my motherly affection for you and of my concern for your advancement. But at last the Lord has revealed to me his will that I should found a new spiritual building in this city, the ancient stronghold of faith. It will form an asylum for women of your rank who have generously resolved to forsake all worldly allurements.

> I am ready to do what the Lord wants. But without you, my sisters, what can I do? You are the foundations of the building, the first stones of the new spiritual house of Mary, his mother. You are the seed from which a plentiful harvest is to spring. Earthly cares, the temporal affairs of life, must no longer take up your time. He summons you to a retreat, where you will live in his presence, imitate his example and copy the virtues of Mary, where you will pray for Rome, and turn away his wrath from this degenerate and guilty city.

After Lorenzo died in 1436, Frances joined the Oblates and became their superior. During the last half of her life she received frequent visions and ecstasies. It is said that for twenty-three years her guardian angel was visible to her, aiding her in her service. She died in Rome in 1440.

Frances of Rome should be named patron of wishes that don't come true. By submitting faithfully to God, she received even more than she had wanted—the blessings of both married and religious life.

Take delight in the Lord and he will give you the desires of your heart.

—Psalm 37:4 *RSV*

MARCH 9 / PATRON OF MOTORISTS
Care of the Sick; Leading Women; Married Saints; Vocation

219. Colette
(1381–1447)

Renewing religious institutions is not easy. We would expect a person chosen to reform convents and monasteries to be formidable. Maybe even physically tall, overbearing, and somewhat threatening. God, however, doesn't seem to agree. For example, in the fifteenth century he selected St. Colette, a young woman the opposite of these characteristics, to call Franciscans to strict observance of the rules of **St. Clare** and **St. Francis**.

Not that Colette was unimpressive. She was a beautiful woman whose radiant inner strength attracted people. However, her spirituality, her commitment to God, and her heart for souls, not her physical qualities, suited her for her reforming mission.

At seventeen, upon her parents' death, Colette joined the Franciscan Third Order. She lived for eight years as a hermit at Corbie Abbey in Picardy. Toward the end of this time, St. Francis appeared to her in a vision and charged her to restore the Poor Clares to their original austerity. When Friar Henry de Beaume came in 1406 to confirm her mission, Colette had the door of her hut torn down, a sign that her solitude was over and her work begun. And she then prayed her commitment:

> I dedicate myself in health, in illness, in my life, in my death, in all my desires, in all my deeds so that I may never work henceforth except for your glory, for the salvation of souls, and towards the reform for which you have chosen me. From this moment on, dearest Lord, there is nothing which I am not prepared to undertake for love of you.

Colette's first efforts to reform convents met vigorous opposition. Then she sought the approval of the Avignon pope, Benedict XIII, who professed her as a Poor Clare and put her in charge of all convents she would reform. He also appointed Henry de Beaume to assist her. Thus equipped, she launched her reform in 1410 with the Poor Clares at Besançon. Before her death in 1447, the saint had founded or renewed seventeen convents and several friaries throughout France, Savoy, Burgundy, and Spain.

Like Francis and Clare, Colette devoted herself to Christ crucified, spending every Friday meditating on the passion. She is said to have miraculously received a piece of the cross which she gave to **St. Vincent Ferrer** when he came to visit her.

St. Joan of Arc once passed by Colette's convent in Moulins, but there is no evidence that the two met. Like Joan, Colette was a visionary. Once, for instance, she saw souls falling from grace in great numbers, like flakes in a snowstorm. Afterward she prayed daily for the conversion of sinners. She personally brought many strays back to Christ and helped them unravel their sinful patterns.

At age sixty-six, Colette foretold her death, received the sacrament of the sick, and died at her convent in Ghent, Flanders.

Blessed be the hour in which our Lord Jesus Christ, God and man, was born. Blessed be the Holy Spirit by whom he was conceived. Blessed be the glorious Virgin Mary of whom the God-man was born.

May the Lord hear our prayers by the intercession of the glorious Virgin Mary and by the remembrance of the most sacred hour in which the God-man was born, that all our desires may be accomplished for your glory and our salvation.

O good Jesus! O Jesus our Redeemer, do not abandon us nor punish us as our sins deserve, but hear our humble prayer and grant what we ask, by the intercession of the Blessed Virgin Mary and for the glory of your holy name. Amen.

—Colette

MARCH 6 / CANONIZED IN 1807
Catholic Reformers; Intercession; Leading Women; Vocation

220. John of Capistrano

(1386–1456)

Imagine living in a country where deadly plague and civil wars have decimated the population and continued for years to threaten the living. Envision, too, suffering the confusion of a church in which two and sometimes three men claimed to be pope. Finally, pretend having responsibility for a religious order bitterly divided into opposing camps. These troubled circumstances provide a backdrop for the life of St. John of Capistrano and give us some perspective on his actions.

John studied law at Perugia, Italy, where he married the daughter of a leading citizen and, in 1412, became the governor.

In 1416, while in jail as a political prisoner, he experienced a conversion and decided to become a religious. Somehow he got his wife to release him. He paraded through Perugia seated backward on a donkey and wearing a paper hat that listed all his sins. Having humiliated himself in this bizarre repentance, he applied to the Franciscans of the Strict Observance and they accepted him.

Immediately, the order put John on the fast track. Ordained in 1420, the Observants commissioned him to preach all over the Italian boot. With his remarkable gift for speaking, he revived the hope of thousands whose faith had eroded in the chaotic fourteenth century. He preached repentance to laity and clergy alike, as the following exhortation to priests shows:

> Those who are called to the table of the Lord must glow with the brightness that comes from the good example of a praiseworthy and blameless life. They must completely remove from their lives the filth and uncleanness of vice. Their upright lives must make them be the salt of the earth for themselves and for the rest of the human family. The brightness of their wisdom must make them the light of the world that brings light to others. They must learn from the eminent teacher, Jesus Christ, what he declared not only to his apostles and disciples, but also to all the priests and clerics who were to succeed them, when he said, "You are the salt of the earth. But what if salt goes flat? How can you restore its flavor? Then it is good for nothing but to be thrown out and trampled underfoot" (see Matthew 5:13).
>
> "You are the light of the world" (see Matthew 5:14). Now a light does not illumine itself, but instead it diffuses its rays and shines all around upon everything that comes into its view. So it must be with

> the glowing lives of upright and holy clerics. By the brightness of their holiness they must bring light and serenity to all who gaze upon them. They have been placed here to care for others. Their own lives should be an example to others, showing how they must live in the house of the Lord.

John of Capistrano collaborated with his mentor, **St. Bernardino of Siena** and with **St. Colette** in reforming the Franciscans. He helped them navigate a balanced course between two extremes, disciplining both the overly lax and the overly austere.

Many find two of John's later activities disturbing. The pope sent him as inquisitor to Austria in 1451. Some roundly criticize him for his severity in dealing with recalcitrant Hussites. And in 1456, it fell to John to raise an army and help turn back the Turks from Belgrade. His campaign succeeded, but many believe his involvement in a military action was inappropriate for a cleric.

After the battle at Belgrade so many bodies lay unburied that pestilence spread, and John succumbed to disease on October 23, 1456.

> *Of all divine things, the most godlike is to cooperate with God in the conversion of sinners.*
>
> —St. Denis the Areopagite

OCTOBER 23 / CANONIZED IN 1724
Catholic Reformers; Conversion; Repentance

221. Joan of Arc
(1412–1431)

No other saint has captured the imagination of the world as has St. Joan of Arc. She has starred in many books, poems, and plays. Nationalists and feminists have made her their emblem. But Joan did not see herself as a hero. She was just a simple peasant girl, who tried to do what she thought God wanted.

In 1425, at age thirteen, Joan began to hear mysterious voices that would set the course of her life:

> I heard the voice on the right-hand side, towards the church; and rarely do I hear it without a brightness. . . . The voice was sent to me by God and, after I had heard this voice three times, I knew it was the voice of an angel.

Joan identified the voice as that of St. Michael the Archangel, who spoke to her almost daily. In 1428 the voice instructed her to raise the siege at Orleans. "And me," she said, "I answered it that I was a poor girl who knew not how to ride nor lead in war." But the voice insisted it was God's will, and Joan obeyed.

For years England had waged war against France, pressing its claim to the French throne. Now with the imminent conquest of Orleans, the French cause was nearly lost. Joan believed her mission was to relieve the siege of Orleans and to get Charles, the Dauphin, crowned king at Rheims. A series of small miracles enabled her to reverse the fortunes of France. With the Dauphin's support, in April 1429, Joan led an army that turned the English back from Orleans. The saint's mission was accomplished on July 17, 1429, when she stood beside Charles VII at his coronation in the Rheims cathedral.

A year later, Burgundian enemies of Charles captured Joan and handed her over to the English. Her captors could not execute her for beating them at war, so they had her tried in an ecclesiastical court as a heretic. The trial was stacked against Joan, but she defended herself admirably. For a brief time she seemed to accede to the court's demand that she recant. However, she soon recovered and asserted herself. Thus the court condemned her as a relapsed heretic, and on May 31, 1431, burned her at the stake in the market square at Rouen. An eyewitness left this account of her death:

> She asked me to fetch the cross from the church so that she could have it continually before her eyes until her death. . . .
>
> In the flames until the end she continuously proclaimed and confessed aloud the holy name of Jesus. And she did not cease invoking the help of the saints in paradise. Moreover, as she bowed her head and breathed her last, as a sign of her fervent faith in God, she uttered the name of Jesus.

Twenty years later Joan's family pressed Pope Callistus III to review her case. In 1456 the original judgment was reversed and she was declared innocent. We remember Joan of Arc not as a martyr, for she was killed because of her politics, not her faith. We honor her as a virgin who gave her life because she wanted to obey God.

> *Nearly all the saints had a "religious" task to perform, and they had to leave the world, so as to be free to accomplish it. But Joan breaks through this rule. She doesn't leave the world because of her mission. Because of it she goes into the world, right into its most dangerous places, into the court, into the camp, into war.*
>
> —Ida Coudenhove

MAY 30 / CANONIZED IN 1920 / PATRON OF FRANCE AND SOLDIERS
Angels; Simple Obedience; Visions and Visionaries; World Historical Saints

222. Nicholas of Flue

(1417–1487)

The Swiss affectionately call St. Nicholas of Flue "Brother Klaus." They revere him as a great holy man and political counselor, who contributed significantly to the formation of their peace-loving nation.

From his youth in Unterwalden, Switzerland, Nicholas was a member of a Catholic lay association called the Friends of God. Scattered throughout Switzerland, the Netherlands, and Germany, members sought closeness to Christ through a disciplined life, especially by meditation on his passion.

Though totally dedicated to peace, twice patriotism led Nicholas to fight in wars to defend Unterwalden. He also held some minor public offices, but resisted efforts to make him governor. At age thirty he married Dorothy Wissling, and during twenty happy years she bore him ten children.

At age fifty, however, Nicholas sensed God's call to live a contemplative life as a hermit. Dorothy, also a member of the Friends of God, would not be opposed to such a desire. She believed that Nicholas had a divine commission, and she and the children released him. So Nicholas left his family and spent the next twenty years in a remote cottage at Ranft. He prayed most of the night, but in afternoons he welcomed visitors. It is reported, but not confirmed, that during these years he took no food or drink, only Holy Communion. Although unable to read or write, Brother Klaus had a spiritual gift of counsel and natural good judgment. Even top leaders sought his direction on personal and political affairs.

In 1481, Nicholas played a major role in solidifying the unity of Switzerland. After the cantons secured independence by defeating the German king, Charles the Bold, a dispute threatened to divide the cantons. Representatives meeting at Stans disagreed over admitting Fribourg and Soleure to the confederation. However, at an impasse they consulted Brother Klaus. Within an hour after obtaining his advice, they agreed to include the territories. The Edict of Stans that settled the affair may even have been drafted in his hut.

A document from that period preserved Nicholas's fundamental political wisdom. *Always put God first,* he said, and

> do not extend too widely the country's frontiers that you may live more easily in peace, union and faithfulness to your dearly attained liberties.
>
> Do not mix in the affairs of others or ally yourself with a powerful stranger. Guard against discord and self-interest. Protect your country and do not hold yourself distant from it.
>
> Do not let grow among you self-interest, jealousy, hatred, envy and factions, or these will work against you.
>
> Dear friends, don't let innovations and roguery seduce you. Hold on to the good, all of you together. Stay on the road in the footprints of your pious ancestors. Guard faithfully that which has been assigned to you. If you do that, neither storm nor tempest can harm you and you will overcome much evil.

Six years after the Stans meeting, on December 21, 1487, Nicholas died at Ranft after an illness of eight days.

> *Seek to keep peace. Protect widows and orphans as you have done before. Such care gives the greatest joy possible on earth since it is thanksgiving to God, and it gives God greater joy in heaven. You must also prevent public sins and always personally insist on justice. You should carry the passion of God in your hearts, for it will be your consolation in your last hour.*
>
> —Nicholas of Flue to the People of Berne

MARCH 22 / CANONIZED IN 1947 / PATRON OF SWITZERLAND
Married Saints; Saints and Politics

223. Casimir

(1458–1484)

The third child of King Casimir IV of Poland, St. Casimir grew up under the tutelage of John Dlugosz, a learned and devout canon of Cracow. Dlugosz trained Casimir in piety from age nine, so the youth developed a hearty Christian character. He avoided all softness and self-indulgence and at the same time related to everyone cheerfully and compassionately.

If we scrape away the thin coat of sweetness from Casimir's biography, we meet a young man of real integrity and courage. Here is an excerpt:

> It is difficult to imagine or to express his passion for justice, his exercise of moderation, his gift of prudence, his fundamental spiritual courage and stability, especially in a most permissive age, when men tended to be headstrong and by their very natures inclined to sin.
>
> Daily he urged his father to practice justice throughout his kingdom and in the governance of his people; and whenever anything in the country had been overlooked because of human weakness or simple neglect, he never failed to point it out quietly to the king.
>
> He actively took up the cause of the needy and unfortunate and embraced it as his own; for this reason the people called him the patron of the poor. Though the son of a king and descendant of a noble line, he was never unapproachable in his conversation or dealings with anyone, no matter how humble or obscure.
>
> He always preferred to be counted among the meek and poor of spirit, among those who are promised the kingdom of heaven, rather than among the famous and powerful men of this world. He had no ambition for the power that lies in human rank and he would never accept it from his father. He was afraid the barbs of wealth, which our Lord Jesus Christ spoke of as thorns, would wound his soul, or that he would be contaminated by contact with worldly goods.
>
> Many who acted as his personal servants . . . testify that he preserved his chastity to the very end of his life.

As a young man, Casimir already had the strength to stand up to his father. Once at the request of Hungarian nobles, the king sent Casimir, then barely fifteen years old, at the head of an army against King Matthias Corvinas. When the Hungarian nobles abandoned the cause and Casimir's men began to desert, he bravely defied his father's instructions and retreated. And, wisely, he had backed off at a moment when the Turks were threatening to advance against Europe's eastern borders. Feeling disgraced, however, the king punished his son by confining him at Dobzki castle for three months. But from that time Casimir tenaciously refused to participate in war. Thus his Polish and Lithuanian admirers esteem him as "The Peacemaker."

Casimir had no inclination to politics, but he always involved himself on behalf of his father's impoverished subjects. When his father promoted a strategic marriage between him and a daughter of the emperor, he refused because of his commitment to celibacy. Weakened by his asceticism and afflicted with lung disease, Casimir died in 1484. He was only twenty-three years old.

Our Savior says that a good tree, that is, a good heart as well as a soul on fire with charity, can do nothing but good and holy works. For this reason ***Saint Augustine*** *said: "Love and do what you will." It is as if he had said: "Charity is not able to sin."*

—Angela Merici

MARCH 4 / CANONIZED IN 1521 / PATRON OF POLAND AND LITHUANIA
Courage; Peacemakers; Serving the Poor; Twenty-Something Saints

224. Francis of Paola
(1416–1507)

St. Francis of Paola was an authentic wonder-worker. More than any other saint, he seems to have exerted direct authority over nature just like Christ. With a command "in the name of charity," he moved boulders, opened springs from rocks, healed the lame, blind, and deaf, and raised the dead. Focusing on Francis's miracles, however, gives a false impression of the saint. He was mainly a gifted pastor, evangelist, and Christian statesman. The miracles were secondary to his mission of bringing renewal to a war-torn and spiritually hungry Italy at the turn of the sixteenth century.

In 1435, Francis founded a community of brothers called the Minim, or the "least," modeled on the Friars Minor of **St. Francis of Assisi.** The Minim adopted a severe life pattern, including a perpetual fast and abstinence from meat. Hundreds of men joined Francis, and his communities spread throughout Sicily, Italy, and France. Everywhere they went, the Minim spawned Catholic revival.

Francis performed one of his most extraordinary miracles when a young father brought him a horribly disfigured infant. The saint prayed and touched the faceless baby until his eyes appeared and his face became normal. Years later when the pope was investigating Francis's lifestyle and miracles, handsome young Francis Rocco testified to his wondrous healing.

Francis the statesman counseled and confronted five kings and seven popes. With prophecy and letters he badgered Ferdinand of Naples to stop his civil wars and drive the Turks from south Italy. In 1481 the pope ordered Francis to go to the court of King Louis XI, who was slowly dying in the aftermath of a stroke. Before his departure, Francis addressed the following farewell to his beloved Minim:

> Sons of mine, whom I so love in the charity of Jesus Christ, I am separating myself from you to go to France. Hear the recommendations that I as your father in Jesus Christ leave with you. Love above all else our merciful Father in heaven, and serve him with all your strength and purity of heart.
>
> Maintain and mortify your members with a salutary and discreet penance, which will not permit you to fall victim to the insidious lures of the devil. He cannot triumph except over those who are slothful and

> negligent. In the trials and temptations we face regularly in our daily lives, help one another.
>
> Obey with humility your superiors, for obedience is the backbone of faith. Be sympathetic to the weakness and failings of others. Persevere in your holy vocation, to which the Lord has so obviously called you. Keep in mind that the crown of salvation is won only by those who persevere. It is vain to begin a good action unless you bring it to full completion. Maintain yourselves with holy emulation on the path of virtue which I have so ardently pursued, particularly the practice of charity, humility, and patience.
>
> Good-bye, my priests and brothers. We shall never again see each other on earth! May the Lord unite us in heaven!

Francis received a revelation that Louis XI would not survive his illness and so was not able to heal him. But he became the monarch's friend and helped him die peacefully. The saint remained in the French court for twenty-five years as the trusted adviser to kings and as the pope's representative. St. Francis of Paola died in 1507.

> *Every moment comes to us pregnant with a command from God, only to pass on and plunge into eternity, there to remain forever what we have made it.*
>
> —Francis de Sales

APRIL 2 / CANONIZED IN 1519
Catholic Reformers; Miracles Do Happen; Saints and Politics

225. Osanna of Mantua
(1449–1505)

St. Osanna, the eldest child of a noble family at Mantua, Italy, began to have visions at the early age of five. Her parents seem to have been unimpressed with the miraculous and misinterpreted her unexpected trances as epileptic seizures. But the visions continued lifelong. Once **Mary** appeared to make her a bride of Christ, and Christ placed an invisible ring on her finger. From 1474 through 1484, Christ's wounds were spiritually replicated in her body. Although no one could see the marks, the stigmata caused Osanna great pain. She did her best to hide all of her visionary experiences. But people noticed, sometimes admiring her and sometimes persecuting her.

Visions of the divine touched Osanna so deeply that she could not find words to describe them, as she explains in the following passage:

> To tell you the nature or extent of this unbounded light is utterly impossible. For the faculties of the body do not know or understand it, but the soul united to the God she beholds. She understands after her own spiritual fashion things past, present, and to come, but cannot explain what she sees. All her bodily faculties are put to sleep and cease to operate. But the soul ascends to that unfathomable vision human eye has never seen nor ear has heard. That divine spectacle holds the soul fast at an altitude so dizzy, that it is as though she were in the air, supported only by that intuition of God that draws her to itself in which she remains fixed and which she is enjoying. I would like to tell you how my soul is drawn by God. But I am unable for lack of suitable words.
>
> For although the soul, thus raised on high, at the time sees, understands and knows the divine light, the understanding is incapable of stating it in words. Nor can it grasp what exceeds its capacity. The soul abides rapt by the divine spectacle and the boundless light, and there is held fast unsupported by anything save the heavenly vision that attracts her, fixed in contemplation of the eternal majesty. Naught beside does she experience or think, thus spellbound by the gaze she fixes on the beauty of the light unbounded.

At fourteen, Osanna had entered the novitiate of the Dominican Third Order. But circumstances prevented her from making a full profession until thirty-seven years later. When her parents died, leadership of the family fell to her. Osanna remained in the family palace for the rest of her life, providing for her brothers and their families. Only in 1500 did she become a full-fledged Dominican tertiary.

Like other visionaries, Osanna was known for her prophetic judgment, for her competence in human affairs, and for her charity. Consider these examples: Influenced by Savonarola, she spoke out against the rampant moral corruption of state and church in Italy. Duke Francis II of Mantua appointed her to take charge of his family when he was off on a military campaign and when he returned continued to consult her on the affairs of government. And observers reported that Osanna was apt to interrupt any conversation or activity to feed a hungry beggar.

Osanna endured failing health for the last four years of her life. She died on June 20, 1505, at the age of fifty-six.

His glory, by whose being all things move,
Pervades creation and no more, no less
Resplendent shines in every part thereof.
Within the heaven his brightest beams caress
Was I, and things beheld which none returning
To earth hath power or knowledge to express.

—Dante

JUNE 20
The Light of Christ; Family; Intimacy with the Divine; Visions and Visionaries

226. Catherine of Genoa
(1447–1510)

If of the love my heart feels for God one drop were to fall into hell, hell itself would altogether turn into eternal life.

—St. Catherine of Genoa

The year 1473 significantly changed the life of St. Catherine of Genoa. For the previous decade she had battled a severe depression apparently caused by her marriage that a brother had arranged for family reasons. Julian Adorno, her husband, proved himself a weak character, a spendthrift, a profligate, and an unfaithful spouse. Then, for several decades after the pivotal 1473, she balanced intense contemplation and mortification with selfless humanitarian service to the sick and poor.

Catherine's turning point was a personal invasion of God's love that exploded into her life around March 23, 1473, the feast of **St. Benedict**, whose intercession she had asked. The experience seems to have temporarily immobilized Catherine, leaving her muttering, "No more sins! No more sins!" The impact of that first exhilarating awareness of God's mercy remained ever with her, mixed with her own relentless sense of evil. She described her constant interior tension in her *Spiritual Dialogue:*

> Considering man's sins, the Soul was astonished at the goodness of God, which together with its own defects it saw in a vision. And the Soul said:
>
> "O Lord, never more do I want to offend you, or do anything against your goodness, which has so bound me to you."
>
> Then turning toward her humanity and seeing all its defects and bad instincts, the Soul said:
>
> "Do you think you are clean enough to appear in the presence of God? Do you not see that you are not beautiful but all spattered with mud?"
>
> The suffering of the Soul was so great that it obliterated all other thoughts.
>
> The Soul said:
>
> "Alas, my God, what shall I do with myself? Where can I hide? How can I appear in your presence sullied as I am?"

Because of her evil, which she felt to be irremediable, she almost despaired. Still, trusting in God she said:

"Lord, I make you a present of myself
I do not know what to do with myself.
Let me, then, Lord, make this exchange:
I will place this evil being into your hands.
You are the only one who can hide it in your goodness
and can so rule over me
that nothing will be seen of my own proper self.
On your part, you will grant your pure love,
which will extinguish all other loves in me
and will annihilate me and busy me so much with you
that I will have no time or place for anything or anyone else."

The year 1473 also brought Catherine's husband first to bankruptcy, and then to conversion to an active faith. From that time the couple agreed to remain celibate. They relocated to a small house close to the hospital of Pammantone, where they tended the sick. Finally, they moved into the hospital in 1479, and Catherine became its administrator eleven years later.

The saint competently managed the hospital, one of Europe's largest at the time. She served heroically during an episode of the plague in 1493, almost dying of the disease herself. After Julian died in 1497, Catherine looked out for his illegitimate daughter, providing for her in her will. And notably, she forgave her husband's mistress. Catherine died of an undiagnosed illness in 1510.

We should not wish for anything but what comes to us from moment to moment exercising ourselves nonetheless for good.

—Catherine of Genoa

SEPTEMBER 15 / PATRON OF GENOA AND ITALIAN HOSPITALS
Care of the Sick; Contemplatives in Action; Conversations with God; Intimacy with the Divine; Married Saints; Mercy; Repentance

227. Joan of France
(1464–1505)

Physically deformed from birth—possibly hunchbacked or dwarfed—St. Joan of France all her life endured the hatred of her relatives. For example, her father, King Louis XI, was repulsed by her and once even tried to kill her. When she was twelve he married Joan to his cousin Louis, Duke of Orleans, who also treated her badly. But when her brother, King Charles VIII, was about to execute Louis for rebellion, she pleaded for her husband and saved his life.

However, in 1498, when Louis became the king, he had the pope annul his marriage to Joan, claiming that he had been forced into it. Joan accepted this rejection peacefully, and possibly rejoiced in getting free to pursue her religious interests.

Joan withdrew to Bourges, where she devoted herself to prayer and works of charity. There she formed a community of women dedicated to the Annunciation of the Virgin Mary. She believed she was divinely inspired to give the new order a rule based only on the virtues of Mary presented in the Bible. Franciscan Father Gabriel Mary, her spiritual director, helped her write it.

In 1504, Joan herself was allowed to become a kind of associate member of the order without going through a novitiate. She made her profession with great flair on Pentecost, during a celebration where nobles had gathered to pay homage to her as the duchess of Berry. Wearing her royal insignia, she publicly renounced her title and possessions and became a nun.

Less than a year later, however, she weakened physically and knew her death was imminent. On the feast of Epiphany, she paid a final visit to her sisters, bearing gifts like those the Magi presented to Christ and giving each a spiritual significance:

> Children, gold is the symbol of charity. Always remember to love God above all things. Keep him always in mind, all that you do, do for the love of him. If you so act, never shall you be separated from him, neither in this world or the next. You must love your neighbor too and all your sisters, doing them the good that you can reasonably expect them to do to you, never doing anything to them that you would not wish them to do to you.

I also give you incense. It is the symbol of prayer, fragrant before the face of God. It signifies that you must love to worship God and devote yourself above all things to prayer, if you wish to advance in virtue and the love of God. Prayer is the chief activity in which I would have you occupy your whole life, for which I have placed you here in the Order of the Virgin Mary.

And for myrrh, I give you my little discipline, so that you may be always mindful of the scourging and all the sufferings that Jesus endured in his passion.

Shortly after this visit, Joan of France died on February 4, 1505. Her order, called the Annonciades of Bourges, has survived under the care of the Franciscans.

O Mary, Jesus' mother sweet,
Make me your handmaid true;
And give me grace, in all my days,
To be in grace with you.
Grant me to love the ones I love,
Because of their love for you;
And my love for you be the reason why
They come to love me too.

—Joan of France

FEBRUARY 4 / CANONIZED IN 1950
Difficult Marriages; Mary; The Secrets of Spiritual Success; Suffering

228. John Fisher
(1469–1535)

We associate John Fisher with **Thomas More,** his good friend, and we remember them together. Both were Christian humanists, concerned for serious study of Scripture and the fathers and the reform of the church. As a young Renaissance king, Henry VIII had loved and admired them both. But in the end, when integrity and faith compelled Fisher and More to stand against him, the king had his old friends beheaded.

We know More better than Fisher. Historians say that's because Fisher left us fewer *bon mots* and anecdotes than his witty friend. The personal note most often reported about Fisher is that he kept a skull at his dinner table to remind him of imminent death.

In 1504, John Fisher became chancellor of Cambridge University and was also appointed bishop of Rochester, England's smallest diocese. With the support of Lady Margaret Beaufort, mother of Henry VII, Fisher revitalized Cambridge, founding new colleges and developing the library. And regarding Fisher's pastoral care for his diocese, Henry VIII boasted that no other prince had so distinguished a prelate as the bishop of Rochester.

But Fisher became Henry's most eloquent and determined opponent when the king was contemplating divorce and asserting himself as head of the Church of England. Finally in 1535, Fisher refused to take the oath of succession because it affirmed the king's supremacy over the church. Henry had him arrested and imprisoned. The pope sent him a cardinal's hat, but the king swore he would remove Fisher's head before he could wear it. A farce of a trial convicted him of high treason and condemned him to death. Once sentence was handed down, John Fisher boldly stated his opinion:

> My lords, I am here condemned before you of high treason, for denial of the king's supremacy over the Church of England. But by what order of justice I leave to God who is searcher of both of the king's majesty's conscience and yours. Nevertheless, being found guilty as it is termed, I am and must be contented with all that God shall send, to whose will I wholly refer and submit myself.
>
> And now to tell you more plainly my mind touching this matter of the king's supremacy: I think, indeed, and always have thought, and do

> now lastly affirm, that his grace cannot justly claim any such supremacy over the church of God as he now takes upon him. Never has it been seen nor heard of that any temporal prince before his days has presumed to that dignity. So, if the king will now adventure himself in proceeding in this strange and unwonted case, no doubt but he shall deeply incur the displeasure of Almighty God. And this to the great danger of his own soul and of many others, and to the utter ruin of this realm committed to his charge. Because of this, some sharp punishment will come from God's hand. Thus, I pray God that his grace may remember himself in time and hearken to good counsel for the preservation of himself and his realm, and the quietness of all Christendom.

John Fisher was beheaded on June 22, 1535, just a few days before Thomas More.

On his way to execution, John Fisher opened his little New Testament, looking for a word of comfort. Appropriately, his eyes fell upon John 17, verses 3–4:

> *And eternal life is this:*
> *to know you,*
> *the only true God,*
> *and Jesus Christ whom you have sent.*
> *I have glorified you on earth*
> *by finishing the work*
> *that you gave me to do* (NJB).

JUNE 22 / CANONIZED IN 1935
Martyrs; Saints and Politics

229. Thomas More

(1477–1535)

When fierce temptations threat thy soul with loss
Think on his passion and the bitter pain,
Think on the mortal anguish of the cross,
Think on Christ's blood let out at every vein,
Think of his precious heart all rent in twain;
For thy redemption think all this was wrought,
Nor be that lost which he so dearly bought.

—St. Thomas More

We especially love St. Thomas More because, like most of us, he was a layperson. A family man, happily married with four children, More led a lively household. Both famous scholars and poor neighbors were always welcome at his house. More served as a barrister, a member of Parliament, an officer in local government, and finally, after 1529, as lord chancellor of England. The saint's world also recognized him as a leader of the Renaissance. His best remembered work, *Utopia*, appeared in 1516.

We are comfortable with More because, like us, every morning he had to relate to several teenagers, see to paying a bill, talk to his wife about dinner plans, and see a guest off. Then he spent long days with little leisure tending to the duties of government and to writing. So we admire Thomas More for demonstrating that a person locked into the daily grind—like you and me—can become a saint.

More was devoted to the crucified Christ. Often on Fridays he knelt for hours before a crucifix, meditating on the Lord's passion. To imitate Christ's suffering he always wore a hair shirt hidden beneath his clothes and sometimes scourged himself. We may be relieved that More only advises us to "think on" the cross and not to use his own severe penances.

Thomas More made his way through Renaissance politics with flawless integrity, until it occasioned his martyrdom. When King Henry VIII decided to divorce his wife and declare himself head of the church in England, More opposed him. But he scrupulously obeyed the law, never speaking of "the King's great matter." However, when

Henry required an oath of support, More refused. The king's cronies arrested him and left him to languish in prison.

More's words and behavior in the face of death may help us approach our death more peacefully. From prison he wrote Margaret, his eldest daughter, "Nothing can come but what God allows. And I am very sure that whatever that be, however bad it might seem, it shall indeed be the best." He also told her he was thankful for his circumstances:

> I thank God, Meg, for I think God makes me a wanton and sets me on His lap and dandles me. He forgave the king's men who condemned him to death. I shall pray heartily, he said, "that though your lordships have now here on earth been judges of my condemnation, we may yet hereafter in heaven merrily all meet together to everlasting salvation."

On July 6, 1535, Thomas More was beheaded. Before his death he eloquently characterized his life by declaring that he was "the king's good servant—but God's first."

On More's way to the scaffold, a troubled man greeted him. Years before the fellow had been healed of mental illness when More had promised to keep him in his prayers. Now he feared that without More's prayers he would relapse into severe depression. But More assured him that death would not stop his intercession. He said, "Go your way in peace, and pray for me, and I will not fail to pray for you." More evidently planned to stay busy in heaven.

JUNE 22 / CANONIZED IN 1935 / PATRON OF LAWYERS AND ADOPTED CHILDREN
Facing Death; Family; Married Saints; Martyrs; Saints and Politics; World Historical Saints

230. John Forest

(1474–1538)

At seventeen, John Forest joined the Franciscans of the Strict Observance at Greenwich, England. Nine years later the community sent him to Oxford to study theology and he returned with a reputation for great learning.

At King Henry VIII's court at Greenwich, John became confessor to the queen, Catherine of Aragon. His closeness to the king was a mixed blessing that put him at risk. Because the Observants opposed the king's desire to divorce Catherine, Henry was determined to destroy the order.

In 1525, John Forest dissuaded the king from banning the community, but his success was only temporary. In 1534 the pope refused to annul the king's marriage. Almost immediately Henry ordered the closing of all Observant houses and the dispersal of the friars. All who continued to oppose Henry were imprisoned. Among these was John Forest, who was jailed in London.

In 1538 the friar was under house arrest at Newgate. He was brought to trial because he denounced the oath of supremacy that acknowledged the king as head of the church in England. Apparently John was browbeaten into assenting to several articles, but when they were presented to him to sign he repudiated them entirely. So he was condemned to be burned to death.

While awaiting his martyrdom, Queen Catherine wrote to encourage him. And he responded to his old friend with the following letter:

> Your Majesty's most gracious letter was not only a great consolation to me, but also a fresh encouragement to patience in my affliction and continual expectation of death. For though I plainly see that all this world's miseries are to be despised for the future glory, yet I find my soul was somewhat heavy on the near view of death. But your great charity has enlivened it. You have renewed my contempt of all torments and inspired me with fresh fervor in the hope of future joys.
>
> I humbly beg you not to doubt my constancy, nor to be troubled for the grievousness of the torments appointed for me. For it does not become my gray hairs to be disturbed in God's cause with such childish bugbears. It does not become a man to fly from death basely,

> after he has lived sixty-four years. Much less does it become a religious man not to love God, and with his utmost endeavors not to aspire to heavenly things, after he has been for forty-four years in the habit of St. Francis, learning and teaching the contempt of all that is earthly.
>
> I will be mindful of you, my Sovereign Lady and daughter in Christ, both in this life and in the next. Promise to pray earnestly for me, especially at that hour when I am to be laboring under those dreadful torments prepared for me.
>
> I presume to make you a poor present of my beads, as I have but three days to live on earth.

John Forest was dragged to Smithfield on a hurdle. Given one last chance to recant, he said that even if an angel came to persuade him or if he were cut to bits, he would still remain loyal to the church of Rome. He was then burned at the stake over a slow fire.

Part of the wood for John's holocaust came from a huge statue of seventh-century St. Derfel Gadarn, who was idolized by the people of Wales. Thomas Cromwell, Henry's crony, had removed it to London to destroy Welsh superstitions about the saint. From ancient times it was said that one day the statue would set a forest afire. And so it did.

MAY 22 / BEATIFIED IN 1866
Courage; Eternal Perspective; Martyrs

231. Angela Merici
(1470?–1540)

Women like **St. Teresa of Ávila** and **St. Catherine of Genoa** contributed significantly to the Catholic Reformation. But in the sixteenth-century church perhaps no woman responded more creatively to the need for reform than St. Angela Merici. She built communities that trained single women in Christian living and provided them a secure place of honor in their local societies.

A single lay woman herself, Angela established groups of unmarried women of all classes in Brescia and other northern Italian cities. She wanted the women to be in the world, but not of it. So they consecrated themselves to God and promised to remain celibate. But they lived at home with their families and looked for ways to serve their neighbors. In 1535, Angela organized the groups into the Company of St. Ursula, later called the Ursulines. Unique for its time, her avant-garde association anticipated modern secular institutes and covenant communities.

Angela gave the Ursulines a military structure, dividing towns into districts governed hierarchically by mature Christian women. This design allowed the community to support members in daily Christian living and protect them from spiritually unhealthy influences.

The rule that Angela wrote for the company required members to remain faithful to the Christian basics. In the following excerpt, she explains the importance of daily vocal and mental prayer:

> Each one of the sisters should be solicitous about prayer, mental as well as vocal, that is a companion to fasting. For Scripture says prayer is good with fasting. As by fasting we mortify the carnal appetites and the senses, so by prayer we beg God for the true grace of spiritual life. Thus, from the great need we have of divine aid, we must pray always with mind and heart, as it is written, "Pray constantly" (1 Thessalonians 5:17 *NJB*). To all we counsel frequent vocal prayer that prepares the mind by exercising the bodily senses. So each one of you, every day will say with devotion and attention at least the Office of the Blessed Virgin and the seven penitential psalms (Psalm 6, 32, 38, 51, 102, 130, and 143) because in saying the office we are speaking with God.
>
> To afford matter and some method in mental prayer, we exhort each one to raise her mind to God and to exercise herself in it every day. And so in the secret of her heart, let her say:

"My Savior, illumine the darkness of my heart, and grant me grace rather to die than to offend your Divine Majesty any more. Guard, O Lord, my affections and my senses, that they may not stray, nor lead me away from the light of your face, the satisfaction of every afflicted heart.

"I ask you, Lord, to receive all my self-will that by the infection of sin is unable to distinguish good from evil. Receive, O Lord, all my thoughts, words, and deeds, interior and exterior, that I lay at the feet of your Divine Majesty. Although I am utterly unworthy, I beseech you to accept all my being."

At Angela Merici's death in 1540 she had started twenty-four groups. Over the years the Ursulines have flourished as the oldest and one of the most respected of the church's teaching orders.

To the long list of authorities Ursulines were to obey—Ten Commandments, church, parents, civil laws—St. Angela added "divine inspirations that you may recognize as coming from the Holy Spirit." A refreshing and liberating rule. Also a dangerous one, for when it's obeyed, the Holy Spirit may act in unexpected ways.

JANUARY 27 / CANONIZED IN 1807
Innovative Saints; Catholic Reformers; Leading Women; Prayer; Valiant Women

232. Cajetan
(1480–1547)

St. Cajetan's noble birth and education had poised him for worldly success. In 1506 he launched his secular career as a senator at Vicenza, his hometown. But concern and compassion for the condition of the Christian people persuaded Cajetan to change directions. Ordained a priest in 1516, he devoted the rest of his years to renewing the church.

Like his contemporary Martin Luther, Cajetan recognized that the sixteenth-century church was "sick in head and members." Clergy both high and low had descended into decadence, and laypeople had drifted away from their faith. Cajetan responded to the vast need by doing what little he could. In Rome, Vicenza, and Verona he organized clergy and laity into a confraternity called the Oratory of Divine Love. Like Mother Teresa in our day, he focused his associates on prayer and service to the poorest of the poor. "In the Oratory," he said, "we serve God by worship. In our hospital we actually find him."

At the heart of Cajetan's piety was the sacrament of the Eucharist, which many were neglecting. For example, in 1522 he wrote a letter of encouragement to Elizabeth Porto, his pregnant niece, urging her to receive communion frequently:

> I desire that as the Virgin Mary visited Elizabeth and—through her Jesus—sanctified both Elizabeth and the son in her womb, so may he deign, because of your goodness, to visit you and the fruit of your womb. May he come to you so that you, who are the tree, and the fruit you produce may now and forever live to the joy of the angels and to the glory of blessed Christ.
>
> My daughter, I am a sinner. I hold myself in low esteem, but I take recourse to the true servants of the Lord and to his mother that beseech blessed Christ on your behalf. But I remind you that even all the saints are unable to make you as beloved by Christ as you yourself are able. Will to be so, and if you wish Christ to love you and help you, then love him. Direct your will toward pleasing him always. Never doubt that, even if you are abandoned by all the saints and by all creatures, he will always help you in your need.
>
> We always ought to give him thanks, love him, obey him and remain close to him as often as possible. He has left himself in the form of food—oh, the unhappy Christian that does not know this gift! We are

able to possess Christ, the son of the Virgin Mary, and we do not desire him. Trouble comes to the one who does not care to receive him.

In 1523, Cajetan cofounded the Theatines, an order of reforming priests. They took their name from his cofounder, John Peter Caraffa, then the bishop of Theate and later Pope Paul IV. The Theatines took vows and lived in community, but involved themselves actively in pastoral work—preaching, tending the sick, and reviving frequent participation in the sacraments. But their special concern was the renewal of priests through a call to repentance, spiritual discipline, study of Scripture, and Christian leadership. In their contributions to the Catholic Reformation the Theatines were overshadowed only by the larger and more widespread Jesuits.

Exhausted by his labor and disappointed by the slow pace of reform, Cajetan died in Naples in 1547.

I shall never be content till I see Christians flocking like little children to feed on the Bread of Life, and with eagerness and delight, not with fear and false shame.

—Cajetan

AUGUST 7 / CANONIZED IN 1671
Catholic Reformers; Saints and Sacraments (Eucharist)

233. Anthony Zaccaria
(1502–1539)

A Catholic Reformation predated and proceeded alongside the Protestant Reformation that wrenched the church in the sixteenth century. Famous saints like **Ignatius Loyola** and **Teresa of Ávila** generated a Catholic renewal. Less well known, but not less important, leaders made significant contributions to this effort. Among these Catholic reformers was St. Anthony Mary Zaccaria.

At twenty-two, Anthony graduated from the University of Padua with a degree in medicine. As he tended to the physical needs of the poor, however, he sensed a call also to minister to their spiritual poverty. So while he continued his medical practice, he studied theology to prepare himself for the priesthood. Ordained in 1528, Anthony served for a time near his home at Cremona.

Then he moved to Milan, where he focused his attention on works of mercy. Anthony enlisted the collaboration of Louisa Torelli, Countess of Guastella, who founded a congregation of women devoted to rescuing and protecting prostitutes. In 1530, with several friends he established the Clerks Regular of St. Paul, a community of priests who took vows and lived by a rule, but continued their work in the world. They made it their goal to "regenerate and revive the love of divine worship and a properly Christian way of life by frequent preaching and a faithful ministering of the sacraments." Anthony trained his brothers to preach the gospel in the spirit of **St. Paul**. You can detect the strong Pauline influence in this excerpt from one of Anthony's sermons to members of his community:

> We should love and feel compassion for those who oppose us, rather than abhor and despise them, since they harm themselves and do us good, and adorn us with crowns of everlasting glory while they incite God's anger against themselves. And even more than this, we should pray for them and not be overcome by evil, but overcome evil by goodness. We should heap good works like red-hot coals of burning love upon their heads, as our Apostle urges us to do (see Romans 12:20). So that, when they become aware of our tolerance and gentleness they may undergo a change of heart and be prompted to turn in love to God. . . .

Consider your calling, dearest brothers; if we wish to think carefully about it we shall see readily enough that its basis demands that we who have set out to follow, admittedly from afar, the footsteps of the holy apostles and the other soldiers of Christ, should not be unwilling to share in their sufferings as well. We should keep running steadily in the race we have started, not losing sight of Jesus, who leads us in our faith and brings it to perfection (see Hebrews 12:2). And so since we have chosen such a great Apostle as our guide and father and claim to follow him, we should try to put his teaching and example into practice in our lives. Such a leader should not be served by faint-hearted troops, nor should such a parent find his sons unworthy of him.

In 1533, the church officially recognized Anthony's community. Anthony served for three years as its general, then resigned to start a new branch in Vicenza. In 1539 the congregation made its headquarters at the church of St. Barnabas in Milan, and so its members have come to be called Barnabites. That same year Anthony became ill and died at his mother's house in Cremona.

> *Bless your persecutors, never curse them. . . . Never pay back evil with evil, but bear in mind the ideals that all regard with respect.*
>
> —Romans 12:14 and 17 *NJB*

JULY 7 / CANONIZED IN 1897
Catholic Reformers; Forgiveness; Perseverance

234. Thomas of Villanova
(1488–1555)

When St. Thomas, surnamed Villanova, took possession of his cathedral in 1545, a huge crowd welcomed him. They were cheering the first archbishop to take personal charge of the Valencia archdiocese in 117 years. For the next decade Thomas renewed the Catholic Church in northeastern Spain. While he did not attend the Council of Trent, he urged the Spanish bishops who did to recommend reforming the church as much as opposing Protestantism. And Thomas's reform program implemented the council's ideals and decisions.

Thomas had joined the Augustinians in 1516 and immediately rose to leadership. For twenty-five years after 1518 he was a prior in various houses. In 1533, Thomas sent the first group of Augustinians to North America as missionaries to Mexico.

Thomas's appointment as archbishop did not change his humble friar's demeanor. Dressed in his threadbare habit and hat he had worn since his profession, he walked nearly three hundred miles from Valladolid to claim his see at Valencia. The cathedral canons gave him four thousand gold pieces to furnish his apartments, but he donated the money for the renovation of a hospital. He said, "What does a poor friar like me want with furniture!"

The canons also complained about his shoddy clothing. They wanted him to dress like an archbishop, but he wouldn't budge. "Gentlemen," he said, "I am much obliged to you for the care you take of my person, but really I do not see how my dress as a religious interferes with my dignity as archbishop. You well know that my authority and the duties of my charge are quite independent of my dress, and consist rather in taking care of the souls committed to me." Later, however, at their urging he traded his old hat for a silk one. He would wave the new hat and say merrily, "Behold my episcopal dignity!"

Thomas received all callers without making them wait. "Never mind whether I am praying or studying," he told his assistants. "For although it may be unpleasant to be interrupted, still I am not my own. As a bishop I belong to my flock." Several hundred needy people a day received at his door a meal, a cup of wine, and a coin. Thomas took special care of his priests, many of whom were ill-formed and caught up in sin. On several occasions he brought priests to live with him and gently turned their lives around.

Once a theologian denounced Thomas because he seemed soft on the immorality of both clergy and laity. Thomas responded:

> He is a good man, but one of those fervent ones mentioned by **St. Paul** as having zeal without knowledge. Is he aware of the pains I have taken to correct those against whom he fulminates? Let him inquire whether **Augustine** and John **Chrysostom** used excommunication to stop the drunkenness and blasphemy which were so common among their people. No. For they were too prudent. They did not think it right to exchange a little good for a great evil by inconsiderately using their authority and so exciting the aversion of those whose favor they wanted to gain in order to influence them for good.

After eleven years of such wise governance and generous service, Thomas of Villanova died at Valencia in 1555.

> *If you want God to hear your prayers, hear the voice of the poor. If you wish God to anticipate your wants, provide those of the indigent without waiting for them to ask you. Especially anticipate the needs of those who are ashamed to beg. To make them ask for alms is to make them buy it.*
>
> —Thomas of Villanova

SEPTEMBER 22 / CANONIZED IN 1658
Almsgiving; Catholic Reformers; Great Pastors; Meekness

235. Ignatius of Loyola
(1491–1556)

The saints were of the same frame as I. Why should I not do as they have done?

—Ignatius of Loyola

The life of St. Ignatius of Loyola is an antidote for Christians who exhaust themselves seeking God's plan for their lives. Ignatius founded the Society of Jesus, a religious community that has had earthshaking influence on the modern world. But he did not do it deliberately by searching out God's design. He merely surrendered to God in all the circumstances of his life.

A Basque nobleman and soldier, Ignatius pursued a military career until a cannonball shattered his leg during a war against France in 1521. While recovering at Loyola in northern Spain, he read the only books available—a life of Christ and lives of the saints—and experienced a profound conversion. The next year Ignatius prayed and did penance at Manresa, and there he wrote the first draft of his famous *Spiritual Exercises.* The following passage from that book displays his own typical radicalism:

> Man is created to praise, reverence, and serve God our Lord, and by this means to save his soul. All other things on the face of the earth are created for man to help him fulfill the end for which he is created. From this it follows that man is to use these things to the extent that they will help him to attain his end. Likewise, he must rid himself of them in so far as they prevent him from attaining it.
>
> Therefore we must make ourselves indifferent to all created things, in so far as it is left to the choice of our free will and is not forbidden. Acting accordingly, for our part, we should not prefer health to sickness, riches to poverty, honor to dishonor, a long life to a short one. And so in all things we should desire and choose only those things that will best help us attain the end for which we are created.

To prepare himself to work for souls, Ignatius went back to school. He studied philosophy at Paris, where he gathered six like-minded companions who became the first Jesuits. They formed the "company of Jesus" in 1534 when they took vows of poverty and chastity. Ignatius dreamed that the group would evangelize Muslims in Palestine, but that did not happen. By 1537 all seven had been ordained priests and taken additional vows, one of obedience and another to go where the pope sent them. Rome gave official approval to the Society of Jesus three years later. Ignatius was chosen the first general of his order.

The Jesuits were immediately in demand everywhere. They served as leaders of the Catholic Reformation in Europe. Soon Jesuits were serving as missionaries in India, China, Ethiopia, Congo, South America, and Canada. Perhaps the community's most significant contribution came through their progressive educational system.

After 1540, Ignatius governed the Jesuits from Rome. He died there suddenly on July 31, 1556. By that date, one thousand Jesuits were serving in nine European provinces, not counting those working in foreign missions. Ignatius's surrender seems to have triggered God's action.

> *Receive, Lord, all my liberty, my memory, my understanding, and my whole will. You have given me all that I have, all that I am, and I surrender all to your divine will, in order that you may dispose of me. Give me only your love and your grace. With this I am rich enough, and I have no more to ask.*
>
> —Ignatius of Loyola

JULY 31 / CANONIZED IN 1622 / PATRON OF SPIRITUAL EXERCISES, RETREATS, AND SOLDIERS

Care of the Soul; Catholic Reformers; Leading Men

236. Peter of Alcántara
(1499–1562)

We all talk of reforming others without ever reforming ourselves.

—Peter of Alcántara

St. Peter of Alcántara was a church reformer who started with himself. At sixteen he graduated in law from the University of Salamanca in Spain. But he renounced a worldly career and joined a reformed branch of the Franciscans. He adopted a strict spiritual regimen patterned on the gospel counsels that he followed until his death. His friend, **St. Teresa of Ávila**, says that as an old man he still ate only a hunk of bread every several days, possessed but one garment, and went barefoot.

Ordained a priest in 1524, Peter became well known as a gifted preacher. In 1533 he wrote his *Treatise on Prayer and Meditation*, that he based on a work by **Louis of Granada**. The book became an instant success—a sixteenth-century best seller—and was translated into several European languages. In the following excerpt Peter warns of the hindrances to prayer:

> The first thing that hinders devotion are our sins, not only mortal sins but also venial sins. While little sins do not take away charity, they diminish its fervor, which is the same as devotion. So we should carefully avoid them, if not for the harm they do, at least for the great good that they prevent.
>
> Excessive remorse of conscience that flows from our sins also impedes devotion. It makes the soul restless, depressed, faint and weak for every good practice.
>
> Scruples obstruct devotion for the same reason. They are like thorns that prick the conscience and prevent it from resting in God and enjoying true peace.
>
> Too many cares constitute another hindrance. They are those mosquitoes from Egypt that disturb the soul. They do not allow it to sleep the spiritual sleep that lulls the soul in prayer. What's worse, they disturb the soul and divert it from its spiritual exercise.
>
> Preoccupation with sensual comforts is another block to devotion because a person who indulges too much in worldly delights does not deserve those of the Holy Spirit.

> Too many occupations are also a hindrance because they devour our time and submerge our spirit, leaving us without opportunity or heart to attend to God.
>
> Finally, interruption of spiritual exercises impedes devotion, unless we must omit them for some devout purpose. The spirit of devotion is very delicate. And just as trees and human bodies need their normal food and drink, and wither and die without them, so it is with devotion when it is deprived of spiritual food and drink.

In 1555, Peter founded a community of friars that attempted to restore the ideals of **St. Francis of Assisi**. No house had more than eight brothers. They lived in seven-foot cells, went barefoot, fasted and abstained perpetually, and practiced three hours of mental prayer daily.

However, perhaps Peter's most significant contribution to the Catholic Reformation was the guidance he gave **St. Teresa of Ávila.** In 1560 he assured her that her spiritual experiences were genuine and encouraged her to pursue her reform of the Carmelites.

Peter of Alcántara died in 1562. He is the patron saint of night watchmen, probably because for forty years he is known to have slept in a sitting position for only one-and-a-half hours a night.

*In assessments of the Catholic Reformation, saints like **Ignatius Loyola** and **Robert Bellarmine** overshadow Peter of Alcántara. He would have liked that because he eschewed prominence. But his conviction that renewal must begin with each individual believer is still relevant for the church that is always in need of reform.*

OCTOBER 19 / PATRON OF NIGHT WATCHMEN AND BRAZIL
Catholic Reformers; Celebration of Discipline; Prayer

237. Peter Favre
(1506–1546)

Peter Favre, a farm boy from Savoy, attended the College of Saint Barbara in Paris. He roomed with **Francis Xavier** and became a friend of **Ignatius Loyola.** When Ignatius formed the Society of Jesus, Peter was the first to join him. He was ordained in 1534, and later that year he celebrated the Mass at Montmarte where the original seven Jesuits took their vows.

In 1540, Peter participated in the diets of Worms and Regensburg, abortive meetings of Protestant and Catholic leaders that failed to pacify the religious turmoil in Germany. Favre had little faith in such discussions. Rather, like his Protestant counterparts, he believed the real need was for a re-Christianization of the church. He was convinced that many Catholics were only partially evangelized, converted, and instructed.

So Peter Favre traversed the Rhineland, giving retreats and spiritual counsel to people in Speyer, Regensburg, Mainz, and Cologne. Many responded to his preaching, and he taught them a basic pattern to maintain their renewed Christian life. He urged people to make a general confession, remember past sins as a motive to holiness, memorize a summary of the faith, take a daily prayer time, and receive communion weekly. He especially urged them to examine their conscience at bedtime, as he does in the following exhortation:

> We must continually examine our affections, thoughts, words and deeds, so as to come to an accurate knowledge of our old and of our new man. But I urge on you as a kind of commandment that you make this examination every night before going to bed. You must demand of yourself a strict account of the day. In the presence of your Judge who will one day appear, you must reprove, accuse and convict yourself of what you have done wrong. And give thanks to God through Jesus Christ for what you have done or thought well.
>
> You should faithfully perform the examination and spend fifteen minutes on it. Its form comprises these five points: 1. You should thank God for the benefits you have received that day, recalling and going over them one by one. 2. You should ask God for grace to recognize and feel your sins committed that day. 3. You should turn to your own heart and demand a detailed accounting of your soul for your thoughts, words and actions, noting those which seem deserving of reproof before

God and his representative. 4. You should ask God's mercy on these sins of commission and omission. 5. You should resolve upon some good emendation of these sins and also upon mentioning in confession those that require the confessor's jurisdiction and judgment, such as all certain or doubtful mortal sins. At the end, say an Our Father and a Hail Mary for the remission of your sins.

In 1546, Pope Paul III summoned Peter Favre to Rome to serve as his theologian at the Council of Trent. Peter was sick and the summer heat was overpowering. The exertion of the trip was too much. Shortly after he arrived in Rome, on August 1, he died in the arms of Ignatius. He was only forty years old.

We must hold Protestants "in great affection and love them very truly, excluding all thoughts and feelings tending to discredit them. We must also win their good will and love by friendly conversation about matters on which we do not differ, taking care to avoid all controversial subjects that lead to bickering and mutual recrimination. The things that unite us ought to be the very basis of our approach, not the things that keep us apart."

—Peter Favre

AUGUST 1 / CULT CONFIRMED IN 1872
Care of the Soul; Catholic Reformers; Celebration of Discipline; Christian Unity; Sin

238. Francis Xavier
(1506–1552)

By a series of divinely inspired accidents, St. Francis Xavier abandoned his plan to be a scholar and became instead a great missionary, second perhaps only to **St. Paul.** If you could interview him, he would say that he was unskilled in evangelism and languages, and so a most unlikely candidate to carry the Gospel to foreign lands. Yet in just one decade he introduced Christianity to tens of thousands in the East.

In 1533, Xavier completed his studies at the University of Paris and was about to begin his career as a theologian. Instead, however, he sensed a divine call to join **St. Ignatius Loyola** in the Society of Jesus which was just forming. So in 1534, Francis Xavier became one of the first Jesuits and was ordained a priest three years later.

Ignatius planned to deploy Francis as a teacher, but reluctantly sent him to India in place of a sick brother. En route, Francis, the intellectual, made friends of many rough seamen and evangelized them. He arrived in Goa in 1542 and plunged into his work.

Xavier's mission strategy was simple. When he entered a village, he gathered the idle and the young. He introduced them to Christ and the church, using the Creed, the Lord's Prayer and the Ten Commandments. He won the children with songs and jingles and they helped him reach the village adults. As soon as people expressed faith in the Creed, he baptized them. With this primitive method, Francis Xavier converted thousands of souls and planted the church from south India to Japan.

In the face of hardship, Francis drew strength from his Jesuit brothers in Europe. *For my own great comfort,* he wrote them,

> and that I may have you constantly in mind, I have cut from your letters to me your names written in your own hand, and these I always carry about with me, together with the vow of profession which I made, to be my solace and refreshment.

Xavier exhausted himself trying to meet the needs he saw, and wished that other young people would decide to abandon their own plans and serve on mission. *How many in these countries,* he once wrote to Ignatius,

> fail to become Christians, simply for the lack of a teacher of the Christian faith! Often I think of running throughout the universities of Europe, and principally Paris and the Sorbonne, there to shout at the top of my voice, like one who had lost his senses—to tell those men whose learning is greater than their wish to put their knowledge to good use, how many souls, through their negligence, must lose Heaven and end up in hell. If all, who with so much labor, study letters, would pause to consider the account they must one day render God concerning the talents entrusted to them, I am sure that they would come to say: "Here I am, Lord. Send me where you please, even to India." How much happier and safer they would be, eventually, when facing that dreadful hour from which no man can escape. Then, with the faithful servant of the Gospel they could say: "Lord, five talents you gave me; behold five others I have gained."

Francis Xavier died in 1552 while waiting to be smuggled into China.

> *If anyone wants to be a follower of mine, let him renounce himself and take up his cross and follow me. Anyone who wants to save his life will lose it; but anyone who loses his life for my sake, and for the sake of the gospel, will save it.*
>
> —Mark 8:34–35 *NJB*

DECEMBER 3 / CANONIZED IN 1622 / PATRON OF FOREIGN MISSIONS
Evangelization; Missionaries; Vocation; World Historical Saints

239. John of God
(1495–1555)

Repentance came to St. John of God in stages marked by dramatic incidents. But once he turned his life to God, he embraced the Christian ideal and never let it go.

Young John served in the army of a Castilian count, where he acquired all the immoral habits of a mercenary. He lived dissolutely until age forty, when sorrow for his past struck his conscience. To reform his life he decided to go to Africa as a missionary and perhaps die a martyr. He made a fitful start in that direction by serving a poor outcast family that was headed to Barbary. But he eventually decided that he had mistaken his call and returned to Spain.

In 1538, John opened up a religious bookshop in Granada. Like many Christian booksellers today, he hoped his little business would present him opportunities to lead others to Christ. But that year at Granada's great festival on St. Sebastian's Day, John's life changed dramatically. At the event, **John of Ávila's** preaching stabbed John's heart. Wild with remorse, he gave away his books and, like **Jacopone da Todi,** went about town screaming and performing weird penances. Because he appeared to be mad, he was confined to mental hospital. However, John of Ávila commanded him to quit his unusual penitential practices and advised him to dedicate the rest of his life to some simple Christian service.

That intervention calmed John. He stayed awhile at the hospital, serving the sick. Then he bought a small house and turned it into a hospital. Other men came to work with him, forming the foundation for the Brothers of St. John of God that has spread all over Christendom. For the next fourteen years until his death in 1555, John of God and his associates relentlessly served the poor and the sick.

John of God's reputation for holiness spread throughout Spain. While he did not hold himself in high esteem as a spiritual director, many sought his advice. Here is a letter he wrote to a duchess that reads like his own testament:

Each of us must walk along the road laid down by God. Some are called to be monks, others clerics, others hermits. Again, many are called to the married state. In whatever state of life God calls us, we can save our souls if we wish.

We owe three things to God: love, service, reverence. We must love him as our heavenly Father above all else in the world. We must serve him as our master, not so much because of the reward he promises, but because of his goodness. We must reverence him as our maker, never pronouncing his holy name except to thank him and bless him.

Good Duchess, when you feel depressed, reflect on the passion of Our Lord Jesus Christ and his precious wounds, and you will experience great consolation. Consider his life. What was it but one long round of labor in order to set us an example? By day he preached. And by night he prayed. Why then should we, poor sinners that we are, seek comfort and riches?

If we were masters of the whole world, we should not be any better. If we had more riches, we should not be any more content. He alone is happy who, despising all, sets his heart on Jesus Christ. He gives all for all, as you desire to do. Confess that you love Jesus Christ more than anything in the world. And in him and for him love your fellows. Thus you will save your soul.

MARCH 8 / CANONIZED IN 1690 / PATRON OF THE SICK, HOSPITAL WORKERS, AND BOOKSELLERS
Care of the Sick; Imitation of Christ; Purpose; Repentance; Vocation

240. John of Ávila
(1500–1569)

Come here, then, my soul, and tell me—in God's name, I ask you—what hinders you from following wholly after God with all your strength? What do you love if not God, your spouse? Why don't you have great love for him who has so greatly loved you? Had he nothing else to do on earth except to give himself up for you? And seek your benefit even to his own hurt?

What is there for you to do on earth except to love the King of Heaven? Don't you see that all these things must come to an end? What do you see? What do you hear? What do you touch? Taste? Handle? Don't you see that all these things are but a spider's web that can never clothe you or keep you from the cold?

Where are you when you are not in Jesus Christ? What do you think about? What do you value? What do you seek beyond the one perfect good?

Let us rise, my soul, and put an end to this evil dream. Let us awaken, for it is day, and Jesus Christ, who is the light, has come.

—St. John of Ávila

A young priest once asked St. John of Ávila how to become a good preacher. John, perhaps the most charismatic preacher of sixteenth-century Spain, said the only way he knew was by loving God above all.

After studying theology at Alcalá, John was ordained in 1525. Already recognized as a gifted preacher, he aspired to go as a missionary to Mexico. But the bishop of Seville commissioned him to evangelize Andalusia, Spain's southernmost province, that had been dominated by the Moors. For nine years John proclaimed the gospel there with great success. Thousands flocked to hear him. People of every rank turned their lives around and John set them on the path to holiness. With a vast correspondence, he kept in touch with his converts. The letters, many of which survive, contain much practical wisdom and have established John of Ávila as a significant spiritual writer.

John made powerful enemies by denouncing wickedness in high places. In 1531 they reported him to the Inquisition, charging him with teaching that the rich could not be saved. Imprisoned for a short time, he was completely cleared in 1533.

Then John conducted missions in various cities including Seville and Córdoba. At Granada he was instrumental in the conversion and spiritual healing of **John of God.** Among his friends were **Francis Borgia** whom he had converted, **Teresa of Ávila, Louis of Granada,** and **Ignatius Loyola**.

For his last fifteen years John of Ávila was in constant pain, but his illness did not keep him from his evangelistic work. Always enamored of the Jesuits, at age fifty-nine he decided to enter the community. But the rigorism of the provincial at Andalusia dissuaded him. The Jesuits, however, have always honored him as one of their own. After his death in 1569 he was buried in the Jesuit church at Montilla.

Love him who loved you when he was a child and who suffered cold for you and wept in the manger for you. Love him who loved you. He was only eight days old when he first shed blood for you. He could not speak then, but he could love. And as he grew older, his love grew too and was shown in the works which he did among us. As his body grew, his trials grew, his pains and tortures and crosses. Love, then, him who first loved you and loves you now in heaven.

—John of Ávila

MAY 10 / CANONIZED IN 1970
Great Preachers; Jesus Christ; A Passionate Love

241. Francis Borgia
(1510–1572)

St. Francis Borgia, a relative of Pope Alexander VI, King Ferdinand of Aragon, and Emperor Charles V, joined Spain's imperial court at age eighteen. The next year he married Eleanor de Castro, who bore him eight children. In 1539, shortly after experiencing a religious conversion, Francis left the court but continued in public life as viceroy of Catalonia. At this time under the influence of **Peter of Alcántara** and **Peter Favre**, he progressed in prayer and the spiritual life.

In 1543, Francis succeeded his father as duke of Gandia, but when his wife died three years later he decided to become a Jesuit. He provided for his children and joined the society in 1550. While he preferred a quiet life of solitude, the Jesuits felt differently and promoted him so that he could use his great administrative talents for the church. In 1554, **St. Ignatius** appointed Francis commissary for Spain, where he founded twelve colleges and a novitiate. The Jesuits chose Francis as their general in 1565. His consolidation of the society and expansion of its ministry has caused him to be recognized as the second founder of the order. He established disciplined novitiates in every Jesuit province, writing regulations and books of spiritual instruction for them.

Francis created a new Jesuit base in Poland and strengthened the community's work in Germany and France. Between 1566 and 1572 he launched the Jesuit mission to Spanish colonies in Florida, Mexico, and Peru. He maintained contact with the missioners by letter, advising them about their own spiritual lives and counseling them on strategy. Following is a excerpt from his correspondence:

> We must perform all our works in God and refer them to his glory so that they will be permanent and stable. Everyone—whether kings, nobles, tradesmen or peasants—must do all things for the glory of God and under the inspiration of Christ's example. . . . When you pray, hear Mass, sit at table, engage in business and when at bedtime you remove your clothes—at all times crave that by the pain which he felt when he was stripped just before his crucifixion, he may strip us of our evil habits of mind. Thus, naked of earthly things, we may also embrace the cross.
>
> Wherever our brethren may be, let their first care be for those already converted. Their first aim must be to strengthen these in the faith and

> to help them save their souls. After this they may convert others not yet baptized. But let them proceed prudently and not undertake more than they can carry through. It is not desirable for them to hurry here and there to convert heathen with whom they cannot afterwards keep in touch. It is better to advance step by step and consolidate conquests already made. . . . They are not to risk their lives unnecessarily in excursions among unconquered people. The swift loss of life in God's service may be advantageous for them. However, it is not for the greater good of the many for there are only a few laborers for the vineyard and it is difficult to replace them.

In 1571 the pope sent Francis to Spain and Portugal to help build an alliance against the Turks. He grew increasingly ill on this embassy and died after returning to Rome in 1572.

> *It is not those who commit the least faults who are most holy, but those who have the greatest courage, the greatest generosity, the greatest love, who make the boldest efforts to overcome themselves, and are not immoderately apprehensive of tripping.*
>
> —Francis de Sales

OCTOBER 10 / CANONIZED IN 1671 / PATRON OF PORTUGAL
Evangelization; Leading Men

242. Edmund Campion
(1540–1581)

For the first dozen years of her reign, Queen Elizabeth I did not strictly enforce her anti-Catholic legislation. But for a variety of reasons, after 1570 she intensified the persecution of Catholics. Not least among these was the increasing presence in England of priests trained at the English College in Douai in Flanders, now in France. They kept alive the Catholic faith that the queen hoped would die out. Posing an even greater threat, in 1580, St. Edmund Campion and Robert Parsons initiated a "Jesuit Mission" to sustain English Catholics.

A popular and notable Oxford graduate, perhaps Campion came to be especially despised because he had converted to Catholicism. He became a Jesuit in 1573 and was ordained five years later. In 1580 he arrived in England disguised as a jewel merchant to support English Catholics.

In a bold move he wrote a challenge to the queen's Privy Council. He declared that his mission was "to preach the gospel, to minister the sacraments, to instruct the simple, to reform sinners, to confute errors—in brief to cry a spiritual alarm against foul vice and proud ignorance, wherewith many of my dear countrymen are abused." In the following passage, Campion dared the council to hear him out and be convinced of their errors:

> I doubt not but you her Highness' Council . . . when you shall have heard these questions of religion opened faithfully, . . . will discountenance error when it is divulged, and hearken to those who would spend the best blood in their bodies for your salvation.
>
> Many innocent hands are lifted up to heaven for you daily by those English students [the seminarians at Douai], whose posterity shall never die. . . . They are determined never to give you over, but either to win you heaven, or to die upon your pikes. And touching our Society, be it known to you that we have made a league—all the Jesuits in the world, . . .—cheerfully to carry the cross you shall lay upon us, and never to despair your recovery, while we have a man left to enjoy your Tyburn, or to be racked with your torments, or consumed with your prisons. The expense is reckoned, the enterprise is begun.
>
> It is of God, it cannot be withstood. So the faith was planted: so it must be restored.

> If these my offers be refused, and my endeavors can take no place, and I, having run thousands of miles to do you good, shall be rewarded with rigor, I have no more to say but to recommend your case and mine to Almighty God, the Searcher of Hearts, who sends us his grace, and sets us at accord before the day of payment, to the end we may at last be friends in heaven, when all injuries shall be forgotten.

This document, that came to be called "Campion's Brag," circulated widely and rallied Catholics with renewed hope. Campion seemed to pop up everywhere, his preaching and publications spreading a reinvigorated Catholicism. Unable to ignore such a threat, the government searched him out and arrested him in the fall of 1581. On November 14, a packed jury condemned him to death on the false charge of plotting rebellion. Edmund Campion died a martyr on December 1, hanged, drawn and quartered at Tyburn near the present-day Marble Arch in London's West End.

> *Our friends are all those who unjustly afflict upon us trials and ordeals, shame and injustice, sorrows and torments, martyrdom and death. We must love them greatly for we will possess eternal life because of what they bring upon us.*
>
> —Francis of Assisi

DECEMBER 1 / CANONIZED IN 1970
Courage; Martyrs

243. Teresa of Ávila
(1515–1582)

A friend was once surprised to find St. Teresa gorging herself on a partridge. "What would people think?" she asked. "Let them think whatever they want," said Teresa. "There's a time for penance, and there's a time for partridge." Endearing stories like this reveal the secret of Teresa's life: Heaven invaded her heart, but she never lost her head in the clouds.

Teresa was a spiritual late-bloomer. She said she was a "gadabout" nun for twenty years, not getting serious about her spirituality until she was forty. Then a series of extraordinary encounters with Christ launched her Christian growth. Once while praying the *Veni, Creator Spiritus* she seemed to hear him say, "I will not have you hold conversations with men, but with angels." From that time St. Teresa enjoyed frequent heaven-sent experiences of God's presence. She wrote about a recurring divine invasion of her soul in this famous passage from her *Autobiography:*

> I would see beside me, on my left hand, an angel in bodily form—a type of vision that I am not in the habit of seeing, except very rarely. . . .
>
> It pleased the Lord that I should see this angel in the following way. He was not tall, but short, and very beautiful, his face so aflame that he appeared to be one of the highest types of angel who seem to be all afire. . . .
>
> In his hands I saw a long golden spear and at the end of the iron tip I seemed to see a point of fire. With this he seemed to pierce my heart several times so that it penetrated to my entrails. When he drew it out, I thought he was drawing them out with it and he left me completely afire with a great love for God. The pain was so sharp that it made me utter several moans; and so excessive was the sweetness caused me by this intense pain that one can never wish to lose it, nor will one's soul be content with anything less than God. It is not bodily pain, but spiritual, though the body has a share in it—indeed, a great share. So sweet are the colloquies of love which pass between the soul and God that if anyone thinks I am lying I beseech God, in His goodness, to give him the same experience.

Teresa encourages us to climb the heights of prayer, but at the same time instructs us to stay in touch with the realities of Christian living.

Prayer that displaces charity, said the saint, does not please God, and her own care for others was the proof of her spirituality. She was an activist who helped thousands live their daily lives more Christianly. From 1560 until her death in 1582, she founded seventeen renewed Carmelite convents in Spain and spearheaded a general renewal of Catholic life. Because of her profound and practical books on prayer and her work as a leader of the Catholic Reformation, Teresa of Ávila has been recognized as a doctor of the church.

> *What the Lord desires is works. If you see a sick woman to whom you can give some help, never be affected by the fear that your devotions will suffer, but take pity on her: if she is in pain, you should feel pain too; if necessary, fast so that she may have your food, not so much for her sake as because you know it to be your Lord's will. That is true union with his will.*
>
> —Teresa of Ávila

OCTOBER 15 / CANONIZED IN 1622 / PATRON OF HEADACHE AND HEART ATTACK SUFFERERS

Angels; Catholic Reformers; Contemplatives in Action; Doctors of the Church; Leading Women; Prayer; A Soul Afire

244. Rudolf Aquaviva
(1550–1583)

Ordained at Lisbon, Portugal, at age nineteen, Jesuit Rudolf Aquaviva was sent as a missionary to Goa, India, where for a decade he had only modest success. Then in 1579, the Great Mogul Akbar requested missionaries be sent to his court near Agra. Rudolf got the assignment and was eager to present the Christian faith to the Muslim king. The great mogul showed his openness to Christianity by permitting the construction of churches and the celebration of the liturgy.

Rudolf's goal, however, was winning the king himself to Christ and, through him, his people. But Akbar's apparently keen personal interest was checked by the Muslim proscription of conversion. And sometimes it seemed he was toying with Aquaviva. For example, during explanations of Christian doctrine that he had invited, he dozed or got distracted by his entertainers or his harem.

Rudolf became completely frustrated. As he explained in the following letter to his spiritual mentor, his zeal flagged and he longed for a martyr's death.

> You know how I longed for this mission, and how delighted I was when it was granted me. I have been able to do what I wished for—to bear witness to the name of Jesus Christ before the kings and rulers of this world. And thus to hope for winning the prize of such a death as Scripture calls precious in the sight of the Lord (see Psalm 116:15). You may be sure that many desire for us this death. Meantime, while it is deferred, there is no lack of thousands of opportunities of suffering from within and from without, so that sometimes I grow weary of life.
>
> We cannot speak out the truth for fear that if we go too far we endanger the life of King Akbar. So we neither die because they do not kill us, and yet we do not live for our zeal wears us out. Or we live only by hope, though that is very uncertain whether it may not turn out rather evil than good. Ours is a very uncertain outlook as far as the King's conversion goes.
>
> Still, the Lord makes us realize that our labors are just as pleasing and acceptable to his divine majesty as if we were to obtain that for which we are striving, for God is a witness of inmost feelings and a searcher of the heart (see Wisdom 1:6). The thought of this makes it seem to me—as it did to Jacob when he waited long years for Rachel—but a

> few days because of the greatness of love (see Genesis 29:9). For day and night we are toiling at a work of great service to God, the planting of his faith in a barbarous nation at such peril of our lives.

By 1583 the mission to Akbar had failed. Then Aquaviva was appointed superior of the Jesuit outreach to Hindus at Salsette, north of Bombay. He and four associates decided to build a church in Cuncolim, a village that was the main source of resistance to their work. This frontal attack won Rudolf his desired martyrdom, as the Hindu villagers massacred him and his companions shortly after they arrived.

Many things Christians attempt to do for God seem to fail—as did Rudolf Aquaviva's missionary efforts . . . But the judgment of failure comes from our nearsighted human perspective. However, God, whom we are serving after all, may see our failure as a great success. It may have drawn us closer to him, for example. And, invisibly to us, it may have accomplished a part of his grand scheme.

JULY 27 / BEATIFIED IN 1893
Eternal Perspective; Missionaries; Pursuit of Holiness; Success in Failure

245. Charles Borromeo
(1538–1584)

In 1560, Pope Pius IV appointed his twenty-two-year-old nephew, Charles Borromeo, a cardinal-deacon and administrator of the see of Milan. Then the pope also made him secretary of state and cardinal-protector of Portugal, the Low Countries, the Friars Minor, and others. He also appointed Charles papal legate in Bologna, Romagna, and Ancona.

The pope's choice may seem to have been rank nepotism. But Charles Borromeo, an unusually gifted and accomplished young man, tackled his assignments methodically and with high energy. When Pius IV announced his intent to reconvene the Council of Trent, Charles handled the preparations for its opening in January 1562. The saint's skillful diplomacy contained the forces that threatened to disperse the bishops before their work was done. Charles himself drafted the council's catechism. And he masterminded this final session of Trent that promulgated its most important reforming disciplinary and doctrinal decrees of the Counter-Reformation.

After his uncle's death in 1566, Charles was finally able to take up his duties in Milan, where the church was in disarray. With firmness and creativity he set about repairing it, implementing the council's reforms. He instructed his clergy in a series of pastoral meetings. He founded seminaries that became models for dioceses everywhere. Charles met considerable resistance, but dealt with it wisely. For example, when his cathedral canons resisted his discipline, he founded an order of priests who made a simple promise to work along with him.

Once in an address to this group, Charles revealed his heartfelt concern for souls that motivated his lifelong service:

> Oh! If we could only understand what it means to deliver a soul from hell, I'm sure that many of you would risk any danger in the hope of saving even one person.
>
> How beautiful are the feet of those who preach the gospel of peace. No wonder that the holy virgin, Catherine of Siena, kissed the ground where preachers had walked because they were fellow-workers with Christ. Nothing pleases God more than to be his Son's helpers and to undertake the charge of saving souls. Nothing brings more joy to the church than those who restore souls to spiritual life, thus despoiling

> hell, defeating the devil, casting out sin, opening heaven, making the angels glad, glorifying the most holy Trinity and preparing for themselves a never-fading crown.

Charles personally visited parishes in every quarter of his diocese. He had to be hard as flint to turn things around, but he dealt with offenders with remarkable gentleness. John Peter Giusano, his disciple and biographer, described this typical instance:

> In a certain town of his diocese lived a priest who had grown old in sin, scandalizing all of the inhabitants. When the cardinal visited there he was informed of the priest's bad example. So the saint sent for him. He admonished the priest privately with a father's tenderness and sent him away without imposing any penance. The townspeople were disappointed because they had expected some public demonstration. However, when they noticed that the priest made a sudden and total change in his life, they were filled with wonder. Some thought it quite miraculous that a single meeting with the cardinal could produce such an effect.

Charles Borromeo literally wore himself out working for reform. He died in 1584 at the age of forty-six.

"Blessed are the meek," Jesus said, "for they shall inherit the earth" (Matthew 5:5 RSV*). And Charles Borromeo is an archetype of biblical meekness which means strength under control. Although he was hard as flint when confronting evil, he always approached people with kindness.*

NOVEMBER 4 / CANONIZED IN 1610
Care of the Soul; Catholic Reformers; Great Pastors; Meekness; Mercy

246. Louis of Granada
(1504–1588)

Few saints have extended their influence as widely as Dominican Louis of Granada. He was perhaps the most popular Catholic writer of the sixteenth century, and is still read profitably today. **Charles Borromeo**, **Teresa of Ávila**, **Alphonsus Liguori**, **Vincent de Paul**, and **Louise de Marillac** and other great saints benefited from his books and spread his message.

Like **Francis de Sales**, Louis wanted to make the interior life accessible to laypeople. So his best-known books, *The Book of Prayer and Meditation* and the *Sinner's Guide*, presented a pattern of the inner life for ordinary Christians. Popularly and persuasively, Louis explained that performing certain fundamentals would make believers more Christlike: mental prayer, cultivation of virtue, contempt for the world, contemplation of God in nature, mortification of the flesh, obedience of the commandments, participation in the sacraments, and imitation of the saints.

In the following excerpt from the *Sinner's Guide*, Louis warns us against spiritual complacency:

> You will no sooner have resolved to give yourself to God than hell will send out its forces against you. The flesh, corrupted from its birth by the serpent's poison, will assail you with its insatiable desires and alluring pleasures. The world, as powerful as it is cruel, will wage a fierce war against you. The devil himself, the arch-deceiver, will turn all his forces against you.
>
> Don't be discouraged. Remember that the prize for which you are striving is worth more than all you can ever give to purchase it. Against the assaults of corrupt nature you have God's grace. Against the assaults of the devil you have the almighty power of God. Against the allurements of evil habits you have the force of good habits confirmed by grace. Against a multitude of evil spirits you have numberless angels of light. Against the bad example and persecutions of the world you have the good example and strengthening exhortations of the saints. Against the sinful pleasures and vain joys of the world you have the pure joys and ineffable consolations of the Holy Spirit.
>
> Is it not evident that all that are for you are stronger than all that are against you? Is not God stronger than the devil? Is not grace superior to nature? Are not the good angels more powerful than the fallen legions?

Are not the pure and ineffable joys of the soul more delightful than the gross pleasures of sense and the vain amusements of the world?

A disciple of **John of Ávila,** Louis was equipped as an academic theologian, but he preferred to preach, a ministry he exercised with great success in Cordoba and Portugal. The Cardinal Prince Henry invited him to Portugal in 1555 to serve the royal family and Portuguese elite, and he scarcely ever returned to Spain. He led the Dominicans of Portugal as their provincial from 1556 to 1560. In that period he wrote many of his twelve books on the spiritual life. Louis's emphasis on the interior life and the pursuit of perfection caught the vigilant eye of the Inquisition in 1559 and again in 1568. But both times his name was cleared in a short time.

Court intrigues, a fraudulent stigmatic nun, and blindness combined to cause Louis much suffering in his declining years. He died in 1588.

If all the calamities which have existed in the world since the creation and all the sufferings of hell were put into one side of a scale, and but one mortal sin into the other, it would outweigh all these evils, for it is incomparably greater.

—Louis of Granada

DECEMBER 31
Care of the Soul; Grace; Pursuit of Holiness; The Secrets of Spiritual Success; Sin

247. Catherine dei Ricci
(1522–1590)

We are curious about mystics who experience ecstasies and visions. But we tend to regard them as psychologically unbalanced persons. However, when we get to know a genuine mystic like St. Catherine dei Ricci we must abandon our stereotypical view.

Catherine was a very competent woman who trained nuns and governed a convent for many years. She taught and advised religious and laity with obvious wisdom. She also delighted in nursing the sick. Her contemporaries and modern scholars alike judge that she was psychologically healthy. And Catherine received some most unusual mystical phenomena, including the stigmata.

At age thirteen Catherine entered the Dominican convent at Prato, Italy. As a young nun she became mistress of novices and at thirty she was elected prioress for life. She became famous for her sound teaching, much of which she communicated in letters to nuns, priests, and laity. Here she addressed a "summary of Christian perfection" to a young nun:

1. We must force ourselves to detach our heart and will from all earthly loves, except for the love of God. We must love no fleeting things. Above all, we must not love God selfishly for our own sakes, but with a love as pure as his own goodness.
2. We must direct all our thoughts, words and actions to his honor. And by prayer, counsel, and good example seek his glory solely, whether for ourselves or for others, so that through our actions all may love and honor God. This second thing is more pleasing to him than the first, as it better fulfills his will.
3. We must aim more and more to accomplish the divine will: not only desiring nothing special to happen to us, bad or even good, in this wretched life, thus keeping ourselves always at God's disposal, with heart and soul at peace. But we must also believe with a firm faith that Almighty God loves us more than we love ourselves, and takes more care of us than we could take care of ourselves.

> Let us always remember, never doubting, that it is the eternal, sovereign, all-powerful God who does, orders, or allows everything that happens. Know that nothing comes to pass without his divine will. If, through his mercy, this conviction becomes strongly impressed upon our wills, we shall easily take all things from his sacred hand with well-contented hearts, always thanking him for fulfilling his holy will in us.

For twelve years, from 1542 to 1554, Catherine received an extraordinary ecstasy. From noon on Thursdays through 4 p.m. on Fridays, she experienced in a trance the events of Christ's passion. Although unconscious, her bodily movements coincided with his—she stood solemnly at the scourging, bowed to be crowned with thorns, extended her arms to be nailed to the cross, and so on. The stigmata, the imprints of Christ's wounds, also marked her body. Inconvenienced and embarrassed by these phenomena, Catherine said that they came—uninvited—from God. In 1554 she and her nuns prayed that the ecstasies would cease, and they did.

Catherine died in 1590 after patiently suffering a long illness. The church canonized her not because of her mystical experiences but for her heroic virtue and perfect union with Christ.

> *The mystics have the special role of talking to us of God's love and of helping us to glimpse something of the reality still hidden from our eyes. They are called "mystics" simply because they have had a particularly vivid experience of the Christian "mystery." They are our safest guides in helping us to look into the reality beyond the reality.*
>
> —Raniero Cantalamessa

FEBRUARY 13 / CANONIZED IN 1747
Care of the Soul; Contemplatives in Action; Intimacy with the Divine; A Passionate Love; The Secrets of Spiritual Success; Stigmata; Visions and Visionaries

248. Alphonsus de Orozco
(1500–1591)

In 1552, the Virgin appeared to Alphonsus de Orozco at Seville, Spain. "Write!" she commanded, giving the shortest message ever recorded in a Marian apparition. And write he did. From that time annually he wrote a work about Mary. In addition to his *Confessions* that catalog his own spiritual journey, he also wrote numerous books on prayer and the Christian life that fill seven large volumes. Alphonsus ranks with **Teresa of Ávila** and **John of the Cross** as a great Spanish spiritual writer. In the following selection from his best-known book, *The Mount of Contemplation*, he explained the importance of spiritual reading:

> St. Augustine gave to reading the function of seeking the treasure. Meditation, he said, will find it, prayer digs for it with all its might, and contemplation sets it forth in clear light. The holy doctor bases this on those words of the gospel: "Everyone who searches finds; everyone who knocks will have the door opened" (Matthew 7:8 *NJB*). So that seeking God is part of holy reading, just as worldly reading . . . leads to losing him. . . . If, then, you want to find the Lord of mercy, read learned and spiritual doctors, for St. Lipsianus says: "As in prayer we speak with God, in reading our God speaks to us. . . ."
>
> We owe much to those who in what they wrote enlightened our understanding. . . . But the book which not only speaks to the understanding but also awakens the will to the love of God should be held in high esteem. Hardly ever should we allow it to leave our hands. It should be read with the mind in repose, doing violence to oneself to pay attention, and casting aside every other thought.
>
> Do not go jumping about from one book to another, nor begin by reading the end. For as a philosopher said, we enjoy variety in what we read, but perseverance in reading is what brings us profit. You should always pick out certain passages from what you have read and fix them in your mind. . . . Always have a definite time each day for reading, just as you should have for prayer and contemplation.

Influenced by **Thomas of Villanova,** his teacher at Salamanca, Alphonsus donned the habit of an Augustinian friar in 1522. A simple man who preferred obscurity and solitude, he spent most of his time at prayer. He ate but one small meal a day and allowed himself only three hours sleep. Ironically, however, his vocation involved Alphonsus in an external life of leadership in his order and of ministry to the Spanish nobility. After 1538, he led four Augustinian houses as prior, and in 1554 he assumed responsibility for the community in Valladolid, where King Philip II noticed him.

Two years later Philip appointed Alphonsus as court preacher. And when the king moved the court to Madrid in 1561, Alphonsus went along. His example of austerity presented a sharp contrast to the splendor of official functions that he had to attend. But his simplicity attracted the members of the royal family and many Spanish nobles. Alphonsus became their friend and mentor and exercised a significant spiritual influence in their lives. For thirty-five years they flocked to his sermons, read his books, and queued up at his confessional. When Alphonsus de Orozco died in 1591, they followed his coffin, mourning the loss of their great friend and saint.

Prayer shows the soul the great secrets of God, is the guide of our desires and of so many of our works, and finally is the gate which takes us to the desired garden of contemplation.

—Alphonsus de Orozco

SEPTEMBER 19 / CANONIZED IN 2002
Countercultural Witness

249. Philip Neri
(1515–1595)

For forty-five years St. Philip Neri evangelized thousands of people at Rome, from the poor to the popes. He buttonholed them in life-changing conversations, instructed them in conferences, and mainly drew them to conversion in the confessional. Philip won their hearts with his consistent kindness and jovial sense of humor. He became known as the "Second Apostle of Rome" because his ministry promoted a general return to the Christian living. You can get a feel for the saint's attractiveness in his maxims, like these:

> "He who wishes to pray without mortifying himself is like a bird trying to fly before it has grown its feathers."
>
> "The best preparation for prayer is to read the lives of the saints, not from mere curiosity, but quietly and with recollection a little at a time. And to pause whenever you feel your heart touched with devotion."
>
> "Imagine yourselves to be spiritual beggars in the presence of God and his saints. You should go round from saint to saint, imploring an alms with the same real earnestness with which the poor beg."
>
> "He who does not go down to hell in his lifetime, runs a great risk of going there when he dies."
>
> "In all other temptations, he who fights overcomes. But against lust, he overcomes who runs away."
>
> "The worst tribulation of the true servant of God is to be without tribulation."
>
> "Never try to evade the cross that God sends you, for you will only find a heavier one."
>
> "Very often the fault we commit by too great sadness when we are rebuked is greater than the fault which drew on us the rebuke."

In 1533, after a dramatic personal experience of God, Philip went to Rome, where he lived in poverty. After several years of solitude and study he sold his books and hit the streets to do the grassroots work of leading people to Christ. Ordained in 1551, he went to live with a community of priests at San Giralomo. He and his associates held conferences in their oratory that gathered people for an evening of study and prayer that climaxed in music or a short pilgrimage to one of the ancient basilicas.

Soon Philip gathered about himself a small group of talented priests that he organized into the Congregation of the Oratory. Philip's informality characterized the foundation. For example, members were not required to take vows, but only to adhere to the gospel. "If you want to be obeyed," quipped Philip, "don't make commandments." Officially recognized in 1575, the Oratory spread throughout the world and attracted illustrious members such as **John Henry Newman.**

Like his contemporary **St. Teresa of Ávila,** Philip Neri was a mystic-in-action. He reported that once at prayer in 1544 he saw a globe of fire enter his mouth and set his heart aflame that permanently afflicted him. The saint did his best to hide his mystical phenomena, but sometimes his ecstasies at Mass lasted so long that the acolytes could leave for an hour's break.

Philip Neri died on May 25, 1595, active till the end and celebrated as the most popular person in Rome.

Cast yourself with confidence into the arms of God. And be very sure of this, that if he wants anything of you he will fit you for your work and give you strength to do it.

—Philip Neri

MAY 26 / CANONIZED IN 1622 / PATRON OF ROME
Contemplatives in Action; Joy; The Secrets of Spiritual Success; Sexual Temptation; A Soul Afire

250. Peter Canisius
(1521–1597)

If you have too much to do, with God's help you will find time to do it all.

—Peter Canisius

For a half-century Jesuit Father Peter Canisius led the Catholic Reformation in Austria, Bavaria, and Bohemia. For that reason he is reckoned an apostle to Germany, second only to **St. Boniface.** With stupendous energy he preached and taught in parishes, reformed and founded universities, wrote many books including popular catechisms, restored lapsed Catholics, converted Protestants, preached retreats, and found time to care for the sick. In his last thirty years traveling more than twenty thousand miles on foot or horseback, St. Peter Canisius spearheaded the renewal of the Catholic faith in southern Germany.

Peter Canisius revitalized Catholic life and teaching at universities in Ingolstadt and Augsburg. He founded new ones at Prague and Fribourg. In all four cities his preaching and catechizing won the hearts of Catholics and attracted nominal Protestants to the church. In Vienna his personal care for plague victims made him a most popular figure. Thus, when appointed diocesan administrator, he was in a position to revive the city's long decadent Catholic community.

After 1555, Peter Canisius published his famous *Summary of Christian Doctrine* and two smaller catechisms. These books generated the Catholic Reformation as Luther's catechism had spread Protestantism. Canisius's catechisms also helped launch the Catholic press. During the saint's lifetime they were translated into fifteen languages and reprinted more than two hundred times.

In the late sixteenth century, when open hostility typified relations between Catholics and Protestants, Peter Canisius advised charity and moderation. He opposed theological debates with Protestant leaders and, in general, discouraged discussion of Catholic distinctives such as indulgences, purgatory, and monastic vows with Protestants. He believed such efforts only heightened division and embittered relations. He articulated his views in this letter to his Jesuit superior:

> It is plainly wrong to meet non-Catholics with bitterness or to treat them with discourtesy. For this is nothing else than the reverse of Christ's example because it breaks the bruised reed and quenches the smoking flax. We ought to instruct with meekness those whom heresy has made bitter and suspicious, and has estranged from orthodox Catholics, especially from our fellow Jesuits. Thus, by whole-hearted charity and good will we may win them over to us in the Lord.
>
> Again, it is a mistaken policy to behave in a contentious fashion and to start disputes about matters of belief with argumentative people who are disposed by their very natures to wrangling. Indeed, the fact of their being so constituted is a reason the more why such people should be attracted and won to the simplicity of the faith as much by example as by argument.

In 1591, Peter Canisius suffered a stroke that nearly killed him. But he recovered and devoted himself to writing for six more years until his death in 1597.

> *Let my eyes take their sleep, but may my heart always keep watch for you. May your right hand bless your servants who love you.*
>
> *May I be united with the praise that flows from you, Lord Jesus, to all your saints; united with the gratitude drawn from your heart, good Jesus, that causes your saints to thank you; united with your passion, good Jesus, by which you took away our guilt; united with the divine longing that you had on earth for our salvation; united with every prayer that welled from your divine heart, good Jesus, and flowed into the hearts of your saints.*
>
> —Peter Canisius

DECEMBER 21 / CANONIZED IN 1925
Christian Living; Catholic Reformers; Christian Unity; Doctors of the Church; Peacemakers

251. Alphonsus Rodriguez
(1533–1617)

I would rather be a doorkeeper in the house of my God than dwell in the tents of wickedness.

—Psalm 84:10 *RSV*

Some saints attack the world head-on, like **St. Peter Claver,** the friend and disciple of St. Alphonsus Rodriguez. Others like Alphonsus himself fight personal battles against failure, loss, temptation, and disease. We tend to admire more activist champions such as Peter Claver, who worked among slaves for forty years. But why should we think any the less of saints such as Alphonsus, who was more like us in his ordinariness and suffering? And who showed us how to be faithful in long lasting spiritual and personal struggles?

Alphonsus's early years in Segovia, Spain, are a story of tragedies. When he was fourteen, his father died and he left school to help his mother run the family business. At twenty-three he married, but his wife died in childbirth three years later. Within a few years his mother and son also died. On top of this, his business was failing, so he sold it. Recognizing a late vocation to religious life, he applied for admission to the Jesuits at Segovia, but was refused because he was not educated. Undaunted, Alphonsus returned to Latin school, humbly bearing the ridicule of his adolescent classmates. Finally, in 1571, the Jesuit provincial accepted him as a lay brother. He was sent to Montesione College on Majorca, where he served as doorkeeper for forty-five years.

His post allowed him to minister to many visitors. And he became the spiritual adviser to many students. He exerted wide-reaching influence, most notably in guiding St. Peter Claver into his mission to the slaves.

Alphonsus adhered to a few simple spiritual guidelines that navigated him through his troubles and trials. For example, a method for finding joy in hardship:

> Another exercise is very valuable for the imitation of Christ—for love of him, taking the sweet for the bitter and the bitter for sweet. So, I put myself in spirit before our crucified Lord, looking at him full of sorrow, shedding his blood and bearing great bodily hardships for me.

> As love is paid for in love, I must imitate him, sharing in spirit all his sufferings. I must consider how much I owe him and what he has done for me. Putting these sufferings between God and my soul, I must say, "What does it matter, my God, that I should endure for your love these small hardships? For you, Lord, endured so many great hardships for me." Amid the hardship and trial itself, I stimulate my heart with this exercise. Thus, I encourage myself to endure for love of the Lord who is before me, until I make what is bitter sweet. In this way learning from Christ our Lord, I take and convert the sweet into bitter, renouncing myself and all earthly and carnal pleasures, delights and honors of this life, so that my whole heart is centered solely on God.

In his old age, Alphonsus experienced no relief from his trials. The more he mortified himself, the more he seemed to be subject to spiritual dryness, vigorous temptations, and even diabolical assaults. In 1617 his body was ravaged with disease and he died at midnight, October 30.

Yet God (that hews mountain and continent,
Earth, all, out; who, with trickling increment,
Veins violets and tall trees makes more and more)
Could crowd career with conquest while there went
Those years and years by without event
That in Majorca Alfonso watched the door.

—Gerard Manley Hopkins

OCTOBER 30 / CANONIZED IN 1888 / PATRON OF MAJORCA
Enduring Trials; Success in Failure; True Humility; Vocation

252. Paschal Baylon

(1540–1592)

As a youth at Torra Hermosa at the border of Castile and Aragon, Paschal Baylon tended his family's sheep. He taught himself to read so that he could pray the *Little Office of the Blessed Virgin*, the popular prayer book of his day. Paschal disciplined himself to endure the harshness and loneliness of a shepherd's work. And when his sheep trod on others' vines, he scrupulously paid for the damage out of his own meager resources.

At twenty-one, St. Paschal joined the reformed Franciscans of **St. Peter of Alcántara** at Loreto. As a lay brother, Paschal for many years served as porter and guestmaster with patience and good humor. John Ximenes, his biographer, reports that he was a model friar, always the first at prayer and never once behaving badly in a relationship. "In no single case," said Ximenes, "do I remember to have noted even the least fault in him, though I lived with him in several of our houses and was his companion on two long journeys."

Like other saintly doorkeepers **Brother André** and **Solanus Casey**, Paschal gained a reputation for miracles. For example, Martin Crespo once told how the saint freed him from his determination to take vengeance on his father's murderers:

> One Good Friday there was a lifelike representation of the descent from the cross. Along with everyone else in town, I followed the crucifix borne in triumph through the streets. I did not know what was in store for me. In a last ditch effort to get me to repent, my friends boxed me in and forced me to endure the preacher's address. He concluded his eloquent speech in a pathetic peroration, urging me to forgiveness in memory of our Savior's passion. His fine discourse left me unmoved and cold.
>
> "Quit tormenting me," I exclaimed angrily. "It's no use. I will not forgive them." Brother Paschal, whom I had not noticed before, stepped forward. He took me by the arm and drew me aside.
>
> "My son," he said, "have you not just now seen a representation of our Lord's passion?" Then with a glance that penetrated my soul he said: "For the love of Jesus Crucified, my son, forgive them."
>
> "Yes, Father," I replied, hanging my head and weeping. "For the love of God I forgive them with all my heart." I no longer felt the

same person. As if by some enchantment, a bloodthirsty wolf had been transformed into a lamb.

The crowd anxiously awaited the outcome of our mysterious conference. When Paschal announced that I had forgiven my enemies, they burst into applause.

The preacher appeared mortified, as the words of a poor brother had a greater effect than his rhetoric.

We remember Paschal Baylon most as the "Saint of the Blessed Sacrament." Typically he spent as many hours a day as he could worshiping before the tabernacle. Because of his faithful devotion, the church has named him patron of Eucharistic congresses and conferences. He died in 1592 at the age of fifty-two.

Paschal Baylon was a simple doorkeeper, but he was no doormat. Once, for example, when some ladies wanted his superior to hear their confessions, the priest instructed Paschal to say that he was not in. "I will tell them that you are engaged," said Paschal. "No," insisted the superior, "tell them I am not home." But Paschal with a flash of independence said, "Forgive me father, but I refuse to lie." And he told the women that his superior was busy.

MAY 17 / CANONIZED IN 1890 / PATRON OF EUCHARISTIC CONGRESSES AND CONFRATERNITIES
Christian Living; Miracles Do Happen; Saints and Sacraments (Eucharist)

253. John of the Cross
(1542–1591)

In the 1560s, Father John of St. Matthias considered withdrawing from the Carmelites at Medina del Campo to a spartan Carthusian monastery, where he might pray more deeply. But **Teresa of Ávila** influenced him to stay and join her effort to reform the Carmelite order. In 1568, taking the name John of the Cross, he and four others opened the first men's house of Discalced (barefooted) Carmelites at Duruelo in Spain.

In 1570, St. John of the Cross became rector of the Carmelite house of studies at Alcalá. That year he was subjected to a grave spiritual trial. Dryness, scruples, temptations, and desolation made him feel that God had abandoned him. When deliverance finally came, he felt he was marvelously rewarded with the light of divine love.

Such firsthand experience provided him the wisdom we find in his profound and practical writings on the spiritual life. For example, reflect on these excerpts from "Sayings of Light and Love":

> "The Lord has always revealed to us the treasures of his wisdom and his spirit, but now that the face of evil more and more bares itself, so does the Lord bare his treasures the more."
>
> "Lord God, who will seek you with simple and pure love and not find that you are all he desires? For you show yourself first and go out to meet those who desire you."
>
> "God desires the least degree of purity of conscience in you more than all the works you can perform."
>
> "God desires the least degree of obedience and submissiveness more than all those services you think of rendering him."
>
> "God values in you an inclination to aridity and suffering for love of him more than all possible consolations, spiritual visions and meditations."
>
> "God is more pleased by one work, however small, done secretly, without desire that it be known, than a thousand done with desire that others know of them."
>
> "A bird caught in birdlime must both free and cleanse itself. And he who satisfies his appetite must both detach himself and cleanse himself of what has clung to him."

"The fly that clings to honey hinders its flight, and the soul that allows itself attachment to spiritual sweetness hinders its own liberty and contemplation."

"A soul hard with self-love grows harder. Good Jesus, if you do not soften it, it will ever continue in its natural hardness."

"A soul enkindled with love is a gentle, meek, humble and patient soul."

Older Carmelites resented John's leadership of the reform and they had him arrested in 1577. When he refused to abandon the movement, they imprisoned him at Toledo, where he was treated brutally and tortured. After nine months he escaped. Then he devoted his time to writing the books for which he has always been esteemed—*The Dark Night of the Soul, The Ascent of Mount Carmel, The Living Flame of Love,* and *The Spiritual Canticle.*

After 1590, John suffered persecution at the hands of his own friars. A party that desired a complete break with the Carmelites opposed his more moderate position. They stripped him of all offices and forced him to live as a simple friar. Then a friar he had disciplined conducted a smear campaign against him. In the midst of it, while still under a cloud of accusations, John took ill and died on December 14, 1591.

At the evening of life, you will be examined in love. Learn to love as God desires to be loved and abandon your own ways of acting.

—John of the Cross

DECEMBER 14 / CANONIZED IN 1726

Celebration of Discipline; The Cost of Discipleship; Doubt; The Secrets of Spiritual Success

254. Gregory Lopez
(1542–1596)

As a youth, Gregory Lopez served as a page at the court of Philip II in Madrid. At about age twenty he made a life-changing pilgrimage to the shrine of Our Lady of Guadalupe in Estremadura. During that time he decided that God was prompting him to move to Mexico. So he crossed the sea to Vera Cruz, gave away his possessions, and for fifteen years lived as a hermit in lonely places. In 1577 a Dominican friend persuaded him to enter the Dominican house in Mexico City. He tried community life for a few days, but was not suited for it and returned to his desert hermitage.

Gregory appeared "mysterious" to some people. To allay their concern, the archbishop of Mexico City investigated and gave him a clean bill of spiritual health. As a result, to Gregory's displeasure, numerous people came to consult him. Although he was steeped in biblical wisdom, he was convinced of his own ignorance and often refused to answer questions. For a while he moved to a hospital where he wrote a book on medicines, applying the extensive knowledge of herbs he had acquired in the desert. Finally, in 1589 he and a friend retreated to a hermitage in an obscure place in Michoacán, where they spent their days praying and studying Scripture.

Unlike **Simeon Stylites** and other solitaries, Gregory was not excessive in his penitential practices. Instead of forcing himself to do without things, his poverty involved making simple use of whatever was available. He also differed from **Anthony of Egypt, Hilarion**, and other hermits in that he kept his body and clothing scrupulously clean.

Gregory maintained a consistently deep prayer life. But he did not believe that anyone, no matter how "spiritual," lived continuously at an elevated state of union with God. Once, when questioned about his experience of prayer, he explained:

> I doubt very much whether any mere creature, with the exception of the most holy Virgin, remained always in so sublime a union. In the ordinary union, such as God has bestowed on me, a person may both constantly persevere and even improve to an eminent degree.
>
> Visions, revelations, ecstasies, raptures, and the like, are not the height of perfection. Perfection does not consist in such things, though

God sometimes grants them to people who are "perfect." God works in every soul according to its capacity, necessity, and disposition. Consequently, souls that are experienced in the act of a pure, simple, and perfect love, do not need the suspension of their senses for God to communicate with them. For the senses neither hinder nor disturb divine communications. As for me, I have never had any ecstasy, revelation, or rapture that suspended my senses because these senses never cause me any distraction.

Perfection and merit lie not in acts of enjoyment, but in the soul's effort to use all her forces in loving God perfectly. That means the soul must love him with the most perfect acts possible. This, you see, is rather doing than enjoying, whereas the other is enjoying rather than doing. For the soul that loves God perfectly can give no more than she does. That comprises the whole law and the prophets, and God requires nothing else from her.

Gregory Lopez died on July 20, 1596. His formal beatification has been on permanent hold since 1752.

If I were to die within a few hours, I would do nothing more than I do now. For now I am actually giving to God all that I have. I cannot give more unless God in his mercy bestows it on me.

—Gregory Lopez

JULY 20
Celebration of Discipline; Prayer; Solitude

255. Juvenal Ancina
(1545–1604)

At twenty-four Juvenal Ancina began his career in Turin as a doctor. He acquired an extensive practice because he treated the poor without charge. In his leisure he wrote Latin and Italian poetry, a diversion he pursued lifelong.

Once at a funeral Mass Juvenal was disturbed by the judgment message of the *Dies Irae,* the dirge sung at funeral masses. He realized that God wanted more of him than mere blamelessness. He resigned his post and went to Rome as the personal physician of an ambassador. There, Juvenal studied theology with **Robert Bellarmine.** He placed himself under the direction of **Philip Neri,** who influenced him to join the Oratory.

In 1582, Juvenal was ordained a priest. Four years later he was sent to found the Oratory at Naples. The genial priest soon became one of the city's most popular figures, especially appreciated for his charismatic preaching. Many people claimed that his sermons transformed their lives. For example, **Francis de Sales** reports the testimony of Guglielmo Cramoysi, a priest of the Congregation of Clerks Regular of St. Paul:

> I was 24 years old. I had many indications that God was calling me to the religious life. Yet through weakness I was so overcome by contrary inclinations that I had almost decided to get married. But by God's mercy, one day I happened to hear Father Juvenal preach at the Oratory.
>
> He described the weakness and instability of human nature. And the generosity with which we ought to follow God's leadings. He seemed to probe my inmost heart and rid it of the pitiful sloth that overlaid it. Finally, raising his voice like a trumpet, he urged me to give myself up as vanquished.
>
> Still full of doubts, after the sermon I sought him out. I briefly told him what I was thinking. "It's too late at night," he said, "to discuss this carefully enough. Come back tomorrow and we'll talk. Meanwhile, you should ask God to give you light. That is what you most need."
>
> Next day I returned and told him everything. I said I was hesitant to become a religious because of my delicate constitution. He said, "That's why God has provided a variety of religious orders. If you feel unequal to an austere life, you can enter one where the rule is more gentle. I

> recommend that you join the Congregation of the Clerks Regular of St. Paul. They practice religious perfection so little burdened by austerities that almost anyone can observe their rule." And Father Juvenal did not rest till he saw me admitted into that community.

Juvenal returned to Rome in 1595. Once when he suspected he might be made a bishop, he fled the city and hid for five months. But in 1602, Pope Clement VIII appointed him bishop of Saluzzo in Savoy. "It's time to obey and not to fly," he said, and accepted the post.

Juvenal spent 1603 and 1604 visiting the churches of his diocese. Upon returning to his see, he disconcertingly predicted his own death. A disgruntled friar, whom the bishop had warned to break off his affair with a nun, poisoned him at a celebration of **St. Bernard**'s day. He died a few days later on August 31, 1604.

> *Oftentimes, when we least expect it, when there seems no chance of it, we are suddenly snatched out of this life. Why then do we not follow the saving advice of* ***St. Paul*** *and devote ourselves to living soberly and justly, looking for the blessed hope and coming of the glory of the great God?*
>
> —Juvenal Ancina

AUGUST 30 / BEATIFIED IN 1869
Great Preachers; Vocation

256. John Leonardi
(C. 1542–1609)

St. John Leonardi grew up in Lucca, Italy, during the Age of Reformation. He recognized the great crisis in the church and wished he could do something to help resolve it. He involved himself for a time in a lay confraternity, where he learned fundamental spiritual disciplines that oriented his later work. Then he pursued seminary studies and was ordained in 1572.

As a young priest in the decade after the Council of Trent, John caught its vision for Catholic reform. He believed he could help implement the council's ideal of returning Catholics to the basics of the faith. John thought that true reform had to begin in the heart of each individual Christian. And that kind of personal reform would come only when the church's leaders responsibly modeled Christian living. Here is an excerpt from his letter to Pope Paul V that sums up his views:

> Those who want to work for moral reform in the world must seek the glory of God before all else. Because he is the source of all good, they must wait for his help, and pray for it in this difficult and necessary undertaking.
>
> They must then present themselves to those they seek to reform, as mirrors of every virtue and as lamps on a lamp stand. Their upright and noble conduct must shine before all who are in the house of God. In this way they will gently entice the members of the church to reform. Thus, in the words of the Council of Trent, they will not demand of the body what is not found in the head, and thus upset the whole order of the Lord's household.
>
> They will be skilled physicians taking pains to dispose of all the diseases that afflict the church and require a cure. They will ready themselves to provide suitable remedies for each illness.

Impressed by John's talent and his idealism, the bishop of Lucca commissioned him to preach renewal in all the churches of the city. John also gathered a group of young men who ministered with him in hospitals and prisons. Some of his associates wanted to become priests, which gave him the idea for a new religious order. John decided to establish a congregation of diocesan priests dedicated to clerical reform, education, and the works of mercy.

Inexplicably, John's new congregation met such opposition from people in Lucca that he had to stay away from the city for the rest of his life. But the bishop of Lucca with the pope's concurrence recognized the community in 1583. **St. Philip Neri** supported John's work and gave him the use of some buildings (on condition that John care for his cat!). The cadre of young priests accomplished so much good that in 1595, Pope Clement VIII recognized the society as a formal congregation.

In 1609, John died of plague while caring for the sick. Twelve years later the church allowed his priests to profess solemn vows and they took the name Clerks Regular of the Mother of God. By design the order stayed small, with only fifteen churches in Italy and one elsewhere.

Eternal God, behold me prostrate before your eternal majesty, humbly adoring you, I offer you all my thoughts, words, and actions of this day.

I offer them all to be thought, spoken and done entirely for love of you, for your glory, to fulfill your divine will, to serve you, to praise you and bless you.

I wish and intend to do everything in union with the most pure intentions of Jesus and Mary.

—John Leonardi

OCTOBER 9 / CANONIZED IN 1938
Christian Living; Catholic Reformers; Leading Men

257. Camillus de Lellis
(1550–1614)

St. Camillus was a giant for his times, standing six-feet-six-inches tall. He also became a spiritual giant through his unselfish service of the sick.

At age seventeen, Camillus left his village in Abruzzi, Italy, to fight with the Venetian army in a war against Turkish invaders. While at war his leg became infected with a serious disease that remained with him for life. He was a rebellious youth, with an addiction to gambling that nearly destroyed him. By age twenty-four he had literally lost his shirt to gambling. At twenty-five, however, while working at a Capuchin monastery, he responded to a friar's preaching with radical repentance. He turned his life to Christ and wanted to become a Capuchin, but could not be admitted to the order because of his diseased leg. So he went to work at a hospital for the incurably sick in Rome, where he had spent some time when his leg was first infected. There he devoted himself entirely to the care of the sick. The hospital's administrators were so impressed with his charity and ability that they appointed him bursar. And to prepare himself to assist the sick spiritually he became a priest.

Camillus was appalled by the poor conditions at the hospital and began to surround himself with other young men who were committed to serve the sick. With the support of his adviser, **St. Philip Neri**, he founded in 1585 the Servants of the Sick, a congregation of male nurses. They pledged themselves to care for the plague-ridden, the sick in hospitals and at home, and prisoners. Camillus and his brothers founded and staffed eight hospitals in Italy. In 1595 and 1601 some of them attended the wounded on battlefields in Hungary and Croatia, the first recorded examples of military ambulance units.

Sick and in pain most of the time, Camillus himself served without complaint. A member of his order wrote this moving description of the saint:

> I cannot get it out my mind, that when he was attending on a sick person, he looked like a hen with her chickens or like a mother at the bedside of her sick child. For, as if his arms and hands were not enough for the expressions of his affection, he might generally be seen bent

over the poor man, as though he wished to communicate to him his heart, his breath, and his very soul.

Before leaving the bed, too, he would keep smoothing the pillow and gently removing the bedclothes from the sick man's face and feet and sides. And as if attracted by some invisible lodestone, he seemed as though he could not force himself away. But he hovered about the bed, inquiring how the patient felt, whether he wanted anything else, and giving him some maxim to meditate on for the good of his soul.

I know not what more the most affectionate mother could have done for her only child in his sickness. No one who did not know the holy father would ever have thought that he had gone to the hospital to serve all the sick without distinction. They would have supposed that all his care was wrapped up in the life of that one poor man and that he had nothing else in the world to think about.

Camillus championed some avant-garde medical practices, insisting, for example, on proper diet, fresh air, and isolation of infected patients. He died in 1614.

Christ's words, "I was ill and you visited me," seems to have been engraved on Camillus' heart. He repeated this divine slogan daily, encouraging his brothers to love the sick without thought of themselves.

JULY 14/ CANONIZED IN 1746 / PATRON OF NURSES AND THE SICK
Innovative Saints; Care of the Soul; Enduring Trials; Repentance; Serving the Poor

258. Robert Bellarmine

(1542–1621)

St. Robert Bellarmine was so short that to be seen from the pulpit he had to stand on a stool. But he was an intellectual giant. He taught himself Greek and Hebrew; became a university lecturer, professor, and rector; edited the Latin Vulgate; debated prominent Protestants; served as theologian to two popes; wrote so many books that he was said to publish one a week, and so on.

With Robert we must shed stereotypical notions that academics are often stuffy and self-absorbed. Bellarmine was a friend to all, sacrificing himself to care for others. Once he gave elegant wall-hangings from his apartment as clothing to the poor. "The walls will not catch cold," he said.

At age eighteen Robert Bellarmine became a Jesuit. After three years of study the Jesuits deployed him as an instructor and preacher to several Italian cities. In 1569 the order sent him to Louvain in Belgium to counteract the false teaching of unorthodox professors. Ordained in 1570, he taught at Louvain for six more years.

Ill health forced Robert to return to Rome in 1576, where he served as professor of controversial theology at the Roman College. He was appointed theologian to Pope Clement VIII in 1597 and reluctantly became a cardinal a year later. Unexpectedly, he was designated archbishop of Capua in 1602, where he devoted himself to caring for his people. However, three years later Pope Paul V summoned him to Rome. As the pope's theological adviser, he defended papal supremacy in a controversy with King James I of England. And he advised his friend, Galileo, not to advocate unproved hypotheses as true—advice the scientist did not take.

Robert Bellarmine developed his theology and apologetics with flawless logic. And in his more popular works he fed hungry souls. Here he inspires readers with a reflection on verse one of Psalm 91, "He who dwells in the shelter of the Most High":

> Notice that what is said is not "he who trusts" . . . but "he who dwells." This is to convince us that we are not to fly to the divine protection as men do to a tree or a doorway when it rains, but rather as little boys who rush to their father's arms when anything frightens them. They

know that they have mother and father there who would gladly give their hearts' blood to protect them.

But people who seek refuge from rain under a tree, have a good look round first. It is only when no better shelter is available that they run willy-nilly to the tree. Why is it that some men implore divine assistance without receiving it, and seem to put their trust in God without being protected by him? The reason is that they do not really dwell in the aid of the Most High, nor take shelter under the providence of God as in their Father's house. They rather make sporadic dashes to it in time of trouble, as they do to a tree when there is a sudden shower. It is therefore very necessary for us to get into the way of always and instinctively turning to God.

The chronic sickness that dogged Robert Bellarmine finally caught up to him. He died on September 21, 1621, at age seventy-nine.

The school of Christ is the school of charity. On the last day, when the great general examination takes place, there will be no question at all on the text of Aristotle, the aphorisms of Hippocrates, or the paragraphs of Justinian. Charity will be the whole syllabus.

—Robert Bellarmine

SEPTEMBER 17 / CANONIZED IN 1930
Catholic Reformers; Intimacy with the Divine; Prayer

259. Stanislaus Kostka
(1550–1568)

"I expect great things of him," wrote **St. Peter Canisius** of St. Stanislaus Kostka. He certainly had in mind accomplishments like those of **St. Francis Xavier** and other early Jesuits. But young Stanislaus died before he could *do* anything. Except live for God and become a saint.

Polish nobleman John Kostka was not pleased with the spiritual inclinations of his second son. He did all he could to discourage Stanislaus's desire for Christian service. Paul, a brother two years older than he, bullied him and tried to lure him into more worldly pursuits.

In 1564 the brothers attended the Jesuit college at Vienna, Austria. After two years Stanislaus fell seriously ill and he thought he was going to die. He wanted to receive Holy Communion, but his Lutheran landlord would not allow it in his house. However, Stanislaus reported that two angels appeared and communicated to him. He also said that the Blessed Mother came to him in a vision, encouraging him to become a Jesuit.

Thus, upon recovering, Stanislaus determined to join the Society of Jesus. With Paul in hot pursuit, he fled to Dillingen where Peter Canisius welcomed him. Then to demonstrate his determination, Stanislaus walked the 350 miles to Rome and there Jesuit general **St. Francis Borgia** accepted him.

Stanislaus kept a journal during his novitiate. His notes reflect both a youthful idealism and an adult commitment. Here are a few excerpts:

> Consider how hard it is for a person to be separated from any place he has loved deeply. How much harder the soul will find it when the time comes to leave the mortal body, its companion so dear. And the great fear it will experience in that moment because its salvation is at stake and it must stand in the presence of the one it has so offended. If the just man will scarcely be saved, what about me a sinner?
>
> But think of the great joy the good will feel at the thought of the service they've paid to God. They will be glad because they've suffered something for love of him back there and didn't fix their hope and attention on the things of this world that we leave so soon. Think of the joy that the soul will feel in its escape from the prison of this body.

> So long has it lived in perpetual exile, expelled from its own heavenly home. How much greater its uncontainable joy and complete satisfaction when it arrives in its own country to enjoy the vision of God with the angels and the blessed.
>
> I am so ashamed and confused because I see how many have been lost on account of a single mortal sin, and how many times I have deserved eternal damnation.
>
> I shall reflect on myself and ask: "What have I done for Christ? What am I doing for Christ? What ought I do for Christ?"

However, Stanislaus did not complete his training. Nine months into his novitiate he again became very sick. Early in the morning on the feast of the Assumption, 1568, he told a priest that he saw Mary surrounded by many angels. And shortly afterward he died. Stanislaus was only seventeen years old when he "arrived in his own country to enjoy the vision of God."

John Kostka and many other parents of saints resisted their children's desire to live for God. We should meditate on his example, hoping that we will always have the common sense to encourage each of our sons and daughters in whatever direction God seems to be drawing them.

NOVEMBER 13 / PATRON OF POLAND
Angels; Child Saints; Facing Death

260. Margaret Clitherow
(1556?–1586)

St. Margaret Clitherow became a convert at her hometown of York in 1573, when it was dangerous to be a Catholic in England. Pope Pius V had excommunicated Queen Elizabeth in 1570, provoking an intense persecution of Catholics. Mass was outlawed, priests were regarded as traitors, and harboring them was a capital crime. Margaret disobeyed the law, keeping secret rooms in her house and at a neighbor's house where priests hid and celebrated Mass.

On March 10, 1586, sheriff's men raided Margaret's house. They found a schoolmaster with her children, whom they mistook for a priest, but he escaped through the secret chamber. The officers terrorized an eleven-year-old Flemish boy who lived with the family. The frightened child led them to the priests' room, where they found vessels and books for Mass. So Margaret was taken to prison to await a hearing.

John Mush, Margaret's biographer, reports that she accepted her persecution lightheartedly. She and Anne Tesh, her friend also betrayed by the boy, laughed so much that Margaret said, "Sister, we are having so much fun that I'm afraid unless we are separated we shall be in danger of losing the merit of our imprisonment." And just before she was to appear before the judge, Margaret decided to cheer thirty-five other Catholic prisoners across the hall. "She looked out of a window towards them," writes Mush, "and she made a pair of gallows on her fingers and pleasantly laughed at them."

Margaret was charged with harboring and maintaining priests. When the judge asked her if she were guilty or not, she declined to enter a plea. The judge warned her that the law required the death penalty for anyone refusing to plead. He told Margaret that she would be stripped, arms stretched out and bound to stakes, and pressed to death with a sharp stone in her back. "I am not worthy of so good a death as this is," was her reply.

Margaret believed that her death was inevitable. Had she pled to the charges, her husband and children would have had to testify against her and her neighbor's guilt would have been exposed, possibilities she could not bear. Her love for her family intensified her suffering, but did not deter her. *I love my husband next to God in this world,* she wrote.

> And I have care over my children as a mother ought to have. I trust I have done my duty by bringing them up in the fear of God, and so I trust now I am discharged of them. And for this cause I am willing to offer them freely to God who sent them to me, rather than I will yield one jot from my faith.

Thus, on the Friday in Passion Week, 1586, she was pressed to death under eight hundred pounds of weight. Fittingly, she must have thought, she died like Christ, with her arms extended, as on a cross.

Saints like Margaret Clitherow both charm and mystify us. Margaret was young, beautiful, happily married, mother of several children, loved by everyone who knew her in York, England, always full of fun—and a martyr at age 30. Our brains want us to believe that these elements do not compute, but in them lies the reason we find Margaret so appealing. We admire her as a competent and cheerful woman who did not take herself too seriously, but who was so serious about her faith that she freely gave her life for it. Yet we wonder at her inner strength because we doubt we would have the gumption to do what she did.

MARCH 25 / CANONIZED IN 1970
Countercultural Witness; Courage; Family; Imitation of Christ; Joy; Married Saints; Martyrs; Twenty-Something Saints

261. Robert Southwell
(1561–1595)

St. Robert Southwell wore many hats: priest, Jesuit, servant, scholar, missionary, martyr—and poet. And in his poetry the saint declared the radical love that animated all of his roles and shaped his life.

Robert Southwell was raised as a Catholic in Queen Elizabeth's England, which was hostile to Rome. His parents had him educated by Jesuits at the Catholic enclave in Douai and at Clermont, the famous Jesuit school in Paris. At age seventeen Robert decided to become a Jesuit himself, but was turned down because of his youth. However, to demonstrate his determination, he walked to Rome, where he was admitted to the Jesuit novitiate in the fall of 1578.

Robert was ordained a priest in 1584. Two years later he and Henry Garnet were sent to serve beleaguered Catholics in England. "Lambs to the slaughter," muttered the Jesuit general as he wished them farewell.

From his first days in England, Robert devoted himself to encouraging Catholics incarcerated in London's prisons. He served openly, avoiding all intrigue, and became well known for his gentleness. In 1587 he became chaplain at the home of Anne, Countess of Arundel. And from there he began to write letters of support to her husband and future martyr, St. Philip Howard, who was imprisoned in the Tower. Perhaps during this time, the saint composed his most celebrated poem, *The Burning Babe*. One snowy night the poet met "a pretty babe all burning bright":

"Alas!" quoth He, "but newly born
    In fiery heats I fry,
Yet none approach to warm their hearts

    Or feel my fire but I!
"My faultless breast the furnace is;
    The fuel, wounding thorns;
Love is the fire, and sighs the smoke;
    The ashes, shames and scorns;
The fuel Justice layeth on,
    And Mercy blows the coals,

The metal in this furnace wrought
    Are men's defilèd souls:
For which, as now on fire I am
    To work them to their good,
So will I melt into a bath,
    To wash them in my blood."
With this He vanish'd out of sight
    And swiftly shrunk away,
And straight I callèd unto mind,
    That it was Christmas Day.

In 1592, Robert was betrayed to the authorities. His captor, Richard Topcliffe, tortured the saint brutally, trying without success to force him to inform on his associates. Robert was then locked in solitary confinement in the Tower, until he was condemned to death as a traitor in 1595. At the scaffold he declared that he was indeed a Catholic priest. He prayed for the queen, his country, his fellow Catholics, and for himself. He was supposed to have been hanged, drawn, and quartered, but his demeanor was so impressive that the clamor of the crowd compelled the executioner to let him die by hanging, postponing the butchery until the saint was dead. Thus St. Robert Southwell was martyred at Tyburn on February 22, 1595.

Christ! health of fevered soul, heaven of the mind,
Force of the feeble, nurse of infant loves,
Guide to the wandering foot, light to the blind,
Whom weeping wins, repentant sorrow moves:
Father in care, Mother in tender heart,
Revive and save me, slain with sinful dart.

—Robert Southwell, *Peter's Plaint*

FEBRUARY 2 / CANONIZED IN 1970
The Cost of Discipleship; Martyrs; Poets; A Soul Afire

262. Aloysius Gonzaga
(1568–1591)

Expectations ran high for Aloysius Gonzaga, heir to the marquis of Castiglione, a prince of the Holy Roman Empire. As a little boy his parents prepared him for his rank, immersing him in court life and taking him to military exercises. Once a normal five-year-old Aloysius disrupted an army camp by shooting off a cannon without permission.

But somewhere around age seven, Aloysius made a choice that set him against his parents' plans. Aloysius decided that he wanted to be a saint. He rejected the decadent culture of the Italian courts and created for himself a devotional pattern of prayer and self-denial. At twelve, while recovering from a kidney disease that left him permanently weakened, he read lives of the saints. Impressed with some of their more rigid and excessive practices, Aloysius began to imitate them. For example, he beat himself savagely with a dog whip, fasted three days a week, and rose at midnight to pray. He also always walked with his eyes cast down, so as never to look at a person of the opposite sex.

Aloysius decided at fifteen to join the Jesuits. But his father fought him ferociously. He sent him on a tour of courts to distract him and sent priests and bishops to try to change his mind. However, with a superior strength of will, Aloysius held out for two years. Finally he overcame his father's disapproval. In 1585 he entered the Jesuit novitiate, where wise superiors immediately curbed his excessive mortifications.

St. Robert Bellarmine became Aloysius's spiritual director. He guided the youth to drop his somewhat naïve and priggish attitude to human relations. Bellarmine's direction formed in Aloysius a strong, single-hearted love for God and for others.

In 1591, Aloysius joined his fellow Jesuits in caring for plague victims. He contracted the disease himself, recovered temporarily, but then he died on June 21, 1591. He was only twenty-three years old.

Shortly before his death, Aloysius wrote the following to his mother, who had taught him the faith:

May the comfort and grace of the Holy Spirit be yours for ever, most honored lady. Your letter found me lingering still in this region of the dead, but now I must rouse myself to make my way on to heaven at last and to praise God for ever in the land of the living; indeed I had hoped that before this time my journey there would have been over. . . .

The divine goodness . . . is a fathomless and shoreless ocean, and I confess that when I plunge my mind into thought of this it is carried away by the immensity and feels quite lost and bewildered there. In return for my short and feeble labors, God is calling me to eternal rest; his voice from heaven invites me to the infinite bliss I have sought so languidly. . . .

Take care above all things . . . not to insult God's boundless loving kindness; you would certainly do this if you mourned as dead one living face to face with God, one whose prayers can bring you in your troubles more powerful aid than they ever could on earth. And our parting will not be for long; we shall see each other again in heaven; we shall be united with our savior; there we shall praise him with heart and soul, sing of his mercies for ever, and enjoy eternal happiness. When he takes away what he once lent us, his purpose is to store our treasure elsewhere more safely and bestow on us those very blessings that we ourselves would most choose to have.

JUNE 21 / CANONIZED IN 1726 / PATRON OF YOUTH
Child Saints; Countercultural Witness; Facing Death; Family; Twenty-Something Saints; Vocation

263. Paul Miki

(1564?–1597)

Christianity spread like wildfire in sixteenth-century Japan. By the 1580s, less than forty years after **Francis Xavier** introduced the faith, the church counted two hundred thousand converts. The growth had proceeded despite the opposition of Buddhist priests and many petty rulers. However, in 1587, Emperor Hideyoshi ordered the banishment of all Catholics, forcing the Jesuit missionaries to operate from hiding. But outright persecution did not break out until late 1596, when Hideyoshi rounded up twenty-six Jesuits, Franciscans, and laypeople and prepared to martyr them.

Among the victims was St. Paul Miki, a Jesuit novice who had just completed eleven years of training. Paul's noble family was converted when he was a child and at age five he was baptized. Educated by Jesuits, the gifted youth joined their novitiate at age twenty-two. He had studied intensively the teachings of the Buddhists so as to be able to debate their priests. He welcomed his chance at martyrdom, but may have wished just a little that it would be delayed long enough for him to be ordained a priest.

Hideyoshi had the left ears of the twenty-six martyrs severed as a sign of disrespect and paraded them through Kyoto. Dressed in his simple black cassock, Paul stood out among them. Most onlookers realized that this noble young man could have worn the samurai's costume with two swords on his belt. The whole display had the unexpected effect of evoking compassion from the crowd, some of whom later became converts.

The martyrs were then taken to Nagasaki. They were tied to crosses with their necks held in place by iron rings. Beside each was an executioner with his spear ready to strike. An eyewitness gave this account:

> When the crosses were set up it was a wonderful thing to see the constancy of all of them. Our brother Paul Miki, seeing himself raised to the most honorable position that he had ever occupied, openly proclaimed that he was a Japanese and a member of the Society of Jesus. And that he was being put to death for having preached the gospel. He gave thanks to God for such a precious favor.
>
> He then added these words: "Having arrived at this moment of my existence, I believe that no one of you thinks I want to hide the truth.

> That is why I declare to you that there is no other way of salvation than the one followed by Christians. Since this way teaches me to forgive my enemies and all who have offended me, I willingly forgive the king and all those who have desired my death. And I pray that they will obtain the desire of Christian baptism."
>
> At this point, he turned his eyes toward his companions and began to encourage them in their final struggle. The faces of them all shone with great gladness. Another Christian shouted to him that he would soon be in paradise. "Like my Master," murmured Paul, "I shall die upon the cross. Like him, a lance will pierce my heart so that my blood and my love can flow out upon the land and sanctify it to his name."

As they awaited death the entire group sang the canticle of Zachary (see Luke 1:67–79). The executioners stood by respectfully until they had intoned the last verse. Then at a given signal they thrust their spears into the victims' sides. On that day, February 5, 1597, the church of Japan welcomed its first martyrs.

When Christ calls a man he bids him come and die.

—Dietrich Bonhoeffer

FEBRUARY 6 / CANONIZED WITH TWENTY-FIVE COMPANIONS IN 1862
The Cost of Discipleship; Martyrs

264. Mary Magdalen dei Pazzi
(1566–1607)

I offer you, O Word, for all the members of your holy church, the countless drops of blood that you shed in your cruel scourging. O Word divine! I will only be content when I am wholly consumed with the desire to bring back all stray souls to you.

I wish I had the strength to gather all the unfaithful and lead them into the bosom of your church. I would pray her with her healing breath to purge them of their infidelity and fill them with new life. But I can only deplore my impotence and my ingratitude, which is its cause.

O my God! How can the wickedness of sin be plucked from the hearts of men? If I were only worthy to give my life for the salvation of souls and to destroy this evil, how happy I would be! How great a torment it is to live and to die every moment; to see that I am only useful by giving my life for others and yet unable to do it. O charity, you are a file that little by little wears away both body and soul.

—St. Mary Magdalen dei Pazzi

St. Mary Magdalen dei Pazzi welcomed suffering. And for years she endured severe physical, emotional, and spiritual pain. She was afflicted with a mysterious illness, tormented by temptations to lust and gluttony, marked by the stigmata, and plagued by desolation. Unlike many Christians today whose pain seems to focus them inward, Mary Magdalen singularly directed her suffering outward. "Those who remember Christ's sufferings," she said, "and offer up their own to God through his passion find their pains sweet and pleasant." She wanted nothing more than to share in Christ's passion for the salvation of human beings.

A strikingly beautiful woman born into Florence's upper crust, Mary Magdalen left her wealthy family to become a Carmelite nun. Toward the end of her novitiate in 1584, a violent disease struck her, but she recovered after she professed her vows. The year 1585 brought Mary Magdalen both a succession of extraordinary mystical phenomena and the onslaught of five years of grievous anguish. Rapt in prayer for months at a time, she seems to have participated spiritually in the events of Christ's passion. She believed that God had told her to live on bread and water only, except on Sundays, for the reparation of sins. Her sisters were so moved by her words spoken during ecstasies that they recorded them and published them after her death.

The saint also endured a long period of spiritual dryness. She felt so strongly that God had abandoned her that she was even tempted to suicide. Relief finally came to her at Pentecost, 1590, and from that time she seems to have again enjoyed a sense of God's presence.

The convent gave Mary Magdalen responsibility to teach young nuns. In her service she exercised charismatic gifts of prophecy, healing, and reading of consciences. She became novice mistress in 1598 and subprioress in 1604. However, later that year illness and desolation struck again. For three years Mary Magdalen lay bedridden until she died on May 25, 1607.

Come, Holy Spirit.
Let the precious pearl of the Father
and the Word's delight come.
Spirit of truth,
you are the reward of the saints,
the comforter of souls,
light in the darkness,
riches to the poor,
treasure to lovers,
food for the hungry,
comfort to the wanderer;
you are the one in whom
all treasures are contained.

Come! As you descended on Mary,
that the Word might become flesh
work in us through grace.
Amen.

—Mary Magdalen dei Pazzi

MAY 25 / CANONIZED IN 1669
Holy Spirit; Sin; Stigmata; Suffering

265. John Berchmans
(1599–1621)

A smile always played on St. John Berchmans' lips, and jokes punctuated his conversations. Happy, intelligent, quick-witted, uncomplicated, eager to please—John was a delight to be with. Perhaps God allowed him to die at age twenty-two because he wanted to have that winsome young man near his heavenly throne.

As a boy, John Berchmans determined to become a priest and a saint. His father, a master shoemaker in Brabant, Belgium, could not afford to send him to school, but instead placed him under the tutelage of a priest at a local abbey. Later, straitened circumstances compelled him to hire John out as a servant in another priest's household at Malines, where he was able to take classes at the archdiocesan seminary. At seventeen, John decided to become a Jesuit, a move his parents resisted because they wanted him to be sure he was making the right choice. Indeed, John was sure, as he explained to them in this crisp letter:

> I am very surprised that you—instead of loving and thanking God for his great favor of calling me to the religious life—should counsel me not to listen to our dear Lord and to put off my vocation for five or six months. As you well know, it is not right that in order to obey you, I should disobey God. When our dear Lord called a young man to follow him, he would not let him go to bury his father, though this was a good work and one which needed but a short time (see Luke 9:59–60). And when he called another he forbade him to bid farewell to his friends, saying: "No one who puts his hand to the plow and looks back is fit for the kingdom of God" (Luke 9:62 *RSV*). Why do you think he did this? Was it not to show us that we must follow our vocation then and there without delay?
>
> So then, my ever honored parents, that I may obey God, that I may make my salvation sure, and that I may avoid that fearful sentence, "I called and you refused, so I will also laugh in your destruction" (see Proverbs 1:24 and 26): With God's grace, I mean two weeks from now to share the joy of my brothers in religion. And I trust through God our Lord, through the prayers of my brothers, and through yours also and my own poor petitions, to obtain that he who has given the good will may grant me the perseverance to the end.

As a Jesuit novice, John excelled in his studies and in holiness. In 1618 he and a friend walked from Antwerp to Rome, where he studied philosophy and languages at the Roman College. Three years later he completed his education with distinction and was poised for a great career as a scholar priest. But in the summer of 1621 the young saint was afflicted with a mysterious disease. When a doctor bathed his temples with vintage wine, he joked that it was lucky such an expensive illness would not last long. Asked if there was anything on his conscience, he said, "Nothing at all." He received the sacrament of anointing and died on August 13.

> *I resolved always to prefer labors to comforts, contempt to honors. And, in particular, if on one side a kingdom were offered and on the other the washing of dishes, I would refuse the kingdom and accept the dish-washing so as to be truly like Christ, who humbled himself.*
>
> —John Berchmans

AUGUST 13 / CANONIZED IN 1888 / PATRON OF YOUTH, ALTAR BOYS, AND ALTAR GIRLS

Purpose; True Humility; Twenty-Something Saints; Vocation

266. Francis de Sales

(1567–1622)

In his classic book *The Introduction to the Devout Life*, St. Francis de Sales showed how ordinary people locked daily into worldly routines could live saintly lives. He argued that not only was holiness possible for people in all walks of life, but that living for God made every calling better. He addresses his reader as Philothea, a soul who loves God:

> Very often, under color of an alleged impossibility, people who are obliged to live an ordinary life are not willing even to think of undertaking the devout life. . . . They are of the opinion that, just as no animal dare taste of the herb called palma Christi [castor oil plant], so no one ought to aspire to the palm of Christian piety, while living in the midst of the press of worldly occupations. And I show them that as the mother-of-pearl fish live in the sea without taking in one drop of salt water, . . . so a vigorous and constant soul can live in the world without receiving any worldly taint. . . .
>
> No, Philothea, true devotion does us no harm whatsoever, but instead perfects all things. When it goes contrary to a man's lawful vocation, it is undoubtedly false. "The bee," Aristotle says, "extracts honey out of flowers without hurting them" and leaves them as whole and fresh as it finds them. True devotion does better still. It not only does no injury to one's vocation, but on the contrary adorns and beautifies it. All kinds of precious stones take on greater luster when dipped into honey, each according to its color. So also every vocation becomes more agreeable when united with devotion. Care of one's family is rendered more peaceable, love of husband and wife more sincere, service of one's prince more faithful, and every type of employment more pleasant and agreeable.

Readers will not find any new secrets in Francis's book. What makes it exceptional is his showing how repentance, prayer, the spiritual disciplines, and virtues fit in the lives of laypeople.

St. Francis's father had educated him for a brilliant secular career. Instead, however, he became a priest, missionary, and bishop. Francis de Sales was an outstanding leader of the Catholic Reformation, a European renewal movement that both preceded and responded to the Protestant Reformation. After his ordination in 1593, he evangelized the people of the province of Chablais, winning many back to the Catholic Church and making many converts.

In 1602, Francis was appointed bishop of Geneva. In that office he proved himself to be an able pastor, administrator, and educator. He was also the spiritual director for other saints, including **St. Jane de Chantal,** who became his close friend in 1604. With her he founded the Order of the Visitation in 1610. He died on December 28, 1622. Francis de Sales is a doctor of the church and the patron saint of writers.

> *Ostriches never fly. Hens fly in a clumsy fashion, near the ground, and only once in a while. But eagles, doves and swallows fly aloft, swiftly and frequently. Similarly, sinners never fly up towards God, but hover close to the earth. Good people who are not yet devout, fly toward God by their good works but do so infrequently, slowly and awkwardly. Devout souls ascend to him more frequently, promptly and with lofty flights. In short, devotion is simply that spiritual agility and vivacity by which charity works in us or by aid of which we do good works quickly and lovingly.*
>
> —Francis de Sales

JANUARY 24 / CANONIZED IN 1665 / PATRON OF WRITERS AND THE CATHOLIC PRESS
Catholic Reformers; Celebration of Discipline; Doctors of the Church; Pursuit of Holiness

267. Josaphat
(C. 1580–1623)

In 1595, the Orthodox metropolitan of Kiev in the Ukraine and five bishops met at Brest-Litovsk, Belorussia, to seek reunion with the Roman Catholic Church. As a young monk St. Josaphat committed himself to working for this union and ultimately died a martyr for the cause.

Josaphat Kuncewycz and his friend Venyamin Rutsky, a convert from Calvinism, entered Holy Trinity monastery in Vilna in present-day Lithuania in 1604. Both had caught a vision for reunion with Rome. They worked to achieve it throughout their careers. Shortly after his ordination, Josaphat quickly became a well-known preacher on the subject.

Rutsky was elevated to the see of Kiev in 1614. Three years later Josaphat was appointed bishop of Vitebsk and archbishop of Polotsk. Over six years he conducted a successful reform of clerical and lay Christian life in his large diocese. But many feared that Josaphat would invite Roman interference into their church life. Thus a considerable opposition rose against him. Consequently, a group of dissident bishops appointed Melitius Smotritsky as their archbishop of Polotsk. He stirred already hot feelings against Josaphat, winning allies in towns like Vitebsk and in rural areas.

In October 1623, Josaphat's enemies condemned him to Leo Sapieha, a Catholic, the chancellor of Lithuania. Influenced by them, he charged Josaphat with resorting to violence on behalf of union with Rome. Josaphat forcefully denied the allegations in the following letter to Sapieha:

> God witnesses to my character. He sees into my heart and knows the purpose of my actions. By no evil example or uncompromising actions did I drive away from me any citizen of Polotsk or any other person in my diocese. There is not the slightest indication of severity on my part which might have become the cause for the rebellion. I do not drag anyone against his will into the Union and there is no proof of it. My position as head of the church obliges me to defend the rights of the church which the Schismatics threaten to take from us by force. I do all of this in a legal, peaceful way, taking for my inspiration and ideal **St. Ambrose** and **St. John Chrysostom**, who accomplished so many

> great works for the glory of God unmindful of any obstacles. If these saints had seen in their times as much wrong done to Almighty God as I now see, they would do much more about it than I.
>
> I know of no other motive for the action of the Schismatics except their jealousy and possibly the fact that we sail in the bark of the greatest captain, the successor of Christ himself. This ship never did sail on peaceful waters, but always in the storm.
>
> The Schismatics do the fighting and then complain that they are being beaten. Is this not directly opposed to the love of one's neighbor as preached by Christ?

In November, Josaphat went to Vitebsk to quell the animosity of his opponents. For two weeks he preached in efforts to make peace, but he encountered the threat of violence boiling everywhere. On November 12, Josaphat fell for a trick and locked up a priest who had viciously harassed him. A mob that had awaited this misstep fell on him. In the melee someone brained him with a halberd and another shot him. Then they threw his mangled body in the Dvina River.

Thus Josaphat became a martyr for Christian unity.

> *Christ always gives his Church the gift of unity, but the Church must always pray and work to maintain, reinforce, and perfect the unity Christ wills for her.*
>
> —Catechism of the Catholic Church, 820

NOVEMBER 12 / CANONIZED IN 1867
Christian Unity; Martyrs

268. Roque González
(1576–1628)

"All the Christians among my countrymen loved the Father and grieved for his death because he was the father of us all, and so he was called by the Indians of the Paraná River." So testified Chief Guarecupi after the martyrdom of Jesuit Roque González and his companions in Paraguay in 1628. The Indians loved him because they had felt his love for them and their ways. And they knew that for two decades he had sacrificed everything to improve their lives both materially and spiritually.

At a time when Spanish conquistadors were brutalizing and enslaving natives, Roque helped them become self-sufficient and free. He led the Jesuits who founded the "reductions," independent Indian village communities that excluded European settlers. The economy of the reductions made the Indians self-supporting by combining communal agriculture with private property holding. And the reductions had their own political structure that gave the natives a measure of freedom. Roque González was the innovative social activist who created the model for these avant-garde communities. Here is his description of Saint Ignacio, the first reduction that he established in 1613:

> This town had to be built from its very foundations. In order to do away with occasions of sin, I decided to build it in the style of the Spaniards, so that everyone should have his own house, with fixed boundaries and a corresponding yard. This system prevents easy access from one house to another, which used to be the case and which gave occasion for drunken orgies and other evils.
>
> A church and parish house are being erected for our needs. Comfortable and enclosed with an adobe wall, the houses are built with cedar girders—cedar is very common wood here. We have worked hard to arrange all this. But with even greater zest and energy—in fact with all our strength—we have worked to build temples to Our Lord, not only those made by hands but spiritual temples as well, namely the souls of these Indians.
>
> On Sundays and feast days we preach during mass, explaining the catechism beforehand with equal concern for boys and girls. The adults are instructed in separate groups of about 150 men and the same number of women. Shortly after lunch, we teach them reading and writing for about two hours.

> There are still many non-Christians in this town. Because of the demands of planting and harvesting all cannot be baptized at the same time. So every month we choose those best prepared. . . . Among the 120 or so adults baptized this year there were several elderly shamans.

Roque and other Jesuits built more than thirty reductions with an average population of three thousand.

In 1628, Roque and Jesuits Alonso Rodriguez and Juan de Castillo started a reduction on the Iijui River and another at Caaró on Brazil's southern tip. Somehow they roused the hostility of a shaman who determined to exterminate all Jesuits. On November 15 his men tomahawked Roque and Alonso at Caaró. Two days later at Iijui they stoned Juan to death. In 1934 these three became the first American martyrs to be beatified.

Roque González's creative social action not only made Christianity attractive to the Indians of Paraguay. It also impressed secular sophisticates like Voltaire, who had this high praise for Roque's settlements: "The Paraguayan missions reached the highest degree of civilization to which it is possible to lead a young people. In those missions, law was respected, morals were pure, a happy brotherliness bound men together, the useful arts and even some of the more graceful sciences flourished, and there was abundance everywhere."

NOVEMBER 15 / CANONIZED IN 1988
Innovative Saints; Social Justice

269. Rose of Lima
(1586–1617)

The Americas revere St. Rose of Lima as their first canonized saint. Named Isabel at birth, as a child she was so lovely that she was often compared to a rose. And she took the name Rose at confirmation.

As a young girl Rose modeled her piety on **Catherine of Siena,** imitating the great saint's severe mortification. She fasted often. Sometimes she made herself vomit after meals, which today would probably be regarded as bulimia. She prayed long hours and frequently beat herself with a little whip. However critical we may be of her excessive practices, Rose seems to have done it all out of a simple love for Christ. Consider this note she wrote after reflecting on St. Catherine's giving her clothing to Christ whom she saw in a beggar:

> This year, 1616, I will clothe my divine Jesus, whom the church will soon represent to us as born to us naked, in a manger, exposed to the severity of winter. I will make him an undergarment of fifty litanies, of nine hundred rosaries and of five days of total fasting in honor of the adorable mystery of the Incarnation. I will fashion his swaddling clothes of nine visits to the Blessed Sacrament, of nine Little Offices of the Blessed Virgin and of nine fast days in honor of the nine months he was enclosed in her chaste womb. His coverings shall consist of five days passed without eating or drinking, of five visits to the most Blessed Sacrament and of five rosaries in honor of his birth into this world.
>
> For the fringes of his swaddling clothes I will make thirty-three extra communions. I will assist at thirty-three Masses. I will spend thirty-three hours in mental prayer. I will recite thirty times the Our Father, the Hail Mary, the Creed, the Glory Be to the Father, and the Salve Regina. I will also recite thirty-three rosaries, fast thirty-three days and take three thousand stripes of the discipline in honor of the thirty-three years he spent on earth.
>
> Lastly, I offer as a gift to my dear Jesus, my tears, my groans and all the acts of love that I shall make. With this I offer my heart and soul that there may be nothing in me that is not entirely consecrated to him.

As a teen Rose withdrew to a small hut in the family garden where she lived reclusively. For ten years her parents pressured her to marry.

But she made herself unattractive to suitors by rubbing her beautiful face with pepper. In order to galvanize her will to remain single for Christ, she took a vow of virginity and, like Catherine, became a Dominican tertiary.

When her parents fell on hard times, Rose supported them by selling flowers during the day and by sewing at night. Like her friend Martin de Porres, she served the poor of Lima. She made rooms in the family home an infirmary for the sick—Indian, black, mulatto, or Spanish, caring for all regardless of race. Very sick for her last three years, Rose lived in the home of family friends. She died on August 23, 1617.

Saint-watcher Phyllis McGinley was so repulsed by Rose's piety that she refused to write about her. The revised Butler's Lives of the Saints questions Rose's mental health and counsels that she is not a suitable model for girls. However, we still must honor Rose for her total commitment to Jesus and her selfless service to her parents and the sick poor.

AUGUST 23 / CANONIZED IN 1671 / PATRON OF PERU, SOUTH AMERICA, THE INDIES, AND THE PHILIPPINES
Care of the Sick; Mere Christian Love; Serving the Poor

270. Jane de Chantal
(1572–1641)

Any Christian who has ever been of two minds should take St. Jane de Chantal as a model. If we are being candid, perhaps all of us should regard her as our patron. Jane de Chantal served God generously her entire life. All the while, however, a worm of doubt gnawed at her soul. In her sunset years she told a friend:

> I've had these temptations for forty-one years now—do you think I'm going to give up after all this time? Absolutely not. I'll never stop hoping in God, though he kill me, though he grind me into the dust of eternity.
>
> Most often, there is a confused sort of strife in my soul. Between feelings of being plunged into impenetrable darkness that I am powerless to do anything about, I have a kind of spiritual nausea that tempts me to give up trying. When these trials are at their most severe, they hardly let up at all, and they cause me unimaginable torment, so that I would almost be willing to do anything to be relieved of this torture. On the one hand, I am caught between the excruciating pain, and on the other hand, my love for our holy Faith that is so deep I would die rather than deny the least article of it.
>
> If I can keep from offending God in spite of all this, then I am content with whatever it may please him to allow me to suffer, even if I must suffer for the rest of my life. I want only to do it knowing that he wants me to, and that in suffering I am being faithful to him.

Spiritually, Jane de Chantal seems lifelong to have endured a dark night of the soul. Medically, physicians today might say she appears to have been clinically depressed. Whatever her condition, however, nothing stopped this most competent woman from sailing through her days.

Jane Frances Frémyot doted on her husband, Baron Christopher de Chantal of Bourbilly in Burgundy, whom she married in 1592. She bore him seven children, four of whom survived. Jane's long sadness began in 1601 when the baron died in a hunting accident. To better serve Christ as a widow, the saint took a private vow of celibacy.

Three years later Jane met **St. Francis de Sales.** She identified him as the bishop pictured in a vision as her future spiritual director. The saints became friends, and Francis took responsibility to guide

Jane's life. She thought of becoming a Carmelite nun, but Francis suggested that she collaborate with him in founding a new religious community for women. In 1610, after ensuring care for her children, she founded the Congregation of the Visitation and became Mother de Chantal.

St. Francis designed the community for women who could not endure the rigors of other religious orders. When Mother de Chantal was criticized for accepting so many ill candidates, she replied, "What do you want me to do? I like sick people, myself." The order spread rapidly. When Jane de Chantal died in 1641, there were eighty-seven Visitation monasteries.

O Lord Jesus, I surrender to you all my will. Let me be your lute. Touch any string you please. Always and forever let me make music in perfect harmony with your own. Yes, Lord, with no ifs, ands or buts, let your will be done in this family, for the father, for the children, for everything that concerns us, and especially let your will be done in me.

—Jane de Chantal

DECEMBER 12 / CANONIZED IN 1767
Doubt; Enduring Trials; Married Saints; Temptation

271. Peter Fourier
(1565–1640)

In 1597, St. Peter Fourier, an Augustinian priest, elected to become pastor of St. Evre's at Mattaincourt in Lorraine. He chose the parish because he judged it the neediest of those offered him. When he arrived he met a congregation of poor, worldly, and ill-formed Catholics. He served them for more than thirty years, and left a parish community renewed in the faith.

An innovative pastor, Peter Fourier decided to reach adults by evangelizing children. He anticipated the modern technique of family-based religious education by catechizing children and parents together. He also appealed to adults by presenting dialogues with children as the main speakers. Crowds flocked to a stage he had constructed at the church to hear children dramatize conversations about Christianity, like the following between Penance and a potential penitent:

Penance appears and is met by the question:

"Who are you?"

"I am Penance."

"What do you want?"

"I want to lead people from the path of ruin to salvation."

"Can you really do that?"

"Yes, through the merits of the precious blood of Jesus Christ."

"Well, have you ever set anyone back on the right path?"

"Yes, and several of them have become great saints. Among others, King David, **St. Peter**, **St. Mary Magdalen** and **St. Mary of Egypt**."

"If you have such power, why didn't you bring back Dives and other unfortunates now in hell?"

"They didn't seek me. I don't force any sinner against his will."

"But I hear you prescribe sackcloth, fasts and a hard life. That's why most people are afraid of you."

"True, I myself do those things. But I don't compel anyone who isn't able to imitate me. I don't do violence to anyone. But some who love me occasionally wring these tortures from me and try to possess them in spite of me."

"Don't people encounter great difficulty when they undertake such things?"

"Not at all. Whatever comes from me is sweet as bread from heaven. A person finds more satisfaction there than in the pleasures of the world."

"I think I might like some of that heavenly bread, but I am afraid to ask you for it."

"Talk to my sisters, Contrition, Confession and Satisfaction. Listen to what they say. Believe them. And shortly your courage will rise to embrace what you now fear and all that is good."

Peter Fourier attempted to invest in future evangelization by founding a boys school, but it flopped. However, with volunteers led by Alix Le Clercq, he opened a free school for young women that employed modern teaching methods. With his support, Alix organized the Cannonesses of St. Augustine that quickly spread the schools throughout France.

Among Peter Fourier's many accomplishments was the establishment of a fund to help parishioners recover from financial hard times. And toward the end of his life he reluctantly but successfully accepted a commission to reform the Augustinians in Lorraine and unite them into a single religious community. Peter Fourier died on December 9, 1640.

God's mercy is like an unleashed torrent. It bears away all hearts in its flood.

—John Vianney

DECEMBER 9 / CANONIZED IN 1897
Evangelization; Great Pastors; Raising Christian Youth; Repentance

272. Martin de Porres

(1579–1639)

St. Martin de Porres was a mulatto, the son of a Spanish conquistador and a freed slave woman from Panama. In 1594 he entered the Dominican monastery at Lima, Peru, and became a professed brother in 1603. Martin was trained as a physician, but he also possessed gifts of healing. So he turned the monastery into a dispensary, a ramshackle prototype of a modern clinic.

Hundreds of Lima's poor came to him for help. With medicine or miracles, he healed the sick. At the monastery door he fed several hundred people every day. He collected money and distributed it among the needy. Once he provided dowries for twenty-seven poor young women who could not have married without his aid. And his most significant act of social justice was funding, designing, building, and staffing an orphanage and school for the street children of the city.

Martin always tried to stay little, hidden in the background. For example, he attempted to conceal his healing gift by using some herb or poultice as a decoy when he ministered to the sick. But despite his efforts he became well-known for his healing.

An amusing story is told of Felician de Vega, who was passing through Lima to take up his office as archbishop of Mexico. He was suffering from fever and an immobilizing pain in his chest. So he sent for Brother Martin, the famous healer. The Dominican superior ordered Martin to go to the archbishop immediately, giving him no time to gather his medical paraphernalia. This time Martin wouldn't be able to hide his gift. When he arrived, the archbishop ordered him to extend his hand:

> "But what would a prelate like Your Excellency want with the hand of a poor mulatto?" asked Martin, hoping to keep his cover.
>
> "Didn't the Father Provincial tell you to do whatever I said?"
>
> "Yes, my lord."
>
> "Then put your hand on my chest."
>
> As soon as the saint touched the archbishop the pain went away. Martin tried to remove his hand. "Isn't that enough, my lord?"
>
> "Leave your hand right where it is," said the archbishop, and he held the saint's hand firmly against his rib cage. Miraculously, the fever and all traces of the illness disappeared.

Embarrassed at his exposure, Martin returned to the monastery. He disciplined himself by grabbing a broom to sweep in dark corners of the building and by cleaning latrines.

"Brother Martin," a priest asked him, "wouldn't you be better off in the palace of the archbishop of Mexico?"

Martin answered with a paraphrase of Psalm 84: "'I have chosen to be a slave in the house of my God.' Father, I think one moment spent in doing what I am doing right now is more important than many days spent in the house of the Lord Archbishop."

Such humility and charity were the hallmarks of Martin's life. For half a century he was the servant of all in the monastery and the city. He died in 1639.

Martin de Porres was both a contemplative and an activist, setting us an example of balancing prayer and social action. Martin devoted most of his day to serving others. Much of the night he sacrificed sleep to worship the Lord before a crucifix. Few of us are called to duplicate the saint exactly. But all of us should imitate him by building both prayer and social action into our busy lives. And in our own small ways, keeping them in balance as Martin did.

NOVEMBER 3 / CANONIZED IN 1962 / PATRON OF SOCIAL JUSTICE AND RACE RELATIONS
Care of the Sick; Contemplatives in Action; Generosity; Healing Touch; Love in Action; Serving the Poor; Social Justice

273. Peter Claver

(1580–1654)

The kingdom of Heaven has been subjected to violence, and the violent are taking it by storm.

—Matthew 11:12 *NJB*

St. Peter Claver was both a kind and a violent man. He was kind to tens of thousands of slaves whose abused bodies and souls he affectionately tended. He was violent to himself, using force to overcome his revulsion at the foul afflictions of his beloved Africans.

At twenty Peter Claver became a Jesuit and was sent for training to Montesione College at Palma on Majorca. **St. Alphonsus Rodriguez,** the college's porter and his mentor, influenced Peter to consider service in foreign missions. He predicted that the saint would work among slaves in Cartagena, New Grenada, which is now Colombia.

In 1610, Peter was sent to Cartagena to complete his training and ordained five years later. Cartagena was the center of the slave trade in South America, with thousands arriving every year from West Africa. Deeply moved by their unimaginable misery, Peter Claver vowed that he would be "the slave of the enslaved Africans forever."

Day and night for forty years he fed, bathed, and brought medical aid to slaves chained in sickening hovels or hid in the homes of the rich. He brought them bread, lemons, pomegranates, dates, medicines, brandy, tobacco, and cologne. "We must speak to them with our hands," he said, "before we try to speak to them with our lips."

Preoccupied as we are with health and hygiene, we may be appalled at Peter Claver's extreme expressions of personal care. He regularly showed affection to afflicted slaves by kissing or licking their open sores. The following is based on an eyewitness account:

> Once he was called to the house of a rich ship owner of Lima, Peru. There was a black man in a corner, separated from all the others, as no one could stand the horror of him. Father Claver arrived as usual, a hand over his chest where he kept his wooden crucifix. He entered the dark room, followed by the master of the house and by four other Spaniards who witnessed the event.

> When Father Claver sensed this horrible atmosphere his head swam, he was almost fainting. His will of steel reacted; his companions could see the effort in his face dilating even more the two lines that crossed his forehead. Taking his left arm out of his cassock he uncovered his shoulders and with a whip tipped with small iron balls started to scourge himself, raining lashes upon his body, while he whispered this self-reproach: "So you are refusing to approach your neighbor redeemed by the blood of Jesus Christ? But it is not going to be like that. You are going to pay for it and achieve by charity whatever needs to be done."
>
> And then came the terrible reaction usual in these cases: he approached on his knees the terrified sick African in his miserable bed, he laid his face tenderly on the ulcers and kissed them. After confessing him, he left him in peace.

With the aid of native interpreters Peter Claver evangelized the slaves and indoctrinated them in the faith. He estimated that he baptized more than three hundred thousand people in forty years, an average of about twenty a day. And he heard as many as five thousand confessions in a year.

In 1650, a serious illness incapacitated Peter Claver. He died in 1654.

Peter Claver's example kindly does violence to our complacency. His discipline dismisses our doing-without-dessert notions of self-denial. And his extremism batters our impersonal notions about social action.

SEPTEMBER 9 / CANONIZED IN 1888 / PATRON OF OUTREACH TO BLACKS
Mere Christian Love; Missionaries; Serving the Poor; Social Justice

274. John de Brébeuf
(1593–1649)

How I grieve, my God, that you are not known, that this savage country is not yet wholly converted to faith in you, that sin is not yet blotted out!

—John de Brébeuf

Some saints I feel I know a little better because I have met someone like them. But I have never met anyone like St. John de Brébeuf, the Jesuit missionary and martyr. Large and handsome, his presence commanded attention. A brilliant student, gifted linguist, and competent manager, he could make things happen. I have met others like that, but none like this saint who was willing to endure anything if only he could thank Christ by giving his life for the salvation of others.

Even though weakened by tuberculosis, John joined the Canada mission in 1625. For a quarter of a century with only a four-year interlude, he evangelized the Hurons in Quebec. He lived with them, embraced their customs, mastered their language, and wrote a catechism for them.

At first he had little success because the odds were stacked against him. The Indians viewed him as member of a conquering race. They also blamed him for rampant diseases and everything else that went wrong. But John persevered with the good humor you see in this letter inviting other Jesuits to join the mission:

> When you reach the Hurons, you will find us with hearts full of love. We shall receive you in a hut, so mean that I have scarcely found in France one wretched enough to compare it with. Fatigued as you will be, we shall be able to give you nothing but a poor mat for a bed. Besides you will arrive when fleas will keep you awake most of the night.
>
> Instead of being a great theologian as you may be in France, you must reckon on being here a humble scholar, and then good God! with what masters—exposed to the laughter of all the savages. The Huron language will be your St. Thomas and your Aristotle. Glib as you are, you must decide for a long time to be mute among the barbarians.
>
> Without exaggeration, you will pass the six months of winter in almost continual discomforts—excessive cold, smoke, the annoyance of the savages who surround our fireplace from morning until evening looking for food.

For the rest, thus far we have had only roses. As we have Christians in almost every village, we must expect to make rounds throughout the year. Add to all this that our lives depend upon a single thread. Your cabin might burn down at any moment or a malcontent may cleave your head open because you cannot make it rain.

Here we have nothing that incites toward good. We are among peoples who are astonished when you speak to them of God.

In 1649, the Iroquois attacked the Huron village where John was living. They brutally martyred him, Gabriel Lalement, his companion, and their converts. Their suffering is indescribable: bludgeoned, burned with red-hot hatchets, baptized with boiling water, mutilated, flesh stripped off and eaten, hearts plucked out and devoured. But John de Brébeuf had his prayer answered. He traded his life for the seven thousand souls he had converted and baptized.

My God and my savior Jesus, what return can I make to you for all the benefits you have conferred on me? I make a vow to you never to fail, on my side, in the grace of martyrdom, if by your infinite mercy you offer it to me some day.

—John de Brébeuf

OCTOBER 19 / CANONIZED IN 1930
Evangelization; Martyrs; Missionaries; Success in Failure

275. Isaac Jogues

(1607–1646)

On August 5, 1643, young Jesuit missionary Isaac Jogues wrote from Canada a long letter to his superior in France. At the time he was a prisoner of a Mohawk clan of the Iroquois nation. He wrote with severely mutilated hands, as his captors had pulled out his nails and gnawed off both of his index fingers. The letter was a gut-wrenching description of the captivity and martyrdom of the Jesuit missionaries and their Huron converts.

St. Isaac Jogues relates that in 1642 he had led an expedition to Quebec to bring much needed supplies to the Huron mission. On their return, Iroquois warriors, traditional enemies of the Hurons, ambushed the party. In the following passage, the saint describes his agony over the enslavement of his beloved Hurons:

> Filling the air with jubilant shouts . . . they led us captive into their country. In all there were twenty-two of us, since three . . . had been killed. We suffered many hardships—thanks be to God—on the journey (which took thirty-eight days) from hunger, excessive heat, threats, blows, the cruel hatred of the savages, in addition to the excruciating pain of our wounds which had not healed but were festered so horribly that maggots were developing in them. But what seemed to me the cruelest of all their torments was that, when we were exhausted after five or six days of traveling, they came up to us with no semblance of anger and in cold blood tore out our hair and our beards, and scratched us deeply with their fingernails which they keep sharply pointed, in the most tender and sensitive parts of our bodies.
>
> All these sufferings were external, however. My interior sufferings were much more intense when I saw that sad procession of Hurons, now slaves of the Iroquois. Among them were many Christians, five of them converts of long standing and pillars of the infant Huron church. I will admit naively that from time to time I could not restrain my tears, deploring their lot and that of all my companions, but even more filled with anxiety for the future. For I saw that the Iroquois would forbid the practice of the Christian faith to these Hurons and to innumerable other nations unless God by a special providence should intervene.

For the previous five years, Isaac Jogues and his Jesuit companions had labored among the Hurons. They had baptized only a few hundred converts, but it was a hopeful start. Now all seemed lost.

In 1644, with the help of the Dutch, Jogues escaped to France. But a year later he returned to Quebec, near the settlement of Montreal, to work again with the Hurons. In 1647, at Ossernenon, an Iroquois village, he helped negotiate a peace pact between the French and the Iroquois chiefs. However, he left behind a box of religious articles that became the immediate cause of his martyrdom. The tribe claimed that an evil spirit in the package was responsible for a serious epidemic. For revenge, on October 18, 1646, a Mohawk clan lured Isaac Jogues to their village with an invitation to dinner. And as he approached they tomahawked him, severed his head, and stuck it on a pole.

During his interlude in France in 1644, Isaac Jogues was temporarily prevented from celebrating Mass because of his deformed hands. But Pope Urban VIII gave him special permission, saying that, "It would be unjust that a martyr of Christ should not drink the blood of Christ."

OCTOBER 19 / CANONIZED IN 1930
Martyrs; Missionaries; Suffering

276. Vincent de Paul

(1581–1660)

St. Vincent de Paul spent the early years of his priesthood ministering among the wealthy in the French countryside near Paris. In 1609 he became tutor to the children of the Gondi family, an involvement that taught him a principle for his work: evangelize the rich and direct them to serve the poor. At that time, Vincent observed that many poorly catechized peasants were not making good confessions. He also noticed that inadequately trained priests did not know how to administer the sacrament of Penance. Encouraged by Madame Gondi, in 1617, Vincent preached a parish mission that pointed to his future. He stirred so many people to repentance that Jesuits from a nearby town had to help hear confessions.

In 1625, Vincent founded the Congregation of the Mission, a community of priests with a threefold commitment. Members obligated themselves to pattern their lives on Christ, to take the gospel to the rural poor, and to help educate priests in their practical duties. The priests mainly conducted parish missions, preaching and hearing confessions.

Vincent gave his brothers a rule that displayed his commonsensical application of Scripture. For example:

> Jesus, the Lord, expects us to have the simplicity of a dove (see Matthew 10:16). This means giving a straightforward opinion about things in the way we honestly see them, without needless reservations. It also means doing things without double-dealing or manipulation, our intention being focused solely on God. Each of us, then, should take care to behave always in the spirit of simplicity, remembering that God likes to deal with the simple, and that he conceals the secrets of heaven from the wise and prudent of this world and reveals them to little ones.
>
> But while Christ recommends a dove's simplicity, he also tells us to have a serpent's prudence. He means that we should speak and behave with discretion. We ought, therefore, to keep quiet about matters which should not be made known, especially if they are unsuitable or unlawful. When we are discussing things which it is good and proper to talk about we should hold back any details which would not be for God's glory, or which could harm some other person, or which would make us foolishly smug.

> In actual practice this virtue is about choosing the right way to do things. We should make it a sacred principle, then, admitting no exceptions, that since we are working for God we will always choose God-related ways for carrying out our work, and see and judge things from Christ's point of view and not from a worldly-wise one; and not according to the feeble reasoning of our own mind.

With the collaboration of **St. Louise de Marillac,** in 1633, Vincent founded the Sisters of Charity, the first community of "unenclosed" women dedicated to care of the sick and the poor. To support the sisters, Vincent recruited rich women, who as Ladies of Charity gave their time and money.

In his last years Vincent was confined to an armchair because of his swollen and ulcerous legs. But he remained cheerful, directing his charitable works by writing hundreds of letters. He was nearly eighty years old when he died in 1660.

Vincent de Paul stumbled into his life's work. Thus he is a healthful model for those who suffer stress trying "to find God's plan" for their lives. Vincent did not start with grandiose plans. He began much more simply. When he observed a need, he figured out a Christian way to meet it. If we would do more of that, we would be better Christians with lower blood pressure.

SEPTEMBER 27 / CANONIZED IN 1737 / PATRON OF CHARITABLE SOCIETIES
Christian Living; Repentance; Saints and Sacraments (Reconciliation); The Secrets of Spiritual Success

277. Louise de Marillac
(1591–1660)

St. Louise de Marillac lived most of her adult life conducting mundane affairs in Paris, France, which probably accounts for the practical bent of her spirituality. She married Antony Le Gras in 1613 and they lived happily together for twelve years. They had a son, Michael, for whom Louise took a lifelong concern. When her husband died in 1625, she decided to remain single and undertake some Christian service.

At that time **St. Vincent de Paul** was recruiting wealthy women to serve among Paris's poor. However, these aristocrats were not well suited for the job. He needed peasant and lower-class women who were like the poor and could more readily deal with their harsh circumstances.

When Vincent met Louise he chose her as his partner because he recognized her strengths. He judged correctly that Louise was self-effacing, unflappable, and gracious. These traits made her the ideal leader to train women for streetwise service.

Neither Louise nor Vincent intended to found a religious order, just a gathering of committed women who would work and pray hard. "Your convent" said Vincent, "will be the house of the sick, your cell a rented room, your chapel the parish church, your cloister the city streets or the hospital wards." In 1633, Louise brought the first four women into her home for training. But the community soon evolved into the Sisters of Charity, and within a quarter of a century Louise had established forty convents in Europe.

Louise led her sisters with intelligence and grace, as her extensive correspondence shows. In this refreshing letter, for example, she requires one of her friends to relax her perfectionism:

> I begged God to help you to forget yourself and to mortify your desire for self-satisfaction which in you, hides under the beautiful appearance of striving for great perfection. We are greatly deceiving ourselves if we think that we are capable of it, and even more so if we believe that we can attain this perfection by our own efforts and by constantly and closely watching over all the movements and disposition of our souls.
>
> It is a good thing, once a year, to apply ourselves seriously to this kind of examination while being duly distrustful of ourselves and

recognizing our weaknesses. But to put ourselves through a continual purgatory to analyze our souls and to give an account of all our thoughts is useless, even dangerous. I am repeating to you what I was told long ago.

I beg you, my dear Sister, to help me by your prayers, as I will help you by mine, so that we may obtain from God the grace to walk simply and confidently along the path of his holy love without too much introspection, lest we resemble those persons, who, instead of growing rich, become bankrupt while striving to find the philosopher's stone.

Succinct confessions are always the best. What are we looking for in this sacrament? Grace alone, and we can be certain that the divine goodness will not withhold it from us if we approach the sacrament with the necessary dispositions of simplicity, heartfelt sorrow, and submission.

Louise de Marillac died in 1660, six months before St. Vincent.

Strict, self-propelled Christianity was popular in seventeenth-century France, and today many still take that human willpower approach. But St. Louise's spirituality was more divine and, thus, more realistic: Stop fussing. Don't try too hard. Let God love you. Rest in his grace. Sounds to me like the teaching of Christ, who promised that his yoke was easy and his burden, light.

MARCH 15 / CANONIZED IN 1934 / PATRON OF SOCIAL WORKERS
Christian Living; Grace; Married Saints; Saints and Sacraments (Reconciliation); Serving the Poor

278. John Regis
(1597–1640)

By the 1630s, constant religious and civil wars had wrecked the social structure of the mountainous regions of southeastern France. Poverty, robbery, and general lawlessness were commonplace. Absentee bishops and pastors had left churches, both Catholic and Protestant, untended for more than two decades. Thus, many had lost their faith and were Christians in name only.

To revive the Christian life under such circumstances, the Jesuits adopted the strategy of the parish mission that **St. Vincent de Paul** and **St. John Eudes** had modeled so effectively. Jesuit superiors noticed the holiness and preaching gift of St. John Regis during his novitiate and targeted him for this demanding work.

Immediately after his ordination in 1631, the Jesuits sent John Regis as a missionary to southeastern France. For the last ten years of his life he preached and cared for the poor in towns and rural areas from Montpellier to Le Puy. Everywhere he attracted huge crowds because he avoided fancy rhetoric and spoke simply in the local patois. After preaching, he always spent morning hours hearing confessions and afternoons in the streets and prisons. He brought many Catholics back to the faith and converted many nominal Protestants.

John Regis extravagantly used his personal resources to aid the destitute and rescue prostitutes. In Le Puy, for example, he established a complete social service of prison visitors and nurses that he staffed with his women penitents. He ran a granary for the poor and a refuge for girls and women. John's generous social activism fomented the anger of some who brought false charges against him. While a few of his colleagues entertained doubts about him, others came to his defense. The following letter of an associate persuaded John's superior to stand by him:

> Undoubtedly some have written to you against Father Regis and against the pretended impetuosity of his zeal. Don't allow yourself to be tricked by the false pictures that may have been painted of this holy man. He is an indefatigable worker who breathes only the divine glory. He combats vice with the zeal of an apostle and is not held back in his ministry by any human consideration. This alone has aroused against

> him many scandalous sinners and even some fathers of the College who are alarmed by the rumors these sinners spread through the city.
>
> I assure you truthfully that I see nothing worthy of blame in his person. On the contrary, I see in him many eminent, praiseworthy virtues. He wars against scandals always with as much prudence as zeal, ever pursuing sin and yet treating sinners with all possible gentleness and charity.
>
> Father Regis conducts public catechism classes in the church that is called Sainte-Pierre-du-Monastier, to the admiration of all and with incredible success. In fact, on every Sunday for the past two years, save for Lent and Advent, five thousand persons of both sexes and of all conditions packed in there, filling not only the nave, which is very vast, but also numerous tribunes and the temporary seats that had to be constructed. And even under the portico and at all entrances, heads were held cocked to hear him. I add that he is an obedient religious and that he is commonly called a saint.

John Regis worked ceaselessly until he died while preaching a Christmas mission at the village of La Louvesc in 1640.

> *The proof of love is in the works. Where love exists, it works great things. But when love ceases to act, it ceases to exist.*
>
> —Gregory the Great

JUNE 16 / CANONIZED IN 1737 / PATRON OF MEDICAL SOCIAL WORKERS
Great Preachers; Love in Action; Missionaries; Serving the Poor

279. Joseph of Cupertino

(1603–1663)

The people of Cupertino, Italy, nicknamed young Joseph Desa "the gaper." They disdained the absent-minded boy who aimlessly wandered the village. Unwanted by his widowed mother, Joseph seemed destined to failure. At seventeen he was apprenticed to a shoemaker, but was soon released for incompetence. Then Joseph attempted to join the Franciscans, but was twice dismissed from communities because he could not successfully perform even simple menial tasks. Finally, his mother arranged for him to become a servant to the Franciscans at Grottella.

In this community Joseph was somewhat more successful in his duties. Eventually recognized for his piety, he was admitted to the novitiate in 1625. But he was such a poor student that he would never have been ordained except for two little miracles. At the exam for the diaconate, the bishop randomly chose for exposition the only passage Joseph was prepared to discuss. Then when the bishop reviewed candidates for the priesthood, the first few men did so well that he passed Joseph and all the others without question.

After ordination in 1628, Joseph experienced a sustained series of mystical phenomena at a level unparalleled by any other saint. A glimpse of a statue of **Mary** or a mere mention of God would throw him into rapture. In these ecstasies Joseph would become weightless and hover motionlessly or fly through the air. More than two hundred saints are reported to have levitated, but none more frequently nor with more flair than Joseph of Cupertino. At least seventy of his "flights" have been recorded. Numerous accounts come from eyewitnesses, such as the following:

> In 1645, the Spanish ambassador to the papal court, the high admiral of Castile, passed through Assisi to see Joseph. After speaking with the saint in his cell, he returned to the church and told his wife, "I have spoken with another **Saint Francis**." So his wife also wanted to meet Joseph, and at her request, his superior commanded him to go up to the church and speak with her.
>
> "I will obey," said Joseph, "but I don't know whether I will be able to speak," and he hastened to comply. Scarcely had he entered the church when, looking up to a statue of Mary Immaculate on the altar,

> he flew about twelve paces over the heads of those present to the foot of the statue. After remaining there some time in prayer, he flew back with his customary cry and returned to his cell. The occurrence amazed the admiral, his wife, and their retinue.
>
> Several religious, whom he helped fold a habit worn by St. Francis, saw him hover in the air above their heads. Others saw him suspended on a cornice in the chapel of St. Francis, about 8 feet from the floor. One day, while a priest was preaching in the chapel of St. Ursula, Joseph flew from a balcony that jutted out in front of the altar. He remained suspended in a kneeling position before the tabernacle until at his superior's command he flew back to the balcony.

For thirty-five years church officials and Franciscan superiors kept Joseph in seclusion, preventing him from having contact with the public. "One Saint Francis of Assisi was enough," said one pope who declined to lift the ban. But Pope Benedict XIV, the scholar who articulated the criteria for determining sanctity, regarded the eyewitnesses of Joseph's flights to be of "unchallengeable integrity." After a short illness, Joseph died in 1663 at age sixty.

With an uncharacteristic touch of humor, the church has named St. Joseph of Cupertino patron of both students and air travelers.

SEPTEMBER 18 / PATRON OF STUDENTS AND AIR TRAVELERS
Miracles Do Happen; Success in Failure

280. Charles of Sezze
(1613–1670)

Combine the simplicity of **Solanus Casey** with the spirituality of **Teresa of Ávila**, and you get a picture of St. Charles of Sezze. Less educated than Casey, John Charles Marchionni also struggled at school, barely learning to read and write. But as a Franciscan friar, also like Casey, he performed lifelong the menial services of sacristan and porter. But as a mystic and spiritual writer, this simple friar paralleled the great Teresa.

Charles joined the Franciscans at Rome in 1635. Too sickly for the foreign missionary service he craved, he spent his entire life serving at convents in and around Rome. In his interior life, Charles ascended to the highest stages of contemplative prayer. As it had happened for Teresa, in 1648, a mysterious ray penetrated his heart, marking him with Christ's wound. After his death, doctors examined the scar and judged it as authentic and miraculous.

Although uneducated, Charles of Sezze wrote several acclaimed treatises on the spiritual life. In *The Three Ways of Meditation* and *Interior Journey of the Soul*, he wrote simply and clearly about meditation and the stages of contemplative prayer. These books compare favorably with those of Teresa and **John of the Cross**.

In his *Autobiography*, written under obedience to his superior, Charles described from experience how God allows those who aspire to sanctity to undergo fierce spiritual combat. The following passage illustrates both the severity of Charles' own struggle and his wisdom about letting God win the battle:

> The temptation to lust with a certain woman lasted for five years as a kind of martyrdom. At night . . . , all hell turned on me although I threw the water of devout thoughts on it by imagining that I was within the sacred wounds of our Lord. . . . I was like a slave, tied and unable to defend myself, free only in the act of my will, which did its best to keep united with his Divine Majesty and far removed from the sensual movements of the flesh. With lips and heart I called on the name of Jesus and Mary, telling them I was willing to . . . suffer any kind of martyrdom rather than offend the law of God. . . .
>
> . . . I tried hard to do my part through penances with my spiritual director's permission. I wore a hair-shirt of animal skins but I had to

> stop because it made me too warm if I wore it for any length of time. I wore a kind of vest of good-sized chains for eight to ten years. When I did sleep, it was on a table. I drank water only and ate meat rarely.
>
> These and other penances helped only a little. To think of wanting to chase off temptations by force of arms is vanity and madness, for this is done only by the favor of divine grace. When the time our Lord had set for freeing me had come, he caused the hellish image to disappear as if it had never been.

Like Solanus Casey, Charles had a gift for reading souls and people often consulted him to verify the authenticity of religious experiences. Three popes made him their friend, often seeking his advice on spiritual matters. Charles died at Rome in 1670.

> *Jesus said: "I give praise to you, Father, Lord of heaven and earth, for although you have hidden these things from the wise and the learned you have revealed them to the childlike."*
>
> —Matthew 11:25 *NAB*

JANUARY 5 / CANONIZED IN 1959
Celebration of Discipline; Sexual Temptation; Spiritual Warfare; Stigmata

281. Anthony Grassi
(1592–1671)

Anthony Grassi became a priest of the Oratory at Fermo, Italy, the third oratory founded during **St. Philip Neri's** lifetime. A gifted young man with an encyclopedic memory, Anthony also suffered from scruples until he celebrated his first mass. From that hour these worries left him and he became well known for his imperturbable calmness.

In 1621, while kneeling at prayer at the church at Loreto, lightning struck Anthony, leaving an unforgettable mark on his body and his soul. He wrote:

> I felt shaken and as though I were outside myself. It seemed to me that my soul was separated from my body and that I was in a swoon. . . . Then I was roused by a great crash, like thunder, and I opened my eyes and found that I had fallen head-first down the steps. . . . Then I saw that a piece of skin had been ripped off one of my fingers, and I remembered a story I had heard of a priest at Camerino who was killed by lightning, on whose body there was no mark except some skin off his hand. So when I saw my finger I thought that I too was going to die. And a sort of heat burning my inside made me feel yet more like it. . . . I was afraid that that scorching heat would reach my heart and kill me. I was helpless, and lay without moving on the steps, thinking that if I could not die in the Oratory I should at any rate do so in a sanctuary of the Mother of God. Then someone bent over me, and I told him I could not move; he called for help and a chair was brought and I was put in it, when I fainted again. But I was conscious that my head and arms were dangling uselessly, and my sight and speech had failed, though my hearing was acute. I knew someone was suggesting the holy names of Jesus and Mary to me.

In a few days Anthony noticed that as an unusual side effect, the strike had cured him of chronic indigestion. But the real effect of the shock was profoundly spiritual. Anthony says the closeness of death made him permanently quite indifferent to worldly things. More important, forever after Anthony remembered with gratitude every day that his life belonged to God in a very special way.

In 1635, the Fermo Oratory chose Anthony as its superior. He believed that if he evaluated any trait of a person in the context of his entire character, he would generally find more good than bad. So he exercised his office with unusual gentleness. When asked why he did not correct people with more severity, he said, "I don't think I know how." Then he would mimic a pompous authoritarian attitude, and ask: "Is this the way?" But Anthony's gentleness did not prevent him from being firm. He held the community at Fermo to a strict observance of the Oratory's pattern of life.

After his eightieth year, Anthony's body wore down. He lost his teeth, so he had to cease preaching and hearing confessions because he could not make himself understood. At the end of November 1671, he fell down some stairs and died two weeks later.

Once someone asked Anthony if he wore a hair shirt. He said he did not because he learned from St. Philip Neri that it is better to undertake spiritual mortification. "Humbling the mind and the will," Anthony said, "is more effective than a hair-shirt between your skin and your clothes."

DECEMBER 13 / BEATIFIED IN 1900
Celebration of Discipline; Facing Death; Meekness

282. Marie of the Incarnation
(1599–1672)

Visualize a grandmotherly French woman cuddling an Algonquin child and you have a picture of Mother Marie of the Incarnation, the missionary. Envision the same woman snuggled in God's lap and you have an image of Mother Marie, the mystic. For like **Teresa of Ávila,** this multi-gifted woman was both a mystic and a missionary.

But Marie enjoyed a more diverse worldly experience than Teresa. At seventeen she married Claude Martin, a merchant of Tours, France, and bore him a son. Claude died before their third anniversary, but Marie continued to competently manage his business.

All the while, however, God seems to have made gentle assaults on Marie's soul. In this passage from her *Autobiography* she tells how God startled her with his mercy:

> Suddenly I was stopped in my tracks, both interiorly and exteriorly. In a flash the eyes of my mind were opened and all the faults, sins, imperfections I had ever committed were represented to me both in general and in particular. I saw them with a distinction and clarity more certain than any human effort could produce. At the same moment I saw myself completely immersed in blood. And I was convinced that it was the blood of the son of God and that this precious blood had been shed for my salvation.
>
> If the goodness of God had not sustained me, I believe I would have died of fright. No human tongue can express how horrible and shocking is the sight of sin, however small it may be. Rather, to see a God of infinite goodness and purity offended by a worm of the earth surpasses horror itself. And especially to see a God-made-man die to expiate sin and shed all his precious blood to appease his Father and in this way to reconcile sinners to him!
>
> Finally, it is impossible to tell what the soul comprehends during this prodigy. But to see not only the fact of one's own personal culpability but also the fact that, even if one were the only one guilty of sin, the Son of God would have done for him what he has done for all—this it is that consumes and seems to annihilate the soul.

The saint swiftly ascended in prayer, so that by age twenty-eight she says she experienced a complete, inexpressible union with God.

In 1629, Marie made the painful decision to leave her son with her sister and joined the Ursulines at Tours. A hunger to save souls and a strange vision of a foreign landscape beckoned her to the Jesuit missions in Canada in 1639. For the next thirty-two years she evangelized and instructed native converts in Quebec. For the work she learned several difficult languages and wrote four catechisms, three for the Algonquins and one for the Iroquois.

During this time she progressed in the course of her mystical union with God, charting it in 1654 in a very readable *Autobiography*. Claude Martin, her son, became a famous Benedictine priest and honored his mother by writing her life story. Marie of the Incarnation died in 1672 at age seventy-three.

Visitors at the mission school could not understand how we could dandle on our laps the little orphans, smeared with grease against the cold and covered only by a small, oily rag. But for us all this was unimaginable joy. Thanks to God's goodness, our vocation and love for the natives never diminished. I carry them all in my heart and try very gently through my prayers to win them for heaven.

—Marie of the Incarnation

APRIL 30 / BEATIFIED IN 1980
Contemplatives in Action; Married Saints; Missionaries; Visions and Visionaries

283. John Eudes
(1601–1680)

In 1623, St. John Eudes entered the French Oratory because he admired **St. Philip Neri**, the founder of the Oratorians. Like his ideal, he generated spiritual renewal through preaching, counsel, and service to the poor and sick.

The Oratory recognized early John's superior speaking ability and encouraged him to preach even before his ordination. Thus they started the saint on his lifelong ministry. John was effective in the pulpit because he could move people to change their lives. Listen in your mind's ear, for example, to his oft-repeated instruction about the benefit of suffering:

> We are indebted to God's justice for a hundred thousand bushels of wheat, and he lets us off for a portion of it. O great favor! We merit eternal torments, and he lets us suffer a few small temporal afflictions. Ah, what goodness!
>
> We should take care to make good use of our afflictions. God wants to cleanse us of the filth of our sins by a lye-bath of suffering that seems very strong. But the stronger it is, the more it whitens us. It makes us pleasing in the sight of his divine majesty, provided that we cultivate the necessary dispositions, chiefly these four:
>
> First, we must accept our sufferings from the most adorable Trinity, and not attribute them in any way to our fellow creatures. They are merely the rods our Father uses to punish us.
>
> Second, we must humble ourselves under the mighty hand of God, regarding ourselves not as innocent, but as guilty criminals. The humbler we become, the more will God protect us and convert all things to our welfare.
>
> Third, we must regard sin as the sole author of all our ills, turning all our hatred against this monstrous enemy. We must forcefully destroy sin by true penitence and banish it beyond the doors of our souls. Let's remove the cause, and the effect will cease.
>
> Fourth, we must guard against subscribing to the pagan sentiment of hating those who hate us. We must follow Jesus, our gentle leader, by loving all—including enemies.

After John was done preaching, he always went to hear confessions. "The preacher beats the bushes," he said, "but the confessor catches the birds." Over the years he presented 110 missions, helping to establish that modern form of parish renewal.

Twice John interrupted his preaching ministry to care for plague victims. The second time at Caen, in order to avoid contaminating others, he lived in a large cask in an open field. He also had a special concern for repentant prostitutes. At Caen he founded a refuge for them that provided temporary housing till they could find honest work.

In 1643, John Eudes left the Oratory to work for the renewal of the priesthood. He founded the Congregation of Jesus and Mary, a community of secular priests committed to spiritual revival. To promote priestly reform he founded and staffed three seminaries.

Toward the end of his life John gave impetus to devotion to the Sacred Heart by providing a sound doctrinal basis for it. He also devised a Mass and office for the celebration of the feast. Thus, he augmented and completed the popular work of **St. Margaret Mary Alacoque.** He died at Caen in 1680.

The Christian life is the continuation and completion of the life of Christ in us. We should be so many Christs here on earth, continuing his life and his works, laboring and suffering in a holy and divine manner in the Spirit of Jesus.

—John Eudes

AUGUST 19 / CANONIZED IN 1925
Great Preachers; Repentance; Saints and Sacraments (Reconciliation); Suffering

284. Kateri Tekakwitha

(1656–1680)

We recognize Kateri Tekakwitha as the first native North American saint. Her short life as a Christian was marked with unrelieved suffering. As a Catholic and a virgin, this courageous young woman was persecuted by a pagan society that expected women to marry. To the daily severities of tribal life, Kateri added extreme penances. She seems to have found her only joy in imitating Christ crucified.

Kateri was born in 1656 at Ossernon, now Ariesville, New York. Her mother was a Christian Algonquin and her father, a Mohawk chief in the Iroquois nation. When Kateri was four years old, smallpox wiped out her family and left her disfigured and partially blind.

James de Lambertville, a Jesuit missionary, baptized Kateri at Easter, 1676, when she was twenty years old. Her conversion to Catholicism alienated her relatives and they ostracized her. So in 1677, Kateri fled to a Christian village where her faith could flourish.

The missionaries loved their idealistic convert. They were especially impressed with her extreme penitential practices. "She treated her body with such harshness," said one biographer, "that it would be difficult anywhere else to find such innocence joined with such austere penance. She tortured her body in all the ways she could invent, by toil, by loss of sleep, by fasting, by cold, by fire, by irons, by pointed girdles, and by harsh beatings with which she tore her shoulders open several times a week."

Another biographer tells how Kateri and her friend, Marie Theresa, regularly scourged each other. He said the women would first pray, and then take turns beating each other with rods:

> Then Katherine [Kateri], who always wished to be the first in suffering, knelt down and received the chastisement. She always complained that it was not painful enough, and begged her companion to strike harder, even though as I know, the third stroke drew blood. When they stopped, they said the rosary and divided it at intervals in each of which they gave themselves five strokes more. Towards the end of their devotions they ceased to count the strokes. Katherine revealed the sentiments of her heart in these words: "My Jesus, I must suffer for you; I love you, but I have offended you. It is to satisfy your justice that I am here. Vent on me, O God, your anger." Sometimes she was unable

> to speak further, but finished with eyes bathed in tears, and finally she would say, "I am very affected by the three nails which fastened Our Lord to the cross; they are but a symbol of my sins."

When the Jesuit missionaries discovered Kateri's secret penances, they curbed them. However, it was also from them that she had learned her severe and twisted piety. For example, one adviser made this warped observation: "Together with all the saints, she carried her cross after Him, and the Divine Master, who guided her, having inspired her with a holy hatred of herself, so much recommended by Jesus Christ and so necessary to salvation." Another Jesuit told her about **St. Aloysius Gonzaga** who had slept on thorns. Imitating the boy saint, for three nights Kateri lay naked on thorns she had scattered over her mat. She died of lifelong illnesses a week later on April 17, 1680.

We correctly view Kateri's austerity as excessive and her muscular spirituality as misguided, but these practices have deep roots in the Christian past. Today we take a more sensible and spiritually healthier approach to our bodies.

JULY 14 / CANONIZED IN 2012
Countercultural Witness; Enduring Trials; Twenty-Something Saints

285. Julien Maunoir
(1606–1683)

Rural France in the seventeenth century was "mission" territory. The poor folk of the countryside blended a superficial Christianity with ancient superstitions. So numerous saints like **Vincent de Paul** and **John Eudes** dedicated themselves to "re-Christianizing" the populace by conducting parish missions and reforming the clergy. Among these domestic missionaries was Julien Maunoir, a young Jesuit called to the evangelization of Brittany.

Julien went to work among the Bretons in Quimper in 1640. There he encountered a folk religion as pagan as it was Christian. People used talismans, visited sacred springs, appeased evil spirits, and prayed to the moon. Wives of sailors even threatened to beat statues of the saints if they did not bring the men home safely. In this culture, Julien's task was more akin to planting the faith anew rather than renewing it.

Upon arrival in Brittany, Julien quickly learned the Breton language. Influenced by Father Michael le Nobletz, a gifted local priest, he adopted a unique missionary technique. To rivet the attention of his hearers, Julien employed a variety of teaching aids, including extemporized songs, pictures, processions, and "living" stations of the cross. For example, he instructed small groups, using colorful charts illustrating the passion, the Lord's Prayer, or the seven deadly sins. Some of the charts were more fanciful presentations of the Christian message, such as the tale of the Knight Errant, described in the following outline:

> The Wandering Knight followed the high roads of vice where Dame Folly cut off his hair, as Delilah did to Samson, and despoiled him of his arms. He arrived at Babylon, the seven towers of which were the seven deadly sins. He sojourned there in the castle of King Carnality and Queen Sensuality, who have nine daughters, including Libertinage and Idleness. He also dwelt in the castle of King Worldly Love and Queen Worldly Prosperity, in company with their daughters, Greediness, Avarice and Pride. Their nurse is Negligence, and their dog, Pass-Time.
>
> The Wandering Knight is sunk in the mire of sin. But Divine Grace touches him with a golden rod, and he invokes God's Help. Trial and Expiation come for him. He falls sick of numerous fevers that are vicious customs. An angel cures him, reveals to him his weakness and conducts him to the castle of Penance that is on a very rugged

> mountain. Divine Grace helps him to mount it, presenting to him a crown. There is a woman before the door, very sorrowful and weeping, called Contrition. She shows him a serpent trying to rub off his own skin between two stones. The gate is called Truth and the key Mercy. Finally the Wandering Knight becomes Desiring the Love of God.

When Julien visited a parish he stayed about six weeks, preaching and teaching until all the mission participants had made a general confession. His practice was to return to each community every four to six years. During his forty-three years in Brittany he conducted 375 such missions. Thus, Julien Maunoir spearheaded the Catholic revival in Brittany, one of the most successful re-Christianization movements in the history of the church. At the start of his ministry only two missioners labored among the Bretons. By his death in 1683 a thousand priests had joined the work.

Julien Maunoir, who used the best media of his day to proclaim the gospel, reminds me of Archbishop Fulton Sheen, who did the same in the 1950s. And now when the whole formerly Christian world seems to have become "mission" territory, I think we may be ready for the Julien Maunoir and Fulton Sheen of cyberspace.

JANUARY 28 / BEATIFIED IN 1951
Innovative Saints; Evangelization; Missionaries

286. Marguerite Bourgeoys
(1620–1700)

As a young woman in Troyes, France, Marguerite Bourgeoys wanted to become a nun. But both the Carmelites and Poor Clares inexplicably refused her. Father Gendret, her adviser, told her to found a community of her own that would not be enclosed in a cloister, but would serve in the world. At that time because of a longstanding tradition of protecting nuns from wordly influences, Catholic bishops vigorously opposed unenclosed sisterhoods. They had already dealt failures to similar efforts by **St. Jane de Chantal.** But Marguerite Bourgeoys was an indomitable and resourceful woman. With faith and courage she founded the Congregation of Notre Dame, the first unenclosed missionary order of women.

St. Marguerite attempted in the 1640s to launch such a community in Troyes. From that period comes the following anecdote that depicts the mettle she typically engaged to topple all obstacles:

> Sister Bourgeoys learned that some young men had abducted a young woman. She found out where they had taken her and went, crucifix in hand, to beg these fellows to let her go. They confronted her with a pistol and threatened to kill her. Fearlessly, she reminded them of their duty, that in attacking a servant of Jesus Christ, they attacked Christ himself, that sooner or later they would be punished. She frightened them so much that they gave up the poor girl, whom she is said to have kept with her and brought to Canada.

The Troyes experiment failed. But the governor of Ville-Marie in Canada hired Marguerite as the schoolmistress for his fledgling colony. She saw there the opportunity to realize her vision. She arrived in Quebec in 1653 and quietly laid the groundwork for building her community. Five years later she opened her first school in a converted stone stable.

The colony developed into the town of Montreal, and the school grew. Anticipating even greater expansion, Marguerite twice traveled back to France where she recruited young women to join her. The first bishop of Quebec, Msgr. de Laval, approved the Congregation of Notre Dame in 1676. Then Marguerite's troubles seemed to increase geometrically—the bishop tried to enforce enclosure, the community was desperately poor, and in 1683 fire destroyed her convent and killed two nuns.

In the face of hardship and opposition, however, the saint's educational venture flourished. She opened a boarding school in 1673 and three years later a mission school for the Iroquois. However, it was not until 1698 that Msgr. de Laval's successor finally relaxed the official opposition to the sisters' not being cloistered. By that time Marguerite had retired as superior of the congregation. But she had accomplished her educational mission that ultimately bore fruit in more than two hundred schools.

Late in 1699, with her health failing, Marguerite prayed that God would take her life in place of a critically ill young sister. Her prayer was answered: the nun survived, and Marguerite Bourgeoys in one final generous act died on January 12, 1700.

> *The profit that small acts of generosity gain for us when they are done for God reminds me of a present I gave my father, so small and trivial that it made those who saw it laugh—and my father as well. But seeing that I had made it with such great affection, he carried this present around with him and showed it to everyone. God is pleased with little virtues that are practiced for love of him and he ennobles them in the measure that they are exercised with greater love. I must do everything, therefore, for the greater love of God.*
>
> —Marguerite Bourgeoys

JANUARY 12 / CANONIZED IN 1982
Courage; Purpose

287. Oliver Plunkett

(1629–1681)

St. Oliver Plunkett reminds us of **Thomas More.** Both men exemplified unusual strength of character. Both excelled in law and theology. They performed outstanding service, More for the state and Plunkett for the church. Each was condemned for treason against his king by false testimony. And both More and Plunkett startle us because they faced brutal deaths courageously.

After fifteen years as a professor in Rome, in 1669, Oliver Plunkett had been appointed archbishop of Armagh. Persistent persecution had left the Irish church in disarray. In his first few months Plunkett confirmed 10, 000 of the 50, 000 who had not received the sacrament. His renewal strategy was to promulgate the decrees of the Council of Trent, to tighten the discipline of the secular and regular clergy, and to improve education. He succeeded in spite of internal conflicts—controversy over the supremacy of Armagh versus Dublin and opposition from some Franciscans who resisted his authority.

Plunkett was caught up in the infamous Popish Plot fabricated by Titus Oates, who prompted many people to accuse Catholics of conniving to kill the English King Charles II. As archbishop of Armagh and metropolitan of Ireland, Plunkett became a prime target of anti-Catholic prejudice. In December 1679 he was arrested on outlandish charges. He was moved to Newgate Prison in London and finally tried there and convicted in June 1681. In giving sentence, a biased, dishonorable judge revealed the real reason behind Plunkett's condemnation: "the bottom of your treason was your setting up of your false religion, the most dishonorable and derogatory to God and his glory of all religions." The saint reported his conviction and his confession of faith to his relative, Michael Plunkett, in this letter:

> Sentence of death passed against me on the 15th, without causing me any fear, or depriving me of sleep for a quarter of an hour. I am innocent of all treason as the child born yesterday. As for my character, profession, and function, I did own it publicly. And that being also a motive of my death, I die most willingly. Being first among the Irish, I will teach others, with the grace of God, by example, not to fear death. But how am I so stout—a poor creature—seeing that my Redeemer began to fear, to be weary and sad, and that drops of his blood ran down to the

ground? I have considered that Christ by his fears and passion merited for me to be without fear.

I forgive all who had a hand directly or indirectly, in my death and in my innocent blood.

My accusers swore that I had seventy thousand men in Ireland to promote the Catholic cause, that I had the harbor of Carlingford ready to bring in the French, and that I levied monies upon the clergy in Ireland for their maintenance—such romances as would not be believed by any jury in Ireland.

I daily expect to be brought to the place of execution, where my bowels are to be cut out and burned before my face, and then my head to be cut off, etc. Which death I embrace willingly. I long for the end.

On July 1, 1681, Oliver Plunkett was hanged at Tyburn. The martyr died before he was disemboweled and cut to pieces.

Your penetrating lines stir up my dull heart and weak will to the contemplation of eternal joys. The passage is but short, yet 'tis dangerous, 'tis from time to eternity, it can never be repassed or repeated: your prayers I beg and your brethren's for me.

—Oliver Plunkett to Father Maurus Corker

JULY 1 / CANONIZED IN 1975
Courage; Facing Death; Martyrs

288. Claude la Colombiére
(1641–1682)

All our life is sown with tiny thorns that produce in our hearts a thousand involuntary movements of hatred, envy, fear, impatience, a thousand little fleeting disappointments, a thousand slight worries, a thousand disturbances that momentarily alter our peace of soul. For example, a word escapes that should not have been spoken. Or someone utters another that offends us. A child inconveniences you. A bore stops you. You don't like the weather. Your work is not going according to plan. A piece of furniture is broken. A dress is torn.

I know that these are not occasions for practicing very heroic virtue. But they would definitely be enough to acquire it if we really wished to.

—Claude la Colombiére

St. Claude la Colombiére was one of the most effective preachers of the seventeenth century. Intelligent, practical, and articulate, his preaching helped turn the tide against Jansenism. Against this heretical view that humans could not obey God without the intervention of overpowering grace, he celebrated our freedom to choose submission. Calmly accepting even the tiniest vexations, as he argued above, could be chances to surrender to God.

At seventeen, Claude said, he overcame a temporary revulsion against religious life and joined the Jesuits at Avignon. His earliest assignments included teaching boys grammar and tutoring the sons of J. B. Colbert, finance minister to King Louis XIV.

When he turned thirty-three, Claude made his profession as a Jesuit. Reflecting on the significance of Christ's thirty-third year, he decided he must die more completely to himself. Thus he made a promise to follow exactly the Jesuit rule and to obey his superiors without question. "It seems right, dear Lord," he wrote, "that I should live in you and for you alone, at the age when you died for all and for me in particular."

The next year he was made head of the Jesuit college at Paray-le-Monial, where he met **St. Margaret Mary Alacoque.** As her spiritual director, he assured her of the authenticity of her revelations about the Sacred Heart. His writings provided a sound theological basis for the devotion and his preaching helped spread it.

In 1676, because of his reputation for holiness and oratory, Claude was sent to London as preacher to Mary Beatrice d'Este, duchess of York. He became well-known not only for his finely-tuned sermons, but also for encouraging persecuted Catholics, restoring lapsed Catholics, and converting Protestants. During the Popish Plot, when Titus Oates falsely accused Catholics of planning to assassinate King Charles II, he was imprisoned. King Louis XIV negotiated Claude's release and exile to France, depriving him of martyrdom. But his ordeal in prison made the saint an invalid and he died at Paray-le-Monial in 1682.

Once Claude wrote to a dying nun whose consciousness of guilt made her fear God's wrath:

Do you know what would stir up my confidence, if I were as near to giving account to God as you are? It would be the number and the seriousness of my sins.

Here is a confidence really worthy of God. Far from allowing us to be depressed at the sight of our faults, it strengthens us in the idea of the infinite goodness of our Creator. Confidence inspired by purity of life does not give very much glory to God. Is this all that God's mercy can achieve—saving a soul that has never offended him? For sure the confidence of a notorious sinner honors God most of all. For he is so convinced of God's infinite mercy that all his sins seem no more than an atom in its presence.

FEBRUARY 15 / CANONIZED IN 1992
Facing Death; Perseverance; Simple Obedience; Sin

289. Margaret Mary Alacoque
(1647–1690)

St. Margaret Mary was responsible for the widespread public devotion to the Sacred Heart in the last few centuries. Since she had neither the gift nor the means to create a worldwide religious movement, this was a remarkable accomplishment.

At age twenty-four, Margaret Mary entered the Visitation convent at Paray-le-Monial in France. In 1673 she began to experience apparitions of Christ that occurred over an eighteen-month period. In the first vision, he told her to spread devotion to his Sacred Heart.

> He made me lean for a long time on his divine breast, while he revealed to me the marvels of his love and the inexplicable secrets of his Sacred Heart. He told me things which before he had always hidden from me. Now he disclosed them for the first time. But he did it in so plain and effective a manner as to leave me no room for doubting it. I am always afraid of deceiving myself about what I say has taken place within me. But the results that this grace produced in me made me sure of it. This is what seems to have happened:
>
> He said to me: "My Divine Heart is so in love with people, and with you in particular, that it can no longer contain the flames of its ardent charity. It needs you to spread them. It must manifest itself to people and enrich them with the precious treasures that I will reveal to you. These treasures are the graces of salvation and sanctification, necessary to rescue people from the abyss of perdition."

Six months later Christ showed Margaret Mary how and why his Sacred Heart was to be displayed:

> This divine heart was shown me on a throne of flames. It was more resplendent than the sun and transparent as crystal. The heart had its own adorable wound, and was surrounded by a crown of thorns, signifying the stings caused by our sins. And there was a cross above it.
>
> He told me that his heart was to be honored under the form of a heart of flesh. I was to wear a picture of it on my heart, in order that his heart might impress its love on my heart. He said that he would lavish his graces and blessings wherever this picture was honored publicly.

Then sometime in 1674, Christ spelled out the practices that would become the elements of the modern devotion to the Sacred Heart:

> You shall receive holy communion on the first Friday of each month. And every Thursday night . . . you shall rise between eleven o'clock and midnight, and lie prostrate with me for an hour . . . to appease God's anger and ask mercy for sinners.

Christ also directed Margaret Mary to establish a feast in honor of the Sacred Heart. It was to be held on the Friday after the octave of Corpus Christi. At first the saint met only resistance and ridicule. It was not until **St. Claude la Colombiére** declared her experience to be genuine that she began to be accepted. After 1683 her convent began to celebrate the feast of the Sacred Heart, which soon spread to the Visitation convents throughout France.

Margaret Mary Alacoque died on October 17, 1690.

*When saints like **Lutgarde** and Margaret Mary described their union with the Sacred Heart, they spoke of burning and unbearable pain, mixed with joyful consolation. Perhaps we should be glad that the devotion has been tamed for domestic use. However, what the Lord wants of us has not been reduced: all our love in exchange for all of his.*

OCTOBER 16 / CANONIZED IN 1920
Conversations with God; A Soul Afire; Visions and Visionaries

290. Sebastian Valfré

(1629–1710)

Priests seeking a model might well choose Sebastian Valfré. For nearly sixty years he daily helped the people of Turin, Italy, get closer to Christ. He led worship, preached, held meetings, visited the sick, and heard confessions. But somehow his innate cheerfulness transformed all these activities, making them especially effective. Sebastian's genuine friendliness attracted people. He became their friend and made them friends of God.

In his poor family, Sebastian learned to assume a servant's posture. He worked his way through school because his parents had nothing to give him. He joined the Turin Oratory in 1651 and was ordained a year later.

Sebastian sparked the Turin Oratory to new life. He took charge of the Little Oratory, an association of laypeople that gathered for prayer and study. Immediately successful, his leadership drew young men and women from all levels of society. At forty, he became superior of the community, which he is said to have governed in the kindhearted but firm spirit of the founder of the Oratory, **Philip Neri**.

Sebastian had the power to read consciences, and he used the gift in the confessional to probe souls. His many penitents liked the way he gently compelled them to confront the truth. He could even deal firmly with rough soldiers and criminals because they could feel his compassion.

Widely sought as a spiritual director, Sebastian gave special attention to the sick and suffering. Here is a sample of advice he gave to an invalid in 1691:

> Every illness and every trial is permitted by God as the means whereby we can best ensure our salvation and as the material most fitted for our sanctification. Take your illness as a penance given you by God, who knows the extent of your debts to him as well as the best way in which you can discharge them. You should be content to do as he wishes, for he is satisfied with far less than you owe him.
>
> Read into everything God's explicit will. Suffer with our Lord, uniting your sufferings to his. Don't look for sufferings, but do not refuse them. Value them as precious marks of favor that he bestows on you. Don't desire to exchange them for others, but don't torment yourself

by adding to them. Don't fix your eyes on the lash that scourges you, but kiss and adore the loving hand and heart wielding it.

God is not content to see you merely suffering with patience. He wants you to be grateful and to approve of what he does. So many of the blessed envy you from heaven and would change places with you if they could.

Feel a more lively gratitude towards those who brace you up and invigorate you in your pain than towards those who merely commiserate you. An unpitied pain wins greater merit before God. Never say to God: "Enough!" Simply say: "I am ready." When it's over you will regret having suffered so little and suffered that little so badly. Finally, don't give trouble to those who wait on you, and don't be exacting with your nurses.

In his later years gloom penetrated Sebastian's heart with doubt, fear, and other temptations. But his own spiritual agony did not keep him from his service. Even at eighty in the dead of winter he would gather poor children around him in the street and encourage them with the good news. He died on January 30, 1710.

Grant, O Lord that your sacred body in Holy Communion may be my last refreshment. And your sweet name, Jesus, the last word on my lips.

—Sebastian Valfré

JANUARY 30 / BEATIFIED IN 1834
Doubt; Great Pastors; Joy; Kindness; Suffering

291. Francis di Geronimo
(1642–1716)

Passion to rescue sinners consumed Jesuit missioner St. Francis di Geronimo. Enormously popular in central Italy, he came to be known as the "Apostle of Naples." Hundreds always turned out to hear him preach and then lined up to confess to him.

The following letter Francis wrote to a rebellious teenager reflects his characteristic kindness:

> My very dear child,
>
> I today called upon your father, and not seeing you as I usually do, I asked where you were. Imagine the grief I felt when I heard you had so lately left home, through circumstances upon which it is unnecessary to enlarge, as you know all about them even better than I do. I am not in the least surprised to find that you allowed yourself to be overcome by a sudden impulse, for we are but human, all of us, subject to many failures, and full of debts. But it is high time you should come to yourself, and repair an error committed in haste.
>
> You must remember that your dear father has, in reproving you, no object except your real good. Therefore, I entreat you to return home without delay, and thus to fulfill your duty to God, to myself, and to your father, who at my request has promised to receive you as kindly as if you had not done wrong. Should you feel somewhat embarrassed at the idea of appearing alone in his presence, call at the professed house, and I will accompany you home. You have done wrong, my son, and you are now bound to repair your fault. I feel certain that you will do as I wish, and that before Sunday I shall have the pleasure of seeing you again.

Francis's tender mercy compelled him to seek out people hardened by vice and crime. He frequented prisons and roved back streets, often preaching spontaneously to passersby. One night during a storm, for example, he felt led to preach in an abandoned street. A woman heard him through an open window. Distressed by her sin, she approached him the next morning and repented. Reportedly, Francis annually converted about four hundred "worst cases." Among the most famous of his penitents was Mary Alvira Cassier. She had murdered her father and, then disguised as a man, had served in the Spanish army. Under the priest's direction she not only changed her life but also gained a reputation for holiness.

Francis also worked to improve the circumstances of the poor. For example, he employed out-of-work and sick people in making rosaries of olive-wood beads. Once near the end of his life he thanked a priest who sent him supplies with the following note. It proclaims his persistent life theme:

> Thank you for all the trouble you have taken in procuring me the beads I wanted for my rosaries. See that you take no less trouble in procuring for yourself a good ship of war, well furnished with guns, in order to make war upon sin, and strike terror into the powers of hell.

As a young Jesuit, Francis had begged to be sent as a missionary to Japan. But his superiors told him that the kingdom of Naples would be his Japan and his India. And so for forty years he served there, preaching over a hundred missions and transforming thousands of lives. After a long sickness, he died at the age of seventy-four.

> *Confession heals, confession justifies, confession grants pardon of sin. All hope consists in confession. In confession there is a chance for mercy. Believe it firmly. Hope and have confidence in confession.*
>
> —Isidore of Seville

MAY 11 / CANONIZED IN 1839
Kindness; Mercy; Saints and Sacraments (Reconciliation); Sin

292. Louis de Montfort
(1673–1716)

Some Catholics did not like St. Louis de Montfort and opposed him lifelong. His unconventional and emotional missions to the poor made them uncomfortable. But the poor loved him. They crowded to hear him preach, watch his mini-dramas, sing his hymns, and learn to pray the rosary. And at his urging, to reform their lives. A poor man himself, Louis identified with the impoverished underclass he served. He had a gift to lift their hearts to God.

In 1700, newly ordained, Louis was assigned to a hospital in Poitiers, France, which he reorganized and improved. During his tenure he formed a religious community from the staff and inmates that became the Daughters of Divine Wisdom. But his success bred resentment, so he was forced to resign.

Undaunted, Louis began preaching missions to the poor. However, his enemies denounced him to the bishop, who banned him from Poitiers. Then Louis walked to Rome to get the approval of Pope Clement XI. The pope gave him the title "missionary apostolic" and sent him back to France. Thus authorized, the saint went to his native Brittany, where he evangelized the poor for the rest of his life.

Louis's opponents disdained book burnings he staged, with the devil displayed as a society woman. Or the emotionalism he evoked when he rolled on the ground, portraying a dying sinner for whose soul the devil and a guardian angel competed. But his preaching touched the poor and brought some meaning to their lives. For example, consider this sermon excerpt:

> If you live the same life as Jesus Christ, your thorn-crowned Head, you must expect only thorns, scourgings, nails—you must look only for the cross. For the disciple must be treated as his master, and the member as its head. And if God offered for your choice, as he offered to **St. Catherine of Siena**, a crown of thorns or a crown of roses, without hesitating choose with her the crown of thorns and press it down upon your head that you may resemble Jesus Christ.
>
> You know that you are the living temple of the Holy Spirit. You are to be placed as so many living stones by the God of love in the building of the heavenly Jerusalem. You must expect then to be hewn and cut and chiseled with the hammer and chisel of the cross. Otherwise

> you will remain as rough stones that are good for nothing but to be despised and thrown away.
>
> Don't wince under the hammer that strikes you. Have an eye to the chisel that cuts you and to the hand that shapes you. The skillful and loving Architect may wish to make of you the chief stones of his eternal edifice and the fairest statues in his kingdom. Then let him do it. He loves you. He knows what he is doing. He has had experience. All his blows are skillful and straight and loving. He never misses, unless you cause him to by your impatience.

Louis de Montfort devoted himself to the Blessed Virgin. He always taught his hearers how to pray the rosary. Today, people still use his book, *True Devotion to the Blessed Virgin* which was popular in his own time. And near the end of his life he organized a few associates who shared his devotion to the Virgin into the Company of Mary. He died suddenly in 1716 at forty-three years of age.

Virgin, faithful pure, God's chosen Mother,
Fill me with a measure of your faith;
That way will Wisdom come to me
And all His attendant treasures.

—Louis de Montfort

APRIL 28 / CANONIZED IN 1947
Celebration of Discipline; Evangelization; Mary; Missionaries; Serving the Poor

293. Mary of the Angels
(1661–1717)

Little Mary Fontanella, age six, schemed with her younger brother to imitate the saints and run away to live "in the desert." But on the appointed day they slept in and spoiled their plans. A decade later, however, Mary entered a personal desert when she joined the Carmelite convent of St. Cristina at Turin, Italy. At first she was overcome with homesickness, detested the pattern of life, and did not get along with the novice mistress. But she persevered and was professed as Sister Mary of the Angels.

Then came an even more serious trial. An extended period of spiritual darkness engulfed Mary. And constant attacks from evil spirits and other diabolical manifestations intensified her desolation. But guided by a wise spiritual director, after three years she finally emerged from her struggle to a more peaceful and deeper life of prayer.

Mary did not think the adversities that had overwhelmed her were enough penance for her sins. So she aggressively tortured her body with unusual ascetical practices, including binding her tongue with an iron ring and suspending herself from ropes in the form of a cross. Contemporary Christians judge such things as excessive, and one biographer cautioned that no one ought either to admire or imitate Mary's penances.

Sister Mary of the Angels was elected novice mistress at age thirty and prioress at age thirty-three. She governed the Carmel at St. Cristina competently. If her own piety had its extremes, her direction for her sisters was more balanced, as her meditation in preparation for Christmas demonstrated:

> Purity is so pleasing to God that his divine Son, having resolved to become man by the operation of the Holy Spirit, wished to be born of a virgin mother. We all know with what an abundance of graces and with what extraordinary purity God was pleased to adorn the body and soul of Mary. Thus he made her a dwelling worthy of the Word who was to become flesh in her chaste womb. So if we wish to induce the Incarnate God to be born spiritually in our souls, we must secure purity of conscience for ourselves. The right way to accomplish this is to banish from our hearts even the smallest faults and cultivate in them all the virtues.

> Ah, how great is your goodness, my Jesus! Although I have so deeply offended you, you still wish to clothe yourself with human flesh and to take on yourself all my sins in order to obtain their pardon for me. I deserved to see you sitting in the tribunal of divine justice as a judge angered against one capable of so many failings. And instead I find you in the bosom of Mary, a savior full of indulgence for my sins. O Lamb of God! How efficacious the sweetness of your love should be in softening the hardness of my heart! I detest my sins with all my strength because they are opposed to your infinite goodness. Imprint on my heart such repentance that I may prefer to die rather than ever to offend you again.

When the sisters were about to elect Mary to a fifth term as prioress, she begged God that if it were his will she might soon die. Three weeks later her prayer was answered and she fell ill and died on December 16, 1717.

> *O radiant Lily of Mary, come to dwell in my soul. However unworthy it be, never leave it again, O my good Jesus. O Sun of Justice, come and dispel the darkness in which my soul is plunged.*
>
> —Mary of the Angels

DECEMBER 16 / BEATIFIED IN 1865
Mary; Passion for Purity; Repentance; Suffering

294. John Baptist de La Salle
(1651–1719)

A wealthy nobleman and canon of Rheims cathedral in France, St. John Baptist de La Salle was on track for a life of ease as an endowed clergyman. Circumstances, however, derailed him and put him on a revolutionary course as a Christian educational reformer—a pioneer in education for the working classes, in the training of teachers, and in the rehabilitation of delinquents.

As a young priest de La Salle collaborated with a layman, Adrian Nyel, to found two schools for poor boys. His early attempts to train and discipline his rough-edged schoolmasters drove them away. But he soon gathered more mature men who joined him in his effort to educate and Christianize youths in a society that gave them little opportunity for improvement.

As the work expanded, John Baptist resigned his canonry and distributed all his money for famine relief among the poor. In the 1680s he opened four schools. Then he founded a junior novitiate for teens aspiring to become teachers and training colleges for teachers at Rheims, Paris, and Saint-Denis. From these groups he drew men into a religious community devoted to education, the Brothers of the Christian Schools. To maintain focus on teaching and to prevent distinctions among the brothers, de La Salle decided that none would ever become a priest. And as the following passage shows, he trained them in the pattern of Christian love:

> Adapt yourself with gracious and charitable compliance to all your neighbor's weaknesses. In particular, make a rule to hide your feelings in many inconsequential matters. Give up all bitterness toward your neighbor, no matter what. And be convinced that your neighbor is in everything better than you. This will not be difficult if you keep even a little aware of yourself. It will give you the ability to overcome your feelings of resentment.
>
> Each day look for every possible opportunity to do a kindness for those you do not like. After examining yourself on this matter every morning, decide what you are going to do, and do it faithfully with kindness and humility.
>
> Be sure to be warmly affable toward everyone. Speak to and answer everyone with very great gentleness and deference. Keep in mind the way the Lord spoke and replied to others even when he was most

> harshly treated. Never comment on the faults or the behavior of your neighbors. When others speak of them, put a good interpretation on their actions. If you cannot, say nothing at all.
>
> In short, decide never to speak of the failings of others nor to reprimand them no matter how serious they seem to you. When you see someone fall into some fault, call to mind the gospel saying, "You can see the splinter in your brother's eye, but you cannot see the beam in your own" (see Matthew 7:3).

Secular schoolmasters, Jansenists, and people who did not believe in educating the poor opposed John Baptist's schools, embroiling him with lawsuits and forced closures. But the Brothers of the Christian Schools persisted. By the turn of the eighteenth century they had established schools throughout France and in Rome, including an innovative reformatory for troubled youths in Dijon, France.

John Baptist de La Salle died in 1719 at the age of sixty-eight. Today his Christian Brothers number more than twenty thousand throughout the world.

John Baptist de La Salle helped revolutionize elementary education. His schools grouped children in classes, gave instruction in the vernacular instead of Latin, employed the simultaneous method of older children tutoring younger, and required silence during lessons—an approach that is still successfully pursued.

APRIL 7 / CANONIZED IN 1900 / PATRON OF SCHOOLTEACHERS
Christian Living; Innovative Saints; Raising Christian Youth

295. Veronica Giuliani
(1660–1727)

For fifty years Ursula Giuliani lived as Sister Veronica in the Capuchin convent of Città di Castello in Umbria, Italy. With gritty determination tempered by humility, she led her sisters as novice mistress for thirty-four years and as abbess for eleven. St. Veronica governed the convent with obvious common sense. For example, so that her young novices would not get puffed up with pride, she forbade them to read the elevated works of the great spiritual masters. Instead she required them to study books on Christian basics. And as a most practical woman, she improved her sisters' comfort by enlarging the convent rooms and having water piped inside.

Like **Teresa of Ávila,** another very down-to-earth saint, Veronica enjoyed an unusually profound communion with God. In the following excerpt from her *Diary*, she struggled to put into words her experience of the divine presence:

> While I was about to go to Holy Communion, I seemed to be thrown wide open like a door flung open to welcome a close friend and then shut tight after his entry. So my heart was alone with him—alone with God. It seems impossible to relate all the effects, feelings, leaping delight and festivity my soul experienced.
>
> If I were to speak, for example, of all the happy and pleasant times shared with dear friends . . . , I would be saying nothing comparable to this joy. And if I were to add up all the occasions of rejoicing in the universe, I would be saying that all this amounts to little or nothing beside what, in an instant, my heart experiences in the presence of God. Or rather what God does to my heart, because all these other things flow from him and are his works.
>
> Love makes the heart leap and dance. Love makes it exult and be festive. Love makes it sing and be silent as it pleases. Love grants it rest and enables it to act. Love possesses it and gives it everything. Loves takes it over completely and dwells in it. But I am unable to say more because if I wished to relate all the effects that my heart experiences in the act of going to Holy Communion and also at other times, I would never finish saying everything. It is sufficient to say that communion is a . . . mansion of love itself.

Veronica had a lifelong devotion to Christ crucified that eventually became manifested in physical signs. The marks of the crown of thorns appeared on her forehead in 1694 and the five wounds on her body in 1697. Veronica was humiliated by the stigmata itself and by her bishop's rigorous testing of her experience. He removed the saint from ordinary community life and put her under constant observation. When he decided that the phenomena were authentic, he allowed her to return to normal convent life and continue her service to her sisters. In 1727, Veronica died of apoplexy at the age of sixty-seven.

> *I see an infinite number of crucified persons in the world, but few who are crucified by the love of Jesus. Some are crucified by their self-love and inordinate love of the world. But happy are they who are crucified for the love of Jesus. Happy are they who live and die on the cross with Jesus.*
>
> —John Eudes

JULY 9 / CANONIZED IN 1839
A Passionate Love; Prayer; Stigmata

296. Lucy Filippini
(1672–1732)

Little known outside of Italy, St. Lucy Filippini deserves more widespread recognition. At a time when few women played a significant role in the world or the church, she helped develop an important association of professional laywomen. With Cardinal Marcantonio Barbarigio and several dynamic women, she cofounded the Maestre Pie, the Institute of Religious Teachers. Cardinal Barbarigio shaped the institute at Montefiascone and recruited Lucy to lead it. Lucy's magnetic personality drew women to the association and her energetic leadership spread the institute throughout the country.

Reminiscent of the early work of **St. Angela Merici**, the Maestre Pie arranged for women to live the life of a religious while serving in the world. Thus, members enjoyed the best of both the lay and religious states of life. An instruction for the institute that Lucy disseminated to its branches explained the benefits of the approach:

> The life of our teachers is free from the restrictions of the cloister and the distractions of the world. They thus enjoy the prerogatives of both states of life without being hindered by their disadvantages. Those who are sheltered in a cloister find less occasion for sin and greater assurance of salvation. But they lack the opportunity and merit of working directly for the salvation of souls. Those who live in the world have a greater opportunity to practice the works of mercy, even if their salvation is exposed to greater dangers.
>
> To discover the secret of a middle course is to find a third state of life in which teachers harmonize the duties of the religious life with those of the secular life. They separate whatever is useful and perfect in those two states of life from what is less advantageous for their souls. And they willingly accept the labors and hardships of those states. Deprived of worldly satisfactions, they must live like solitaries. But renouncing the peace and repose of solitaries, they are to dedicate themselves to works of charity.
>
> This sort of life is not new in the church. Christian virgins of the early church followed this mode of life when there were neither convents nor monasteries. These chaste spouses of the Lord lived in the midst of the world. Their own virtue and the respect with which they were surrounded was sufficient protection for their innocence. They wisely divided their time among contemplation, divine worship

and works of charity. So they were neither idle in their solitude nor distracted in their charitable works.

Lucy used her superb teaching and speaking gifts to introduce the institute throughout the country. All the women of a town would come to hear her speak at parish retreats. So the work spread rapidly. In 1707, Pope Clement XI invited Lucy to set up a branch of Maestre Pie in Rome. And in six months she had established a school that attracted more pupils than it could accommodate.

In 1726, Lucy was afflicted with cancer and could not continue her work. She died six years later on March 25, 1732.

Women like Lucy Filippini and Angela Merici pioneered groups that enable laypeople in the world to live a disciplined spiritual life. They paved the way for a great diversity of modern lay associations—secular institutes, pious societies, fraternities, sodalities, covenant communities, prayer groups—that have made the contemporary church more relevant and resilient.

MARCH 25 / CANONIZED IN 1930
Innovative Saints; Contemplatives in Action; Leading Women

297. Peter Sanz
(1680–1747)

Enflamed with a desire to bring China to Christ, around 1711, Peter Sanz, a young Dominican from Spain, set sail for the Philippines to learn Chinese. During thirteen months at sea Peter suffered constant sickness, but when he arrived at Manila he recovered miraculously. In a short two-and-a-half years he mastered the complex Chinese idiom. And in June 1715, Peter and a companion arrived in Fu-Kien.

For thirty-one years till his martyrdom, Peter Sanz, a great-spirited priest, led the Dominican mission at Fu-Kien. An aggressive persecution broke out in 1729, exiling him to Canton for six years. In 1730, Peter was consecrated as a bishop, and five years later he returned to direct the mission until his arrest in 1746. That year a major persecution erupted in Fu-Kien. A man Peter had refused funds brought formal charges against him and his associates, Spanish Dominican Fathers Francis Serrano, Joachim Royo, John Alcober, and Francis Diaz. He accused them of breaking the laws and converting people to Catholicism. All were arrested and brutally tortured, beaten on the face with boards and having their feet crushed in clamps. After suffering in prison for a year, Peter and his companions were taken in chains to Fou-Cheou and condemned to be beheaded. The following account described Peter's martyrdom:

> On the 25th of May, 1747, the Imperial decree commanding Peter Sanz to be beheaded immediately arrived at Fou-Cheou. The prison was invaded by a troop of ruffians shouting "Where is Pe-te-to?" The holy bishop, who was sitting praying his rosary, instantly rose, saying, "Here I am." They took off his handcuffs, and shaved the back of his head. "What does this mean?" asked the bishop of Father Serrano.
>
> "They are shaving your head that the edge of the sword may meet with no obstacle," he answered. "It is well," replied the bishop. "Please give me absolution." He made his confession in few words. . . .
>
> When he reached the prefect's tribunal, he asked which soldier was going to be his executioner, for he had put aside a small sum to reward him. But he was only answered by a kick and told, "Kneel down and be silent."
>
> A tablet was fastened between his arms, declaring, "Pe-te-to has been condemned to death as a warning and example to all because by

> his lies and hypocrisy he has seduced the souls of men." He was then led through the streets to the place of execution.
>
> The procession stopped outside the city by a large stone in the middle of the road and the valiant soldier of Christ knew that his Calvary was reached. "Wait a moment," he said to the executioner, "give me time to recommend my soul to God."
>
> Finishing his prayer, he said to the executioner, "My friend! I am going to heaven!" "Ah, how I wish I were going with you," the man replied. "Well, if you want to save your soul," said the bishop, "you must obey the law of God." Then he lay his head upon the stone and told the executioner to perform his office. With a single blow, he freed the soul of the blessed martyr.

The following year Peter's four Dominican associates were executed in prison.

> *Christianity is a warfare, and Christians spiritual soldiers. In its beginning, our faith was planted in the poverty, infamy, persecution and death of Christ. In its progress, it was watered by the blood of God's saints. And it cannot come to the full growth unless it be fostered with the showers of the martyrs' blood.*
>
> —Robert Southwell

MAY 26 / BEATIFIED IN 1893
Martyrs; Missionaries

298. Leonard of Port Maurice
(1676–1751)

The charism of one person often generates spiritual renewal for many others, as did the gift of St. Leonard Casanova. In the first half of the eighteenth century, from his bases in Rome and Florence, he preached throughout northern Italy, his words gently turning thousands to God. The churches could not hold the crowds that gathered for Leonard's parish missions. So like that other great eighteenth-century evangelist, John Wesley, he often held open-air meetings. He used the stations of the cross as illustrations in his talks and popularized the devotion by installing 571 sets of stations throughout Italy. He even built stations of the cross in the Coliseum, thus reclaiming for the church the place where many early Christians imitated Christ's passion in heroic martyrdoms.

Born in 1676 at Port Maurice on the Italian Riviera, at twenty-one Leonard joined a strict branch of Franciscans called the Riformella. He quickly became a leader in the community. For more than fifty years his lively spirituality and exemplary asceticism inspired his brothers and attracted young recruits to the order.

Many sought out Leonard for spiritual direction. His letters to advisees convey a commonsense Christianity, still fresh today, as the following example demonstrates:

> To speak quite frankly, my dear brother, I believe you are under a delusion. You seem to have got into your head the silly notion that it is impossible for you to live chastely. With this false principle fixed in your mind, at each temptation you immediately give up.
>
> True, without God's grace we cannot live a chaste life. But it is also true that God gives his grace to those who try their best. "From the man who does what lies in him God withholds not grace" (see Psalm 84:11).
>
> So when temptation comes, turn straight to God, and he will help you. He said so, clearly: "Seek and you shall receive" (see Matthew 7:7). With God's help you will keep from sin.
>
> Impress, then, on yourself this great truth. Even if all hell's devils came against you to tempt you, you won't sin unless you want to—provided that you trust not in your own powers, but in the assistance of God. He doesn't refuse help to those who ask it with a lively faith.

> This is the only way to get clear of the labyrinth you are in. Of course, you must avoid dangerous occasions and keep guard over your eyes. Try it, and you will see the good results. Meanwhile, I recommend you to God, that he may give you the true spirit of penance and mortification without which it is no easy thing to triumph over so degrading a vice. May God bless you.

Leonard's declining years were marked with failures. Sent by the doge of Genoa to preach peace in Corsica, Leonard was rebuffed by unruly crowds of young men brandishing arms. Six months of strenuous effort on the island wore him down and his health declined. His last missions in Lucca and other towns met indifference, resistance, and hostility. With his voice faltering, he continued to preach until his death at Rome on November 26, 1751.

Once at the port of Civitavecchia, Leonard preached for three weeks to hard-bitten seamen, soldiers, galley slaves, and convicts. Many stony hearts were softened, including those of several English sailors. "The poor fellows," he said, "had been more touched by what they saw than what they heard, for they hardly understood the language at all—which only shows that grace is the prime mover in stirring the heart."

NOVEMBER 26 / CANONIZED IN 1867 / PATRON OF PARISH MISSIONS
Christian Living; Grace; Great Preachers; Passion for Purity; Sexual Temptation

299. Gerard Majella
(1726–1755)

Frail and sickly from childhood, St. Gerard Majella lived only twenty-nine years. But all during that short time he enjoyed a remarkable closeness to God. Once, for example, kneeling before the altar, he was overheard shouting, "Lord, I beg you to let me go. I have work I must do!"

Gerard spent his youth as a hardworking tailor's apprentice and as a bishop's servant. From 1745 to 1752 he ran his own tailor shop to support his mother. Then in 1752 he became a Redemptorist lay brother in Caposele, Italy, where he served three years as infirmarian, tailor, traveling companion, and porter.

Gerard manifested unusual miraculous powers that attracted much attention. He used his gifts of healing, prophecy, and reading consciences to make many people whole. But his reputation as the eighteenth century's greatest wonder-worker stems from his ability to bilocate. On numerous occasions witnesses reported that he was seen ministering to people in two places at once.

Even before he became a Redemptorist, Gerard practiced extreme forms of mortification. Once at the direction of his superior, he wrote this summary of his penitential disciplines:

> Mortifications for every day. I take the discipline once. I wear a chain nine inches broad and eighteen long as a cincture. Upon rising and going to bed, I make nine crosses on the floor with my tongue. With one portion of my lunch and dinner I mix bitter herbs or wormwood. I wear on my breast a heart studded with iron points. At least three times a day I chew bitter herbs or wormwood. I say in the morning and evening six Hail Marys with my face on the ground.
>
> Wednesdays, Fridays and Saturdays, and on all vigils, I eat my meals kneeling. Moreover, at lunch as well as dinner I make nine crosses with my tongue on the floor. And on all these days I leave untouched the fruit that is served. On Fridays at noon, I partake only of two courses, and at supper of one. On Saturdays I fast on bread and water.
>
> On Wednesdays, Fridays and Saturdays during sleep, I gird my forehead with a little chain. I put another about my waist. I lie upon the same heavy chain that serves as my belt during the day. I always wear a chain around my arm.

> During all novenas that precede feasts of Our Lord, our Blessed Mother and of other saints, besides all the previously listed penances, I scourge myself to blood during the novena and on every ordinary day in it.

In a religious culture that admired such practices, the Redemptorists did not seem to find Gerard's self-abnegation excessive. But some of Gerard's letters in which he complained about agonizing depression and desolation may indicate some connection between his self-torture and his mental anguish.

Two popes praised Gerard Majella as a model for lay brothers and young men. However, the church calls us to imitate his piety, service, and generosity. Not his wonders or his disciplines. The saint wore himself out serving his brothers and the poor at Caposele. He died there in 1755.

> *Be courageous, do not be cast down. Trust in God and hope that he will grant you every grace. Do not rely on yourself, but rather on the Lord, and if you imagine that all is calm, then be assured that the enemy is quite near. Do not put too much confidence in peace, for in the midst of rest war may break out.*
>
> —Gerard Majella

OCTOBER 16 / CANONIZED IN 1904 / PATRON OF EXPECTANT MOTHERS
Miracles Do Happen; Twenty-Something Saints

300. John Baptist de Rossi
(1698–1764)

On a superficial level St. John Baptist de Rossi's life was uneventful. A simple priest, for forty years he worked in the capacity of an assistant pastor in Rome. On a spiritual level, however, he touched thousands of needy people—the sick, the homeless, prostitutes, transient cattle drivers who came to market in Rome, and other rough sorts. By day he devoted himself to the sick poor in Rome's hospitals. By night he ministered to street people at a refuge.

Caregivers can look to John Baptist as a model. Before he would speak to a dying person about salvation, he did all he could to relieve their suffering. No service for the sick, no matter how repugnant, repulsed him. And his selflessness won people's hearts. Once, for example, a young man dying of syphilis rebuffed de Rossi's attention until the priest emptied his bedpan. Touched by John Baptist's humble care, the fellow finally listened to him and made a good confession before he died.

Other priests and penitents were amazed by John Baptist's persuasiveness in the confessional. With a few gentle words he turned people's lives. Once a young man came to him who was sexually entangled with a woman who kept coming to his house under the pretense of washing and mending his clothes. A brief conversation with John Baptist broke the youth's addiction. As a sign of his cure, the next day he brought the priest a pile of his clothes he had taken from the woman.

John Baptist exhorted others to follow his example in caring for souls. Here is an excerpt from one of his sermons to his fellow priests:

> Ignorance is the leprosy of the soul. How many such lepers exist in the church here in Rome, where many people don't even know what's necessary for their salvation? It must be our business to try to cure this disease.
>
> Like the child Jesus, we also must be about our Father's business—the saving of the souls of our brothers and sisters. The souls of our neighbors are in our hands, and yet how many are lost through our fault? The sick die without being properly prepared because we have not given time or care enough to each particular case. Yet with a little

> more patience, a little more perseverance, a little more love, we could have led these poor souls to heaven.
>
> Many of us shrink from going to the hospitals from fear of infection or from the sights and smells that await us there. Courage! We are not in the world to follow our own will and pleasure, but to imitate the Lord. If we experience some repugnance in our work, either from its nature or from the unwillingness of the poor to listen to us, let's remember the example of **St. Francis de Sales**. He shrank from no labor, no fatigue, and was rewarded by the return to the church of seventy thousand people. When reproached for having shortened his life by these means, he said: "It's not necessary that I should live, but that souls should be saved." This must also be our motto.

John Baptist de Rossi, himself worn out by his unselfish service, suffered a stroke in 1763 and died a year later.

> *The poor come to church tired and distracted by their daily troubles. If you preach a long sermon they can't follow you. Give them one idea that they can take home, not half a dozen, or one will drive out the other, and they will remember none.*
>
> —John Baptist de Rossi

MAY 23 / CANONIZED IN 1881
Care of the Sick; Care of the Soul; Evangelization; Saints and Sacraments (Reconciliation)

301. Marguerite d'Youville
(1701–1771)

Name the trouble, and St. Marguerite d'Youville of Quebec, Canada, suffered it: her father's early death, poverty, an unfaithful husband, a nasty mother-in-law, infant deaths, bankruptcy, fire, ridicule, persecution, and more. Yet Marguerite seems joyfully to have trusted God to carry her through these terrible circumstances.

When Marguerite's father died in 1714, she left school to help her mother support her family. At twenty-one she entered a disastrous arranged marriage with François d'Youville, a dashing but irresponsible young fur trader. He got Indians drunk and ripped them off, slept around, and squandered the family fortune. On top of this, four of Marguerite's six babies died. However, sometime in 1727, Marguerite had an extraordinary personal experience of God the Father's love for her. That grace enabled her to endure François and his domineering mother without complaint, until his death in 1730 released her.

Marguerite devoted the rest of her life to caring for the poor of Montreal. In 1737, she and three companions made a private commitment to serve the destitute. They rented a house as a place to welcome indigent boarders. When fire destroyed the building in 1745, Marguerite knelt in the ashes, prayed a thankful *Te Deum*, and promised the poor that she would never abandon them. Shortly after, she and her companions signed the "Original Commitment" which became the basis for her religious order. Here is an excerpt from that document:

> We, the undersigned, for the greater glory of God, the salvation of our souls and the relief of the poor, sincerely desiring to leave the world, renouncing everything we own to consecrate ourselves unreservedly to the service of the poor, have joined together in the bonds of the purest charity. . . . We have unanimously agreed and have freely promised. . . :
>
> To live together for the remainder of our lives in perfect union and charity, under the guidance of those superiors who will be given to us, in the practice and faithful observance of the rule prescribed for us; . . . in poverty and complete renunciation, . . . placing everything we now own and will own in common, not retaining ownership nor any right to dispose of it, making a pure, simple and irrevocable gift of it to the poor by this document. . . .

> To devote unreservedly our time, our days, our effort, our life itself to work, and, putting the income in common, to provide for the support and maintenance of the poor.
>
> To shelter, feed and support as many poor people as we can either by our own means or by the alms of the faithful.
>
> All those who will be taken into the house will bring everything they own with them—linens, clothing, furniture and silver, to put everything in common not excepting or retaining anything, renouncing all rights of ownership and of retention, by the voluntary and irrevocable gift they will make of it to the members of Jesus Christ. . . .

So Marguerite began to formalize her little band of associates into a religious community. In 1755 the bishop of Quebec approved the congregation as the Sisters of Charity. They adopted a gray habit and so were called the Grey Sisters. Because drunks often flopped on their doorsteps, persecutors mockingly tagged them "the tipsy sisters," as the French word *gris* could mean "drunk" as well as "gray." After Marguerite's death in 1771, the Grey Sisters extended her ministry throughout the world, especially to the Inuit people of North America.

Sometimes we hold to the mistaken idea that when God puts his hand on us everything will move forward with ease. The life experience of saints like Marguerite d'Youville should dispel that false notion once and for all.

DECEMBER 23 / CANONIZED IN 1990
Difficult Marriages; Serving the Poor; Suffering

302. Paul of the Cross

(1694–1775)

Paul Danei focused himself entirely on the passion of Christ. The sufferings of Christ consumed him like fire, illumined his mind, and directed his actions. "Single-hearted devotion to the cross" sums up his entire life in a few words and justifies his name.

With the exception of a year in the Venetian army fighting the Turks, Paul spent his youth in Menoa, Italy, acquiring the spiritual disciplines. In 1720 the Blessed Mother appeared to him wearing a black habit with a white emblem bearing Christ's name and a cross. She directed him to establish a community dedicated to preaching the passion.

In 1727, with his brother and best friend, John Battista, Paul was ordained and founded a new religious order, now called the Passionists. From the start they garbed themselves in the habit Mary had worn in Paul's vision. He viewed his brothers as monk activists. They obligated themselves both to extreme personal austerities and to preaching to the poor. The Passionists soon became known for their parish missions and were in high demand throughout central Italy.

We know the spirituality of St. Paul of the Cross through more than two thousand of his letters. Mostly he concerned himself with prayer and asceticism. Paul sometimes used the traditional imagery of being consumed by fire to describe the soul's union with God. But he also compared growing deeper in Christ with going fishing, as he does in the following composite drawn from several letters:

> Besides, I want you to go fishing sometimes. How? I will tell you. The most holy passion of Jesus is a sea of sorrows but, at the same time a sea of love. Pray to God that he teach you to fish in this sea. Then dive into its depths. No matter how deep you go, you will never reach bottom.
>
> And if, in this solitude in which you are reborn to a new holy life, the Divine Spouse brings you to fish in the sea of his passion, then fish. Allow yourself to be penetrated completely by sorrow and love. In this way, you will thoroughly appropriate the passion of Christ and make his sufferings your own. In this vast sea of the sacred passion, fish for the pearls of all the virtues of Jesus. This divine fishing trip in the sorrows of the Son of God is accomplished without words in pure faith, without leaving solitude or interior silence.

> I have a lively confidence that your Spouse will teach you this divine method of fishing. He will teach it to you if you keep yourself in interior solitude, your mind free from all distraction, detached from all earthly affections, from every created thing, in pure faith and holy love.

Paul became famous as an outstanding preacher, exciting crowds with his words about the cross and sometimes by scourging himself publicly. People regarded him as a living saint because of his austerity and spiritual gifts of healing, prophecy, and reading consciences.

In his declining years Paul founded a cloistered community of Passionist nuns. He died at Rome in 1775 at the age of eighty. After 1840 the Passionists spread to Belgium and England, and then gradually throughout the world.

> *If you cannot spend much time at prayer, no matter: to act well is always to pray well. Be attentive to your duties, and at the same time be attentive to God by frequently purifying your heart in the immense ocean of divine love.*
>
> —Paul of the Cross

OCTOBER 19 / CANONIZED IN 1867
Great Preachers; Intimacy with the Divine; Prayer

303. Benedict Joseph Labre
(1748–1783)

From childhood, St. Benedict Joseph Labre felt called to dedicate himself to God. Recognizing their son's pious disposition, his parents sent him at age twelve to live with an uncle, a pastor who could train him for the priesthood. But Benedict was more inclined to monastic life and dreamed of entering La Trappe, the famous Trappist abbey near Dijon, France.

When his uncle died, he returned home. In 1766, Benedict walked sixty miles to La Trappe, only to be turned away because of his youth. Then he made several attempts to join Carthusian monasteries and further appeals to La Trappe, but all failed. In 1769 the Carthusians at Neuville allowed Benedict to spend six weeks with them as a postulant. But in a short time they judged him unsuitable for communal life and sent him on his way. Upon his dismissal, Benedict wrote this charming letter to his parents:

> This is to tell you that the Carthusians find me unsuited to their life, and that I left them on the second of October; I look on this as a command from God calling me to something more perfect still—they said themselves that it was the hand of God taking me from them. I am therefore setting out for La Trappe, where I have always so longed to go.
>
> I ask your forgiveness for all my disobedience, and for all the sorrow I have caused you. I ask both of you to give me your blessing so that the Lord will be with me. I shall pray for you every day of my life; please do not worry about me. . . . I am glad to be able to feel quite sure that God is leading me.
>
> Be sure you instruct my brothers and sisters carefully, especially my godson; please God I shall not cost you any more, nor cause you any more suffering: pray for me. . . . Thank you for all your goodness to me, for all you have done for me, God will reward you. Give my brothers and sisters the same upbringing you gave me; that is the way to make them happy in heaven; they cannot be saved unless they are taught. . . .
>
> The Lord, whom I received before I left this place, will help and direct me in this undertaking which he has inspired. I will have the fear of him always before me, and love of him in my heart. . . .

Benedict tried to join the Cistercians at Sept-Fons in 1769, but they did not accept him. With that failure, Benedict decided to walk as a pilgrim to Rome. On the way Benedict believed he finally realized what God wanted him to do. He had thought he was supposed to abandon the world by becoming a monk. Now he decided he was to shun the world's allurements while remaining in it.

From that time Benedict imitated the circumstances of the homeless. He never begged, shared alms forced upon him with others, ate what he scrounged from garbage heaps, and never bathed, his body becoming tormented with lice. For three years he made pilgrimages on foot to holy sites. Then in 1774 he went to Rome, where he spent his days praying in churches and his nights sleeping in the Coliseum. The whole city regarded him as a saint and turned out to honor him upon his death in 1783.

Some critics judge that Benedict Joseph Labre suffered from mental illness. Perhaps so, but he seems to resemble the much admired solitaries who shunned the world for the desert—like the great ***Anthony*** *(who did not bathe for eighty years!)—except that Benedict sought his solitude while living in the world.*

APRIL 16 / CANONIZED IN 1883 / PATRON OF THE HOMELESS AND THE MENTALLY ILL
Solitude; Suffering

304. Junípero Serra
(1713–1784)

Franciscan friar Junípero Serra began his professional life as a Spanish university professor. A gifted scholar, even before his ordination in 1738, he was assigned to teach philosophy in his community. After he received his doctorate in theology in 1743, for five years he held the Duns Scotus chair of philosophy at Lullian University in Majorca. But Fra Junípero's heart's desire was to become a missionary. And in 1749 he was dispatched to serve at the Apostolic College of San Fernando in Mexico City.

From 1750 to 1758, Fra Junípero governed the five missions to the Pame Indians in the Sierra Gorda mountains. There the learned scholar trained himself in missionary skills and methods. He decided that to bring the natives to Christ he would have to become one of them. So he mastered their language, treated them as equals, and daily worked side-by-side with them in the fields. Then beginning in 1758 he spent eleven years working at missions throughout Mexico and Lower California.

When the Spanish undertook the conquest of Upper California in 1769, Junípero Serra accompanied the military expedition. That year he established his first mission at San Diego. Between 1770 and 1782, Fra Junípero founded eight more missions, including San Francisco and San Carlos at Monterey-Carmel, which became his base.

The spiritual well-being of the Indians dominated Serra's concerns. Following is a representative letter he wrote from the San Antonio mission in 1771:

> All the missionaries are groaning. We all deplore the vexations, the hardships and the delays that we have to endure. But no one desires or thinks of leaving his mission. The fact is that, hardship or no hardship, many souls are saved in heaven, and souls converted in Monterey, San Antonio and San Diego. Perhaps also in San Gabriel, though I have not heard of any yet. Quite a considerable number of Christians praise God. His holy name is in the mouth of these pagans more often than in that of many Christians. Some have declared that these apparently gentle lambs will some day turn into tigers and lions. However, speaking of our several years' experience with those of Monterey and San Antonio, we can say that every day they grow better.

> Above all, I have personally experienced God's promise to **St. Francis** that pagans merely have to look upon his sons in order to be converted to our holy Catholic faith. For if any here are not Christians, in my judgment it is simply because of our ignorance of the language. I have little grace for learning a new language and interpreters will not be available until some of these people learn Castilian. This difficulty has already been overcome in San Diego, where adults are being baptized and marriages celebrated. We are preparing to do the same here, as the young men are beginning to explain things in Castilian.

At the California missions Fra Junípero baptized six thousand Indians and confirmed five thousand.

He also improved the material welfare of the natives. For example, his introduction of agricultural methods and tools afforded them a better quality of life. He also defended them against the abuses of the military expedition. In 1773, for instance, he went to Mexico City and persuaded the viceroy to implement his "memorial" of thirty-two points to regulate the power of the military and improve the conduct of mission affairs in California.

Junípero Serra died at Carmel in 1784.

You will be my witnesses not only in Jerusalem but throughout Judea and Samaria, and indeed to the earth's remotest end.

—Acts 1:8 *NJB*

AUGUST 28 / BEATIFIED IN 1988
Evangelization; Missionaries

305. Alphonsus Liguori
(1696–1787)

During sixty years of Christian service in central Italy, opposition of every sort stalked St. Alphonsus Liguori. His bullheaded father resisted his ordination. Powerful anticlericals battled the Redemptorists, his religious order. Jansenists denounced *Moral Theology*, his book that sought to correct them. People of rank threatened him because of his reforms as bishop of Sant' Agata. Rheumatism bent his head into his chest, a deformity he suffered for his last twenty years. A controversy between the pope and the king of Naples over the Redemptorist rule resulted in his exclusion from the community he founded. And for two years just before he died, Alphonsus was assailed with a dark night of doubt, fear, and scruples.

A successful lawyer before age 20, Alphonsus used his legal skills lifelong in his writing and the governance of his order and his diocese. He was ordained in 1717 and immediately became well-known as a compassionate confessor and down-to-earth preacher. "I have never preached a sermon," he said, "that the poorest old woman in the congregation could not understand." You can hear his gentle voice in the following excerpt that also suggests the secret behind his perseverance:

> We are now at the end of 1761. Today the New Year of 1762 has begun. How many saw the beginning of the year that has just gone but did not live to see its end! We should give thanks to God that we are allowed to see its conclusion. But do we know whether we shall see the end of this year? Certainly, many will not see it. Who knows if we shall not be among this number? A year must dawn for us that will be our last.
>
> We should awaken our faith and strive for the remainder of our lives to live according to the maxims of our faith. Why should we wait until death overtakes us and finds us living according to the maxims of the world? Let us awaken our faith to realize that this earth is not our true home but that we are merely here as pilgrims.
>
> Our faith will give us confidence in our difficulties, teaching us that whoever prays will be saved. May our faith make us always live with the thought of eternity. Let's keep ever before our eyes this great thought—everything in this world comes to an end, whether it be prosperity or adversity. Eternity alone never ends.

In 1748, St. Alphonsus published his acclaimed *Moral Theology* that steered a middle way between the rigorism of the Jansenists and an irresponsible laxity. At age sixty-six, he reluctantly accepted appointment as bishop of Sant' Agata and worked hard for thirteen years to renew his flock. His resignation in 1775 brought the saint no rest, as he had to fight to protect his community from the state. External politics threatened to divide and destroy the Redemptorists. But the community endured and today has missioners serving throughout the world. Exhausted by a life of extraordinary industry, St. Alphonsus Liguori died on August 1, 1787, two months before his ninety-first birthday.

> *Contradictions, sickness, scruples, spiritual aridity, and all the inner and outward torments are the chisel with which God carves his statues for paradise.*
>
> —Alphonsus Liguori

AUGUST 1 / CANONIZED IN 1839
Doctors of the Church; Enduring Trials; Eternal Perspective; Perseverance

306. Theresa Margaret of the Sacred Heart
(1747–1770)

In 1764, at age seventeen, Anna Maria Redi entered **St. Teresa of Ávila**'s convent at Florence, Italy. Her heart's desire was to imitate the famous foundress, and she got her wish. Anna Maria invaded the convent, refreshing the nuns with her friendliness, service, and purposefulness. And God seems to have invaded Anna Maria, hastening her growth to Christian maturity.

When we read the saint's writing we feel that we are communicating with someone much older. Someone with a wisdom distilled from many years' experience, not a young adult barely twenty years old. Consider this expression of the saint's life theme:

> To possess ourselves of Holy Love, we must call to mind the presence of God and place ourselves in that presence. Just as one in the world loving someone of the world often has him in his thoughts, so we must frequently remind ourselves that God is always present, and that he always has us in his thoughts for our good and happiness. In loving, one must render love for love. Therefore, if God has loved us always and so much, regardless of our merit, what must we, who have been so loved, do to requite him for his love? We must make ourselves like . . . Jesus in humility, kindness, sweetness, saying to ourselves whenever we experience the weariness and repugnance that can come to anyone, "Without complaint everything shall I suffer, for in the love of God, nothing have I to fear."

As a Carmelite, Anna Maria took the name Theresa Margaret, but she wanted to be called "of the Sacred Heart" to express her desire to return God's love with all her might. "Yes, my God," she resolved, "know that no other longing have I than to be a victim of your Sacred Heart, entirely consumed as a holocaust in the furnace of your holy love."

God honored her desire, for shortly after Pentecost, 1767, the saint began to feel the love of God burning like a fire in her heart. She seems to have received the same mystical experiences as St. Teresa of Ávila, who says her heart was divinely wounded and set afire by his love. These mysterious phenomena drew Theresa Margaret closer to God until her death in 1770.

Like Teresa of Ávila, the saint's nearness to God drove her to love others. Even when she was ill herself, for example, Theresa Margaret tenderly cared for her elderly sisters. She has left us *Maxims* on Christian relationships that described the kindness with which she conducted all of her own relationships:

> Let us do everything for love and, remembering that love longs for love alone, nothing can appear hard to us.
>
> If the actions of our neighbors have a hundred sides, we ought always to look at them on the best side.
>
> When an action is blameworthy, we should strive to see the good intentions back of it.

Theresa Margaret died at age twenty-three, having spent only five short years as a Carmelite nun. Yet her life seems to have been full and complete. "Do you not see," as the saint once wrote, "how God helps us so that, at the journey's end, everything is finished?"

> *I desire to love you, O my God, with a love that is patient, with a love that abandons itself wholly to you, with a love that acts, and most important of all, with a love that perseveres.*
>
> —Theresa Margaret

MARCH 11 / CANONIZED IN 1934
Love in Action; A Passionate Love; A Soul Afire; Twenty-Something Saints

307. Joseph Pignatelli
(1737–1811)

Obedience is somewhat out of fashion today. We don't like it much, finding the virtue prickly and hard-to-take when we are expected to obey. However, obedience even in the worst circumstances may bear good fruit, as the life of St. Joseph Pignatelli demonstrates.

By the eighteenth century, the Society of Jesus had made many enemies. For example, anticlerical political leaders in Portugal and France regarded the Jesuits with their pledge of loyalty to the pope as powerful opponents under a foreign influence. So they suppressed the order.

Shortly after Joseph Pignatelli was ordained as a Jesuit priest, Charles III also expelled the society from Spain. Some Jesuits had found temporary refuge in Corsica, until the French drove them out. Then Pignatelli helped arrange a center for them at Ferrara, Italy.

In 1773, Pope Clement XIV yielded to political pressure and suppressed the Jesuits entirely. When the vicar general of the order asked the men at Ferrara whether they would obey and disband the order, they said, "Yes, willingly." The result was to secularize Father Pignatelli and twenty-three thousand other Jesuits.

For twenty years Father Pignatelli devoted himself to study and aiding other Jesuits. However, in the 1790s the tide began to turn. The Duke of Parma invited three Jesuits to establish themselves there. With the pope's permission, Pignatelli established a novitiate at Colorno, sending men for training to Russia, where the government had not promulgated the suppression. After 1804, under the most difficult conditions, Pignatelli became provincial for Naples. Then, after the French drove the Jesuits out of Naples, he became provincial at Rome for all Italy. In these very straitened circumstances, Pignatelli apparently had the help of divine intervention. Miracles seemed to accompany him, like the following described by an archbishop during his canonization process:

> I called at St. Pantaleon's to confer with the provincial on business. I was seated at the side of his small desk, with not more than a foot between us. The procurator came in and said he needed immediately a certain sum of money. The provincial opened the top desk drawer

> where I saw right under my eyes a loose assortment of money. He gave the procurator the entire amount, which left the drawer empty.
>
> The procurator came right back, saying that he was still short of funds. I wish to emphasize the position I was in at the time. I was as close to the desk drawer as he was himself. My view of the interior was unobstructed. Then I witnessed a prodigy that I shall never forget. The saint paused momentarily. He seemed to withdraw from us, entering into himself and forgetting our presence.
>
> After a brief thought, he raised his eyes upward and moved his lips. I shall always remember the serene smile that lighted his face at that moment. Had he been in communion with the Invisible? I don't know. But I watched him open the drawer he had just emptied. There in the identical location as before was, for all appearances, the same money he had already given to the procurator. The thing was so manifestly supernatural and I was so struck with wonder, that I cried out: "A miracle!" At my shout, the holy man humbly bowed his head. The he abruptly turned to the subject of our interrupted conference.

During the French occupation of Italy in the first decade of the 1800s, St. Joseph Pignatelli worked quietly to conserve the reorganization of the Jesuits he had achieved. He deserves recognition as the restorer of the Jesuits, although the full restoration of the society occurred in 1814, three years after his death.

The cross represents the inversion of all human values. The human is put to death and out of the death comes life.

—John Courtney Murray

NOVEMBER 28 / CANONIZED IN 1954
Miracles Do Happen

308. Julie Billiart
(1751–1816)

Many faithful Catholics resisted the French Revolution's anticlericalism and the destruction of the church. But perhaps the most outstanding opponent of the Jacobins, and certainly the most unusual, was St. Julie Billiart, for she was paralyzed and conducted her defiance from her bed.

Julie Billiart was a born teacher. Already as a child she liked to teach catechism to her playmates in the village of Cuvilly, Picardy. When her wealthy family slid into poverty, Julie had to work long hours, but she always made time to instruct others in the faith.

One day in 1774 someone fired a shot at her father. The bullet missed, but the traumatic event plunged Julie into a mysterious illness and she was immobilized by a debilitating paralysis. From her bed, however, she continued to catechize the village children.

In 1790 a schismatic priest who had sworn loyalty to the revolution took over the Cuvilly church. He tried to visit Julie but she refused to admit him. And singlehandedly the invalid persuaded the entire village to boycott him. She was very clear that no compromise with the state church was allowable or necessary, as she told a friend:

> I congratulate you, my dear good friend, that God gives you the opportunity of being useful to souls. But walk with caution because present circumstances make this work difficult for you. You say it seems to you better to be schismatic rather than to be utterly without religion. But my dear friend, you cannot have weighed the matter. For, in conscience, we must not leave our brethren in error. If they go to the instructions of an intruder, they are automatically out of the way of salvation. . . .
>
> All those good people, who find it utterly impossible to get into touch with their legitimate pastors, will not be punished for it. And it is better for them to remain all their lives without instruction, without Mass. . . . God will send an angel from heaven to them rather than allow them to perish forever.

Enraged by Julie's opposition, revolutionary authorities sought to silence her, so she fled in a hay wagon and went into hiding. At Amiens she met Frances Blin, a viscountess who became her friend and companion. The women went to Bettencourt, where they taught catechism classes and restored the entire village to the practice of the faith. Julie and Frances returned to Amiens where they founded the Institute of Notre Dame, a community of women dedicated mainly to the care and instruction of poor girls.

In 1804 during a novena, a priest exhorted Julie to take a step in faith and on the spot she was miraculously healed. With her restored strength, Julie together with Frances spent her last years establishing fifteen Notre Dame convents throughout France. She died at Namur in 1816.

However severe God's guidance may seem to us at times, it's always the guidance of a Father who is infinitely good, wise and kind. He leads us to our goal by different paths. And after all, my dear good friend, let's be honest—Isn't it true that we tend to spoil the work of grace in us? So it's to our advantage to experience the withdrawal of grace and abandonment by God. Then we must act as little children do in the dark—clasp the hand of father or mother and go where we are led.

—Julie Billiart

APRIL 8 / CANONIZED IN 1969
Angels; Countercultural Witness; Miracles Do Happen; Raising Christian Youth

309. Clement Mary Hofbauer
(1751–1820)

The tumultuous politics and wars of the late eighteenth century continuously hampered St. Clement Mary Hofbauer's ministry. But like his contemporary **St. Joseph Pignatelli**, he succeeded because of his faith and meekness. Through a series of serendipitous accidents that some might call divine appointments, he established the Redemptorist order north of the Alps. And that at a time when anti-Catholic monarchs in Germany and Austria seemed bent on exterminating religious orders.

With simple spiritual wisdom, Clement Hofbauer dominated seemingly impassable obstacles. He summed up the ideals that governed his conduct in maxims like these:

> We must not force ourselves too much to maintain a pure intention. If we make it in the morning in the best way we can, let us then go quietly to our daily duties without anxiety or scruples. We should be like a little child who goes simply on its way and only cries out for its mother when it meets with some grave difficulty. God will find the means for our progress to perfection, if only our will be right.
>
> When impure thoughts come into our minds we should think of them as little as we do of the leaves that fall from the trees. We must not dwell on them for a moment and without heeding such suggestions from the enemy of souls, go quietly on our way.
>
> When we are conscious of having failed and done wrong, we must humble ourselves before God, implore his pardon, and then quietly move ahead. Our defects should make us humble, but never cowardly.
>
> We cannot obtain divine grace by violence. Everything should be done gently. Mary, the Mother of God, suffered a greater martyrdom than any other woman, but she was always quiet and calm.
>
> The best way to become a saint is to plunge ourselves in the will of God, as a stone is immersed in the water. We must allow ourselves to be tossed like a ball here and there according to his good pleasure.

The image of a divine ball toss suitably describes the course of Clement's life. First he tried the life of a hermit but decided he had a missionary call. He wanted to be a priest, but could not afford an education. However, one day he casually assisted two wealthy women who returned his little favor by paying for his seminary education in Rome. He joined the Redemptorists there in 1784. Then, after ordination, he tried to open a Redemptorist house in Vienna, but Joseph II's anticlerical laws blocked him.

On his way to missionary work in Courland in 1787, Clement Hofbauer got sidetracked in Warsaw. He stayed there twenty years, caring for Germans and Poles. His preaching, counsel, and educational and charitable projects stirred a spiritual renewal. But when Napoleon invaded Poland in 1808, he returned to Vienna.

First he worked quietly in the Italian quarter, but soon his preaching and counsel attracted the attention of the whole city. He contributed enormously to the Catholic revival in Austria, even helping defeat a proposal at the Congress of Vienna to set up an independent German church. The imperial chancellor tried to expel Clement, accusing him of spying. But the emperor, influenced by the good report of the archbishop, protected him.

In 1819, Clement contracted a fatal illness and he died a year later on March 15.

Nothing in life is accidental. He who believes in accident does not believe in God.

—Alexander Yelchaninov

MARCH 15 / CANONIZED IN 1909 / PATRON OF VIENNA
Christian Living; Meekness; The Secrets of Spiritual Success; Sexual Temptation

310. Elizabeth Ann Seton
(1774–1821)

Elizabeth Ann Seton lived two lives. First, she was a much-loved wife and mother. Then, she had a second life as founder of a religious order and many schools. Between the two periods she left her Protestant heritage to become a Catholic. During both periods Elizabeth Ann Seton was a saint.

In 1794, Elizabeth married William Magee Seton, a wealthy New York merchant. They were very much in love and demonstrated it with little tendernesses. Once she slipped her picture into his shaving kit, which he proudly showed to everyone on his travels. Within nine years they had five children, three girls and two boys. William died of tuberculosis in 1803 while the couple was traveling in Italy. Elizabeth stayed on six months with a Catholic family and she returned home desiring to become a convert. On March 14, 1805, she was received into the Catholic Church. Some friends and family members were so appalled by her decision that they shunned her.

For several years Elizabeth struggled to support her family. However, in 1808 a priest invited her to open a school for girls in Baltimore. A group of like-minded women joined Elizabeth there, forming a small community. In 1809 the women established themselves as a religious order. They moved to a house in nearby Emmitsburg, Maryland, which became their base of operations.

From that time Elizabeth was known appropriately as Mother Seton. Not only was she caring for her infant community of the Sisters of Charity, but she also had some of her own children with her and never stopped looking after those who were away at school or work.

Elizabeth and her sisters set up schools and orphanages along the East Coast. They are credited with launching the parochial school system which became a mainstay of Catholicism in the United States.

An abscess in her breast eroded Elizabeth's health, but not her spirit. As death drew near, she wrote eloquently about her desire to rest and simply enjoy union with God:

> For at last, how much more good can we do by staying with God, than by most zealous speculations. Plenty of people in this world to mind planning and opinions, but how few to build in God and be silent, like our Jesus.

Link by link, the blessed chain
One Body in Christ—He the head we the members
One Spirit diffused thru' the Holy Ghost in us all
One Hope—Him in heaven and Eternity
One Faith—by his Word and his Church
One Baptism and participation of his sacraments
One God our dear Lord
One Father We his children—he above all through all and in all.

Who can resist, all self must be killed and destroyed by this artillery of love—one, one, one, one. Who could escape this bond of unity, peace, and love? O my soul be fastened link by link, strong as death, iron and Hell as says the sacred Word.

Elizabeth Ann Seton died at Emmitsburg on January 4, 1821. Pope Paul VI canonized her in 1975, the first native-born American citizen to be recognized as a saint.

Our misery is not to conform ourselves to the intentions of God as to the manner in which he will be glorified. What pleases Him does not please us. He wills us to enter in the way of suffering, and we desire to enter in action. We desire to give rather than receive—and do not purely seek his Will.

—Elizabeth Ann Seton

JANUARY 4 / CANONIZED IN 1975
Facing Death; Leading Women; Married Saints; A Passionate Love

311. Joan Antide-Thouret
(1765–1826)

Failure, criticism, inadequacy, anticlericalism, petty church politics—none of these prevented St. Joan Antide-Thouret from pursuing her vocation. Like **Anne-Marie Javouhey,** she accomplished a significant work during the turbulence of the French Revolution.

After Joan's mother died, from age sixteen she managed her father's household at a village near Besançon, France. In 1787 a compelling divine call prompted her to join the Sisters of Charity at Paris. There two serious illnesses impeded her religious training. The revolution dispersed the community in 1793, before Joan had made her profession. She returned to her hometown, where she ran a school for the village children.

When political conditions had improved, the vicar general of Besançon invited Joan to open a school. Reluctant at first because she did not feel she had been adequately prepared for the work, Joan overcame her reticence and started the school in April 1799. Six months later she added a soup kitchen and dispensary. Critics denounced her for not returning to her original community. But she had not taken vows and had acted in obedience to the bishop.

Joan also ran the female asylum at Belleveaux, which housed orphans, criminals, the homeless, and the mentally ill. Her sisters labored there under hopeless conditions, and opponents criticized and persecuted them for undertaking this work. In the following letter, Joan encouraged the sister in charge at Belleveaux:

> Hello, my dear daughter Elisabeth! How are you? Still holding on firmly to the handles of the plow? Is the ground hard and dry? Is the corn growing well? The weeds not stifling it? If so, dig out the weeds with a hoe, without damaging the corn. Have courage. The good corn of the elect will ripen and will nourish you for eternal life. Prune the vine well. You will drink the good wine in long draughts in paradise.
>
> But to merit this happiness let's not tire of fighting during this exile. Let's despise the world and its false gods. Let's despise its honors. In vain would we seek our happiness in them. It will benefit us greatly to receive nothing from the world but ingratitude and opposition. This will detach us from it and attach us closely to God alone.

> You face many troubles in serving the poor unfortunates entrusted to your care. I am sure that you do so from charity and the love of God. That you treat your dear companions as you would like them to treat you. That you do justice to them all.
>
> I have also the quiet assurance that you love and carefully practice our holy rule. That you make the rest respect and practice it. That you love peace and that you do everything you can to preserve it among you all, as well as mutual respect, good manners and gentle kindness, which unite all hearts in accordance with the spirit of God.

By 1810 the community had spread to Switzerland, Savoy, and Naples, where Joan herself moved to administer a hospital. In 1819 the pope approved the order as the Daughters of Charity. Because the pope removed the sisters from the authority of the bishop of Besançon, he detached all the convents of his diocese from the rest of the community. In order to maintain control over the sisters in his diocese, he banned St. Joan from visiting her convents in France, a painful separation that troubled her for the rest of her life. She died at Naples in 1826.

When God gives us a job to do, we may imagine that he makes the way easy for us. However, the experience of saints like Joan Antide-Thouret prove that notion false. And un-Christian, as it contradicts Christ's example and teaching.

AUGUST 24 / CANONIZED IN 1934
Perseverance; Suffering

312. Seraphim of Sarov
(1759–1833)

We unconsciously expect modern saints to show some signs of modernity. In the 1800s, for example, **St. Madeleine Sophie** founded a community known for its avant-garde educational practices. But St. Seraphim, a nineteenth-century Russian monk, was not modern at all. He would have been at home in a fourth-century hermitage.

In 1778, he entered the monastery at Sarov, near Moscow, in western Russia. Two years of excessive mortification devastated his health, and he was bedridden for three years. In 1783 the Virgin Mary, in one of a dozen appearances to Seraphim, healed him.

At age twenty-five he became a hermit, living in a hut a few miles from the monastery. There in 1804 brigands beat him with his own ax. Although afterwards his body was permanently bent, he upgraded his penitential practices. Imitating the ancient stylites, he stood in prayer day and night for three years. Then in 1807 he pledged himself to absolute silence so as to achieve inner peace and finally conquer the devil. For the next eighteen years he spoke to no one.

In 1825, the Virgin appeared again to Seraphim. She released him from his silence and opened a healing spring near the monastery. For the remainder of his life the saint served as a spiritual adviser and healer, ministering to hundreds of seekers. Most notably, in 1831 he healed Nicholas Motovilov of chronic rheumatism and the young nobleman became his disciple. Nicholas wrote a conversation with the saint summarizing Seraphim's teaching. The following capsulizes Seraphim's instruction on receiving the Holy Spirit:

> The true goal of our Christian life consists in the acquisition of the Holy Spirit of God. Fasting, vigils, prayers, alms-giving and all good deeds done for the sake of Christ are but means for the acquisition of the Holy Spirit of God.
>
> "But what is 'acquiring?'" I asked.
>
> "'Acquiring' is the same as 'gaining,'" he replied.
>
> You understand, surely, what is meant by acquiring money? Acquiring the Holy Spirit of God is the same thing. The aim of the worldly life of ordinary people is the acquisition or the making of money. The acquisition of the Spirit of God is also capital, but a capital that dispenses grace and that is eternal.

And since it is very like monetary, social and temporal capital, it is obtained in similar ways.

God the Logos, our Lord the God-Man Jesus Christ, compares our life with the marketplace. He calls our activity on earth trading, and says to us: "Trade till I come" (see Luke. 19:13), "redeeming the time, because the days are evil" (see Ephesians 5:16). In other words, make the most of your time to obtain heavenly blessings through earthly goods.

Of course, every good work done for the sake of Christ gives us the grace of the Holy Spirit, but prayer provides it most of all, for prayer is always at hand. But acquire the grace of the Holy Spirit also by practicing all the other virtues for Christ's sake. Trade in them spiritually, trade with those of them that give you the greatest profit.

On January 14, 1833, Seraphim was found dead in his cell, his face turned toward an icon of Mary and his garment burnt by a candle he was holding.

God freely pours out his Holy Spirit on us. But as Seraphim taught, we must at least do our part to receive the divine gift. Receiving the Spirit is not a passive event but an active acquisition. Thus, we accept God's gift of his Spirit by prayer, by fasting, by serving others—by whatever works best for us.

JANUARY 2

Grace; Healing Touch; Holy Spirit; Pursuit of Holiness; The Secrets of Spiritual Success

313. Anne Mary Taigi
(1769–1837)

A model lay woman, Anne Mary Taigi managed a large household in Rome for nearly half a century. She handled finances with little money, patiently cared for a cantankerous family, and entertained a constant stream of guests who came to consult her. She did all this full of faith and good cheer. Even though Anne Mary was blessed with charisms of prophecy and healing, it was not these gifts, but her resilient leadership of her family through poverty and trouble that earned her a saint's crown.

An impoverished servant girl herself, at age twenty-one she married Domenico Taigi, a servant in the Chigi Palace. They had seven children, two of whom died at childbirth. Early in her marriage, Anne Mary experienced a religious conversion. She took a Servite priest as a spiritual guide. Under his direction, she simplified her life, initiating practices of prayer and self-denial that she pursued the rest of her life.

Anne Mary took the spiritual lead in her family. The day began with morning prayer and mass and ended with reading lives of the saints and the rosary. The Taigis had little of their own, but she always found ways to provide for those who had less. She also took in her hard-to-get-along-with parents and her widowed daughter, Sophie, with her six children.

Domenico had a violent temper that often disrupted the family. But somehow Anne Mary was always able to calm him and restore peace. In his old age, Domenico gave this touching tribute to his wife:

> Often I came home to a house full of people. Immediately, Anne Mary would leave anyone who was there—maybe a great lady or a bishop—and would hurry to pay affectionate attention to me. You could tell she did it with all her heart. She would have taken off my shoes if I had allowed her. In short, she was my comfort and the consolation of everyone.
>
> With her wonderful tact she was able to maintain a heavenly peace in our home. And that even though we were a large household full of people with very different temperaments. For example, when my son Camillus was living with us early in his marriage, my daughter-in-law was a disturbing element. She always wanted to play the mistress of the

> house. But my wife knew how to keep everyone in his place and she did it with a graciousness that I can't describe.
>
> I often came home tired, moody and cross, but she always succeeded in soothing and cheering me. And due to her, I corrected some of my faults. I am not good at expressing myself, for I am old. But if I were a young man and could search the whole world to find such a wife, it would be vain. I believe that God has received her into heaven because of her great virtue. And I hope that she will pray for me and our family.

Reportedly, Anne Mary had a permanent vision that gave her insight into the causes of evil in the world and dangers that threatened the church. She also had a gift of healing. For example, with a sign of the cross she anointed cancer victims and epileptics and they were cured.

After seven months of sickness and spiritual trials, Anne Mary Taigi died on June 9, 1837.

> *The practices of mortification should be moderated by prudence and a wise director's advice because the devil often urges a soul to excessive penances to tire her and render her unfit for the service of God and the fulfillment of her duties.*
>
> —Anne Mary Taigi

JUNE 9 / BEATIFIED IN 1920

Celebration of Discipline; Family; Married Saints; Peacemakers; The Sign of the Cross

314. Dominic Barberi
(1792–1849)

Dominic Barberi, eleventh child of a peasant family in Viterbo, Italy, joined the Passionist Order in 1814. From his earliest days in the community he entertained a burning desire to minister in England, where the Passionists had not yet gone. And once during his novitiate, while kneeling at the Blessed Virgin's altar, he received a revelation that he would someday work as a priest in northern Europe and in England.

Ordained in 1818, Dominic taught for ten years and eventually became provincial of the order. He opened the first Passionist retreat in Belgium in 1840. Two years later he established the Passionists in England, thus fulfilling both strands of his 1814 prophecy.

Dominic immediately began to preach missions, employing the typical fire-and-brimstone message of the day. People ridiculed his broken English and shabby dress, and nicknamed him Paddy-Whack. But his exemplary poverty, from which he liberally gave alms, and reports of his miracles soon won him respect and a reputation for holiness. When he walked down a street, people would fall silent and mothers would hold out their babies for his blessing.

In 1845, Dominic received **John Henry Newman,** Britain's leading Anglican theologian, into the church and became famous overnight. In an article in the *Tablet,* he wrote about the event:

> When they told me that I was to receive Mr. Newman into the church, this news filled me with joy, and made me soon forget the rain, that had been pelting upon me for the last five hours. From Oxford we drove in a chaise to Littlemore, where we arrived about eleven o'clock. I immediately sat down near a fire to dry my clothes, when Mr. Newman entered the room, and throwing himself at my feet, asked my blessing, and begged me to hear his confession and receive him into the church. He made his confession that same night, and on the following morning the Reverend Messrs. Bowles and Stanton did the same.
>
> In the evening of the same day these three made their profession of faith in the usual form in their private Oratory, one after another, with such fervor and piety that I was almost out of myself for joy. I afterwards gave them all canonical absolution and administered to them the sacrament of baptism, conditionally. On the following morning I said Mass in their Oratory, and gave communion to Messrs. Newman, St. John, Bowles, Stanton and Dalgairns. After mass, Mr. Dalgairns took

> me to the house of Mr. Woodmason, Esq., a gentleman of Littlemore; I heard his confession, and that of his wife and two daughters, and received all four into the church. . . .
>
> All that I have suffered since I left Italy is well compensated by such a happy event as this.

Dominic had also become instantly infamous, as some suspected that he had been sent from Rome to use cunning arguments to ensnare Newman. But Newman himself later explained that Barberi had little to do with his conversion and until the last moment was unaware that Newman wanted him to receive him into the church.

Having performed rewarding service all his life, Dominic Barberi died in 1849 at the age of fifty-seven.

God has created me to do Him some definite service.
He has committed some work to me which He has not committed to
another. . . .
I am a link in a chain, a bond of connection between persons. . . .
I shall do good; I shall do his work. I shall be an angel of peace,
a preacher of truth in my own place, while not intending it
if I do but keep his commandments.

—John Henry Newman

AUGUST 27 / BEATIFIED IN 1963
Purpose; Visions and Visionaries

315. Anne-Marie Javouhey
(1779–1851)

Imagine a Mother Teresa in the France of Napoleon's day and you will have a picture of Anne-Marie Javouhey. Nanette, as she was called, was a "velvet brick," a thin layer of gentleness covering her determined core. A competent leader, Nanette dominated every scene in her adventurous life.

In 1800, she tested her vocation with the Sisters of Charity at Besançon. One night she heard a voice say, "You will accomplish great things for me." A few nights later, **St. Teresa of Ávila** with black, brown, and bronze children appeared to her. "God wants you to found a congregation to care for these children," said the saint.

In 1801, Nanette and her three natural sisters opened a school for poor children near Chamblanc. During the next decade she ran two day schools and an orphanage. In 1812 she founded the Sisters of St. Joseph of Cluny. Then the dam burst, with demand for her sisters' services clamoring throughout France.

Nanette, now Mother Javouhey, held her sisters to a high ideal of community life that she articulated in the following communiqué:

> As we are joined together in community, we should live in unity with all its members, having one heart and soul. We should be always willing to labor and suffer privations without troubling others. We must possess nothing of our own, aware that everything belongs to the community according to the spirit of community life.
>
> If we find that we are in want for certain things—and surely we will be often—we should rejoice because holy poverty does not imply that we should want nothing. But rather it means that we should be happy to do without anything for the sake of God and the sake of others.
>
> Each sister should be prepared to accept willingly the duties assigned to her, no matter how hard or how menial they may appear.
>
> Do not fail to tell new members that they must be ready to go wherever the superior decides to send them. Those who are sent to remote places where the sick-poor have no care should visit them and provide for their spiritual and temporal needs as far as possible but above all should prepare them for the last sacraments.

In 1817, Mother Javouhey sent sisters to the African island of Reunion to open her first missionary outpost. It wasn't long before she had sisters serving black, brown, and bronze people at remote places in Africa at Senegal, Sierra Leone, and Gambia, and in South America at French Guiana. With dogged faith the sisters battled extreme hardship everywhere.

At the government's request, Mother Javouhey undertook some very unusual tasks. For example, she spent four years supervising the establishment of a colony for blacks at Mana, French Guiana. Then in 1834 she accepted the most remarkable assignment of her life. Six hundred slaves were to be liberated in Guiana, and she was asked to prepare them for emancipation by training them in the ways of religion and civilized society. As each family was ready to be freed, Mother Javouhey arranged for them to have money, some land, and a cottage.

Anne-Marie Javouhey spent the last years of her life in France directing the work of her burgeoning congregation. When she died in 1851, her sisters were in thirty-two countries and colonies.

Anne-Marie Javouhey was a spiritual entrepreneur. God gave her ten talents that she invested and returned to him with more than a hundredfold interest. She forces us to think about what we will say when God looks at our balance sheet.

JULY 15 / BEATIFIED IN 1950
Innovative Saints; Community; Leading Women; Serving the Poor; Social Justice; Vocation

316. Philippine Duchesne

(1769–1852)

Perhaps God wants his missionary nuns to sanctify themselves on failure.

—Philippine Duchesne

When St. Philippine Duchesne looked back over her life, she judged herself a failure. As a girl in Grenoble, France, she had dreamed of evangelizing American Indians. She got her desire, but the reality of life in America was nothing like her romantic notion of saving the souls of "savages." In Philippine's view, everything went wrong because of her inadequacies, yet she stuck it out for thirty-four years. Everyone else saw things differently, praising Philippine for her work and especially for her prayer.

Failure was Philippine's constant companion. At eighteen, she joined the Visitation sisters at Ste-Marie-d'En-haut. But before she could make her vows, the French Revolution expelled the order. However, under Napoleon's rule in 1801, she got possession of St. Marie's convent and tried to restore the Visitation community there. But the effort failed.

In 1804, **St. Madeleine Sophie Barat** accepted Philippine into the Society of the Sacred Heart. For fourteen years she campaigned to be sent to America. Finally in 1818, Madeleine Sophie sent five sisters to Louisiana with Philippine as the superior.

The bishop established the nuns in St. Charles, Missouri, where they opened the first free school west of the Mississippi. In the next few years Philippine opened a novitiate, founded an orphanage in St. Louis, and started several other schools in neighboring communities.

But Philippine had no sense of success. Everything seemed to go wrong. Money was short. Food and firewood were scarce. Nuns were always sick. No Indians came to the schools. The children who enrolled were unruly. Parents did not seem to care. She was unable to learn English and so could not teach. You can almost hear Philippine's sighs of frustration in the following excerpts from her letters home:

> There is no one in the community who is not suffering. It is heartbreaking, after such ardent desires, to see our success hindered or slowed up and to realize that I am the obstacle.
>
> The dear Lord has prepared much suffering for me, since the days when we opened our convent here with such a promise of success. The scarcity of money has caused the withdrawal of the majority of our boarding pupils—only 10 remain. But the hardest of all has been the fact that practically all the pupils who have left us and who seemed so fervent, have fallen back into their former neglect of religion. I still hope that their faith is not dead and that age, reverses, and other trials from the hand of God will someday bring them to repentance.
>
> I carry in my heart a great fear of spoiling things wherever I shall be, and this because of words I heard in the depths of my soul: "You are destined to please Me, not so much by success as by bearing failure."

At age seventy-two, Philippine got her youthful wish and was sent to serve the Potawatomis at the Jesuit mission at Sugar Creek, Kansas. The Native Americans loved her, nicknaming her "The Woman Who Prays Always." But she had no stamina and could not learn the language, so her superiors brought her back to St. Charles after only a year. She spent the next decade there, interceding before the Blessed Sacrament for the work of her sisters. She died peacefully in 1852.

Evangelization is never easy, and always seems somewhat hampered by failure. What makes it work is passion, perseverance, and prayer. The church regards Philippine as a successful missionary because she excelled in all three.

NOVEMBER 18 / CANONIZED IN 1988
The Cost of Discipleship; Enduring Trials; Missionaries; Success in Failure

317. John Vianney
(1786–1859)

Do you think of St. John Vianney, the Curé of Ars, as a priest of low intelligence who only by extraordinary grace in his confessional converted thousands of people? If so, think again. The saint's reputed ignorance is greatly exaggerated. Yes, he was an ill-educated farm boy who had difficulty learning Latin and passing his seminary exams. But he possessed superior moral intelligence and Christian wisdom, as shown in these aphorisms from his sermons:

> "To content his love, God must give himself to us separately, one by one."
>
> "A pure soul is with God, as a child with its mother. The child caresses and embraces her, and its mother returns all its endearments."
>
> "We have nothing of our own but our will. It is the only thing that God has so placed in our own power that we can make an offering of it to him."
>
> "Our Lord takes pleasure in doing the will of those who love him."
>
> "You must accept your cross. If you bear it courageously it will carry you to heaven."
>
> "The way to destroy bad habits is by watchfulness and by doing often those things that are the opposites to one's besetting sins."
>
> "God commands you to pray, but he forbids you to worry."
>
> "Prayer is the conversation of a child with his Father. Of a subject with his King. Of a servant with his Lord. Of a friend with the Friend to whom he confides all his troubles and difficulties."
>
> "To approach God you should go straight to him, like a bullet from a gun."
>
> "The interior life is like a sea of love in which the soul is plunged and drowned. Just as a mother holds her child's face in her hands to cover it with kisses, so does God hold the devout person."

The care of souls obsessed John Vianney. Appointed in 1817 as pastor to Ars, he soon converted most of the 230 people who lived in the little French village. A few minutes in his confessional was enough to turn hardened sinners into saints. People said he could read their consciences, see their past sins, and predict the future. For many years three hundred penitents a day came to him by train from Lyons, which had to maintain a ticket office just for Ars. He spent twelve to seventeen hours a day hearing confessions, stopping only to preach at 11:00 a.m. And the saint disciplined himself harshly as prayer for the conversion of sinners. For example, he ate one meal a day, often only boiled potatoes.

The devil seemed to take notice of the Curé of Ars. For thirty years day and night he put up with intrusions he regarded as diabolical, including poltergeists, noises, personal violence, and even the mysterious burning of his bed. "The *grappin* and I are almost mates," he would say.

John Vianney blended strictness and gentleness. He upheld the commandments with uncompromising severity and loved people with motherly tenderness. His preaching, for example, emptied the pubs of Ars and restored the Sunday observance. And when he wasn't in the confessional, the curé was rescuing abandoned children. He crowded orphans into the homes of his friends. Once he brought a child to an associate who objected, "But there's no bed." "There's always yours," he said, and left the child at the door.

Worn out by the constant stream of visitors and by his lifelong austerity, St. John Vianney died at the age of seventy-three.

Here is a rule for everyday life: Do not do anything which you cannot offer to God.

—John Vianney

AUGUST 4 / CANONIZED IN 1925 / PATRON OF PARISH PRIESTS
Care of the Soul; Saints and Sacraments (Reconciliation); The Secrets of Spiritual Success; Spiritual Warfare

318. Mary Euphrasia Pelletier
(1796–1868)

Apparently any woman called to found a religious community must be tough. All whom I have encountered not only had to fight for survival on worldly terms, they also had to navigate dangerous rapids within the church. St. Mary Euphrasia Pelletier did not escape the rule. But like her contemporary, **Anne-Marie Javouhey**, she succeeded because she was truly spiritual, competent, and bold. Critics might also say "bullheaded." Maybe so, but properly directed, a strong will may produce both virtue and success.

In 1641, to provide care for prostitutes, **John Eudes** had founded the Institute of Our Lady of Charity. In 1814, Rose Virginia Pelletier entered that community at Tours, taking the name Mary Euphrasia. When she was twenty-nine the community chose her as superior.

Once in office Mary Euphrasia attempted to create a new religious foundation at Angers. She successfully assumed leadership of the Good Shepherd House of Refuge, which had existed there for many years. However, disputes with clergy and others compelled her to return to Tours. But with hard negotiation, Mary Euphrasia fought her way to become prioress of the house at Angers.

These painful controversies persuaded Mary Euphrasia to establish a centralized organization that would serve and govern all of the community's houses. She realized that difficulties would persist if each refuge remained independent. She wanted to start a new order that would benefit from having a common novitiate and a superior with translocal authority. Over bitter opposition from among her sisters and from bishops and clergy, she balanced doggedness with humility to succeed. At Angers she created the Institute of Our Lady of Charity of the Good Shepherd.

Frequently accused of rash innovation, personal ambition, and insubordination, Mary Euphrasia always conducted herself with the charity and trust she prescribed for her sisters in the following instruction:

> Oh, how happy are the souls who live by love. It is true that they may have sorrows. But love delights in suffering. Nothing is hard to one who loves.
>
> A soul who ardently loves God no longer runs, she flies along the path of perfection. We should try to live by love. Fear should never be

allowed to disturb and oppress our hearts. It is not in the spirit of fear that the Good Shepherd wishes us to serve him. He who fears is not perfect in love. Love inspires confidence, joy and peace, while fear is marked by anxiety. . . .

Faith is love that believes. Hope is love that expects. Adoration is love that worships. Prayer is love that petitions. Mercy is love that pardons. Charity is love that sacrifices itself. Mortification is love that immolates self. We can make more progress in one year by love than we could in ten through fear.

According to Saint Clement, there is no more perfect image of the Deity than a soul that, whether in prosperity or in adversity, always maintains its interior peace. Remember that here below, everything is passing. Nothing should really afflict us except sin. Go straight on. Be like the fisherman who keeps casting his net always hoping to catch a fish. Then allow God to do the rest. He knows better than we do what is for our good.

We are only feeble instruments in his hands.

The pope approved the new foundation in 1838. By Mary Euphrasia's death in 1868, 2,760 Good Shepherd sisters covered the globe. So spiritual success depends both on God and grit.

Virtue that is gloomy, morose, sour, hard, is virtue only in name. It is not inspired by God's Spirit and it does not become a Christian soul.

—Mary Euphrasia Pelletier

APRIL 24 / CANONIZED IN 1940
Love in Action; Pursuit of Holiness; The Secrets of Spiritual Success

319. Michael Garicoits
(1797–1863)

St. Michael Garicoits encouraged many young people to persevere in their religious vocations. Obstacles, he said, come from God as a test of faith and grit, and God always gives enough grace to conquer them. Read this letter he wrote to a young socialite whose father doubted her calling:

> I have read repeatedly the letter from your father that you kindly sent me. It should not prevent your carrying out inspirations that are plainly divine. On the contrary, pain and trouble render such an enterprise more dear. Even more sacred.
>
> What would have become of the divine work entrusted to **St. Vincent de Paul**, **St. Francis de Sales**, and **St. Francis Xavier**, had they let obstacles bar their way? The crosses their vocation brought convinced them it was divine, and they held to it with all the strength of their soul.
>
> To oppose a real religious vocation, such as yours appears to me, would be to risk anathema both from heaven and the world. God alone gave you the idea and wish to consecrate yourself to him. To him alone you owe the feelings that make it easy to reach the goal.
>
> He allows you to meet obstacles only to try your fidelity. Obstacles are not insuperable, and your father is not a tyrant. He seems to me to be a very good father, an excellent father, although I have not the pleasure of knowing him. And I don't doubt but that kindness alone has made him take what he calls an irrevocable decision. I probably would have done the same thing if I believed what he believes. The thing is to drive away his mistaken ideas and show him how wrong his judgment is. Then all will come out fairly.

When Michael wrote such letters, he was probably reflecting on his own experience. Obstacles blocked both his vocation and his spiritual work. But he slowly pushed his way through them to success.

The Garicoits were a poor peasant family dwelling in the Lower Pyrenees. They were too poor to pay for the education of their eldest son, Michael, who desperately wanted to become a priest. So young Michael was hired out as a shepherd to a local farmer. But his grandmother appealed to a parish priest who had been saved by the Garicoits family, and he arranged for Michael to work his way through seminary by doing odd jobs. One obstacle down.

Ordained in 1823, Michael served two years as a curate and then as professor and superior of Bétharram seminary. But the bishop soon merged the seminary with another, and Michael was out of work. Another obstacle, but Michael moved through it.

He sensed a divine leading to establish an order of priests to do parish missions. With his bishop's encouragement, he gathered a handful of men into an informal community and began to train them. All was quite promising, when a new bishop rejected his plans. This time a big obstacle. The bishop confined the community's activity to his diocese and ruled it directly. Although he was crushed, Michael willingly complied with the limitations. He died in 1863 without seeing his order free to serve as he thought God intended.

Michael Garicoits never stopped believing that obstacles to divine initiatives came from God himself as a test. And his perseverance brought him success. Fourteen years after Michael's death the pope approved the Society of Priests of the Sacred Heart of Bétharram on the lines the founder had laid down.

MAY 14 / CANONIZED IN 1947
The Secrets of Spiritual Success; Success in Failure; Vocation

320. John Gabriel Perboyre
(1802–1840)

O my Divine Savior,
transform me into yourself,
May my hands be the hands of Jesus.
May my tongue be the tongue of Jesus.
Grant that every faculty of my body
may serve only to glorify you.
Above all transform my soul and all its powers
that my memory, my will and my affections
may be the memory, the will and the affections of Jesus.
I pray you to destroy in me all that is not of you.
Grant that I may live but in you, and by you, and for you
that I may truly say with Saint Paul:
"I live now, not I, but Christ lives in me" (see Galatians 2:20).

—St. John Gabriel Perboyre

"I mean to be a missioner!" announced fifteen-year-old John Gabriel Perboyre after hearing a sermon on foreign missions. From that time his determination grew firm and specific. John Gabriel believed God was calling him to take the gospel to China. One year later, in 1818, he joined the Congregation of the Mission, the Lazarists, and entered their seminary at Montauban, France.

John Gabriel was ordained a priest in 1826, champing at the bits to be sent on mission. However, because he was an excellent teacher, the Lazarists deployed him as a seminary professor at Saint-Flour and trainer of novices in Paris. Finally after nine years of pleading, in 1835, John Gabriel was sent to the China mission. The saint was a quick study. After four months of training in China, he could speak enough of the language to be sent to the mission station at Honan. He wrote to his brothers at Paris:

> If you could see me now in my Chinese "get up," you would see a very curious sight: my head shaved, a long pig-tail and mustaches, stammering my new language, eating with chopsticks. They tell me that I don't make a bad Chinese. That is the only way to begin making oneself all things to all men: may we be able thus to win all men to Jesus Christ!

For two years at Honan, John Gabriel rescued street children and taught them the faith with engaging stories. In 1839 he was sent to teach catechumens at Hupeh, where a persecution unexpectedly erupted. John Gabriel hid in a nearby forest, but was betrayed by a new convert and captured.

For the next year John Gabriel Perboyre patiently endured the unendurable. He was dragged in chains before judges who demanded that he inform on his associates and stomp on the crucifix. Twenty times he was confronted. Twenty times he refused. And twenty times he was brutally tortured. Once he was branded on his face with four characters that proclaimed he was "a teacher of false religion." Near the end his body was a mass of open wounds with bones exposed.

John Gabriel wrote his prayer for Christlikeness, quoted above, when he was twenty-three years old, and prayed it often. The answer seems to have been yes both in his life and in his death. At last on September 11, 1840, John Gabriel was strangled along with five criminals, a martyrdom fitting for a saint who wanted so much to be like Jesus.

Many people have difficulty in finding a meditation book. But I have found nothing so good as my own heart and the heart of Jesus. Why is it that we so often change the subject of our meditation? Only one thing is necessary: Jesus Christ. Think unceasingly of him.

—John Gabriel Perboyre

SEPTEMBER 11 / CANONIZED IN 1996
Courage; Imitation of Christ; Martyrs; Missionaries

321. Frederic Ozanam
(1813–1853)

As a teenager in Lyons, France, Frederic Ozanam had immersed himself in the anti-Catholic literature of the French Revolution. Doubts tested his Christian commitment, but emerging from them, he promised Christ to devote himself to defending the faith.

In 1831, Ozanam enrolled at the Sorbonne, the famous Parisian university. Appalled by many lectures against Catholicism, he urged students to let no attacks go unanswered. He also organized a discussion club that sponsored public debates with atheists and doubters. One night an opponent hit Frederic with a personal challenge. "Mr. Ozanam," he said, "what do *you* do besides talk to prove the faith you claim is in you?"

The taunt struck deep. After examining his life, Frederic decided that he must back up his words with actions. He began to visit the poor, providing them fuel, food, and clothing out of his own resources. Seven other students joined him, and he organized them into a group that became the first conference of the St. Vincent de Paul Society. By 1837, Ozanam's little association had mushroomed into a national movement with two thousand members.

Ozanam insisted that Christian service to the poor must be personal, as he explained in this passage:

> Help is humiliating when it appeals to men from below, taking heed only of their material wants. It humiliates when there is no reciprocity. When you give a poor man nothing but bread or clothes, there is no likelihood of his ever giving you anything in return.
>
> But help honors when it appeals to him from above. It respects him when it deals with his soul, with his religious, moral and political education, and with all that emancipates him from his passions. Help honors when, to the bread that nourishes, it adds the visit that consoles, advice that enlightens, the friendly handshake that lifts up flagging courage. It esteems the poor man when it treats him with respect, not only as an equal, but as a superior, since he is suffering what perhaps we are incapable of suffering. After all, he is the messenger of God to us, sent to prove our justice and our charity, and to save us by our works.
>
> Help then becomes honorable, because it may become mutual. Every person who gives a kind word, good advice, a consolation today, may tomorrow need a kind word, advice, or consolation. The hand that

> you clasp clasps yours in return. That indigent family whom you love loves you in return, and will have largely acquitted themselves towards you when they shall have prayed for you.

Ozanam married Amelie Soulacroix on June 23, 1841. A priest who thought Frederic should have chosen the religious life told Pope Gregory XVI that Ozanam had fallen into the "trap of marriage." "Oh!" replied the pope. "I always thought we had seven sacraments. Not six sacraments and a trap!" Perhaps Frederic's greatest happiness was the birth of his daughter Marie in 1845.

Just before his marriage, Ozanam was appointed professor of literature at the Sorbonne. With his prestige and through his writing he exerted considerable influence on French public affairs in the tempestuous 1840s. And he lost no opportunity to spread the work of the St. Vincent de Paul Society. After 1846 he was constantly ill. He died in 1853 at the age of forty.

On the twenty-third day of every month, Frederic presented Amelie with a bouquet of flowers to commemorate their wedding day. He was a wise husband, to invest such tenderness in his marriage relationship. Such little things mean a lot.

SEPTEMBER 8
Defending the Faith; Married Saints; Serving the Poor; Social Justice

322. Dominic Savio
(1842–1857)

As a father who has endured the adolescences of seven children, I am convinced that the notion of a "teen saint" is an oxymoron. Yet teenager Dominic Savio, a remarkable exception, proves me wrong. Spiritually mature beyond his fifteen years, he lived the Christian life with as much commitment and with more balance than many adult saints. The real test of Dominic's holiness was the joy he expressed in his wonderful sense of humor. We get a taste of what this engaging youth was like in this letter to his friend, John Massaglia, written shortly before he died:

> I was very pleased to receive your letter, for as we had no news of you since you left, I was uncertain whether I should say a "Glory Be to the Father" or the funeral psalm (Psalm 130) for you! You will receive the things you asked for today. I only remind you that, good friend as Thomas à Kempis is, yet being dead he cannot move. You must therefore seek him out, shake him, and after reading him, put what you have read into practice.
>
> You say you miss our religious devotions here. When I was at Mondonio I felt the same, but I tried to pay a daily visit to the Blessed Sacrament, taking with me as many of my friends as possible. As well as the Imitation I read "The Treasure Hidden in the Holy Mass" by **St. Leonard of Port Maurice**. If you think it good, do the same. . . .
>
> As for me, my poor body is anything but strong. Everything leads me to believe that I am fast nearing the end both of my studies and of my life. But anyhow, let's continue to pray for each other, and ask God the grace of a happy death. Whichever of us goes first to Paradise shall prepare a place for the other, who, when his turn arrives, will be welcomed with open arms by his friend into the kingdom of heaven.
>
> May God keep us in his grace and help us to become saints. But may it be soon, for I have a feeling that we are near the end.

At age twelve, Dominic came under the care of **John Bosco** at his oratory in Turin. Don Bosco immediately discerned the extraordinary qualities of the boy and carefully formed him in the Christian life. Dominic was inclined to severely mortify himself, but the priest forbade him to undertake any penance without permission. He also insisted that Dominic participate in recreation with all the other boys.

Dominic quickly emerged as a leader among his fellows. He inspired younger boys with his entertaining storytelling. His friendliness helped older teens conform to Christian principles. Dominic also organized the Company of the Immaculate Conception, a group of teens who did whatever menial service Don Bosco needed and helped misfits feel at home in the oratory. In 1859, when Don Bosco established the Salesians, he selected all the members of the company in the core group. All except Dominic Savio. The youth suffered with tuberculosis and, according to the medical practice of the day, was bled to excess. He had died at his parents' home in 1857.

> *Religion must be like the air we breathe, but we must not weary boys with too many devotions and observances. . . . The penance God wants is obedience. There is plenty to put up with cheerfully—heat, cold, sickness, other people's tiresome ways. There is quite enough mortification for boys in school-life itself.*
>
> —St. John Bosco

And for adults in work-life, we might add.

MARCH 9 / CANONIZED IN 1954
Celebration of Discipline; Child Saints; Mere Christian Love; Purpose

323. John Neumann
(1811–1860)

On the night before his consecration as the fourth bishop of Philadelphia, Pennsylvania, St. John Neumann wrote a short autobiography. I found his no-frills account refreshing because he simply reported facts without the saccharine piety that I expect in saints' biographies.

John Neumann was a realist who recognized the quiet movements of God's hand in ordinary events. For example, he tells how he discovered his call to be a missionary when he was a seminarian at Prague, Bohemia, in 1832:

> In the second year of theology we had the New Testament in Latin and Greek together with Exegesis and Canon Law. What appealed to me most were the Letters of the Apostle, **St. Paul**, which the professor knew how to explain very well. About this time I began to read the reports of the Leopoldine Society, especially the letters of Father Baraga and other missionaries among the Germans in North America. This is how there arose in one of my fellow students, Adalbert Schmidt, and in myself on the occasion of a walk along the Moldau River, the determination to devote ourselves to North America as soon as we acquired some experience after ordination. From that moment on my resolution was so strong and lively that I could no longer think of anything else.

So the missionary journeys of **St. Paul** and those of Frederick Baraga to Germans and Native Americans beckoned John Neumann to North America.

The saint completed his seminary education in 1835. With his bishop's blessing he undertook his own missionary journey in 1836. Bishop John Dubois was happy to receive him into the New York diocese. He ordained Neumann and assigned him to work in the Buffalo-Rochester area, where he served German and Native American Catholics for four years.

In 1840, Neumann felt the need for community support and joined the Redemptorists. Because of his outstanding pastoral work and pragmatic holiness, he became the Redemptorist vice-provincial in 1847. From his base at St. Alphonsus Church in Baltimore he continued his energetic service. Among his achievements was the support of a community of black sisters devoted to educating African-American children.

In 1852, Pope Pius IX named him bishop of Philadelphia, a sprawling diocese of 35, 000 square miles with 170, 000 German, Irish, and Italian Catholics. From day one John Neumann was a bishop of the people—his welcome parade was canceled and the money used to build a school. His episcopal style was personal contact. Before the end of the year he had visited more than half of his parishes, talking to people, preaching, celebrating Mass, and hearing confession for hours. To make himself more accessible he had learned Italian and Gaelic. "Thanks be to God!" exclaimed an Irish woman. "We now have an Irish bishop!"

Bishop Neumann exhausted himself tending to the physical and spiritual needs of his flock. He constructed churches and schools. To staff them he brought in religious orders and founded others. He encouraged the growth of lay confraternities and established the practice of Lenten devotions and parish missions. He introduced the Eucharistic adoration of Forty Hours and personally scheduled it throughout the diocese.

Literally, John Neumann worked himself to death. On January 5, 1860, while walking to perform some errands, he collapsed on the street and died.

Many think that being "spiritual" has to be supernatural, preternatural, exotic, and even weird. But a person who is truly spiritual simply asks the Holy Spirit to inspire, guide, and direct him in the natural things of life and then goes about his business. Like John Neumann.

JANUARY 5 / CANONIZED IN 1977
Missionaries; Simple Obedience; Vocation

324. Joseph Cafasso
(1811–1860)

St. Joseph Cafasso's body was twisted with curvature of the spine. Yet in a society that looked down on the disabled, this shriveled little priest became a successful teacher, preacher, and confessor. His life tells us to value people with physical deformities. And his example signifies hope to all disabled persons.

Ordained in 1833, Joseph Cafasso first became a popular lecturer and then, in 1848, the rector of the church and Institute of St. Francis in Turin, Italy. There he prepared many young priests for lives of prayer, pastoring, and preaching. A dynamic preacher himself, he taught his pupils to speak colloquially. "Be like Jesus Christ," he said, "who, in his infinite wisdom, always used the words and idioms of his hearers." However, Don Cafasso became best known as a confessor. He had a gift for releasing penitents from scruples. "When we hear confessions," he wrote, "the Lord wants us to be loving, merciful and fatherly to all." As people had flocked to **John Vianney,** people from all over Europe queued up at his confessional.

Don Cafasso also conducted an extensive prison ministry. He visited violent men who were herded together in barbarous conditions. And he taught them the Christian faith and brought them to repentance. His friend and biographer **John Bosco** told this story:

> Forty-five hardened criminals had promised to go to confession on the vigil of a feast of Our Lady. But when the day came, none of them would confess his sins.
>
> Don Cafasso's ingenious charity and courage found a way out of the difficulty. With a smile, he approached the biggest and strongest prisoner. Without a word Don Cafasso grabbed his long, flowing beard. Thinking the priest was fooling around, the man said, "Take anything else you like, but leave me my beard!"
>
> "I won't let you go until you go to confession," replied Don Cafasso. "But I don't want to go to confession," said the prisoner. "You may say what you like," said the priest, "but you won't escape until you confess." "I am not prepared," said the prisoner. "Then I will prepare you," said Cafasso.
>
> If the prisoner had wished, he could have easily freed himself. But whether it was by respect for the priest or by God's grace, the man surrendered. He allowed himself to be led to a corner of the room. Don

> Cafasso sat on a bundle of straw and prepared his friend for confession. Shortly there was a commotion. The prisoner was so moved by Don Cafasso's exhortation that his sighs and tears almost prevented him from telling his sins.
>
> Then he who had been most vehement in refusing to make his confession went to his companions. He told them he had never been so happy in his life. And his experience persuaded them all to go to confession.

Over the years Don Cafasso accompanied sixty condemned men to their public executions. His regarded these "hanged saints" as his favorite parishioners.

As a teenager John Bosco idolized Joseph Cafasso, and the two became close friends. Cafasso influenced John Bosco to undertake his work with youth. Lifelong he mentored and supported him. Although John Bosco established the Salesians several years after Cafasso's death, the order reveres him alongside their founder. Joseph Cafasso died on June 23, 1860, and John Bosco preached at his funeral.

> *You're troubled about your preparation for communion? Don't make any. You should always be ready to receive Communion. Just see if you have any venial sins, make an act of contrition, kiss a crucifix and receive without fear.*
>
> —Joseph Cafasso

JUNE 23 / CANONIZED IN 1947 / PATRON OF PRISONERS
Mercy; Saints and Sacraments (Reconciliation)

325. Théophane Vénard
(1829–1861)

One day, nine-year-old Jean-Théophane Vénard read about a priest who had been beheaded in Tonkin, Indochina, which is in present-day Vietnam. Perhaps because the martyr was from Poitiers, his home town in France, the story affected him profoundly. "Me, too! I want to go to Tonkin!" he shouted. "Me, too! I want to be a martyr!" By coincidence or by grace, his wish would come true twenty-two years later.

St. Théophane Vénard came from a close-knit family. But at age twelve he was sent away to school at Douai, from that time returning home only occasionally. He completed his seminary education in 1850 and a year later joined the Society of Foreign Missions in Paris. His decision caused his family great pain, as the society was a factory for martyrs.

Théophane was ordained in 1852. That same year he went to Hong Kong for training, where he was sick a great part of the time. Originally he was to serve in China. However, circumstances changed and he was sent to Indochina in 1854. Thus the stage was set for the realization of his childhood wish.

A general persecution of Christians was under way in Indochina, but for five years the saint worked secretly with other priests to care for tens of thousands of converts. In 1859, when the persecution intensified, he was forced to hide in the home of an elderly woman. *What an enviable situation!* he wrote a friend:

> Three missionaries, one of whom is a bishop, lying side by side, day and night, in a space a yard-and-a-half square, getting a dim light from three holes the size of a little finger, made in the mud wall, which a poor old woman conceals with some sticks thrown down outside. Under our feet is a brick cellar, constructed with great skill by one of my catechists. We have enjoyed the old woman's hospitality for three weeks, during which time I am afraid you would have been rather scandalized at our gaiety.

Betrayed by a visitor, the priest was arrested on November 30, 1859. While awaiting execution, he was imprisoned for two months in a small cage. He wrote these words in a farewell to his father:

> All those around me are civil and respectful, and a good number love me. From the great mandarin down to the last soldier, they all regret that the laws of the country condemn me to death. I have not had to endure any torture, like so many of my brothers. One light saber blow will separate my head from my body, like a spring flower that the master of the garden picks for his pleasure. We are all flowers planted on this earth for God to pluck when he will, some sooner, some later. One is a blushing rose, another a virginal lily, a third a humble violet. Let us all try to please our sovereign Lord and Master by the gift and the fragrance he has given us.

However, Théophane's decapitation at the hands of an executioner was a gruesome event. He died, a martyr of Indochina, on February 2, 1861.

The best word to describe Théophane Vénard is "happy." He was happy at home, happy at school and seminary, happy when he was sick, happy to be sent to Vietnam. And he was happy in his hiding hole, happy in his cage, and happy to bend his neck for the executioner's saber. We may not wish for martyrdom, but undoubtedly we would like to be infected with a joy like Théophane Vénard.

DECEMBER 4 / CANONIZED IN 1988
Eternal Perspective; Joy; Martyrs; Missionaries

326. Gabriel Francis Possenti

(1838–1862)

Hagiographers make sanctity seem impossible for us when they tell fanciful stories about a saint's early life. How little saint so-and-so was always rapt in prayer, worked miracles, undertook severe mortifications, never had a sexual thought, and so on. Thank God for St. Gabriel Francis Possenti and his biographers, who report that he had a normal childhood. The eleventh child of a famous lawyer in Spoleto, Italy, Francis was characteristically cheerful. Although a diligent student as a teenager, he also enjoyed reading novels and attending plays. And his friends called the handsome youth *damerino*, a "ladies' man."

As a teen at the Jesuit school in Spoleto, Francis felt a call to the priesthood. But he procrastinated deciding to act on it. Twice when he was ill he promised to become a priest if he recovered. But still he delayed. Finally in 1856, motivated by the death of a favorite sister, he entered the Passionist novitiate, taking the name Gabriel-of-Our-Lady-of-Sorrows.

Everyone who met Gabriel was impressed with his joyful submission to the humdrum routine of daily circumstances. No great achievement marked his short life, except that he did all that was expected of him with extraordinary patience and kindness. The following prayer displays the tenor of his bright spirit:

> Behold me at your feet, O my Lord, begging your mercy. What will you lose by granting me a deep love for you, a profound humility, a great purity of heart, mind and body, a brotherly charity, a sincere sorrow for having offended you, and the grace to offend you no more? What will you lose by enabling me to receive worthily your beloved Son in Holy Communion? By assisting me to act through love for you in all my thoughts, words, penances and prayers? By bestowing on me the favor of loving most tenderly the holy mother of your Son? By giving me the grace of final perseverance in my vocation and of dying a good and holy death?
>
> I am a beggar covered with wounds and rags, asking for alms. Behold, O Lord, all my wretchedness! See my proud intellect, my stony heart! See my mind filled with worldly thoughts, my will disposed to evil and my body rebellious to every good work.
>
> Help me, O my God, to correct myself. This grace I beg through your own infinite goodness and mercy. To obtain it, I offer you the

> merits of your Son, Jesus Christ, our redeemer. I have no merits of my own. I am destitute of all good, but his wounds are my hope. Had I shed my blood for love of you, like your Son, would you not grant me this favor? How much more ought you hear me now, since he shed his blood for me.

Gabriel's Passionist superiors wisely restrained his youthful eagerness for self-abnegation. Once when he asked permission to wear a chain with sharp points, his director refused. "You want to wear the little chain!" he said. "I tell you what you really ought to have a chain on is your will." When Gabriel repeated his request, the superior required him to wear the chain outside his habit. Such curbs helped the saint maintain a healthy piety.

Before he reached ordination, Gabriel contracted tuberculosis. He died in 1862 at the age of twenty-four.

Gabriel Possenti's life paralleled that of his contemporary, ***Thérèse of Lisieux****. Both had normal childhoods, displayed cheerful dispositions, sought holiness in doing little things lovingly, and died young of tuberculosis. Had Gabriel not destroyed all his personal notes just before his death, we may have had the male counterpart of* A Story of a Soul.

FEBRUARY 27 / CANONIZED IN 1920 / PATRON OF CLERICS AND YOUTH
Celebration of Discipline; Mere Christian Love; The Secrets of Spiritual Success; Twenty-Something Saints

327. Madeleine Sophie Barat

(1779–1865)

In her long career as an educator, St. Madeleine Sophie founded many schools for girls. But perhaps because of the way she was instructed, she should be named patron for home schoolers.

In 1789, Louis Barat, her older brother and godfather, came home from seminary as a deacon to be schoolmaster of Joigny in Burgundy. The Madeleine Sophie he encountered upon return was an ebullient and talented ten-year-old. He believed God had destined her for some significant work and determined to prepare her. Louis took responsibility for her spiritual formation. And he "home-schooled" her with a classical education—Greek, Latin, physics, history, and mathematics.

The French Revolution interrupted Madeleine Sophie's instruction. In 1793, Louis, then a priest, was imprisoned for two years for refusing to cooperate with the new government. But after 1795 he was released and brought his sister to Paris, where he taught her Scripture, the fathers, and theology.

By 1800 the first revolutionary wave had dissipated and the church was rebuilding what had been destroyed. Especially needed were Christian schools. It was in this context that Madeleine Sophie discovered her calling. A priest named Varin invited her to start an association of religious women committed to educating girls. In 1800 at Amiens, France, the saint formed a small community with several other young women. Two years later she was appointed the superior of this group that became the Society of the Sacred Heart.

Over the years Madeleine Sophie and her sisters established 105 schools throughout Europe and sent a team to start schools in North America. The saint was a forward-thinking educator, insisting that her sisters stay up-to-date with contemporary methods. Madeleine Sophie also championed the education of women:

> How rare it is to find a valiant woman! It is perhaps necessarily so, since Scripture says that they are more precious than pearls and diamonds. Let us however work to train a few. For in this century we must no longer count on men to preserve the faith. The grain of faith that will be saved will hide itself among women. A woman cannot remain neutral in the world. She too is set for the fall and resurrection of many. How different are God's thoughts from ours!

> Between women and God is often arranged the eternal salvation of husbands and sons. But for this she must be the valiant woman. Strong to uphold purity of life. Strong to keep inviolate the treasure of faith. Strong in every battle of life. Great-souled in the face of calumny, persecution and death. And remember, sorrow is the training ground of strong souls.

The saint founded boarding schools for wealthy girls, but she also set up many day schools for the instruction of poor girls for whom she had a special concern. Madeleine Sophie led her community for sixty-three years. She died in 1865 at eighty-six years of age.

Parents, teachers, and others who feel frustrated in their efforts to educate and evangelize children may well take counsel from St. Madeleine Sophie: "Give of your superabundance to the children. Fill your hearts with the love of God, and then you will always be able to instill it into them. If we are united to God we shall be able to do wonders for them. I cannot exaggerate the effect produced upon children's souls by the spirit of prayer and union with God. I would have founded the society for the soul of one child."

MAY 25 / CANONIZED IN 1925
Leading Women; Love in Action; Raising Christian Youth; Valiant Women

328. Francis Xavier Seelos

(1819–1867)

Redemptorist Father Francis Xavier Seelos radiated cheer and mercy everywhere he served. From Bavaria to the United States. From Pittsburgh to New Orleans, and from Detroit to Baltimore. Like **Joseph Cafasso**, another extraordinarily gifted priest of the nineteenth century, Father Seelos attracted large numbers of people to his confessional. They came because they felt his mercy and because his advice seemed to release them from sin and scruples. He exposed his compassionate heart in sermons, like this one:

> Oh, if only all the sinners of the whole wide world were present here! Yes, even the greatest, the most hardened, even those close to despair. I would call out to them. "The Lord God is merciful and gracious, patient and of much compassion" (see Exodus 34:6). I would show them why the Apostles call God the Father of Mercy, the God of all consolation. I would tell them that the prophet in the Old Testament even said that the earth is full of the mercy of God and that mercy is above all his works.
>
> Oh how can I make this clear to you? First, that God is filled with pity and invites us lovingly to come to him? That God waits for the conversion of the whole world with patience? And thirdly, that God receives the repentant sinner with all love.
>
> Oh Mary, Mother of Mercy! You understood the mercy of God when you cried out in the Magnificat: "His mercy is from generation to generation." Obtain for all sinners a childlike confidence in the mercy of God.
>
> Oh, you sinners who have not the courage to confess your sins because they are so numerous or so grievous or so shameful! Oh, come without fear or trembling! I promise to receive you with all mildness. If I do not keep my word, I here publicly give you permission to throw it up to me in the confessional and to charge me with lying.

To fulfill his childhood dream of becoming a priest, Xavier had to leave his poor but close-knit family to pursue his studies. And ultimately he exiled himself from his Bavarian homeland by applying to join the Redemptorists and go to the United States as a missionary. He achieved his goal in 1844 when the bishop of Baltimore ordained him a priest. He began his twenty-three years of priestly work at

St. Philomena's Parish in Pittsburgh, serving under the exemplary leadership of its pastor, **John Neumann**.

On top of full-time parish duties, Father Seelos held numerous responsible positions in his Redemptorist community. For sixteen of his twenty-three years as a Redemptorist, in various places, he cared for his brothers as superior. As novice master he was both criticized and applauded for mercifully instructing his charges in their vernacular instead of Latin. The seminarians loved him, as one said, "more than I loved my own mother!"

From 1863 to 1865, Father Seelos led the Redemptorist mission team. After crisscrossing the United States several times, curing souls from the pulpit and in the confessional, he was assigned to parishes first in Detroit and then in New Orleans.

Shortly after Father Seelos became pastor of St. Mary's Parish in New Orleans, an epidemic of yellow fever hit the city. While he was tending to the sick, the deadly virus struck him. He died on October 4, 1867, at the age of only forty-eight years.

If mercy were a sin, I believe I could not keep from committing it.

—Bernard of Clairvaux

OCTOBER 4

Kindness; Mercy; Saints and Sacraments (Reconciliation); Sin

329. Korean Martyrs

(1839–1866)

In the late eighteenth century, laymen brought the Catholic Church to Korea. Yi Sung-hun, a young scholar in Seoul, pored over Catholic books imported from China. In 1784, he visited a Catholic church in Peking and was baptized. He recruited and baptized family and friends, organizing the first Catholic community in his country.

Government persecution began in 1785 and continued sporadically for a century. Each time the growing Catholic community smuggled in a foreign priest, the government arrested believers and tortured them in order to find him. Lay leaders besieged Rome with requests for a bishop. Finally in 1831, a Korean vicariate was established and the Society of Foreign Missions at Paris was put in charge. In 1837, Bishop Laurent Imbert finally slipped into Korea, setting off waves of persecution that lasted from 1839 to 1866. Thousands from the infant Korean church were brutally tortured and beheaded during those years.

During the Korean church's centennial celebration in 1984, Pope John Paul II canonized 103 martyrs of that period. Many women and men who gave their lives were novice Catholics engaged in evangelization and catechesis. The government arrested and interrogated suspected Catholics. When victims refused to recant, they were bludgeoned, scourged, and twisted till their bones broke and protruded from their skin.

Those condemned to death were suspended from a huge cross on an oxcart, and with their bodies hanging in midair, were carried outside the city. After the painful journey, the prisoners were taken down from the cross, stripped naked, and beheaded.

The martyrs who were canonized in 1984 included 93 Koreans and 10 French clergy; 47 women, 54 men, and 2 children. The Koreans came from all walks of life, both married and single. Many were lay leaders in the church. Among the martyrs were:

- Chong Ha-sang Paul. Tortured and beheaded in 1839. Paul had worked for church renewal and had successfully lobbied Rome for a Korean vicariate.

- Father Kim Tae-gon Andrew. Beheaded in 1846 at twenty-six years old and ordained just one year. "In this difficult time," he wrote from prison, "to be victorious, we must be steadfast, using all of our strength like brave soldiers fully armed in the battlefield. You must love and help one another, and wait hopefully for the time when our Lord in his mercy will relieve our sufferings. Whatever happens behave in such a way that God will be glorified."
- Nam Myong-hyok Damian, a catechist, and Yi Yon-hui Mary, his wife. Tortured and beheaded in 1839. Guards tried to break Mary by molesting her and torturing her twelve-year-old son. Damian encouraged Mary to be brave: "This world is nothing but an inn we pass through. Our real home is heaven. Follow me and become a martyr. I want us to meet again in the kingdom of eternal glory."
- Yu Tae-ch'ol Peter. Thirteen-year-old boy. Strangled in 1839. Tortured fourteen times, he bore 600 lashes and 45 cudgel blows. "I believe in God," he told his persecutors. "I am not afraid of being hit."
- Bishop Siméon Berneux who served the Korean church for twelve years. He built a seminary and published Catholic books. Tortured and beheaded in 1866, along with three newly ordained French missionaries.

In 1839, there were 9,000 Catholics in Korea. In 1866, after the persecutions which took 8,000 lives, there were 23,000. A century later in 1954, there were 160,000. Now the Catholic Church in Korea, one of the fastest-growing communities in the world, has 1.6 million members. The blood of the Korean martyrs was not spilt in vain.

SEPTEMBER 20 / CANONIZED IN 1984
Countercultural Witness; Martyrs

330. Peter Julian Eymard
(1811–1868)

"Those two hours seemed a moment," said St. Peter Julian Eymard of his experience carrying the Blessed Sacrament in a Corpus Christi procession. "I laid the church in France and throughout the world, everybody, myself at the Lord's feet. My eyes filled with tears. My heart seemed under the wine press." That event confirmed Eymard's desire to spread devotion to Christ in the Eucharist.

At that time Father Eymard was provincial of the Marists at Lyons. Gradually he became convinced that he was called to leave that order to found a congregation of priests totally dedicated to Eucharistic adoration. In 1851 he proposed the idea of such a community to his superiors, but they asked him to take time to discern carefully his intention. Encouraged by Pope Pius IX and John Colin, the Marist founder, he finally moved ahead in 1856. He submitted his plan to the archbishop of Paris, who approved it and gave him a house as a center.

Thus, with only one other priest, Eymard launched the Priests of the Blessed Sacrament. By 1862 the community had opened three houses and established a regular novitiate. The congregation's sole purpose was worshiping Christ in the Eucharist, as Eymard explained to new members in the following address:

> The Lord has different types of servants. While some work for his glory among their brothers and sisters, others devote themselves exclusively to his worthy person. You have been numbered among the latter. But remember that you must belong to him unconditionally. You must rely on him for everything.
>
> The law of your life, the perfection of your sanctity consists in serving Christ personally. You have not come here primarily to sanctify yourselves in solitude or to be apostles. Neither do you come to lead souls to God by your prudent and zealous directions. You have come here only to serve the Lord. Your duty is to attend continually to the Lord in the Blessed Sacrament.
>
> When you first came here did anyone ask you, "Are you talented, or have you brought any money?" No, never have I even given such a question a thought. You were simply asked, "Do you wish to serve?" The only condition required of a servant is that he should take to heart the interest of the Master whom he wishes to serve.

Thus you were admitted to the Congregation. You were told to have but one end in view—the service of the Lord's person. To have but one desire—to please him and work for him alone.

Are you willing to kneel on this prayer stool to consume your life as a candle on the altar? Are you willing to be a servant in the full sense of the word. If so, come in.

In 1858, Father Eymard established the Servants of the Blessed Sacrament, a community of women entirely engaged in perpetual adoration. He also formed associations of priests and laypeople who committed themselves to pray an hour a day in Christ's presence at the tabernacle. Owing much to Eymard's work, by the mid-twentieth century such groups had spread to parishes throughout the world.

After a long illness, Peter Julian Eymard died on August 1, 1868.

To us, serving Christ usually means sharing his actions—feeding the hungry, housing the homeless, announcing the good news, counseling the depressed. St. Peter Julian Eymard, however, expands our concept of Christian service to include simply paying personal attention to the Lord in prayer.

AUGUST 1 / CANONIZED IN 1962
Intimacy with the Divine; Prayer; Saints and Sacraments (Eucharist); Worship

331. Anthony Mary Claret
(1807–1870)

By nature St. Anthony Mary Claret was an irrepressible evangelist. Thoroughly modern in his outlook and methods, he spread the gospel creatively by establishing institutions with wide-ranging impact—an international religious order, a museum, publishing ventures, libraries, professional associations, schools, and cultural centers.

Frustrated as a young priest in his effort to join a missionary order, in the 1840s Anthony plunged himself into the evangelization of Catalonia, his home province in Spain. He wove ancient Christian wisdom into fresh, contemporary strategy and tactics for evangelization that he articulated in his *Autobiography*. In the following excerpt, for example, he explains why evangelizers must temper zeal with meekness:

> Jesus told his disciples, "Learn from me, for I am gentle and humble in heart, and you will find rest for your souls" (Matthew 11:29 NJB). Humility is like the root of the tree, and gentleness is its fruit. We please God by humility and our neighbor by gentleness.
>
> No virtue is so attractive as gentleness. If you throw little pieces of bread into a pond, the fish will come fearlessly up to your feet. But if you throw rocks, they will swim away and hide. Jesus Christ was gentleness itself, and because of this virtue he is called the Lamb. The prophets foretold that he would be persecuted and yet remain silent. But by his suffering and silence he redeemed us and taught us how we must act to save the souls he has entrusted to us.
>
> Bad temper and anger—the lack of gentleness—often masquerade as zeal. I have studied the distinction between them, so as not to make a crucial mistake. The function of zeal is to abhor, flee, renounce, combat and overthrow everything that is contrary to God.
>
> But zeal is an ardent and violent love that needs to be wisely controlled. Otherwise it might go beyond the limits of modesty and discretion. Moved by anger it fails to keep within the bounds of reason and pushes the heart to disorder.
>
> My God, give me a zeal that is discreet and prudent so that I may do everything strongly yet sweetly, gently yet thoroughly.

Apostolic zeal impelled St. Anthony himself. Lifelong he preached ten thousand sermons and published two hundred books and pamphlets.

In 1847 he founded the very successful Religious Library, a publishing venture that distributed five million books and four million leaflets in two decades. At the same time Anthony organized his priest collaborators as the Missionary Sons of the Immaculate Heart of Mary, now called Claretians.

Appointed archbishop of Santiago, Cuba, in 1850, St. Anthony set about reforming a diocese that had been untended for fourteen years. His intensive efforts to revitalize the church on the island met considerable resistance. Once he was even seriously wounded by a man whose mistress he had converted.

In 1857 he resigned his post and returned to Spain, where he served the rest of his life as chaplain to Queen Isabella II. His position at court repressed his impulse to evangelize, but he channeled his energy into founding a scientific laboratory, music and language schools, and a museum. He also worked with the Claretians, reorienting his community to continue his work in the contemporary world.

Revolution in Spain in 1868 drove the saint into exile with the queen. He died in Rome in 1870.

O my God, I give you my word that I shall preach, write and circulate good books and pamphlets in abundance, so as to drown evil in a flood of good.

—Anthony Mary Claret

OCTOBER 24 / CANONIZED IN 1950
Innovative Saints; Evangelization; Meekness

332. Catherine Labouré

(1806–1876)

Like her contemporary **Bernadette** and other visionaries, St. Catherine Labouré was a simple, uneducated young woman. In 1830, having cared for her father's household for a decade, she joined the Sisters of Charity of St. Vincent de Paul at Châtillon-sur-Seine, France. After her postulancy, she went to a convent in the rue du Bec, Paris, for her novitiate. Only four days after her arrival, Catherine began to experience the series of visions that made her famous. On July 31, for example, late at night a shining child awakened her and escorted her to the chapel. There Mary spoke with her for two hours, telling her she would have a difficult task to perform and predicting future events.

On November 27, Mary appeared to give Catherine her mission. She saw Mary standing on a globe, with rays of light flooding from her hands. Later Catherine gave this account of the vision:

> While I contemplated her, the Blessed Virgin lowered her eyes and looked upon me. Then I heard a voice saying to me: "The ball that you see represents the entire world . . . and each person in particular." I cannot now express what I then saw and felt. Oh! The beauty and the splendor of those rays! "These rays symbolize the graces that I shed on those who ask for them." With this I understood how agreeable to the Blessed Virgin are the prayers addressed to her. I discovered how generous she is toward those who invoke her, what precious graces she would give those who would ask them of her and with what joy she would grant them.
>
> At this moment I scarcely knew where I was. All I can say is that I was immersed in supreme delight, when a panel of oval shape formed around the Blessed Virgin. On it traced these words: "O Mary conceived without sin, pray for us who have recourse to thee!" Then a voice said to me: "Have a medal struck on this model. All those who wear it will receive great graces. It should be worn around the neck. Great graces will be the portion of those who wear it with confidence." All at once the picture appeared to turn and I saw the reverse of the medal. Solicitous about what should be inscribed on the reverse, one day I seemed to hear a voice saying: "The M and the two hearts are enough."

Catherine spoke about the apparitions only to Father M. Aladel, her confessor, who determined that they were genuine. With the permission of the archbishop of Paris, Aladel had fifteen hundred medals struck in 1832. His book about the "miraculous medal" —so-called because of its origins, not its properties—became an international best-seller translated into seven languages. The conversion of Alphonse Ratisbonne, an Alsatian Jew who had reluctantly worn the medal and then had the same vision as Catherine, enormously increased its popularity.

Catherine herself maintained her anonymity. She even refused to appear at the archbishop's investigation in 1836 that declared the visions authentic. She lived quietly for the rest of her life at a convent in Enghien-Neuilly, answering the door, raising poultry, and tending the sick. But when Catherine died in 1876, an outburst of popular veneration exploded at her funeral. And the healing of a twelve-year-old girl, crippled from birth, at her grave helped spread her fame widely. Though little is known of her personal life, Catherine Labouré has become one of the most esteemed of all the saints.

I knew nothing. I was nothing. For this reason God picked me out.

—Catherine Labouré

NOVEMBER 28 / CANONIZED IN 1947
Mary; Pursuit of Holiness; Visions and Visionaries

333. Bernadette Soubirous

(1844–1879)

St. Bernadette Soubirous's humdrum life would have gone unnoticed except for a luminous two-month interlude. She was the oldest daughter of an impoverished miller in Lourdes, France. At fourteen, Bernadette was undersized, afflicted with chronic asthma, uneducated, and had not yet received her first communion. But on February 11, 1858, while she was scavenging for wood in a remote area, the Virgin Mary appeared to her in a rocky cave. "Within the opening of the grotto," said Bernadette:

> I saw a girl in white, no bigger than myself, who greeted me with a slight bow of the head. She stretched out her arms slightly away from her body, opening her hands, as in pictures of Our Lady. Over her right arm hung a rosary.
>
> Raising my eyes again, I saw the girl smiling at me most graciously and seeming to invite me to come nearer. But I was afraid. It was not however a fear such as I have had at other times, for I would have stayed there forever looking at her. Whereas, when you are afraid, you run away quickly.

Then Bernadette tried to pray, but could not lift her hand to make the sign of the cross until the girl in white crossed herself and took up her rosary.

> While I was saying the rosary, I watched as hard as I could. She was wearing a white dress reaching down to her feet of which only the toes appeared. The dress was gathered very high at the neck by a hem from which hung a white cord. A white veil covered her head and came down over her shoulders and arms almost to the bottom of her dress. On each foot I saw a yellow rose. The sash of the dress was blue, and hung down below the knees. The chain of the rosary was yellow; the beads, white, big and widely spaced.
>
> The girl was alive, very young and surrounded with light. When I had finished my rosary, she bowed with a smile. She withdrew into the grotto and all of a sudden disappeared.

From February to April the Virgin appeared to Bernadette eighteen times. She directed the saint to pray and do penance for sinners and to have a church built at the grotto. She led Bernadette to a spring where there had never been one before. From that time twenty-seven thousand gallons of water have flowed from it every week. When Bernadette asked the girl to identify herself, she said, "I am the Immaculate Conception."

The aftermath of the apparitions caused Bernadette considerable pain. With courage and integrity she withstood interrogations by skeptical civil and church officials. Curious visitors harassed her for years. In 1866 she entered a convent of the Sisters of Notre Dame of Nevers, where in spite of constant illnesses she patiently performed domestic duties.

By her own choice Bernadette had nothing to do with the development of Lourdes as an international pilgrimage center. She did not even attend the dedication of the basilica in 1876. She was thirty-five years old when she died in 1879.

The church recognizes Bernadette as a saint not because she experienced apparitions and ecstasies. Rather we celebrate her for her simple faith, her quiet perseverance, and her unblemished integrity. As ***Mary's*** *song has it, God "has pulled down princes from their thrones and raised high the lowly" (Luke 1:52* NJB*). So, if we take Bernadette's example, we won't long for special spiritual experiences, but we will compete for the lowest places.*

APRIL 16 / CANONIZED IN 1933
Mary; True Humility; Visions and Visionaries

334. Mary Mazzarello
(1837–1881)

St. Mary Mazzarello stumbled into her ministry. As a girl she worked on her father's farm in Mornese, Italy. At seventeen she became active in a new Marian sodality that **John Bosco** had inspired. During a typhoid epidemic in 1860, Mary and the sodalists cared for victims, and Mary got sick and almost died.

Upon recovery Mary found herself too weak for farmwork, so she and a friend began to work as seamstresses. Their business flourished. Soon they involved young girls as their apprentices. Thus almost by accident Mary Mazzarello found what was to become her life's work—the care and education of poor girls.

Don Bosco wanted a community of women to parallel for girls his work for boys. Under his influence, in 1872 the local Mornese parish built a home where Mary and the sodalists formed a new religious order. Don Bosco appointed Mary Mazzarello, the country seamstress, as superior of the congregation that came to be called the Salesian Sisters.

Under Mary's gentle leadership the order grew steadily. In 1878 she sent six sisters on a Salesian mission to Indians in Argentina. Mary communicated by letters to her sisters there, and the following excerpt expresses her typical wisdom, faith, and joy:

> I am sorry that the new house at Las Piedras is not going well. Sister Giovanna is too young and not settled enough to act as the superior. There is no need for you to worry, however. You must be convinced that there will always be defects. You must correct and remedy what you can, but always with calm and leaving the rest in the hands of the Lord. Sometimes by making too much of little things we let the big things pass. I do not mean that you should not pay attention to little failings. That is not what I mean.
>
> Don't pretend that the sisters have no defects. And never pretend that they correct them all at once! Correct, advise always, but in your heart always have compassion and charity toward everyone. We must study inclinations and know how to use them. To succeed you must inspire confidence.
>
> But with prayer, patience, vigilance and perseverance, little by little you will succeed in everything. Trust in Jesus, place all your troubles

> in his heart. Let him do everything. He will fix everything. Be always happy and full of good spirits!
>
> I am very happy that you have a lot of work because work is the father of all the virtues. When we work our little whims fly away and we are happy. While I want you to work, I also want you to take care of your health and also to work without ambition, solely to please Jesus.

In February 1881, Mary became very ill. She asked Don Bosco if she would survive, and he said no. Cheerfully, Mary faced her death. When she received the last anointing, she said to the priest, "Now that you've given me my passport, I can go any time, can't I." However, just before her death, Mary Mazzarello endured a severe temptation to despair. But she emerged from it singing "Those who love Mary shall be happy." She died on May 14, 1881.

Paradoxes abound in saints' lives. For example, the scholar ***Francis Xavier*** *took the gospel to the ordinary people of the East. And Mary Mazzarello, an uneducated peasant woman, founded an order that now educates girls from fourteen hundred houses all over the world. I think both saints were successful at tasks they did not seem well suited for because of their innate friendliness.*

MAY 14 / CANONIZED IN 1951
Care of the Soul; Raising Christian Youth; Serving the Poor

335. Paola Frassinetti

(1809–1882)

As a young woman, St. Paola Frassinetti for health reasons moved from Genoa to Quinto to join her brother, the pastor of the village's church. There, while she recovered her strength, she busied herself teaching poor children. And in that experience she discovered her vocation. With her brother's counsel, she organized a few women who had gathered around her into the Sisters of St. Dorothy, a religious institute dedicated to educating the poor.

Paola faced big obstacles in establishing her community. Not the least of which was her complete lack of resources. However, she built her success on a joyful acceptance of God's will in all circumstances. Paola did not believe in "resignation," but in "uniformity" to the divine will, as she explained in this letter to a sister:

> My dear child, I will tell you something I have never told anyone else. I was at one time so overwhelmed with miseries that I felt myself to be an incarnate demon. In desperation, I made a supreme act of uniformity to the will of God. Thus I severed at one blow the chains that abound me a slave to myself.
>
> Uniformity to the will of God closes the door to every desire and vain anxiety. It enables one to go freely to God and gives real peace in the midst of the greatest sorrow. I do not claim to have arrived at such uniformity to the will of God. If I had, I should be a saint. But this exercise has helped me, and would have helped me more had I practiced it better.

Paola seems to have been gifted in developing sound human relationships. She possessed considerable practical wisdom that benefited her sisters and made the rigors of religious life more endurable. For example, she did not encourage physical penances, but recommended disciplines of the will like patience and self-control. Listen in as she teaches a sister a Christian approach to feelings and humility:

> My dear Sister, you tell me that you have brought your pride with you. I assure you that I was quite aware of that! If you had left all your passions behind you and were just an unfeeling lump, how could you prove your love and faithfulness to God? Therefore don't worry about your feelings but fight bravely, leaning on God. And if sometimes

the old feelings get the better of you, don't lose courage, but rise up humbly and go on with renewed vigor.

No one falls from the valleys, but many from the heights. When we started the congregation we had certainly no idea of founding anything great. We only wished to do the holy will of God. So however things may go, we will be content.

Don't permit your miseries or defects to depress you. Rather let them be steps by which you descend the deep mine where we find the precious gem of holy humility. Learn that it is our littleness that buys this unique and true treasure that alone renders the soul that possesses it blessed in time and in eternity.

Officially recognized in 1863, the Sisters of St. Dorothy spread throughout Italy, Portugal, and Brazil. After a series of strokes, Paola Frassinetti died peacefully on June 11, 1882.

Paola Frassinetti did not set out to do something big for God. Or even to be a saint. She saw in Quinto the need of the poor children there and threw herself into teaching them. Thus, her compassion occasioned the creation of a community that benefited many. And ultimately it resulted in her becoming a saint.

JUNE 11 / CANONIZED IN 1984
Humility; Leading Women; Simple Obedience

336. Charles Lwanga and Companions
(D. 1886)

In the 1880s, Catholic and Protestant missionaries introduced Christianity into the Ugandan kingdom of Buganda. The spread of the faith caused witch doctors and chiefs to fear for their power. So they persuaded young King Mwanga that the new religion would undermine his authority.

The eighteen-year-old ruler was unstable, alcoholic, and addicted to sexual relations with boys. When Joseph Mukasa, the Catholic captain of the king's pages, rebuked him for his debauchery and for slaughtering a Protestant missionary, he determined to uproot Christianity from Buganda. Because Mukasa protected Christian pages from his advances, Mwanga had him beheaded in November 1885.

In May 1886 the king tried to seduce a page and discovered that another young man had been instructing him in the faith. Livid with rage, he drove a spear through the catechist's neck. Then he demanded that all the Christian pages renounce their faith or face death. They chose death, and Mwanga obliged. He rounded up the Christian pages, Catholic and Protestant alike. On June 3, 1886, he had them executed at Namugongo, a place of ritual sacrifice.

Charles Lwanga, a young Catholic leader, had succeeded Mukasa as majordomo of the pages. Like his predecessor, he encouraged the faith of the Christians and insulated them from Mwanga's perversions. So he was one of the first to be martyred. A page who was mysteriously pardoned at Namugongo described Charles' death:

> Then we set out from the square walking in single file, a rope from neck to neck joining the prisoners. As we went every one of us prayed in his heart, but not aloud. When we arrived in the valley we were ordered to halt where the high executioner, Senkole, and a big crowd waited.
>
> Senkole separated Charles Lwanga from the others, saying: "This is the man of my choice. He'll be my victim."
>
> Lwanga said to us: "Friends I am staying here. Good-bye! We shall meet again in heaven." With one voice we answered, "Yes, before the throne of God. Au revoir."

Charles was laid on a pyre under which the fire was kept low. The flame slowly charred the martyr's legs without touching the rest of his body. Later, an assistant provided these details:

> Senkole said to Charles: "Let's see whether Katonda (God) will come to deliver you from the fire."
>
> Bearing his agony without a murmur, Charles said: "Poor, foolish man, you don't know what you say. You are burning me, but it is as if you were pouring water on my body. I die because of the religion of Katonda. But you, you will see trouble. Katonda, whom you insult, will one day plunge you into real fire. Sir, if only you would also become a Christian."

Charles prayed quietly while the fire slowly did its work. Just before the end, he cried out, "*Katonda wange!*" (My God!) and died.

Then the other pages were stripped, wrapped in reed mats, piled on a huge pyre, and burnt alive. "*We have killed many people,*" said one executioner, "*but never such as these. On other occasions, victims did nothing but moan and weep. There was not a sigh, not even an angry word. All we heard was a soft murmur on their lips. They prayed until they died.*" That day, thirteen Catholics, eleven Protestants, and eight unbaptized seekers, ranging in age from thirteen to twenty-five, offered their lives in the flames.

One of the martyrs said prophetically, "A well that has many sources never runs dry. When we are gone, others will come after us." Already by 1890, the number of Christians in Buganda was estimated at ten thousand.

JUNE 3 / CANONIZED IN 1964
Child Saints; Martyrs; Passion for Purity; Twenty-Something Saints

337. John Bosco
(1815–1888)

God must have laughed heartily at the joke he played when he gave St. John Bosco to the nineteenth century. Don John Bosco was a man of great faith in an age of great unbelief. He was a wonder-worker who routinely performed miracles, was guided by dreams, read people's consciences, and accurately predicted the future.

However, Don Bosco was mainly an evangelist, educator, and leader of men. He used all of his gifts, both spiritual and natural, for others. For nearly half a century he catechized and cared for homeless youths in Turin, Italy. And he founded a religious order that has extended his ministry throughout the contemporary world.

In 1841 a newly ordained priest, he came to Turin to study theology. Soon he had gathered about himself hundreds of street youths. First they flocked to his Sunday events for fun, games, food, catechism, and worship. Over the next fifteen years he collected abandoned youths in a ragtag but impressive community. With nothing but faith he built them residences, workshops, schools, and churches.

But the most valuable thing Don Bosco gave his boys was love. Most soaked up his affection and responded by getting their lives on track. In a letter to a colleague, the saint explained the role of charity in his educational method:

> . . . It is more fitting to be persistent in punishing our own impatience and pride than to correct the boys. We must be firm but kind and patient with them.
>
> I give you as model the charity of **Paul** which he showed to his new converts. They often reduced him to tears and entreaties when he found them lacking docility and even opposing his loving efforts.
>
> See that no one finds you motivated by impetuosity or willfulness. It is difficult to keep calm when administering punishment, but this must be done if we are to keep ourselves from . . . spilling out our anger.
>
> Let us regard those boys . . . as our own sons. . . . Let us not rule over them except for the purpose of serving them better.
>
> This was the method Jesus used with the apostles. He put up with their ignorance and roughness and even their infidelity. He treated sinners with a kindness and affection that caused some to be shocked, others to be scandalized, and still others to hope for God's mercy. And so he bade us to be "gentle and humble of heart."

> They are our sons, and so in correcting their mistakes we must lay aside all anger and restrain it so firmly that it is extinguished entirely.
>
> There must be no hostility in our minds, no contempt in our eyes, no insult on our lips. We must use mercy for the present and have hope for the future, as is fitting for true fathers who are eager for real correction and improvement.

A small band of priests joined Don Bosco. In 1854, at a time when Italian anticlericals were banning religious orders, he successfully organized them into a community. He named them Salesians after **St. Francis de Sales,** his favorite saint. He had an incredible vision in 1883, showing him that his brothers would travel to the ends of the earth via automobiles, freeways, and airplanes! A dream that has come true, as now there are about two thousand Salesian communities in 113 countries.

Anger and impatience are little volcanoes in me, waiting to erupt at an unsuspecting bystander, usually a family member. Reflecting on John Bosco reminds me to let Christ replace those explosive tendencies with the grace to be humble and kind.

JANUARY 31 / CANONIZED IN 1934 / PATRON OF APPRENTICES AND LABORERS
Leading Men; Mere Christian Love; Raising Christian Youth

338. Damien the Leper (Damien de Veuster)
(1840–1889)

I make myself a leper with the lepers to gain all for Christ.

—Damien de Veuster

In 1873, Belgian priest Damien de Veuster volunteered to serve the lepers at Molokai. Shortly after the young missionary had arrived in Hawaii eight years before, a leprosy epidemic struck the islands, and victims were herded into isolation. Even though he had a premonition that he would die a leper, he undertook his assignment with excitement. "I—I want to go there!" he had told his bishop. "I know many of these unfortunate souls and I ask only to share their lot and their prison."

And Damien found that Molokai was indeed a prison—of degradation, suffering, and death. Although engulfed by hopelessness, he refused to submit to it. Immediately Damien set out to restore the dignity of the lepers. He treated them not as victims, but as ordinary human beings. He organized them into work groups that constructed roads, cottages, and clinics. He established a cemetery and built coffins for them, improving their lives by making their deaths respectable. For the sports-loving Hawaiians he organized footraces, even though some competitors had lost their feet. He cheered the island by forming a choir and a band. Two organists who had ten fingers between them played at funeral masses.

Damien took no personal precautions in caring for his people. Though often sickened by the overwhelming stench of their rotting flesh, daily he touched, hugged, and bathed them. "I have seen him," said a visitor, "dress the most loathsome sores as if he were arranging flowers."

Father Damien never rested. When he was not tending to the needs of his beloved lepers, he was pressuring the government for more money and medical resources for the colony. He finally contracted the dreaded disease and died at Molokai on April 15, 1889.

The saint was always gentle with others, but like **St. Peter Claver,** hard on himself. We admire his self-abnegation, but recoil from the thought of doing what he did. We don't easily understand such selflessness, but perhaps Damien's "personal rule," quoted below, explains something of the force that drove him:

The memory of your past infidelities must move you at each present moment to acts of humility and contrition, with the renewing of firm vows for the future. Be severe toward yourself, indulgent toward others. Have a scrupulous exactitude for everything regarding God, that is, in prayer, meditation, celebration of mass and the sacraments.

Unite your heart with God. And especially, in the midst of temptation, protest ceaselessly that you prefer to die instantly rather than consent to the least venial sin. May passion lead you continually to whisper these words: "I wish to be dissolved and to be with Christ." To stave off consent to sin, remember the invisible judgment of God, who watches and knows all the actions of your free will.

Be good. Be vigilant. Remember always your three vows by which you are dead to the things of the world. All that you have is only for you to use, not your personal property. Death to the pleasures of the flesh: purity makes you like an angel. Impurity makes a devil out of a priest. No sensuality, no looking for ease. Death to all the caprices of your own will. As with the corpse, let your superiors do what they think best with you.

Remember always the immutability of God, and imitate it by a patience in the face of all tests. Remember always that God is eternal. Work courageously in order one day to be united with him forever.

APRIL 15 / BEATIFIED IN 1995
Celebration of Discipline; Love in Action; Sin; Suffering; Temptation

339. Mary Teresa De Soubiran
(1835–1889)

Young Sophie de Soubiran La Louvière had her heart set on the cloistered life of Carmel. But in 1854 she yielded to the wishes of an uncle who wanted her to head up a *béguinage*, a group of laywomen who took no vows and performed some Christian service. Taking the name Mary Teresa, she assumed leadership of the béguine community at Castelnaudary, France, her hometown. Under her guidance, the little group of women opened an orphanage and flourished in their Christian commitments.

But Mary Teresa still longed for something more, and on an Ignatian retreat she heard God's call to start a new community. In 1864 she founded the Society of Mary the Helper at Toulouse. Dedicated to saving souls through practical work, Mary Teresa wanted her sisters to do the lowly work that others neglected. She outlined her rationale for this in the congregation's constitution:

> Nothing is small when it is a matter of helping souls saved by Our Lord. Nothing is hard when we remember what we have cost him and recall his words inviting our help and accepting our services as if rendered to himself: "In so far as you did this to one of the least of these brothers of mine, you did it to me" (Matthew 25:40 *NJB*).
>
> In order to reproduce in the active life the same character of humility as in the interior life, we must choose, like Our Lord at Nazareth, obscure and unrecognized work, with no external showiness and often even without success. We must also be wholly satisfied in pleasing God and doing his will whatever it may be. To be more sure of not deviating from this humble and hidden life, that brings us close to God, we should prefer the lack of human means, not only from indifference to creatures, but from a sincere desire to be deprived, like Our Lord, of all human aid. Thus, we can lean upon God alone, and expect everything from his good pleasure.
>
> We must be fully persuaded that this complete detachment can and should be constantly practiced in the work entrusted to us. We must bring to our service a real freedom from all purely human and personal preoccupations. We must subordinate our own needs to those of others so that we may exercise charity and humility and self-denial very perfectly and in the sight of God alone.

For almost a decade the society flourished. The sisters found their special vocation in establishing homes for working girls in industrial cities. But in 1874 a bizarre series of events unfolded. Mother Mary Frances, a trusted assistant to the superior, had pushed the community into financial troubles, but blamed Mary Teresa. This clever, unprincipled woman maneuvered things so that Mary Teresa was finally expelled from her order. She left her congregation as a laywoman and had to begin her life over. Rejected by the Carmelites, she joined the Sisters of Charity at Paris in 1877, where she lived till her death in 1889.

Mother Mary Frances ultimately met her demise. The order chafed under her arbitrary rule, and in 1889 she resigned and left the society when the general chapter rebuffed her. After her death in 1921 it came to light that she was actually a married woman who had abandoned her husband. Thus she was never validly a nun, and none of her decisions were canonical. And so Mary Teresa was vindicated: she had never really ceased to be a member of the order she founded.

The great truth that God is all, and the rest nothing, becomes the life of the soul, and upon it one can lean securely amid the incomprehensible mysteries of this world.

—Mary Teresa de Soubiran

OCTOBER 20 / BEATIFIED IN 1946
Success in Failure; Suffering

340. John Henry Newman
(1801–1890)

Early in his career as an Oxford don, Anglican John Henry Newman grew convinced that the Church of England needed a reformation. He thought the Anglican communion should reshape itself on the pattern of the "catholic" elements that characterized the church in the first five centuries. After 1833, Newman acted as the leader of the Oxford Movement that advocated this ideal of reform. He fueled the movement with his *Tracts of the Times* and with books like *Lectures on the Prophetical Office of the Church*.

Newman's sermons, published in 1837 as *Parochial and Plain Sermons*, popularized the Oxford Movement. His followers, impressed by his personal devotion, loved him as a man who practiced what he preached. No ivory-tower intellectual, Newman taught an appealing practical wisdom, as he did in this sermon excerpt:

> When persons are convinced life is short . . . and that eternity is the only subject that really can claim or can fill our thoughts, then they are apt to undervalue this life altogether, and to forget its real importance. They are apt to wish to spend the time of their sojourning here in a positive separation from active and social duties: yet it should be recollected that the employments of this world, though not themselves heavenly, are after all the way to heaven . . . but it is difficult to realize this. It is difficult to realize both truths at once, and to connect both truths together. . . . In various ways does the thought of the next world lead men to neglect their duty in this; and whenever it does so we may be sure that there is something wrong and unchristian, not in their thinking of the next world, but in their manner of thinking of it. . . .
>
> The Christian will feel that the true contemplation of his Savior lies in his worldly business; that as Christ is seen in the poor, and in the persecuted, . . . so is he seen in the employments he puts upon his chosen . . . ; that in attending to his own calling he will be meeting Christ; that if he neglect it, he will not on that account enjoy his presence at all the more, but that while performing it, he will see Christ revealed to his soul amid the ordinary actions of the day, as by a sort of sacrament.

After 1840 Newman gradually embraced the view that the Roman Catholic Church was the fullest embodiment of the ancient church. Suspecting Newman's drift, an Anglican bishop banned the *Tracts of the Times*. Chagrined, Newman resigned from Oxford University and withdrew to his place at Littlemore, where he finally decided to convert to Roman Catholicism. There in 1845, **Dominic Barberi**, an Italian missionary, received him into the church of Rome.

Newman had a somewhat rocky beginning as a convert. Powerful clerics like H. E. Manning, archbishop of Westminster, unfairly suspected him of undermining the faith. In 1864, in response to an unjust attack on his integrity, Newman published his famous autobiography, the *Apologia pro Vita Sua*, that won him respect and renewed his popularity.

For half a century as a Catholic, Newman devoted himself to prayer and writing. His books like *An Essay on the Development of Christian Doctrine* and *A Grammar of Assent* helped shape modern Catholic theology. In 1879, Pope Leo XIII made him a cardinal. He died in 1890 at age eighty-nine.

Lead, kindly Light, amid the encircling gloom,
Lead thou me on!
The night is dark, and I am far from home,
Lead thou me on!
Keep thou my feet! I do not ask to see
The distant scene; one step enough for me.

—John Henry Newman

AUGUST 11 / DECLARED VENERABLE IN 1991
Christian Living; Conversion; Eternal Perspective

341. Thérèse of Lisieux
(1873–1897)

From obscurity as a young, idealistic Carmelite, Thérèse of Lisieux has emerged as one of the best-loved saints. Her simplicity attracts us because she puts holiness within our reach.

Thérèse was the daughter of Louis and Zélie Martin. When she was four years old, her pleasant childhood was interrupted by Zélie's untimely death. Then Thérèse's older sister, Pauline, took responsibility for raising her in the faith. In 1882, Pauline entered the Carmelite convent at Lisieux, igniting a desire in Thérèse to do the same.

Thérèse's fourteenth year was pivotal. Her sister, Mary, joined Pauline at the convent. And at Christmas, the young saint had an experience she described as her "conversion." Later, in *A Story of a Soul*, her autobiography, Thérèse described it as a release from depression and oversensitivity:

> Jesus flooded the darkness of my soul with torrents of light. I got back for good the strength of soul lost when I was four and a half. Love filled my heart, I forgot myself, and henceforth I was happy.

In spite of Thérèse's youth, the next year the bishop allowed her to become a Carmelite at Lisieux.

From childhood Thérèse aspired to become a missionary and a martyr. It soon became clear to her, however, that neither option was open to a cloistered nun. So she sought the Holy Spirit and searched the Scripture for another way to excel:

> We live in an age of inventions. We need no longer climb laboriously up flights of stairs. And I am determined to find an elevator to carry me to Jesus, for I was too small to climb the steep stairs of perfection. So I sought in Holy Scripture some idea of what this lift I wanted would be, and I read, "Whoever is a little one, let him come to me" (see Luke 8:16). I also wanted to know how God would deal with a "little one," so I searched and found: "You shall be carried in her arms and fondled in her lap; as a mother comforts her son. . . ." (Isaiah 66:12–13 *NAB*)
>
> It is your arms, Jesus, which are the elevator to carry me to heaven. So there is no need for me to grow up. In fact: just the opposite: I must become less and less.

In 1897, Thérèse thought her dream of becoming a missionary was about to come true. The Carmelites at Hanoi in Indochina, now Vietnam, had invited her to join them. But on the early morning of Good Friday she began to hemorrhage from the mouth. She had contracted tuberculosis, which tortured her for several months before it took her life on September 30, 1897.

Thérèse learned to do the loving thing in every situation, which she discovered was the fuel that fired the faith of martyrs and saints. That was the secret of her "little way" of perfection that has captivated our hearts. "Great deeds are forbidden me. I cannot preach the gospel nor shed my blood—but what does it matter? My brothers toil instead of me and I, a little child, keep close by the throne of God and I love for those who fight. Love proves itself by deeds. I will scatter flowers, perfuming the Divine Throne, and I'll sweetly sing my hymn of love. These flowers are every little sacrifice, every glance and word, and the doing of the least of actions for love."

OCTOBER 1 / CANONIZED IN 1925 / PATRON OF FOREIGN MISSIONS, FRANCE, AND OUTREACH TO RUSSIA
Doctors of the Church; Mere Christian Love; Pursuit of Holiness; The Secrets of Spiritual Success

342. Maria Goretti
(1890–1902)

In 1900, two farm laborers relocated their destitute families to an old barn near Nettuno, Italy. Luigi Goretti, his wife, Assunta, and their six children moved in with Giovanni Serenelli and Alessandro, his teen-aged son. Soon after the move, Luigi died, leaving Assunta to carry on his work. Maria, her oldest child, who was ten, assumed the household duties and cheerfully supported her mother.

At twelve Maria was already a beautiful young woman. Alessandro, then nineteen, twice made advances toward her. She rebuffed him and kept his propositions secret because he had threatened to kill her. On July 5, 1902, Maria sat atop the hovel's stairs, mending Alessandro's shirt. He stormed past her, ordered her into a bedroom, grabbed her, and attempted to rape her. "No! No! No!" Maria cried. "Don't touch me, Alessandro! It's a sin!" She resisted him with all her strength. Angered beyond control, he stabbed her fourteen times.

Maria survived a pain-filled twenty-four hours in the hospital. She showed more concern for where her mother would sleep in the hospital than for herself. Before she died she forgave Alessandro and prayed for God to have mercy on him.

Alessandro was sentenced to thirty years' hard labor and imprisoned at Noto, Sicily. One night in 1910 he dreamed that Maria handed him a bouquet of lilies and he began to feel remorse. Soon after, Bishop Blandini of Noto visited him, explaining that Maria had forgiven him and that God would also forgive him. The message struck home. A few days later Alessandro sent the bishop this letter:

> I cannot tell you what comfort has come to my sorrowing soul through the conversation with your Excellency, for which I send my most heartfelt gratitude.
>
> It is indeed true that in a moment of mental aberration I was led to commit a barbarous murder which the law has already punished. But I can never accuse myself of doing it with the sole and firm purpose of committing so great a wrong. The fact that I was very young and knew little about life was the primary cause which brought me to such a step which I regret bitterly.
>
> I regret doubly the evil I have done, because I realize that I have taken the life of a poor, innocent girl. Up to the last moment she

> wanted to protect her honor, sacrificing herself rather than give in to my wishes. This it was that drove me to so terrible and deplorable a deed. Publicly, I detest the evil that I have done. And I ask God's forgiveness and that of the poor, desolate family for the great wrong I committed. I hope that I too, like so many others in this world, may obtain pardon.
>
> I declare this to your Excellency with the hope that you also will pardon me this great crime of my inexperienced youth. May your prayers united to mine obtain for me the forgiveness of him who governs all things, and the calm and the blessing of the poor departed one.

Alessandro was released from prison early for good behavior. He reformed his life and ultimately joined the Franciscan Third Order. Pope Pius XII canonized Maria Goretti in 1950. Assunta was present for the event, the first time a mother was present when her child was declared a saint.

On Christmas eve, 1936, Alessandro visited Assunta and asked her to forgive him, which she did. And together they attended Midnight Mass in the church where Maria lay buried. Alessandro was also present in St. Peter's Square in 1950, probably the first murderer to attend the canonization of his victim.

JULY 6 / CANONIZED IN 1950 / PATRON OF TEENAGE GIRLS
Child Saints; Forgiveness; Passion for Purity; Repentance

343. Gemma Galgani
(1878–1903)

St. Gemma Galgani was an Italian counterpart of **Thérèse of Lisieux.** Like Thérèse, she was remarkable for her faithfulness in little things. From childhood both were entirely devoted to Christ, and at age fifteen both also aspired to become nuns. And both young women suffered from tuberculosis, which ultimately took their lives.

Gemma, like Thérèse, was adept at prayer and had visions of Christ. Gemma described her sense of Christ's presence in this way:

> When I begin to pray I do not see Jesus with my eyes, but I know he is there before me, and my soul finds rest in his presence. I hear his voice which at times is as piercing as a sword, and penetrates into the inner senses of my spirit. His words are words of life. When I see him in this manner and hear his voice, it is not a beautiful corporeal form that I see. Nor do I hear the sound of a human voice, but I see a light, great and infinite. I hear a voice, inarticulate yet strong, that to the soul is more powerful than the loudest sound of storm or wind.
>
> Try to think of a light that fills the whole universe, that penetrates and kindles it. At the same time, a light that gives life and animation to all things, so that all things that exist are imbued with, or encircled in it, and in it and through it have life. Thus I see God and in him all creatures. He is a burning fire. It burns but does not consume. On the contrary, it gives light and warmth and joy. The more it burns, the more happy and perfect it makes those encircled by its rays. And the more anxious do they become to be burning in his fire. Thus do I see the souls in God.

Where Thérèse was successful, popular, and uncontroversial, Gemma was the opposite. Her persistent efforts to become a Passionist nun failed because of her chronic illnesses. Gemma's extraordinary ecstasies and apparitions made her a mockery among her family, friends, and neighbors.

In 1898, Gemma nearly died of nephritis and tuberculosis of the spine. Doctors despaired of any remedy. But **St. Gabriel Francis Possenti**, a Passionist to whom Gemma was devoted, appeared to her and she was instantaneously healed. Even her healing caused dissension because some attributed it to autosuggestion.

Most controversial, however, was Gemma's stigmata. From June 1899 through February 1901, the wounds of Christ mysteriously appeared on her body every Thursday evening and stayed until three o'clock on Friday afternoon. They bled freely and immobilized the saint with extreme pain. Witnesses described the wounds in detail, testifying that by Sunday only tiny white traces remained in their place. Gemma concealed her condition as much as she could. All the while experiencing these unusual graces, she performed her regular household duties. And she returned kindnesses to those who scoffed at her.

Gemma's miraculous cure was not permanent. Her disease flared up again, and after a long final time of suffering, the saint died in 1903 at the age of twenty-five.

> *We, who believe that God is ever with the world he has created, and that even in our materialistic age his arm is not shortened—however much our vision is restricted—should thank him for this powerful manifestation of his grace in Gemma Galgani. Her life demonstrates so clearly that the supernatural world is as sure, as real and as near to us as the world about which our senses tell us.*
>
> —Aidan Gasquet, OSB

APRIL 11 / CANONIZED IN 1940 / PATRON OF TUBERCULOSIS AND PHARMACISTS
Conversations with God; The Light of Christ; Stigmata; Success in Failure

344. Assunta Pallotta

(1878–1905)

We expect big things of saints. They defend the faith, found religious orders, convert thousands, write theological books, die heroically as martyrs. While we admire their achievements, the same accomplishments distance them from us. Such saints seem so great that we believe we could never be like them.

But saints like Assunta Pallotta bring sanctity back to earth. They show that anyone who aspires to holiness can become a saint.

Because her father was often unemployed and absent, Assunta helped support her impoverished family in Force, Ancona, Italy. She worked hard for little money first as a mason's assistant then as a tailor's apprentice. Always serious and quiet, Assunta used solitude on her jobs as a chance to pray.

One year at a carnival dance before Ash Wednesday, Assunta had to resist the advances of a young man. That experience precipitated her decision to become a nun and perhaps to become a saint. In her late teens she joined the Franciscan Missionaries of Mary. As a postulant in Rome, Assunta worked in the kitchen. And during her novitiate in Grottaferrata, she worked in the fields. Always cheerful and generous, when she finished her work she often helped others complete their tasks.

Like many of us, Assunta struggled with scruples and doubts. She spoke about these problems in the following letter:

> I have had some scruples since I entered the Institute, but now it seems that I have even more. When I went to confession and Father asked me if I were sure that I had committed a certain fault, I did not know what to say. I was in doubt, and I answered that I did not think I had committed any fault voluntarily. He replied, "Go to Holy Communion, and obey." He sent me away without even letting me recite the act of contrition. May the will of God be done always.
>
> I have also had doubts about my vocation; it seems to me I have not corresponded with its graces and done enough penance.
>
> I hope God permits this for his greater glory and the good of my soul. I wish only what God wishes.
>
> I ask only for the grace never to offend him. Then he may do with me whatever he wills.

> I am quite confused to have these doubts about my vocation after the great grace of having been admitted into the Institute out of charity.

With the advice of such a wise confessor, Assunta's doubts and scruples seem to have propelled her forward in the Christian life.

In 1904, Assunta's community sent her on a mission to China. She performed domestic service in the orphanage at Tong-eul-koo, cooking, taking care of the children, and studying Chinese. She made a set of resolutions at the beginning of 1905 that began: "I came to the convent to become a saint. What good will it do to live long if I do not attain my goal?" In February a typhus epidemic broke out at the mission. Assunta contracted the disease while caring for victims and she died on April 7. An aroma of incense mixed with violets lingered in her room, which prompted many Chinese converts to declare her a saint.

On her way to the Chinese mission, Assunta wrote:

> *We saw four of these poor people bowing down in worship before a large stone painted red, and then dabbing their foreheads with some of the red varnish.*
>
> *I thought of how they could put to shame some of us Christians who are so filled with human respect that we cannot even make a sign of the cross openly.*

APRIL 7 / BEATIFIED IN 1954

Mere Christian Love; The Sign of the Cross; Twentieth-Century Saints; Twenty-Something Saints

345. Elizabeth of the Trinity

(1880–1906)

Elizabeth Catez offers hope to any parent who struggles with a strong-willed child. A holy terror as a toddler, she once embarrassed her mother by shouting out at mass, "Bad priest! Bad priest! That's my doll!" The priest had secretly borrowed her doll to be used as the Christ Child in his creche. But gradually Elizabeth channeled her willfulness into a determination to become a saint.

Elizabeth's first communion and confirmation at age ten touched her deeply without quelling her rambunctiousness. But from that time she opened up to an interior prayer life that slowly matured into the infused contemplation of a mystic. At fourteen she felt drawn to choose Christ as her spouse. Without hesitating she made a private vow of virginity. And having been intrigued by visits to the local Carmelite convent at Dijon, France, since childhood, she was determined to become a Carmelite.

Marie, her mother, was horrified at the thought. She did all she could do to prevent it. She sent Elizabeth to parties in hopes that these might distract her and arranged for suitors to pursue her. But she could not in the end resist her daughter's strong will. She gave up and allowed Elizabeth to enter the Dijon Carmel in 1901.

Appropriately, she took the name Elizabeth of the Trinity, for the focus of her life became her immersion in the Godhead, or rather the Trinity's immersion in her. This letter from Elizabeth to a friend typifies her spirituality:

> I love to penetrate beyond the veil of the soul to this inner sanctuary where we live alone with God. He wants us entirely to himself, and is making there within us a cherished solitude. Listen to everything that is being sung . . . in his heart. It is Love, the infinite love that envelops us and desires to give us a share . . . in all his blessedness. The whole Blessed Trinity dwells in us, the whole of that mystery which will be our vision in heaven. Let it be our cloister. You tell me that your life is passed there. So is mine. I am "Elizabeth of the Trinity"—Elizabeth disappearing, losing herself, allowing herself to be invaded by the Three.
>
> Let us live for love, always surrendered, immolating ourselves at every moment, by doing God's will without searching for extraordinary

things. Then let us make ourselves quite tiny, allowing ourselves to be carried, like a babe in its mother's arms, by him who is our all. . . .

In the morning, let us wake in Love. All day long let us surrender ourselves to Love, by doing the will of God, under his gaze, with him, in him, for him alone. . . . And then, when evening comes, after a dialogue of love that has never stopped in our hearts, let us go to sleep still in love. And if we are aware of any faults, let us simply abandon them to Love, which is a consuming fire, and so do our purgatory in his love!

Like **St. Theresa Margaret of the Sacred Heart,** another Carmelite, Elizabeth delighted the other sisters in the cloister with her simple and joyful service. However, in 1903, she contracted Addison's disease. She suffered intensely and joyfully until she died in 1906. St. Elizabeth of the Trinity was only twenty-six years old.

During painful times, when you feel a terrible void, think how God is enlarging the capacity of your soul so that it can receive him—making it, as it were, infinite as he is infinite. Look upon each pain as a love token coming to you directly from God in order to unite you to him.

—Elizabeth of the Trinity

NOVEMBER 8 / BEATIFIED IN 1984
Intimacy with the Divine; A Passionate Love; Prayer; Purpose

346. Raphael Kalinowski
(1835–1907)

Sometimes we find lives of saints more distressing than encouraging. We read that Saint So-and-So from age three to ninety was always faithful, never doubted, never had a sexual thought, never sinned, and prayed day and night. That kind of story puts sanctity beyond our reach. But the life of Joseph Kalinowski, later as a Carmelite called Raphael, makes holiness possible for us.

By his death in 1907, Raphael was regarded as a great saint throughout Poland and Lithuania. But he progressed slowly on the road to sainthood, drifting away from the faith as a youth and struggling with doubts and hesitations during his gradual conversion.

Joseph began his career as a lieutenant in the Polish corps of engineers. In 1858 he was dispatched to supervise the planning of a trans-Russian railroad. He worked alone, and in his isolation he began to turn to God. *This continuous work on myself,* he wrote in 1859,

> far away from people, has made a great change in me—for the better. I came to realize the necessity of acquiring certainty in my religious convictions and finally I have turned towards them. I look at life more calmly now and have become indifferent to its pleasures. In my solitude I cultivated the interior life. Here it was that I recognized the great need there is for inalienable religious convictions and at last I made such convictions my own. It was here that I drank deeply of this new life.

Joseph had taken a big step, but he had a distance to go before his conversion was complete. In 1863 he resigned from the corps of engineers to become a leader in the Polish insurgency against Russia. That year he progressed further in his Christian life. *After ten years of defection,* he wrote to a friend, *I returned to the bosom of the church. I went to confession, and it was so exhilarating. I boast of this to you because I consider this turn in my religious conviction as a very important event in my inner life.*

Then in 1864 the Russians arrested Joseph and deported him to Siberia. For nearly nine years he was forced to work in the salt mines. And during that time he advanced significantly in his faith. He wrote the following about his deepening relationship to God and others:

> I keep my eyes fixed on Eternity, and from this source I draw constancy in the midst of the confusion of daily life. Freedom in my relationships with others and joy in spirit. God empties my heart of all natural attachments, probably to fill it with things more pure, of which nothing surpasses the desire to do good to my neighbor.
>
> I like to find at least a few moments each day spent in doing good for others out of love for God. These few moments, almost unnoticeably used, bring something like rays of peace and comfort behind them. They unite us with people and God with purity and sweetness.

Released in 1873, Joseph returned home to Poland. It seemed clear to him that he was called to the monastic life. But characteristically he postponed action until 1877, when he joined the Carmelite order at Graz, Austria. Raphael was ordained a priest in 1882. In his last twenty-five years he held various leadership positions among the Polish Carmelites. He aimed to renew the spirit of prayer in the community and worked for the reunion of Christians. He died in 1907.

God gave himself fully for us, how can we not dedicate ourselves fully to God?

—Raphael Kalinowski

NOVEMBER 15 / CANONIZED IN 1991
Conversion; Doubt; Twentieth-Century Saints

347. Mary McKillop
(1842–1909)

St. Mary McKillop smiles beautifully at us from photographs, her bright eyes and wide mouth projecting intelligence and strength. In her day, Catholics, Protestants, and the unchurched esteemed her for her service to the poor. Today feminists claim her as a pioneer. And the Australian church celebrates Mary McKillop as its first native-born saint.

At twenty, Mary aspired to join a religious order. But Father Julian Woods, her spiritual director, influenced her to start a new community in South Australia to care for the poor. Together they founded the Sisters of Saint Joseph of the Sacred Heart, the Josephites. Mary and her sisters opened schools, orphanages, refuges, and hostels. The nuns lived austerely and welcomed all, regardless of religious background.

Mary McKillop battled lifelong opposition to her work. For example, misguided and arrogant bishops obstructed her way with excommunications, depositions, and dispensations. Mary was feisty in these conflicts, but always responded obediently. She balanced submission with determination.

In the early 1870s, Father Woods occasioned one famous controversy by unwisely supporting several visionaries among the Josephites at Adelaide. Priests, who wanted Woods out because of his insistence on absolute poverty, used this indiscretion to denounce him. In 1871 a complex tangle ensued during which the bishop excommunicated Mary for alleged disobedience. However, a year later the bishop restored Mary, apologizing for having taken bad advice.

The Vatican appointed a commission to investigate this affair in 1873. Mary went to Rome, where Pope Pius IX received her warmly. The commission exonerated Mary. It also required Father Woods to step down as spiritual director of the Josephites, a decision he deeply resented. Mary knew that her testimony had played a big part in Father Woods's removal, so she wrote him a letter of encouragement. You will see in the following excerpt the saint's typical blend of respect and forcefulness:

> If your sorrow tonight is great as I know it is, what must not mine be at the great share I have had in causing it? Let it at least console you,

> dear Father, to know that I have but endeavored to put into practice lessons which you have long since over and over again given to me. Do you remember how much you used to fear that when higher duties might withdraw you from my reach, I would lose heart and fail perhaps in giving to God what he would have a right to expect? Do you remember too, dear Father, how earnestly you used to remind me of acting always with a pure intention of pleasing God and not minding creatures?
>
> I think what has been proposed to you is the will of God. You are our Founder: God inspired you with the desire of establishing the Institute. He enabled you to draw out the rules for it, and now I think he wants you in your own lifetime to see how the work he inspired you to commence can be conducted according to its rule and without your immediate direction. He wants you in your own example to teach your children the lesson of detachment you have so often imparted. He wants you to make them think less of the creature through whom he directs them than of himself who actually directs the creature.

For nearly forty years Mary McKillop prevailed through similar obstacles as she built and governed the Josephites. She died of a stroke in 1909.

Everest-sized obstacles did not stop Mary McKillop from following what she believed was God's will. We take courage from saints like her when molehills in our way seem impassable.

MAY 25 / CANONIZED IN 1995
Leading Women; Serving the Poor; Twentieth-Century Saints; Valiant Women

348. Pius X

(1835–1914)

For the first seventeen years of his priesthood, Italian Giuseppe Sarto cared for souls in parishes. He then spent nine years as diocesan chancellor and seminary director at Treviso. Next, for nine years as bishop of Mantua he used his pastoral and administrative skills to rejuvenate that moribund diocese. In 1893, Pope Leo XIII named him cardinal and patriarch of Venice. Ten years later when Leo XIII died, he was elected pope, taking the name Pius X.

St. Pius X's motto—"to restore all things in Christ"—guided his papacy. Unlike his more philosophical predecessor, who focused on the church in the world, Pius X directed his energies to the church itself. Simpler and more pastoral than Leo XIII, but no less strategic, Pius X accomplished many things for the spiritual revitalization of Catholicism. For example, he sponsored a reform of church music that gave impetus to the liturgical movement. He chartered a codification of canon law and restructured the papal government. He encouraged and reoriented the involvement of laity in the church, pointing Catholic political activists in a more spiritual direction.

Pope Pius X revolutionized Catholic spirituality by encouraging frequent reception of Holy Communion. And he opened the way for children to participate in the Eucharist. In the following talk to first communicants we hear him exhort the children to take advantage of the sacrament to get closer to Christ:

> My dear children, you have received Our Lord for the first time. But it is not enough. Every day we ask God for the bread to sustain the life of our body. So, too, we have need of heavenly Bread that gives life to our soul.
>
> My advice is that you receive holy communion frequently—if you cannot do so daily—and unite yourself to the Savior. Make frequent visits to him in the solitude and silence of his tabernacle. Then you will hear him speak to you his invitation, full of love: "Come to me, you who hunger, and I will refresh you. All you who have been burdened and weighed down—and I will give you comfort, peace and consolation" (see Matthew 11:28–29).
>
> My last desire, dear children, is that the love of Our Lord dwell in you so that it will change you into so many apostles, zealous for his

> glory. You will be the treasure of your families. You will make them happy by your good conduct.
>
> Your example alone will win them to receive holy communion frequently. At school you will bring your companions to imitate your piety. In the parish, all will look on you as good angels.
>
> Finally, everywhere about you, by your prayers, by your prudence, by the attraction of your modesty, you will contribute to the conversion of sinners. And to the return of unbelievers and the indifferent to Jesus Christ.

In 1907, Pius X condemned Modernism, which he regarded as a subversive heretical movement. Modernism was a loosely organized intellectual movement that tried to bring traditional Catholic belief into line with modern philosophical ideas. In 1910, he required all priests teaching theology or engaged in pastoral ministry to take an antimodernist oath. His effort to uproot error unintentionally spawned an age of zealous anti-intellectualism that lasted until the 1950s.

Pius X worked hard diplomatically to avert World War I, but lived just long enough to see his efforts frustrated. He died on August 20, 1914, a few days after the war broke out.

Simplicity and poverty marked Giuseppe Sarto, even as pope. "Look how they have dressed me up," he once said to a friend and burst into tears. And in his will he wrote, "I was born poor. I have lived poor. And I wish to die poor."

AUGUST 21 / CANONIZED IN 1954
Care of the Soul; Great Pastors; Saints and Sacraments (Eucharist); Twentieth-Century Saints

349. Elizabeth Leseur

(1866–1914)

After Elizabeth Leseur's death, Felix, her husband, found her notebooks that revealed a passionate spiritual life that she had concealed beneath her genteel, pleasant demeanor. Her simple application of Christian truths to her soul touched him deeply, as did his discovery that she had quietly offered years of great suffering for his conversion. Felix was so moved that he not only embraced Christ, but also became a Dominican priest who traveled throughout Europe speaking about his wife's spiritual writings.

Felix, a medical doctor, had abandoned his faith when he read the fashionable atheistic literature of the late-nineteenth century. Ironically, his attempt in 1899 to get Elizabeth to read Renan's *Life of Jesus* occasioned her spiritual awakening. From that time she kept a journal in which she recorded her progress in making her life a purer and better instrument for serving God and others. God seems to have invaded her soul, giving her a profound awareness of the interdependence of Christians. Isolated from Christian conversation in her marriage, Elizabeth participated by prayer in the communion of saints. And in her social contacts she made it her preference to show kindness particularly to the irksome people who bored her. "I want to have boundless charity," she wrote, "especially toward those who do not attract me."

Sick all her life with hepatitis, Elizabeth's condition worsened after 1908. And in 1911 she was diagnosed with cancer. She calmly accepted the disease's intense pain, and understood it as a form of prayer. She explained her view in this letter to a woman who was facing blindness:

> I know all that suffering means, the fine and mysterious power it possesses, what it obtains and what it accomplishes. After all, our activity is of little importance. When Providence prefers to work by means of suffering, we should not complain too much. Then we can be sure that the work will be well done and not mixed up with all the misery of egotism and pride which sometimes spoil so much of our outward activity. I know by experience that in hours of trial certain graces are obtained for others which all our efforts had not previously obtained. I have thus concluded that suffering is the higher form of action, the best

expression in the wonderful communion of saints. In suffering one is sure not to make mistakes, sure to be useful to others and to the great causes one longs to serve.

The Stoics said, "Suffering is nothing." They were wrong. Illuminated by a clearer light we Christians say, "Suffering is everything!" It demands, it obtains, everything. Through it God consents to accomplish everything. Suffering helps Christ to save the world and souls. When I am overwhelmed by the immensity of my desires for those I love, . . . it is toward suffering that I turn. It is through suffering that I ask to be allowed to serve as an intermediary between God and souls. It is the perfect form of prayer, the only infallible form of action. . . . Through the cross to the Light.

After enduring a long agony, Elizabeth Leseur died in 1914 at the age of forty-eight.

I believe that there circulates among souls—those here below, those expiating their sins, and those who have obtained true life—a vast and ceaseless stream of the sufferings, merits and love of all these souls. And that through the divine action even our slightest pains, our least sorrows, can reach out to souls both dear and distant and bring them light and peace and holiness.

—Elizabeth Leseur

MAY 3
Intercession; Married Saints; Suffering

350. Charles de Foucauld

(1858–1916)

Wealthy and lazy, Viscount Charles de Foucauld wasted his youth. At fifteen he declared himself an agnostic. Seven years later Charles had failed at school and been discharged from the army for his dissolute life. "I rent by the day, not by the month," he had told a string of discarded mistresses.

After 1881, however, his life slowly turned. He returned to military service and led his men bravely against an uprising in Algeria. Then he resigned his commission to explore Morocco, where the solitude of the desert seems to have touched his soul. When he returned to France he renewed his relationship with his cousin, Marie de Bondy. A wise and holy woman, she gently precipitated his conversion. Marie did not nag Charles, but wooed him to Christ by her example. "The moment I realized God existed," he said, "I knew I could not do otherwise than live for him alone." He returned to the church in 1886.

For the next decade Charles experimented with community life in several Trappist houses. However, believing he had a different calling, in 1897 he withdrew to Nazareth to live as a hermit. Imitating the hidden life of Jesus at Nazareth became one of Charles' life themes. Ordained in 1901, Charles de Foucauld set up a base on the Algerian-Moroccan border from which he hoped to evangelize the desert tribes. Influenced both by his cousin's evangelistic method and by circumstances, he determined to bring Christ to Muslims not by preaching, but by example. Charles developed a concept of friendship evangelization that he explained to a priest friend:

> Our work for the conversion of unbelievers ought not to be limited merely to material gifts, but rather ought to lead to the settlement among them of agricultural workers, businessmen, skilled workers, property owners and so on. Good Christians of all kinds would be valuable support for the missionaries, drawing unbelievers to the faith by their example, goodness and friendship.
>
> The work to be done here, as among all Muslims, is one of moral uplift: raising them morally and intellectually by all possible means, coming close to them, having contact with them, tying the bonds of friendship with them, breaking down their prejudices against us through daily friendly relations, and changing their ideas by the

> manner and example of our lives. Then we must concern ourselves with real education—in a word, we must educate them completely. By means of schools and colleges, we must teach them standard subjects and courses. Through daily and close contact with them we must also instruct them in the things one learns through one's family—we must become their family.
>
> When this objective has been gained, their ideas will be completely changed, and at the same time their customs will have improved. It will then be easy to bring them to the gospel. God could, of course, do all this. If it were his will, he could convert the Muslims by his grace in a moment. But up till now it has not been his will.

In 1905, Charles migrated farther into the Sahara Desert and settled at Tamanrasset in Algeria. There his witness as the "little brother of Jesus" made many friends among tribal people. While he attracted no permanent disciples, after his death his vision and example inspired the formation of the Little Brothers of Jesus and the Little Sisters of Jesus. A marauding band of a Muslim sect murdered him on December 16, 1916.

> *The more we lack in this world, the more surely we discover the best thing the earth has to offer us: the cross.*
>
> —Charles de Foucauld

DECEMBER 16 / BEATIFIED IN 2005
Conversion; Evangelization; Repentance; Solitude; Twentieth-Century Saints

351. Frances Xavier Cabrini
(1850–1917)

As a child Frances Cabrini determined to go on mission to China. She dressed her dolls as nuns. On a stream she floated paper boats manned by violets, pretending they were missionaries off to foreign lands. She abstained from sweets because she could expect none in China. And she added Xavier to her name in honor of the great patron of foreign missions. A missionary she would become, but not to China. Instead she was guided from Italy to the United States of America, where she would become a citizen and the first canonized American saint.

Twice as a young woman she applied to religious orders, but they both refused her on grounds of poor health. However, a priest in Codogno in Italy asked her to form into a community the women who were running an orphanage in his parish. When that effort failed, the priest encouraged Frances to found a missionary order of women. In 1880 she established the Missionaries of the Sacred Heart to run schools and orphanages for the poor.

St. Frances Xavier Cabrini attracted women like a magnet, and her community grew rapidly. She was affectionate but firm, practical but motivated by an eternal perspective, as shown in this letter she wrote to a sister in 1885:

> Why, dearest daughter, do you waste time in sadness when time is so precious for the salvation of poor sinners? Get rid of your melancholy immediately. Don't think any more about yourself. Do not indulge in so many useless and dangerous reflections. Look ahead always without ever looking back. Keep your gaze fixed on the summit of perfection where Christ awaits you.
>
> He wants you despoiled of all things, intent only on procuring his greater glory during this brief time of your existence. For the short time that remains, is it worthwhile to lose yourself in melancholy like those who think only of themselves, as if all were to end with this life?
>
> Ah, no. We must not even desire that our pilgrimage on this earth be a short one because we do not yet know the infinite value of every minute employed for the glory of God. Carry your cross then but carry it joyfully, my daughter. Think that Jesus loves you very much. And in return for such love, don't lose yourself in so many desires, but accept daily with serenity whatever comes your way. May the heart of Jesus bless you and make you holy not as you want but as he desires.

In 1889, Frances led a contingent of her order to New York to work among fifty thousand Italian immigrants, most of whom were unchurched. Obstacles galore blocked her path, but none big enough to stop her. "Are *we* doing this?" she would ask, "or is the *Lord*?" Soon she had other foundations in New York; Managua, Nicaragua; New Orleans, and later in Chicago and Buenos Aires, Argentina. By the time of the saint's death in 1917, fifteen hundred women were working as Missionaries of the Sacred Heart in eight countries. In all, sixty-seven houses of sisters devoted themselves to education, nursing, and care of orphans—an achievement well beyond the saint's original goal of aiding Italian immigrants.

Lord, you are the one who acts. I am not even an instrument in your hands, as others say. You alone are the one who does all, and I am nothing more than a spectator of the great and wonderful works that you know how to accomplish.

—Frances Xavier Cabrini

NOVEMBER 13 / PATRON OF MIGRANTS, HOSPITAL ADMINISTRATORS, AND ORPHANS

Eternal Perspective; Leading Women; Missionaries; The Secrets of Spiritual Success

352. Matt Talbot
(1856–1925)

For sixteen years Matt Talbot was a daily drunk. Then one day an unanticipated conversion transformed him and he became a model penitent.

As a child of a poor family in Dublin, Matt had to forgo school for a job. After a year of basic education, in 1868 he started working as a messenger for a wine seller. Matt's father was already an alcoholic, so the job environment played on a family weakness, and Matt started drinking heavily at the early age of twelve.

His father beat him, made him change jobs—but nothing could stop Matt's habit. After work he and his buddies went straight to the pub. Matt spent every penny on drink and once pawned his boots for a pint. Remarkably, his drinking did not prevent his putting in a good day's work. And he said that when he was intoxicated he occasionally thought about the Blessed Mother and prayed an off-handed Hail Mary. Matt speculated later that she may have had something to do with his conversion.

One day in 1884 everything suddenly changed. Matt had been out of work several days and expected his buddies to take him drinking. When they snubbed him, he made a decision that transformed his life irrevocably. Mary Andrews, his sister, reported what happened when Matt came home that day:

> My mother said, "You're home early, Matt, and you're sober!" He replied, "Yes, mother, I am." After dinner he remained in the house which was not usual, and finally he remarked to my mother. "I'm going to take the pledge." She smiled and said, "Go, in God's name, but don't take it unless you are going to keep it." He said, "I'll go, in God's name."
>
> As he was going out mother said, "God give you strength to keep it." He went to Clonliffe, made his confession, and took the pledge for three months. He had been a couple of years away from the sacraments then. Next morning—Sunday—he went to Holy Communion. On Monday he went to 5 a.m. Mass in Gardiner Street and was at his work as usual at 6 a.m. This he made a regular practice from that time on. But after his work, to keep away from his companions, he used to walk to a distant church, either St. Joseph's, Berkeley Road, or St. Peter's, Phibsboro, and remain there until bedtime.

> Once or twice—possibly on a Saturday—he went with the men to the public house, but he drank only minerals, and he usually spent Saturday afternoons away from where he might meet his old companions, and generally in a church. He had a bad time of it at first and sometimes said to my mother, that, when the three months were up, he would drink again.

But Matt extended the three months into forty-one years. His new behavior flabbergasted everyone. Matt supported his sobriety with traditional Catholic disciplines such as prayer, frequent communion, weekly confession, spiritual reading, fasting, and service. He also seems to have taken guidance from a wise spiritual director, but the person's name is not known. In 1891, Matt found community support by joining the Franciscan Third Order. He lived the rest of his life quietly, working and praying and encouraging others to quit drinking.

Matt Talbot died walking to Mass on Sunday, June 7, 1925.

Matt Talbot wrote this note to himself in one of his books: Three things I cannot escape: the eye of God, the voice of conscience, the stroke of death. In company guard your tongue. In your family guard your temper. When alone guard your thoughts.

JUNE 7 / CAUSE OF BEATIFICATION AND CANONIZATION INTRODUCED IN 1947
Conversion; Twentieth-Century Saints

353. Pier-Giorgio Frassati
(1901–1925)

In post–World War I Italy, Pier-Giorgio Frassati became a beloved hero in Turin. His life was an intriguing balance of opposites that, like a magnet, drew people to the supernatural. Pier-Giorgio was wealthy but lived in poverty, giving everything imaginable to the poor. Handsome and strong, he devoted himself to the weak and malformed. He was gregarious, yet a lover of solitude. Pier-Giorgio was rambunctious, the life of every party and a practical joker. But at prayer he was solemn, recollected, and quiet.

Even when Pier-Giorgio felt depressed no one would have noticed because he always behaved cheerfully. The secret of his personality was his constant joy. *My life is monotonous,* he once said, *but each day I understand a little better the incomparable grace of being a Catholic. Down, then, with all melancholy. That should never find a place except in the heart which has lost faith. I am joyful. Sorrow is not gloom. Gloom should be banished from the Christian soul.*

As a teenager the saint made friends of the poor in Turin's filthy backstreets and gave them whatever he had—his money, his shoes, his overcoat. "Jesus comes to me every morning in Holy Communion," he replied to a friend who asked why the hovels did not repulse him. "I repay him in my very small way by visiting the poor. The house may be sordid, but I am going to Christ."

At school Pier-Giorgio became the leader of groups that organized outreach to the needy. He set a high standard, his investment of time and money far exceeding that of his friends. On Sunday, galoshes for a barefoot child; Monday, a room for a homeless woman; Tuesday, boots for an unemployed laborer; Wednesday, payment of a girl's school bill; Thursday, relocation for a blind veteran; Friday, groceries for a hungry family; Saturday, medicine for an old man with bronchitis. The catalog of his giving seems endless. At the same time he was the organizer of student parties, games, and fund raisers to finance ski trips to the Alps—Pier-Giorgio was addicted to mountain climbing!

Once after visiting a badly disfigured leper he explained to a friend his rationale for his selfless ministry:

> How rich we are to be in good health. The deformation of that young man will disappear in a few years when he enters Paradise. But we have the duty of putting our health at the service of those who haven't it. To act otherwise would be to betray the gift of God.
>
> No human being should ever be left abandoned. But the best of all charities is that consecrated to the sick. That is an exceptional work: few have the courage to face its difficulties and dangers; to take on themselves the sufferings of others, in addition to their own needs and their own precautions and cares.

Pier-Giorgio was famous in Turin, but his family regarded him as a problem. His father, Alfredo Frassati, editor of the daily *La Stampa*, seems to have resented his largesse. And his mother was inconvenienced by his frequent absences and his lateness to meals. Only after his death did they come to appreciate their son.

A virulent form of poliomyelitis attacked Pier-Giorgio in July 1925, and he died within a week. He was twenty-four years old.

Once a friend observed that when Pier-Giorgio finished praying in church, he waved a little farewell towards the tabernacle. I like to imagine the scene when this jovial saint said hello to Christ in heaven.

JULY 4 / BEATIFIED IN 1990
Generosity; Joy; Serving the Poor; Twentieth-Century Saints; Twenty-Something Saints

354. George Matulaitis
(1871–1927)

Should we not infiltrate every place, especially the big cities, the universities, among the youth, in order to bring Christ there?

—George Matulaitis

Lithuanian-born George Matulaitis was ordained a priest in 1898 in a world nearing the brink of war. Aging European empires were collapsing, nationalisms were boiling, and Marxism was on the rise. Amid the turmoil that unfolded into World War I and the Russian revolution, Fr. George worked quietly—sometimes subversively—to advance the cause of Christ. An intellectual, an activist, and a zealot, he inspired seminarians, organized workers, led fellow priests, and revived a persecuted religious order. And all the while he was suffering with tuberculosis of the bone that had afflicted him since his youth.

Armed with a PhD in sociology from the University of Fribourg, the young priest taught at seminaries in Kielce and Warsaw, Poland. With other activist priests in Warsaw, George established support groups for workers that mushroomed into a movement of fifty thousand members. In 1904 his disease flared up and he nearly died. However, friends nursed him back to health and upon recovery, he vowed to do something to honor Mary in thanksgiving.

In 1907 in St. Petersburg, Russia, George found a way to keep his promise. He decided to revive the community of the Marian Fathers that the tsar had suppressed. The last living Marian priest received him into the order. And in 1910 he moved to Fribourg, Switzerland, where he began to rebuild the community. In this excerpt from his diary, George described his expansive vision for the Marians:

> Thoroughly imbued with the spirit of Christ, it should be our concern to gather and organize around ourselves people of good will, train them, prepare them for the work, and then together with them and through them to bring in Christ in order to renew all in Christ, to accept all things for Christ, to draw all things to Christ.
>
> Laboring for the glory of God and the benefit of the Church, we need not fear that some project or work will not succeed. We must risk it, for with God there is no losing. He accepts our good will, our

> intention. Neither should we fear people: they cannot deprive us of heaven or God, consign us to perdition, or crowd us off the earth. And what is there to fear from worldly governments? Do we wish them any untoward harm? It is not our desire to overthrow their thrones; neither is it our intention to collaborate with or take sides with any one political or national party. It is not our mind to destroy the social order. There is only one thing to fear: "To die not having suffered anything, not having borne hardships, not having labored for the church and the salvation of souls, and all this for the greater glory of God."

In 1918, George became bishop of Vilnius, Lithuania. The conflicting religious and national loyalties of his flock stymied him, forcing him to resign in 1925. But the pope immediately appointed him as an archbishop delegated to straighten out affairs in the Lithuanian church, a task that he accomplished only with strenuous effort.

After an unsuccessful operation, George Matulaitis died in 1927. By that time the revived Marian Fathers already had two hundred fifty priests scattered at centers all over the world.

Many saints like George Matulaitis were always sick and in pain. Their selfishness disappeared in their love for God, like a droplet in the ocean. They worried not about themselves, but about God's concerns and the needs of others.

JANUARY 27 / BEATIFIED IN 1987
Courage; Eternal Perspective; Suffering; Twentieth-Century Saints

355. Miguel Pro
(1891–1927)

In 1909, twenty-year-old Miguel Augustin Pro joined the Jesuits as a novice in Mexico. A year later a revolution erupted and by 1914 the Jesuits were forced to flee. Via Texas, California, Nicaragua, and Spain, Miguel received his seminary training en route to Belgium, where he was ordained in 1925.

The Jesuits sent Padre Pro to Mexico City in 1926, hoping a return home might relieve the priest's chronic stomach ailment. Just twenty-three days after Padre Pro arrived, President Calles banned all public worship. Since he was not known as a priest, Padre Pro went about clandestinely—sometimes in disguise—celebrating Mass, distributing communion, hearing confessions, and anointing the sick. He also did as much as he could to relieve the material suffering of the poor. In a letter he gave this faith-filled account:

> We carry on like slaves. Jesus help me! There isn't time to breathe, and I am up to my eyebrows in this business of feeding those who have nothing. And they are many—those with nothing. I assure you that I spin like a top from here to there with such luck as is the exclusive privilege of petty thieves. It doesn't even faze me to receive such messages as: "The X Family reports that they are twelve members and their pantry is empty. Their clothing is falling off them in pieces, three are sick in bed and there isn't even water." As a rule my purse is as dry as Calles's soul, but it isn't worth worrying since the Procurator of Heaven is generous.
>
> People give me valuable objects to raffle off, something worth ten pesos that I can sell for forty. Once I was walking along with a woman's purse that was quite cute (the purse not the woman) when I met a wealthy woman all dolled up.
>
> "What do you have there?"
>
> "A lady's purse worth twenty-five pesos. You can have it for fifty pesos which I beg you to send to such-and-such a family."
>
> I see God's hand so palpably in everything that almost—almost I fear they won't kill me in these adventures. That will be a fiasco for me who sighs to go to heaven and start tossing off arpeggios on the guitar with my guardian angel.

In November 1927, a bomb was tossed at Calles's car from an auto previously owned by one of Miguel's two brothers. All three brothers were rounded up and condemned to death. The youngest was pardoned, but Padre Pro and his brother Humberto were executed by a firing squad. Calles had news photographers present, expecting the Pros to die cowardly. But Padre Pro refused the blindfold and welcomed the bullets with his arms extended in the form of a cross, crying out, "Viva Cristo Rey!" Although Calles outlawed any public demonstration, thousands of Mexicans defiantly lined the streets, honoring the martyr as he was carried in procession to his grave.

Once while walking with Concepcion, his favorite sister, Miguel noticed in a window an especially gaudy statue of the Virgin. She thought it was "hideous." To tease her, he ran to the owner's door and knocked. "Hello," he said, "my sister loves your beautiful statue. Will you sell it?"

"Sorry," was the answer. "That madonna is a family treasure."

Quick-witted and lighthearted Miguel played similar practical jokes all his life. He also played them in death. President Calles thought executing Padre Pro publicly would demoralize Catholics, but it had the opposite effect. Miguel even promised to joke in heaven. "If I meet any long-faced saints there," he said, "I will cheer them up with a Mexican hat dance!"

NOVEMBER 23 / BEATIFIED IN 1988
Facing Death; Joy; Martyrs; Serving the Poor; Twentieth-Century Saints

356. André Bessette
(1845–1937)

When André Bessette died, a million people reportedly came to the Oratory of St. Joseph in Montreal to bid him farewell. They honored him because his ministry had touched them, their relatives, or their friends. And because they regarded him as a saint.

At age fifteen, André entered the Congregation of the Holy Cross as a working brother. The community almost dismissed him at the end of his novitiate because he was sickly. But the archbishop of Montreal intervened and the congregation permitted André to stay. Because he was frail and uneducated, the community assigned him as the doorkeeper of the College of Our Lady of the Snows, a boys' school in Montreal. "My superiors showed me the door," he joked, "and I stayed there forty years."

Traditionally the Holy Cross brothers were devoted to **St. Joseph**, and Brother André became St. Joseph's ambassador extraordinaire. He encouraged sick people to ask St. Joseph to intercede for their healing. He anointed the ill with oil from a lamp that burned before St. Joseph's image and sometimes massaged men (not women) with a medal of the saint wrapped in cloth.

Over the years many people were healed through Brother André's ministry. As his reputation grew, so many seekers came that they disrupted the school. So on a hill nearby, Brother André constructed the Oratory of St. Joseph, where he could receive petitioners. News coverage in 1910 exploded him into international prominence. And hundreds more came to him for help.

The following is an example of a healing that a doctor verified.

> Mrs. Marcoux was dying. She had been constantly watched for five days. She had frequent weak spells and the doctor said that she would pass away in one of these crises.
>
> Learning that Brother André was passing through Quebec, Mr. Marcoux sought him out at the residence of the Holy Cross Fathers, Sante-Famille St., and induced him to return home with him. At the very moment when the husband was requesting the favor of Brother André, Mrs. Marcoux suddenly felt her strength return. Getting up, she dressed herself and went into another room, where on

> his arrival, Mr. Marcoux, much to his astonishment, found her sitting. The happiness of the family may be easily imagined.
>
> —From a letter of Mr. Joseph Marcoux to The Annals of St. Joseph, July 1921.

> I, the undersigned, solemnly certify that Mrs. Joseph Marcoux has been under my medical care since December 27, 1920; that she was afflicted with heart disease of a very serious nature; that her legs were swollen; and that she was succumbing to progressive feebleness. I looked upon her case as hopeless. She is at present quite well, her heart beats regularly, her pulse is good, and her legs have resumed their normal condition. I consider her cure to be a wonderful grace obtained by Frere André, of St. Joseph's Oratory.
>
> —From a certificate of M. A. Falardeau, MD

From 1910 through 1937, an estimated ten thousand people received healing through Brother André's ministry—at least one every day. He died in 1937 at the age of ninety-one.

Brother André was kind, but he was not always nice. "Go away, I'm busy," he would snap, dismissing a persistent petitioner. He claimed that no one could truly appreciate the pain caused him by the daily press of hundreds of visitors, each expecting a healing. Thanks, Brother André, for showing that holiness and crotchetiness are not always mutually exclusive.

JANUARY 6 / BEATIFIED IN 1982
Healing Touch; Feisty Saints; True Humility; Twentieth-Century Saints

357. Katharine Drexel
(1858–1955)

Contemplation and generosity vied for first place in St. Katharine Drexel's life. The heiress from Philadelphia, Pennsylvania, wanted most to withdraw to a cloister, but her circumstances and gifts pulled her to Christian service.

Francis A. Drexel, a world-renowned banker and a man of faith, provided his family a life of ease. And Emma Bouvier, her stepmother, trained Katharine and her two sisters in generous giving. Mrs. Drexel believed God gave wealth to the family to aid others, and regularly involved her daughters in distributing food, medicine, clothing, and rent money to the poor. The experience shaped Katharine's future.

Both parents died by 1885, leaving Katharine and her sisters to share the annual income from a fourteen-million-dollar estate. Right away Katharine began to donate thousands of dollars to the Bureau of Catholic Indian Missions for the construction and staffing of schools for Native American children, which became her life's passion.

At this time, however, Katharine's spirit was in turmoil. Bishop James O'Connor, her spiritual director, thought she should remain a single woman serving in the world. But she wished to become a contemplative nun. *My heart is very sorrowful,* she wrote him in 1886, *because like the little girl who wept when she found that her doll was stuffed with sawdust and her drum was hollow, I, too, have made a horrifying discovery and my discovery like hers is true. I have ripped both the doll and the drum open and the fact lies plainly and in all its glaring reality before me: All, all, all (there is no exception) is passing away and will pass away.*

> European travel brings vividly before the mind how cities have risen and fallen, and risen and fallen; and the same of empires and kingdoms and nations. And the billions and billions who lived their common everyday life in these nations and kingdoms and empires and cities, where are they? The ashes of the kings and mighty of this earth are mingled with the dust of the meanest slave.
>
> Day succeeds day and, as Byron so beautifully expresses it, when the heavens grow red in the western sky, "The day joins the past eternity." How long will the sun and moon, the stars continue to give forth light? Who can tell? Of one thing alone we are sure. In God's own time—

> then shall come the Son of Man in great power and majesty to render to each according to his works.
>
> The question alone important, the solution of which depends upon how I have spent my life, is the state of my soul at the moment of death. Infinite misery or infinite happiness! There is no half and half, either one or the other. And this question for me is to be decided at most in seventy years, seventy short years compared with eternity.

In 1891, Katharine resolved the tension by founding a new religious community, the Sisters of the Blessed Sacrament for Indians and Colored People, that combined prayer and social action. By 1904, 104 sisters had joined her. Katharine established 145 Catholic missions and twelve schools for Native Americans and fifty schools for blacks. During her lifetime she gave away about twenty million dollars, mostly for these causes.

In 1935, Katharine suffered a severe heart attack. Two years later she retired and got her heart's desire—eighteen years of quiet contemplation before she died in 1955 at age ninety-seven.

Katharine's vast inheritance was distributed among her father's twenty-nine favorite charities. Not a penny went to her own community. She wanted her sisters to live by faith, trusting God—not money—for everything.

MARCH 3 / CANONIZED IN 2000
Contemplatives in Action; Eternal Perspective; Generosity; Serving the Poor; Twentieth-Century Saints

358. Faustina Kowalska
(1905–1938)

Helena Kowalska was the third of ten children of a peasant family who lived in Glogowiec, Poland. She was simple, uneducated, and attractive. As a child she began to sense God's call, but she was twenty before she found it irresistible. In 1925, Helena entered the Congregation of Sisters of Our Lady of Mercy. She took the name Faustina and was assigned to domestic service.

On the evening of February 22, 1931, Jesus appeared to St. Faustina. He wore a white robe, and two rays, one white and one red, flowed from his breast. In this and subsequent visions, Christ directed Faustina to propagate devotion to the Divine Mercy. He instructed her to make a painting of his image, promising that anyone who honored it would be saved. He also told Faustina that he wanted the whole church to celebrate the first Sunday after Easter as the Feast of Mercy.

Faustina's first efforts met with ridicule, doubt, and only lukewarm support. However, after 1933, with the aid of her spiritual director, Father Michael Sopocko, she made good but slow progress. By 1935 thousands in Poland were participating in the Divine Mercy movement.

The Divine Mercy meant not only receiving mercy, but also giving it. With Faustina we can pray that we too might become merciful:

> O Most Holy Trinity! As many times as I breathe, as many times as my heart beats, as many times as my blood pulsates through my body, so many thousand times do I want to glorify your mercy.
>
> I want to be completely transformed into your mercy and to be your living reflection, O Lord. May the greatest of all divine attributes, that of your unfathomable mercy, pass through my heart and soul to my neighbor.
>
> Help me, O Lord, that my eyes may be merciful, so that I may never suspect or judge from appearances, but look for what is beautiful in my neighbors' souls and come to their rescue.
>
> Help me, that my ears may be merciful, so that I may give heed to my neighbors' needs and not be indifferent to their pains and moanings.
>
> Help me, O Lord, that my tongue may be merciful, so that I should never speak negatively of my neighbor, but have a word of comfort and forgiveness for all.

> Help me, O Lord, that my hands may be merciful and filled with good deeds, so that I may do only good to my neighbor and take upon myself the more difficult and toilsome tasks.
>
> Help me, that my feet may be merciful, so that I may hurry to assist my neighbor, overcoming my own fatigue and weariness. My true rest is in the service of my neighbor.
>
> Help me, O Lord, that my heart may be merciful so that I myself may feel all the sufferings of my neighbor. I will refuse my heart to no one. I will be sincere even with those who, I know, will abuse my kindness. And I will lock myself up in the most merciful heart of Jesus. I will bear my own suffering in silence. May Your mercy, O Lord, rest upon us.

Faustina died of tuberculosis in 1938. After her death the Divine Mercy devotion has grown steadily. With the support of Pope John Paul II, it became popularly established throughout the entire church.

*Faustina, and other saints like **Margaret Mary Alacoque**, **Joan of Arc**, and even the **Virgin Mary**, were simple and unassuming young women. What makes them extraordinary is God's grace. He seems to favor ordinary folks with his mercy, which is very good news.*

OCTOBER 5 / CANONIZED IN 2000
Mercy; Twentieth-Century Saints; Visions and Visionaries

359. Maximilian Kolbe
(1894–1941)

"Herr kommandant, I wish to make a request, please," stated Father Maximilian Kolbe.

"What does the Polish swine want?" asked the Nazi officer. The scene is Auschwitz, 1941. The Nazi commander has just designated ten men for execution as revenge for the escape of a prisoner from their cell block.

Kolbe pointed at Francis Gajowiniczek and answered: "I am a Polish Catholic priest. I am old. I want to take his place because he has a wife and children."

"Out!" shouted the officer, who traded the priest for the married man. Father Kolbe and nine companions were herded into a starvation block and left to die.

As a young Franciscan, St. Maximilian Kolbe had conceived of himself as a "knight" of **Mary.** He saw his mission as fighting at her side to reverse the dark tides that were engulfing the world. Kolbe's charism attracted numerous followers, whom he organized into a movement. And now he was directly engaged in the battle.

The saint was a communications genius. To propagate his vision, in 1922 he launched *Knights of the Immaculate* magazine that in twenty years had a worldwide circulation of one million. In 1927, near Warsaw, Kolbe and a few friars began construction of a center he called the City of the Immaculate. A decade later he had made it a state-of-the-art media complex, with 762 friars staffing a printing press, radio station, college, and an airfield. Kolbe suffered from chronic tuberculosis, which slowed him down, but never stopped him.

Kolbe was an outspoken critic of the Nazis. So in 1939 they turned the City of the Immaculate into a concentration camp. They arrested the saint in February 1940 and sent him to Auschwitz in May.

During the months before his death, Kolbe's spirit never flagged, and he gave the other prisoners hope. Mieczyslaus Koscielniak, an artist, remembered this conversation with the saint:

> Father Kolbe began to speak quietly about . . . the great and all-mighty God, about the suffering he sends us to make us ready for a better life. He urged us to endure and take heart because the time of trial must

> pass. "God's justice will prevail," he said, "and all will plainly see it, so there is no reason to despair."
>
> We listened spellbound, temporarily forgetting our hunger and degradation. He continued: "No, no they will never kill our souls. We prisoners are different from our persecutors. We are Catholics and Poles. They cannot kill our dignity. No, we will never give in, we will hold out to the end, their terror will never kill the Polish soul. If we die, we will die in holiness and peace, accepting the will of God."

Early in August, Kolbe was thrown into the starvation block. For two weeks the saint encouraged his fellows, leading them in singing hymns and praying the rosary. By the third week all were dead except Kolbe and four others. On August 14, the eve of the Assumption, the commandant had Kolbe and the others killed with injections of carbolic acid. Father Maximilian Kolbe had prayed to die on a feast of Mary and his prayer was answered.

The godless say to themselves:]
"For if the upright man is God's son, God will help him
and rescue him from the clutches of his enemies.
Let us test him with cruelty and with torture,
and thus explore this gentleness of his
and put his patience to the test.
Let us condemn him to a shameful death,
since God will rescue—or so he claims."

—Wisdom 2:18–20 *NJB*

AUGUST 14 / CANONIZED IN 1982 / PATRON OF DRUG ADDICTS
Innovative Saints; Countercultural Witness; Martyrs; Twentieth-Century Saints

360. Edith Stein
(1891–1942)

On July 20, 1942, the Dutch hierarchy condemned the Nazis for deporting Jews to concentration camps. The Nazis quickly sought revenge by sending Jewish Catholics from the Netherlands to certain death. Among the victims was St. Edith Stein, a Carmelite nun, who was gassed and her body burned in the ovens at Auschwitz in August 1942.

Edith Stein was a high-powered professional, yet she never hid behind self-important pretenses. All who met this lovely woman instantly felt she had been their lifelong friend. If you had visited her, she would have served you and joked with you. You would never have guessed she was a famous scholar.

In 1916, Edith completed a PhD in philosophy at Freiburg University, where she became an assistant to the renowned philosopher Edmund Husserl. Over the next decade her writing and speaking established her scholastic reputation throughout Europe.

Edith had been raised in a devout Jewish family, but abandoned her faith in her youth. As a student, however, Edith had discovered Catholicism. She became a convert in 1921 after reading **Teresa of Ávila**'s *Autobiography*.

In 1932 she was appointed lecturer at the Educational Institute in Muenster. But when the Nazis came to power a year later, she was fired because she was a Jew. Edith viewed her dismissal as an opportunity to act on a long-standing desire to become a nun, and she entered the Carmelite community at Cologne.

Edith realized that the Nazi menace would ultimately touch her. For her protection the Carmelites moved her to a house at Echt in the Netherlands. Edith, threatened but courageous, remained confident in God, as she explained in this letter:

> It is good to remember, these days, that poverty implies being ready to leave our home in our dear convent. We have bound ourselves to the enclosure, but God has not bound himself to protect me in the enclosure-walls forever. He does not need to, because he has other walls with which to protect us.
>
> The situation is parallel to the use of the sacraments; for these are the preordained means of grace, and we can scarcely be too eager to receive

> them. But God is not restricted by them. At the moment in which we are cut off from the sacraments by external power, he can more than compensate us in some other way; and he will do so the more surely, the more faithfully we have gone to the sacraments beforehand.
>
> Similarly it is our solemn duty to observe the precepts of the enclosure as conscientiously as possible so as to live undisturbed, hidden with Christ in God. If we have done so faithfully, and if we are driven out onto the street, then our Lord will send his angels to encircle us, and their invisible wings will enfold us in a peace more secure than that of the highest and most solid convent walls. Certainly we ought to pray that we shall be spared the experience, but only with the deeply sincere addition: "Not mine, but thy will be done."

Just as the Carmelites were arranging Edith's relocation to a Swiss convent, the Nazis struck. On August 2, 1942, SS men seized her with other Jews, a reprisal for the bishops' public defiance. Edith Stein was executed at Auschwitz a week later.

We don't easily fathom why God does not seem to protect good people from the violence of evil people. Mysteriously, he seems to have a preference for martyrdom. As the psalm says, "Precious in the sight of the Lord is the death of his saints" (Psalm 116:15 RSV*).*

AUGUST 10 / CANONIZED IN 1999
Countercultural Witness; Martyrs; Twentieth-Century Saints

361. Jacob Gapp
(1897–1943)

Austrian Father Jacob Gapp, SM, saw things in terms of either/or. Either you were for the truth. Or you were against it. His extremism tolerated no accommodation with evil. So when Hitler annexed Austria in 1938, Father Gapp publicly condemned the Nazis. "I could have contented myself," he said, "with a purely interior rejection of National Socialism, as many priests did. But I told myself that it was my duty as a Catholic priest to teach the truth and combat error."

Youthful hardships molded Jacob Gapp's steely character. The seventh child of a poor family, he was wounded in World War I and spent a year as a prisoner. Later he joined the Society of Mary (Marianists) and was ordained a priest. As a teacher at Graz, Austria, he organized his students to help the poor and often gave the coal for heating his room to impoverished families.

Gapp observed firsthand the evils of National Socialism at Graz, which became a Nazi stronghold. He compared Nazi writings with critical Catholic publications, especially Pope Pius XI's encyclical, *Mit brennender Sorge*. Thus he firmed up his resolve:

> More than all earthly well-being, more than all earthly goods, I consider eternal life that which ought to be earned here on earth. Because of that I am convinced that it is a greater evil for an individual or for a people to lose their soul rather than be required to renounce as a loss of war their possessions and their earthly well-being.

The Nazis took active interest in Father Gapp after he rebutted another teacher's proclamation of hatred for Czechs and Jews. He became a dangerous embarrassment to the Marianists, who had decided to go along with the government in order to protect their schools. So they shuffled the outspoken priest to houses in the Tyrol, France, and Spain, hoping to protect him and avoid confrontation with the Nazis.

However, in Spain he was betrayed. A couple posing as Jews asked him for instructions in the Catholic faith. One Sunday afternoon they invited him to a picnic on the French border, then occupied by the Nazis. There the Gestapo arrested him and transferred him to Berlin, where he was tried and condemned to death for treason. On August

13, 1943, the day of his execution, he wrote the following in moving letters to his superiors and relatives:

> Last year I was arrested on French soil on November 9. I was brought to Berlin and was finally condemned to death on July 2, the feast of the Sacred Heart of Jesus. The sentence will be carried out today. At seven o'clock this evening I will go to our dear Savior, whom I have always ardently loved. Do not mourn for me. I am completely happy. After such a difficult struggle, I am now at the point of my life where I consider the present day to be the most beautiful of my life. Do not be sad. Everything passes, only heaven remains. We will someday be together again and then there will be no separation.

That evening Jacob Gapp was beheaded by guillotine at the Ploetenzee prison in Berlin.

The saint's judge reported an intriguing remark made by Heinrich Himmler, the head of Hitler's special forces. Germany, he said, would be winning the war if a million Nazis had been as committed as Jacob Gapp.

> *A man may very well lose his head and yet come to no harm—yea, I say to unspeakable good and everlasting happiness.*
>
> —St. Thomas More

AUGUST 13 / BEATIFIED IN 1996
Countercultural Witness; Eternal Perspective; Martyrs

362. Titus Brandsma
(1881–1942)

It seems almost axiomatic that the closer the saints draw to God in prayer the more likely they are to undertake bold public action in his name. Along with many like **Teresa of Ávila** and **Bridget of Sweden,** Titus Brandsma illustrates the point.

For nineteen years Carmelite Father Brandsma taught philosophy and mystical theology at the Catholic University of Nijmegen, which the Dutch bishops had founded in 1923. A widely respected scholar-activist, he organized Carmelite schools for boys, reformed the Carmelite seminary curriculum, and edited a journal on spirituality. He also established a library of medieval spiritual manuscripts, including three hundred editions of the *Imitation of Christ*.

However, Father Brandsma made his most significant contribution at age sixty as a steely opponent of the Nazis. Johannes De Jong, archbishop of Utrecht, commissioned him to unite the Catholic press against the Nazi invaders. He drafted a letter urging all editors to refuse to publish Nazi propaganda at whatever cost and personally delivered it to fourteen of the most important Catholic papers. Then the German security forces arrested him and jailed him at Scheveningen. He appeared before one official who said he respected Titus's firm convictions, but regarded him as a "very dangerous person." Confined to a dark, windowless cell, Father Brandsma gathered spiritual strength in its solitude. He wrote:

> I am completely at home in this little cell. I haven't been bored once. On the contrary, I am alone, yes, but never has the Lord been so near to me. I could shout for joy that he has allowed himself to be found by me, without me meeting people or people being allowed to meet me. He is now my sole refuge and I feel safe and happy. I am willing to remain here always, if he will allow me to. Rarely have I been so happy and content.

Finally the Nazis sent Titus to Dachau where they forced him to work from 5:30 a.m. 7:00 p.m. He was sick with uremic poisoning and a severe foot infection, but his captors did not cut him any slack. Repeatedly they punched, beat, and gouged him, leaving him bloody and unconscious in the mud. But Titus frustrated his jailers with his forbearance. "Don't yield to hatred," he told other prisoners. "We are here in a dark tunnel but we have to go on. At the end, the eternal light is shining for us."

Because of his disease the Nazis ultimately put Titus in the camp hospital, where he endured degrading medical experiments. When they found him too weak for further tests, they killed him with a lethal injection on July 16, 1942.

Six months before, anticipating his martyrdom, Titus Brandsma wrote the following poem, which inspired many people throughout Holland:

Dear Lord, when looking up to Thee,
I see thy loving eyes on me;
Love overflows my humble heart,
Knowing what faithful friend Thou art
A cup of sorrow I foresee,
Which I accept for love of Thee.
Thy painful way I wish to go;
The only way to God I know.
My soul is full of peace and light;
Although in pain, this light shines bright.
For here Thou Keepest to Thy breast
My longing heart to find there rest.
Leave me here freely alone,
In cell where never sunlight shone,
Should no one ever speak to me,
This golden silence makes me free!
For though alone, I have no fear;
Never were Thou, O Lord, so near.
Sweet Jesus, please, abide with me;
My deepest peace I find in Thee.

JULY 27 / BEATIFIED IN 1985
Contemplatives in Action; Countercultural Witness; Martyrs

363. Solanus Casey
(1870–1957)

By human standards, Solanus Casey was a failure. A mediocre student, he was dismissed from a diocesan seminary, and he barely made it through the Capuchin seminary. When the Capuchins finally ordained him in 1904, they made him a "simplex priest," limiting his ministry to celebrating the Mass. He was not allowed to hear confessions, preach formally, or even wear the Capuchins' distinctive hood. Solanus spent his fifty-three years as a priest in menial service as a sacristan and porter. Had we been treated this way, we may have bolted in anger. But Solanus humbly accepted every decision that put him in lower places.

However, by spiritual standards, Solanus Casey was a great success. As the porter of St. Bonaventure's Monastery in Detroit, Michigan, he became a twentieth-century **John Vianney**. Thousands discovered that Solanus was a good listener and they benefited from his sage advice and spiritual insight. Thousands, also, received divine healing through his ministry. So many people were miraculously touched, that Solanus Casey ranks among the most prodigious wonder-workers in church history.

In 1921, Solanus was given responsibility for enrolling people in the Seraphic Mass Association. Capuchins all over the world interceded at daily Mass for people who were members. When people came to Solanus for help, he would encourage them to sign up in the "S. M. A." and to put their trust in God. And after he enrolled people in the association, they often experienced some miraculous intervention. So many healings occurred that in 1923 the Capuchin superior directed Solanus to keep a log, which he did for many years. Here is a sampling of his notes:

> JULY 26, 1926—Russell Jay, just 17 years old tomorrow and 49 inches tall is enrolled in S. M. A today (non-Catholic). Asks Fr. S to "make me grow." . . . JAN, 2nd. 1927—Today Russell Jay reported he grew 4 1/2 inches—1st change in 12 years—Now developing normally.
>
> JULY 29, 1932—Jen Dorothy Wards—6—had convulsions since 3 months old, as many as 20 a day—when taken here and enrolled. Since that time two years ago has not had a spell.

> DEC. 29, 1937—John Charles Kulbacki—6—blind since 3 weeks old; was enrolled in Ser. Mass A. 6 weeks ago. On Xmas Day when at "Crib" here in church, was almost frightened as he exclaimed—pointing to the lighted "crib" "Look, Mama." Deo Gr. [Deo gratias, thanks to God.]
>
> AUGUST 6, 1944—James Lee Kiser—6—in Highland Park General Hospital—diagnosed as infantile paralysis and brain tumor. Operation was to take place yesterday. Mother phoned to enroll day before when child was on way to the hospital. A 2nd x-ray showed nothing wrong. Child home and O. K. Deo Grat.

When Solanus died in 1957, twenty thousand passed by his casket in one-and-a-half days. They came to say thanks to the saint through whom God had worked marvels in their lives. And had Solanus Casey been an ordinary priest—had he not been a "failure" consigned to the lowest places—he may not have had the opportunity he had to serve so many so well.

> *Sometimes listening to people becomes monotonous and extremely boring, till one is nearly collapsing; but in such cases it helps to remember that even when Jesus was about to fall the third time, he patiently consoled the women-folk and children of his persecutors, making no exceptions. How can we ever be as grateful as we ought for such a vocation?*
>
> —Solanus Casey

JULY 31 / DECLARED VENERABLE IN 1995
Healing Touch; Miracles Do Happen; Success in Failure; Twentieth-Century Saints

364. Padre Pio

(1887–1968)

Today Padre Pio shares top billing with **Thérèse of Lisieux** as the most popular twentieth-century saints. Preternatural phenomena marked the life of this southern Italian priest—miracles, prophecy, bilocation, reading of consciences, and the stigmata that he bore for fifty years. His extraordinary gifts touched thousands of people who became his loyal followers.

Padre Pio's human side also touched them. He endured physical and spiritual torments all his life, yet always lightened others' burdens with a joke. And his sense of humor was his self-defense against detractors. Once, for example, a psychologist said that he "meditated neurotically" on the passion, causing his body psychosomatically to reproduce replicas of Christ's wounds. "Right," Padre Pio responded, "now you go meditate like that on a bull and see if you grow horns."

Like **John Vianney,** Padre Pio's heart for souls led him to spend many hours each day hearing confessions. Penitents appreciated his mercy and spiritual insight and believed his words brought healing to their souls. No rigorist, sometimes in his compassion Padre Pio excused behavior others saw as seriously wrong. For instance, once he was asked his opinion of a thief who had stolen jewels from a church's painting of Mary. "What do you want me to say?" he asked. "That poor young man was probably hungry and went to Our Lady to say: 'Of what use are these stones to you?' And probably Our Lady gave them to him. Silly him to get caught with the goods in his pocket."

The saint often found his own trials unbearable. But his spiritual teaching helped many understand the reasons God allowed their pain, as he does in these sayings on finding meaning in suffering:

> There's a woman who is embroidering. Her son, seated on a low stool, sees her work, but in reverse. He sees the knots of the embroidery, the tangled threads. He says, "Mother, what are you doing? I can't make out what you are doing!" Then the mother lowers the embroidery hoop and shows the good part of the work. Each color is in place and the various threads form a harmonious design. So, we see the reverse side of the embroidery because we are seated on the low stool.
>
> Religion is a hospital for spiritually sick people who want to be healed. To be healed they submit themselves to suffering. That is, to

> the lance, to the scalpel, the fire and bitter medicine. In order to be spiritually cured they must submit to all the painful procedures of the divine Physician.

Francesco Forgione, "Franci" to his family, became a Capuchin priest in 1910. A strange illness prevented his staying permanently in friaries for nearly a decade until he was sent to the isolated monastery of San Giovanni Rotondo in southern Italy, where he lived for half a century. There on September 20, 1918, the stigmata became visible on his body, a source of torture and embarrassment until his death. Padre Pio died on September 23, 1968. One hundred thousand people crowded into the little village at San Giovanni Rotondo to pay their last respects and attend his funeral. Because he displayed holiness and gifts similar to **Francis of Assisi**, his namesake, Padre Pio is sometimes called the Second Saint Francis.

> *No pilgrim soul can worthily love God. But when a soul does everything possible and trusts in divine mercy, why would Jesus reject such a spirit? Has he not commanded us to love God according to our strength? If you have given and consecrated everything to God, why be afraid?*
>
> —Padre Pio

SEPTEMBER 23 / CANONIZED IN 2002
Stigmata; Suffering; Twentieth-Century Saints

365. Teresa of Calcutta

(1910–1997)

Teresa of Calcutta won the admiration of the entire world for her service to the poorest of the poor. No other saint has ever achieved the global popularity that she did during her lifetime. Not even **St. Francis** nor her namesake, **St. Thérèse of Lisieux.** And no other saint had the opportunity to exploit the media as effectively as Mother Teresa did for the causes of Christ. Small in stature, but big in savvy, she knew how to take advantage of TV's evening news, as she did in 1994 when millions watched her rebuke the president of the United States to his face for failing to defend unborn babies.

However, Mother Teresa made it her hallmark always to perform the humblest services to the helpless poor. Here she tells a story that symbolized her ministry:

> My sisters also work in Australia. On the reservation, among the Aborigines, there was an elderly man. I can assure you that you have never seen a situation as difficult as that poor old man's. He was completely ignored by everyone. His home was disordered and dirty.
>
> I told him, "Please let me clean your house, wash your clothes and make your bed." He answered, "I'm okay like this. Let it be."
>
> I said again, "You will be still better if you allow me to do it."
>
> He finally agreed. So I was able to clean his house and wash his clothes. I discovered a beautiful lamp, covered with dust. Only God knew how many years had passed since he last lit it.
>
> I said to him, "Don't you light that lamp? Don't you ever use it?"
>
> He answered, "No. No one comes to see me. I have no need to light it. Who would I do it for?"
>
> I asked, "Would you light it every night if the sisters came?"
>
> He replied, "Of course."
>
> From that day on the sisters committed themselves to visiting him every evening.
>
> Two years passed. I had completely forgotten that man. He sent this message: "Tell my friend that the light she lit in my life continues to shine still."
>
> I thought it was a very small thing. We often neglect small things.

Both a simple woman of prayer and a gifted spiritual entrepreneur, Mother Teresa presided over a rapidly growing community at a time when other religious orders were waning. She founded the Missionaries of Charity in 1950, and in rapid succession opened a home for the dying, a novitiate, a children's home, and a leper's village. By 1971 she had fifty homes scattered over India, Africa, Australia, Europe, and England.

Even more dramatic growth occurred after she won the Nobel Prize for Peace in 1979 and journalist Malcolm Muggeridge told the world about her in *Something Beautiful for God*. Between 1980 and 1983 she established forty-four new centers in all parts of the world. And in the late 1980s, because of Mother Teresa's universal acceptance, her order made inroads into countries previously closed to missionaries—Ethiopia, Yemen, and Russia.

In the 1990s, Mother Teresa suffered heart disease and contracted malaria. A fatal heart attack took her from us on September 5, 1997. At that time four thousand Missionaries of Charity served in 107 centers all over the globe.

A mere smile, a short visit, the lighting of a lamp, writing a letter for a blind man, carrying a bucket of charcoal, reading the newspaper for someone—something small, very small—may, in fact, be our love of God in action.

—Teresa of Calcutta

SEPTEMBER 7 / BEATIFIED IN 2003

Innovative Saints; Leading Women; Love in Action; Serving the Poor; Twentieth-Century Saints

Themes

You may read Voices of the Saints topically. Choose any subject below and go to the saints listed.

Almsgiving
Caesarius of Arles
Cyprian of Carthage
Hedwig
Lawrence
Maximus of Turin
Peter Chrysologus
Severin of Noricum
Thomas of Villanova

Angels
Cecilia
Gall of Clermont
Joachim and Anne
Joan of Arc
Julie Billiart
Kevin
Pachomius
Peter
Stanislaus Kostka
Teresa of Ávila
Vincent of Saragossa

Care of the Sick
Camillus de Lellis
Catherine of Genoa
Elizabeth of Hungary
Fabiola
Frances of Rome
Hedwig
John Baptist de Rossi
John of God
Martin de Porres
Rose of Lima

Care of the Soul
Catherine dei Ricci
Charles Borromeo
Clare of Assisi
Honoratus of Arles
Ignatius of Loyola
John Baptist de Rossi
John Ruysbroeck
John Vianney
Louis of Granada
Mary Mazzarello
Pelagia
Peter Favre
Pius X
Vincent Ferrer

Catholic Reformers
Angela Merici
Anthony Zaccaria
Benedict of Aniane
Bernardino of Siena
Cajetan
Charles Borromeo
Colette
Dunstan of Canterbury
Francis de Sales
Francis of Paola
Ignatius of Loyola
John Leonardi
John of Capistrano
Malachy
Odo of Cluny
Peter Canisius
Peter Favre
Peter of Alcántara
Robert Bellarmine
Teresa of Ávila
Thomas of Villanova
Vincent Ferrer

Celebration of Discipline
Anne Mary Taigi
Anthony Grassi
Benedict
Charles of Sezze
Damien the Leper (Damien de Veuster)
Dominic Savio
Elizabeth of Hungary
Francis de Sales
Gabriel Francis Possenti
Gregory Lopez
Honoratus of Arles
John of the Cross
Louis de Montfort
Maximus of Turin
Melania

Peter Chrysologus
Peter Favre
Peter of Alcántara
Sabas
Valerian

Celtic Saints

Brendan the Navigator
Brigid
Caedmon
Columba
Columban
Cuthbert
Flannan
Hilda
Kentigern
Kevin
Patrick
Wilfrid
Willibrord

Child Saints

Agnes
Aloysius Gonzaga
Charles Lwanga and Companions
Dominic Savio
Eulalia of Mérida
Maria Goretti
Stanislaus Kostka

Christian Living

Ambrose
Athanasius
Barnabas
Caesarius of Arles
Clement Mary Hofbauer
Clement of Alexandria
John Baptist de La Salle
John Cassian
John Climacus
John Henry Newman
John Leonardi
Leonard of Port Maurice
Louise de Marillac
Martin of Braga
Nicetas of Remesiana
Paschal Baylon
Peter Canisius
Syncletica
Vincent de Paul

Christian Unity

Bonaventure
Clement I
Cyril and Methodius
Dionysius of Alexandria
Ignatius of Antioch
Irenaeus
James the Just
Josaphat
Leander of Seville
Malachy
Martin of Braga
Peter Canisius
Peter Favre
Proclus

Community

Ammon
Anne-Marie Javouhey
Basil the Great
Brigid
Dominic
Eusebius of Vercelli
Hilda
Honoratus of Arles
Marcella
Martin of Tours
Pachomius
Sabas

Contemplatives in Action

Aldobrandesca
Angela of Foligno
Catherine dei Ricci
Catherine of Genoa
Catherine of Siena
Hedwig
Henry Suso
Katharine Drexel
Lucy Filippini
Marie of the Incarnation
Martin de Porres
Philip Neri
Teresa of Ávila
Titus Brandsma

Conversations with God

Catherine of Genoa
Catherine of Siena
Gemma Galgani
Gertrude of Delft
Gertrude the Great
Henry Suso
John Ruysbroeck
Lutgarde of Awyières
Margaret Mary Alacoque
Margaret of Cortona
Mechtild of Helfta
Mechtild of Magdeburg

Conversion

Alban
Charles de Foucauld
Cyprian of Carthage
Hilary of Arles
John Henry Newman
John of Capistrano
Justin

Mary of Egypt
Matt Talbot
Norbert
Pelagia the Penitent
Philip Benizi
Raphael Kalinowski

The Cost of Discipleship

Andrew
Apphian
Eusebius of Vercelli
Francis of Assisi
John of the Cross
Paul Miki
Philippine Duchesne
Robert Southwell
Theodore the Studite

Countercultural Witness

Aloysius Gonzaga
Alphonsus de Orozco
Anthony of Egypt
Apphian
Edith Stein
George of Lydda
Jacob Gapp
Julie Billiart
Kateri Tekakwitha
Korean Martyrs
Margaret Clitherow
Martin of Tours
Maximilian Kolbe
Perpetuas
Titus Brandsma
Vincent of Saragossa

Courage

Agnes
Edmund Campion
Casimir
Clotilda
Flora
George Matulaitis
Gregory VII
John Forest
John Gabriel Perboyre
Margaret Clitherow
Marguerite Bourgeoys
Mary Magdalen
Oliver Plunkett
Theodore the Studite

Defending the Faith

Alexander
Ambrose
Amphilochius
Athanasius
Basil the Great
Cyril of Alexandria
Ephrem
Eusebius of Vercelli
Faustus
Frederic Ozanam
Fulgentius of Ruspe
Germanus of Auxerre
Germanus of Constantinople
Gregory Nazianzen
Gregory of Nyssa
Hilary of Poitiers
Hippolytus
Irenaeus
John Damascene
Justin
Leo the Great
Marcella
Martin I
Methodius of Olympus
Polycarp
Proclus
Stephen
Vincent Ferrer
Vincent of Lérins

Difficult Marriages

Clotilda
Fabiola
Joan of France
Marguerite d'Youville
Monica
Radegund
Rita of Cascia

Doctors of the Church

Alphonsus Liguori
Ambrose
Anselm
Athanasius
Augustine
Basil the Great
Bede
Bernard of Clairvaux
Bonaventure
Catherine of Siena
Cyril of Alexandria
Cyril of Jerusalem
Ephrem
Francis de Sales
Gregory Nazianzen
Hilary of Poitiers
Isidore of Seville
John Chrysostom
Peter Canisius
Peter Chrysologus
Teresa of Ávila
Thérèse of Lisieux

Doubt

Henry Suso
Jane de Chantal
John of the Cross
John the Baptist
Raphael Kalinowski
Sebastian Valfré
Thomas

Dreams
Caedmon
Euthymius
Joseph
Leoba
Martin of Tours

Enduring Trials
Alphonsus Liguori
Alphonsus Rodriguez
Ambrose
Camillus de Lellis
Fina
Fulgentius of Ruspe
Jane de Chantal
Kateri Tekakwitha
Philippine Duchesne
Rita of Cascia

Eternal Perspective
Alphonsus Liguori
Diana d'Andalo
Columban
Eulogius of Cordoba
Frances Xavier Cabrini
George Matulaitis
Hippolytus
Jacob Gapp
John Forest
John Henry Newman
Jordan of Saxony
Katharine Drexel
Macrina
Pachomius
Paulinus of Nola
Rudolf Aquaviva
Théophane Vénard

Evangelization
Alban
Anthony Mary Claret
Augustine of Canterbury
Charles de Foucauld
Cyril and Methodius
Euthymius
Francis Borgia
Francis Xavier
Germanus of Auxerre
Giles of Assisi
Gregory the Wonderworker
John Baptist de Rossi
John de Brébeuf
Jordan of Saxony
Julien Maunoir
Junípero Serra
Justin
Leander of Seville
Louis de Montfort
Martin of Braga
Peter Fourier
Sturm
Vedast
Willibrord

Facing Death
Aloysius Gonzaga
Anthony Grassi
Athanasius
Braulio
Claude la Colombiére
Elizabeth Ann Seton
Ephrem
Felicity
Hilarion
Hugh of Lincoln
Macrina
Miguel Pro
Oliver Plunkett
Paulinus of Nola
Paul the Hermit
Stanislaus Kostka
Thomas More

Faith Seeking Understanding
Anselm
Justin
Prosper of Aquitaine
Rabanus Maurus
Severinus Boethius
Thomas Aquinas

Family
Aloysius Gonzaga
Anne Mary Taigi
Joseph
Macrina
Margaret Clitherow
Monica
Osanna of Mantua
Scholastica
Thomas More

Fasting
Cyprian of Carthage
Kevin
Melania
Peter Chrysologus

Feisty Saints
André Bessette
Cyril of Alexandria
Hilary of Arles
Hippolytus
Jerome
Margaret of Hungary
Shenoute
Thomas Becket

Intercession
Anthony of Padua
Catherine of Siena
Colette
Cyprian of Carthage
Cyril of Alexandria
Dominic
Elizabeth Leseur
Felix
Gall of Clermont
Gaudentius of Brescia
Lutgarde of Awyières
Mary
Mary of Egypt
Monica
Scholastica
Thomas Aquinas

Intimacy with the Divine
Augustine
Bruno
Catherine dei Ricci
Catherine of Genoa
Elizabeth of the Trinity
Eucherius
Gertrude of Delft
Gertrude the Great
John Cassian
Mary
Mary Magdalen
Mechtild of Magdeburg
Osanna of Mantua
Paul of the Cross
Peter Julian Eymard
Robert Bellarmine

Jesus Christ
Alexander
Amphilochius
Andrew of Crete
Dionysius of Alexandria
John of Ávila
Leo the Great
Nicetas of Remesiana

Joy
Margaret Clitherow
Miguel Pro
Philip Neri
Pier-Giorgio Frassati
Sebastian Valfré
Théophane Vénard

Kindness
Elizabeth of Hungary
Francis di Geronimo
Francis Xavier Seelos
John Kolobos
Jordan of Saxony
Joseph
Nicholas
Proclus
Sebastian Valfré
Ubald of Gubbio

Leading Men
Aelred of Rievaulx
Benedict
Benedict of Aniane
Bernard of Clairvaux
Dominic
Francis of Assisi
Francis Borgia
Ignatius of Loyola
Honoratus of Arles
Humbert of Romans
John Bosco
John Leonardi
Jordan of Saxony
Macarius the Great
Odo of Cluny
Raymond of Penyafort
Theodore the Studite

Leading Women
Angela Merici
Anne-Marie Javouhey
Brigid
Clare of Assisi
Colette
Elizabeth Ann Seton
Frances of Rome
Frances Xavier Cabrini
Leoba
Lucy Filippini
Madeleine Sophie Barat
Mary McKillop
Paola Frassinetti
Paula
Syncletica
Teresa of Ávila
Teresa of Calcutta

The Light of Christ
Gemma Galgani
Gregory Nazianzen
Hildegard of Bingen
Osanna of Mantua
Simeon the New Theologian
Vincent Ferrer

Lights in the "Dark Ages"
Bertilla
Boniface
Caedmon
Clotilda
Columba
Cuthbert
Fridiswede

Hilda
Leoba
Rabanus Maurus
Sturm
Vedast Wilfrid

Love in Action

Barnabas
Damien the Leper (Damien de Veuster)
Genevieve
John Regis
Louis IX
Madeleine Sophie Barat
Martin de Porres
Mary Euphrasia Pelletier
Teresa of Calcutta
Theresa Margaret of the Sacred Heart

Married Saints

Anne Mary Taigi
Balthild
Catherine of Genoa
Clotilda
Elizabeth Ann Seton
Elizabeth Leseur
Elizabeth of Hungary
Frances of Rome
Frederic Ozanam
Gregory of Nyssa
Hilary of Poitiers
Jane de Chantal
Joachim and Anne
Louis IX
Louise de Marillac
Margaret Clitherow
Margaret of Scotland
Marie of the Incarnation
Nicholas of Flue
Olympias
Paulinus of Nola
Stephen of Hungary
Thomas More

Martyrs

Alban
Apphian
Cecilia
Charles Lwanga and Companions
Edith Stein
Edmund Campion
Eulalia of Mérida
Eulogius of Cordoba
Felicity
Flora
The Forty Martyrs of Sebaste
George of Lydda
Ignatius of Antioch
Isaac Jogues
Jacob Gapp
James the Great
John de Brébeuf
John Fisher
John Forest
John Gabriel Perboyre
Josaphat
Korean Martyrs
Lawrence
Margaret Clitherow
Martin I
Maximilian Kolbe
Miguel Pro
Oliver Plunkett
Paul Miki
Perpetua
Peter Sanz
Polycarp
Robert Southwell
Stephen
Théophane Vénard
Thomas Becket
Thomas More
Titus Brandsma
Vincent of Saragossa

Mary

Bernadette Soubirous
Catherine Labouré
Germanus of Constantinople
Ildefonsus of Toledo
Joan of France
John Damascene
Louis De Montfort
Mary of Egypt
Mary of the Angels
Peter Damian
Theodore the Studite

Meekness

Anthony Grassi
Anthony Mary Claret
Charles Borromeo
Clement Mary Hofbauer
Hugh of Lincoln
Odo of Cluny
Thomas of Villanova

Mercy

Anthony of Padua
Bridget of Sweden
Catherine of Genoa
Charles Borromeo
Cyril of Jerusalem
Faustina Kowalska
Francis di Geronimo
Francis Xavier Seelos
Fulgentius of Ruspe
Gertrude the Great
James the Just
John Chrysostom
Joseph Cafasso
Luke
Wenceslaus

Mere Christian Love

Aelred of Rievaulx
Assunta Pallotta
Clement I
Dominic Savio
Gabriel Francis Possenti
Gregory the Great
John
John Bosco
Joseph
Peter Claver
Rose of Lima
Thérèse of Lisieux
Venantius Fortunatus

Miracles Do Happen

Alban
Apphian
Caedmon
Cuthbert
Fina
Francis of Paola
Genevieve
Gerard Majella
Gregory the Wonderworker
Hilarion
John
Joseph of Cupertino
Joseph Pignatelli
Julie Billiart
Kentigern
Lutgarde of Aywières
Malachy
Martin of Tours
Maurus
Odoric of Pordenone
Paschal Baylon
Peter
Scholastica
Severin of Noricum
Shenoute
Solanus Casey
Theodore of Sykeon
Vedast

Missionaries

Augustine of Canterbury
Boniface
Brendan the Navigator
Columba
Columban
Cuthbert
Cyril and Methodius
Frances Xavier Cabrini
Francis Xavier
Isaac Jogues
John de Brébeuf
John Gabriel Perboyre
John Neumann
John Regis
Julien Maunoir
Junípero Serra
Louis de Montfort
Marie of the Incarnation
Nicetas of Remesiana
Odoric of Pordenone
Paul
Peter Claver
Peter Sanz
Philippine Duchesne
Rudolf Aquaviva
Sturm
Théophane Vénard
Timothy
Wilfrid
Willibrord

A Passionate Love

Bernard of Clairvaux
Catherine dei Ricci
Elizabeth Ann Seton
Elizabeth of the Trinity
Jacopone da Todi
John of Ávila
Julian of Norwich
Lutgarde of Aywières
Richard Rolle
Theresa Margaret of the Sacred Heart
Veronica Giuliani

Passion for Purity

Agnes
Ammon
Augustine
Charles Lwanga and Companions
Fridiswede
Irenaeus
Leonard of Port Maurice
Margaret of Cortona
Maria Goretti
Mary of the Angels
Methodius of Olympus
Sabas

Peacemakers

Anne Mary Taigi
Casimir
Epiphanius
Flannan
Germanus of Auxerre
Hedwig
Irenaeus
Monica
Peter Canisius
Philip Benizi
Theodore of Canterbury

Perseverance

Alphonsus Liguori
Anthony Zaccaria
Braulio
Claude la Colombiére
David
Gall of Clermont
Gregory the Wonderworker
Joachim and Anne
Joan Antide-Thouret
Malachy
Timothy
Vedast
Henry Suso
John Cassian
John Ruysbroeck
John the Silent
Luke
Macarius the Great
Pachomius
Paul of the Cross
Peter Julian Eymard
Peter of Alcántara
Robert Bellarmine
Teresa of Ávila
Thomas Aquinas
Veronica Giuliani
Clare of Assisi
Eucherius
Eulogius of Cordoba
Felix
Francis de Sales
Hildegard of Bingen
John Climacus
Louis of Granada
Mary Euphrasia Pelletier
Rudolf Aquaviva
Seraphim of Sarov
Simeon Stylites
Thérèse of Lisieux
Valerian

Poets

Caedmon
Columba
Ephrem
Jacopone da Todi
John Damascene
Mechtild of Magdeburg
Paulinus of Nola
Rabanus Maurus
Robert Southwell
Venantius Fortunatus

Prayer

Albert the Great
Angela Merici
Angela of Foligno
Bonaventure
Brendan the Navigator
Caesarius of Arles
Cyprian of Carthage
Cyril of Alexandria
Dominic
Elizabeth of the Trinity
Giles of Assisi
Gregory Lopez
Gregory of Sinai

Prophets

Bridget of Sweden
Hildegard of Bingen
John the Baptist
Philip Benizi
Vincent Ferrer

Purpose

Barnabas
Dominic Barberi
Dominic Savio
Elizabeth of the Trinity
The Forty Martyrs of Sebaste
Francis of Assisi
Ignatius Loyola
John Berchmans
John of God
Marguerite Bourgeoys

Pursuit of Holiness

Athanasius
Benedict of Aniane
Bernard of Clairvaux
Catherine Labouré

Raising Christian Youth

Anselm
John Baptist de La Salle
John Bosco
Julie Billiart
Madeleine Sophie Barat
Mary Mazzarello
Peter Fourier

Repentance

Ammon
Andrew of Crete
Angela of Foligno
Augustine
Bertilla
Bernardino of Siena
Camillus de Lellis
Catherine of Genoa
Charles de Foucauld
Columba
Jerome
John Eudes
John of Capistrano
John of God

John the Baptist
Margaret of Cortona
Maria Goretti
Mary of Egypt
Mary of the Angels
Matthew
Peter Fourier
Theodore of Canterbury
Vincent de Paul

Saints and the Bible

Alcuin
Bede
Dominic
Humbert of Romans
Jerome
Luke
Mark
Matthew
Norbert
Paula
Vincent of Lérins

Saints and Politics

Ambrose
Balthild
Basil the Great
Daniel the Stylite
Dunstan of Canterbury
Epiphanius
Francis of Paola
Gregory the Great
Gregory VII
Hugh of Lincoln
Ildefonsus of Toledo
John Fisher
Leo the Great
Louis IX
Nicholas I
Nicholas of Flue
Olaf
Severinus Boethius
Stephen of Hungary
Thomas Becket
Thomas More
Vedast
Wenceslaus
Wilfrid

Saints and Sacraments

Baptism
Aphraates
Faustus
Felicity
Gaudentius of Brescia
Gregory Nazianzen
Ildefonsus of Toledo
Eucharist
Cajetan
Ignatius of Antioch
Margaret of Scotland
Paschal Baylon
Peter Damian
Peter Julian Eymard
Pius X
Reconciliation
Francis di Geronimo
Francis Xavier Seelos
John Baptist de Rossi
John Eudes
John Vianney
Joseph Cafasso
Louise de Marillac
Vincent de Paul

The Secrets of Spiritual Success

Catherine dei Ricci
Clement Mary Hofbauer
Frances Xavier Cabrini
Gabriel Francis Possenti
Joan of France
John of the Cross
John Vianney
Louis of Granada
Mary Euphrasia Pelletier
Mechtild of Helfta
Michael Garicoits
Philip Neri
Seraphim of Sarov
Simeon the New Theologian
Thérèse of Lisieux
Vincent de Paul

Serving the Poor

Anne-Marie Javouhey
Basil the Great
Brigid
Camillus de Lellis
Casimir
Clement of Alexandria
Frederic Ozanam
Genevieve
Hedwig
John Regis
Katharine Drexel
Louis de Montfort
Louise de Marillac
Marguerite d'Youville
Martin de Porres
Mary Mazzarello
Mary McKillop
Miguel Pro
Odo of Cluny
Paulinus of Nola
Peter Claver
Pier-Giorgio Frassati
Rose of Lima
Teresa of Calcutta

Sexual Temptation

Aldobrandesca
Augustine
Benedict
Charles of Sezze
Clement Mary Hofbauer
David
Jerome
Leonard of Port Maurice
Macarius the Great
Margaret of Cortona
Philip Neri

The Sign of the Cross

Aldobrandesca
Anne Mary Taigi
Anthony of Egypt
Assunta Pallotta
Caesarius of Arles
Christopher
Cyril of Jerusalem
Euthymius
Gall

Simple Obedience

Claude la Colombiére
Joan of Arc
John Neumann
Mary
Maurus
Paola Frassinetti

Sin

Bridget of Sweden
Caesarius of Arles
Claude la Colombiére
Damien the Leper (Damien de Veuster)
Francis di Geronimo
Francis Xavier Seelos
Fulgentius of Ruspe
Louis of Granada
Mary Magdalen dei Pazzi
Maximus of Turin
Pelagia
Peter Favre

Social Justice

Anne-Marie Javouhey
Frederic Ozanam
Martin de Porres
Peter Claver
Roque González
Wenceslaus

Solitude

Anthony of Egypt
Aphraates
Benedict Joseph Labre
Bruno
Charles de Foucauld
Eucherius
Euthymius
Gregory Lopez
Hilarion
John the Silent
Julian of Norwich
Paul the Hermit
Sabas

A Soul Afire

Bruno
Clare of Assisi
Margaret Mary Alacoque
Mechtild of Magdeburg
Philip Neri
Richard Rolle
Robert Southwell
Simeon the New Theologian
Teresa of Ávila
Theresa Margaret of the Sacred Heart

Spiritual Warfare

Anthony of Egypt
Boniface
Charles of Sezze
Christopher
Daniel the Stylite
David
Gall
George of Lydda
Giles of Assisi
Gregory of Nyssa
John Vianney
Macarius the Great
Patrick
Peter
Syncletica

Stigmata

Catherine dei Ricci
Charles of Sezze
Francis of Assisi
Gemma Galgani
Gertrude of Delft
Mary Magdalen dei Pazzi
Padre Pio
Rita of Cascia
Veronica Giuliani

Study

Albert the Great
Alphonsus de Orzoco
Bede
Benedict Biscop
Columba
Isidore of Seville
Leoba

Marcella
Radegund
Thomas Aquinas

Success in Failure

Alphonsus Rodriguez
Gemma Galgani
John de Brébeuf
Joseph of Cupertino
Mary Teresa de Soubiran
Michael Garicoits
Philippine Duchesne
Richard Rolle
Rudolf Aquaviva
Solanus Casey
Willibrord

Suffering

Benedict Joseph Labre
Catherine of Siena
Damien the Leper (Damien de Veuster)
Elizabeth Leseur
Fina
George Matulaitis
Henry Suso
Isaac Jogues
Joan Antide-Thouret
Joan of France
John Eudes
Marguerite d'Youville
Martin I
Mary Magdalen dei Pazzi
Mary of the Angels
Mary Teresa de Soubiran
Padre Pio
Raymond of Penyafort
Sebastian Valfré

Temptation

Aldobrandesca
Ammon
Athanasius
Damien the Leper (Damien de Veuster)
David
Gregory of Nyssa
Jane de Chantal
John Cassian

True Humility

Alphonsus Rodriguez
André Bessette
Balthild
Bernadette Soubirous
Bonaventure
John Berchmans
Paul

Twentieth-Century Saints

André Bessette
Assunta Pallotta
Charles de Foucauld
Edith Stein
Faustina Kowalska
George Matulaitis
Katharine Drexel
Mary McKillop
Matt Talbot
Maximilian Kolbe
Miguel Pro
Padre Pio
Pier-Giorgio Frassati
Pius X
Raphael Kalinowski
Solanus Casey
Teresa of Calcutta

Twenty-Something Saints

Aloysius Gonzaga
Apphian
Assunta Pallotta
Casimir
Cecilia
Charles Lwanga and Companions
Elizabeth of Hungary
The Forty Martyrs of Sebaste
Gabriel Francis Possenti
Gerard Majella
John Berchmans
Kateri Tekakwitha
Margaret Clitherow
Perpetua
Pier-Giorgio Frassati
Theresa Margaret of the Sacred Heart
Wenceslaus

Valiant Women

Angela Merici
Bridget of Sweden
Fridiswede
Hilda
Madeleine Sophie Barat
Mary Magdalen
Mary McKillop
Perpetua
Radegund

Visions and Visionaries

Angela of Foligno
Bernadette Soubirous
Catherine dei Ricci
Catherine Labouré

Dominic Barberi (prophetic revelation)
Faustina Kowalska
Gertrude the Great
Hildegard of Bingen
Joan of Arc
Julian of Norwich
Margaret Mary Alacoque
Marie of the Incarnation
Osanna of Mantua

Vocation

Aloysius Gonzaga
Alphonsus Rodriguez
Andrew
Anne-Marie Javouhey
Anthony of Egypt
Colette
Frances of Rome
Francis Xavier
Gall of Clermont
Hilary of Arles
John Berchmans
John Neumann
John of God
Juvenal Ancina
Margaret of Hungary
Michael Garicoits

World Historical Saints

Bede
Benedict
Boniface
Clotilda
Columba
Cyril and Methodius
Dunstan of Canterbury
Francis Xavier
Gregory the Great
Isidore of Seville
Joan of Arc
Nicholas I
Patrick
Paul
Severinus Boethius
Thomas More

Worship

Andrew of Crete
Dominic
Pachomius
Peter Julian Eymard

A Calendar of the Saints

While this list is based on the calendar of the Roman Rite of the Catholic Church, it includes only the saints that are contained in this book. Names of saints who are celebrated liturgically in the universal church are capitalized. Names of saints celebrated liturgically only in certain areas are italicized. Saints traditionally remembered on certain days but who are not in the liturgical calendar are in lower-case letters.

January

1 SOLEMNITY OF MARY, MOTHER OF GOD; Fulgentius of Ruspe.

2 BASIL THE GREAT and GREGORY NAZIANZEN; Seraphim of Sarov.

3 Genevieve.

4 *Elizabeth Ann Seton.*

5 *John Neumann;* Syncletica; Simeon Stylites; Charles of Sezze.

6 Gertrude of Delft; André Bessette.

7 Raymond of Penyafort.

8 Severin of Noricum.

12 Aelred of Rievaulx; Benedict Biscop; Marguerite Bourgeoys.

13 HILARY OF POITIERS.

14 Felix of Nola; Kentigern; Odoric of Pordenone.

15 PAUL THE HERMIT; Macarius the Great; Maurus.

16 Honoratus of Arles.

17 ANTHONY OF EGYPT.

18 Margaret of Hungary.

20 Euthymius the Great.

21 AGNES; Epiphanius.

22 VINCENT OF SARAGOSSA.

23 Ildefonsus of Toledo.

24 FRANCIS DE SALES.

25 Henry Suso.

26 TIMOTHY and TITUS; Paula.

27 ANGELA MERICI; George Matulaitis.

28 THOMAS AQUINAS; Julien Maunoir.

30 Balthild; Sebastian Valfré.

31 JOHN BOSCO; Marcella.

February

1 Brigid.

4 Joan of France; Rabanus Maurus.

6 PAUL MIKI AND COMPANIONS; Vedast.

10 SCHOLASTICA.

11 Caedmon.
12 Benedict of Aniane.
13 Catherine dei Ricci.
14 CYRIL AND METHODIUS.
15 Claude la Colombiére; Jordan of Saxony.
21 PETER DAMIAN; Robert Southwell.
22 Margaret of Cortona.
23 POLYCARP.
26 Alexander.
27 GABRIEL FRANCIS POSSENTI; Leander of Seville.
28 Angela of Foligno.
29 John Cassian.

March

1 David.
3 Katharine Drexel.
4 CASIMIR.
6 Colette.
7 PERPETUA and FELICITY.
8 JOHN OF GOD.
9 FRANCES OF ROME; Gregory of Nyssa; Dominic Savio.
10 The Forty Martyrs of Sebaste.
11 Eulogius of Cordoba; Theresa Margaret of the Sacred Heart.
12 Fina; Simeon the New Theologian.
15 Louise de Marillac; Clement Mary Hofbauer.
17 PATRICK.
18 CYRIL OF JERUSALEM.
19 JOSEPH.
20 Martin of Braga; Cuthbert.
22 Nicholas of Flue.
25 Lucy Filippini; Margaret Clitherow.
26 Braulio.
30 John Climacus.

April

2 FRANCIS OF PAOLA; Apphian; Mary of Egypt.
4 ISIDORE OF SEVILLE.
5 VINCENT FERRER.
7 JOHN BAPTIST DE LA SALLE; Aphraates of Persia; Assunta Pallotta.
8 Julie Billiart.
11 Gemma Galgani.
13 MARTIN I.
15 Damien the Leper. (Damien de Veuster)
16 Benedict Joseph Labre; Bernadette Soubirous.
21 ANSELM.
22 Theodore of Sykeon.
23 GEORGE OF LYDDA; Giles of Assisi.
24 Mary Euphrasia Pelletier.
25 MARK.
26 Aldobrandesca.
28 Louis de Montfort.
29 CATHERINE OF SIENA.
30 Marie of the Incarnation.

May

2 ATHANASIUS.
3 JAMES THE JUST; Elizabeth Leseur.
5 Hilary of Arles.
9 Pachomius.
10 John of Ávila.
11 Francis di Geronimo.
12 Germanus of Constantinople.

13 Robert Bellarmine; John the Silent; Julian of Norwich.
14 Michael Garicoits; Mary Mazzarello.
16 Ubald of Gubbio; Brendan the Navigator.
17 Paschal Baylon.
19 Alcuin.
20 BERNARDINO OF SIENA.
22 Rita of Cascia; John Forest.
23 John Baptist de Rossi.
24 Vincent of Lérins.
25 BEDE; GREGORY VII; MARY MAGDALEN DEI PAZZI; Madeleine Sophie Barat; Mary McKillop.
26 PHILIP NERI; Peter Sanz.
27 AUGUSTINE OF CANTERBURY.
30 Joan of Arc.

June

1 JUSTIN.
3 CHARLES LWANGA AND COMPANIONS; Clotilda; Kevin.
5 BONIFACE.
6 NORBERT.
7 Matt Talbot.
9 Columba; Anne Mary Taigi; Diana d'Andalo.
11 BARNABAS; Paola Frassinetti.
13 ANTHONY OF PADUA.
16 Lutgarde of Aywières; John Regis.
18 Ephrem.
20 Alban; Osanna of Mantua.
21 Aloysius Gonzaga.
22 PAULINUS OF NOLA; JOHN FISHER; THOMAS MORE; Nicetas of Remesiana.
23 Joseph Cafasso.
24 THE BIRTH OF JOHN THE BAPTIST.
25 Prosper of Aquitaine; Maximus of Turin.
27 CYRIL OF ALEXANDRIA.
28 IRENAEUS.
29 PETER and PAUL.

July

1 Shenoute; Gall of Clermont; Oliver Plunkett.
3 THOMAS.
4 Andrew of Crete; Pier-Giorgio Frassati.
5 ANTHONY ZACCARIA.
6 MARIA GORETTI.
9 Veronica Giuliani.
11 BENEDICT.
14 CAMILLUS DE LELLIS; Humbert of Romans; *Kateri Tekakwitha.*
15 BONAVENTURE; Anne-Marie Javouhey.
19 Macrina.
20 Gregory Lopez.
22 MARY MAGDALEN.
23 BRIDGET OF SWEDEN; Valerian.
25 JAMES THE GREAT; *Christopher.*
26 JOACHIM AND ANNE.
27 Rudolf Aquaviva; Titus Brandsma.
29 Olaf.
30 PETER CHRYSOLOGUS.
31 IGNATIUS OF LOYOLA; Germanus of Auxerre; Solanus Casey.

August

1 ALPHONSUS LIGUORI; Peter Favre; Peter Julian Eymard.
2 EUSEBIUS OF VERCELLI.
4 JOHN VIANNEY.
7 CAJETAN.
8 DOMINIC.
10 LAWRENCE; Edith Stein.
11 CLARE OF ASSISI; John Henry Newman.
13 HIPPOLYTUS; Radegund; John Berchmans; Jacob Gapp.
14 Maximilian Kolbe.
15 ASSUMPTION OF MARY.
16 STEPHEN OF HUNGARY.
19 JOHN EUDES.
20 BERNARD OF CLAIRVAUX.
21 PIUS X.
22 QUEENSHIP OF MARY.
23 ROSE OF LIMA; *Philip Benizi.*
24 Joan Antide-Thouret.
25 LOUIS IX.
27 MONICA; Caesarius of Arles; Dominic Barberi.
28 AUGUSTINE; Junípero Serra. 29 THE PASSION OF JOHN THE BAPTIST. 30 Juvenal Ancina.

September

3 GREGORY THE GREAT.
7 Teresa of Calcutta.
8 BIRTH OF MARY.
9 PETER CLAVER.
11 John Gabriel Perboyre.
13 JOHN CHRYSOSTOM.
15 Catherine of Genoa.
16 CYPRIAN OF CARTHAGE.
17 ROBERT BELLARMINE; Hildegard of Bingen.
18 *Joseph of Cupertino;* Methodius of Olympus.
19 Theodore of Canterbury; Alphonsus de Orozco.
21 MATTHEW.
22 *Thomas of Villanova.*
23 Padre Pio.
27 VINCENT DE PAUL.
28 WENCESLAUS; Faustus of Riez; Leoba.
29 Richard Rolle.
30 JEROME; Korean Martyrs.

October

1 Thérèse OF LISIEUX.
4 FRANCIS OF ASSISI; Ammon; Francis Xavier Seelos.
5 Raymond of Capua; Faustina Kowalska.
6 BRUNO.
8 Pelagia the Penitent.
9 JOHN LEONARDI.
10 *Francis Borgia.*
12 Wilfrid.
15 TERESA OF ÁVILA.
16 HEDWIG; MARGARET MARY ALACOQUE; Gall; Gerard Majella.
17 IGNATIUS OF ANTIOCH; John Kolobos.
18 LUKE.
19 ISAAC JOGUES; JOHN DE BRÉBEUF; PAUL OF THE CROSS; Fridiswede; Peter of Alcántara.
20 Mary Teresa de Soubiran.
21 *Hilarion.*
23 JOHN OF CAPISTRANO; Severinus Boethius.
24 ANTHONY MARY CLARET; Proclus.

25 Gaudentius of Brescia.

30 Alphonsus Rodriguez.

November

1 ALL SAINTS.

3 MARTIN DE PORRES; Malachy.

4 CHARLES BORROMEO.

5 Bertilla.

6 Théophane Vénard.

7 Willibrord.

8 Elizabeth of the Trinity.

10 LEO THE GREAT.

11 MARTIN OF TOURS; Theodore the Studite.

12 JOSAPHAT.

13 Frances Xavier Cabrini; Nicholas I; Stanislaus Kostka.

15 ALBERT THE GREAT; Roque González; Raphael Kalinowski.

16 MARGARET OF SCOTLAND; GERTRUDE THE GREAT; Mechtild of Helfta; Eucherius.

17 ELIZABETH OF HUNGARY; *Gregory the Wonderworker;* Dionysius of Alexandria; Hilda; Hugh of Lincoln.

18 Odo of Cluny; Philippine Duchesne.

19 Mechtild of Magdeburg.

22 CECiLIA.

23 CLEMENT I; COLUMBAN; Amphilochius; Miguel Pro.

24 Flora.

26 Leonard of Port Maurice.

27 Gregory of Sinai.

28 Catherine Labouré; Joseph Pignatelli.

30 ANDREW.

December

1 Edmund Campion; Charles de Foucauld.

2 John Ruysbroeck.

3 FRANCIS XAVIER.

4 JOHN DAMASCENE.

5 SABAS; Clement of Alexandria.

6 NICHOLAS.

7 AMBROSE.

8 IMMACULATE CONCEPTION OF MARY.

9 Peter Fourier.

10 Eulalia of Mérida.

11 Daniel the Stylite.

12 JANE DE CHANTAL.

13 Anthony Grassi.

14 JOHN OF THE CROSS; Venantius Fortunatus.

16 Mary of the Angels.

17 Olympias; Sturm.

18 Flannan.

21 PETER CANISIUS.

23 Marguerite d'Youville.

25 Jacopone da Todi.

26 STEPHEN.

27 JOHN; Fabiola.

28 THOMAS BECKET.

31 Melania; Louis of Granada.

Sources

Abbreviations

ACW *Ancient Christian Writers;* ed. Walter J. Burghardt and Thomas C. Lawler. New York: Newman Press.

ANF *The Ante-Nicene Fathers;* ed. Alexander Roberts and James Donaldson. Grand Rapids, Michigan: Wm. B. Eerdmans Publishing Company.

BLS *Butler's Lives of the Saints;* ed. Herbert Thurston, SJ, and Donald Attwater. London: Burns & Oates, Ltd., © 1956; 4 vols.

CWS *The Classics of Western Spirituality.* New York: Paulist Press.

FC *The Fathers of the Church;* ed. Joseph Deferrari. Washington, D. C.: The Catholic University of America Press.

LTC *The Lessons of the Temporal Cycle and the Principal Feasts of the Sanctoral Cycle.* St. Meinrad, Indiana: St. Meinrad's Abbey, 1943.

NAB *The New American Bible.* Nashville, Tennessee: Catholic Bible Press, 1987.

NBLS *Butler's Lives of the Saints: New Full Edition;* ed. David Hugh Farmer. Collegeville, Minnesota: The Liturgical Press.

NJB *The New Jerusalem Bible.* New York: Doubleday & Company, Inc., 1985 and 1999.

NPNF *Nicene & Post-Nicene Fathers of the Christian Church;* ed. Philip Schaff and Henry Wace. Grand Rapids, Michigan: Wm. B. Eerdmans Publishing Company.

OR *The Office of Readings According to the Roman Rite.* Boston: Daughters of St. Paul, 1983.

RSV *Revised Standard Version of the Bible.* © 1946, 1952, 1971 by the Division of Christian Education of the National Council of Churches in the U. S. A.

TWC Gerard MacGinty, OSB, ed. *Today We Celebrate.* London: Collins Liturgical Publications, 1986.

References

Aelred of Rievaulx: Aelred Squire, *Aelred of Rievaulx: A Study*. Kalamazoo, Michigan: Cistercian Studies, 1981.

Agnes: *The Principal Works of St. Ambrose. NPNF* (Second Series, Vol. X; 1983).

Alban: *The Venerable Bede's Ecclesiastical History of England and the Anglo-Saxon Chronicle*; ed. J. A. Giles. London: Bell and Daldy, 1870.

Albert the Great: Albert the Great, *On Union With God,* 7. Flelinfach: Llanerch Publishers, 1915.

Alcuin: G. F. Browne, *Alcuin of York*. London: SPCK, 1908.

Aldobrandesca of Siena: *Life of the Blessed Aldobrandesca of Siena* in Elizabeth Petroff, *Consolation of the Blessed*. New York: Alta Gaia Society, 1979.

Alexander: *Christian Conversation: Catholic Thought for Every Day of the Year;* ed. Ann Fremantle. New York: Stephen Daye Press.

Aloysius Gonzaga: *OR*.

Alphonsus de Orozco: *The Mount of Contemplation,* 7, in Kathleen Pond, *The Spirit of the Spanish Mystics*. London: Burns & Oates, © 1958.

Alphonsus Liguori: Frederick M. Jones, CSSR, *Alphonsus de Liguori*. Westminster, Maryland: Christian Classics, 1992; Nancy Fearon, IHM, *Never Stop Walking*. Monroe, Michigan: Sisters, Servants of the Immaculate Heart of Mary, © 1977.

Alphonsus Rodriguez: Angel Valtierra, SJ *Peter Claver: Saint of the Slaves*. London: Burns & Oates Ltd., © 1960; *NBLS*, October.

Ambrose: *The Principal Works of St. Ambrose. NPNF* (Second Series, Vol. X; 1983;) *Collected Hymns, Sequences and Carols*. London: Hodder & Stoughton, 1914.

Ammon: *Letters from the Saints*. New York: Hawthorn Books, © 1964.

Amphilochius: M. F. Toal, ed., *The Sunday Sermons of the Great Fathers*, 2. Swedesboro, New Jersey: Preservation Press, 1996. André Bessette: C. Bernard Ruffin, *The Life of Brother André*. Huntington, Indiana: Our Sunday Visitor, © 1988.

Andrew: *LTC*.

Andrew of Crete: *Christian Readings 3, Year 1*. New York: Catholic Book Publishing Co., 1972.

Angela Merici: Sr. M. Monica, *Angela Merici and Her Teaching Idea*. New York: Longmans, Green & Co., © 1927.

Angela of Foligno: *Angela of Foligno: Complete Works. CWS* (1993).

Anne-Marie Javouhey: Glenn D. Kittler, *The Woman God Loved.* Garden City, New York: Hanover House, 1959. Anne Mary Taigi: *BLS.* Anselm: Eadmer, *The Life of St. Anselm.* Oxford: Oxford University Press, 1972; Enzo Lodi, *Saints of the Roman Calendar.* New York: Alba House, 1992.

Anthony Grassi: *BLS.*

Anthony Mary Claret: St. Anthony Mary Claret, *Autobiography,* 25. Chicago: Claretian Publications, 1976.

Anthony of Egypt: St. Athanasius, *Life of St. Anthony* in *The Paradise or Garden of the Holy Fathers.* Seattle, Washington: Saint Nectarios Press, 1978.

Anthony of Padua: Mary Purcell, *St. Anthony and His Times.* Garden City, New York: Hanover House, 1960.

Anthony Zaccaria: *OR.*

Aphraates of Persia: *OR.*

Apphian: *Eusebius: Church History* [and other works]. *NPNF* (Second Series, Vol. I; 1986).

Assunta Pallotta: *The Theme Song of Assunta.* Franciscan Missionaries of Mary, 1956.

Athanasius: *The Paradise or Garden of the Holy Fathers.* Seattle, Washington: Saint Nectarios Press, 1978.

Augustine: *Confessions, in NPNF* (Vol. I; 1983).

Augustine of Canterbury: *The Life of St. Augustine of Canterbury, Apostle of the English.* London: James Toovey, 1845.

Balthild: *Sainted Women of the Dark Ages.* Durham, North Carolina: Duke University Press, 1992.

Barnabas: *The Apostolic Fathers: With Justin Martyr and Irenaeus; ANF (Vol. I; 1987).*

Basil the Great: *Basil the Great,* Gateway to Paradise. Brooklyn, New York: New City Press.

Bede: *The Venerable Bede,* ed. Benedicta Ward, S. L. G. Harrisburg, Pennsylvania: Morehouse Publishing, 1990; Bede, *A History of the English Church and People.* Baltimore, Maryland: Penguin Books, 1970.

Benedict: *The Life of Our Most Holy Father S. Benedict.* Rome, 1895.

Benedict Biscop: Clinton Albertson, SJ, *Anglo-Saxon Saints and Heroes.* New York: Fordham University Press, 1967.

Benedict Joseph Labre: Agnes de la Gorce; *Saint Benedict Joseph Labre.* New York: Sheed & Ward, 1952.

Benedict of Aniane: *Soldiers of Christ.* University Park, Pennsylvania: The Pennsylvania State University Press, 1995.

Bernadette Soubirous: Francis Trochu, *Saint Bernadette Soubirous, 1844–1879.* New York: Pantheon, 1958.

Bernard of Clairvaux: *Bernard of Clairvaux: Selected Works. CWS* (1987).

Bernardino of Siena: Maisie Ward, *St. Bernardino: The People's Preacher.* St. Louis, Missouri: B. Herder, 1914.

Bertilla: *Sainted Women of the Dark Ages.* Durham, North Carolina: Duke University Press, 1992.

Bonaventure: *Bonaventure: The Soul's Journey into God; The Tree of Life; The Life of St. Francis. CWS* (1978).

Boniface: Willibald, *The Life of Saint Boniface.* Cambridge: Harvard University Press, 1916.

Braulio: *Iberian Fathers,* Vol. 2. *FC* (63).

Brendan the Navigator: *Bethada Náem Nérennn; Lives of Irish Saints.* Oxford: Oxford University Press, © 1922.

Bridget of Sweden: *Birgitta of Sweden: Life and Selected Revelations. CWS* (1990).

Brigid: Alice Curtayne, *St. Brigid of Ireland.* Dublin: Browne & Nolan, Ltd., 1933.

Bruno: André Ravier, SJ, *Saint Bruno: The Carthusian.* San Francisco: Ignatius Press, © 1995.

Caedmon: *The Venerable Bede's Ecclesiastical History of England and the Anglo-Saxon Chronicle;* ed. J. A. Giles. London: Bell and Daldy, 1870; *BLS.*

Caesarius of Arles: *Saint Caesarius of Arles: Sermons,* Vol. 1. *FC* (31).

Cajetan: *Theatene Spirituality: Selected Writings. CWS* (1996); *BLS.*

Camillus de Lellis: *St. Camillus of Lellis (by Sanzio Ciccatelli).* Milwaukee, Wisconsin: The Servants of the Sick, 1926.

Casimir: *OR.*

Catherine dei Ricci: F. M. Capes, *St. Catherine de' Ricci.* London: Burns & Oates, 1905.

Catherine Labouré: Edmond Crapez, CM, *Venerable Catherine Labouré.* Emmitsburg, Maryland: St. Joseph's, 1918.

Catherine of Genoa: *Catherine of Genoa: Purgation and Purgatory; The Spiritual Dialogue. CWS* (1979).

Catherine of Siena: *St. Catherine of Siena: The Dialogue. CWS* (1980).

Cecilia: *The Golden Legend of Jacobus de Voragine.* New York: Arno Press, 1969.

Charles Borromeo: John Peter Giusano, *The Life of St. Charles Borromeo.* London: Burns & Oates, 1884.

Charles de Foucauld: *Spiritual Autobiography of Charles de Foucauld.* Denville, New Jersey: Dimension Books, © 1964; Ann Ball, *Modern Saints: Their Lives and Faces*; Vol. 2. Rockford, Illinois: TAN Books and Publishers, © 1983.

Charles Lwanga and Companions: J. P. Thoonen, *Black Martyrs.* London: Sheed & Ward, 1942; *NBLS*, June.

Charles of Sezze: St. Charles of Sezze, *Autobiography.* London: The Catholic Book Club, 1963.

Christopher: Jacobus de Voragine, *The Golden Legend.* Cambridge: Cambridge University Press, 1914.

Clare of Assisi: *The Legend and Writings of Saint Clare of Assisi.* St. Bonaventure, New York: The Franciscan Institute, 1953.

Claude la Colombiére: George Guitton, SJ, *Perfect Friend: The Life of Blessed Claude la Colombiére.* St. Louis, Missouri: B. Herder Book Co., © 1956; *BLS.*

Clement I: *The First Epistle of Clement to the Corinthians.* London: SPCK.

Clement Mary Hofbauer: Michael Haringer, *Life of the Venerable Servant of God Clement Maria Hofbauer.* New York: Fr. Pustet & Co., 1883.

Clement of Alexandria: *The Writings of the Fathers Down to AD 325. ANF* (Vol. II; 1987).

Clotilda: Gregory of Tours, *The History of the Franks*; Vol. II. Oxford: Oxford University Press, 1927.

Colette: Mother Mary Francis, P. C. C., *Walled in Light: St. Colette.* Chicago: Franciscan Herald Press, 1985.

Columba: Lucy Menzies, *Saint Columba of Iona.* London: J. M. Dent & Sons, Ltd., 1920.

Columban: George Metlake, *The Life and Writings of Saint Columban.* Philadelphia: The Dolphin Press, 1914.

Cuthbert: Clinton Albertson, SJ, ed. *Anglo-Saxon Saints and Heroes.* New York: Fordham University Press, © 1967.

Cyprian of Carthage: *The Writings of the Fathers Down to AD 325. ANF* (Vol. V, 1986).

Cyril and Methodius: *OR.*

Cyril of Alexandria: *TWC.*

Cyril of Jerusalem: St. Cyril of Jerusalem, *Catechetical Lectures. NPNF* (Second Series, Vol. VII; 1983).

Damien de Veuster: Gavan Daws, *Holy Man: Father Damien of Molokai.* New York: Harper & Row, © 1973; Omer Engelbert, *The Hero of Molokai.* Boston, Massachusetts: St. Paul Editions, 1954.

Daniel the Stylite: *Three Byzantine Saints.* Crestwood, New York: St. Vladimir's Seminary Press, 1977.

David: *Rhigyfarch's Life of St. David;* ed. J. W. James. Cardiff: University of Wales Press, 1967.

Diana d' Andalo: E. I. Watkin, *Neglected Saints.* San Francisco: Ignatius Press, 1994.

Dionysius of Alexandria: *Christian Conversation: Catholic Thought for Every Day of the Year.* New York: Stephen Daye Press.

Dominic: *Saint Dominic: Biographical Documents.* Washington, D. C.: The Thomist Press, 1964.

Dominic Barberi: Denis Gwynn, *Father Dominic Barberi.* Buffalo, New York: Desmond & Stapleton, 1948.

Dominic Savio: John Bosco, *Ven. Dominic Savio.* St. Louis, Missouri: B. Herder Book Co.

Dunstan of Canterbury: Eleanor Shipley Duckett, *Saint Dunstan of Canterbury.* New York: W. W. Norton & Company, 1955.

Edith Stein: Sister Teresia de Spiritu Sancto, ODC, *Edith Stein.* New York: Sheed Ward, 1952.

Edmund Campion: E. Waugh, *Edmund Campion, Jesuit and Martyr.* New York: Doubleday, 1956.

Elizabeth Ann Seton: Annabelle M. Melville, *Elizabeth Bayley Seton.* New York: Pillar Books, 1976.

Elizabeth Leseur: Lucy Menzies, *Mirrors of the Holy.* London: A. R. Mowbray & Co., 1928.

Elizabeth of Hungary: Count de Montalembert, *The Life of Saint Elizabeth.* New York: P. J. Kenedy & Sons, n. d.

Elizabeth of the Trinity: *Sister Elizabeth of the Trinity: Spiritual Writings.* New York: P. J. Kenedy & Sons, 1962.

Ephrem: *Select Metrical Hymns and Homilies of Ephraem Syrus.* London: Blackader, 1853.

Epiphanius: *The Life of Saint Epiphanius by Ennodius.* Washington, D. C.: The Catholic University of America Press, 1942.

Eucherius: *Christian Conversation: Catholic Thought for Every Day of the Year.* New York: Stephen Daye Press.

Eulalia: *The Poems of Prudentius. FC* (43).

Eulogius of Cordaba: Justo Pérez de Urbel, *A Saint Under Moslem Rule.*

Milwaukee, Wisconsin: The Bruce Publishing Company, © 1937.

Eusebius of Vercelli: *OR.*

Euthymius the Great: Cyril of Scythopolis, *The Lives of the Monks of Palestine.* Kalamazoo, Michigan: Cistercian Publications, 1991.

Fabiola: *Silent Voices, Sacred Lives.* New York: Paulist Press, © 1992.

Faustina Kowalska: *The Diary of Sr. Faustina Kowalska: Divine Mercy in My Soul (Diary,* 163). Stockbridge, Massachusetts: Congregation of Marians of the Immaculate Conception, © 1987.

Faustus: *OR.*

Felicity: *The Acts of the Christian Martyrs.* Oxford: Oxford University Press, © 1972.

Felix of Nola: *The Poems of St. Paulinus of Nola. ACW* (No. 40; 1975). Fina: Giovanni Di Coppo, *The Legend of the Holy Fina, Virgin of Santo Gimignano.* New York: Cooper Square Publishers, Inc., 1966.

Flannan: *Life of Saint Flannan.* Dublin: James Duffy and Co, 1902. Flora: Justo Pérez de Urbel, *A Saint Under Moslem Rule.* Milwaukee, Wisconsin: The Bruce Publishing Company, © 1937.

The Forty Martyrs of Sebaste: *BLS;* Anne Fremantle, *A Treasury of Early Christianity.* New York: New American Library, 1953.

Frances of Rome: Lady Georgiana Fullerton, *The Life of St. Frances of Rome.* New York: D. & J. Sadlier & Co.

Frances Xavier Cabrini: *Letters of St. Frances Xavier Cabrini.* Milan: Ancora, 1970.

Francis Borgia: Margaret Yeo, *The Greatest of the Borgias.* Milwaukee, Wisconsin: The Bruce Publishing Company, © 1936.

Francis de Sales: St. Francis de Sales, *Introduction to the Devout Life.* Garden City, New York: Doubleday Image Books, 1972; *Introduction to the Devout Life.* London: Burns, Oates & Washbourne, 1924.

Francis di Geronimo: *The Life of St. Francis di Geronimo.* New York: Benziger Brothers, 1891.

Francis of Assisi: *Writings of St. Francis of Assisi.* Chicago: Franciscan Herald Press.

Francis of Paola: Gino J. Simi and Mario M. Segreti. *St. Francis of Paola.* Rockford, Illinois: TAN Books and Publishers, Inc., 1977.

Francis Xavier: James Broderick, SJ, *Saint Francis Xavier (1506–1552).* New York: The Wicklow Press; 1952; Mary Purcell, *Don Francisco: The Story of St. Francis Xavier.* Westminster, Maryland: The Newman Press, 1954.

Francis Xavier Seelos: "Sermons and Instruction A," 21, Redemptorist Archives Baltimore Province (RABP), III; Zimmer, Leben, 228 and 230, RABP, III.

Frederic Ozanam: Kathleen O'Meara (Grace Ramsay), *Frederic Ozanam.* New York: Catholic School Book Company, n. d.; Boniface Hanley, *Ten Saints.* Notre Dame, Indiana: Ave Maria Press, © 1979.

Fridiswede: James Parker, *The Early History of Oxford.* Oxford: At the Clarendon Press, 1885.

Fulgentius: Fulgentius, *Selected Works. FC* (95).

Gabriel Francis Possenti: Camillus [Hollobraugh], C. P., *Saint Gabriel, Passionist.* New York: Catholic Book Company, 1953.

Gall: Walahfrid Strabo, *The Life of St. Gall.* Llanerch Publishers, 1927.

Gall of Clermont: *Vita Patrum: The Life of the Fathers by St. Gregory of Tours.* Platina, California: St. Herman of Alaska Brotherhood, © 1988.

Gaudentius of Brescia: M. F. Toal, ed., *The Sunday Sermons of the Great Fathers,* 3. Swedesboro, New Jersey: Presentation Press, 1996.

Gemma Galgani: Leo Prosperio, SJ, *St. Gemma Galgani.* Milwaukee, Wisconsin: The Bruce Publishing Company, 1940.

Genevieve: *Sainted Women of the Dark Ages.* Durham, North Carolina: Duke University Press, 1992.

George Matulaitis: Anthony Kucas, *Archbishop George Matulaitis.* Chicago, Illinois: Marian Fathers of the Immaculate Conception, © 1981.

George of Lydda: I. Hill Elder, *George of Lydda: Soldier, Saint and Martyr.* London: The Covenant Publishing Co., Ltd., 1949; *Eusebius: Church History* [and other works]. *NPNF* (Second Series, Vol. I, 1986).

Gerard Majella: Charles Dilgskron, CSSR, *Life of Blessed Gerard Majella.* New York: The Redemptorist Fathers, 1892.

Germanus of Auxerre: *The Western Fathers,* Sheed & Ward, © 1954.

Germanus of Constantinople: M. F. Toal, ed., *The Sunday Sermons of the Great Fathers,* 4. Swedesboro, New Jersey: Preservation Press, 1996.

Gertrude of Delft: *Christian Conversation: Catholic Thought for Every Day of the Year.* New York: Stephen Daye Press.

Gertrude the Great: *The Life and Revelations of St. Gertrude.* Westminster, Maryland: Christian Classics, 1987.

Giles of Assisi: *The Little Flowers of St. Francis.* Garden City, New York: Doubleday Image Books, 1958.

Gregory VII: *The Correspondence of Pope Gregory VII.* New York: Octagon Books, Inc.

Gregory Lopez: Canon Doyle, OSB, *The Life of Gregory Lopez.* London: R. Washbourne, 1876.

Gregory Nazianzen: *Select Orations of Saint Gregory Nazianzen. NPNF* (Vol. VII, 1983).

Gregory of Nyssa: *Select Writings and Letters of Gregory, Bishop of Nyssa. NPNF* (Vol. V, 1954).

Gregory of Sinai: *Writings from the Philokalia on Prayer of the Heart.* London: Faber and Faber, 1951.

Gregory the Great: *Be Friends of God: Spiritual Reading from Gregory the Great.* Cambridge, Massachusetts: Cowley Publications, © 1990.

Gregory the Wonderworker: Johannes Quasten, *Patrology.* Westminster, Maryland: Christian Classics, Inc., 1992; *BLS.*

Hedwig: *OR.*

Henry Suso: *Henry Suso: The Exemplar and Two German Sermons. CWS* (© 1989); *Breakfast with the Saints.* Ann Arbor, Michigan: Servant Publications, 1996.

Hilarion: St. Jerome, *Life of St. Hilarion. FC* (15).

Hilary of Arles: *Early Christian Biographies. FC* (15).

Hilary of Poitiers: *TWC; Breakfast With the Saints.* Ann Arbor, Michigan: Servant Publications, 1996.

Hilda: *The Venerable Bede's Ecclesiastical History of England and the Anglo-Saxon Chronicle*; ed. J. A. Giles. London: Bell and Daldy, 1870.

Hildegard of Bingen: *Hildegard of Bingen: Scivias. CWS* (1990).

Hippolytus: *The Writings of the Fathers Down to AD 325. ANF* (Vol. V, 1986).

Honoratus of Arles: *Early Christian Biographies. FC* (15).

Hugh of Lincoln: David Hugh Farmer, *Saint Hugh of Lincoln.* Kalamazoo, Michigan: Cistercian Publications, © 1985.

Humbert of Romans: *Early Dominicans: Selected Writings. CWS* (1999).

Ignatius of Antioch: *The Apostolic Fathers.* Grand Rapids, Michigan: Baker Book House, 1984.

Ignatius of Loyola: *The Spiritual Exercises of St. Ignatius.* Garden City, New York: Doubleday Image Books, 1964.

Ildefonsus of Toledo: *The Life and Writings of Saint Ildefonsus of Toledo.* Washington, D. C.: The Catholic University of America Press, 1942.

Irenaeus: *St. Irenaeus' The Preaching of the Apostles.* Brookline, Massachusetts: Holy Cross Orthodox Press.

Isaac Jogues: *An Autobiography of Martyrdom.* St. Louis, Missouri: B. Herder Book Company, © 1964; *NBLS,* October.

Isidore of Seville: *TWC.*

Jacob Gapp: Text of Interrogation, January 21–27, 1943, and farewell letters, no copyright claimed.

Jacopone da Todi: George T. Peck, *The Fool of God.* Birmingham, Alabama: The University of Alabama Press, © 1980.

James the Great: *LTC; NJB.*

James the Just: *NAB.*

Jane de Chantal: André Ravier, SJ, *Saint Jeanne de Chantal: Noble Lady, Holy Woman.* San Francisco: Ignatius Press, 1989.

Jerome: *The Principal Works of St. Jerome. NPNF* (Second Series; Vol. VI, 1983).

Joachim and Anne: Jacobus de Voragine, *The Golden Legend,* Vol. 2. Princeton, New Jersey: Princeton University Press, © 1993.

Joan Antide-Thouret: Francis Trochu, *Saint Jeanne Antide Thouret.* London: Sands & Company, Ltd., 1966.

Joan of Arc: Régine Pernoud, *Joan of Arc: By Herself and Her Witnesses:* New York: Stein and Day, 1969.

Joan of France: Ann M. C. Forster, *The Good Duchess.* New York: P. J. Kenedy & Sons, © 1950.

John: *NJB.*

John Baptist de La Salle: *The Letters of John Baptist de La Salle.* Romeoville, Illinois: Lasallian Publications, 1988.

John Baptist de Rossi: *St. John Baptist De Rossi.* New York: Benziger Brothers, 1906.

John Berchmans: Albert S. Foley, SJ, *A Modern Galahad: St. John Berchmans.* Milwaukee, Wisconsin: The Bruce Publishing Company, © 1937.

John Bosco: *OR.*

John Cassian: *John Cassian: Conferences. CWS* (1985).

John Chrysostom: *On the Priesthood* [and other works]. *NPNF* (Vol. IX, 1983).

John Climacus: John Climacus, *The Ladder of Divine Ascent. CWS* (1982).

John Damascene: John of Damascus, *Exposition of the Orthodox Faith, 16. NPNF* (Second Series, Vol. IX; 1983).

John de Brébeuf: *The Jesuit Relations and Allied Documents: Travels and Explorations of the Jesuit Missionaries in New France, 1610–1791,* Vol. 10; ed. Reuben Gold Thwaites. Cleveland, Ohio: The Burrows Brothers, 1897; NBLS, October.

John Eudes: Saint John Eudes, *Letters and Shorter Works.* New York: P. J. Kenedy & Sons, 1948.

John Fisher: T. E. Bridgett, *Life of Blessed John Fisher.* London: Burns, Oates & Washbourne, Ltd., 1911.

John Forest: Fr. Thaddeus, OSF, *Life of Blessed Father John Forest, OSF* London: Burns & Oates, 1888.

John Gabriel Perboyre: G. de Montgesty, *Two Vincentian Martyrs.* Maryknoll, New York: Catholic Foreign Mission Society of America, 1925.

John Henry Newman: *English Spiritual Writers.* New York: Sheed Ward, © 1961.

John Kolobos: Benedicta Ward, SLG, ed., *The Sayings of the Desert Fathers: The Alphabetical Collection.* Kalamazoo, Michigan: Cistercian Publications, © 1975.

John Leonardi: M. Basil Pennington, *Through the Year with the Saints.* Spencer, Massachusetts: Cistercian Abbey of Spencer, Inc., © 1988; Anthony F. Chiffolo, *At Prayer with the Saints.* Liguori, Missouri: Liguori, © 1998.

John Neumann: *The Autobiography of St. John Neumann, CSSR.* Boston, Massachusetts: Daughters of St. Paul, © 1977.

John of Ávila: E. Allison Peers, *Studies of the Spanish Mystics,* Vol. 2. London: The Sheldon Press, 1930.

John of Capistrano: M. Basil Pennington, *Through the Year With the Saints.* Spencer, Massachusetts: Cistercian Abbey of Spencer, Inc., © 1988.

John of God: Norbert McMahon, *St. John of God.* Dublin: M. H. Gill Sons, Ltd., 1952.

John of the Cross: *The Collected Works of St. John of the Cross.* Garden City, New York: Doubleday & Company, Inc., 1964.

John Regis: Albert S. Foley, SJ, *St. Regis: A Social Crusader.* Milwaukee, Wisconsin: The Bruce Publishing Company, © 1941.

John Ruysbroeck: Evelyn Underhill, *Ruysbroeck.* London: G. Bell and Sons, Ltd., 1915.

John the Baptist: *NJB.*

John the Silent: Cyril of Scythopolis, *The Lives of the Monks of Palestine.* Kalamazoo, Michigan: Cistercian Publications, 1991.

John Vianney: W. M. B., ed. *Thoughts of the Curé d'Ars.* Rockford, Illinois: TAN Books and Publishers, Inc., 1984.

Jordan of Saxony: Gerald Vann, OP, *To Heaven With Diana!* New York: Pantheon Books, 1960.

Josaphat: Theodosia Boresky, *Life of St. Josaphat.* New York: Comet Press Books, © 1955.

Joseph: *NJB; The Life of Teresa of Jesus.* Garden City, New York: Doubleday/ Image Books, 1960.

Joseph Cafasso: St. John Bosco, *The Life of St. Joseph Cafasso.* Rockford, Illinois: TAN Books and Publishers, Inc., © 1983.

Joseph of Cupertino: Angelo Pastrovicchi, OMC, *St. Joseph of Copertino.* Rockford, Illinois: TAN Books and Publishers, Inc., 1980.

Joseph Pignatelli: D. A. Hanly, PA, *Blessed Joseph Pignatelli.* New York: Benziger Brothers, 1937.

Julian of Norwich: Juliana of Norwich, *Revelations of Divine Love.* Garden City, New York: Doubleday Image Books, 1977; Julian of Norwich, *Revelation of Love.* New York: Doubleday Image Books, 1996.

Julie Billiart: Malachy Gerard Carroll, *The Charred Wood.* London: Sands & Co., 1950.

Julien Maunoir: Martin P. Harney, SJ, *Good Father in Brittany.* Boston, Massachusetts: St. Paul Editions, © 1964.

Junípero Serra: *Francisco Palou's Life and Apostolic Labors of the Venerable Father Junípero Serra.* Pasadena, California: George Wharton James, 1913.

Justin: *The Apostolic Fathers: With Justin Martyr and Irenaeus. ANF* (Vol. I; 1987).

Juvenal Ancina: Charles H. Bowden, *The Life of B. John Juvenal Ancina.* London: Kegan Paul, Trench, Truebner & Co, Ltd., 1891.

Kateri Tekakwitha: *The Positio of the Historical Section of the Sacred Congregation of Rites on the Introduction of the Cause for Beatification and Canonization and on the Virtues of the Servant of God Katherine Tekakwitha.* New York: Fordham University Press, 1940.

Katherine Drexel: Sr. Consuela Marie Duffy, SBS, *Katharine Drexel: A Biography.* Cornwells Heights, Pennsylvania: Sisters of the Blessed Sacrament, © 1966.

Kentigern: Jocelyn of Furness, *Life of St. Kentigern*, 42, in W. M. Metcalfe, *Pinkerton's Lives of the Scottish Saints.* Paisley, 1889.

Kevin: *Bethada Náem Nérennn; Lives of Irish Saints.* Oxford: Oxford University Press, © 1922.

Korean Martyrs: Kim Chang-seok Thaddeus, *Lives of 103 Martyr Saints of Korea.* Seoul: Catholic Publishing House, 1984.

Lawrence: *The Poems of Prudentius. FC* (43).

Leander of Seville: *Iberian Fathers. FC* (62).

Leo the Great: *The Letters and Sermons of Leo the Great. NPNF* (Second Series, Vol. XII; 1983); Anthony E. Chiffolo, ed., *At Prayer With the Saints.* Liguori, Missouri: Liguori, 1998,

Leoba: C. H. Talbot, *The Anglo-Saxon Missionaries in Germany.* London: Sheed & Ward, 1981.

Leonard of Port Maurice: Dominic Devas, OFM, *Life of St. Leonard of Port-Maurice, OFM.* London: Burns, Oates & Washbourne, Ltd., 1920; *BLS.*

Louis IX: John of Joinville, *The Life of St. Louis.* New York: Sheed & Ward, 1951.

Louis de Montfort: *Life and Select Writings of Louis-Marie Grignon de Montfort.* London: Thomas Richardson & Son, 1870.

Louis of Granada: Louis of Granada, OP, *Sinner's Guide.* Rockford, Illinois: TAN Books and Publishers, 1985.

Louise de Marillac: *Vincent de Paul and Louise de Marillac: Rules, Conferences and Writings. CWS* (1995).

Lucy Filippini: Pascal P. Parente, *Schoolteacher and Saint.* St. Meinrad, Indiana: Grail Publications, © 1954.

Luke: *NJB.*

Lutgarde: Thomas de Cantimpré. *The Life of Lutgarde of Aywières.* Saskatoon: Peregrina Publishing Co., 1987.

Macarius the Great: Benedicta Ward, SLG, ed.; *The Sayings of the Desert Fathers: The Alphabetical Collection.* Kalamazoo, Michigan: Cistercian Publications, 1975.

Macrina: *St. Gregory of Nyssa: Ascetical Works. FC* (58).

Madeleine Sophie Barat: Maud Monahan, *Saint Madeleine Sophie.* New York: Longmans, Green & Co., 1925.

Malachy: Bernard of Clairvaux, *The Life and Death of Saint Malachy the Irishman.* Kalamazoo, Michigan: Cistercian Publications, 1978.

Marcella: *Handmaids of the Lord.* Kalamazoo, Michigan: Cistercian Publications, Inc., 1996.

Margaret Clitherow: Mary Claridge, *Margaret Clitherow.* New York: Fordham University Press, 1966.

Margaret Mary Alacoque: Monsginor Demimuid, *Blessed Margaret Mary.* New York: Benziger Brothers, 1914.

Margaret of Cortona: *The Revelations of Margaret of Cortona.* Franciscan Institute, 1952.

Margaret of Hungary: S. M. C., *Margaret, Princess of Hungary.* London: Blackfriars Publications, 1954.

Margaret of Scotland: *Saint Margaret* (Turgot's *Life of Margaret, Queen of Scotland*). Edinburgh: Floris Books, 1993.

Marguerite Bourgeoys: Patricia Simpson, *Marguerite Bourgeoys and Montreal, 1640–1665.* Montreal: McGill-Queen's University Press, © 1997.

Marguerite d'Youville: *From the Fatherhood of God to the Brotherhood of Mankind.* Philadelphia, 1976.

Maria Goretti: Marie Cecilia Buehrle, *Maria Goretti, Saint and Martyr.* Dublin: Clonmore & Reynolds, Ltd., 1952.

Marie of the Incarnation: *The Autobiography of Venerable Marie of the Incarnation, OSU.* Chicago: Loyola University Press, 1964. *Marie of the Incarnation: Selected Writings.* New York: Paulist Press, 1989.

Mark: *NAB.*

Martin I: *BLS.*

Martin de Porres: Giuliana Cavallini, *Saint Martin de Porres: Apostle of Charity.* Rockford, Illinois: TAN Books & Publishers Inc., 1979; J. C. Kearns, OP, *The Life of Blessed Martin de Porres.* New York: P. J. Kenedy & Sons, 1937.

Martin of Braga: *Iberian Fathers,* 1; *FC* (62).

Martin of Tours: Sulpicius Severus, *Life of St. Martin,* in *FC* (7).

Mary: *NJB.*

Mary Euphrasia Pelletier: Gaetan Bernoville, *Saint Mary Euphrasia Pelletier.* Westminster, Maryland: The Newman Press, 1959.

Mary Magdalen: *NJB; The Prayers and Meditations of St. Anselm.* New York: Penguin Books, 1979.

Mary Magdalen dei Pazzi: Pierre Pourrat, *Christian Spirituality,* Vol. III. Westminster, Maryland: The Newman Press, 1953. *Traditional Catholic Prayers;* ed. Charles J. Dollen. Huntington, Indiana: Our Sunday Visitor, © 1990.

Mary Mazzarello: Peter Lappin, *Halfway to Heaven.* New Rochelle, New York: Don Bosco Publications, © 1981.

Mary McKillop: George O'Neill, SJ, *Life of Mother Mary of the Cross.* Sydney, Australia: Pellegrini & Co., 1931.

Mary of Egypt: Benedicta Ward, SLG. *Harlots of the Desert.* Kalamazoo, Michigan: Cistercian Publications, Inc., 1987.

Mary of the Angels: George O'Neill, SJ, *Blessed Mary of the Angels.* London: R. & T. Washbourne, Ltd., 1901.

Mary Teresa de Soubiran: *Marie-Thérèse de Soubiran, A Study in Failure.* Fr. Monier-Venard, SJ, ed. Privately published, 1944.

Matt Talbot: Mary Purcell, *Matt Talbot and His Times.* Westminster, Maryland: The Newman Press, 1955.

Matthew: *LTC; RSV.*

Maurus: *LTC.*

Maximilian Kolbe: Desmond Forristal, *Kolbe: A Saint in Auschwitz.* New Rochelle, New York: Don Bosco Publications, © 1982; Boniface Hanley, OFM, *Ten Christians.* Notre Dame, Indiana: Ave Maria Press, 1979; Patricia Treece, *A Man for Others.* San Francisco: Harper & Row Publishers, © 1982.

Maximus of Turin: *The Sermons of St. Maximus of Turin,* in *ACW* (No. 50; © 1989).

Mechtild of Helfta: Mary Jeremy Finnegan, OP, *The Women of Helfta.* Athens, Georgia: The University of Georgia Press, © 1991.

Mechtild of Magdeburg: *The Revelations of Mechtild of Magdeburg.* London: Longmans, Green & Co., Ltd., 1953.

Melania: *The Paradise or Garden of the Holy Fathers.* Seattle, Washington: Saint Nectarios Press, 1978; *Handmaids of the Lord.* Kalamazoo, Michigan: Cistercian Publications, Inc., 1996; *BLS.*

Methodius of Olympus: St. Methodius, *The Symposium,* in *ACW* (No. 27; © 1958).

Michael Garicoits: *Life of Blessed Michael Garicoits.* London: Sands & Co., 1935.

Miguel Pro: Fanchón Royer, *Padre Pro.* New York: P. J. Kenedy & Sons.

Monica: *The Confessions of St. Augustine.* New York: New American Library, © 1963.

Nicetas of Remesiana: Nicetas of Remesiana, *The Names and Titles of Our Saviour,* in *FC* (7), 11–12; English translation of *Te Deum Laudamus* by the International Consultation of English Texts in *Bless the Lord!* Notre Dame, Indiana: Ave Maria Press, 1974.

Nicholas: *The Golden Legend of Jacobus de Voragine.* New York: Longmans, Green & Co., © 1941.

Nicholas I: Jules Roy, *Saint Nicholas I.* New York: Benziger Brothers, 1913.

Nicholas of Flue: Marie McSwigan, *Athlete of Christ.* Westminster, Maryland: The Newman Press, 1959.

Norbert: Cornelius J. Kirkfleet, Ord. Praem., *History of Saint Norbert.* St. Louis, Missouri: B. Herder, 1916.

Odo of Cluny: *The Makers of Christendom.* New York: Sheed & Ward, © 1958.

Odoric of Pordenone: Anselm M. Romb, OFM. Conv., *Mission to Cathay.* Paterson, New Jersey: St. Anthony Guild Press, 1956.

Olaf: Sigrid Undset, *Saga of Saints.* New York: Longmans, Green & Co., 1934.

Oliver Plunkett: Alice Curtayne, *The Trial of Oliver Plunkett.* New York: Sheed & Ward, 1953.

Olympias: *Silent Voices, Sacred Lives.* New York: Paulist Press, © 1992.

Osanna of Mantua: E. I. Watkin, *Neglected Saints.* San Francisco: Ignatius Press, 1994, 145.

Pachomius: *The Paradise or Garden of the Holy Fathers.* Seattle, Washington: Saint Nectarios Press, 1978.

Padre Pio: C. Bernard Ruffin, *Padre Pio: The True Story.* Huntington, Indiana: Our Sunday Visitor, Inc., © 1982.

Paola Frassinetti: Joyce Umfreville, *A Foundress in Nineteenth Century Italy.* Staten Island, NY: The Sisters of St. Dorothy, © 1939.

Paschal Baylon: Oswald Staniforth, OSFC, *The Saint of the Eucharist.* London: R. & T. Washbourne, Ltd., 1908.

Patrick: John Healy, *The Life and Writings of Saint Patrick.* Dublin: M. H. Gill & Sons, 1905.

Paul: *NJB; NAB.*

Paul Miki: *Christian Readings 3, Year 1.* New York: Catholic Book Publishing Co., 1972; Francis J. Corley, SJ, and Robert J. Willmes, SJ, *Wings of Eagles.* Milwaukee, Wisconsin: The Bruce Publishing Company, © 1941.

Paul of the Cross: Martin Bialas, *The Mysticism of the Passion in St. Paul of the Cross.* San Francisco: Ignatius Press, © 1990; *Flowers of the Passion: Thoughts of St. Paul of the Cross.* New York: Benziger Brothers.

Paul the Hermit: *Early Christian Biographies. FC* (15).

Paula: *Handmaids of the Lord.* Kalamazoo, Michigan: Cistercian Publications, Inc., 1996.

Paulinus of Nola: *The Poems of St. Paulinus of Nola. ACW* (No. 40; 1975).

Pelagia: *Holy Women of the Orient.* Berkeley, California: University of California Press, 1987.

Perpetua: *BLS;* F. J. Sheed, ed., *Saints Are Not Sad.* New York: Sheed & Ward, 1949.

Peter: *NJB.*

Peter Canisius: James Broderick, SJ, *Saint Peter Canisius.* Chicago: Loyola University Press.

Peter Chrysologus: St. Peter Chrysologus, *Sermon 43*, in *FC* (17).

Peter Claver: Angel Valtierra, SJ, *Peter Claver: Saint of the Slaves.* London: Burns & Oates Ltd., © 1960.

Peter Damian: Owen J. Blum, OFM, *St. Peter Damian: His Teaching on the Spiritual Life.* Washington, D. C.: The Catholic University of America Press, 1947.

Peter Favre: *The Spiritual Writings of Pierre Favre.* St. Louis, Missouri: The Institute of Jesuit Resources, 1996.

Peter Fourier: Edmund Kreusch, *Life of St. Peter Fourier.* Milwaukee, Wisconsin: The School Sisters of Notre Dame, 1932.

Peter Julian Eymard: Martin Dempsey, *Champion of the Blessed Sacrament.* New York: The Sentinel Press; *NBLS*, August.

Peter of Alcántara: *The Treatise on Prayer and Meditation*, 3, in Kathleen Pond, *The Spirit of the Spanish Mystics.* London: Burns & Oates, © 1958.

Peter Sanz: *Catholic Biographies,* Vol. IX. London: Catholic Truth Society, 1894.

Philip Benizi: Peregrine Soulier, *Life of Saint Philip Benizi.* London: Burns & Oates, 1886.

Philip Neri: Alfonso Capecelatro, *The Life of Saint Philip Neri.* London: Burns & Oates, 1882.

Philippine Duchesne: Louise Callan, RSCJ, *Philippine Duchesne.* Westminster, Maryland: The Newman Press, 1965.

Pier-Giorgio Frassati: Robert Claude, SJ, *The Soul of Pier-Giorgio Frassati.* New York: Spiritual Book Associates, © 1960.

Pius X: Francis Thornton, *The Life of Pope Pius X.* New York: Benziger Brothers, Inc.

Polycarp: *The Acts of the Christian Martyrs;* tr. Herbert Musurillo. Oxford: Oxford University Press, © 1972.

Proclus: *Christian Readings 3, Year 1.* New York: Catholic Book Publishing Co., 1972.

Prosper of Aquitaine: St. Prosper of Aquitaine, *The Call to the Nations,* I, 8. *ACW* (No. 14; 1952).

Rabanus Maurus: *Hymns for the Year* (1896).

Radegund: *Sainted Women of the Dark Ages.* Durham, North Carolina: Duke University Press, 1992.

Raphael Kalinowski: Monk Matthew, *Saint from the Salt Mines.* Privately published, © 1986.

Raymond of Capua: Hyacinth M. Cormier, OP, *Blessed Raymund of Capua.* Boston: Marlier Callanan & Co., 1900.

Raymond of Penyafort: *OR.*

Richard Rolle: *Richard Rolle: The English Writings. CWS* (1988).

Rita of Cascia: Agostino Trapé, *The Message of Saint Rita of Cascia.* Augustinian Press, 1989.

Robert Bellarmine: James Broderick, SJ, *Robert Bellarmine: Saint and Scholar.* Westminster, Maryland: The Newman Press, 1961.

Robert Southwell: Christopher Devlin, *The Life of Robert Southwell: Poet & Martyr.* New York: Greenwood Press, 1969.

Roque González: C. J. McNaspy, SJ, *Conquistador Without Sword.* Chicago, Illinois: Loyola University Press, © 1988; *NBLS,* November.

Rose of Lima: Leonhard Hansen, *The Life of Saint Rose of Lima.* New York: P. J. Kenedy & Sons, 1847.

Rudolf Aquaviva: Francis Goldie, *The First Christian Mission to the Great Mogul*. Dublin: M. H. Gill & Sons, 1897.

Sabas: Cyril of Scythopolis, *The Lives of the Monks of Palestine*. Kalamazoo, Michigan: Cistercian Publications, 1991.

Scholastica: *The Life of Our Most Holy Father S. Benedict*. Rome, 1895.

Sebastian Valfré: Lady Amabel Kerr, *The Life of Blessed Sebastian Valfré*. London: Catholic Truth Society, 1896.

Seraphim of Sarov: Constantine Cavarnos and Mary-Barbara Zeldin, *Modern Orthodox Saints,* Vol. 5. Belmont, Massachusetts: Institute for Byzantine and Modern Greek Studies, © 1980.

Severin of Noricum: Eugippus, *The Life of Saint Severin, in FC* (55).

Severinus Boethius: Boethius, *The Consolation of Philosophy*. New York: Penguin Putnam, Inc., 1969.

Shenoute: Besa. *The Life of Shenoute*. Kalamazoo, Michigan: Cistercian Publications, 1983.

Simeon Stylites: Theodoret of Cyrrhus, *A History of the Monks of Egypt*, 12. Kalamazoo, Michigan: Cistercian Publications, 1985.

Simeon the New Theologian: *St. Symeon the New Theologian: The Discourses. CWS* (1995).

Solanus Casey: James Patrick Derum, *The Porter of Saint Bonaventure's: The Life of Father Solanus Casey*. Detroit: The Fidelity Press, 1968.

Stanislaus Kostka: Joseph E. Kearns, SJ, *Portrait of a Champion: A Life of St. Stanley Kostka*. Westminster, Maryland: The Newman Press, 1957.

Stephen: *NJB*.

Stephen of Hungary: *OR*.

Sturm: C. H. Talbot, ed. *The Anglo-Saxon Missionaries in Germany*. London: Sheed & Ward, 1981.

Syncletica: Benedicta Ward, ed. *The Sayings of the Desert Fathers; The Alphabetical Collection*. Kalamazoo, Michigan: Cistercian Publications, 1975.

Teresa of Ávila: *The Life of Teresa of Jesus*. Garden City, New York: Doubleday Image Books, 1960; St. Teresa of Ávila, *Interior Castle*. Garden City, New York: Doubleday Image Books, 1961.

Teresa of Calcutta: *The Mother Teresa Reader*. Ann Arbor, Michigan: Servant Publications, 1995.

Theodore of Canterbury: William Reany, *St. Theodore of Canterbury*. St. Louis, Missouri: B. Herder Book Co., 1944.

Theodore of Sykeon: *Three Byzantine Saints.* Crestwood, New York: St. Vladimir's Seminary Press, 1977.

Theodore the Studite: M. Basil Pennington, *Through the Year with the Saints.* Spencer, Massachusetts: Cistercian Abbey of Spencer, Inc., © 1988.

Théophane Vénard: *A Modern Martyr: Théophane Vénard.* Boston: Society for the Propagation of the Faith, 1906; Christian Simmonnet, *Théophane Vénard: A Martyr of Vietnam.* San Francisco: Ignatius Press, 1988.

Theresa Margaret of the Sacred Heart: James F. Newcomb, *St. Theresa Margaret of the Sacred Heart.* New York: Benziger Brothers, 1934.

Thérèse of Lisieux: St. Thérèse of Lisieux, *The Autobiography of St. Thérèse of Lisieux.* New York: Doubleday, 1957.

Thomas: *LTC.*

Thomas Aquinas: *Summa Contra Gentes. CWS* (© 1988).

Thomas Becket: Richard Winston, *Thomas Becket.* New York: Alfred A. Knopf, 1970.

Thomas More: R. W. Chambers, *Thomas More.* Ann Arbor, Michigan: University of Michigan Press, 1982.

Thomas of Villanova: *The Lives of St. Thomas of Villanova* [by Claude Maimbourg, 1659] *and of St. Francis Solano.* London: Thomas Richardson and Son, 1847; *BLS.*

Timothy: *NJB.*

Titus: *NJB.*

Titus Brandsma: Joseph Rees, *Titus Brandsma: A Modern Martyr.* London: Sidgwick & Jackson, © 1971.

Ubald of Gubbio: Michael L. Gaudoin-Parker, *A Window on the Mystery of Faith.* New York: Alba House, © 1997.

Valerian: St. Valerian, *Homily 19*, in *FC* (17).

Vedast: *The Life and Legend of Saint Vedast;* eds. Gertrude Simpson and W. Sparrow Simpson. London: privately published, 1896, 54–56.

Venantius Fortunatus: *Collected Hymns, Sequences and Carols.* London: Hodder & Stoughton, 1914.

Veronica Giuliani: Michael L. Gaudoin-Parker, *A Window on the Mystery of Faith.* New York: Alba House, © 1997.

Vincent de Paul: *Vincent de Paul and Louise de Marillac: Rules, Conferences and Writings. CWS* (1995).

Vincent Ferrer: S[ister] M[ary] C[atherine], *Angel of the Judgment: a Life of Vincent Ferrer.* Notre Dame, Indiana: Ave Maria Press, 1954.

Vincent of Lérins: *The Commonitory of Vincent of Lérins,* II, 4–6. *NPNF* (Second Series, Vol. XI; 1986).

Vincent of Saragossa: *The Poems of Prudentius; FC* (43).

Wenceslaus: *TWC.*

Wilfrid: *The Anonymous Life of Wilfrid* in Clinton Albertson, SJ, ed. *Anglo-Saxon Saints and Heroes.* New York: Fordham University Press, © 1967.

Willibrord: *Alcuin's Life of Willibrord* in Clinton Albertson, SJ, ed. *Anglo-Saxon Saints and Heroes.* New York: Fordham University Press, 1967.

Copyright Acknowledgments

The author and publisher wish to thank the following for permission to reprint selections from books on which they hold copyrights:

Aloysius of Gonzaga; Anthony of Zaccaria; Aphraates of Persia; Casimir; Cyril and Methodius; Eusebius of Vercelli; Faustus; Hedwig; John Bosco; Raymond of Penyafort; Stephen of Hungary: The English translation of the office writings of the saints from *The Liturgy of the Hours*, © 1974, International Committee on English in the Liturgy, Inc. All rights reserved.

Alphonsus de Orozco; Peter of Alcántara: Kathleen Pond, *The Spirit of the Spanish Mystics*. London: Burns & Oates, © 1958. Used by permission.

Alphonsus Rodriguez; Peter Claver: Angel Valtierra, SJ *Peter Claver: Saint of the Slaves*. London: Burns & Oates, © 1960. Used by permission.

Amphilochius; Gaudentius of Brescia; Germanus of Constantinople: M. F. Toal, ed., *The Sunday Sermons of the Great Fathers*. Swedesboro, New Jersey: Preservation Press, 1996. Used by permission of Ignatius Press, the current copyright holder.

Andrew; James the Great; Matthew; Maurus; Thomas: *The Lessons of the Temporal Cycle and the Principal Feasts of the Sanctoral Cycle*. St. Meinrad, Indiana: St. Meinrad's Abbey, 1943. Used by permission.

Andrew of Crete; Paul Miki; Proclus: Reproduced with permission from *Christian Readings 3, Year 1,* © 1972, Catholic Book Publishing Co., New York, N. Y. All rights reserved.

Anne Mary Taigi; Anthony Grassi; Martin I: *Butler's Lives of the Saints;* ed. Herbert Thurston, SJ, and Donald Attwater. London: Burns & Oates, © 1956. Used by permission.

Bede; Benedict Biscop; Wilfrid; Willibrord: Clinton Albertson, SJ, *Anglo-Saxon Saints and Heroes*. New York: Fordham University Press, 1967. Used by permission of the author.

Bertilla; Balthild; Genevieve; Radegund: *Sainted Women of the Dark Ages,* ed. and tr. Jo Ann McNamara, John E. Halbourg, and Gordon Whatley. Durham, N. C.: Duke University Press, © 1992. Reprinted with permission. All rights reserved.

Bonaventure: *Bonaventure: The Soul's Journey into God; The Tree of Life; The Life of St. Francis*, ed. Ewert Cousins. *The Classics of Western Spirituality*. New York: Paulist Press, Inc., © 1978.

Brendan; Kevin: *Bethada Náem Nérennn; Lives of Irish Saints*, ed. Charles Plummer. Oxford University Press, © 1922. Used by permission.

Diana d'Andalo; Osanna of Mantua: E. I. Watkin, *Neglected Saints*. San Francisco: Ignatius Press, 1994. Used by permission of Mrs. Magdalen Goffin, daughter of the author.

Daniel the Stylite; Theodore of Sykeon: *Three Byzantine Saints*, tr. Elizabeth Dawes and Norman H. Baynes. Used with permission of St. Vladmir's Seminary Press, 575 Scarsdale Road, Crestwood, NY 10707.

Eulalia; Lawrence; Vincent of Saragossa: *The Poems of Prudentius* in *The Fathers of the Church*, Vol. 43; ed. Joseph Deferrari. Washington, D. C.: The Catholic University of America Press. Used by permission.

Felicity; Polycarp: *The Acts of the Christian Martyrs*, introduction, texts, and translations by Herbert Musurillo. Oxford: Oxford University Press, © 1972. Used by permission.

Felix of Nola; Paulinus of Nola: *The Poems of St. Paulinus of Nola*, 135 and 149, in *Ancient Christian Writers;* ed. Walter J. Burghardt and Thomas C. Lawler. New York: Newman Press, © 1975. Used by permission of Paulist Press, now holder of the copyright.

Eulogius; Flora: Justo Pérez de Urbel, *A Saint Under Moslem Rule*. Milwaukee, Wisconsin: The Bruce Publishing Company, © 1937. Reprinted by permission of the superior of the Missouri Jesuit Province and Burns & Oates.

Euthymius the Great; John the Silent; Sabas: Cyril of Scythopolis, *The Lives of the Monks of Palestine,* tr. R. M. Price. Kalamazoo, Michigan: Cistercian Publications, © 1991. Used by permission.

Faustina Kowalska: *The Diary of Blessed Faustina Kowalska: Divine Mercy in My Soul,* © 1987 Congregation of Marians of the Immaculate Conception, Stockbridge, MA 01263. All world rights reserved; printed with permission.

Francis of Assisi: *Writings of St. Francis of Assisi,* tr. Benen Fahy, OFM. Chicago: Franciscan Herald Press. Reprinted by permission of the Franciscan Press of Quincy University, Quincy, Illinois.

Hilarion; Hilary of Arles; Honoratus of Arles: *Early Christian Biographies* in *The Fathers of the Church,* Vol. 15; ed. Joseph Deferrari. Washington, D. C.: The Catholic University of America Press. Used by permission.

John of Capistrano; Theodore the Studite: M. Basil Pennington, *Through the Year with the Saints.* Spencer, Massachusetts: Cistercian Abbey of Spencer, Inc., © 1988. Used by permission of the author.

John Kolobos; Macarius the Great; Syncletica: from Benedicta Ward, SLG, ed., *The Sayings of the Desert Fathers: The Alphabetical Collection.* Kalamazoo, Michigan: Cistercian Publications, © 1975. Used by permission.

Leander of Seville; Martin of Braga: *Iberian Fathers* in *The Fathers of the Church,* Vol. 62; ed. Joseph Deferrari. Washington, D. C.: The Catholic University of America Press. Used by permission.

Leoba; Sturm: *The Anglo-Saxon Missionaries in Germany.* London: Sheed & Ward, © 1953, 1981.

Louise de Marillac and Vincent de Paul: *Vincent de Paul and Louise de Marillac: Rules, Conferences and Writings in The Classics of Western Spirituality.* New York: Paulist Press, Inc., © 1995. Used by permission.

Marcella; Melania; Paula: Joan M. Peterson, tr. *Handmaids of the Lord.* Kalamazoo, Michigan: Cistercian Publications, Inc., 1996. Used by permission.

Martin of Tours; Nicetas of Remesiana: *The Fathers of the Church,* Vol. 7; ed. Joseph Deferrari. Washington, D. C.: The Catholic University of America Press. Used by permission.

Peter Chrysologus; Valerian: *The Fathers of the Church,* Vol. 17; ed. Joseph Deferrari. Washington, D. C.: The Catholic University of America Press. Used by permission.

Ubald of Gubbio; Veronica Giuliani: Michael L. Gaudoin-Parker, *A Window on the Mystery of Faith.* New York: Alba House, © 1997. Used by permission.

Glossary

Abbess—the head of a community of nuns, and sometimes of nuns and monks.

Abbot—the head of a community of monks.

Albigensians—a religious sect based in southern France during the late twelfth and thirteenth centuries; taught a dualism, affirming two eternal principles of good and evil.

Arianism—heresy based on teachings of Arius, a priest of Alexandria, who held that Christ was not truly God; that the Son was a creature and capable of sin. Condemned at the Council of Nicea in 325 and at the Council of Constantinople in 381.

Augustinians—communities following the monastic rule of St. Augustine.

Avignon Papacy—Under the powerful influence of the French kings, from 1309 to 1377 popes resided in the southern French city of Avignon. The rest of Europe regarded these popes as tools of France and described the situation as the "Babylonian Captivity" of the church.

Béguines—sisterhoods of celibate women who lived in common households, prayed together, and dedicated themselves to works of mercy; they could own property and leave to marry.

Canon—a member of a religious community living according to a canon or rule; a priest serving in a cathedral or collegiate church, usually supported by an endowment.

Capuchins—offshoot of the Friars Minor; founded in 1552 by Matteo di Bassi of Urbino, Italy, in order to return to the primitive simplicity of the Franciscan order.

Carmelite order—the Order of Our Lady of Mount Carmel, founded in the twelfth century in Palestine by St. Berthold; Carmelite communities of men and women spread throughout Europe in the thirteenth and fourteenth centuries.

Catechumen—a person who is receiving instruction in basic Christianity in preparation for baptism.

Cenobium—a community of monks who live, worship, and work together.

Chapter—an assembly or meeting of the canons of a cathedral; a meeting of the leaders or representatives of a religious order.

Cîteaux—the central house of the Cistercian order, a strict Benedictine monastic community founded in the eleventh century, located south of Dijon, France.

Cluniac reform—a general church reform in the eleventh and twelveth centuries generated by the influence of the monastery of Cluny in Burgundy.

Council of Trent—the Nineteenth Ecumenical Council (1545–1563) called as a response to Protestantism and to the great need for moral and administrative reforms in the church.

Diocese—the geographical district under a bishop's supervision.

Doctor of the church—an honorary title given to saints to recognize significant contributions to faith and understanding of the Christian life.

Dominican—See Friars Preachers.

Fathers of the church—early Christian writers whose authority on doctrinal matters carried special weight.

Franks—Germanic tribe that after 486 under Clovis consolidated a kingdom stretching from east of the Rhine in Germany to the Pyrenees bordering Spain.

Friars Minor—the religious community of men founded by Saint Francis of Assisi in the thirteenth century; Franciscans.

Friars Preachers—the religious community of men founded by Saint Dominic in the thirteenth century; Dominicans.

Host—the consecrated bread of the Eucharist.

Hours—see Liturgy of the Hours.

Hussites—followers of John Huss, fifteenth-century Bohemian reformer whose preaching and doctrine helped prepare the way for the Protestant Reformation.

Iconoclasm—heresy that denounced the veneration of icons (images). The Iconoclastic controversy agitated the church of the East from 725 to 842.

Jansenism—teaching of Cornelius Jansen, seventeenth-century author of the Augustinus, in which he held that without a special grace from God it is impossible to obey his commandments. He also taught that the operation of grace is irresistible, so that human beings are subject to a supernatural determinism.

Laura—a settlement of hermits living in huts and caves around a church.

Lectionary—a book containing extracts from Scripture appointed to be read at public worship.

Lent—the penitential season observed in preparation for Easter.

Liturgy of the Hours—the public prayer of the church; consisting of psalms, hymns, and Scripture; arranged so that it covers the entire day at specified intervals; required of priests and religious men and women and open to the participation of all.

Manichaeism—a religious dualism originating in third-century Persia; taught the release of the spirit from matter through asceticism.

Mass—the official public worship of the Catholic Church, consisting of the Liturgy of the Word (the proclamation of Scripture) and the Liturgy of the Eucharist (the representation of Christ's sacrifice and communion).

Matins—the Liturgy of the Hours for night that originated in the vigil celebrations of the early church; according to the Rule of St. Benedict, celebrated at 2 a.m.

Metropolitan—archbishop of the principal see, an archdiocese, in an ecclesiastical province consisting of several dioceses. He has full power in his own diocese and limited authority and influence over the other dioceses in the province.

Minster—a large or important church, often having cathedral status.

Mitre—a tall ornamental cap with peaks in front and back, worn by abbots, bishops, and popes as a sign of their office.

Monophysitism—fifth-century heretical doctrine that in the person of Christ there was a single divine nature, as opposed to the orthodox teaching of a double nature, divine and human; condemned at the Council of Chalcedon in 451.

Monothelitism—a seventh-century heresy holding that Jesus had only a divine will and, therefore, was not fully human; condemned at the Council of Constantinople in 680.

Montanism—late second-century enthusiastic movement generated by Montanus in Phrygia (in Asia Minor). Montanists expected the immediate and experiential outpouring of the Holy Spirit, which they saw manifested in their own prophets and prophetesses.

Nestorianism—fifth-century heretical doctrine of Nestorius, the patriarch of Constantinople, who taught that there were two separate persons in Christ, one divine and one human, as opposed to the orthodox teaching that Christ was a single person, at once God and man; condemned at the Council of Ephesus in 431.

Novice—a person on probation while taking training in a religious community and before taking vows.

Novitiate—the training program for new members of a religious order.

Oratory—a private or institutional chapel for prayer.

Oratory of St. Philip Neri—a congregation of secular priests living in community without vows, those with private means supporting themselves; founded by Philip Neri in 1564, taking its name from the oratory at St. Girolamo, Rome, where they held their meetings.

Order—a religious community of men or women who live according to a rule of life.

Ostrogoths—Eastern Goths from the region of the Black Sea, a Germanic tribe that settled in central Europe in the mid-fifth century. Theodoric, the Ostrogoth king, conquered Rome in 493.

Papacy—the term used for the government or office of the pope.

Passionists—religious congregation founded in 1720 by St. Paul of the Cross; they stress the contemplative life, and in addition to vows of poverty, chastity, and obedience, they vow to further the memory of Christ's passion.

Pelagianism—heresy that denied the freedom of the will in choosing to receive salvation.

Pentateuch—the first five books of the Hebrew Scriptures (Genesis, Exodus, Leviticus, Numbers, and Deuteronomy).

Porter—doorkeeper and greeter at a monastery.

Postulant—a candidate for membership in a religious order in the period before the probationary period of the novitiate.

Prelate—a bishop or an abbot.

Prior—the second in command under an abbot in a monastery; also the head of a priory, a subordinate unit of a monastery.

Provincial—the governor of a province, a geographical unit of a religious order.

Rogation Day—one of three days of prayer for the harvest formerly observed three days before the feast of the Ascension.

Roman martyrology—the official list of saints honored by the Catholic Church.

Sacramentary—a liturgical book containing the celebrant's part of the Mass and the rites for the administration of the sacraments.

Sacristan—attendant responsible for the vessels and vestments used during the liturgy and sacraments.

Scholasticism—the philosophy and theology of the medieval universities that characteristically integrated faith and reason.

Semi-Pelagianism—fourth- and fifth-century heretical doctrines of theologians who, while not denying the necessity of grace for salvation, held that the first steps of the Christian life were taken by the will, with grace intervening only later.

Sodality—an association or guild formed to advance some religious purpose by mutual action or assistance.

Spiritual director—a pastor or counselor who governs the Christian life of another person.

Stigmata—the reproduction of the wounds of Christ's passion in the human body.

Synod—a local council of bishops convened for regulating doctrine and practice.

Tertiary—a member of a Third Order.

Third Order—an association of laypeople who pattern their lives on the rule of a religious community, but who continue to lead ordinary secular lives.

Trappists—the popular name for the main branch of the Cistercians of the Strict Observance; derived from its center at the abbey of Notre Dame de la Trappe near Soligny, France.

Vespers—evening prayer in the liturgy of the hours.

Visigoths—West Goths, a Germanic tribe that became the first independent barbarian nation in the Roman Empire after 378. Under Alaric, the Visigoths sacked Rome in 410.

Index of Saints Names